Also from The Mountaineers:

Trekking in Tibet, by Gary McCue
Definitive guidebook of one-day to ⟨...⟩ tance
and route highlights, with detailed ⟨...⟩ and
language. Maps, photos. $16.95

Himalayan Passage: Seven Months ⟨...⟩ *y of Tibet, Nepal,*
China, India, and Pakistan by Jeren⟨...⟩ ⟨...⟩ut, with photographs by Patrick
Morrow
Winner of the first Barbara Savage Memorial Award. Two couples who cir-
cumnavigated the base of the Himalayas by bike, foot, taxi, and donkey cart
share their adventures and experiences of a vast, varied region. $22.95

South America's National Parks: A Visitor's Guide, by Bill Leitch
Unique guide to 32 parks and their varied climates, recreational opportunities
and amenities, with information on trails, flora and fauna, and geology. Color
photos, maps. $16.95

The Galapagos Islands, by Marylee Stephenson
Complete, practical guide to touring isolated archipelago off Ecuador. History,
necessary travel information, and descriptions of plants' and animals' unique
adaptations to environment. $12.95

Mount Everest National Park: Sagarmatha, Mother of the Universe, by
Margaret Jeffries
Reference and guide to the Khumbu, a World Heritage site. Covers the region's human history, biology, geography and geology, plus access and visitor
facilities. Color photos. $18.95

Royal Chitwan National Park: Wildlife Sanctuary of Nepal, by Himanta R.
Mishra and Margaret Jeffries
Reference and guide to this World Heritage site, the last refuge for much of
Asia's rarest wildlife. Covers park's human history, biology, geography and
geology, region's people and conservation efforts, plus access and visitor facil-
ities. Color photos. $18.95

**Available from your local book or outdoor store, or from The Mountain-
eers Books, 1011 SW Klickitat Way, Seattle, WA 98134.
1-800-553-4453**

Nepali for Trekkers: Language Tape and Phrase Book, by Stephen Bezruchka

" . . . trekkers constantly tell me how their attempts to speak Nepali even when trekking with guides provide intimate, unforgettable experiences with the country that others, who don't make the effort, miss," says author Stephen Bezruchka.

A basic knowledge of the Nepali language can make the difference between a good trip to Nepal and a truly memorable, meaningful one. Start down the road to fluency with this comprehensive phrase book (reprinted from The Mountaineers *Trekking in Nepal*) and easy-to-use language tape.

The phrase book includes pronunciation, grammar notes, practice sections, and common Nepali words and phrases. The tape is ninety minutes and covers not only the material in the phrase book, but additional Nepali terms and place names as well. Accuracy and authenticity are guaranteed because words and phrases are spoken by a native Nepali. Pauses allow the listener time to repeat them.

Use *Nepali for Trekkers: Language Tape and Phrase Book* to expand your understanding of a complex, fascinating land, and to give the people of Nepal a good impression of yours.

Available from your local book or outdoor store, or from The Mountaineers Books, 1011 SW Klickitat Way, Seattle, WA, 98134. 1-800-553-4453.

Trekking in
Nepal

A Traveler's Guide

Sixth Edition

Trekking in Nepal

A Traveler's Guide

Sixth Edition

STEPHEN BEZRUCHKA

The Mountaineers • Seattle

First edition 1972; second edition 1974; third edition, 1976; all by Sahayogi Press, Kathmandu, Nepal

Fourth edition, 1981; fifth edition, 1985; sixth edition, 1991, published in the United States, by The Mountaineers, Seattle, Washington.

5   4
5   4   3   2

Published by The Mountaineers
1011 SW Klickitat Way, Seattle, Washington 98134

Published simultaneously in
    Canada by Douglas & McIntyre, Ltd., 1615 Venables Street, Vancouver,
        British Columbia V5L 2H1
    Great Britain by Cordee, 3a DeMontfort Street, Leicester, England LE1 7HD
    Nepal by Sahayogi Press, Tripureshwar Kathmandu

Manufactured in the United States of America

Edited by Richard C. May
Cover photo: Dharapami and Gurja Himal by Patrick Morrow
Frontispiece: The west face of Dhaulagiri, from Jaljala
All photographs by the author unless otherwise indicated.
Cover design by Betty Watson
Book layout by Constance Bollen

Library of Congress Cataloging-in-Publication Data

Bezruchka, Stephen.
    Trekking in Nepal: a traveler's guide / Stephen Bezruchka. – 6th
    ed.
        p.   cm.
    Rev. ed. of: A guide to trekking in Nepal. 5th ed. 1985.
    Includes bibliographical references and index.
    ISBN 0-89886-279-5 : $16.95
    1. Hiking—Nepal—Guide-books.   2. Nepal—Description and travel-
-Guide-books.   I.Bezruchka, Stephen. Guide to trekking in Nepal.
II. Title.
GV199.44.N46B49   1991
915.496--dc20   91-771
                                                                    CIP

Contents

Mount Everest, from Kala Pattar, first climbed in 1953 by Sir Edmund Hillary and Tenzing Norgay

Foreword

Stephen Bezruchka's book has proved a resounding success. Many of the trekkers I see each year in the Himalaya carry a much-used copy as a guide and friend.

Since 1976 when I first wrote a foreword to *A Guide to Trekking in Nepal,* I have seen many changes in the country—both good and bad. Population pressure has relentlessly increased and the growth of tourism has been quite remarkable. Many of the walking tracks and campsites are cleaner now as trekking agencies make greater efforts to tidy up behind them. But in the mountains the climbing expeditions still leave piles of rubbish around. There has been a determined effort to increase reforestation but the steep hillsides are frequently barren and scarred with great slips carrying soil down into the flooded rivers.

But despite the devastation Nepal is still very beautiful. The mountains are as superb as ever and the people just as friendly. Trekking in Nepal is an experience never to be forgotten. Those of us who have been around a long time can see the changes but the newcomer sees only the drama and the beauty. Perhaps it is better that way. We must desperately battle for environmental protection but not lose our ability to absorb the remaining beauty of the mountains and the valleys. It is the responsibility of all of us to encourage reforestation and make a determined effort to leave the country at least as tidy as we found it—or maybe a little bit better.

Sir Edmund Hillary

Nepal is there to change you, not for you to change it. Lose yourself in its magic. Make your footprints with care and awareness of the precarious balance around you. Take souvenirs in your heart and spirit, not in your pockets. Nepal is not only a place on the map, but an experience, a way of life from which we all can learn.

Preface

Nepal is on the map for the adventure traveler, and even the casual tourist. Adventure used to be for the elite or crazy, but now "adventures" are undertaken by ordinary people—perhaps a disease of the complex, modern, post-industrial society.

Trekking in its various styles is an increasingly popular activity, with over 50,000 participants annually. Especially along the popular routes, there have been many changes over the span of more than twenty years that I have been fortunate to be involved with Nepal.

Trekking is so popular because of the land forms in this remarkably varied country, and because of the nature of the Nepali spirit. What can be done to enhance the experience of both the visitor and the Nepali host? Clearly it is understanding on both sides that is necessary. With the remarkable quality of Nepali tolerance, there is little that needs to be said about that aspect. But for the visitor, there is much to be learned about the way of Nepal if you want to be respected by your hosts. That is the purpose of this book. Whether you are going with an agency, organizing your own portered trip, or going it alone, this book will help you have an experience that is remarkable, memorable, and close to the heart of Nepal. For even though you might surmise that the larger numbers of tourists will dilute the hospitality of the Nepali people, the opposite is true. The more you are sensitive to the ways of Nepal, the more intimate and wonderful your experience. This will set you apart from the others. Countless letters from users of this book attest to that.

My orientation is to help you learn about the real Nepal, not just the tourist corridor, be it the trekker trail through the lodges to Jomosom, or the inns of Manang, but also the less visited areas, including the Kangchenjunga and Makalu regions, and the wild west. This is a never ending process, which will delight you in the coming years.

I have also written an appendix on the Nepali language. It is also sold separately in a pocket-size version, together with a language tape, to help you study the *baasaa* before you go, and to learn it as you trek. There is no more important advice I can give you to enjoy Nepal than to study Nepali, and use it in the country. Nothing else will set you apart from the other trekkers as easily.

Many people have helped me in updating this edition. Thanks to: Tom Arens, Jan Balut, Rochelle Bell, Miriam Bender, Tika Bhattarai, Barry Bishop, Cherie Bremer-Kamp, Kevin Brosan, Jeff Buckwalter, Bob Campbell, Brian Chomica, Steve Conlon, David Cummings, Catherine Dalton, Alfred Dougherty, Polly Fabian, Jill Fleming, Deb Foden, Hannelore Gabriel, Elinor Graham, Mithra Gorter, Barbara Guss, Ane Haaland, Peter Hackett, Louis Helbig, William Holland, Robin Houstin, Frances Klatzel, Christine Kolisch, David Kulka, Suzanne Kurtz, Chris Leach, Kathleen Learned, Bill Liske, David Marmorek, Bob Matthews, Cecilia Meagher, Mike Moore, Patrick and Baiba Morrow, Nancy and Tony Parinello, Jeremy Polmear, Pam Poon, Mark Porter, George Povey, Charlie Pye-Smith, Michele Richard, Anne

Rodman, Hans Sauter, Gyalgen Sherpa, Penny Dawson Sherpani, David Shlim, Hugh Swift, Puru Thapa, Rosemary Valen, Neil Vigilante, Claire Waddoup, Risa Weber, Simon Whitney, Dave Yospe, and Cindy Zikmund. Special thanks to Daniel Schelling and Carol Inskipp, who have provided a new chapter on natural history. Thanks also to Mary Lynn Hanley, who suggested the format for the language book. I appreciate the efforts of Rick May and Marge Mueller of The Mountaineers Books in producing this edition. I am grateful to His Majesty's Government for granting me permission to trek. I am indebted to Mr. Ramesh Kumar Sharma, who first undertook to publish this book in 1970, and he continues to support its development after all these years. Many thanks to Margaret Jefferies for going through the text painstakingly, making corrections, and giving helpful suggestions. My porters continue to teach me most of what I know about Nepal. I am especially grateful to Chandra Pal Rai, Hari Bahadur Rawal, and Hasta Bahadur Pakrin.

Nepal is currently undergoing many changes in its political process, in one of the most remarkable periods of recent world history. Tourism has brought many changes to this country. The people of Nepal will now be able to make more decisions about the future of their country themselves. It is an exciting time to have the privilege of traveling through this Himalayan wonderland.

This guidebook, faced with a landform that is constantly changing, is bound to be out of date in some places, and in error in others. Over the years, many trekkers have sent information to me, and this has resulted in substantial improvements to the book. Many are acknowledged above. Please keep the comments and letters coming.

A NOTE ABOUT SAFETY

Safety is an important concern in all outdoor activities. No guidebook can alert you to every hazard or anticipate the limitations of every reader. Therefore, the descriptions of roads, trails, routes, and natural features in this book are not representations that a particular place or excursion will be safe for your party. When you follow any of the routes described in this book, you assume responsibility for your own safety. Under normal conditions, such excursions require the usual attention to traffic, road and trail conditions, altitude, weather, terrain, the capabilities of your party, and other factors. Keeping informed on current conditions and exercising common sense are the keys to a safe, enjoyable outing.

Political conditions may add to the risks of travel in Nepal in ways that this book cannot predict. When you travel, you assume this risk, and should keep informed of political developments that may make safe travel difficult or impossible.

The Mountaineers

SECTION I

ABOUT TREKKING

Dhaulagiri and the Kali Gandaki Valley, from the trail to North Annapurna Base Camp (photo by Peter Banys)

Light streams into a Sherpa home as breakfast is cooked.

What to Expect

A hundred divine epochs would not suffice to describe all the marvels of the Himalaya.

Sanskrit proverb

What kind of experience will you have in Nepal? Think of waking up early one morning and directing your gaze to the north. It is quite cloudy, but for some reason you lift up your eyes. There it is—the triangular rock-and-snow face of Machhapuchhre, glistening in the sun through a hole in the clouds. But it is not even 23,000 ft (7000 m) high! How could it look so big? Or you are walking along the trail when you suddenly hear, "Good morning, sir," spoken in perfect English. You turn around, astonished, to see an ordinary-looking Nepali. Yes, the speaker is a Gurkha soldier, retired from the British Army. The two of you pass many miles talking together. Or it is the day's end and you are resting after the walk, looking at a Western book or magazine that you carry. Soon you are surrounded by children who gaze intently at the pictures. You want to tell them that the world those pictures represent is not better than theirs. Or after you have walked for eleven days, you reach the top of a hill and suddenly see Mount Everest and Ama Dablang. Everest is over 6000 ft (1800 m) higher, but you hardly notice it; Ama Dablang dazzles you all the time you are near it. Or it is spring and you have toiled to get far above the valley. The rhododendrons make the mountains look like a paradise. The blooms are red in many places, yet the colors can be light, and even beautifully white. Every day there will be many times like these when you will forget the miles you have yet to go, the vertical feet yet to climb, the load on your back. And you will vow to return.

Nepal is a land of unparalleled variety. Imagine a rectangle, 500 mi by 150 mi (800 km by 240 km), divided lengthwise into three strips. The northernmost strip is the Himalaya, meaning "abode of snow." It includes eight of the ten highest mountains in the world. The Himalayan region is sparsely settled by people who speak languages of the Tibeto-Burman family and practice Tibetan Buddhism. The southernmost region, which is the narrowest of the three strips, is called the Tarai. It is an extension of the Gangetic plain of northern India, a jungle with elephants, rhinoceroses and tigers. These inhabitants contrast markedly with the yaks and snow leopards less than 100 mi (160 km) to the north. This area is populated by people who speak Indo-European languages and practice Hinduism. Between the two outer strips lies an interface region of hills and valleys. The inhabitants speak languages of both the Tibeto-Burman and Indo-European families and generally practice Hinduism with many Buddhist and shamanistic influences. This region is the unexpected treasure of Nepal.

Climatically, the country has subtropical, temperate, and alpine regions, determined by elevation. It contains examples of most of the vegetation zones of the world.

The economy is basically subsistence agriculture. Nepal has most of the statistical characteristics of the world's poorest countries in terms of per capita income, literacy, and infant mortality. The World Bank ranks Nepal close to the poorest country in the world. The high rate of population growth—doubling time is about thirty years—threatens to outstrip food production. Another serious problem is deforestation by clearing land for marginal agricultural use to feed the increasing population. The result is erosion and loss of topsoil. Nepal's population is over 18 million, and its annual growth rate is approximately 2.7 percent. Although I returned from Nepal in 1970 with a doomsday outlook, I have seen many positive changes over the years, as well as some negative ones, so the situation does not seem hopeless. Historically, the Nepali people have worked through their problems satisfactorily, and I see no reason to doubt their ability to continue to do so, as long as we visitors don't interfere.

Nepal was the world's only Hindu monarchy in recent times. The King, Birendra Bir Bikram Shah Dev, is a direct descendant of Prithvinarayan Shah who unified the country in the 1760s. For over a hundred years, until 1951, Nepal was ruled by a sequence of hereditary prime ministers, the Ranas. During this period Nepal was essentially cut off from outside influences. Because of its forbidding mountains to the north and deadly malaria endemic in the Tarai to the south, Nepal was never successfully invaded by a major power.

After the Chinese occupied Tibet in 1959, many Tibetans fled to India and Nepal where they settled in refugee camps. The northern border of Nepal was closed for some time, but restrictions now have been relaxed somewhat so that trade goes on, though it is not the extensive commerce it once was. Most Tibetans in Nepal have successfully adapted to their new environment.

After an attempt at democracy in 1959, the country was ruled by a system of participatory councils but with real power vested in the King. In the spring of 1980 a popular referendum was held to determine if the country should allow multiple political parties. The proposal was defeated. In early 1990, popular support for democracy again surfaced. Although initial demonstrations were suppressed with violence, the Nepal Congress Party, supported by the quest for democracy throughout the world, was allowed to form an interim government. In November 1990 a new constitution was adopted, with the King as a constitutional monarch and head of the army. It gives power to the people through free elections and a multiparty democracy centered around a parliament of two houses. The first elections were held in May 1991.

Nepal was closed to foreigners and foreign influence until 1951 and did not officially open its doors to tourists until a few years later. But by 1988, almost 200,000 non-Indian tourists were visiting the country each year, and massive amounts of foreign aid has started Nepal on the road to modernization and development. Major contributors of aid are India, Japan, Germany, France, China, the Soviet Union, and the United States. It remains to be seen whether this economic assistance will improve the lot of Nepali farmers. In the past, most aid has been given primarily for political reasons, although Nepal is a nonaligned country and has declared itself a zone of peace. So far, most of Nepal remains largely untouched by the ways and ideas of the West.

A trade embargo was imposed by India in 1989, after a trade and transit treaty expired. This caused great economic hardship to the developing industries, but has little affected the hill peasant, who continues to be relatively self-sufficient. Trade is now back to normal.

It is this land of contrasts that beckons those who are willing to travel, as the Nepalis do, on foot. Indeed, walking is the only means of reaching most destinations, since Nepal still has the fewest miles of roads in proportion to area of population of any country in the world. The trails that trekkers use are the public transportation and communication routes for the local people.

Trekking, as described here, means travel by foot for many days. During this time, travelers can spend nights either in the homes of local people or in recently constructed simple hotels, or they can camp by themselves. They can eat either local food, or food they have brought with them. In fact, on many journeys through populated areas to lonely heights, it is customary to try all of the above variations. Most of Nepal is not wilderness as the term is understood in the West. Trekking routes pass through rural, sparsely settled areas, the homeland of the Nepali people. Visitors need to be cognizant of the local values and culture, a subject expanded upon in chapter 4.

In recent years the number of tourists visiting Nepal has leveled off, but the number of trekkers continues to increase. In 1988, almost 50,000 trekking permits were issued. If this number discourages you from going, realize that by choosing one of the rarely visited areas (see end of chapter 2) you can almost be assured of not meeting another trekker.

Trekking is a very healthy activity, although not without its hazards. It is strenuous and burns calories, so that many overweight people shed their excess load along the trail. Smokers may cut back on their consumption of cigarettes. And everyone feels his or her muscles strengthen and firm up. To be sure, there are hazards and lower standards of hygiene. Furthermore, modern health care is not available in the hill and mountain areas. But when sensible precautions are taken, few get sick in Nepal. To the contrary, most people find it physically and spiritually enlightening.

How to Use this Book

To pursue an interest in trekking, some basic decisions need to be made early. Chapter 1 outlines the most important one, namely whether or not you want to go with an agency, and when. You must decide this early on. If you go with an agency headquartered outside Nepal, most of your arrangements will be made with them. If you decide to go on your own, or with a Nepali agency, then more preparations are needed, including the obvious one of getting to Nepal. Flights to Kathmandu are usually heavily booked during the major tourist seasons, so the sooner you start this process the better. If you plan to go with a Nepali agency, you should contact them soon too. It helps to try to work with several and choose one that fits your needs and seems responsible. See the list of trekking agencies in appendix A.

The material in chapters 2, 3, and 5 should be considered next. Begin exercise, both mental (see chapter 4) and physical. I hope you will want to learn some Nepali, so obtain the language tape and accompanying pocket reference from your bookstore. At your leisure, look at Section III, and the routes in Section II. You may wish to follow specific interests, perhaps through appendix B.

Most likely, on your return home, or even sooner, you will be looking at appendix D, and considering other treks. It will no longer be hard to understand why this tiny country has had such a profound impact on foreigners.

Morning along the Mayagdi Khola

1 Trekking Styles

It's the richest banquet imaginable. For anyone with an appetite for fantastic legends, a thirst for color (especially red), and a general craving for utter theological wonder, visiting Nepal is a case study in all-you-can-eat.

Jeff Greenwald, *Shopping for Buddhas*

There are three basic approaches to trekking, but within each there are many variations as well as some related activities that can be enjoyed during or between treks. The style you choose depends on your budget, time available, and personal preferences. The areas you wish to visit dictate certain choices. Finally, your choice depends on what you want from your trek.

Trekking without a Guide

This mode, also known as the "live on the land" approach, is very popular among budget-conscious travelers as well as those who wish to live among the people of Nepal during their treks. This is a good way to learn Nepali, if traveling off the popular routes. You can sleep and eat with the local people, or in areas where there are no inhabitants, carry your own food and shelter. Food can often be purchased at the last inhabited place on your route, but be sure to check availability beforehand. Along the popular routes, your main human contacts usually are with other, similar-minded trekkers. Local porters can usually be hired anywhere along a trek. If you have porters, they can keep you on the right trails.

Along the popular trails, enterprising Nepalis have established hotels that provide rooms for trekkers and offer international menus. Villagers are very likely to run after you or at least shout if you take the wrong turn on a trail. While this has diminished the sense of adventure, it has made it easy for people to travel without a guide, carrying their own small loads. Of course, by avoiding these popular trails, it is still possible to experience Nepal as it was before trekking tourism became popular.

Such travel, especially on the standard treks described in this book, can be very rewarding and expenses can be quite low. Daily costs, not including any porters, can be less than U.S. $5 per person. This is the way that I prefer to trek.

Disadvantages of this mode of travel can include spending considerable time in Kathmandu organizing affairs, getting lost occasionally—especially when traveling off the standard routes—and being limited in the areas you can travel to.

Recognize that the more trekkers in the party, the less interaction there will be with the local people, and the less intimate your experience with Nepal will be. Two trekkers is probably the limit for a close interaction with the people, unless most participants speak Nepali.

Trekkers who choose to travel without a guide are more likely to be disappointed in some of their expectations than those who have their treks catered through a professional agency, although most people seem to manage quite well. But the advantage of trekking without a guide is that learning to deal without the cultural props you grew up with can be a very educational and enlightening experience. Attempting to view the world through Nepali eyes may be the best lesson trekking in Nepal has to offer.

Trekking with a Guide

This mode of travel can mean arranging and outfitting a large trek just as a professional agency would do. Or it might mean simply hiring a guide to accompany a small group. A guide can keep the party on the correct trails and may sometimes cook, carry a load, or attend to other chores. Many guides are quite knowledgeable and can be a valuable resource to explain things seen, and what is not seen. Porters—that is, people hired strictly for load-carrying—can be taken on along the trail when necessary, or hired in Kathmandu before starting a trek. The guide can take care of this. Parties may camp all the way; or they may eat and sleep in local homes or hotels and camp only where necessary. Those camping all the way must carry considerable food and equipment. This is a good way for older people and those wishing less uncertainty about the quality of food and accommodation to travel, providing they bring along enough equipment and food for comfort.

Recognize that if you have a staff of more than say, four, it is unlikely that fast times can be made over long distances. The larger the party, the more likely that it will move at the customary pace for specific treks (see Guides and Porters in chapter 3).

A guide can be hired either privately, or through a trekking agency. The agency can also make other arrangements, such as providing equipment and porters. Agencies tend to either offer a self-sufficient camping trek or a "tea house" trek without intermediate options. Nevertheless, you can often talk your way into other possibilities with them if you try. Guides can often be hired at points along the trek for difficult portions and high passes, although this can't be assured in advance.

Parties wishing more of a spirit of adventure—and a savings on wages— can hire an inexperienced guide. Such a person may be an older Sherpa who has been a porter for treks and mountaineering expeditions, or a youngster eager to break into the business. Such people can be excellent and will often do much more than guide—they can cook, carry things, and help in other ways. On my first trek in Nepal in 1969, I hired a young inexperienced Sherpa. We both learned a great deal and enjoyed ourselves immensely.

The advantage of trekking with a guide is that it allows considerable flexibility in the choice of route, diversions, and scheduling. There is also a greater opportunity for interacting with the local people encountered en route, especially if the party is small. However, arranging all this after arriving in Nepal can be time-consuming, frustrating, and somewhat difficult, and it is sometimes helpful to seek the assistance of a local trekking agency.

Trekking in a modest style is a good means of getting money into the hands of people in the hills of Nepal, since the villagers, who provide food, run the inns, and work as porters, benefit directly. This may be a more effective means of economic assistance than international aid. Costs for this style are less than for professionally arranged treks, and depend on the number of assistants hired.

Trekking with a Professional Agency

While initially only Mountain Travel, founded in 1965 by the indomitable Himalayan veteran, Lieutenant Colonel James Roberts, was able to offer comprehensive trekking arrangements for the traveler, many similar business operate today.

Many travel agencies and organizations based in other countries operate treks for groups to various regions of Nepal. The actual arrangements for the treks are customarily handled by one of the approved trekking agencies in Nepal. No listing of non-Nepali agencies is given here, but information about them can be obtained from travel agents in your own country. Even though a particular trekking agency in Nepal works with an affiliated agency in your country, you can usually deal directly with the Nepali agency if you prefer. A list of these is provided in appendix A.

This mode of travel is expensive, but it offers a degree of luxury that is not available in the others. Treks are organized for both large and small groups and are usually conducted by Sherpa guides called Sirdars, who are often famous for their mountaineering exploits on Himalayan expeditions. The guides speak sufficient English to allay fears of language difficulties. A large retinue of porters ensures that nothing essential to the comfort and well-being of trekkers is left behind. The parties usually camp in tents near villages and skilled cooks prepare fine meals. Most of the necessary equipment is provided. These parties often have someone with medical expertise along and emergencies can usually be handled more quickly than in less experienced groups. There is also no need to spend time planning for all these arrangements in Kathmandu. Trekking with an agency means there is a company to complain to if there are problems, something that is important to some visitors.

Agency trek parties usually have to stick to a predetermined route and schedule, so there is less leeway for interesting diversions or layovers. Members of large parties generally keep together. Trekkers in these professionally organized parties are usually rather insulated from the local people encountered en route. Indeed, the participants tend to relate exclusively to one another, to the guides, and to other employees of the trek.

Certain areas, such as the regions around Kangchenjunga and southern Dolpo, are only open to trekkers going through an agency. This is an attempt by the government to lessen the environmental impact.

If going with an agency, ask how many rest days are built into the schedule at high altitude. Also ask how flexible the schedule is should a member of the party develop altitude illness. Be aware that it appears that most of the serious cases of altitude illness develop among group trekkers, because these parties try to stick to a predetermined schedule, and peer pressure seems to push people beyond their limits. If the party will sleep above 14,000 ft (4270 m), do they carry oxygen, and do they have a Gamow Bag™? (For details, see Altitude Illness in chapter 5.)

Ask if all the cooking, including meals for the porters, is done on kerosene. Ask if porters are provided with sufficient equipment so they don't need to huddle around fires at night to keep warm, and can deal adequately with the conditions. Inspect the porters' equipment. Given the scarcity of firewood in Nepal, it is necessary for the trekker going with an agency to choose one that minimizes its impact on the environment.

Some agencies are offering tea house/trekker lodge-style treks. In these, accommodation and food is contracted out to the various establishments en route. This results in a cheaper trek, compared to the traditional camping style. A guide is along to take care of logistics, and interpret features about the countryside. This mode is suitable for small groups. With the competition among the numerous agencies increasing, many will negotiate various arrangements for trekkers.

Arrangements are usually made, either directly or through agents, before leaving your own country. However, many trekkers wait till they come to Nepal and then go visit various agencies and shop around to see what can be organized for them at short notice. It is preferable to arrange this in advance, but for one or two trekkers not planning a route far off the beaten path, this can work out fine.

The costs, exclusive of air fares and charters, run from about U.S. $35 to $100 per person per day and vary according to the length of the trek and the number of people in the party. This kind of travel is especially suited for those who have neither the time nor the desire to make their own arrangements, but wish to enjoy the scenery of the country. In contrast to people who prefer other styles of trekking, those who embark on this type of trek are paying for comfort and security.

Some people argue that an agency trek is preferable since your food is carried from Kathmandu and does not deplete local resources. On such treks, however, all of the food for the porters is purchased along the route, and some food for trekkers may be purchased locally as well. The argument that Sirdars for trekking groups will get the best prices for local foods does not always hold up. When the primary concern is that the trek go well, cooks and Sirdars can pay high prices for food items. As a consequence, the price for villagers goes up too. Traveling on your own or with only a few employed people reduces the impact on the local food economy.

Finally, much of the money to support an agency trek leaves Nepal to pay for imported food and equipment. There is little sharing of profits with the locals. An estimated 80 percent of Nepal's dollar earnings from tourism is spent to import goods and services required by visitors. This figure seems high, but it does spell out the situation. I don't mean to discourage travel with agency treks. It is best to decide what your hopes, needs, and means are and to travel accordingly.

Choosing a Trekking Style

It is basically true that "anybody" can trek in Nepal—if they try to match their level of experience to the difficulty of the journey they plan. Given the tremendous travel expense, time commitment, and for many, a once-in-a-lifetime opportunity, ambition can easily outstrip ability. Trekking in the Himalaya was once considered at the high end of the spectrum of walking, backpacking, and mountaineering. Often, mountaineers experienced in ranges such as the Alps, Rockies, or Sierra become "mere" trekkers in the Himalaya, where routes carry them thousands of feet above the summits of their home ranges.

But these days, a disturbing trend is changing the nature of trekking in Nepal. Less experienced hikers are electing to undertake harder treks. Walking in the mountains is a skill that requires some training and experience. Recently, the number of tourists who have fallen from trails (fatally and nonfatally) is up dramatically. Inexperienced hikers are becoming incapacitated by severe musculoskeletal problems that could have been prevented by adequate training.

Trekking should be regarded as an expedition: you are often days from any form of outside help, and unless you are experienced and confident of your self-sufficiency skills, first treks should be on established tourist trails that offer a minimum of difficulty and no dangerous passes. The scenery in Nepal is no less exotic because other outsiders have seen it before you. As your experience, skills, and confidence grow, you can plan more challenging, isolated, and adventurous treks.

Trekkers should be aware that there is now a worldwide movement afoot to promote what is variably known as "alternative tourism," "discerning tourism," "gentle tourism," or "tourism with insight." Advocates try to promote travel that is consistent with local needs, and attempt to maintain local cultural values and remain environmentally sensitive.

MORE TIME THAN MONEY

If you crave adventure, have plenty of time but limited money, want to adapt your schedule to circumstances, and want to interact with local people as much as possible, then organize your own trek, especially if you want to travel one of the popular routes.

MORE MONEY THAN TIME

An organized trek with one of the well-known agencies may be for you if you have a limited amount of time yet want to cover a major route and can accept limitations in flexibility. An agency trek may be an attractive option if you enjoy the idea of camping in Nepal with food prepared to familiar tastes and with all arrangements made for you. One disadvantage of such treks is the relative lack of close contact with the local people.

Of course, the dichotomy is not quite so cut and dried. Many agencies allow some flexibility in scheduling, and with increasing competition they try to adapt treks to your needs.

Another "decision tree" for the first-time trekker to Nepal is the following: If you are on a tight budget, basically go trekking on a popular route and stay in local inns and tea houses. If you enjoy carrying a pack, then don't hire a porter—but if you don't want to carry anything heavier than a day pack, hire a local porter. Those with more funds, and perhaps more anxiety about doing it themselves, often hire a guide and porters, usually through an agency in Kathmandu, and stay in local hotels.

If you have more money to spend, and have your own group, organize a trek through an agency, and stay in tents. If you don't have a group, and are willing to travel with strangers, join an organized group through one of the agencies in Kathmandu. Those with a lot of money and wanting as few hassles as possible should join an organized trek from their home country.

Trekking Alone

Those trekking alone would be wise to hire a guide or a porter, especially on trails with few foreigners. If traveling alone along the popular trails, you will find it easy to meet up with similar-minded people. Plan to touch base with them periodically for support. It is also easy to meet and join up with other trekkers in Kathmandu; people advertise for trekking partners on bulletin boards in tourist-frequented places.

Women should not travel alone but should try to find a female guide or porter. Nepalis find it difficult to understand why foreigners, especially women, would travel alone—indeed, Nepali women wouldn't. Local people seem to consider a woman walking alone to be a witch or person of low morals. The same caution applies to men, although it is more common to see a Nepali man traveling alone. On a recent trek in which I went with three porters, Tupi Pasang, a yak herder, remarked to me: "You must be a poor man in your country; you're traveling alone and with few porters or supplies." Nevertheless, I find traveling alone the best way to get to know Nepal.

There have been rare instances of attacks on trekkers, usually those who are alone, camping in remote areas. I can no longer state that you are perfectly safe from human harm in Nepal, but if you follow the principles outlined in chapter 4 and are sensitive to your hosts, you should have no problems. Travel in Nepal is certainly safer than in almost every other country, including your homeland.

Trekking with Small Children

Small children need not be left at home in order for the adults of a family to enjoy a trek in Nepal. Certainly a trek with children will be different from one without children, but it need not be any less enjoyable or memorable. In fact, children can be real icebreakers in an alien land; they provide a common

Trekking infants never lack for a babysitter in Nepal.

link with which the local people can identify.

When I first came to Nepal in 1969 no one trekked with children except occasional expatriates working there; now you can often see families along the trails, especially those more popular with tourists. The Nepali village people are open and friendly for the most part, and the sight of a trekking family will interest them. Indeed, while you eat, they will often care for the child, holding, comforting, and playing with it. Although a small child may initially be overwhelmed by the interest of outsiders, an exciting cultural exchange can be encouraged if the child becomes accustomed to the local people. Flexibility in the itinerary is particularly important if the family hopes to achieve this communication. Many of the difficulties encountered in trekking with children in Nepal can be overcome if the family tries some overnight trips near home. In fact, I would not recommend that a family attempt trekking in Nepal if they have not done overnight hikes at home. In chapter 5 there is an important section on health care for children. It should be read concurrently with this section.

It is probably best not to travel with very young children, perhaps those under five years of age, unless parents have prior trekking experience in Nepal. If a child is over five, it is advisable to have more than one child along for companionship. Families who wish to trek independently of an agency will find it easiest to take one of the popular routes where lodges cater to trekkers.

Don't assume that treks must be modest in scope. One family with children aged four and six trekked with another family with a child of six. They covered almost 500 mi (800 km) in fifty-five days, from Pokhara to Baitadi in the extreme western part of Nepal. This trek was more ambitious than most people would choose to undertake with children of that age, but for them it was a wonderful experience that none of them will forget. The two families, by carrying moderate packs themselves (30 to 50 lb, 13 to 23 kg) and living off the land insofar as possible, were able to get by with only two porters. They never carried any of the children except across streams or rickety bridges. Thus the pace was slower than that of normal adults, but they compensated for this by increased attention to peripheral activities, such as photography and bird-watching. The children appeared to thrive on the physical exercise. They received lots of personalized attention from their parents and were constantly stimulated by new sights and activities. At the end of the day, they had little energy left and usually fell asleep soon after dinner.

It may not be inappropriate to consider taking older children out of school for a trek. Understanding school officials will probably agree that what the children learn on the trip far outweighs any loss in class room learning. Parents can help children keep journals of their activities and adventures, which will aid them with their writing and provide a resource for later use.

Younger children need not be left at home. Infants can trek, though I would recommend that only breast-fed infants be taken. One trekking family with a two-year-old found it most convenient that the child was still breast feeding. In Nepal children nurse at their mother's breasts until they are quite old. Certainly this is the most sanitary method of feeding, and it has many other health benefits.

Families with younger children have carried them in a back- or front-style pack carrier. A back carrier with an elevator seat is probably best. Other families hire a porter, the best being a woman—a Sherpani or hill Nepali. It will be difficult to hire just one woman. Two together could porter and help take care of the child. Most such women have children themselves and enjoy singing and playing with the child. They usually prefer carrying the child in a *Doko,* a conical wicker basket, using a tumpline. A foam pad for the inside and an umbrella attached to the basket rim for shade keep the child comfortable. It is not unreasonable to carry a child up to 44 lb (20 kg) in this manner. Some children, especially active ones, may not tolerate being carried in a basket by a stranger. The method you choose depends on your personal preferences. Certainly carrying your child can contribute to an important relationship with him or her.

Children in diapers need not be a problem. Use cloth diapers, which either you or the porters wash. It is not a chore that a porter can be expected to do, but an arrangement can be worked out beforehand. Your porter will probably prefer to wash the diapers away from town, and out of sight of the villagers. Try to avoid pollution of streams when washing diapers. Bring a string for a clothesline, soap, and clothespins. Drying diapers would be very difficult in the monsoon. In fact, it is probably not advisable to trek with young children at that time. Nepali children never use diapers as we know them. A few disposable diapers may come in handy in case of diarrhea, even for a toilet-trained child. Disposable diapers are not available in Nepal except in the new supermarkets in Kathmandu. Burn them out of sight of others and bury the ashes. A "potty" or chamber pot for toilet-trained children may be helpful. Otherwise, unfamiliar surroundings may make defecation difficult for them.

Food for children can vary a great deal. The children of one trekking family soon became willing consumers of *daal bhaat,* the local rice-and-lentil dish. Those on treks organized by professional agencies have few problems if the cook prepares familiar foods. A great deal depends on the parents' attitude and their children's food fussiness. It may be wise to keep some favorite snacks handy.

Parents who have hiked with their children under various conditions should have no difficulties choosing clothing for them. The new synthetic-pile garments, worn over a zippered pajama suit, may be the best choice for cold days. Such clothes are warm, light in weight, and quick drying.

Useful ideas include discussing each day's plans with the children, what the trail might be like, the kind of people they'll meet, their fears, and how to interact with Nepalis. Rules for youngsters on the trail should include: no running downhill, no getting out of sight, no rock-throwing, drink plenty of liquids, and put on extra clothing right away when stopping in the high, cold regions.

Most children, like many adults, find it difficult to be continually stared at. This is the case when staying in a Nepali home that is not set up as a hotel, with separate rooms for trekkers. To avoid this problem, take a tent or choose one of the popular treks with lodges or hotels along the way. A tent gives your children a familiar place to go, away from the prying eyes of the crowds that always assemble to stare at the funny little white kids. Children may find it reassuring to sleep between their parents when in unfamiliar surroundings.

Your children may be surprised to see that Nepali children have few toys. It is wise to bring a few items to keep your children amused since they won't be as inspired by the beauty of the countryside as you. Playing with toys with the Nepali children could be fascinating for your children, but avoid setting an unfortunate precedent by indiscriminately giving out toys to local children. Nepali children are quite happy with the toys they have, and they could become quite envious if they knew about the toys they don't and can't have. Getting your children to play with the simple toys that Nepali children use could be an important formative experience.

Be aware of the physical hazards in Nepal. There are plenty of places inside homes, along the trails, and in the fields where a slip or fall could be disastrous for a child. Dogs (particularly rabid ones) represent an occupational hazard for trekkers in Nepal, and even more so for children. Exercise extreme caution around all dogs and villages, as options after being bitten are few and unpleasant. Children should avoid petting stray dogs. Although they are not known to be carriers of rabies, water buffalo frequently have surly dispositions and delight in charging small children. I would advise getting the pre-exposure rabies vaccine for your children.

Altitude may affect children more than adults. Also, it may be difficult to ascertain whether it is altitude or some other illness that is causing symptoms in infants and young children. (See Altitude Illness in chapter 5.) Like most aspects of trekking in Nepal, the experience of going as a family can be rewarding and enlightening if you prepare yourself adequately.

Trekking in the Monsoon

In Nepal all paths and bridges are liable to disappear or change at no notice due to monsoons, act of Gods, etc.
Note on trekking map, 1972

Although many consider it out of the question, trekking during the rainy season has been discovered by a select few "Nepalophiles." There are several reasons to consider joining these eccentrics. Many people can come to Nepal only during the Western summer holidays, which correspond to the monsoon. Some want to trek when popular trails are not packed with foreigners, or are interested in the plant and animal life that is most spectacular at this time. It is undeniably a most beautiful time of the year. Everything is lush and green. The clouds perform dramatically, and periodically part to reveal the splendor of spectacular vistas. Mist-shrouded mountain views during the monsoon may be unforgettable. The high country is alive with activity as people pasture their animals on the upper slopes.

During the monsoon, Nepal is much like it was years ago, except that now there are better bridges, portable radios, more supplies available, and children who may remember to beg when they see you. You can plan your route either to get behind (north of) the Himalaya (north of Pokhara), or to the far west (RaRa), or into the Himalaya (Khumbu) to experience less rainfall. See the climatological data in the next chapter.

There are many problems, however. Everything tends to get soaked. Trails are often very muddy, always wet, and sometimes treacherous. It is always hot and muggy at low altitudes, though more comfortable higher up. Distant views are clouded most of the time. Bridges sometimes wash out, necessitating time-consuming and difficult detours. What may have been a trickle in the dry season becomes a deep, fast torrent in the monsoon. Travel often involves fording rivers. At times you may have to wait a day or two for the water level to drop enough for a safe ford. To make matters worse, leeches populate

Nepalis and their animals camping near lush vegetation during the monsoon

the forests at higher altitudes (see chapter 5), while mosquitoes abound at lower elevations.

Yet, just as you adjust to trekking in Nepal during the dry season, so you can adapt your lifestyle to the monsoon. Certain items of equipment are essential: a waterproof cover for your pack, sheets of plastic for the porter loads, an umbrella, and footwear with good traction, preferably new waffle-soled training flats or boots with flexible Vibram soles. Light skirts for women, preferably with a hem about calf length, and shorts for men are the most practical clothing. Most waterproof rain parkas and cagoules are not very useful—if you do not get wet from the outside, you will soak in sweat from the inside. Gear made from Gore-Tex™, a fabric that breathes yet is waterproof if kept clean, may be suitable for the monsoon when at higher altitudes. Gore-Tex™ jackets with underarm zips allow considerable ventilation, as do pants with side zips. Pile clothing or garments of synthetic, downlike material are useful in the wet high altitudes.

In planning a monsoon trek, do not plan on covering too much distance in a short time. It is hard to equal dry-season trekking times. Many of the trails will be different during the monsoon. Drier ridges are usually taken instead of the flooded valley bottoms. Take time to enjoy village life, to sample the fruits and vegetables in season, and to enjoy the prodigious plant life. And do not tell too many people how much you enjoyed it!

Himalayan Weight-Loss Treks

Are you in adequate physical shape but want to lose ten to twenty pounds, never be hungry while doing so, and want to keep the weight off? Undertake a twenty-day trek along a popular trail, carry your own pack, and eat as much *daal bhaat* twice a day as you wish. It works!

*Ascending to Shipton Pass, en route to Makalu Base Camp
(photo by Pat Morrow)*

2   Choosing A Trek

Just go on and on. . . . Do you see the mountain ranges there,
far away? One behind another. They rise up. They tower. That
is my deep, unending, inexhaustible kingdom.

                                             Henrik Ibsen, *The Master*
                                             Builder

In choosing a trek, many factors must be considered. Among them are the time available, the strength and ability of the members of the party, and the desires of the trekkers. Certain treks offer majestic mountain scenery; others a glimpse of hill life in Nepal; still others spectacular floral displays. Routes can be linked to provide many different experiences. Some entail entering potentially dangerous mountain terrain. Finally, the time of year is very important, as certain treks are difficult if not impossible during heavy snowfalls. Others are very uncomfortable in the pre-monsoon heat.

Weather

The usual trekking season lasts from October to May. During the remainder of the year, the monsoon makes traveling wet and offers little in the way of mountain views. In addition, leeches abound.

During October and November the skies are generally clear and good views can be expected. Occasional short storms may occur and the temperature often goes below freezing at night above 10,000 ft (3050 m). This is the most popular time for trekking.

December and January are the coldest months, but there is little snowfall. Again, excellent clear views are common, though there seems to be more haze in recent years, at least around Kathmandu. Temperatures constantly plunge below freezing at night above 10,000 ft (3050 m) and below 0° F (−18° C) at altitudes above 14,000 ft (4300 m). Some inhabitants of the northern Himalayan region head south for the winter at this time. It can be a hauntingly beautiful time of the year to trek.

February and March bring warmer weather, but more frequent storms and considerable snowfall at higher altitudes. Birds and flowers, especially the rhododendrons, are seen at the lower altitudes. Toward the end of March, haze—caused by dust from the plains of India—and smoke from local fires often obscure distant views. In addition, it becomes much warmer in the regions below 3000 ft (1000 m).

April and May are less suitable for trekking because of the heat—sometimes 100° F (38° C)—at altitudes below 3000 ft (1000 m). Also, the haze mars distant views of the peaks. During these months, however, you encounter

CLIMATOLOGICAL DATA FOR SELECTED TREKKING TOWNS

(First line: Precipitation [mm]. Second line: Temperature—Max/Min [°C])

Town (Altitude [meters/feet])	Jan.	Feb.	March	April	May	June	July	Aug.	Sept.	Oct.	Nov.	Dec.
Kathmandu (1336/4383)	18 19/2	11 21/3	33 25/7	54 28/10	83 30/14	270 29/18	383 28/19	338 28/19	160 27/17	62 27/12	7 23/7	2 20/2
Trisuli (541/1775)	20 22/7	23 25/8	29 30/13	57 34/17	90 33/19	319 33/21	463 32/20	474 32/20	265 31/18	107 30/15	14 27/12	5 23/8
Langtang (3500/11483)	2/-11	3/-10	8/-6	14/-2	17/2	18/7	19/9	18/8	16/7	15/2	9/-8	8/-10
Pokhara (827/2713)	26 19/6	25 21/8	50 26/12	87 30/15	292 30/18	569 29/20	809 29/21	705 29/21	581 28/20	224 26/17	19 23/11	1 20/7
Lumle (1615/5300)	28 13/5	45 14/6	52 19/10	194 22/13	318 22/14	902 23/17	1522 22/17	1339 23/17	932 21/16	294 20/14	23 16/9	2 13/6
Marpha (2667/8750)	14 10/-1	13 12/0	27 15/3	22 18/5	26 19/7	44 21/11	63 21/12	58 21/12	45 20/11	58 17/7	7 14/2	2 12/0
Jomosom (2713/8900)	20 12/-3	18 13/-1	23 16/2	15 20/4	11 23/7	17 25/12	41 25/14	54 25/14	35 23/11	37 19/5	2 15/1	2 13/-2
Chame (2615/8580)	3 9/-3	71 13/1	72 14/1	— 20/7	50 19/6	106 21/11	182 21/10	65 21/10	145 19/10	59 17/6	8 14/1	24 11/-3
Jumla (2329/7640)	32 11/-2	40 13/-3	43 17/0	27 22/3	40 24/6	70 24/13	162 23/15	173 24/15	92 23/12	39 24/6	1 19/-4	4 15/-5
Jiri (1905/6250)	18 13/0	20 15/1	47 19/4	71 22/8	139 22/12	381 23/16	599 23/17	605 23/17	337 22/15	93 20/10	15 17/4	3 14/1
Namche Bazaar (3446/11300)	26 7/-8	23 6/-6	34 9/-3	26 12/1	41 14/4	140 15/6	243 16/8	243 16/8	165 15/6	78 12/2	9 9/3	39 7/-6
Tengboche (3867/12887)	13 4/-9	24 5/-9	23 9/-6	25 12/-4	29 14/-1	95 14/3	280 14/5	265 14/4	140 13/2	72 12/-2	9 8/-7	2 6/-7
Taplejung (1783/5850)	15 14/4	32 15/6	55 19/9	111 22/2	243 23/14	335 24/17	448 24/18	400 24/7	271 23/16	82 22/13	14 18/8	4 15/5
Ilam (1300/4265)	10 16/9	8 18/10	18 23/14	62 25/16	139 25/17	321 25/18	463 25/18	280 25/19	215 25/17	81 25/16	8 21/12	2 18/8

many species of plant and animal life not seen at other times. As the season progresses, the magnificent rhododendrons bloom at higher and higher altitudes until the flowers reach the treeline. Occasional pre-monsoon storms clear the haze and cool the atmosphere for a few days. While temperatures below freezing can be encountered above 12,000 ft (3600 m), it becomes quite warm below 8000 ft (2500 m) and almost oppressive below 3000 ft (1000 m).

Depending on the year, travel in the high country can be difficult because of heavy snowfalls, especially during January, February, and March. Passes, such as the Thorung La, Trashi Labsta, the one near Gosainkund, the high route from Pokhara to Jumla, and the Ganja La heading north into Langtang are best attempted in autumn through December or in late spring.

Trekking in the monsoon (June to the end of September) can be undertaken by the keen or experienced. Rain, mist, and fog can be expected almost daily, but occasionally clouds part to give spectacular views of the mountains. The flora are usually at their most colorful.

It is important to keep in mind that mountain weather is highly unpredictable. Classical signs of a storm approaching, such as a cirrus-clouded sky or a fall in barometric pressure, can be misleading. Occasionally, unexpected heavy storms can wreak havoc. In October 1987, a surprise storm dumped several feet of snow in all the high areas, resulting in some trekker deaths among those who were unprepared.

The table on page 32 gives precipitation and maximum and minimum temperatures for various trekking locations. You can estimate temperatures for other nearby locations by a simple formula. For a rise of 100 m the temperature falls 0.65° C; or for a rise of 1000 ft, it falls 3.5° F. Metric units are used with conversion scales below.

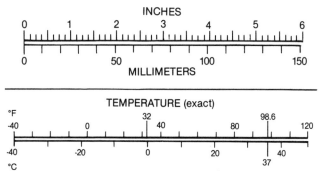

Helambu, Gosainkund, and Langtang

The trekking most accessible to Kathmandu is in Helambu, Gosainkund, and Langtang, all north of the capital city. There are trails linking the three regions, and as many can be visited as time and conditions permit. The minimum time for a brief visit is a week. Two weeks would allow you to combine two of the regions, and in three weeks you could enjoy the entire area. The ethnic groups encountered are: the Hindu castes, lower down; *Tamang,* in the middle elevations; and people who call themselves Sherpa in the Helambu region and *Gurung* in the Langtang, higher up.

Helambu is the region closest to Kathmandu. It is best approached from the northeast rim of the Kathmandu Valley. The name refers to a region at the north end of the Malemchi Khola (river). It is inhabited by people calling themselves Sherpas, though they are not closely related to the famed Sherpas of the Everest area. This region south of the main Himalayan chain provides an example of typical hill life in Nepal. A circuit can be made through the area with minimal backtracking if snow does not prevent travel on one high-level stretch. The trails are fairly good and only a few sections are difficult to follow. Cooked food and lodging are easily available, except on the high-level stretch. The route begins in areas of Hindu influence and goes through Buddhist villages. Side trips are possible and linkups can be made with Gosainkund and Langtang, weather conditions permitting. There are distant views of the Himalaya on the high-level stretch in good weather, except during late spring when they may be obscured by the haze. Rather than backtrack to Kathmandu you could vary your exit to reach the Kathmandu–Kodari road, either at Panchkhal if you head south from Tarang Marang.

Gosainkund is the site of several lakes that lie south of a major ridge between Helambu and the Trisuli River to the west. The area is uninhabited for the most part, but every August as many as 50,000 pilgrims crowd into the area for a festival near a lake that figures prominently in Hindu mythology. Trekkers may wish to visit this area from Dhunche reached by road from Kathmandu, and, if conditions permit, cross a moderate pass to link up with Helambu. In the spring when rhododendrons are in bloom, it is a spectacular area. Trekkers heading into this area may now find accommodations for most if not all of the journey.

Langtang is a Himalayan valley that lies north of both Helambu and Gosainkund. It is inhabited by Tibetan people and provides a glimpse of mountain life. Trails are straightforward, yet you can head east in the Langtang Valley beyond the last habitation to spectacular remote mountain areas, taking various side trips. Food and lodging are available for the most part. Linkups with Gosainkund are reasonably simple; but those with Helambu require crossing a substantial pass, for which you must be self-sufficient. There is a little-used airstrip in the Langtang Valley at Kyangjin where planes can be chartered. They can be used to leave the area, but should not be taken in because the altitude gain is too abrupt. Most of Langtang and Gosainkund has been included in Langtang National Park in an attempt to preserve their beauty.

North of Pokhara

The area north of Pokhara is popular both with trekkers new to Nepal and with veterans. Expect to meet people from many different countries. The mountain scenery is as spectacular as any in Nepal, especially on the high

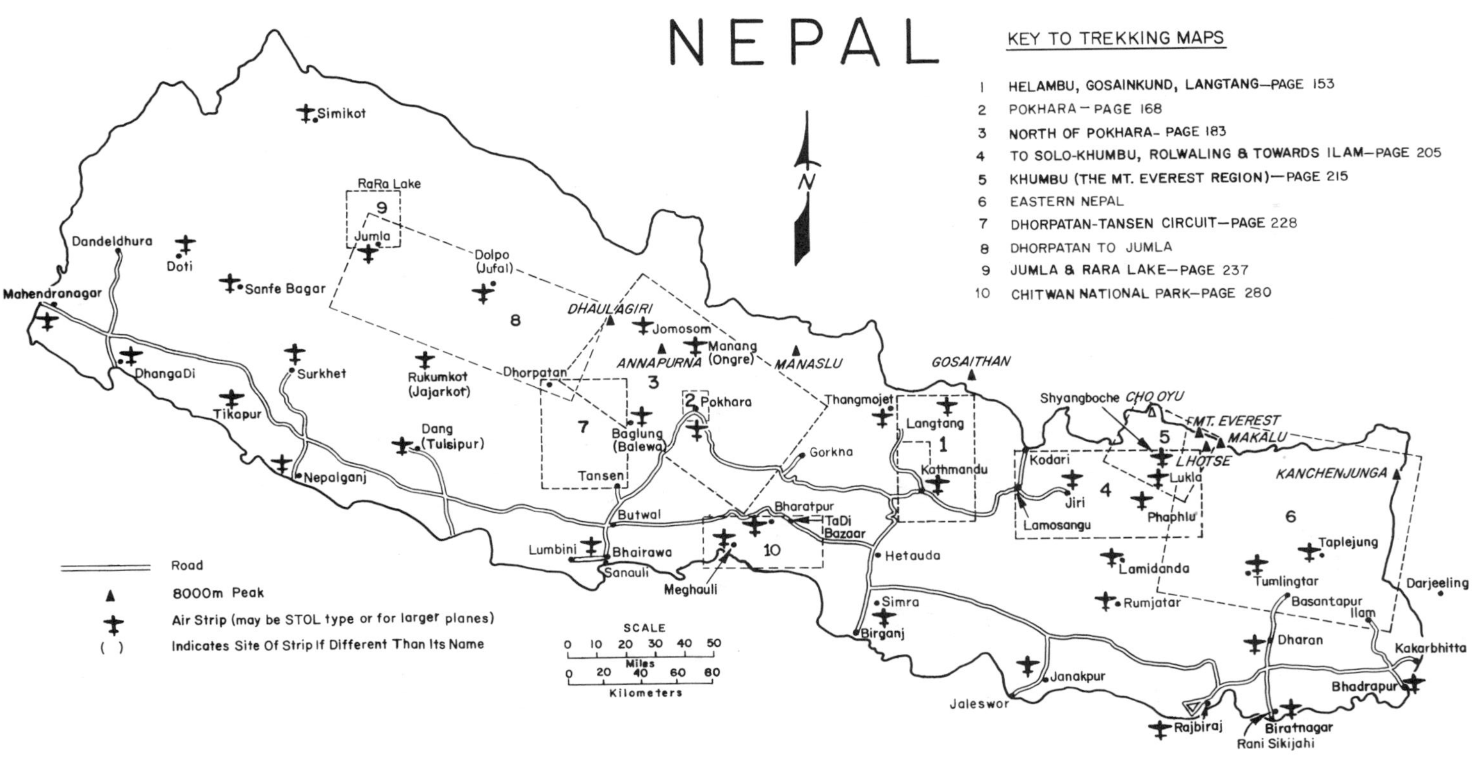

NEPAL
KEY TO TREKKING MAPS
1 HELAMBU, GOSAINKUND, LANGTANG—PAGE 153
2 POKHARA—PAGE 168
3 NORTH OF POKHARA- PAGE 183
4 TO SOLO-KHUMBU, ROLWALING & TOWARDS ILAM—PAGE 205
5 KHUMBU (THE MT. EVEREST REGION)—PAGE 215
6 EASTERN NEPAL
7 DHORPATAN-TANSEN CIRCUIT—PAGE 228
8 DHORPATAN TO JUMLA
9 JUMLA & RARA LAKE—PAGE 237
10 CHITWAN NATIONAL PARK—PAGE 280
N
Simikot
RaRa Lake
Jumla
Dandeldhura
Doti
Sanfe Bagar
Mahendranagar
DhangaDi
Surkhet
Tikapur
Nepalganj
Dolpo
(Jufal)
Rukumkot
(Jajarkot)
Dang
(Tulsipur)
DHAULAGIRI
Jomosom
Manang
(Ongre)
ANNAPURNA
MANASLU
Dhorpatan
Baglung
(Balewa)
Tansen
Pokhara
Gorkna
Butwal
Lumbini
Bhairawa
Sanauli
Meghauli
Bharatpur
TaDi
Bazaar
GOSAITHAN
Thangmojet
Langtang
Kathmandu
Hetauda
Simra
Birganj
Jaleswor
Janakpur
Shyangboche
CHO OYU
MT. EVEREST
MAKALU
LHOTSE
Kodari
Lamosangu
Jiri
Lukla
Phaphlu
KANCHENJUNGA
Taplejung
Lamidanda
Tumlingtar
Rumjatar
Darjeeling
Basantapur
Ilam
Dharan
Kakarbhitta
Bhadrapur
Rajbiraj
Biratnagar
Rani Sikijahi
Road
8000m Peak
Air Strip (may be STOL type or for larger planes)
( ) Indicates Site Of Strip If Different Than Its Name
SCALE
0 10 20 30 40 50
Miles
0 20 40 60 80
Kilometers

routes. The many different ethnic groups are as interesting, if not as famous, as the Sherpas of Khumbu. Those encountered include the Hindu castes lower down, *Magar, Gurung,* and *Thakali* at middle elevations, and *BhoTiya* higher up. Some of the areas provide perhaps the finest native cuisine in rural Nepal. One ethnic group, the *Thakali,* runs numerous inns and hotels in the area. They have adapted their menu in many cases to the palates of foreign trekkers and can provide food and accommodations for those who wish to avoid local diets and the lodgings used by hill Nepalis.

Finally, and perhaps most significantly, most of the treks in this region traverse through many different ecological zones. They begin with the customary terraces of the hills, encounter rain and deciduous and pine forests, pass through arid desertlike country similar to the Tibetan Plateau, and even reach alpine areas. Remarkable transitions through different areas, each with its customary animal life, can be made in a week or less.

Perhaps the most famous trek is from Pokhara to the Kali Gandaki river and up it to the Thak Khola region and to Jomosom, the administrative center of Mustang District. This route does not go higher than 10,000 ft (3048 m) and is not too strenuous. Along the way there are plenty of inns and hotels that cater to single trekkers or small parties. The trek is quite suitable for those traveling without guides or porters. The trail goes through an incredible variety of vegetation and follows one of the deepest gorges in the world—that between Annapurna and Dhaulagiri. On this route you are likely to encounter colorful mule caravans made musical by the tinkling of neck bells. Several side trips out of the Kali Gandaki valley are possible. They are strenuous, but they reward tired hikers with spectacular views and give trekkers a sense of the size of the valley. This is a justifiably popular trek, and the only way to avoid meeting other trekkers all along the trail is to take the side trips. Ten days is the minimum time for a round trip to Jomosom. Most parties prefer to take two weeks and travel up to Muktinath (12,475 ft, 3802 m), an ancient pilgrimage site a day beyond Jomosom.

The Annapurna Sanctuary, the basin southwest of Annapurna that is the source of the Modi Khola, is a fine objective for those who wish to trek only a short time, yet include a trip into alpine country. There is not quite the same variety in vegetation as on the trek up the Thak Khola since you never get north of the main Himalayan chain. The *Gurung* villages en route are particularly colorful. Ten days is the minimum time. Snowfall and avalanche hazards may make it difficult, if not impossible, to reach the sanctuary in winter. During the peak season, cooked food and shelter may be available for the entire journey.

Both the Annapurna Sanctuary and the Thak Khola route toward Jomosom are very popular, because there are plenty of lodges and restaurants conveniently set up for trekker traffic. Expect to meet many foreigners, as well as friendly Nepalis, and get wonderful mountain views.

Manang, the region north and east of the Annapurna massif, is a third worthwhile objective north of Pokhara. This area was not opened to foreign travel until 1977, and gets less trekker traffic. The people of the villages of Manang are traders and, many of them, world travelers. The scenery north of the main Himalayan chain is spectacular. It takes over a week to reach the town of Manang if you walk the entire way from Dumre or Pokhara, though most trekkers now take a vehicle to Besisahar, shortening the walk by two days. There are no *Thakali* here running the kind of hotels and lodges for tourists that you find on the trail to Jomosom. But the local people have set up comparable inns and hotels that cater to Western tastes. Beyond, a high pass, the Thorung La, leads over to Muktinath. This pass can be difficult or impossible in the winter and early spring because of snow. But for those able to cope with the high altitudes, the pass allows a complete circuit of the Annapurna massif without backtracking. You can usually travel across the Thorung La during the popular season without using your own food or shelter.

The classic trek in this region, combining Manang and Thak Khola in a circuit, covers more than 150 mi (240 km) and requires at least three weeks. The Thorung La pass is best crossed from Manang to Thak Khola in order to allow enough time for acclimatization. Crossing this pass is a major undertaking, and is not for those without adequate clothing. Crossing in the winter (generally December through March) is equal to a winter climb in the Himalaya. Don't even consider it unless you have the requisite experience and equipment. It is feasible to include the Annapurna Sanctuary on the circuit. There are airstrips at Jomosom and Hongde, so scheduled or charter flights from Kathmandu can shorten treks. You should not fly up and then attempt the pass without acclimatizing first. The altitude gain is too abrupt for safety. Many trekkers with little time make a circuit from Pokhara to GhoRepani, down to the Kali Gandaki, to Baglung, and then to Pokhara. Other such circuits include: to Ghandruk via Chandrakot and return via Dhampus; to GhoRepani and return via Ghandruk. There are many other fine possibilities. A road is being built from Pokhara to Beni and Baglung, and this will change access to the area north of Pokhara. This area provides great ethnic and geographic diversity together with spectacular mountain scenery. A trek here can be as easy or as difficult as you wish.

The Annapurna Conservation Area Project (ACAP) is a nongovernmental organization set up to balance the effects of trekking tourism in this entire region with sustainable development for its residents. ACAP has improved trails in the area, built toilets and garbage pits, organized litter collection in the Annapurna Sanctuary, standardized menus and set prices at lodges, and produced useful publications. They have also printed a Minimum Impact Code for trekkers to help preserve the wonderful experience visitors have here for future generations. Their headquarters and visitors center are in Ghandruk. Regional offices are in GhoRepani, and others are planned. Trekkers should also visit the Annapurna Regional Museum at the Prithvi Narayan Campus of Tribhuvan University in Pokhara.

Pokhara can be reached from Kathmandu by foot, road, or air, or from India by road or air. If traveling from Kathmandu, it is currently much easier to fly, as the road is in a state of disrepair. Flight delays to or from Pokhara may be common during the peak tourist season, so it is best to make reservations as far in advance as possible.

Solu-Khumbu

Solu-Khumbu is the district south and west of Mount Everest. It is populated by Sherpas, an ethnic group that has achieved fame because of the exploits of its men on mountaineering expeditions. Khumbu is the name of the northern half of this region, which includes the highest mountain in the world and many of the 8000 m (26,247 ft) summits. Most of Khumbu is part of Sagarmatha National Park. Solu, the southern portion, is less rugged but it has many interesting monasteries and villages.

The attractions are the majestic mountains, the villages in the high mountain valleys, the associated monasteries, and the legendary inhabitants. The area is popular, and, outside of the monsoon, many trekkers are encountered. Some potential visitors might be put off by this, but where else can you find so many of the world's highest mountains together with communities of people living among them? Twenty-five times more tourists crowd into Yosemite Valley on an average summer *day* than into Khumbu in a *year* (9000 in 1987)! While you can count on meeting many trekkers on the standard route to the base of Mount Everest (except in the monsoon), it is quite possible to spend time in Khumbu and its environs and meet few other trekkers.

A survey of trekkers conducted in October 1978 rated the following trails according to number of trekkers (in order from highest to lowest): Namche Bazaar to Pheriche; Pheriche to Lobuche; Namche Bazaar to Khumjung-Kunde; Namche Bazaar to Thami; Lobuche to Kala Pattar; Namche Bazaar to Gokyo, to Phortse, to Chhukhung, to Gokyo's Kala Pattar, to Everest Base Camp, to Island Peak, to Trashi Labsta, to Pass 5420 m.

Travel to and from Khumbu can pose logistic problems. Royal Nepal Airlines (RNAC) has scheduled flights from Kathmandu to Lukla, an airstrip located one to two days south of Namche Bazaar, the entrance to Khumbu. While getting flights to Lukla can be a problem, finding a seat back to Kathmandu can be even more trying since weather sometimes delays landings for weeks! Several hundred trekkers can be stranded there, with patience wearing thin. There are other airstrips in the region, but the one at Shyangboche, close to Namche Bazaar, is even higher. However, it is not useful for flights out, as there are currently no scheduled flights. Trekkers who land at high altitudes such as at Lukla and venture into the rarefied altitudes are at greater risk of altitude illness. It is preferable to walk to Khumbu, and to fly out if you can tolerate delays. Part of the pleasure of walking to Khumbu lies in enjoying the beautiful countryside of hill Nepal and in anticipating your arrival in Khumbu as you follow the footsteps of many mountaineering expeditions.

Two weeks is the minimum time I would recommend spending in Khumbu if your goal is the foot of Everest. If you walk from Lamosangu on the Kathmandu–Kodari road and fly back, the entire trip takes three to four weeks. Most people shorten the trip by taking a bus to Jiri from Kathmandu, three days farther in from the main road. Walking to and from Khumbu makes that part of the trip two weeks. By walking in, the trekker samples midland Nepal as well as the Sherpa country. Many trekkers find the walk to Khumbu from Jiri better than the destination itself. Ethnic groups encountered along the way include the Hindu castes, *Tamang, Jirel,* and *Rai.* Other approaches to Khumbu on foot include walking to Rolwaling either from Barabise on the Kathmandu–Kodari road, or from Charikot on the Lamosangu–Jiri road, and crossing the Trashi Labsta Pass. Another attractive route is to walk to or from the southeast and the Arun drainage. Also you can enter and leave from the Tarai. Finally, airstrips at Phaphlu in Solu, and at Rumjatar and Lamidanda in the south, can shorten approaches or exits. Flying to or from Phaphlu is an especially attractive alternative.

For those planning to trek on their own, there should be few problems obtaining cooked food and shelter on the standard route to Khumbu, except for the last day of the trek to the base of Mount Everest. However, shortages do occur at times, and it is best to carry some food in reserve. While a Sherpa guide or porter may not be absolutely necessary, one whose home is in Khumbu can often give you a hospitable base of operations.

The Khumbu trekking area offers a visit to the homeland of the Sherpas, a chance to get close to the highest mountain in the world, as well as the feeling that you are surrounded by peaks.

Western Nepal

Generally, the part of Nepal west of the Kali Gandaki river is not often visited by trekkers. The facilities for trekkers are few and distances are great. There are very few roads suitable for launching treks and, unless you charter a plane, air transportation is difficult. Food is sometimes impossible to obtain. Except for the treks near the Dhaulagiri Range, there are few trails that provide views of spectacular mountains. In fact, Dhaulagiri is the only 8000 m peak in Nepal west of the Kali Gandaki. The feeling of being right in the mountains that is common in, say, Khumbu is rare here.

In spite of the difficulties, the rewards are many. The hills of western Nepal are characterized by majestic forests and interesting vegetation. Population pressures have yet to contribute to extensive deforestation. The country is very rugged and, in the northern reaches, has a feeling of openness. The people are also very interesting. The farther west you go, the less contact they have had with Westerners. This can create difficulties in getting their cooperation.

The main trekker destination in the west used to be a circuit from Jumla to RaRa Lake, the site of a national park. Jumla is reached by scheduled planes from Kathmandu, but getting a seat on a return flight direct to Kathmandu can be difficult due to weather problems. Most flights are now "rice charters" from Nepalganj that return mostly empty. In addition, there is more frequent service to Nepalganj than Kathmandu. Hence it is easier to get from Jumla to Nepalganj, and then to take a scheduled flight from there back to Kathmandu. Food and shelter must be carried on the week-long circuit. Finding the way can be a challenge, so those on their first trek in Nepal should hire a guide if they are not on a professionally organized trek. Very few trekkers visit this region, even now. In 1981, only ten trekking permits were issued for RaRa. Ethnic groups encountered on this trek include *BhoTiya, Thakuri,* and the Hindu castes.

A contemplative spot during the monsoon in Western Nepal

In 1989, restrictions were lifted on trekkers passing through most of Dolpo District. This too has enabled a classic strenuous trek to be done from Pokhara to Jumla, crossing several high passes, and visiting Shey Phoksumdo National Park. Regulations stipulate that treks through Dolpo must be organized through a trekking agency, and that food and fuel must be carried. There are no hotels such as those around Annapurna, or through Khumbu, that cater to the trekker. It is a difficult, rewarding journey through one of the most remote areas of Nepal. Ethnic groups met along the way include *Magar, Chantel, Tarali,* and *BhoTiya.*

Another trek is a circuit from Pokhara to Dhorpatan, returning via Tansen, the capital of an old kingdom. It can be walked in less than two weeks.

From Tansen you can either return to Kathmandu by road via Pokhara, or motor to Bhairawa in the Tarai and fly from there. The trek can be shortened using regular RNAC flights to Balewa near Baglung. Food and lodging are available along most of the route. There are excellent views of the Dhaulagiri Range and you can take side trips into more mountainous country. Fewer than a hundred trekkers a year currently visit Dhorpatan.

In general, if this is your first visit to Nepal, choose one of the other treks unless you have some specific reason for wanting to trek in western Nepal. On the other hand, if you are a veteran trekker and are looking for new, exciting, interesting experiences, go west and enjoy them.

Eastern Nepal

The region around Kangchenjunga has recently opened up for treks organized through an approved agency. Only 500 trekkers per year will be allowed permits, issued on a first come, first served basis, as a trial policy. This policy attempts to lessen the environmental impact of trekking on the frail ecology of this mountain region. The area has been little affected by trekking tourism, as most of the visitors were on mountaineering expeditions. How it will develop is unclear, and will partly depend on whether it becomes popular with trekkers, and whether the government relaxes its restrictions. Trekkers will encounter the Hindu castes, *Tamang, Rai,* and *Limbu* as well as *BhoTiya,* some of whom call themselves Sherpa, and others *Wallungi.*

Once you leave the region near Taplejung, the district center for the most northeastern district in Nepal, and head into the mountains, the lifestyle is much as I remember during my earliest treks in 1969. That is, there are as yet no trekker lodges, few if any tea shops, many difficult trail sections, and pristine forests. If not camping, and cooking for yourself, the only other way to get along is to walk up to people's homes and offer to pay for food and lodging. However, just as the area was opened up for trekkers in 1988, some children had begun to beg—the result of the first few trekkers' behavior modification techniques! Also, toilet paper now litters the formerly pristine trails in the high country.

Three weeks to a month is an appropriate time to get to and explore either the North Kangchenjunga Base Camp or the south, or even both. The walk in and out has much to offer, and a circuit of sorts can be made to avoid much backtracking. The "grand tour" encircling Kangchenjunga done by Freshfield's party in 1899 (he sneaked into forbidden Nepal from Sikkim and India) is currently not allowed either, and the chances of escaping detection are nil. Maybe someday, when borders are mere lines on a map and nothing more, we will be able to entertain this notion.

The routes described in this book make several journeys possible. I describe flying to Tumlingtar on the Arun Khola from Kathmandu, since that is currently the easiest predictable access. There is an airstrip at Taplejung that puts the trekker even closer to Kangchenjunga, but there are few flights from Kathmandu, and these are often canceled. There are also flights there from Biratnagar at present. It is also much harder to get out of Taplejung by air.

The other major access would be by road, usually from Kathmandu. The long journey is not as formidable as it used to be, on account of regular, almost pleasant, night bus service from Kathmandu to Dharan, Biratnagar, or Ithari (on the East–West Highway, at the junction to Dharan). Seats can be reserved, and it is even possible to get enough leg room for my 6-foot-5-inch (196 cm) frame! Once in Dharan, another bus can be taken to Basantapur and foot travel begun there. Another access would be via the road that leads to Taplejung, passing through Ilam. Currently the road leads to Ghopethar, and service is irregular.

How future road construction will change the access and affect trekker choices is unclear. I would continue to recommend the route as described here, since it traverses interesting eastern hills, which are generally more wealthy and better developed than in western Nepal. Furthermore, reaching the ridge that Gupha Pokhari sits on and walking along it is an idyllic walk in itself, affording views of the massive Kangchenjunga Range, as well as the entire Everest, Lhotse, and Makalu group. Where else can you gaze upon five (Cho Oyu is there, too) of the world's fourteen 8000 m peaks all at the same time?

It is difficult to travel here without using porters and carrying food. Close to Kangchenjunga, the villages are scattered, and often have little food to spare; and it is not cuisine up to the standards of hill Nepal, where the *Thakali* run *bhaTTi* in central Nepal. Furthermore, in places the trails are narrow and often very exposed, and require caution.

In addition to the Kangchenjunga route, a description is given of another way to get to Khumbu from the east, this one (unlike the exit over the Trashi Labsta) suitable for all trekkers. This is the walk from Tumlingtar to Karikhola. It takes about five days and is best done during the winter when there is little haze from the plains of India to obscure the view. Also the weather in the lowlands is coolest at this time.

Another trek that is becoming more popular is to ascend the Arun Khola from Tumlingtar to reach the Makalu Base Camp in the upper Barun Khola valley. Ethnic groups encountered include the Hindu castes, *Tamang, Rai,* and Sherpa. Once you leave Tashigaon, the last inhabited place where food can be obtained, it takes about five days to reach the base camp, so food and porters are necessary.

Other Treks

The treks described in chapter 11 include an exit from Khumbu across the Trashi Labsta, a high pass to the west (18,885 ft, 5775 m), and through Rolwaling to the Kathmandu–Kodari road. The pass is strenuous and hazardous, and unsuitable for neophyte trekkers. Sir Edmund Hillary once said it was one of the hardest passes he had ever crossed. Some mountaineering experience is required, and food and shelter must be carried. The trek takes a minimum of ten days. It is best attempted in the early autumn or late spring. During the winter, the crossing would be a formidable Himalayan climb. Don't even consider it unless you have the requisite experience and equipment. The route can be followed in reverse to visit the Rolwaling Valley, an incredibly steep-walled

Camping below the west side of the Trashi Labsta (photo by Mary Lynn Hanley)

valley inhabited by Sherpas. It is a fine objective in its own right, although it is not advisable to cross from Rolwaling to Khumbu because of the abrupt altitude gain. Careful parties can do it successfully if they take time to acclimatize.

Consider linking several treks. Some wanderers head from Kathmandu to Khumbu, then to Makalu, and on to Kangchenjunga. You could essentially traverse all the Himalaya in Nepal, as has already been done.

In contrast to treks to hill and mountain regions, a trip to Chitwan National Park provides an example of the country, people, animals and vegetation of the Tarai. Like other treks described in this book, it can be done economically. About five days is an appropriate time to spend on the round trip from Kathmandu.

Areas you might consider include the Arun Valley in the east, and to the Hongu Basin. Areas in central Nepal include the Bara Pokhari Lekh north of Chiti, the upper Chepe and Darondi Kholas, and the area south of Ganesh Himal as well as crossing the Rupina La. Some trekkers consider the mountain panorama from the Singla Pass, below Ganesh Himal, to be the finest in Nepal. Encircling Manaslu by crossing the Lakya La after traveling up the Buri Gandaki is an exciting new option. There are many possibilities in the west, among them heading up the Mayagdi Khola to French Col, then to Thak Khola via Dhampus Pass. Consider visiting Khaptad National Park in the west. But before trying one of these, get some experience on the more popular treks.

All of Nepal is now open for trekking, though most areas such as Mustang, Humla, Mugu, and Dolpo require organizing your journey through a trekking agency. There are regulations that must be followed, in addition, for these areas.

Many of the former restrictions were imposed due to the disdain for the prevailing rules and limits shown by earlier travelers. If all trekkers abide by the regulations, there may be fewer restrictions imposed on travel due to the transgressions of a few.

After gaining some basic experience in Nepal on some of the treks described in this book, the person yearning for adventure can easily strike out to visit places where few outsiders have been. The opportunities are endless.

Travel From Nepal To Tibet

In the autumn of 1988 there were irregular flights from Kathmandu to Lhasa, depending on the season and popularity. To get a month's visa in Kathmandu to visit the Tibetan Region of the People's Republic of China, you must go on a prearranged tour with a travel agency. These tours are relatively informal but rather expensive. It appears that you can leave the tour and travel on your own at some point, perhaps returning to Nepal overland, which is permitted when crossing at Kodari. You can also go overland via this route to Tibet, but currently only on a prearranged tour. If you wish more freedom to travel independently, get a visa to China at another Chinese embassy (easiest in Hong Kong) and travel to Tibet through China. The political situation in China has recently restricted independent travel in Tibet. Trekking from Humla to Kailash is currently permitted. All this information is subject to change, based on political and bureaucratic considerations.

Summary of Treks

Easiest

Chitwan National Park
Pokhara to Jomosom

Moderate

Dhorpatan circuit
Gosainkund
Helambu
Jumla to RaRa Lake circuit
Langtang
Kangchenjunga Base Camp
Makalu Base Camp
North of Pokhara to Jomosom
Rolwaling Valley

More Difficult

Pokhara to Jumla, through Dolpo
High-altitude wanderings north of Pokhara, in Khumbu, and beyond Rolwaling
High passes such as the Ganja La, Trashi Labsta (most difficult and hazardous), and Thorung La

Shortest (a few days)

Initial part of most any trek
Flying to Lukla, Hongde, or Jomosom, walking a day or two without altitude gain, and flying back

Around a week

Gosainkund
Helambu
Khumbu—flying in and out, but not going to Everest Base Camp or Kala Pattar
Langtang
Pokhara to Ghandruk circuit
Pokhara to GhoRepani circuit
RaRa Lake circuit

Two weeks or more

Dhorpatan circuit
Combining two areas north of Kathmandu

Pilgrim at a Buddhist shrine

Khumbu—flying in and out, and visiting Everest Base Camp and Kala Pattar
To Manang and back from Pokhara
To Kangchenjunga Base Camp, flying (or driving) to Taplejung
Rolwaling
To Thak Khola heading north from Pokhara, returning the same way

Three weeks or more

Dhorpatan circuit with side trips
Helambu, Gosainkund, and Langtang
Khumbu with plenty of side trips or walking from Kathmandu and back
North of Pokhara with a lot of side trips or the Annapurna circuit
Pokhara to Jumla
Kangchenjunga Base Camp
To Makalu Base Camp

Most spectacular mountain scenery

Annapurna circuit
Khumbu
Upper Langtang Valley
Manang
Side trips north of Pokhara, such as Annapurna Sanctuary, Annapurna Base
     Camp, Dhaulagiri Icefall, Tilicho Tal, or Dhampus Pass
Kangchenjunga Base Camp
Makalu Base Camp
Upper Rolwaling Valley

Good springtime introduction to flora, especially rhododendrons

Eastern Nepal (Kangchenjunga or Makalu Base Camp)
Dhorpatan circuit
Gosainkund, Helambu, and Langtang
RaRa Lake circuit
Rolwaling
Solu-Khumbu

Greatest cultural and geographic diversity

Pokhara to Muktinath or Jomosom
Pokhara to Jumla (through southern Dolpo)
Annapurna circuit

For those seeking new adventures

Monsoon treks—even in areas you have visited before
Far west or far east treks
Re-walk a trek you did ten or more years ago
Trek with few if any other trekkers on a less popular route
Take your family (spouse, parents, children)
Don't go with an agency if you have done so previously
Don't hire any guides or porters who speak English

Focus on a specific interest (flowers, birding, local crafts, photography, architecture, etc.)

Go on a pilgrimage at the time Nepalis visit pilgrimage sites

Climb a trekking peak if you have the requisite mountaineering experience

Check appendix D, After Trekking, What Next?

Most popular treks in decreasing order (based on number of trekking permits issued in 1987)

North of Pokhara (30,914)
Khumbu (8998)
Helambu, Langtang, Gosainkund (6107)
Others (1256)

Most popular time to trek (in decreasing order based on number of permits issued)

October
November
March
April
December
February
January
September
May
August
June
July

Treks with few other trekkers

Dhorpatan circuit
Khumbu to Ilam
RaRa Lake
To Rolwaling
Kangchenjunga Base Camp
Makalu Base Camp
Pokhara to Jumla

Table of Treks

	Ghorepani or Tatopani and return	Annapurna Sanctuary	Pokhara to Jomosom and return	Dumre to Manang and return	Around Annapurna	Chitwan Park	Langtang loop	Helambu loop	Gosainkund and Helambu	Langtang, Gosainkund	Ganja La	Lukla to Kala Pattar	Jiri to Kala Pattar	Cho La in Khumbu	Tesi Lapcha	Tumlingtar to Khumbu	Makalu Base Camp	Kangchenjunga Base Camp	Dhorpatan Circuit	Pokhara to Jumla via Dolpo	Rara Lake
Comfortable lodges	x	x	x	x	x	x	x	x	x	x	x	x	x	x	x						x
Mountain passes		x			x						x			x	x	x	x	x	x	x	x
Hill passes	x	x	x	x	x				x	x		x	x	x	x	x	x	x	x	x	x
Hill terrain	x	x																			
River valley bottoms	x	x	x	x	x	x	x		x	x	x	x	x		x		x	x	x	x	x
High altitude pastures	x		x	x	x		x		x	x	x	x	x	x		x	x	u	x	x	
Road travel used			u	u	u	u	u		u	u		u	u			u		u		u	u
Airstrips used												x	x			u	u	x		u	u
Distant mountain views	x	x	x	x	x	x	x	x	x	x	x	x	x	x	x	x	x	x	x	x	x
Close mountain views	x	x	x	x	x		x		x	x	x	x	x	x	x	x	x	x			
Being inside mountain ranges	x	x	x	x	x		x		x	x	x	x	x	x	x	x	x	x			
Tarai Jungle						x															
Meet many trekkers	x	x				x	x	x	x	x		x	x								
See few other trekkers	m	m	x	x	m		m	m	m	m	x	m	m	x	x	x	x	x	x	x	x
Be amongst Sherpas											m	x	x	x	x	x	x	x			
See a variety of Nepali cutlures		x	x	x	x							s	s			x	x	x	x		
See rhododendrons												s	s	s	s	s	s				
Cross high passes		x		x	x		x	x	x	x	x	x	x	x	x	x	x	x	x	x	x
Want to stay warm	x	x	x	x	x			x		w		w	w					x			w
Objective danger, altitude illness, frostbite, exposure	w								w			w	w	x	x	x	x	x	w	x	x

x = present anytime   w = winter   s = spring   m = monsoon   u = usually

Setting out delicious meals of daal bhaat *in a* bhaTTi

3   Preparations

All obstacles are blessings of the guru.
A *BhoTiya* saying

Remember this saying when in Nepal, for, despite all your careful preparations, some "serendipitous accident" may occur. The message in this chapter is "be prepared," but most of all, be prepared to be flexible and to make the best of all circumstances. Trekking in Nepal, like any other activity, is usually more successful if the participants are ready, and if they have some idea of what to expect.

Visas and Permits

Most travelers to Nepal need a visa. This can be obtained from one of the Nepali Embassies and Consular Services in eighteen countries throughout the world. The visas are valid for up to one month. Two passport-size photographs are necessary for the application, and travelers should bring a dozen or so to Nepal for use in formalities.

Visas valid for fifteen days only are issued at entry points to Nepal. The main entry points are: (1) Kathmandu, for those arriving by air; (2) Kodari along the Nepal-Tibet border (open only to those in organized groups; you can often join a group through a travel agent in Kathmandu); (3) Birgunj across from Raxaul, India, on the main road from India to Kathmandu; and (4) Sunauli across from Nautanwa, India, near the town of Bhairawa on the road from India to Pokhara. Other border points with India, less used by tourists, are: DhangaDi, Jaleswor, Kakarbhitta, Koilabas, Mahendranagar, Nepalganj, and Rani Sikijahi. Travelers coming by road need a *carnet de passage* for their vehicles. There is also bus service on the main roads.

Nepali Embassies and Consular Services are located in Edgecliffe, Australia; Vienna, Austria; Dacca, Bangladesh; Brussels and Antwerp, Belgium; Rangoon, Burma; Peking and Lhasa, Peoples Republic of China; Cairo, Egypt; London, England; Bonn, Dusseldorf, Frankfurt, and Munich, Germany; Paris, France; Hong Kong; New Delhi and Calcutta, India; Tokyo, Japan; Beirut, Lebanon; Islamabad, Pakistan; Bangkok, Thailand; Washington, New York and San Francisco, United States; Toronto, Canada; and Moscow, Soviet Union. There may be honorary consuls in other locations from time to time.

Trekking regulations also change from time to time, so it is wise to check by writing to one of the trekking agencies. At present, permits are required for all areas except the Kathmandu and Pokhara valleys and Chitwan National Park. All of Nepal has been opened to trekking. Specific regulations apply in the formerly restricted areas. See page 44.

Under current regulations, trekking permits are issued at the Central Immigration Office of the Home Ministry, His Majesty's Government (HMG), at Tridevimarg (Thamel) in Kathmandu, and in Pokhara near the airport. A visa extension is issued first, then a trekking permit for one trek at a time. The places that you are permitted to go are stated on the permit and are standardized for the popular treks. In applying, state the northernmost town in each major valley as well as names of towns with police check posts. Two passport-size photographs are required and a fee is levied. Bring a supply of passport photographs with you to Nepal and a negative to print more if necessary. If you forget, there are several shops supplying instant passport photos near the Immigration Department in Kathmandu. The trekking permit must be presented at all police check posts along the route and annotated by the post nearest to the destination. It is a good idea to have the permit annotated at all check posts to verify that you have in fact traveled with the permit. This procedure may be helpful in getting visa extensions. With the increasing number of incidents occurring to trekkers, it is especially important to check in at police posts in case you end up missing or being sought in an emergency. A trekking agency can handle many of the formalities.

The limit for tourist visas is four months in any twelve-month period. Extensions for one month at a time can be obtained through the Central Immigration Office in Kathmandu for the first three months. For the fourth month, you have to apply to the Home Ministry. An initial visa for one month can be obtained from Nepali embassies abroad, or at an entry point to Nepal. Extensions can usually be granted only in Kathmandu or Pokhara, though occasionally it may be possible to obtain one-week extensions at a police post.

Visas and trekking permits now can usually be obtained the same day if you apply early. All government offices are closed on Saturday, the weekly holiday, and on other holidays, which are frequent.

It cannot be stressed too strongly that you should attempt to put forward a pleasant image in dealing with the immigration officials. Be considerate, dress neatly, and try to minimize the element of distrust that Nepali officials may have of foreigners. You will have fewer problems if you do so.

National Parks and Conservation Areas

Seven areas of Nepal have been designated national parks. They include the Shey Phoksumdo, Langtang, RaRa, Royal Bardiya, Khaptad, Royal Chitwan, and Sagarmatha (Everest) national parks. Foreigners must pay a fee and obtain a park permit at the entrance. Buying wood from locals or taking it from the forests is illegal in the parks. All travelers are required to carry non-wood stoves and fuel. Violators can be arrested and fined. The flora and fauna are protected. Enquiries can be directed to the Department of National Parks and Wildlife Conservation at Babar Mahal, near the Department of Forests, in Kathmandu.

In addition to national parks, there are wildlife reserves and conservation areas. These are alternatives to designating an area as a national park. Trekkers visiting the Annapurna Conservation Area pay a fee to the King Mahendra Trust for Nature Conservation at the time they obtain their trekking permit. The funds collected are spent on sustainable development projects for the residents of the region, as well as the conservation of natural resources. Unlike the situation with national parks, where the park entrance fee goes into the general government treasury, the fee you pay to visit this region is spent on local community development.

Maps

Modern topographical maps suitable for trekking are difficult to find for many areas of Nepal. Nevertheless, there is a variety of maps available and I have provided a fairly complete listing here that may be of use to aficionados.

The maps in this book are intended to help the reader visualize the route descriptions. They are drawn to scale and show the towns and trails described in the text. Except for major ridge features and drainage systems, little else is depicted. Trekkers not especially interested in maps should find them adequate, but those who appreciate good maps should try to obtain the Schneider maps and may also enjoy the book *Maps of Nepal,* by Harka Gurung, listed in appendix B.

The series of maps most used by trekkers is produced by Mandala Maps. Trails, towns, and some contours are shown on most of them, but these features are not always correct, as they were drawn by people who haven't trekked. They are usually poor dyeline copies of artwork, though recently improved versions are being printed. Nevertheless, they are sufficient for most trekking purposes. Maps to cover most of the commonly trekked areas are available sporadically. Titles include: *Kathmandu, Helambu, Langtang, Gosainkund; Pokhara to Jomosom, Manang; Pokhara to Round Dhaulagiri Himal; Lamosangu to Mount Everest; Kathmandu to Pokhara; Jomosom to Jumla and Surkhet; Jumla to Api & Saipal Himal; Jugal Himal; Khumbu Himal; Dhankuta to Kangchenjunga, Mt Everest, Makalu and Arun Valley;* and *Jumla to RaRa.* The series is also called "Latest Trekking Maps." Expect other local publishers to continue to produce similar maps.

Because of extensive mountaineering interest in the Khumbu region, there are excellent maps of it and of some nearby areas. Currently the best available are published by Kartographische Anstalt Freytag-Berndt und Artaria, Vienna, Austria. The *Tamba Kosi–Likhu Khola Nepal* sheet covers about five days of the hill portion of the trek to Khumbu. The *Shorong/Hinku* sheet covers the next portion to just below Namche Bazaar. The *Khumbu Himal Nepal* sheet covers the region from Namche Bazaar north. The *Lapchi Kang Nepal* and *Rolwaling Himal (Gaurishankar) Nepal* sheets cover the trek from the Kathmandu–Kodari road to Rolwaling and beyond. The *Dudh Kosi* sheet covers the southern part of Solu. These modern topographic maps on the scale of 1:50,000 (one inch = 0.8 mi) are produced by the Research Scheme Nepal Himalaya and are accurate in almost all respects. An earlier version of the *Khumbu Himal* sheet was published in 1957 as *Mahalangur Himal.* It covers only an area close to Mount Everest and has a scale of 1:25,000 (one inch = 0.4 mi). Heading further west, the *Helambu–Langtang* sheet covers the appropriate area north of Kathmandu on the 1:100,000 scale. This map is less accurate than the others in the series. The region south of it is on the *Kathmandu Valley* sheet on the 1:50,000 scale. All that remains for popular trekking routes is the region north of Pokhara, but that area won't be mapped by this group for some time yet.

These maps are usually available in Kathmandu. They can also be purchased from the mail order sources listed below. They are expensive, but map lovers will find them hard to resist. In this text, they are often referred to as the Schneider maps after the original map maker.

A map titled *Mount Everest,* of both the north and south sides of the mountain, was published by the National Geographic Society in November 1988. On a scale of 1:50,000, it has details not present on the *Khumbu Himal* sheet of the Austrian series and is helpful for trekkers heading from Pangboche on up. Order it (#20033) from the National Geographic Society, Box 2806, Washington, DC 20013. It is often available for sale in Kathmandu.

The King Mahendra Trust for Nature Conservation has published a topographical map, *Annapurna Conservation Area,* on a scale of 1:125,000. This is available in Kathmandu and is the best map currently available of the country's most popular trekking area. Although the lay of the land seems well depicted, the trails and town placements are often inaccurate.

The country was surveyed between 1924 and 1927 by clandestine workers for the Survey of India. They ventured through the country with concealed survey instruments and did a creditable job. While the altitudes on their maps are not usually correct, the relative features of the topography south of the Himalaya are portrayed well. But the trails are not always marked accurately. The 1:250,000 series (one inch = 3.9 mi) of this survey is not generally available. Like most Indian cartographic materials, its distribution used to be restricted to official agencies. In the United States, the U.S. Army Map Service, Corps of Engineers, has recently printed these maps under the title Series 1501. Copies of these maps in the older U502 series are sometimes available from the sources listed at the end of this section. The sheets most useful to trekkers are:

NG 45— 3 *Kangchenjunga* (toward Darjeeling)
NG 45— 2 *Mount Everest* (Kathmandu to Khumbu and Rolwaling)
NH 45— 14 *Tingri Dzong* (north of above sheet)
NG 45— 1 *Kathmandu* (Gorkha to Kathmandu and north)
NH 45— 13 *Jongkha Dzong* (north of Kathmandu)
NH 44— 16 *Pokhara* (north and west of Pokhara)
NH 44— 4 *Tansing* (south of above sheet)
NH 44— 11 *Jumla* (Jumla to RaRa Lake, and east)

These and other useful maps can be seen at major map libraries, including those of the Library of Congress, and at universities. Some government offices in Kathmandu have maps from this series on display. Generally, unless someone is quite interested in cartography, the trekking maps available in Kathmandu and mentioned below will suffice for most people.

A scaled-down version of the Survey of India maps on the scale of 1:506,880 (one inch = 8.0 mi) is available to the public. These maps, Series U462, are published by the British Ministry of Defence. They can be seen at His Majesty's Government (HMG) Tourist Office in Kathmandu. A blue non-topographical version with recently built roads and airstrips is also sometimes available. A further scaled-down version on the scale of 1:780,000 (one inch = 12.3 mi) is available from American-Nepal Maps, c/o M.S. Holloway, 5831 Hampton Court, San Diego, CA 92120. Either of these versions gives general impressions of the topography, but few towns are marked and the delineation of the trails is not quite accurate. Nevertheless, they are the best general maps of Nepal available.

A map has been produced from land satellite imagery covering Nepal on the 1:500,000 scale. It is available from International Mapping Unlimited, 4343 39th Street NW, Washington, DC 20016. Although not too helpful for trekking, it depicts the country very well.

Maps produced for aircraft navigation are available from: DMA Combat Support Center, Attn: Docs, Washington, DC 20315-0010. They portray the topography well, but do not show most villages or trails. In the 1:500,000 (one inch = 7.9 mi) series, four sheets cover Nepal—TPC-H-9A, 9B, 9C, and 9D. In the 1:1,000,000 (one inch = 15.8 mi) series, ONC-HO-9 covers all of Nepal.

The Survey of India completed an aerial survey of Nepal in the early 1960s to produce maps on a scale of 1:63,360 (one inch = 1.0 mi). They are excellent, but almost impossible to find because of restrictions on distribution. The same is true for a more recent Nepali government series in the 1:50,000 scale.

There is a series of ecological maps published by the Centre National de la Recherche Scientifique (CNRS), and can be ordered from Librairie de vente du CNRS, 295 rue Saint-Jacques, 75005 Paris, France, or SMPF, 16 East 34th Street, 7th floor, New York, NY 10016. They are useful because they show vegetation zones and contain some ethnographic information. Presently available are:

Carte Ecologique du Nepal Region Annapurna–Dhaulagiri 1:250,000 (one inch = 3.9 mi)
Carte Ecologique du Nepal Region Jiri–Thodung 1:50,000 (one inch = 0.8 mi)
Carte Ecologique du Nepal Region Kathmandu–Everest 1:250,000
Carte Ecologique du Nepal Region Tarai Central 1:250,000
Carte Ecologique du Nepal Region Ankhu Khola–Trisuli 1:100,000 (one inch = 1.6 mi)
Carte Ecologique du Nepal Region Biratnagar Kangchenjunga 1:250,000
Carte Ecologique du Nepal Region Jumla Saipal 1:250,000
Carte Ecologique du Nepal Region Butwal–Mustang 1:250,000
Carte Ecologique du Nepal Region Dhangarhi–Api 1:250,000
Carte Ecolo gique du Nepal Region Nepalganj–Dailekh 1:250,000

Many accounts of mountaineering expeditions include maps that are useful to trekkers. Map sellers handling many of the maps (including sometimes those published in Nepal) are: Edward Sanford Limited, 12-14 Long Acre, London WC2E 9LP, England; Geo Center GmbH, Honigwiesenstrasse 25, Postfach 80 08 30, D-7000 Stuttgart 80, West Germany; Geo Buch, Rosental 6, D-8000 Munchen 2, West Germany; Reise und Verkehrsverlag, Gutenbergstrasse 21, Stuttgart, West Germany; Zumsteins Landkartenhaus, Liebkerrstrasse 5, 8 Munchen 22, West Germany: Libreria Alpina, Via C. Coronedi-Berti 4, 40137 Bologna, zona 3705 Italy; Bradt Enterprises Inc., 95 Harvey Street, Cambridge, MA 02140, USA; and Michael Chessler Books, P.O. Box 2436, Evergreen, CO 80439, USA, (800) 654-8052.

Finally, don't expect most Nepali people to be able to read maps, even the roughly 20 percent who are literate. They do have a superb spatial sense of the land, a quality few of us possess. Tapping this resource, should it be necessary, is one of the joyful challenges of traveling independently.

Equipment

Although much of the equipment used is the same, trekking in Nepal is different from backpacking as the term has come to be known in North America and Western countries. Here you are traveling in populated regions for the most part. My equipment preferences are based on considerable and varied experience in Nepal. Readers' suggestions from previous editions are also included. Much of the equipment described is current "state of the art" gear. Sophisticated designs are not really necessary for trekking, but it is important to have equipment adequate for the conditions. I have used many different types of gear while trekking in Nepal, sometimes going quite simply, though never as simply as the local Nepalis. There is considerable detail here, since many trekkers these days are not experienced backpackers.

To minimize customs hassles and delays, trekkers should carry equipment with them into Nepal, rather than shipping it separately.

Camping and mountaineering equipment used by Sherpas, other trekkers, and climbers on Himalayan expeditions is often available for sale or rent in Kathmandu, Pokhara, and Namche Bazaar. The number of shops selling and renting a variety of equipment has proliferated greatly in recent years. Much of it is new gear unused on expeditions. Prices vary from cheap to outrageous, and the quality is not uniform. Some trekkers sell their equipment after their treks by means of notices in restaurants and hotels. The variety of equipment available, like everything else in Kathmandu, is never constant. Some people are able to pick up everything they need in the city, but it is safer to come at least minimally prepared.

If you don't own items such as good down sleeping bags, jackets, foam pads, and packs, or if you have other travel plans that make it difficult to bring your own equipment, plan to rent. I would not advise renting footwear, so do bring your own shoes and boots, first wearing them at home to break them in before they "break you" on the trail. When renting equipment, don't leave your passport as collateral—you may need it. Cash, either Nepali rupees or hard currency (U.S. dollars, etc.), is usually left as a deposit.

FOOTWEAR

Comfortable footwear is a must, but opinions vary widely on what types are best. The requirements in footwear are: good traction, shock absorbency, waterproof, breathable, good foot and ankle support, light weight, durable, and with a separate insole. No single design works best for all situations. There are many choices for footwear, and a variety of good and bad designs appear in trekking stores in Kathmandu. But do not wait till you get there to buy.

Running shoes are popular and quite suitable below the snowline. But make sure they provide adequate traction. For this reason, the new "walking shoe," mainly designed for the city sidewalk, is not ideal. Running shoes, with good shock-absorbing heels, are excellent for downhill travel. Those with waffle soles, if new, provide excellent traction during the monsoon. However, this type of footwear is not suitable for snow. If you plan to cross high passes, take along substantial boots for snow and cold. Trekkers with inadequate footwear have suffered serious frostbite. The current substantial leather and fabric hiking boots with shock-absorbing heels are good for the hills—if they are strong enough to last. Individuals prone to ankle sprains should always wear boots that go over the ankle and provide support. Those troubled with knee problems, especially when going downhill, should wear boots or shoes with shock-absorbing heels. Sorbothane heel pads sold for running shoes may be helpful. Trekkers planning to carry a heavy pack are better off with a more substantial boot. As with any footwear, be sure to try it out at home on terrain similar, if in lesser scale, to that in Nepal.

For high-altitude treks, it makes sense to carry two pairs, a light, flexible pair, and a more substantial pair for rugged terrain. If they have removeable insoles, bring spares.

Do not bring an old, worn-out pair of boots or shoes to Nepal to trek in. They will have less shock-absorbing capacity in the soles, and the uppers are often coming apart. On long treks there may be considerable wear, especially to the uppers. Bring stitching material and Barge cement or epoxy glue for the soles. In snow or wet weather, appropriate waterproofing material is needed.

I prefer a Vibram-soled mountaineering boot for the high country where snow, ice, or rock is anticipated. But at most other times I wear a pair of light, flexible Vibram-soled boots with uppers above the ankles, or waffle-soled running shoes, the latter especially during the monsoon. I find one-piece leather uppers the most durable in boots, as there are no stitched seams to come apart. I also find the new rubber sandals, made by Teva, with velcro-attached straps that do not come between the toes, ideal to change into at the end of the day. They can also be used for some limited trail walking, and are unexcelled for wading streams. I wear wool socks over a light, thin pair of synthetic socks.

It cannot be overstressed that your footwear must be comfortable and remain so for days on end. Boots and shoes must be broken in before you come to Nepal. This can only be done by wearing them enough. Nothing makes a trek as miserable as uncomfortable boots or shoes.

If boots or shoes are irritating your feet, determine what the problem is. Does the foot move relative to the shoe or boot and create friction? If so, try using the laces in a creative way to decrease the movement. Try lacing loosely to the instep, then tying a knot and lacing tightly the rest of the way, especially for downhills. Boots with locking lace hooks make this easier. On some boots, avoiding some of the first lacing holes and lacing diagonally may prevent painful infolding of the leather. Try adding padding, such as moleskin, in layers to the area where friction is occurring to redistribute the stresses. If your footwear has removeable insoles, carry a spare pair and change them frequently. Bring spare laces or nylon cord.

Once you have a well-fitting, comfortable shoe, the secret of foot care is in the socks. The outer pair, which should be soft and woolen to absorb the moisture, should be changed frequently. Thick outer socks made of synthetic material (acrylic or nylon) should be avoided since they do not absorb sweat well and often lead to blisters. Wick dry socks are preferred by some. Synthetic socks as thin inners are excellent. Worn under heavier ones, they allow the feet and the inner socks to slip around inside the outer socks, decreasing stress and preventing blisters. (For prevention and care of blisters, see chapter 5.) A plastic bag over the inner sock may prevent the inside of the boot from getting wet from sweat and help keep feet warm in cold, snowy conditions. Some people advocate changing socks twice a day or more, keeping a pair drying outside the pack. Try this if you are having trouble with your feet. Be sure to take enough pairs, say four to six, for the journey. Also take some wool for darning. There is usually a good selection of ex-expedition wool socks for sale in trekking shops around Thamel in Kathmandu. In the high snowy regions, gaiters can be useful in keeping snow out of boot tops.

CLOTHING

Loose trousers for men, long skirts for women, and shirts with pockets are good basic garments. To understand why skirts are *de rigeur* for women, see the dress section of the next chapter. There is good advice there on the type of skirts to bring.

Wool clothing is traditionally chosen for the cold because it feels warm when wet. Knickers, also called plus-fours, are versatile for men since they can be ventilated easily. Long thermal underwear is good at higher altitudes, especially during the winter months. Wool has traditionally been considered best for these garments, but new synthetic fabrics such as polypropylene keep moisture away from the skin and are more comfortable when the wearer sweats. Sweaters, worn with an outer nylon shell to provide wind protection, provide variable degrees of warmth depending on the number of layers. A down jacket is a light, efficient alternative to a sweater, but down is useless when wet. Synthetic, fiber-insulated clothing works well in wet weather, and also dries quickly. A pile jacket with underarm zippers that allow me to remove my arms from the sleeves while walking, is, for me, the ultimate insulator. But there is almost nothing available currently in synthetic pile that has this feature. If you tend to overheat, modify a garment to provide this.

Some advocate down pants for sitting around in the cool high campsites; synthetic pile pants are also good. Perhaps most important is a windproof pant.

Appropriate dress for female trekkers

Even inside homes in the high country you will find drafts that make you cold. Currently I carry a Gore-Tex™ outer pant with leg zippers that can be put on over existing pants. Women can wear this under a skirt. Garments that can be easily put on over existing clothing are the most versatile. A layered system with polypropylene underwear and pile pants and jacket, covered with a Gore-Tex™ jacket and zippered pants, provides versatility for almost all conditions. Wear the underwear and the Gore-Tex™ outer for the active situations, adding the pile in severe cold.

A hat is important on cold days since considerable heat can be lost from the scalp because of its particularly good blood supply. A balaclava is versatile, especially when you face the wind. A hat with a wide brim is best at high altitudes in order to shade the eyes from the sun. I like a visor for this and can use it with my balaclava. Other trekkers like a local shawl. Dark glasses or goggles are also essential at high altitudes, especially on snow where the sunlight is exceptionally intense. Such eye protection should have eye shields to prevent light from coming in from the sides. They should absorb all ultraviolet light and at least 90 percent of visible light. If you or someone else is stuck on snow without them, jury-rig a pair by poking little holes in paper or cloth and wrapping it around the eyes. Long hair combed over the eyes can also help. If you wear eyeglasses or contact lenses, bring a spare pair and a copy of the refraction prescription. Consider bringing disposable contact lenses to solve the problem of cleaning them in Nepal.

Mittens are better than gloves for cold weather. Fingerless gloves, or ones made of thin silk or synthetic material, are good for operating cameras or attending to other intricate details in the snow. Thermolactyl™ mitts (not gloves) I find excellent; they are thin enough to allow fine touch for various tasks. Finally, for snow or winds up high, a waterproof or at least wind-resistant outer mitt is necessary. An unexpected snowfall, falling and getting mittens wet, and numerous other situations can result in finger and toe loss from frostbite. If you are stuck, and inadequately equipped, use spare socks as mittens, and cover them with plastic bags or stuff sacks, to save digits.

It is difficult to stay dry while walking in rainy weather. Those wearing waterproof garments tend to sweat inside them. The Gore-Tex™ fabrics are a definite improvement over the old coated nylon gear because they are waterproof if kept clean, yet breathe better than other waterproof fabrics. Jackets and pants with zippered areas under the arms and down the legs are preferable, since they have better ventilation. In the 100 percent humidity of an intense rainfall, no clothing can breathe so you will probably get wet from the inside no matter what. In those circumstances, light clothes and an umbrella or loose-fitting poncho may be the best compromise. Serviceable bamboo-shafted umbrellas are available in Kathmandu. Trekkers often use them for shade in the hot sun as well as for excretory privacy, and they are essential for the monsoon.

Men should bring shorts for the hot, low altitudes. Skirts for women should be light synthetic or cotton fabrics for the lowlands, but wool for the high country. A bathing suit can be useful and modesty should prevail there.

Since individuals vary, it is difficult to give specific details regarding how many garments of a particular type will give the required warmth at a particular temperature range. Many of the temperature ranges encountered are familiar. Most people can expect to be reasonably comfortable at high altitudes with thick wool pants, two sweaters, a wind jacket, mittens, a hat, wool socks, and heavy boots. You may feel chilly in the morning, when it could be well below freezing, yet sweat later in the day, as you exercise in the sun. The climatological data in chapter 2 should help you plan what to bring.

SLEEPING GEAR

A good sleeping bag is essential for those who contemplate going to the cold, high elevations. A down or synthetic-fiber mummy bag is usually necessary for comfort at temperatures below freezing. Recently, bags have been produced with a silvery reflective lining material that improves efficiency. A bag with a full zipper is more versatile because it is comfortable at cool, high altitudes and in warm, low country. A washable sleeping bag liner solves some hygiene problems, and the liner alone may be all you'll need during the monsoon season at low altitudes.

An air mattress or foam pad provides a comfortable night's sleep, and to me at least, is worth the extra effort needed to carry it. Some like an inflatable pillow. I find the Thermarest™ pad by Cascade Designs to be the most comfortable and durable. The short, rubberized nylon models, extending from the knees to the shoulders, weigh little and are sufficient. Bring a repair kit for it. Some prefer a simple foam pad. A sheet of plastic under the sleeping bag helps keep equipment clean and dry and stops dampness from coming up from the ground. This is a good item on the floors of village houses and even in hotels. In lodges along the popular trekking trails, you can usually get a foam mattress to sleep on, so carrying a mattress may be unnecessary then. Sometimes they will have cotton comforters as well, but I would not count on this.

Those who plan to sleep outside or in a tent at low temperatures (below freezing, or on snow or ice) should be aware that a sufficient thickness of insulation is necessary under you as well as over. Most sleeping bags do not provide enough since the filler compresses under the weight of the body. Anything that can trap air and provide a quarter- to a half-inch of insulation is sufficient. An ideal item is a closed-cell foam pad or an inflatable foam pad. Of course, jackets, clothing, rope, rugs, packs, or other items can serve as well.

At night, sleeping up high, where it is quite cold, put your boots and water bottle in the sleeping bag with you, to keep them from freezing. Place the boots in your sleeping bag stuff sack.

The lightest, most versatile combination for all but the highest elevations may be a light rectangular sleeping bag with a full zipper and a removeable bottom sheet with slots for an air mattress or pad. The combination bottom sheet, zipped to the top bag, makes a light comfortable bed for two, especially when the air bed or pad is installed. The unzipped bag, with sheet attached, can be used as a blanket for two in the warmer zones. The bottom sheet can be zipped to make a single cool cloth bag for low elevations. This cloth bag can be installed in the regular sleeping bag as a liner for individual use up high. Wearing plenty of clothing in this case can make it suitable at higher elevations, if you choose a bag size large enough.

SHELTER

Your route and preferred style dictate whether you need a tent. If you prefer to camp, or desire privacy even occasionally, a tent is necessary, except along certain routes where hotels with private rooms are common. A tent is a must at high altitudes if there is no shelter. A lightweight nylon tent good enough to withstand high winds and snow is necessary for the high passes, but a lean-to made from a sheet of plastic and some cord can weather some of the heaviest of storms if properly pitched. There are many models of tents available. Generally, having one large enough to house other people such as porters in an emergency is best. Check out the erection instructions, and practice before you depart.

Bivouac sacs used by mountaineers are light, efficient shelter good for occasional use. In some areas you can stay in herding huts call *goTh*. Shelter can sometimes be found in caves or beneath overhanging rocks. Be sure you have enough adequate shelter for *all* the members of your party if you are going to high altitudes. It is not unheard of for porters to die of exposure and hypothermia in the parties of thoughtless trekkers. My relationship with porters has always improved after showing them the tent they would use on the high passes.

Campsites can be quite variable. Near villages, terraces that are harvested or in fallow make ideal campsites. Schoolyards make good campsites and sometimes you can stay inside a school house. In this case, it is good to make a donation to the school for upkeep and supplies, if you can find a responsible person. Clearings in the forest, monastery courtyards, and *dharmsala* (resting houses for native travelers) are all possible sites. In western Nepal, where there are flat-roofed houses, you can often pitch your tent on a roof! Be sure to obtain permission to use people's land. Finding a place to camp is usually not a problem for a small group, but finding water may be difficult. Ridges and hillsides may lack water, especially before the monsoon. Trek descriptions in later chapters indicate where I know water to be a problem.

PACKS

Traditionally, the most suitable and comfortable carrying device for trekking was the contoured pack frame made of aluminum or a light alloy. The load is placed in a bag that attaches to the frame. Packs with padded waistbands allow you to transfer the weight from your shoulders to your hips by tightening the waistband and loosening the shoulder straps a bit. Waterproof nylon bags with outside pockets are best since they allow easy access to selected items during the day. The sleeping bag is usually stuffed in another bag and attached to the frame below the pack bag. Today's models of internal frame packs and soft packs are equally suitable. As with much outdoor gear, recent models are ergonomic, that is, designed to be very efficient. If you carry a heavy load, and your pack has a plastic buckle on the waistband, carry a spare as it seems easy to inadvertently step on the buckle and break it. Don't carry a heavy pack with very loose shoulder straps that require you to lean forward; shoulder pain could result. With soft packs, the load must be arranged carefully in order to be comfortable. Equipment and supplies that the porters carry can be packed in sturdy, bright-colored duffel bags, preferably ones that can be locked. Belt or fanny packs, worn in front, can keep needed items easily accessible.

While I understand the "carry it all yourself" philosophy, it makes little sense to burden yourself down like a pack animal and then wear yourself out carrying the load. There may be little for you to enjoy except the feeling that you did it. Porters are quite inexpensive, and by hiring them, you contribute directly to those who need it. I, for one, feel I must always carry something. I once limited myself to 40 or 50 lb (I weigh 190 lb), but I reduced this when going above 12,000 ft (3657 m). I did make the mistake of starting off on my first trek with 50 or 60 lb on my back, and, after some days, I developed back strain that didn't disappear for quite a while. Now I carry 25 to 30 lb. I'm learning as I get older! So start off light and gradually get accustomed to carrying a load. Members of mountaineering expeditions do this.

COOKING GEAR

Light nesting pots are available in Kathmandu. Two or three should suffice for a small group cooking together. Spoons are the ideal general purpose utensil, and pocket knives are a good accessory. A combination salt and pepper shaker is useful if you season your food. Plastic scouring pads are handy for cleaning pots, but steel pads are easier to find in Kathmandu.

Because travelers have placed great pressures on the scant forests remaining in the high-altitude areas, regulations require that all trekkers and their porters, cooks, and guides be self-sufficient in the national parks. And I strongly recommend that trekkers use kerosene stoves at all times, especially in the high-altitude areas. One group, crossing the Thorung La after a heavy snowfall on the last day of November, was wise in bringing a kerosene stove. They were able to melt snow and have a hot drink up high. On the same day, another trekker sustained serious frostbite there. So even if you are eating in lodges, carrying a kerosene stove can be a life saver in the high country.

Kerosene is the only fuel available in the hills. Even then its availability is sporadic outside of popular places like Namche Bazaar. Furthermore, its quality is low and at times unsuitable for burning in some stoves. So fuel must sometimes be carried from Kathmandu. The quantity needed depends on whether snow must be melted for water, the efficiency of the stove, and the number in the party. About three liters will last a party of four for a week if snow must be melted. Plastic jerry cans for fuel are available in Kathmandu.

Kerosene stoves of Indian manufacture are readily available in Kathmandu; though adequate, they are generally bulky and heavy. The lighter Swedish stoves are sometimes found in stores selling trekking and climbing gear. In my experience, the older Swedish stoves seem to operate well at high altitudes on the impure kerosene found in the hills. However, they are heavy, and with some models it can be easy to lose crucial parts. The MSR G/K stove, the most efficient kerosene design, used to be finicky on impure kerosene. If you are experiencing difficulties operating this model on dirty kerosene, remove the surge damper. The current model, X-GK, is better, while the new MSR Whisper Lite Internationale Stove is more suitable for those needing to control the burner flame in order to simmer. Be sure to carry appropriate spare parts (MSR produces maintenance kits for their stoves) and a funnel containing a wool filter. Try the stove out before you leave.

MISCELLANEOUS

A medical kit is essential (see chapter 5).

Food is best packed in plastic bags and then put into labeled cloth bags tied with string. Plastic bags can be purchased in Kathmandu, although some trekkers prefer Ziploc™ bags brought from home. Be sure to take extras. Sheet plastic is also available. It is a good item for protecting porters and loads in the rain as well as putting under your sleeping bag if lying on a mud floor, the typical *bhaTTi* arrangement. Cotton bags can be sewn by a local tailor, but nylon stuff sacks are, perhaps, a better choice.

Take enough enough stuff sacks to store all your gear so it is easier to keep track of your goods. I like light, zippered nylon bags in various colors to store small items. They can be packed in a duffel bag or a porter's *Doko* (basket). A sturdy, zippered duffel bag that locks is ideal for a porter to carry. Get a heavy nylon or canvas model—light nylon wears too quickly. For security reasons, it is not advisable to leave loose items in the basket. Another lockable piece of luggage in which to store your extra gear at your hotel when you trek is a good idea. I find the small combination locks easiest to use. A bright-colored bag makes it easy to spot from afar, and can help locate your porter. Some people find large plastic garbage bags (brought from home) useful. On long treks during the monsoon, I use them to protect the contents of those duffel bags that don't need to be unpacked too often. Small plastic bags inside stuff sacks are useful for gear in the monsoon.

It is important to consider what might break down and carry appropriate spare parts. A sewing kit is indispensable and a sewing awl for heavier items may be useful. Epoxy glue can repair most things if used discriminately. In Kathmandu ask for the brand Aryldite, in stores carrying Indian products. A more flexible contact cement, such as Barge cement, would also be useful. A pair of pliers can be good to have; the combination wrench, pliers, and screwdriver originally made for ski troops is ideal. A pocket knife with a few gadgets on it will also come in handy.

Ski poles, ice axes, walking sticks, etc. are favorites, especially with older European trekkers. The telescopic ski poles adjust to various lengths and collapse to a small size. People customarily use them for steep descents to ease the trauma on their knees, and to help maintain balance on difficult trails. Experienced practitioners feel it gives them four legs and increases efficiency in rugged terrain. Constant use of ski poles wastes energy and tires the arms and shoulders. In difficult, extremely steep situations, you are better off holding onto the rock for support and balance. But ski poles seem ideal for crossing streams on ice-covered rocks, for snow drifts on high passes, on slippery monsoon trails, and on icy trails after snowfalls. An ice ax is advisable for steep snow, or glacier travel, but only if you know how to use this potentially lethal weapon.

Bring several handkerchiefs for colds and upper respiratory infections, or learn to blow your nose Nepali style. The use of toilet paper for nose blowing creates insolvable disposal problems. Petrolatum jelly is good for cold-weather chapping. Tampons for women should be the variety that can be inserted without an applicator that then must be discarded.

A water bottle of at least one quart (liter) capacity should be carried for each person in the party. Visit your local hospital emergency department and pick up a few empty one-liter plastic bottles that were used to hold irrigation fluids. They are ideal for water, kerosene, or just about any liquid, and the price is right. Water is often scarce and must be treated before use. The plastic jerry cans and bottles with stoppers and screw tops available in the Kathmandu bazaar provide an alternative. Some trekkers find a wide-mouth "pee bottle" useful in a tent at night. Take biodegradable soap in a container. A washcloth or towel and a toothbrush are good to have. A small flashlight or torch is very useful—the plastic kind is warmer to handle in cold weather. A headlamp is a pleasant luxury. I like one with a low-wattage bulb and a lithium battery, so I can read and write at night. Battery and bulb life can be over 100 hours. Carry spares. Indian D-cell batteries are about the only kind usually obtainable outside of Kathmandu, though you may be able to find other sizes in popular trekking areas these days. Take candles to read by at night, matches in a water-proof container (or a lighter), and toilet paper. I bring interlocking folding toilet paper from home, the kind that you find in public washrooms and buy from sanitary supply houses. Consider earplugs for noisy hotels. A combination lock is useful to secure hotel room doors without keys and allow several people to enter independently. Such locks can also be used for duffel bags.

It is wise to have at least one compass in the party. Magnetic declination in Nepal is less than two or three degrees west in most places and can be over-looked for most map work. My compass has a clinometer to measure angles of elevation. This can be used either with a trigonometric calculator or a small slide rule (yes, these can still be useful) to help decide if peaks in certain com-pass directions are in fact specific summits on the map. I first did this in 1969, before I could believe the mountain above me at Khobang was Dhaulagiri, its summit very foreshortened and an incredible 20,000 ft (6095 m) above me. Of course I had no trig slide rule then and had to rely on my recall of identities, facts that are too far away from me now. A pair of binoculars, an altimeter, and a thermometer can be helpful. For those wishing to have a convenient multi-purpose instrument, there are now two watches that I know of that combine an altimeter with the time keeper. The Casio Alti-Depth model is limited to 13,120 ft (4000 m), while the bulkier Citizen Altichron registers up to 17,000 ft (5000 m). Both have a chronograph and can help you compare your walking times with those in this book. A star chart can help you identify constellations in the clear night air.

Trekkers wearing contact lenses are advised that the risks of infectious complications are probably greater than at home. Bring plenty of sterilizing/disinfecting solutions and don't exceed advised recommended wearing times. Use boiled water for cleansing when water is called for. At the first sign of any problems, remove the lenses and wear glasses. Use the treatment for conjuncti-vitis outlined in chapter 5. Don't despair. I have worn my extended-wear con-tacts without problems while trekking. The new disposable extended-wear contact lenses are probably the easiest to care for on a trek and are highly rec-ommended.

Insects are not usually a problem in the high country, but those trekkers traveling extensively in the lowlands during the warmer months or during the monsoon should use mosquito netting while sleeping and insect repellents (the ones with N, N-diethyl-meta-toluamide are the best) while traveling. Insecti-cide sprays and powders may help in the sleeping bag and applied to the net-ting. The safest are probably those containing pyrethrins or permethrin. I personally only use netting in hotel beds where it is provided, or when I am living in the lowlands. I well remember one sleepless night in Tatopani in May, being abused by no-see-ems while I was lying naked on top of my sleeping bag. Finally, I was able to cover my body with a sheet and get to sleep.

Consider taking a portable tape recorder to capture the local music and other sounds of Nepal. Cassette tapes of various manufacture and D, C, and AA batteries are available in Kathmandu. Realize that you might spend a month or more and hear few sounds of civilization, such as motor vehicles, motors running various things, etc., except for the now ubiquitous radio. You may find yourself learning to hear the sounds of nature: the various cacophonous insects, animals, wind, and water, as well as people, and that rare sound in the West, *silence*. On occasion I carry a quality tape recorder and a professional stereo microphone to capture these memorable treasures, the sounds of Nepal. If your recorder has a built-in microphone, get a separate one, preferably with a low-pass (voice) filter and a windscreen. Key techniques to getting good recordings are to use a windscreen on the microphone, use the voice setting, get it as close as possible to the sound source, and don't jiggle it!

You might consider using a dictation recorder, for your voice impressions as you walk. I now do this for trail descriptions, and have sewn an "office holder" for my pack strap that carries the recorder, notebook, pencil, and altimeter in separate pockets.

If you are a musician who plays a portable instrument, consider bringing it along. A harmonica, recorder, or flute can help break the ice in a village and elicit "good vibrations." Porters may balk at carrying a piano, but Jonathan Miller, cello recitalist and Boston Symphony musician, took a compact, battery-operated cello that enriched everyone he played for. Consider other social and entertainment skills that you may have that you could share with special people in Nepal. Perhaps you juggle, or can play games with string, or perform magic tricks.

Most trekkers carry reading matter and writing materials. Rereading years later a journal kept on a trek can be a most rewarding experience. Bring a picture book about your country to show to special Nepali people you encounter. Rural Nepali folk especially appreciate looking at pictures of farm scenes, horses, cows, sheep, goats, and produce. Photographs of your family are great fun to share. Obtain the language tape and book. And bring this book, an essential item. If its weight seems too great, remove the trail descriptions that don't apply to your trek.

For the rare situation in which you may have to deal with the bureaucracy in rural Nepal, a supply of business cards and letterhead stationary can be valuable. Rubber stamps and, especially, embossed seals can also help you to get things done.

For anything absolutely indispensable, that you could not replace on the trail, consider taking a spare. You might also bring items to barter or trade on your trek. Warm clothes, booties, almost any kind of clothing, including designer labels, are valuable currency, particularly along the well-trekked trails. The well-known U.S. brand of jeans is especially sought after. See chapter 4 for gift suggestions and appropriate circumstances.

The equipment game can be, and often is, carried to extremes. Naturalist

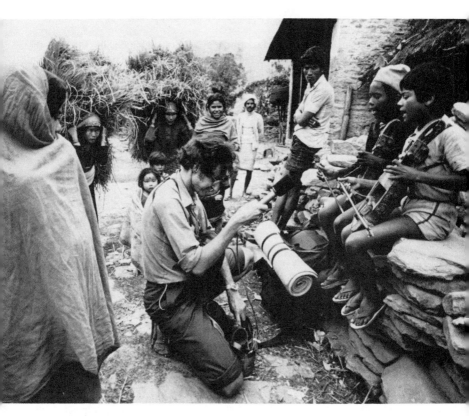

Author recording folk minstrels near Pokhara (photo by Mary Lynn Hanley)

Ed Cronin describes how, relying on the Boy Scout spirit of preparedness, he emerged from the plane at a remote airstrip on his first trip to Nepal. He was dressed in his custom-designed field jacket, complete with dashing epaulets and eleven pockets, offering precise space for various necessities from compass to moleskin to a waterproof container of matches. Around his neck he carried two camera bodies, and a host of lenses and light meters as well as a pair of binoculars and a tripod. Descending laboriously from the plane, he noticed that all eyes were on him. "I thought at the time this was because I was new and lacked a sunburn, but later realized it was because I carried more wealth on my person than the average porter. . . could accumulate in a lifetime," he said. He later described all the difficulties he had walking with this paraphernalia.

For many reasons, including some important reasons to be discussed later, be reasonable in what you bring and keep most of it packed until needed. Trekkers who carry their own equipment often find they return having lugged many nonemergency items they never used. Often they end up leaving things along the way. Review your equipment list, and pare it down beforehand.

Photography in Nepal

"Photography is a magical process that has given Sahibs all over the world the chance to rest under the guise of business," states Cronin. This is most certainly true, but I also find it valuable as an art form expressing my impressions of Nepal and as a means of sharing my experiences with others. And years later it helps me remember.

Inexperienced photographers should bring a small, simple 35 mm zoom automatic camera. Models with fill-in flash can be quite useful in enabling you to get better results if you must photograph people in the harsh midday light. An instant picture or self-developing camera may make you popular with some people, but I would be cautious in its use. Often, after I snap the shutter on my 35 mm camera, people along the popular trails wait thirty seconds and approach me for the photograph. If you use an instant camera, everybody will pester you for their photograph. Avid photographers will do best bringing 35 mm single lens reflex equipment. It is especially suited to candid photography, and with a suitable array of lenses, a flash, and a tripod, you can handle most situations. Large-format cameras can provide incredibly sharp images that come close to doing justice to Nepal's scenery.

A trekker once remarked that if you are walking along a trail in Nepal with a camera, lose your step, and fall, and in the process accidentally trip the camera shutter, you will get a good photograph. It does take a little more work, a lot more if you want top images, but Nepal is very photogenic. Problems in getting good results stem from the immense scale of the terrain, contrasty light, and poorly lit interiors.

Wide-angle lenses help capture the grandeur of the mountain landscape, but their use demands attention to the foreground for good results. Choosing a suitable foreground, with color and action, together with an appropriate background with good lighting, is the key to good wide-angle photographs. Details of mountains, especially if shrouded in cloud, can be dramatic studies if taken with a suitable focal-length lens. The range of light intensities in bright sun makes good results almost impossible except in the early morning or late in the day. So either restrict your photography to the oblique filtered light close to sunrise and sunset, or consider using polarizing and split-density filters and fill-in flash, and bracketing the exposures. The last process means making exposures above and below what your light-meter reading shows and choosing the best result later.

It is most important to know which exposure conditions will throw the built-in light meter in your camera off and to adjust accordingly. When the background is very bright, as with the sky or snow, the camera meter reading will be too low and the subject will be dark and underexposed. When the background is too dark, in a forest for example, the opposite may occur. In these circumstances take a meter reading at very close range, directly off the subject's face, or, if on bright snow, use the flat of your hand for a reading. With automatic-only cameras, exposure compensation, if available, will help surmount this problem. Lacking that option, adjust the film speed (increasing film speed to decrease the exposure, and vice versa). Another problem commonly occurs when taking portraits in the midday sun. When the face is positioned so the overhead sun casts strong shadows across the eyes, there is little except fill-in flash that will help. If possible, orient the subject to avoid these shadows. Practice before your trip so you won't lose good pictures or waste film.

Battery-dependent cameras will cease to function if the battery fails. Carry plenty of spares. If your camera operates mechanically without the battery and you have no spare, the following principle for determining exposure will help. When shooting in the midday sun, unobscured by clouds, a setting of f:16 and a shutter speed close to the ISO (also called ASA in the old terminology) film speed will produce good results. For example, with ISO 64 film, set the camera to f:16 and 1/60th second. If on snow, set it to one stop less, e.g. f:16 and 1/125th. In hazy conditions, open up one stop to f:11 and 1/60th. On cloudy days, open up two stops to f:8 and 1/60th. On overcast days or in open shade, open up three stops over the basic reading for bright sun to f:5.6 and 1/60th. Any combination of lens opening and shutter speed that produces the needed exposure will work. Alas, this will not work for the totally battery-dependent camera.

The fascinating activities in the dark interiors of Nepali homes are difficult to photograph. Long exposures using a tripod and fast film can work, while a carefully used flash can handle other situations. The harsh light of direct on-camera flash rarely produces pleasing effects. Creative use of bounce light is better. Even a piece of white paper held obliquely to the flash head and positioned to reflect light on the subject can work. Flash equipment should be chosen with bounce versatility in mind. Fast film and bare-bulb flash produces the softest light and best results. Old-fashioned flashbulbs used this way are ideal. To capture the striking art on dark monastery walls, two flashes from either side at a 45° angle to the camera are necessary to avoid light reflections. A flash meter, off-the-film flash metering, and experience are necessary to get good results with this technique.

Accept the challenge of varied photographic conditions in Nepal. Subjects in mist or fog often produce striking images. Overexposing slightly may help under such conditions. The monsoon season is ideal for capturing moody landscapes, and even photographing in the rain can produce rewarding results. An umbrella can keep you and the camera dry. A macro lens allows striking close-ups of the prodigious monsoon flora and insects. Long exposures at night in the unelectrified villages of Nepal can provide interesting images.

The camera I use is a Pentax LX, chosen because it is rugged, is well sealed for the monsoon, and provides off-the-film metering in the automatic mode, yet functions mechanically when the battery fails. Off-the-film flash metering is also useful, not only in difficult interior situations but also for macrophotography. The lenses I find useful in Nepal are 20 mm, 28 mm, 50 mm, f:1.2 for low light situations, 100 mm macro, 70–210 mm zoom, and 400 mm. Of course I often go light with one body and two lenses (a 28 mm and a 100 mm) but the above is my burden when I so choose.

A chest pack to hold the camera and several lenses keeps my equipment close at hand. I often carry a substantial tripod with a reversing center piece, but a camera clamp attached to a pack, ice ax, or stick can double as a tripod. I use polarizing filters and carry a split filter, hoping one day to get the ideal rhododendron in bloom sharply framed against a mountain scene. A winder is useful in capturing the smile that follows the shutter release in posed pictures of Nepalis. Lens cleaning equipment and spare batteries are a must. I find Kodachrome™ film excellent for outdoor photography and use the 200 film indoors. The new Fuji Velvia™ film is worth considering as well. E-6 and C-41 processing is available in Kathmandu.

The video revolution has come to Nepal too. A video camera can enable you to capture many scenes and events that you experience. It can also serve as a kind of diary. The major problem is that most cameras run on rechargeable battery packs, and there is little or no opportunity to restore them outside of Kathmandu and big centers with electricity, which is 220 volts/50 cycle in Nepal. So you must carry extra charged battery packs. Be aware that North American equipment conforms to a different standard than that found in Asia (PAL), which is not the same as that in Europe. Hence you won't be able to play your tapes recorded on equipment purchased in one area on playback units and monitors used in another. While I question the ethics of displaying another source of wealth to the rural Nepali people, something that they can't have, it probably makes little difference compared to the other equipment we carry there.

Food

Some people are surprised to discover that Nepal has no large-scale organized food distribution network with supermarkets and the like. However, in Kathmandu many Western processed and packaged foods are now available in the new shopping areas set up mainly to cater to the new Nepali middle class and in more traditional "cold stores." The Bluebird Supermarket near the Blue Star Hotel has a large variety these days. Other big cities, such as Pokhara, carry some processed foods. The type of food available in the hills varies depending on the place and the season. It is also somewhat dependent on who has gone before you. Many locally grown items are available during the autumn harvest time, but in late spring vegetables and other commodities may be scarce. Fruits, a real treat, are available in season. On the more popular routes, such as in Khumbu, Helambu, Langtang, Thak Khola, and some parts of Manang, many items normally only available in large cities can be purchased. Cooked meals available at inns are described in the next chapter.

Below, the starred (*) items are sold in most hill bazaars, and can sometimes be purchased in people's homes. Also, (#) means the item is also probably available along the popular trails. The remainder, except as noted above, can only be bought in Kathmandu, Pokhara, or cities in the Tarai. Although the metric system has been introduced and is the legal standard, the traditional system of measure given here is still used in distant locales. The metric measures used in the hills have variable standards. The Nepali beer bottle, holding about 700 ml, is passed off as a liter. You may find it best to just accept this. Volume is measured in *maanaa*. One *maanaa* equals twenty ounces or 2½ cups (0.7 l). Eïght *maanaa* equal a *paathi*. The basic unit of weight is the *paau*, about half a pound (0.2 kg). Four *paau* equal a *ser* and three *ser* equal a *dhaarni* or six pounds (2.7 kg). Be sure to bring containers with you on a trek to carry the foods you might buy. Small cloth bags are ideal.

Rice* is the staple food of richer Nepalis, but it is not easily obtainable in the northern regions. It is traditionally measured by volume. Most Nepalis eat large quantities of rice daily. Try to buy the kind with unbroken grains. Other grains are occasionally available. Popcorn can now be purchased in Kathmandu.

Lentils*, or chickpeas, are made into a soup called *daal*. It is poured over rice to make the staple meal. A *maanaa* of lentils should last two or three people for about three meals.

Assorted vegetables* are obtainable locally. They are eaten in comparatively small amounts by the Nepali people, except in the mountains where entire meals may consist of potatoes.

Noodles (#) once were not often found outside of Kathmandu, Namche Bazaar, Langtang, and other areas of Tibetan influence. They have become more commonplace in shops, especially if there is chance a trekker might pass through. A quick-cooking brand from India, called Maggi, has become the generic term for a thick instant noodle soup in the east, but RaRa is the term north of Pokhara. Try asking for some to be cooked for you, hopefully with some added condiments or vegetables. In a pinch you can eat the noodles uncooked.

Tea* is the staple drink, usually taken sweet with milk. Five hundred grams should last two or three people most of a month. In Khumbu and other areas of Tibetan influence, Tibetan tea is served with butter and salt. It is delicious, but it is an acquired taste. You might enjoy bringing herbal teas from home.

Coffee (#) is sold usually only in the instant variety from India. However, coffee beans, grown in Nepal, are available in Kathmandu now.

Sugar* is sold either by weight or volume. It is a comparative luxury and is sometimes hard to find in the hills. About twenty *paau* should last a small party for almost a month.

Milk (#) is best carried in powdered form. If mixed dry with sugar before adding hot tea or coffee, it should dissolve well. Several kilograms should last a month. Cans of condensed sweetened milk are sometimes sold in the hills. Milk powder is often sold along the popular trekking trails, though sometimes only infant formula is available and is used in tea shops. Fresh milk should be heated to the boiling point before being consumed.

Salt* of the finely granulated iodized variety is available in Kathmandu. Only coarse rock salt is available in the hills.

Pepper* and other spices should be bought in Kathmandu. Many unfamiliar, exotic spices are used in the hills. Try them!

Oats (#) are another item that lend variety to a diet.

Making tsampa *from roasted barley flour*

Cheese (#) is usually available from "cold stores" in Kathmandu. The variety is always increasing and includes imported canned cheese. Cheese can be purchased at certain times at plants in Langtang, at Thodung, at Tragsindho, and at Sing Gomba near Gosainkund.

Butter can also be purchased at the dairies in Kathmandu. It does not keep long if unrefrigerated. Indian butter is available in cans. In the hills, clarified butter called *ghiu** is available.

Oil in the hills is usually processed mustard oil, though other varieties are available in Kathmandu.

Peanut butter (#) and various **jams** are a treat, but the ones that come in glass jars should be repackaged.

Biscuits made in Nepal are quite good if fresh, and fairly available. The original brand was packaged in metal tins twenty years ago, in order to have them survive the long carry into the hills. These tins became a common building material for roofs and the like. Oil tins have replaced the biscuit tins, as boxes are now used for portering them.

Candy is a source of quick energy during the day. Try the milk bonbons made by Nebico. Buy them in the kilogram package. Chocolate bars of Indian manufacture are available at times, as are Swiss varieties and other junk food snacks.

Roasted flour is a common food in the hills. It may be of wheat, barley *(tsampa)*, corn, or millet. Mixed with water and spices, it is sometimes the only food you can get.

Soup mixes, cooked and poured over rice, make a good substitute when *daal* is not available. Stores in the popular tourist areas of Kathmandu often stock well-known European and Southeast Asian brands.

Eggs are available wherever there are laying chickens. This includes most places except the high mountain areas (above 10,000 ft, 3050 m).

Dehydrated foods produced in Kathmandu, suitable for trekking and mountaineering expeditions, are available. These foods are of good quality, are quite reasonably priced, and require less fuel to cook than many other foods. They are available in many supply stores in Kathmandu and some in Pokhara, as well as occasionally in major trekking towns.

Many luxury items, such as Indian-canned fruits, vegetables, and meat, are sold in Kathmandu, but they are quite heavy. Shops in areas of the city frequented by tourists sometimes carry imported foods. Foods taken on mountaineering expeditions find their way into shops in the appropriate areas—for instance, around Namche Bazaar, north of Pokhara, and near Langtang. The variety and quality vary greatly.

You may want to bring other items from home that aren't usually available in Nepal—drink mixes, instant soup mixes, freeze-dried meats, vegetables, mustard powder, and desserts. Of course, none of them are necessary, but it may be enjoyable to celebrate at certain times during the trek.

Any nonburnable containers (metal, glass, plastic) that you carry into the hills must be compacted and carried out.

Note that few meat items are mentioned. Most Westerners are used to meals centered around meat, but this is not so in Nepal, and is even changing in the West for health reasons. Occasional bits of meat may turn up among the vegetables and you can ask to have a small dish of meat served to you with your *daal bhaat*. It is often dried goat meat, but may be buffalo, or yak. You can buy a chicken in the hills and have it cooked. Be aware that it will likely be a road runner and not at all like the tender, juicy, chemical-fed variety you may be accustomed to. Where meat is available, it must be requested separately—at a small extra cost. If you are in good health, you can survive and remain quite healthy without any meat. For more on nutrition, see chapter 5.

Guides and Porters

Porters are the culture of Nepal.
Bill O'Connor, *The Trekking*
Peaks of Nepal

The trekker who does not travel with porters is missing out on the perfect opportunity to get to know the amazing people of this country. If you are traveling on an agency-organized trek, you should read most of this section for general information and to understand your responsibility for their safety.

Sherpas are an ethnic group who have become famous for their exploits on mountaineering expeditions. The term Sherpa, as commonly used by Nepalis, does not stand for a specific job description, but for a group of people who originally migrated from eastern Tibet and settled in the Solu-Khumbu region of Nepal. They have often been employed by trekkers as guides (Sirdars), cooks, and porters. But the term sherpa, especially when used by foreigners, and increasingly by Nepalis, at times refers to anyone of any ethnic group who does those tasks. People of ethnic groups other than Sherpas—*Tamang, Gurung,* and Tibetans, for instance—are working as guides. Many of them are quite capable.

People trekking in Nepal for the first time, especially if off the popular routes, will generally have fewer problems if they have a guide or Sirdar. This is especially true for a group of people who are planning to hire a number of porters for a long trek. It may be difficult to hire a good Sirdar during the busy autumn season. The rate of pay for guides, porters, etc. varies depending on where they are hired (rates are highest in Kathmandu, on the side of a high-altitude pass, and in western Nepal), where you are going (more is expected when you will go up high, be on snow, etc.), the time of year (rates are higher in times when there is plenty of trekking or village work), the experience and language capabilities of the guide, and whether the trekker provides food (they usually do for Sirdars). Find out the current rates for Sirdars and porters from other trekkers, and inquire at trekking stores and agencies. It is wise to ask several people to get a good estimate. For a small group of, say, two trekkers and two porters, eating locally, it is more efficient to have the Sirdars and porters eat with the trekkers than it is to hire them with food provided.

Take your time in the hiring process. Do not immediately hire the first person who approaches you. Trust your impressions of people, and talk to several to find those you can get along with. Send word out that you are looking for people. I prefer to hire porters who have not worked mostly for trekking groups, and who dress in native clothes.

Guides sometimes demand excessive amounts of equipment and I would seek another person in this circumstance, if possible. Experienced Sirdars do not carry loads, and usually do not cook either; they confine their activities to guiding, hiring porters, and attending to various logistical matters. Most guides speak some English, and some speak varying degrees of French, German, Japanese, and other languages due to their close contacts with foreigners on treks and mountaineering expeditions.

Sometimes younger people with little experience or knowledge of English, who are nevertheless enthusiastic and quite capable, can be hired for less. Such people are, in a way, more desirable, especially for the trekker who wants as few assistants as possible and wants to learn some Nepali. Sometimes these workers may carry a porter's load and do some cooking in addition to guiding.

Be aware that in the Annapurna Conservation Area region and in Sagarmatha National Park there appears to be a requirement that guides (Sirdars) be hired from recognized trekking agencies. This is monitored at police check posts, where a guide might be asked to produce a letter from an agency. Trekkers who have hired independent guides might do well to be processed apart from their guides at check posts, and to state that they are their own guides, if this regulation appears to be enforced. Alternatively, if you have hired a guide with the help of a trekking agency, then be sure to have a letter stating his connection with that company.

The guide will make many decisions about routes and stops for the night. His choices may be dictated by personal factors, such as where he has friends or other business to do, and often this will not be discussed with the trekkers. Trekkers may find that they did not visit areas they had wished to, for poorly understood reasons. It is important to read the trail descriptions and decide for yourself.

For a large party not eating locally, a cook, and perhaps a helper, are needed, in addition to the porters, who are hired strictly for load carrying. The guide can usually suggest a cook. Porters are also hired by the guide, or by you if you do not have a guide. It is often possible to make a contract with a porter to carry the load a certain distance, an arrangement that may work out to be cheaper than a daily wage. Porters usually carry their own food. Guides and porters can be hired through the trekking agencies in Kathmandu, in other areas at airstrips, restaurants, and hotels frequented by foreigners, or at staging areas for treks. Some trekkers prefer to bring reliable people with them from Kathmandu. Porters hired locally may be Sherpas or Tibetans in Khumbu, Tibetans in Pokhara, *Gurung* north of Pokhara, *Tamang* in Kathmandu, or people of other ethnic groups, depending on the area. I find the Hindu caste porters less satisfactory than the hill ethnic groups. Others have found this true for guides as well. Women as well as men can be good porters; a few women have become guides. Some porters on the large treks prefer the companionship of their friends to that of the trekkers. Look for porters who might enjoy close contact with trekkers.

Porters carry their loads—usually around 65 lb (30kg)—by means of a tumpline or *naamlo*, a band going around the load and around the forehead. You might need only to put the load in a sack or duffel bag, hopefully one that

you can lock. Or porters use a *Doko,* a conical basket available for a few rupees throughout much of Nepal. Anything can be carried in it, and an outer
wrapping of plastic can keep the load dry when it rains. Even if you give your
porters a modern pack to carry, some may disregard the straps and waist belt in
favor of a tumpline, which supports the weight from their foreheads. Indeed,
for those accustomed to it, this may be the most efficient and comfortable way
to carry a heavy load. Try a tumpline with your pack and gradually increase the
weight it supports. Items carried by porters receive rough treatment, and it is
best to carry fragile items yourself.

All transportation costs such as bus or plane fares to the actual beginning
of the trek are the responsibility of the trekker. In addition, if the trek does not
leave an employee at his home or point of hiring, you are obligated to pay for
his return, usually at half the daily rate. Travel is faster on the return trip, so
the number of days the journey will take should be agreed upon in advance.

With numerous mountaineering expeditions and large groups requiring
many porters along the major trails, especially to Everest, it may be difficult to
find porters at the start of a trek, or several days into it. And you may have to
pay quite an inflated rate. While you can sometimes hire people in remote
places such as at the last settlement below a pass, their rates may also be quite
expensive. You have few options at this point, and the porters looking for work
likely have many. Economics works in Nepal!

If you have a large group of trekkers that you are organizing on your own,
and need quite a few porters, consider hiring a guide, Sirdar, or head porter in
Kathmandu, or other staging point. It is difficult for a person new to Nepal to
hire and manage a group of porters. Send the Sirdar to the starting point a day
or two ahead to hire the needed porters and make other arrangements. It is best
to recognize one person in the group of trekkers as the leader, and have the Sirdar deal with him or her.

Large groups organized by trekking agencies commonly follow day-to-
day itineraries or "camps," stopping at agreed-upon points. Porters hired for
such routes may insist that you pay them the daily rate for the usual stages—a
fixed sum for the distance to be covered—instead of the days you actually
walk. In such circumstances I would advise trying to find other porters who are
more flexible, since it is often likely that a small, fit group will cover ground
faster than at the camp rate. Sometimes you may not be able to get around paying the camp rate, but since this amount often does not include pay for the return journey, it may work out to be similar to a daily rate.

Do not give an unknown guide a large advance, perhaps two or three
days' wages at the most. Even if your guide is looking after the porters, you
should, at the start of a trip, make the wages clear with them yourself to avoid
possible misunderstandings later. An advance of two or three days' wages may
be paid to the porters so that they can purchase needed items. Have the guide
keep an account book. Also do not loan your guide or porters money in con-
trived circumstances if you expect to get it back. If you feel insecure about
your potential guide, ask for references and try to verify them.

When you hire porters and guides, you are taking responsibility for them.
If they get sick or injured, see to it that they get suitable medical attention.
Many lowland porters have never been on snow or in below-freezing tempera-

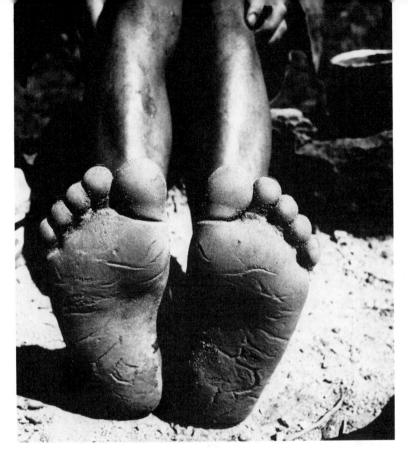

The tough soles on a porter's feet never wear out.

tures. They may not be aware of conditions in the places you want to take them. Provide them with footwear, clothes, bedding, and shelter if necessary. Equipment for porters can be rented in Kathmandu. Make sure the porters understand that the equipment is a loan, not a gift. Bring old clothes and out-of-style hiking gear from home to loan or give to your porters who don't have enough. (Take inventory at home—you will be surprised at what you have that you will never use.) If you go through a trekking agency, give the equipment directly to the needy porters, rather than to the staff of the company.

The following scene is all too common. The sahib is in his tent, comfortable and warm in his down sleeping bag sitting on a thick foam pad. His down jacket and pants are stuffed in the corner. Outside, huddled together by some rocks used as a windbreak, his wet, shivering porters do not sleep a wink all night. The sahib wonders why they are so slow the next day.

If you have a guide, it is his responsibility to see to the needs of the porters, but this does not relieve you of responsibility. Time and time again, porters have died needlessly on high passes in storms after they were abandoned by guides. In a storm, it is wise to sit low and wait it out rather than to cross a pass to keep on schedule.

If you have a group of porters and feel that they are taking too many rests, check to see that their loads are not too heavy. Sometimes, rather than staying with them, shadowing them, so to speak, it may turn out to be more efficient to agree on a destination for lunch or that evening, and walk independently of them, especially after a trusting relationship has developed. You might also travel ahead and arrange to have food cooked for them at a hotel or *bhaTTi*. Then it is ready when they arrive.

Some people advise trekkers to give guides and porters cigarettes occasionally, or even regularly. Smoking is well established in Nepal, but I feel that it is unethical to further this unhealthy habit, especially for those trekkers who don't smoke. If you do smoke, it may be unreasonable not to share your cigarettes. But don't make a habit of buying cigarettes for the employees. There are other ways to share your satisfaction with them on the trip and to show your appreciation for their efforts at its end. English lessons are much valued. You could buy some appropriate language materials in Kathmandu, or bring them from home. Good gifts include used clothing, pocket knives, pencils, crayons, paper notebooks, discarded containers, sewing needles, and strong thread.

Do not overlook the possibility of using animals to carry loads. This is especially feasible in Khumbu and other northern regions. I have used a yak and a *zopkio*—the sterile male offspring of a cow mated with a yak. The animals are remarkably sure-footed, but the *zopkio* has a much better disposition than the yak, which requires pulling and pushing at times. However, the yak can withstand more cold than the *zopkio*. Either can carry 100 pounds or more. In some areas horses can be used. Their use depends on the availability of fodder, so high passes such as the Jangla would not be feasible during the late fall and winter, but quite appropriate in the monsoon. Sometimes a person whom you may want to hire as a porter will carry nothing, but use a pack animal. In this case, the person is paid as a porter, or two, depending on the load carried by the animal. Be sure that the arrangement is clear beforehand.

SLEEPING COOLIE

On his back a fifty-pound load
spine bent double
six miles straight up in the January snow,
naked bones,
two rupees worth of life in his body
to challenge the mountain.

Cloth cap black with sweat
and worn to shreds,
body swarming with lice and fleas,
mind dulled.
It's like sulphur, but how tough
this human frame.

The bird of his heart panting,
sweat and breath.
On the cliff his hut, kids trembling:
hungry griefs!
No greens to eat; his wife combs the woods
for weeds and nettles.

Beneath the snow peak
of this more than human hero's mountain,
conquering nature, with a hoard of pearls—
the sweat on his forehead—
and above only the lid of night
bright with stars:
in this night he is rich with sleep.

Laxmiprasad Devkota, 1958
(1909–1959) Nepal's foremost poet

Aircraft

The anthropologist Ralph Beals once wrote that as an effective
agent of change, one road is worth a thousand schools. The
same might be said for one STOL (short-take-off-and-landing)
airstrip.

James Fisher, *Sherpas*

Flying in Nepal is exciting for many reasons. The pilots are especially skilled at landing in remote airstrips, and fly in seemingly impossible monsoon weather without benefit of IFR beacons. The old adage that they don't fly when there are clouds because "the clouds have rocks in them" doesn't seem to hold these days, especially where the route is reasonable. Their safety record is enviable.

Small STOL (Short Take Off and Landing) aircraft can be chartered to small airstrips in many parts of Nepal. Some airstrips built in the past are currently unusable due to lack of maintenance. Helicopters can also be chartered for travel to trekking sites, although this is rare for most tourists. Helicopters are used more commonly for sightseeing and rescue. The planes are single-engine Pilatus Porters carrying 900 to 1100 lb (400 to 500 kg) or Twin Otters carrying more than twice that load. There may not be any Pilatus Porters available in the future (too unprofitable), limiting this option. Charters are arranged in Kathmandu through the offices of Royal Nepal Airlines (RNAC) or any of the new private airlines. These are usually cheaper than charters, but you can only be sure of the reservations from Kathmandu to the place in question. Reservations for the return trip can be made in Kathmandu, but this is usually not very helpful, and everything has to be rearranged at the remote airstrip. For example, it is notoriously difficult to get a reservation back to Kathmandu from the STOL strip in Jumla.

Some suggestions for minimizing hassles with flights in Nepal include making sure you have a return reservation back home before you arrive in Nepal. If you do, then once you arrive, reconfirm it in person at that airline's office, and get the ticket so stamped. Otherwise make sure you book a flight back before you leave on your trek. Trekking agencies in Kathmandu can take care of many of the hassles dealing with domestic flights, and with international carriers. They will also work hard to get you back to Kathmandu if your return flight was canceled on account of weather or other reasons.

If you are on your own, go to a travel agent to arrange the local flights. Reservations are only made when you purchase the ticket. Mr. Karki, the Chief District Officer in Surkhet, once remarked to me, when the plane I was scheduled to leave on actually arrived, and I was buckled in my seat ready to go, "Your flight is confirmed." This is the rule for internal flights in Nepal. To increase your chances, try to make return reservations for your flight back to Kathmandu in the capital before you leave. When you arrive at the remote location, take time to reconfirm at the airline's local station, and see that your name is on the passenger list. If your flight is bumped, then patiently go daily to the office and try to make arrangements to get back. Be aware that each flight has seats reserved for government officials. Travelers with legitimate, documentable reasons can sometimes get clearance from government officials to be issued these seats. This process is begun by writing a letter explaining the reason to the responsible official.

By making arrangements to fly, it is possible to complete treks in a shorter time and occasionally to prevent backtracking. In addition, the views are often

The landing at Lukla is unforgettable.

incredible, and the thrill of a spectacular landing is not quickly forgotten. However, this mode of travel is more expensive.

Tickets for foreigners must currently be paid in hard currency. Sometimes, however, agents at some airstrips will accept Nepali currency if presented with a recent bank receipt showing that a significant amount of hard currency has been changed. Be sure to bring some small denomination U.S. cash or travelers checks with you if you might fly back from some remote strip in Nepal.

Charters are usually arranged to bring a party into a high-altitude area. The quick gain in elevation can be very fatiguing and the time lost recuperating from the sudden rise can sometimes equal the time necessary to trek to the area. Even more important for quite a few trekkers, such rapid elevation gain has resulted in death from altitude illness, especially high-altitude pulmonary edema. Hence, given the choice, it is better to arrange a charter to return from the area and to acclimatize by walking in.

Trekking parties are cautioned not to wave at low-flying helicopters as this is an invitation to be rescued. Such activity has confused rescue pilots trying to locate the stricken party.

Cars, Buses, and Trucks

> *A fast approach by plane robs the journey of anticipation; a slow approach by road always begins with the hope of a pleasant trip, and continues with the hope of simply reaching the destination.*
>
> George Schaller, *Stones of Silence*

In the 1970s studies showed road building in Nepal to have a negative effect on economic development. The debate is now forgotten and there is currently a frenzy of road building, though there is little budgeted for maintenance. Roads are planned to Jumla, to Beni, to Num, almost completed to Taplejung, and perhaps someday there will be a road to Namche Bazaar. This is in addition to the current spur roads to Jiri, Gorkha, Syabrubensi, Besisahar, and KAARe, and the major access roads to Kathmandu, Kodari, Pokhara, and the network in the Tarai. What effect this will have on trekking is certainly unclear. In describing the treks, roads are taken into account to the extent their status is known. Landslides and washouts will continue to be common, and perhaps the old trails will continue to be used. So be aware that any road described in this book may not be motorable at the time you access it.

With the building of roads in popular trekking areas of Nepal, returning trekkers have an opportunity to sense what the early mountain adventurers in the Rockies, Coast Range, and Alps must have sensed when they returned to find a road built where they had struggled to travel before.

Private bus companies provide service over Nepal's main roads. The routes most often used by trekkers are Kathmandu to Lamosangu and then to Jiri for treks east; Kathmandu to Trisuli, and then to Dhunche for treks north;

Kathmandu to Pokhara for treks north of Pokhara; and Bhairawa to Pokhara for western treks. Feeder roads, such as from Pokhara to KAARe, and from Dumre to Besisahar, or Dharan to Basantapur, are also popular. Further information is given in the route descriptions. Riding on these buses often taxes the trekker as much as two weeks' walk with a pack. Most trekkers are willing to put up with the slow, pitching buses in order to save time. There are night bus services between Kathmandu and many points in the Tarai. This odyssey begins in the late afternoon, and you arrive bedraggled in the morning. As the seats in most buses are small, and the space very cramped, consider buying two seat reservations for one person where seats are reserved in advance.

Trekkers may sometimes be able to purchase rides on trucks transporting goods; this may even be preferable to the crowded buses. If you find yourself in the back of a pitching truck, try to get your center of gravity as low and forward as you can. In dusty situations, ride as high and far forward as you can. In trucks or buses, try to get seats up close to the driver. Vehicles often charge extra from trekkers for transporting their equipment. It may make sense for a large party wishing to transport all its gear, porters, and trekkers to the start of a trek to hire taxis or other private vehicles. Trekking agencies, of course, usually make these arrangements and provide pickup services.

You can shorten treks by taking jeeps and buses that travel on the now numerous spur roads off the main routes. In certain places you may find this preferable to taking the trail. I sometimes describe alternative routes that avoid the roads. It is up to you to decide whether to see Nepal from a bone-jerking vehicle or by sauntering along a trail.

Money

Nepali currency is the medium of exchange in Nepal. In the not-too-distant past, bartering was the common means of trade and commerce in the hills, although Indian coins were occasionally accepted. Now I recommend taking one-, two-, five-, ten-, twenty-, and fifty-rupee *(rupiyAA)* notes. For a group paying bills together, 100-rupee notes are also convenient. There are 100 *paisaa* in a rupee but with inflation it seems pointless to carry this denomination (except for the one lucky *paisaa* coin I always have with me). A rupee is equal to about three cents (U.S.) at the 1991 exchange rate. In Solu-Khumbu, Thak Khola, and other areas of wealth, 1000-rupee notes can sometimes be changed. I would advise against using large bills (Rs. 100 or more) for small payments. If you must, don't flash them, but handle them discreetly and try to only use them if little change is to be made. In wealthy areas some trekkers manage to do business with foreign currency such as U.S. dollars, but this is illegal except at certain locations. It is easiest to exchange currency at banks in Kathmandu and Pokhara. While banks do have branches in most of the district centers and a few towns, exchanging foreign currently at them can be time-consuming and difficult, if not impossible. But like most encounters with Nepali bureaucracy, it is fascinating. Credit cards are not useful in the rural areas! Some facilities in Kathmandu take them presently, and at least one bank, Nepal Grindlays Bank in Kathmandu, will issue travelers checks against a Visa or Mastercard. The exchange rate for this may be quite unfavorable. There is an American Express office in Kathmandu as well.

Hard currency (U.S. dollars, etc.) is necessary for purchasing air tickets, as well as for paying for trekking permits to certain areas. I cannot be specific regarding the latter as this is in a state of flux. Bring some hard cash and travelers checks in small denominations to Nepal, especially if not trekking with an agency.

Many trekkers barter clothes and equipment for Nepali crafts, meals, and lodging. Western goods can also be exchanged for cash at times. The local people like to obtain useful foreign goods in this way. I usually travel with minimal gear that is difficult to replace in Nepal and do most of my commerce with cash. Some who are in Nepal for short periods of time exchange, sell, or give away much of their clothing and equipment toward the end of their trek.

It is best to take new currency on your trek. Exchange worn tattered notes for crisp new ones in Kathmandu. People in the hills will often refuse a ragged, torn note or coins that are worn thin. As for the amount of money to take, it depends on your style of trekking. If everything has been arranged by a prepaid trekking company, little money is needed. If you are traveling without porters or guides and eating food locally, U.S. $3 to $5 per person per day takes care of the necessities. In the Annapurna region, and Khumbu where there are more sophisticated hotels, you can spend a great deal more. Carry enough funds for contingencies. Generally you get a great deal of value for the money spent in Nepal. Don't lose that perspective.

The prices throughout this book are based on 1990 rates. Although you may well find the prices higher when you reach Nepal, you'll at least have some idea of what to expect.

Addresses for Receiving Mail in Nepal

The best, in order of preference are: (1) a friend living in Nepal, (2) your trekking agency, if you have one, (3) your embassy, (4) American Express, if you use their travelers checks, and (5) Post Restante (General Delivery, Kathmandu, Nepal).

Equipment List

R   *items you may be able to rent in Nepal*
P   *items you can hope to purchase in Nepal, though you may not be able to count on the quality*

Essential for all trekkers

      walking shoes, well broken-in, and spare insoles if appropriate
P   socks; several pairs of heavy wool outer socks and a few pairs of nylon inner socks
P   skirts: mid-calf to above the ankle
P   pants; baggy ones are best (for women, only between settlements)

P	shirts, blouses, T shirts
P	hat with wide brim
R,P	sleeping bag adequate for temperatures encountered
	repair kit to deal with all your gear
P	water-purification materials (see chapter 5)
P	water bottle; at least 1-liter capacity
R,P	backpack with outside pockets to handle smaller items
P	stuff sacks (nylon is best) for organizing equipment
P	medical kit (see chapter 5)
P	flashlight (torch) with spare batteries and bulbs (consider headlamp)
P	handkerchief
P	toiletries (soap, washcloth, towel, toothbrush and paste, dental floss, comb, shampoos)
	trekking permit
	this book
	Nepali for Trekkers
P	rupees in small bills and coins
P	pen or pencil, ink, paper, and envelopes (to write an emergency message should the need arise) pocket knife, perhaps with can opener and scissors
P	plastic bags; several sizes with rubber bands or twist ties
P	nylon line (parachute chord)
	blister-prevention materials (see chapter 5)
P	feminine hygiene materials (imported varieties now available at supermarkets in Kathmandu)
	plastic trowel to bury feces
P	matches or cigarette lighter
	sunglasses
	spare eyeglasses or contact lenses if you wear them
P	umbrella if traveling in warm sunny lowlands
	smiles

For treks to cold, snowy, and high places

P	wool or pile hat; balaclava
R,P	wool sweaters or pile or down jacket
P	wool or pile pants
	long underwear of polypropylene and wool
	mitts (possibly gloves) with water-resistant shell and warm, light inner lining for dexterity
P	windproof outer garments, pants and jacket
	boots, well broken in and waterproofed
P	gaiters to keep snow out of boots
P	ice ax, rope, and crampons for glacier travel
P	glacier goggles with spares, including enough for Nepali employees
P	sunscreen; zinc oxide for lips

If trekking with an agency (check with the manager regarding items in the other categories)

P   duffel bag; sturdy, zippered, lockable with all your gear stowed inside; to give to your porter

If trekking independently, where hotels catering to trekkers exist all the way

P   toilet paper
P   makeshift shelter (plastic sheeting or bivouac shelter)
P   some food for contingencies

If trekking independently and relying on *bhaTTi*

R,P   air mattress or foam pad
P   toilet paper
P   plastic ground sheet
P   some food for contingencies

If trekking independently where you may camp and rely on your own food at times

R,P   tent
P   toilet paper
P   sturdy duffel bags, zippered and lockable, for gear
P   kerosene stove
P   fuel containers, fuel filter
P   nesting pots
P   cups, plates, spoons
P   scouring pad
P   alcohol in a plastic container (for priming stove if your model requires this)
R,P   shelter, warm clothing, and cooking facilities for your employees if you will be in remote areas
P   food, packed appropriately

Monsoon treks

    running shoes with new waffle soles
P   umbrella
    waterproof (Gore-Tex™) jacket with underarm zips, or a rain poncho or cape (latter now made in Kathmandu and good value)
    waterproof rain chaps or pants (optional)
    large, heavy-duty plastic bags and several smaller ones
P   plastic sheeting for covering porters' loads, and other uses
    insect repellent, permethrin spray
    patience
    adaptability

Optional gear

       specialty food items
       bathing suit
       shorts for men
       shaving paraphernalia for men (battery operated or safety razor)
       altimeter
       compass
       thermometer
       watch with a chronograph and alarm (and possibly an altimeter)
       binoculars
       spotting telescope and tripod

P   maps
       star chart
       ear plugs (for sleeping despite barking dogs)
       headlamp
       candle lantern

P   candles
P   reading material
P   journal, diary, or pocket notebook to record observations
P   stationery, air letters, post cards, stamps
P   English-language learning materials to use with porters (buy in Kathmandu)
       a picture book or post cards about your country or favorite activities
       a picture book of farms, farm activities, and animals
       photographs of your family, friends, and activities
       photographic equipment, film, appropriate spare batteries
       tape recorder, batteries, blank tapes
       prerecorded tapes
       headphones
       microphone
       cellular phone
       hair dryer
       language tape and book
       musical instrument
       games
       belt bag or fanny pack for easy access to selected items while walking
       collapsible ski poles

4 Interacting with Nepal

*Madam, this is Nepal. In America you can be a bird in a gilded
cage. Here the bird is free. And for that there is a price.*
A Nepali to an inconvenienced
and angry trekker

For many years, few indulged in trekking in Nepal, and their impact on the
country was rather small. But the large numbers of people who have begun
trekking in recent years are causing many changes, good and bad, in the landscape and the people of Nepal. Generally, trekkers are unaware of these
changes until, reflecting later, they wonder what is happening.

This chapter provides not only basic information on day-to-day trekking,
but also food for thought on how to help preserve the character of trekking in
Nepal. This type of tourism is now being called "tourism with insight," "alternative tourism," etc. I am pleased to see several Nepali agencies now es-
pousing the cross-cultural attitudes first presented in this book in 1976. Such
information is now included in mainstream guidebooks as well.

Trekking Life

Variables such as the type of trek, the size of the party, and the area visited all affect the way you organize your daily trekking activities. Those on an
organized camping trek follow a personalized daily routine, usually with hot
tea served in your tent before you get up. Breakfast follows, then you hike till
around midday, eat lunch prepared by an advance cook team, then continue till
the evening stop. Those traveling in areas where there are plenty of trekker-
oriented hotels can structure the day much as they wish. Trekkers employing
Nepali assistants are advised to adhere to a schedule compatible with their employees. Trekkers traveling in areas where there are few foreigners and who
wish to eat local food must also adhere to the local schedules.

Though local schedules vary depending on the area and the village, the
following general outline gives you some idea of what to expect. In the hills,
Nepali people get up around sunrise, sometimes have a brief snack, then work
until the mid-morning meal around 10:00 A.M. Work then continues until the
late afternoon, and is followed by the second meal of the day. A snack immediately preceding this meal is not uncommon. Since activities coincide with period of daylight, people tend to go to sleep soon after sunset. In the mountains,
people wait until it warms up a little before engaging in much activity. They
generally eat three meals a day.

En route to Khumbu and in Khumbu, Langtang, Helambu, Gosainkund,
and north of Pokhara, many establishments cater specifically to trekkers. They
often sell foods carried in from big towns and bazaars, and hoteliers will gener-

ally cook meals for you at other than the usual Nepali times. Popular places often have hired cooks from Kathmandu. These places have signs. A variety of non-Nepali meals are available, depending on local supplies. Often a book is available for you to write in what you have ordered and received, in order to account for it later on the honor system. This is not gourmet cooking, and the local people do not eat it. If you find you do not like the native cuisine, you can avoid it by staying on the popular trails and eating in such hotels. Those who sample local foods, however, may be surprised by the tasty variety and become converts to this simple cuisine.

Seek out less popular lodges, and private homes, or *bhaTTi* rather than patronizing the most frequented places. This distribution of income will have a significant overall economic impact in the area. It is not uncommon to go through a popular trekking stop and find everyone trying to stay at one facility, not necessarily because it is the best, but because everyone else is there. Avoid this herd mentality.

It is important to realize that innkeepers, in spite of their lengthy menus, often only have one stove to cook on. Try to size up the situation and adjust your order to what is already being cooked or, even better, learn some tips from the Nepalis on patience. Fast food hasn't yet arrived in rural Nepal. Be aware that to cook almost anything other than traditional *daal bhaat* is more difficult for the Nepalis, and also uses up more of the scarce wood supply. Trekkers should limit their use of scarce fuel resources by trying to eat the local diet as much as possible.

Thus, a reasonable schedule for trekkers not too insulated from the Nepali lifestyle is to arise around sunrise, or just before. After a snack or hot drink, begin walking in the cool morning until 9:00 or 10:00 A.M. Then stop at a *bhaTTi* (local inn) for food or cook your own along the trail. If traveling away from the trails frequented by foreigners and eating in the local inns, the food is *daal bhaat,* a large quantity of rice, with a lentil soup poured over it. There are usually some cooked vegetables available, and occasionally you may be able to get an egg or some meat. Unlimited quantities of *bhaat* (rice) are included in the meal, but the *daal* (lentils) and vegetables are rationed. Some hotels or *bhaTTi,* especially those along roads, in some popular trekking areas, and up high, are beginning to charge for extra helpings of rice, *daal,* and vegetables, essentially a "plate rate." The food requested in a *bhaTTi* is usually not cooked until after you order, so the entire food stop takes approximately two hours. However, if you ask for the typical Nepali *daal bhaat* at 9:30 to 10:00 A.M., in a popular *bhaTTi* or sometimes in a lodge, it may be essentially already cooked. This can be valuable for small parties needing to cover long distances quickly.

If you eat in traditional inns or *bhaTTi,* or even in hotels, lodges, and tea shops (the last three terms are used interchangeably) that cater to Westerners, please realize that the standards of hygiene do not compare to those in restaurants at home. They don't even come close. That is the price you pay to reap the benefits of being in Nepal. The sanitation on treks run by professional guides also varies considerably, but you may be able to exercise some influence there.

Lodge owners along the popular trekking routes are especially eager to please tourists. By asking about toilets and rubbish disposal, use of kerosene, boiled water, and hygiene, a trekker can influence future directions for the lodges. Compliment lodge people for the many things they do well.

Sometimes, away from the popular trekking areas, rice is not available, and you may have to eat *saatu, dherdo,* or *piTho,* terms for roasted flour (corn, millet, or wheat) made into a thick paste by adding boiling water. Eat it with a spicy sauce and vegetables if available.

Spoons are seldom available in a traditional *bhaTTi* frequented by Nepalis. You must either provide your own or eat with your right hand as Nepalis do. It is not considered impolite to make slurping noises while eating, and a burp is often taken as an appreciation of the meal. Sometimes, while waiting for a meal to be cooked, you can obtain a snack *(khaajaa)* such as roasted corn (it does not pop like the Western variety). Often tea is available too, but the farther north you go along trails frequented mostly by Nepalis, the more scarce it becomes. In many areas of Buddhist influence in the northern regions, only Tibetan tea served with butter and salt is available. Along the less-trekked routes, it is served as a part of normal hospitality, without expecting payment. When I asked Thupi Pasang if I could pay once, I got the reply, "If you want to pay 1000 rupees, I'll take it, otherwise it is free." Along certain northern routes frequented by trekkers, tea with milk and sugar is often available.

In Khumbu as in most mountain areas, the traditional diet can be mostly potatoes. They are made into a stew *(shakpa)* or pancakes *(riki kur),* or mashed and served with a spicy sauce *(riltok sen),* but most often they are boiled and eaten after peeling the skin off. Other features of the Sherpa diet, also common to other *BhoTiya,* are *thukpa,* a noodle soup, and *tsampa* (roasted barley flour). *Tsampa* is eaten either as a watery porridge *(chamdur),* made by pouring tea over it, or as a drier form *(pak)* poured into the tea.

Just as tea shops can only be found in certain areas, local inns are often limited to regions settled by *Thakali,* the traditional innkeepers, though people of other ethnic groups also run them. *BhaTTi* are especially scarce in the west. When you cannot find one, villagers are often willing to provide food and shelter in their own houses. This generally is not possible, however, in Brahman and *Chhetri* dwellings with some exceptions. Brahmans may arrange to feed you and let you sleep in some place where you won't pollute their homes. *Chhetri* may do this in a veranda or porch part of the house. To ask, you must first attract the attention of someone inside the house (never go in without being invited). Call out a suitable term of address and wait for someone to appear. Then make your request.

With the first meal of the day in your stomach, the rest of the day's trail awaits your feet. Along the way you pass tea shops and stop for refreshment. Trekkers may pass pastures and shepherds in the high country, and may be able to obtain some fresh milk, yoghurt *(dhai),* or whey *(mAI).*

During the day's walk, you may pass through several villages and farming areas, cross major rivers, climb to the crest of one or more ridges, and descend down into the valleys again. When trekking without a guide, it is necessary to constantly ask the name of the current village and the way to the next village. Except along the most popular trekker routes, there are few trail signs in Nepal, and finding the route is a matter of asking the way as the Nepalis do. Indeed, Nepali people traveling in unknown areas are constantly asking the way and exchanging news. Often you may be confused by the answers Nepalis give to your questions. If so, repeat the question or phrase it differently until you are satisfied with the response. The problem may be your pronunciation. Ask the next person on the trail, too. It's all part of the fun of trekking and finding your way in Nepal. Along the more popular routes local people make a commotion when they think you are on the wrong trail. This can create problems when you deliberately wish to take a side trip. When asking the way, keep in mind both the next town's name as well as a larger, well-known town farther along. Often the names of small settlements may not be known, but everyone knows the names of big centers, even though they may be a few days' walk away. Because of the lack of standardized spelling, names on many maps may lead to improper pronunciation.

Nepalis are eager to please Westerners and, in their enthusiasm to do so, often give incorrect answers to questions. For example, a Nepali might say that a particular destination you ask about is close when it is actually a long way off. Or he might say that the trail you are on goes to the place you are asking for, rather than upset you by telling you the truth. And people who don't understand your questions sometimes answer nevertheless. Learning to get around these problems is all part of the experience. It isn't insurmountable or fraught with hazard.

Trails in the high country where there are no settlements are a different matter. Travel along these is seasonal. Most Nepalis go there only during the monsoon when few trekkers are afoot. Animal trails may be confused with human trails. Forest, fog, or whiteout may make finding the route difficult or impossible. Trekkers have often become lost in such circumstances, and it is easy to remain lost for several days, especially if trying to bushwhack to a trail you don't know. If lost, backtrack to a point you know, rather than trying to push onward. It is prudent to travel with a guide in such country. Often one can be hired locally for a few days.

Trails vary considerably with the seasons. During and soon after the monsoon, when the rivers are still swollen, travelers take ridge trails rather than those following the valley floors. But in the dry season, November through May, many trails on ridges are abandoned in favor of more indirect river routes. In addition, shortcuts across dry paddy fields are favored over the well-worn trails. These shortcuts can be numerous and at times misleading, but they are still preferable in most cases.

During the day you may pass many Nepalis who ask where you are coming from and where you are going. The accepted form of greeting or taking leave of a person is to place the palms of your hands together in front of your face as if to pray and say *namaste* or *namaskaar*. The latter is more respectful and formal. Both have the connotation of "I salute the god within you." Children will often badger you with endless greetings. Always use the less formal greeting with children.

Trail signs at Shey Phoksumdo National Park; such signs are becoming more common.

In the late afternoon or sooner, look for a place to stay. Asking for a meal in the evening is equivalent to asking for a place to sleep. Along the popular routes, there is usually a hotel fee for sleeping in places that cater to foreigners. But in *bhaTTi* in the rest of the country, a place for the night is included in the charge for a meal. Hotels for foreigners often have separate rooms with beds and mattresses. Some places have wood stoves or fireplaces for warmth and hot showers. Charges are reasonable in view of the wood used, but I feel it is appropriate to limit your use of these scarce resources. In the more typical *bhaTTi*, you sleep on the floor, often with many other travelers. Sometimes when the *bhaTTi* is particularly crowded, you may be shown a hayloft or other simpler accommodation. I sometimes prefer to sleep on porches outside the houses, as chimneyless and windowless interiors are often quite smoky. This is obviously impractical in most high, cool areas. Establish the prices for items when you order so you will not be surprised at the bill. Most lodges catering to foreigners have a menu with prices listed.

If stopping to cook your own food along the trail during the day, expect to take two hours. Setting up camp in the evening takes 30 minutes, and breaking it the next morning takes almost an hour. Trekkers on trips organized through an agency will tend to have customary meals at the usual times. Lunch is usually prepared by the cooking staff who then go on ahead. The staff sets up and breaks camps and makes sure that the trekker keeps to the correct trail. The Sirdar and other staff may be able to enrich the experience by explaining things seen, and also things not seen.

Trekkers traveling in the high country often stay at *goTh,* temporary shelters used by shepherds. Some are quite substantial structures, while others are only four walls or just the frames for the walls. When the shepherds bring their animals up to graze during the hot monsoon months, they bring bamboo mats or yak wool roofs to cover the frames. *Yersa* in Khumbu are groups of *goTh* used by those who pasture yak and sheep. If there is any doubt about whether these shelters will be available or if privacy is desired, it is best to carry a tent. For other details on campsites, read the section on tents in chapter 3.

It is especially important to check in at police posts along the way, should you need to be traced in an emergency. To get a small group processed at a police check post may take up to 30 minutes, but check posts along the popular trails have become much more efficient than in the past. For a group, carry copies of a list of everyone's name, age, sex, address, passport number, nationality, and trekking permit number. Leave these with check posts, and it will take less time. The official will usually make a note in your trekking permit. Do not produce your passport unless absolutely necessary or there may be further delays. If you are carrying binoculars, keep them discreetly out of sight, or the officials may suspect you have motives other than bird-watching. Be patient and courteous in dealing with officials.

Don't always be in a hurry, eager to cover as much ground as possible. Sometimes, stop at noon and watch village life or explore the surroundings. Consider spending an entire day in some place that is *not* the highest, the most spectacular, the most beautiful, and just let things happen.

Cross-Cultural Clues for the Survival of Trekking in Nepal

To expect Nepalis to conform to and accept outsiders' ways is the most extreme form of cultural arrogance.
Donald Messerschmidt

The fullest enjoyment of Nepal in all its myriad aspects comes to those who attempt to transcend the cultural and linguistic differences between themselves and their Nepali hosts. Such people are more easily accepted into the social framework of Nepal and there are many rewards.

In the past, many trekkers have offended their Nepali hosts. They have also misunderstood the actions and feelings of Nepalis, and the foreigner's reactions have made a bad situation worse. Others have taken great advantage of traditional hospitality without considering the consequences. Still others, realizing how much further their money will go in this country, have made a big display of their wealth. They have handed out large (for Nepal) sums of money, and given away many of their possessions. Trekkers have disgraced religious customs and shown great disrespect for their hosts' beliefs. The local people have adapted somewhat to this breach of courtesy and ethics by these

Weaving cloth is a common cottage industry in the hills.

foreign travelers. Indeed, Nepalis along the popular routes expect foreigners to behave in this manner. Partly for this reason, traditional Nepali hospitality is less obvious along these trails. Some trekkers complain that Nepal isn't all that it was billed to be and search for new unspoiled places to desecrate. The Nepali people will not let you know of their displeasure—it isn't their way. But amongst themselves they will have less respect for you and less desire to treat you as an honored guest. But should you make the effort to stand apart from the other trekkers, to respect the Nepali people and their customs, they will relate to you in positive ways you couldn't have imagined. You will find yourself more respected in turn.

This section, the most important part of this book, is an attempt to provide you, the guest in Nepal, with the understanding to act in ways that constitute reasonably acceptable behavior to your hosts. Most of the information has been subtly gleaned from Nepalis, or from the experiences of sensitive visitors to Nepal. If your attitudes are right, and your practices are acceptable, then a few faux pas will be overlooked. All of us in Nepal have, at times, acted incorrectly. How do you think I've obtained most of the information presented here? But once you have learned acceptable norms of behavior, the benefits should make all the effort worthwhile. Encourage others who have your confidence to do likewise. This is essential if trekking in Nepal is to continue to be one of the supreme experiences in social-cultural peregrination.

When talking to trekkers in Nepal, I compare the experience of those who are behaving in a fashion sensitive to Nepali customs with those who aren't so considerate. The thoughtful trekker has invariably had a more intimate relationship with the Nepali people and has encountered fewer problems.

Nepal is a complex social mosaic, with Hindu and Buddhist traditions overlaying animistic and shamanistic beliefs. Many of the customs stem from Hindu concepts of purity and ritual pollution. As hill Nepal becomes increasingly Sanskritized, these concepts have become more important. While the *BhoTiya*—Buddhist highlanders of Nepal—have their own customs that must be respected, they too are becoming increasingly affected by Hindu religion. There are basic rules governing acceptable behavior in Nepal that have knit the social fabric together over centuries. These rules are not difficult. Basically, you need only observe what Nepalis around you are doing and act accordingly. What follows classifies and expounds on this.

LANGUAGE

Along the popular trails, Nepalis who deal with trekkers have learned basic English and other foreign languages to enable them to please their guests. Even off the trekker trails, some English is spoken; but in remote areas, you are less likely to find translators to help communicate.

Everyone who attempts to learn some rudimentary Nepali will find his experience in the country much richer. You will be more welcome, people will be friendlier, and they will go out of their way to help if you try to speak some Nepali.

Nepali is an Indo-European language that is easy to learn. It is used as the second tongue by half of Nepal, so people commonly hear many variations in how it is spoken. Hence your efforts to speak the national language will immediately make you welcome and help you stand out from other visitors. It is the first step in transcending cultural differences to make for a more rewarding interaction.

To help you learn the language, the text of my language book has been added to this book as appendix F. The best, most convenient way to learn Nepali is to order the pocket-size book *Nepali for Trekkers,* published by The Mountaineers Books, and practice with the accompanying language tape (see appendix F for ordering information).

DRESS

The dress code for men is as important as that for women but is often neglected. For example, men wearing shorts have low status in Nepal. Men should never bare their chests, except when bathing discreetly. Wear a shirt at all times.

Women should attempt to wear full, long skirts, mid-calf at least, as often as possible. It is important that women do not expose their legs. Wearing long underwear is helpful if your skirt is shorter than mid-calf. In fact, you can put long underwear, pile pants, and the like on when it gets cold, and take it off quite discreetly when it warms up. Shorts are not acceptable for women. If women wear shorts, Nepali men and women make rude remarks about them amongst themselves. Attire appropriate for the beaches of Cannes is not appropriate for Nepal, just as attire for Papua New Guinea Highlands is inappropriate in Perth. Skirts can allow a woman to urinate with some privacy if there aren't enough bushes around, especially if she doesn't wear underpants.

For women, a *lungi* or tube of material can be purchased in any cloth shop in Nepal and custom-sewn in 10 minutes into a suitable garment. Have a pocket or two sewn in. An elastic waistband or drawstring is helpful for washing discreetly. Perhaps easier to wear is the *AAgi,* or *chubaa,* a long sleeveless *BhoTiya* dress that ties in back. In Kathmandu you can sometimes purchase a ready-made cotton one. Or it can be made from wool or polyester. Long skirts brought from home are also excellent. Some women have made them of denim, or with beautiful patterns. Skirts should be full (not tight), and in a lightweight fabric will be as cool as shorts, and definitely cooler than trousers. If you must wear baggy pants for the arduous part of the day's walk, change into your skirt in the evening when in a village or when dealing with Nepali people.

Several women on one trek reported a phenomenal difference in acceptance by Nepalis depending on whether they wore skirts, pants or shorts. One woman in another group of women decided to not wear a skirt while her companions did. She wrote me that her friends received all the attention from Nepalis and she was ignored. This all changed after a visit to the tailor along the way when in desperation she had one made and wore it ever since. One woman who started trekking in a skirt decided it wasn't necessary and changed into shorts. In an hour she was accosted by a Nepali man. Another changed from wearing shorts into a skirt and found that, rather than being stared at as a curiosity, she felt more accepted by Nepalis. A Nepali hillsman who married a

trekker reported that he was attracted to her in distinction to other women because she wore a skirt.

Trekkers who have questioned Sherpas or other Nepalis about appropriate
attire have countered my arguments by quoting their answers. The Nepalis
always answer to please, even though their feelings are offended. Donald Messerschmidt, the author of chapter 13, was talking with a shopkeeper in Tirkhe-
dhunga when a French couple walked by, dressed as if on the Riviera, the man
in a tiny brief, the woman in a skimpy bikini. The shopkeeper asked Don what
country they came from. Don, having heard them speak, replied France. The
shopkeeper then asked, "What's the matter, don't they have cloth in their
country?" Consider how you might feel if a Papua New Guinea highlander
male, wearing only a penis shield, walked near your home and spoke to you.
Would you treat him in a friendly manner and invite him inside? Nepalis feel
equally put off by the dress of many foreigners.

BATHING

Trekkers often like to relax in hot springs or swim in rivers or lakes.
Nepalis are usually very shocked if this is done with genitals exposed. Women
should not bare their breasts, especially those who have not borne children.
Men may go bare-chested only while swimming or bathing. If you wish to
swim in the nude, do so out of sight of Nepalis. Also be modest while washing
yourself within view of others. Women wearing skirts can bathe discreetly
when not alone by hitching the skirt up, using it as a tent. Clothes can be
changed under it too, and an elastic waistband or drawstring makes it easy
if your skirt is not too bulky. A tank suit underneath the skirt makes it easier
to swim.

BARGAINING

To understand the custom of bargaining, which is almost universal in
Asia, one must realize that it is a game, not an impediment to friendship. Westerners, by contrast, often harbor bad feelings after the bargaining process. Yet
once a price is agreed upon, it is "fixed." Language trouble can also create
misunderstandings. I can well remember bargaining with a taxi driver to take
me to the start of a trek out of the Kathmandu Valley. He named a price and I
began to bargain with him, but named a higher price, as my command of numbers in Nepali in 1970 was poor. He quickly agreed, and it was only as the
ride began that I realized my mistake. Nevertheless, I paid the price I had
agreed upon.

Try to find out the going price for an item before you begin bargaining.
Failure to do so hurts everyone. As an example, if a Nepali will sell an egg to
his neighbor for Rs. 2, but finds he can get Rs. 3 from a trekker, he will be less
likely to sell that egg to his neighbor. Thus the price of eggs goes up. The
Nepali is hurt, but not the trekker, to whom the difference in price is negli-
gible. Such inflation has become quite common, and it behooves the trekker to
always pay the lowest going price in any transaction.

In many places, people want Western gear, such as down jackets, wind-
breakers, and other items of apparel or equipment, more than they do your

money. So you can either plan to bring extra to trade, or barter unneeded items toward the end of your trek.

Bargaining effectively takes time, so be leisurely and relaxed. Don't show too much interest in the item and certainly don't begin by offering the top price you are willing to pay. If you are hung up over the last stages of the bargaining process, remember the monetary exchange value of the amount in dispute. Sometimes it may just be a few cents and not worth the haggle for something a local wouldn't buy. Also remember that prices are fixed for certain items, usually food and commodities, especially along well-traveled routes, and bargaining is not appropriate.

EATING

Hindus are concerned about ritual pollution of food when it is touched by anyone outside their caste or religion. As a foreigner, you are outside the caste system. Often you are considered an outcaste or untouchable. Thus, do not touch any cooked foods on display, though it is usually all right to handle uncooked foods such as fruit and raw vegetables. When drinking from a container used by others, avoid touching your lips to it; pour the liquid into your mouth. Similarly, when drinking from a water bottle, do not touch your lips to it—at least not in sight of your hosts. Wait for food to be served to you rather than helping yourself. Do not give leftovers to your hosts, even though they may be rare delicacies brought from home. Do not offer a person anything from which you have taken a bite or sip. This is the *juTho* concept of food—if any food is touched by someone's mouth the entire plate is contaminated and the utensils must be washed before anyone else uses them. By the same token, all leftover food or drink must either be thrown away or fed to animals. The only exception is that a wife may eat from her husband's plate. Hence, do not accept more food than you can eat, and in a tea shop, make sure you put your empty glass where the Nepalis put theirs. Furthermore, since Westerners are considered outside the Hindu caste system, trekkers who visit Brahman houses or villages can expect to be served apart from others, usually outside their host's house. They will not be allowed to sleep in a Brahman house. In general, don't offer to share food in a group of Nepalis unless you have enough for everyone.

Don't touch food with your left hand. Nepalis use the left hand for cleaning after defecating, and it is offensive for them to see food in it. Eat with your right hand and use your left for picking up a glass or holding something nonedible. Before and after meals, you will be offered water and a place to wash your hands and rinse your mouth. Wash your hands separately, or your left one not at all. Your right hand may be used to wipe your mouth, never your left. Give and receive items with your right hand. In eating *daal bhaat* and vegetables, the meal is served in separate containers, so keep them that way, except for small portions that you mix on your plate prior to eating. It is, of course, possible to eat with a spoon or chopsticks, which may be available along the more popular trekking trails. But try eating with your right hand. It's fun! It's also the most popular way of consuming food in the world.

The above is the way food is handled in the traditional Nepali way. The norm in hotels that cater to trekkers is less well defined, and behavior like that you are accustomed to back home is more commonplace. All the same, the more a trekker is aware of the usual Nepali manners, and the more he or she uses them in everyday behavior, the more comfortable a Nepali host will be with that person.

GIFT-GIVING AND GENEROSITY

In dealings with people, pay the going rate. Never walk off without paying. In tipping people for their services, be reasonable. Routine tipping is not a Nepali custom. Some people tip much more than the salary or cost of the service they are paying for. This only reinforces the belief that the sahib does not know the value of his money, and thus should be relieved of as much of it as possible.

Bringing small gifts for people who have helped you along the way is a good idea. However, bringing gifts for routine distribution every time you stay

Share the pictures in this book with villagers along the way (photo by Anne Rodman).

in someone's house is to be frowned on, since the Nepalis themselves don't do this. People you wish to be generous to may appreciate a look through your camera or binoculars or at the pictures in this book, *Birds of Nepal,* or *Flowers of the Himalaya.* Nepalis really do enjoy looking at the paintings and pictures of familiar and unknown birds and flowers. Their knowledge about their own environment will impress you. Allowing people to look through picture books from home (those with farm scenes are most appreciated), post cards of temples and other sights of Nepal, or to see photographs of your family, will be a welcome gesture. Or sing songs for them, dance with them, or play a musical instrument. Bring a sketch book and share drawings with them. Let them draw for you. One trekker suggests bringing string and playing string games with children and adults, something that is imaginative, cheap, and portable. Displays of generosity should be limited to appreciation for something extraordinary that has been done for you.

Gifts should emphasize the transcendent values of friendship, knowledge, and health over material wealth. Read the next section to understand why. But beware of the long-term repercussions of anything you do. When a friend of mine who was working in family planning in Kathmandu in 1969 suggested that I distribute condoms during my treks, it seemed a great idea. Reluctant to demonstrate their proper use to adults, I blew them up as balloons for children. This was a highly successful public relations gesture, but I learned later that people following my path were besieged with requests for condoms and balloons. Currently such litter abounds. Bring small useful items like strong sewing thread, needles, cloth, and rope. Whether or not you travel with small children, baby clothes will be appreciated. Consider bringing your older clothes that are out of style, or camping or trekking equipment that is no longer "state of the art" to give to porters and people as gifts, again within the grounds noted above.

BEGGING, AND DEALING WITH CHILDREN

> *Give me one pen,* miThai, *bonbon. Give me one rupee.*
> The sounds of Nepali children
> the trekker hears today

Trekkers may sometimes encounter beggars to whom it is appropriate to give. There are few traditional beggars in the hills, but occasionally saddhu, or holy men, travel through begging as part of their lifestyles. Monks and nuns occasionally beg. Food such as rice is an appropriate gift item for them. Sometimes destitute people are encountered and gifts of clothing, food, and occasionally money are appropriate. Note the actions of Nepalis around you when deciding whether to give.

It is instructive to watch patterns of begging develop along the trekking trails over the years. When I first came to Nepal in 1969 there was no begging in the hills. Yet children and others along the trekking trails are now constantly begging for candy, money, pens, and cigarettes. A few hours' walk off these trails, people do not beg at all. In areas such as Thak Khola where many types of trekkers are seen, people who beg tend to approach those who appear to be well-to-do. When I visited Manang after only a few rather lavishly organized treks had been through that area I was constantly besieged. Yet over the pass in Thak Khola the pressure to give was much less, presumably because the children and others realize their requests will be better rewarded by trekkers in large groups.

Why do trekkers give money, pens, cigarettes, candy, and other items to children? Clearly they like the happy smiles they receive. And in Nepal, foreigners can feel generous without having to give very much. Others feel guilty about the great gulf in material wealth between themselves and Nepali people. If you are one of these, realize that you are making beggars out of children who once were spontaneously happy. To encourage and support begging is an example of the cultural arrogance that characterizes many tourists. Do you want everyone in Nepal to lose their self-respect, a quality that you probably admire so much? If everyone stopped reinforcing inappropriate begging, it would cease in a generation or less. To sample the experience without begging, take a trek away from popular areas. You'll be convinced.

Nepalis have had good dental hygiene in the past, due mostly to their low consumption of sugar. Don't work against this by giving candy. Indeed, the amount of tooth decay in the Khumbu area from recent consumption of sugar in the form of candies has increased dramatically. There are plans for remedial dental work there. Heavy cigarette smoking is a major factor contributing to the high rate of lung disease in Nepal. Don't encourage smoking by handing out cigarettes, especially to children. A few enlightened Nepalis will not allow smoking inside their inns! Handing out money to everyone who asks or giving money for posing for pictures is not a good idea. Parents of Nepali children are usually quite ashamed to learn that their children have been begging, and they try to stop it, except in areas where begging has been so reinforced that parents have become a type of pimp.

You will find many other trekkers giving to begging children. Suggest tactfully to them that they not do so and explain the reasons. This will be a significant step in trying to help the Nepalis maintain their self-respect. It will help return Nepal to the trekking paradise it once was.

When approached by a beggar, either walk away disinterested, or, for begging children, use one of the phrases in Appendix F. I don't find talking to Nepali children about begging very effective. It might be if everyone said the same thing. Don't taunt or ridicule the beggar. Sarcasm is not understood in Nepal.

Sometimes trekkers are approached to donate large sums of money for village construction projects such as schools, trails, and bridges. That is probably legitimate and if Nepalis also contribute, then the trekker might too. In some places Nepalis will approach you to plant a *Tikaa* (red mark) on your forehead or garland you with flowers for which they expect you to pay. Avoid such people if you don't want the product. Sometimes trekkers will spend several days with a family and then decide to be generous with that family in some special way. That is perfectly appropriate, it is a part of normal social human behavior. It certainly doesn't encourage the kind of begging that has sprung up on the shoulders of trekker tourism.

"Oh money come to me." This may become the mantra of the future in Nepal if we who are fortunate enough to travel here don't exercise care and sensitivity.

THEFT AND OTHER INCIDENTS

> *Tourism is thus not only the goose that lays golden eggs, but it also fouls its own nest.*
>
> Dr. Kamal Kumar Shrestha, Nepali chemist

When the first trekkers came to Nepal, the reaction among the hill people was uniform. The visitors were given hospitality and respect, and their actions were watched carefully. With the passage of time and many travelers, patterns of interaction developed. As the kinds of people who came to trek changed, so did the Nepalis' reactions.

The first travelers were interested in mountaineering or research. Some people, generally well-to-do, came just to see the country. All traveled similarly, with large numbers of porters, much equipment, and imported food. They tended to be quite generous, both with their money and their equipment. Lavish tips and presents were offered. More often than not, local feelings were not respected, and customs were violated. Travelers began to be viewed as a source of income and goods. Since they were usually able to pay outrageous prices for Nepali goods and services, this came to be expected. Traditional hospitality remained and has to this day, but it is much less spontaneous and more dependent on money, especially along the more frequented routes.

At the other extreme, in the late 1960s and early 1970s, very budget-conscious travelers and "hippies" came onto the scene. Their actions and customs were different from those of the earlier travelers. Often they lived and kept themselves in a dirtier state than many Nepalis. Their drug habits were also viewed with suspicion. While Nepalis have used marijuana and hashish for years, it is used in moderation and only among some older people in society. The new travelers would sometimes run off without paying for food or services. Occasionally, they would even steal precious items. Indeed, once Nepalis realized that art objects had value other than religious, they too began to steal them to sell on the black market.

The result of all this is that trekking in many areas has become essentially a commercial venture in which attempts are made to relieve travelers of their goods and money. Nepal was once renowned as a place where travelers had absolutely no worries about theft and violence. Now some trekkers complain of theft. Petty vandalism and thievery of packs and luggage left on tops of buses is no longer rare. Tents left unattended have been robbed, and some have even been slit open and robbed while occupied. Misunderstandings have resulted in attacks, robberies, and a few deaths. Among the incidents have been attacks on trekkers camping alone in areas with few people, attacks by porters, and instances where trekkers enjoying a view from an exposed area have been pushed off a precipice. Perhaps there is no increase in the incidence of such episodes, but as the number of trekkers increase they are no longer unheard of.

However, clearly some trekkers have been insensitive to local customs, have mistreated their porters, and have behaved in a manner outside the norms of Nepali experience. The increasing numbers of trekkers have made such behavior more visible. In the past, Nepalis would not steal because others would see them with the item and everyone would know, especially if it was imported. But now, in popular trekking areas, theft is more common because there is greater display of wealth, everyone is more mobile, and it is easier to get rid of stolen property. There has been a considerable change in cultural values among some people living in the areas most heavily influenced by trekking, in part because our display of wealth is often greater than a Nepali could ever accumulate in a lifetime. The Nepalis believe that trekkers don't value their money because they don't try to get the best prices. Since they are so willing to pay too much, others try to relieve them of their seemingly unvalued money and possessions. Remember, however, that the risk of attack and robbery in Nepal is much less than in your home country. But I can no longer state that it will not happen. In case of theft or an incident, be sure to make a report with the police or local official.

Try to prevent petty thievery by keeping a watchful eye on your possessions. Carry around exposed to view only the equipment you expect to use a great deal. Try to have all your gear stowed inside your pack and duffel bag, and keep the pockets done up. Lock items whenever possible. Discreetly inventory your gear in the morning and afternoon; it will be less likely to disappear through porter mishap. When traveling by bus with your belongings in the luggage rack on top, either have someone in the party ride with them, or be watchful of people climbing on top when the bus stops. It helps to keep all easily removed items buried deep inside the luggage. In populated areas, don't leave your tents unattended.

Be sure to register with your country's embassy or consulate when you arrive in Nepal. This is advisable for all trekkers, even those on organized treks. Let the embassy officers know your dates and itinerary, and give them a contact person should they need to follow up.

Another aspect of travel in Nepal that contributed to its popularity was the availability of cheap labor. Porters could be hired for very low rates. Trekkers who could not afford it at home could have servants do many of the distasteful and laborious chores of camping and backpacking. Porters and assistants were sometimes thought of as less than human. This was evident in the lack of responsibility that many took toward their employees.

Treat your porters with respect. Make sure they have equipment and food sufficient for the undertaking.

In lodges and hotels where the honor system is used, be honest, and never run off without paying. Where this has happened too many times, the lodge has the trekker pay for each item as it is ordered.

MEDICAL TREATMENT OF LOCAL PEOPLE

In the past, medical facilities were very scarce in Nepal, and foreigners were almost the only source of Western medicines. It became traditional to consider each passing traveler a doctor, and indeed, many people, both medical and nonmedical, devoted a considerable part of their energies to treating the ills of the local people. I feel that this effort is probably not warranted, and may even do more harm than good. To begin with, it helps destroy confidence in health care services developing in rural areas. Besides the facilities staffed by doctors along the trails, there are many health posts manned by auxiliary health workers. It is very doubtful that ephemeral medical care such as a trekker could dispense would result in a cure or significant benefit to the sufferer. Furthermore, the idea that a little medicine might help a sick person and enable him or her to get to proper medical aid just does not hold up. Based on my personal experience as a doctor working in a remote area of Nepal and on discussions with other medical personnel, giving medicine to someone whom you wish to refer to another facility is almost certain to deter that person from acting on the referral. Finally, the idea that a little aspirin won't hurt anyone is untenable because, since it will not effect a cure, it may help destroy confidence in Western medicine. In a country with many different medical practices, it is best to introduce those aspects of medicine that definitely work. This may seem like a very inhumane and hard-nosed attitude, especially for a physician, but it is in Nepal's best interests, and several important Nepali organizations have publicly concurred.

However, this advice does not apply to your porters and other employees. If a problem presents itself that you can confidently manage, you should treat them to the best of your abilities. Otherwise, if the condition is serious, you are responsible for obtaining proper medical care for that person. In other situations, exercising normal humanitarian instincts and helping your fellow man is also appropriate. That is, don't walk away from the scene of an accident without rendering assistance in any way that you can.

MISCELLANEOUS CUSTOMS

The fire and hearth are considered sacred in Sherpa homes, and in those of most other *BhoTiya*. Thus do not throw any refuse, including cigarettes, into a hearth. This is also the case in high-caste Hindu homes. Sherpas and other *BhoTiya* believe that burning or charring meat offends the gods. Even if you have the opportunity, do not roast meat on an open fire.

Shoes are considered the most degrading part of your apparel, so keep them on the floor or ground. Remove them before putting your feet up on anything. Shoes, especially leather ones, should always be removed before entering any kind of temple, *gomba,* or monastery. Do not touch anyone with your shoes. The greatest insult you can give a Nepali is to kick him or her with your shoe. Follow the example of your host in deciding whether to remove shoes before entering a Nepali home. If in doubt, remove them. When sleeping in a temple or *gomba* don't point your feet at the images.

Don't wash your feet in water that will flow into a water-driven prayer wheel. If you must wash your feet in such a stream, do it after the water has passed through the entire series of prayer wheels. The head of an adult Nepali is the most sacred or ritually clean part of the body. You should never touch it. Similarly, don't touch anyone with your left hand.

Before sitting down on the ground, you will almost always be offered a mat to sit on. When sitting, do not point the soles of your feet at anyone. Nepalis will not step over your legs and feet. Be sure to draw them up to make a path for anyone coming or going. If you and your porters, or Nepali hosts, have to sleep on the floor together, sometimes around a fire, the arrangement should be sure to avoid anyone's feet being pointed at a Nepali person's head. As you go further north, these concepts of purity and pollution become more relaxed. Watch your hosts and adjust your habits accordingly.

While traveling, you may pass Buddhist *mani* walls containing tablets with prayers carved on them in handsome Tibetan script. Walk by them, keeping them on your right, as Buddhists would do as a sign of respect. Similar treatment is given to the *chorten* and *stupa,* commemorative mounds sometimes modeled after those at Swayambhu or Baudha. If in doubt as to whether a structure is one of these, keep it on the right as you walk by. When visiting a monastery or *gomba,* a donation of money for the upkeep is expected as a gift. In paying respects to the abbot of a monastery, offer him a ceremonial scarf, or *kata,* obtained from another monk. Note that many Hindu temples will be out-of-bounds for non-Hindus.

Many Western habits are offensive to Nepalis. Some, such as shaking hands, using dry toilet paper, carrying around a used handkerchief, and eating without washing, seem unsanitary to them.

OTHER CONCERNS FOR THE TREKKER

Respect people's desires not to be photographed. Think how you would feel if hordes of invaders would regularly descend into your life, not say a word to you, but plunge long lenses into the midst of your daily routine, and occasionally into your most private affairs. Many, especially elderly villagers, believe that being photographed can shorten their lifespans. Sometimes if you talk with them a while, they will consent. After you show them pictures of your family, they may be more willing to be photographed. Or let a recalcitrant subject take a photograph with your camera. After he snaps the shutter, he may change his mind and let you photograph. If I want a photograph badly enough, these techniques, just basically respecting human dignity, work. Don't promise to send copies of photographs to people unless there is a reasonable chance that you can do so. Sending photographs through the mail in Nepal used to be completely unreliable unless the letters were registered, but the mails are becoming more reliable. You could send them with another traveler, or through your trekking agency in Kathmandu. Recently, I have on occasion sent photographs via ordinary mail and had them arrive!

Some people who come to Nepal are attracted by the freely available marijuana and hashish. The plant grows as a weed in much of the country. Traditionally, older shopkeepers consumed it now and then at the end of the day. Young Nepali people never used it when I first came to Nepal in 1969. Now in their desire to copy foreign habits they indulge. Nepal now has a considerable drug problem among its natives! Some trekkers smoking marijuana on the trails will offer it to wide-eyed young children. Consumption of this drug is a personal adult decision. It is illegal to carry and sell it. It is wrong to try to entice youngsters to use it.

Many trekkers purchase art and craft objects in the hills. Sometimes they buy valuable old art objects, usually at modest prices. This is expressly illegal; it is prohibited to remove any valuable old items from their origins. Even transporting idols and artifacts can result in imprisonment, and this has happened to trekkers. Steadfastly deny any interest in old art, for if you don't, you encourage Nepalis to steal objects from sanctuaries, monasteries, or temples in order to sell them to foreigners.

Some Nepalis have taken to fraudulently "antiquing" art. The old-appearing *thangka* (scroll painting), brought out of a chest in Helambu and sold as an antique, is common. So-called old jewelry peddled by *BhoTiya* is another example. It may even be difficult to obtain government permission to export fraudulently antiqued works of art or objects of religious value. Permission must be obtained from the Archaeological Department in Thapathali in Kathmandu.

Beware of other amazing items for sale. Once in Manang I was shown what appeared to be a huge (ten-carat or more) diamond that its owner said he found lying on the ground near a mountain glacier. He went to great lengths to "prove" to me that it was not glass and said he wanted only Rs. 300 for it. I was entertained, but not convinced. There are many good locally made craft

Tarali *look through a trekker's camera, a good way to break the ice.*

items in certain areas. Purchasing these at the going prices is certainly beneficial to the local economy.

Finally, and perhaps most important, consider this aphorism on the wall
of the police check post in Jomosom:

> *A smile costs nothing, but gives much. It enriches those who re-
> ceive without making poorer those who give. It takes a moment, but the
> memory of it lasts forever. None is so rich or mighty that he can get
> along without it, and none is so poor but that he can be made rich by it.
> A smile creates happiness in the home, fosters good will in business, and
> is the countersign of friendship. It brings rest to the weary, cheer to the
> discouraged, sunshine to the sad, and it is nature's best antidote for
> trouble. Yet it cannot be bought, begged, borrowed or stolen, for it is
> something that is of no value to anyone until it is given away. Some
> people are too tired to give you a smile, give them one of yours, as none
> needs a smile so much as he who has no more to give.*

Conservation

Take nothing but pictures, leave nothing but footprints.
Sierra Club motto

In addition to the effect trekkers have on the people of Nepal, they may
have a profound impact on the countryside. Nepal's limited supply of firewood
is being rapidly consumed and there are few reforestation projects. As a result,
Nepal's biggest export is probably the extremely valuable topsoil being eroded
away into rivers to be washed into India. Trekkers increase the demand for
wood, especially in alpine areas where forests are being cut down near treeline
to provide it. In addition, *goTh*, temporary herding huts, are sometimes dis-
mantled by trekkers or their porters who need firewood for warmth or cooking.
Use of wood for trekking, especially in the high-altitude areas, must stop if
trekking is to be a resource-conserving activity. Some may argue that wood is a
renewable resource, while kerosene is a nonrenewable fossil fuel. True, but in
Nepal the deforestation problem is far too severe to be further worsened by
trekkers. The local people need the wood for themselves, and even for them, it
won't last forever. In the hills, wood is just as scarce. For those on agency
treks, choose an agency that uses only kerosene as a fuel for all members and
staff.

Trekkers should bring kerosene stoves, and use them. It is difficult to get
innkeepers to do this. However, trekker pressure can exert a significant effect:
if they cook your food on kerosene, patronize them, even though it might cost
a little more. Suggest to others (who don't) how important it would be to their
business to do so. In addition, porters build fires to keep warm unless you provide them with enough warm clothes and shelter up high.

Try to eat the more simple Nepali *daal bhaat* rather than the less fuel-
efficient foreign menus that hotels try to prepare. This will have a significant
effect on conserving Nepal's fuel supply. Hotels often offer hot showers for

trekkers. Usually the water is heated in a wood fire—if so, consider showering less often to conserve fuel wood. Patronize hotels that use solar heaters for showers. Hotels burn considerable quantities of wood in heaters to keep trekkers warm. Consider the effect of this, and put on more clothing to keep warm.

When camping, especially in the frail alpine meadows, be careful not to add to erosion problems. It takes many decades to produce the vegetation that can be carelessly torn away by a boot or killed by a tent. Similarly, when following trails, stay on the path and do not cut switchbacks. If the vegetation surrounding the trail erodes, it is much more likely that the trail will wash out during the torrential monsoon.

The difference in waste along trekker-frequented and unfrequented trails is obvious, especially today with more consumer goods more widely available. On the trails not taken by trekkers, you see candy, biscuit, and cigarette wrappers, and matchboxes. Along the trekker trails, there are all types of detritus, including tampons, condoms, toilet paper, and that offering to the great Western god, Feces. Indeed, trekkers often discard litter in Nepal in a way they would never do at home. Is this how Nepalis should remember us?

For some popular trails, the route description might as well read, "Follow the line of sahib's garbage—film boxes, food wrappers, foreign cigarette boxes, tin cans, toilet paper, tampons—for a week to reach the superb alpine pastures and majestic viewpoint." Many parties have so littered areas of Nepal that they are reminiscent of the overused campsites, trails, and countryside of North America. Carry your wrappers and other items throughout the day, and burn them in the evening.

Along popular trekking trails you may see litter containers. Rarely, the paper contents of these are burned, and the metal discarded. Usually, the contents are just pitched off the back of the lodge or shop; these litter areas are all too easy to spot. Talk to the lodge owners and operators about this, and give your preference for incineration and then burial. You can influence them, since they want to be liked, and to do the "right thing" to get your business.

A number of trekkers have begun collecting garbage around inns or as they walk along, burning it when they stop. This practice is to be encouraged. Bring a sealable plastic bag to collect litter as you walk. It will not only help reduce the litter, but perhaps also provide a good example for the Nepalis. Remember, however, not to throw any items into your host's hearth fire. Giving metal and glass containers to villagers is no longer as appreciated as it once was because of the abundance of containers and trekkers offering them. Consolidate and carry out noncombustible items (metal, glass, and plastic). Burial is not an option.

I do not feel that the consumption of bottled mineral water that is now available along the popular trekker routes is ecologically sound, unless you can carry all the empty bottles back home, or at least to Kathmandu. The empty plastic bottles in various stages of destruction create a new category of litter that is totally despicable.

Those trekkers with guides and porters should not leave them in charge of garbage disposal. If you do, it will routinely be discarded either in your sight, or if you make a fuss, out of your sight. Garbage disposal and pollution doesn't mean the same thing to them as it does to us.

Trekkers and mountaineers can contribute to "light pollution" in a different sense, especially in areas such as the Khumbu, through which pass expeditions bound for the heights. Often they carry along stickers with expedition logo which they affix to walls, counters, and windows in hotels. Many, plastered on windows, results in less light getting inside the inn. There is considerable wall paper of unconventional sorts in these places, which seems a part of their decorative scheme. It makes sense to keep it off the glass windows.

Disposing of body wastes is another problem facing trekkers. Those on large organized treks often erect enclosed latrines at campsites. The feces and other material are then buried. This commendable practice avoids the unsightliness and potential for disease of piles of feces, each with a topping of toilet paper. Travelers who are not on organized treks that provide portable toilets should ask if there are communal latrines *(chaarpi)* in the villages, or if a family has one. One of the many positive changes over the past decade has been the establishment of latrines in certain heavily trekked areas. In addition, public health campaigns have resulted in the erection of latrine structures by many individuals near their homes. There are latrines in many of the villages of Manang, Thak Khola, Solu-Khumbu, and other areas. Although not always maintained, they are often excellent facilities. Most homes in Khumbu have traditionally had a convenient latrine arrangement on top of the hay pile situated in an alcove off the second floor, or more recently, a separate latrine near the house. However, in much of Nepal, you will have to do as the Nepalis do. Usually, they perform their eliminations before dawn or after sunset in various places near the village that are obvious to inspection. They carry a *loTaa,* or container of water, to wash themselves. You never see adult Nepalis defecating along the trail.

I recommend that you find a corner of a field or other sheltered spot away from running water and bury your feces, or at least cover them with stones. Carry a little plastic trowel for this. Burn the toilet paper. Keep a cigarette lighter or matches in a bag with your toilet paper. I prefer the interlocking folding toilet paper often used in institutions and parks. It can be purchased in bulk from sanitation supply houses in the U.S. Some people, unable to defecate squatting, have taken small portable toilets for their personal use. (It is rare, but trekkers have developed a dropped foot due to nerve compression from squatting.) The results must be buried after cremation. Sadly, so much of the countryside next to the popular trails is festooned by Western prayer flags: soggy, brightly colored toilet paper, or tampons and other feminine hygiene materials. Always burn and bury them. Used tampons have been turning up as children's toys. (Feminine hygiene products are not available in the hills but are now found in Kathmandu.) Bring the type of tampon that inserts without a special applicator that must be discarded.

Often you will find pariah dogs that eat feces—indeed, these are often summoned by villagers to clean up after young children. Disgusting as it may seem to non-Nepalis, it is certainly preferable to some alternatives. Whatever you do, be sure to exercise appropriate modesty and get out of sight of others. You never see a Nepali in an act of defecation. Nepali women and men often urinate discreetly by hunkering in their skirts. Some women trekkers find this quite appropriate if wearing long skirts with no underpants. If women separate their inner labia before urinating, it often does away with the need for toilet paper and solves other hygiene problems. Indeed, this simple, ingenious method, suggested to me by a lady trekker, has given the women who have tried it much freedom.

Many wild animals and plants are being seriously threatened by illegal commercial trade. To combat this serious threat, many countries, including Nepal, have become signatories to CITES (Convention on International Trade in Endangered Species of Wild Fauna and Flora). Don't be tempted to buy the fur of a spotted cat, an orchid, a tortoise shell, or other animal or plant parts. To do so not only undermines Nepal's natural heritage, but means you are breaking international laws. Many of the spotted cat skins you see in stores in Kathmandu and elsewhere are endangered in the wild. One person noted that 86 percent of the stores he visited carried coats made from protected species. In this survey, it was found that 700 protected cats had been killed to stock the fur coats in Kathmandu shops. Let store or hotel owners know your feelings if you see illegal furs for sale.

Finally, in whatever you do, realize that you are not alone. If you carry off one *mani* stone from a prayer wall, saying that one less will make no difference, realize what would happen if everyone did so. Think of how you would like this country to be when you come to visit again, or when your children or grandchildren do. If we who travel in this exotic country respect its culture and customs, perhaps its spectacular countryside and the experience that we have found so worthwhile can be preserved for the benefit of Nepal and the enjoyment of future trekkers.

Essential Do's and Don'ts

Do

- register at your embassy, let them know your itinerary, especially if not traveling through an agency
- verify the phone numbers for rescue on page 151
- wear a shirt if you are a man
- wear a long skirt if you are a woman
- take responsibility for your employees
- keep your valuables secure; locked up if possible
- keep prayer walls and *chorten* on the right when passing them
- pay the going price for food and other goods
- give away useful containers to villagers
- burn combustible garbage
- carry out unburnable garbage
- bury your feces and burn all toilet paper used
- draw up your legs while sitting on the floor so Nepalis can pass by you
- leave donations when visiting monasteries
- use kerosene stoves whenever you can

- patronize hotels and eating establishments that cook on kerosene; encourage others to do so
- patronize hotels that have solar-heated showers
- eat Nepali food for the most part
- compliment lodge and *bhaTTi* owners for the good aspects of their facilities
- smile—Nepalis tend to smile to relieve possible embarrassment; a return smile quickly eases tensions

Don't

- give to beggars unless Nepalis also do so, and give the amounts they do
- give money or items to people who have not done special favors for you
- give medicines to local people
- point the soles of your feet at anyone
- touch anyone with your shoes
- touch any Nepali's head
- give or receive food with your left hand
- eat off another's plate
- give food to Nepalis if you have touched it
- touch your lips to a drinking container that is to be used by others
- accept more food on your plate than you can eat
- walk out of a hotel or *bhaTTi* without paying your bill
- throw garbage in your host's fire
- photograph someone against their wishes
- defecate or urinate indiscreetly
- offer recreational drugs to Nepali children or adults
- travel alone, if a woman
- be sarcastic to a Nepali

5   Health Care

I suffered increasingly from mountaineer's foot—reluctance to put one in front of the other.

H. W. Tilman, *Nepal Himalaya*

Trekking in Nepal need not be a great risk to your health in spite of what many Westerners may think. If the preventive measures described here are strictly followed before and during your stay in Nepal, you should enjoy reasonably good health. (It is likely that you will have a bout of diarrhea and get a cold.) Field treatments and procedures are given for the medical problems you may commonly encounter in the hills. These are based on my own experiences as a physician who has worked and trekked in Nepal, as a specialist in travel medicine who has written a lay book on the subject, and on discussions with other experienced trekkers.

What follows may seem frightening to would-be trekkers who are used to the professional medical care available in modern society. In Nepal you may be a week's walk or more from a doctor. Tens of thousands of trekkers have followed precautions similar to those outlined here and have led a most enjoyable and healthy journey. Awareness and prevention are the keys. But it is better to have advice available should it be needed, rather than to disclaim any potential for illness, and to avoid liability on my part. For most people, trekking is not dangerous; it is the beginning of a new vitality.

Preparations and Post-Trek Precautions

Many people come to Nepal with no hiking experience and, though in poor condition, take on their first trek, walk 100 mi (160 km) or more, and thoroughly enjoy themselves. Some treks are more conducive to doing this successfully than are others. Still, I strongly recommend that those planning to trek undertake a conditioning program. Running several miles a day is about the best single conditioner. Taking hikes uphill with a heavy pack is a good activity to put variety into the regimen. Bicycling, cross-country skiing, swimming, and other aerobic activities are also excellent. But all of them must be started months ahead of time and carried on regularly with increases in the amount of exercise each week. Toughen your feet and break in your footwear through progressively longer hikes. Applying tincture of benzoin to your feet over pressure points where blisters may occur may toughen the skin.

Before you leave for Nepal, visit your physician and get necessary inoculations. The following immunizations are recommended: Sabin trivalent polio, typhoid, meningococcal meningitis, and tetanus-diphtheria. These vaccinations should be recorded on a World Health Organization-approved International Certificate of Vaccination that can be obtained from the health department in your country's national government offices. The live oral typhoid vaccine now available in parts of Europe and America may be preferable to the dead vaccine given by injection elsewhere. Immunization against measles, mumps, and rubella is recommended for those not previously infected or vaccinated.

Rabies exists in Nepal and you may wish to get the expensive human diploid cell vaccine. I have not heard of a trekker contracting rabies, but animal bites do occur and the risk is there. If you are bitten when you are far from anyplace where you could get the rabies shots, you face a dilemma. Should you abandon your trek and get to Kathmandu for the series of injections? A matter of time, inconvenience, and money. If you have had the pre-immunization prophylaxis, then you need only get two doses of the human diploid cell vaccine, three days apart. If not, then you are looking at five injections over a month, together with another shot, the very expensive agent rabies immune globulin. It all depends on your level of risk assumption. Approximately 4 trekkers per 100,000 get post-exposure rabies prophylaxis in Kathmandu. Children sometimes get bitten and don't tell their parents, so you might especially consider it for the youngsters traveling with you. If in doubt, I recommend the vaccine. If you have had it before, then you should either get your antibody blood levels tested, or get a booster dose. There is a new dosage scheme (0.1 ml intradermally on days one, seven, and twenty-one or twenty-eight) that is cheaper than the older one.

The cholera inoculation was required in the past, but it was not particularly effective, and the World Health Organization has withdrawn it. Decline it if offered. Typhus is present in Nepal and you may wish to be immunized against it. This vaccine is no longer available in the U.S. Other vaccinations that might be appropriate for specific groups include influenza, and pneumococcus (for those with chronic lung and heart disease, or over age sixty-five), as well as haemophilus B (children under age five). Several cases of meningococcal meningitis occurred in Westerners in Kathmandu during the mid-1980s. Get the single-injection meningococcal polysaccharide vaccine. Obtain a tuberculin test and consider the BCG immunization against tuberculosis. (I do not recommend it for trekkers.)

A knowledgeable physician can time all of these inoculations properly. They should begin several months before departure. Have a thorough physical examination and let your physician know the nature of the activities you will be engaged in and the altitudes you hope to reach. Visit a dentist to have potentially disabling dental problems cared for. There has been no easily accessible good dental service in Nepal outside of Kathmandu. Women taking oral contraceptives should not stop them while trekking in Nepal. There appears to be no additional risk associated with their use while trekking.

Those with active chest and heart diseases that limit physical activity should avoid going to high altitudes. Individuals with the following conditions definitely should *not* go to high altitudes: primary pulmonary hypertension, cyanotic congenital heart disease, absence of the right pulmonary artery, chronic pulmonary disease with arterial unsaturation, coronary artery disease with severe angina or cardiac failure, congestive failure with arterial unsaturation, and disablingly symptomatic cardiac arrhythmias. These conditions are described in specific medical terms so the risks can be accurately assessed by your physician. Show this list to your doctor if you believe you have one of these conditions.

Occasionally, people who had serious preexisting diseases have died while trekking. Those with sickle cell disease or sickle cell trait greatly increase their risk at high altitudes. People with recurrent deep vein thromboses and pulmonary emboli should also avoid high altitudes, but those with essential hypertension tolerate high altitudes well. Our knowledge of the effect of high altitudes on people with mild or moderate chronic disease, as well as on the elderly, is woefully inadequate. Information on drug effects at high altitudes is similarly lacking. Certainly many people in their sixties and seventies have trekked at high altitudes in Nepal with no problems. If you are in that age range or older and enjoy good health and physical conditioning, by all means consider trekking in Nepal, at least at moderate altitudes. You could later consider trying the high passes. Anyone with chronic diseases not discussed here should seek the advice of a knowledgeable physician, and, if given the go-ahead, should first make supervised visits to high altitudes in his or her home country. Similarly, those who wonder if they have the physical stamina for trekking should first take backpack trips in hilly areas before planning a trek in Nepal.

There is somewhat of a debate in the medical community regarding whether individuals who have had coronary artery bypass surgery for ischemic heart disease should trek in Nepal. I side with the proponents of going trekking, since the benefits of a trek on the body and psyche outweigh the possible increased risk of a cardiac event. However, this is a personal decision that the individual should make in consultation with his or her physician. This question was reviewed in *Journal of the American Medical Association,* 261, 1046–1047, February 17, 1989.

Pregnant women have trekked and ascended to high altitude. We know something about the effects of high altitude on long-term residents there, in terms of its effect on the fetus and baby. However, there is no data on trekkers who venture there for a short time. There is an increased risk of problems, but it is probably small. The risk is greater at the beginning of pregnancy and toward term. I recall one instance where a pregnant trekker decided not to go. She had tried to conceive for years, and was finally successful, and did not want to undertake the risk of having something happen and then wonder if she might have avoided it by not trekking.

Those with stable chronic diseases who can undertake strenuous exercise can certainly trek. Some such people may wish the security provided by an organized trek with a doctor along. Others may have enough self-confidence to trek in small groups without a physician. To my knowledge, people with diabetes, recurrent cancer, amputations, arthritis, and even blindness have enjoyed trekking.

Diabetics who are insulin dependent should be adept at regulating their own insulin dose based on blood glucose determinations. The exercise in-

Shamans, the commonest healers in Nepal, will chant and drum to drive the evil spirit from a sick child; traditional and modern medicine coexist in Nepal.

volved in trekking will usually result in lower insulin requirements, and this must be monitored en route. It is wise to carry snacks, as well as glucagon for insulin reactions. Companions should be well versed in dealing with these problems.

Many physicians are not too familiar with travelers' health problems. If yours isn't, state and local public health departments usually have knowledgeable people whom you can consult.

Ask your physician about taking malaria suppressants. Malaria was once endemic in the Tarai, but today it has been somewhat controlled in most areas. Nevertheless, incidents of malaria continue to occur. The usual form of protection is to take the suppressant chloroquine, 500 mg weekly. Except during the monsoon, the chances of contracting malaria while trekking in the hills and mountains is slight, especially above 4000 ft (1200 m). Malaria transmission is thought to occur sporadically in Nepal at altitudes above 4000 ft (1200 m), perhaps up to 6500 ft (2000 m), but I am not aware of trekkers who have contracted malaria at these heights. I do not take chloroquine prophylaxis while trekking. But you may wish to take the drug as an additional protection, especially if trekking in the monsoon. If so, start taking the pills one week before you reach the first area where there is a chance of getting malaria. Do not discontinue them until one month after you have left all infected areas and until you are in an area where good medical care is available in case an attack occurs after you stop the drug. Rather than take it for prophylaxis, I would advise the trekker going outside of the monsoon season to carry some chloroquine for treatment of suspected attacks of malaria if his travels will involve a considerable stay below 4000 ft (1200 m). There is occasional chloroquine-resistant *falciparum* malaria in the southwest and southeast corners of Nepal. I do not consider this a threat to trekkers on the popular routes. Alternatively, if carrying ciprofloxacin, or norfloxacin, this can be used to treat suspected cases; see Fever, later in this chapter.

Discuss the medical supplies mentioned here with your physician. Drugs and most supplies can be bought cheaply in Kathmandu. Moleskin, iodine water-purification tablets, and modern sunscreens may only be available in developed countries. Moreover, a few items available in Kathmandu, such as elastic or adhesive bandages, are inferior to those made in the West.

Finally, arrange to get an immune globulin (gamma globulin) injection before you leave home. This provides partial protection against infectious hepatitis (Hepatitis A), long feared by travelers to Asia. Currently, the U.S. Centers for Disease Control advises a dose of 0.02 ml per kg body weight for a stay of two months or less, or 0.06 ml per kg body weight for up to five-month protection. If traveling for more than five months, you can get an immune globulin injection at 1:00 P.M. on Monday, Wednesday, and Friday at the Kalimati Clinic in Kathmandu (phone 214743). They also offer the meningitis, typhoid, and rabies vaccines. Gamma globulin does not offer complete protection, but lessens the risk remarkably, so that if you follow other safeguards mentioned below while in Nepal, you will probably not end up with hepatitis.

Some people are expressing concern about AIDS and the possibility of contracting it from an immune globulin injection. There is absolutely no risk. On the other hand, people do die from hepatitis. As to other concerns about

AIDS in Nepal, blood at the blood bank in Kathmandu is routinely screened for the virus as of 1991. There have been only a few HIV-positive blood samples found to date, usually related to Nepali prostitutes from India.

In summary, every trekker should have current immunization status for polio, typhoid fever, tetanus, diphtheria, measles, mumps, rubella, and meningococcal meningitis, and should obtain immune globulin. I recommend rabies vaccine but suggest that malaria prophylaxis not be taken, except possibly for lowland treks during the monsoon.

Consider obtaining travel and evacuation insurance in addition to standard medical insurance. This will not prevent you from having to arrange payment for a helicopter rescue should it be necessary, but it can help recover the substantial costs involved. Travel agents and insurance brokers can provide policies. Make sure the policy you obtain covers trekking travel in Nepal.

Traditional advice is to have a stool exam for ova and parasites after you return home. I recommended this in previous editions and some people wrote thanking me for this advice, as the test turned up a parasite in them for which they were treated. However, I no longer do this for myself if I have had no symptoms. Only do so if you have had diarrhea, or vague abdominal pain, or are worried. You should also repeat your tuberculin skin test if it was previously negative.

Health Care of Children

For those trekking with children, it is essential that a knowledgeable physician or other health professional be consulted before you leave home in order to get specific information appropriate to your children and their needs. See this person well in advance—several months may be necessary—to ensure that the required immunizations can be obtained in time. Your doctor might wish to consult the two papers listed in appendix B regarding international travel for the child younger than two, if that applies. If it is decided that your children should take chloroquine as a malaria prophylactic, pills of appropriate size can be obtained at stops en route, in Hong Kong for example, or sometimes in Nepal. Small-dose tablets are not easily available in the United States or Canada.

The greatest health risk for children trekking in Nepal is the hazard of fecal-oral contamination. Children at oral stages tend to put everything into their mouths. Human and animal feces are everywhere, and tend to get into the hands and mouths of children. The problem is compounded because children with diarrhea and vomiting can get dehydrated quickly. Since there are essentially no medical care facilities in the hills, each family is on its own. Take solace in knowing that most trekking families have no problems.

Prevention is the key. Watch what your child puts in his mouth. Iodize or boil all water for drinking and feed your child only cooked food. Keep materials for making oral rehydration solution on hand in case diarrhea or vomiting develops. If the liquid losses in stool or vomitus are replaced gradually, no serious problems should result. Oral rehydration powder has been formulated by the World Health Organization and provides the substances lost. In Kathmandu, this oral rehydration powder, called Jeevan Jal (meaning life-liquid), can be purchased in drug shops. Mix one packet with four cups (one liter) of boiled or iodized water, and feed it to the child a little at a time by spoon or cup. Try to get the child to drink at least as much liquid as he has lost. Check for signs of adequate hydration, such as normal frequency and amount of urination, moisture on the lips and mouth, and fairly normal behavior. If in doubt, get the child to take more fluids. Do not use opiates or other similar drugs to "plug up" diarrhea in children. Do not use tetracycline drugs in children under age eight. If you lack a commercial oral rehydration powder such as Jeevan Jal, a substitute can be made up almost anywhere. Add one three-finger pinch of salt, and a three-finger scoop of sugar to one *maanaa* (2½ cups or 570 ml) of boiled or iodized water. Add some orange or lime juice if available.

Colds and other upper respiratory infections are very common in Nepal, and your children may get their share. One family found a bulb syringe handy for clearing their two-year-old's snotty nose.

Children's doses for drugs are not given here. They vary, of course, with the age and weight of the child. They are listed in my book *The Pocket Doctor,* which you may find helpful. Be sure to discuss which drugs to take, and confirm their doses, with your doctor. Liquid doses are best for young children.

The hazards of high altitudes are no less for children than for adults, except that it may be even more difficult to determine whether a particular child's health problem is due to altitude or to some other cause. One family took their twenty-one-month-old child to 16,500 ft (5000 m) without difficulty, after appropriate acclimatization. I have seen Sherpa mothers carry their one- or two-month-old babies over 19,000 ft (5800 m) passes. And a woman who was six months pregnant ascended to 24,000 ft (7300 m). Such extremes are not recommended. Families should limit their treks to 13,000 ft (4000 m). With infants, 10,000 ft (3050m) might be a safe limit. Little is known about altitude illness in infants and young children. But the general consensus is that unless born at high altitude, children probably tolerate ascent to heights less well than do adults. All people with children who venture to high altitudes should descend immediately if there is any difficulty with acclimatization. The safety margin in waiting out the minor symptoms of altitude illness is significantly less in children than in adults.

The Medical Kit

A very basic medical kit is proposed here so that trekkers will be reasonably prepared for problems. Most of the items can be purchased quite cheaply in Kathmandu. Since the greater part of its contents will remain unused, it can be considered a kind of insurance. In most developed countries, prescriptions are required for some of the drugs. An understanding physician should give you these if you carefully explain why you need them. Do not use these medications when medical assistance is available nearby. In most cases, the procedures outlined here are only field approximations, and proper diagnosis is very important. However, when you are sick and there are appropriate treatments, it makes sense to use them.

Among many trekkers, there seems to be a fear of self-treatment. By following the suggestions in this chapter, the chances are excellent that you will recover, and the benefits of treatment far outweigh the risks. If you are not getting better in spite of self-treatment, then consider other alternatives, especially if the situation seems grave.

Names of drugs are always a dilemma. While the official or generic names are generally the same throughout the world, the advertising or brand names vary greatly from place to place. The generic names are used here whenever possible.

My recommended medical kit—enough for a party of two—includes:

Moleskin—Felt or foam (molefoam) padding (about 1 mm thick for felt, 2 or 3 mm for foam) with adhesive backing, used for the prevention of blisters. About half a square foot per person should be enough. It is not available in Kathmandu, but adhesive tape or zinc oxide strapping can be used as a substitute. See the foot care section for other alternatives.

Bandages—One roll of 2-inch adhesive tape, and five to ten adhesive bandages per person for small wounds.

Elastic Bandage—One 3-inch roll for relief of strains and sprains.

Thermometer—One that reads below normal temperatures (for diagnosis of hypothermia) as well as above (for fever).

Miscellaneous—Scissors, needle or safety pin, and forceps or tweezers.

Plastic Dropper Bottles—One-ounce (30 ml) size for iodine. This is best brought from home, as the ones available in Nepal tend to leak. If your pharmacy no longer carries empty plastic dropper bottles for dispensing compounded ear, eye, or nose drops, buy a plastic dropper bottle of nose drops and dump the contents.

Water Purification Chemicals—Tetraglycine hydroperiodide or iodine in various forms (see next section).

Iron Pills (Optional)—Ferrous gluconate tablets, for women only. Take one per day, and discontinue after your trek.

Nose Spray or Drops—Phenylephrine HCL (0.25 percent) for stuffed noses and sinuses. Put two drops in each nostril two or three times a day when symptomatic and when changing altitude. An alternative is oxymetazolone, used no more than twice a day.

Nasal Decongestant (Optional)—For those accustomed to taking these tablets for colds.

Antihistamine—For treating symptoms of colds and hay fever. If you do not have a favorite, try chlorpheniramine maleate tablets (4 mg). Terfenadine and astemizole are expensive, nonsedating antihistamines you could try, but they are often less effective.

Aspirin or Similar Drug—Twenty-five tablets (5 grain, 325 mg) of aspirin for relief of minor pain, for lowering temperatures, and for symptomatic relief of colds and respiratory infections. Ibuprofen (200 mg) is an appropriate substitute for those who can't tolerate aspirin. Acetaminophen (paracetamol) is another alternative.

Codeine—Fifteen tablets (30 mg) for relief of pain, cough, and diarrhea. A good multipurpose drug.

Anti-motility Agent—Codeine as mentioned above, or loperamide (2 mg), or diphenoxylate compound tablets. Take twenty.

Antibiotic—The current trekkers' wonder drug is probably ciprofloxacin, in 500 mg tablets. Expensive, but adequate for most of the infectious bacterial causes of illnesses that might befall the trekker, as well as malaria. Take twenty capsules at least; the dose is one capsule twice a day. An alternative that is also available in Kathmandu is norfloxacin, 400 mg tablets, taken twice a day. Another choice is a cephalosporin (cefaclor, cefuroxime, and cefadroxil are the choices in the U.S.). Carry ten days' supply of a 250 mg cephalosporin. The dose for the cephalosporin is either one or two every 8 hours (cefaclor) or 12 hours (cefuroxime or cefadroxil). If allergic to penicillin, you might also be allergic to a cephalosporin, but this is relatively rare. Erythromycin (250 mg capsule) would be the best choice for allergic individuals. Take forty. In the past, I have recommended co-trimoxazole (trimethoprim 160 mg and sulfa-methoxazole 800 mg) in so-called double-strength tablets (abbreviated TMP/SMX later in this chapter). But there is considerable resistance now to this drug treating diarrhea in Nepal. For other choices, especially in diarrhea, read the section later in this chapter.

Antiprotozoan—Tinidazole is the best drug to self-treat presumed *Giardia* infections while trekking. It is not currently available in the U.S. but can be purchased in Nepal. Take twelve to twenty 500 mg tablets.

Antihelminth (worm medicine)—Six 100 mg tablets of mebendazole. One tablet taken morning and evening for three days will take care of most worm infestations in a porter. You won't be there long enough to require treatment in Nepal.

Oral Rehydration Solution (ORS, Jeevan Jal)—A mixture of salts and glucose, this powder is added to a liter of water to provide the appropriate drink to rehydrate in almost any situation, but especially from diarrhea. Not easily available in the U.S.—buy it in Nepal.

Altitude Medicines—Acetazolamide 250 mg tablets, take twenty (or the 500 mg sustained release, take ten), and also dexamethasone 4 mg tablets, take five. The first is to treat symptoms of mild altitude illness, and the second is to take if someone has the serious, cerebral symptoms. The first drug is appropriate to use for prevention in suitable situations. Read the section on altitude illness, below.

Gamow Bag™—A hyperbaric chamber for treatment of serious altitude illness. Enquire to Portable Hyperbarics, Inc., P.O. Box 510, Ilion, NY 13357 or Altitude Technologies, Box 622, Avon, CO 81629.

Anti-inflammatory Agent—To be considered if you are prone to arthritic conditions or tendonitis. Aspirin or ibuprofen are good choices; acetaminophen is not effective. If you've had such problems before, ask your doctor about indomethacin, or meclofenamate. The latter is a good all-purpose pain medicine.

Sunscreen Preparation—One with a Sun Protection Factor (SPF) of at least 15 in order to get adequate protection from the sun on snow slopes at high altitudes. Zinc oxide, an opaque ointment, may be the only effective sunscreen available in Nepal, although some of the others may occasionally be available in shops carrying supplies for trekkers. Sunscreens are best applied one or two hours before exposure, and reapplied after heavy sweating. Be sure to apply them over all areas that can receive direct or reflected sunlight, especially under the nose, chin, and eyebrows. Lip balms containing effective sunscreens should also be used.

Topical Ophthalmic Antibiotic—For instance, 10 percent sodium sulfacetamide (15 ml). Many antibiotic products are made for treatment of conjunctivitis or eye infections, but in choosing one, avoid all penicillin products since the chance of being sensitized to them is great if they are used on the skin. The same goes for any antibiotic if you may want to take the active ingredient internally. Good choices of ophthalmic antibiotics are those that contain bacitracin, gentamicin, polymyxin, or tobramycin. Avoid any that contain steroids such as betamethasone, cortisone, dexamethasone, hydrocortisone, prednisolone, or others. If you wear contact lenses trekking, be sure to bring antibiotic eye drops.

Malaria Suppressant (optional)—Chloroquine, for instance, if you and your doctor think it is necessary.

These items are considered a bare minimum by some, too much by others; they are clearly adequate for most situations. Other items are mentioned in the next section and can be added if desired. I pack my kit in a zippered nylon bag. First I put the pills into small labeled plastic bags, such as the tiny bags that your airline cutlery is packed in, and then assemble all these together inside a small plastic bottle. The whole kit never weighs more than a pound (½ kg). I would never go into the hills without an antidiarrheal, aspirin, iodine, a sunscreen, moleskin, and an antibiotic. Physicians accompanying a group to high altitudes might find a stethoscope and perhaps an ophthalmoscope useful. I don't carry them.

Pregnant women should consult a physician regarding medical problems they might encounter and the use of these or other drugs.

Nepalis have their own remedies for many illnesses. If you don't seem to be getting better, in spite of my recommendations, you might consider their suggestions. While working as a doctor in Nepal, I have occasionally been frustrated by my inability to help some unfortunate sick person, and then later discovered that the individual was cured by a folk remedy or a session with a shaman!

Health and Medical Problems

The vast majority of diseases that plague the trekker in Nepal are transmitted by food or water contaminated by infected human or animal feces. You should assume that all water and uncooked foods in Nepal are contaminated. This holds true in Kathmandu as well as along the trails. Prepare food and water properly to render them harmless.

WATER

Boiling. The safest procedure is to bring drinking water to the boil and let it cool before drinking. Boiling for an extended time is not necessary to render water safe for drinking even at altitude. All prolonged boiling does is kill bacterial spores, none of which cause disease by drinking. I feel that boiling water on a trek, especially if wood is used, wastes scarce resources. Better to use a chemical disinfectant. Water from the hot-water faucet, if allowed to run for a few minutes, might be safe, a consideration where there may be *no* other alternative. In any case, allow the water to cool in the container in which it was boiled, unless it can be transferred to a known sterile or noncontaminated vessel.

Filtering. Several commercial devices now exist to filter out the harmful organisms. These are all rather bulky, and expensive, and need occasional cleaning, which may result in contamination of water. However, the ones advertised for this purpose in the U.S. have undergone some testing to verify the sometimes limited claims made for them. They may only filter parasites, perhaps also bacteria, but not viruses, which limits their usefulness in Third World situations. They specifically do not remove the hepatitis virus. Consider all these factors before you invest in one. The water filters you commonly see in restaurants in Kathmandu, and can purchase there, contain ceramic candles inside. They only filter out silt and other sediment and cannot be relied upon to render water potable.

Chemical Disinfection. Elemental iodine is the best agent, added by one of several means. The dose stated here is for clear water; double it for cloudy water. Once the chemical is added, the waiting time depends on the temperature of the water. Ten minutes is adequate for warm water; 20 to 30 minutes should suffice for cold water. For very questionable very cold water, double the dose and wait 30 minutes or more.

Iodine tablets (tetraglycine hydroperiodide, or Potable Aqua™, Wisconsin Pharmacal), are most useful for water bottles. Use one tablet per quart (liter) of water, and wait 10 minutes after it has dissolved.

Tincture of iodine (USP) has several uses. Add five drops per quart (liter) or, conveniently, two drops per glass (250 ml). I carry this in an opaque plastic dropper bottle, obtained by purchasing nose spray or drops, discarding the contents, and pouring in the tincture. I use this technique almost exclusively; it is easy to carry the bottle to add to water in restaurants, *bhaTTi,* and people's homes. I tell them it is medicine for the water if they ask, and will explain why. If water doesn't taste like iodine, it isn't water (unless I know it has been boiled). In Nepal, it may be difficult to know the exact contents of a solution called tincture of iodine. In the U.S., or elsewhere, look for the USP designation (United States Pharmacoepia) which indicates that the product is compounded to the correct standard, with 2 percent free iodine. Other names of similar products that might be found in Nepal are given below. I find this material also useful for removing leeches and with it, I can disinfect the skin around a wound (do not put it directly into a wound).

Strong Iodine Solution (BP) (British Pharmacoepia) should be used in one-fifth the dose, that is, one drop per quart of clear water. It contains 10 percent free iodine. The Indian Pharmacoepia (IP) formulation is the same.

Weak Iodine Solution (BP) is used in the same dose as Tincture of Iodine (USP). The Indian Pharmacoepia (IP) formulation that is available in Kathmandu is used in the same dose as the BP.

Lugol's Solution does not have a standardization that makes it reliable to use for water disinfection. However, you might be able to learn the percent concentration of free iodine present in a particular formulation and adjust the dose. If it is labeled Lugol's Solution (Aqueous Iodine Solution BP), then two drops can be added to a quart (liter) of water. Many countries will have their own pharmacopoeia and standards for iodine solutions and tincture. See if they are equivalent to the British or U.S. ones before using, or else inquire locally for efficacy. Better still, bring tincture of iodine from home.

Iodine solution, made by adding the supernatant of crystalline iodine carried in a glass bottle. This method is potentially lethal if crystals are ingested, and there are now commercial preparations (Polar Pure™) available to make this unlikely.

Alcoholic iodine solution. Most of the tinctures and solutions mentioned above contain free iodine (the active agent), and a salt of iodine that is not active but contributes to the dose of iodine ingested, and adds to the taste. Those who find the taste of iodine objectionable could compound their own iodine solution. Prepare 2 grams of iodine in l00 ml of 95 percent ethanol. Then follow the same dose guidelines as listed above for tincture of iodine. It is probably wise to discard this solution each year and make a fresh one, since the alcohol will evaporate and increase the concentration of iodine, making the dose less accurate. Most people will find it easier to purchase tincture of iodine than to make their own.

Povidone iodine solution. This is used for surgical disinfection, and usually comes as a 10 percent solution (do not get the scrub, which has a detergent added). It has not been studied for water disinfection, but should probably be effective in a dose of eight to sixteen drops per quart (liter) of water, the higher amounts used in cold or cloudy water. The major advantage of this form of iodine is that it is less irritating than tincture of iodine when used around and in wounds, and thus would be a useful adjunct to the medical kit.

Iodine or activated charcoal resin in devices through which the water passes results in safe water that lacks the iodine taste. The water should probably stand for 10 to 15 minutes after filtering through those units containing iodine to allow time for the material to work. They are effective but slow and tedious to use.

Rare individuals may be allergic to iodine. These people would usually have a long-standing skin rash when taking iodine. They should not use this chemical for water purification. Pregnant women should have no problem with these chemical methods of water treatment. Persons with thyroid disease might conceivably have problems with the iodine ingested in the chemical treatment of water as outlined above. Discuss this with your doctor. The best plan would be to experiment at home before you leave by treating your water to observe if any changes in thyroid function occur.

Finally, those who find the taste of their chemically treated water objectionable might add some powdered drink mixes to flavor the water. However, don't do this until the proper time has elapsed to render the water potable.

On organized treks, trekkers are sometimes told the water they are given has been boiled when in fact it hasn't. I always assume that "boiled water" has not been boiled unless I have supervised it.

All water should be purified, including that used for brushing your teeth and that found in ice. If water is cloudy or murky, let it stand to clarify. (Alternatively, you could add a three-finger pinch of alum to a quart/liter of water, stir it well initially and then occasionally over 1 hour, and let it settle for several hours to clarify it.) Water used for cleaning open wounds is best boiled first and left to cool. However, if cleansing a wound concerns me, I will use any water available. It is unlikely that contaminated water poured in a wound could injure a normally healthy person. Similarly, if concerned about rehydrating someone who has lost plenty of fluids and is severely dehydrated, and thereby in danger of dying, I will use untreated water if there are no other choices. With very cold water and iodine treatment, allow the water to stand twice as long, even up to an hour, before consumption. Bottled soft drinks and beer of well-known brands are considered safe.

Chlorine (halazone) is widely used as a water purification agent, but it is not as effective as iodine against amebic cysts. Most trekkers will probably decide to add iodine to their water rather than boil it.

Bottled Water. There is now bottled mineral water available on the popular treks. It comes in sealed plastic bottles and is reputed to be safe. It is expensive and its use results in the profusion of empty plastic bottles scattered about. You can't depend on its availability everywhere on the popular trails. I advise that you use iodine instead. There are bottled carbonated beverages (soft drinks) available along the popular trails. These refillable glass bottles can be seen making the return journey, empty, on a porter's back. Consumption of these drinks makes more ecologic sense.

FOOD

Thoroughly cooked foods can be considered safe, but only if they are eaten soon after cooking. Fruits and vegetables that are eaten uncooked must first be washed and peeled under sanitary conditions. Leafy vegetables must be cooked, since it is not clear how effective it is to wash them in an iodine solution. Thus, peel it, cook it, or forget it.

Food prepared by Nepalis can be assumed to be safe if it has just been cooked and not allowed to be contaminated by flies. Contamination is possible from the plates the food is served on, but this is very difficult to control.

Milk should always be heated just to the boiling point and allowed to cool before drinking, unless it is known to be already pasteurized. Curds are made from boiled milk and can be assumed to be safe unless recontaminated. This can easily occur, especially if flies have been allowed to sit on the surface. Scraping off the top layer should then be sufficient. If milk has been diluted with water, it is necessary to bring the mixture to a boil. Buttermilk and cottage cheese, especially when prepared by herdsmen in their alpine huts, can be considered fairly safe. The dairy in Kathmandu pasteurizes its milk. Most of the ice cream in Kathmandu is risky.

It is difficult to follow rigorous advice concerning homemade alcoholic drinks. To be safe avoid them all. *Rakshi,* distilled from a fermented mash, is perhaps the safest since it has been boiled. The *Thakali* frequently serve *daru*, a *rakshi* that is very much like sake. The common fermented drink is called *chang* by the Sherpas and Tibetans, and *jAAR* by other Nepalis. Unless the water from which it is made is known to be pure, it is possible to get sick from it (a hangover notwithstanding). Finally, in the east, there is *tomba*, a fermented millet mash that is served in a bamboo canister with a straw. Hot, hopefully boiled, water is poured over it and the leach sucked up with the straw. Partly safe, except for the mash, container, and straw. Wonderful! Many trekkers will find it very difficult to abstain from alcohol.

Honey is often obtained in the hills from beehives located on cliffs. The bees are smoked out by Nepalis dangling on primitive ladders made out of reeds. If this honey is from rhododendron flowers, it may contain a potent neurotoxin (poison). Locals are often aware of this. Cooking the honey is reputed to destroy the toxin. On one of my treks in a remote region, we obtained some cliff honey and later consumed part of it. An hour later, my companion began to feel ill and then became comatose. He required rescue but later fully recovered. We subsequently cooked the honey, but days later his Nepali companion ate some and developed similar, though less severe, symptoms. Be careful of unknown local honey.

NUTRITION

A survey of trekkers' diets in Nepal showed that many are inadequate in protein and caloric intakes. Rice and lentils *(daal bhaat)* in large quantities are a reasonable source of calories and balanced protein. Trekkers should make sure that they periodically eat green vegetables and pigmented fruits and vegetables to get sufficient vitamins A and C. Those worried about their protein intake because of the relatively meatless diet should ask at Nepali homes for some roasted soybeans *(bhaTmaas)*. These are pleasant to munch on along the trail and they contain more protein per unit weight than any other food, including meat. Eggs are also available at the lower altitudes.

Learn a lesson from your porters, who consume vast quantities of rice. This is necessary to provide the calories needed for walking, and the protein for repair. Sometimes ascents are measured in the amount of rice needed to carry a certain load up a specific hill. So eat plenty and then some!

For insurance, some trekkers might want to take a vitamin pill daily. Women might also want to take an iron pill daily, as the local diets do not contain much iron. Women do lose a significant amount of iron monthly through menstruation. However, neither of these supplements should be necessary for healthy trekkers who spend a few months walking around in the hills.

DIARRHEA AND DYSENTERY

It's a brave man that farts in Asia.

Diarrhea and dysentery are the most common problems among trekkers. In fact, it is safe to say that almost every trekker will have a bout of diarrhea during his stay in Nepal. The term diarrhea as used here means frequent passage of loose stool. Dysentery means forms of diarrhea in which the stool often contains blood and mucus. Sufferers may also have stomach cramps and fever. Diarrhea is much more common among trekkers than dysentery and can be caused by toxin-producing intestinal bacteria, or parasites, such as *Giardia lamblia* or other bugs.

I will give a number of options for trekkers in dealing with diarrhea, then state my current personal treatment regimen. I have been following this since 1974, with excellent results.

General principles in either situation are to note the number and nature of the stools and to begin taking clear fluids such as water, weak tea with sugar, juice, clear soup, or soda pop that has been left to stand until the carbonation is gone. Avoid dairy products. Drinking lots of fluids is necessary to avoid dehydration. Perhaps the best liquid to take is an oral rehydration solution. Jeevan Jal, a powder manufactured in Nepal by Royal Drug Company, contains the needed salts. Mix one small bag with a quart (liter) of water and drink it in small sips. The diet should match the stool form. If you have watery diarrhea, drink plenty of liquids; if it is loose, eat soft foods. If the diarrhea is particularly bothersome, take an anti-diarrheal, loperamide, codeine, or diphenoxylate with atropine. Treatment with opiates and synthetic anti-motility agents may actually prolong illness in those afflicted with certain forms of dysentery, so don't take them indiscriminately. The one time I would be sure to use them if suffering from diarrhea is before a long bus or plane ride.

If these medications relieve the symptoms, return to solid food gradually. If you continue to have two or three loose stools a day with no blood or mucus but feel well enough to continue, omit taking the anti-diarrheal and go on. Usually the diarrhea will subside of its own accord. On the other hand, if you have dysentery, especially with nausea, vomiting, and fever, rest and begin the antibiotic. Co-trimoxazole (TMP/SMX), ciprofloxacin, or norfloxacin are good choices. Take one tablet every 12 hours for five days. People with such symptoms will rarely be able to continue at the time, but with rest and constant intake of fluids, the symptoms should disappear in a few days. It is important to continue fluids, even if only small portions can be taken at any one time.

Another effective remedy for non-*Giardia* diarrhea is bismuth subsalicylate suspension, as in Pepto-Bismol™. It has also been shown to work as a prophylactic agent, with all the studies having been done in Mexico. No side effects have been reported. The dosage of 60 ml (4 tbsp) taken four times a day is effective for either purpose, but this necessitates carrying enough for a cup a day. But ½ lb (225 g) a day (not counting the weight of the container) works out to some 15 lb (7 kg) for a month's trek. Tablets work for prevention (dose of two tablets three or four times a day), but apparently not as well for treatment.

If your diarrhea is accompanied by burps of rotten-egglike gas, then the protozoan parasite *Giardia lamblia* may well be the cause. This parasite seems to be perhaps more prevalent on treks around and north of Pokhara, though it is common elsewhere in Nepal too. It generally takes a longer time to acquire this infection than the bacterial ones, usually two weeks, and sometimes longer, after ingesting the cysts. Stools will often contain mucus and smell like rotten eggs or sulfur, as will expelled gas. Trekkers presenting at clinics with diarrhea for two weeks or longer are more likely to have *Giardia*. If your symptoms persist for several days, and you are far from help, it makes sense to treat yourself presumptively for giardiasis. Take 2 grams of tinidazole (which is not available in North America but can be purchased in medical halls in Kathmandu) as a single dose. The dosage may have to be repeated in 24 hours. Some trekkers have developed *Giardia* neuroses, thinking that each loose stool has been caused by this comical-looking flagellate. There are other causes of loose stools and foul-smelling burps. For these people, taking tinidazole every few days could be risky.

Another way of treating the common, non-*Giardia* diarrhea that trekkers get is to take an antibiotic. The current best choice is one of the quinolones: ciprofloxacin, norfloxacin, or ofloxacin. In the past, tetracycline and doxycycline were used, as well as co-trimoxazole (trimethoprim and sulfamethoxazole), but there is now considerable resistance to the latter, so I don't recommend it. I would start by taking one dose of the antibiotic, and if the diarrhea persists, continue taking it for up to three days. If you combine this with an anti-diarrheal listed above, you'll get better slightly faster. The dose for doxycycline is 100 mg every 12 hours, for tetracycline 250 mg every 6 hours, for norfloxacin 400 mg every 12 hours, for ciprofloxacin 500 mg every 12 hours, and for ofloxacin 400 mg every 12 hours. Be aware that tetracycline and doxycycline can cause an increased sensitivity to sunlight, resulting in a pronounced rash and sunburn. Tetracycline, doxycycline, norfloxacin, and ciprofloxacin should be avoided by children and pregnant women. Be aware that naladixic acid, a relative of the "floxacins," is also being used.

There are many other treatment regimens for diarrhea and dysentery. In fact almost every traveler knows of several. One old favorite, the widely touted iodochlorhydroxyquin (marketed under the name Entero-Vioform™), is not effective, and has been implicated in causing eye and nerve damage. I would not recommend it, nor a related preparation marketed as Mexaform™.

My personal regimen for treating my diarrhea is to (1) rehydrate if necessary, (2) decide if it might be *Giardia,* (3) if not, take a single dose of an antibiotic, (4) resume solid foods in a few hours.

Drugs have been used for prophylaxis of travelers' diarrhea. Sulfa drugs and neomycin, as well as bismuth subsalicylate, have been shown to be of some benefit in controlled studies. Studies have shown that doxycycline, 100 mg, or norfloxacin, 400 mg, or ciprofloxacin, 500 mg, taken once a day is effective. Use of a drug for prevention for longer than three weeks is not recommended, and in general I would not recommend using them at all, but rather to follow the advice given above for treatment of diarrhea once it occurs. Of course, you should also follow the food and water hygiene steps to prevent diarrheal diseases. The only class of people for whom taking medicine to prevent diarrhea would be appropriate are those with no acid production in the stomach. Such people would have either achlorhydria or surgical removal of the stomach. Once again, doxycycline should not be used by children under eight years of age, or pregnant women, and attention should be paid to the increased risk of sun sensitivity. Also, women often find that taking this drug greatly increases their chances of getting vaginal yeast infections.

ALTITUDE ILLNESS

> *If you are not feeling well at altitude, it's altitude illness until*
> *proven otherwise.*
> > David Shlim, M.D.

Problems with altitude can strike anyone, even at relatively low altitudes such as 8000 ft (2450 m). Indeed, some have died from altitude illness at this level. But in general, trekkers going to higher altitudes quickly are more severely affected. People who fly to a high altitude and then proceed to an even higher area or cross a pass should be especially wary. Examples include flying to Lukla and Shyangboche and going to Everest Base Camp; flying to Jomosom and crossing the Thorung La; or flying to Langtang and crossing the Ganja La. Statistically, some symptoms will be felt by two-thirds to three-fourths of those going to high altitudes, especially to 14,000 ft (4200 m) or above. Those hiking up will have fewer problems than those flying up. Serious illness occurs in perhaps less than 2 percent of people who go to high altitudes.

Altitude illness can be prevented by acclimatization; that is, by a graduate rate of ascent, allowing sufficient rest at various intermediate altitudes. It is a totally preventable problem. The proper amount of rest and rate of ascent vary greatly from individual to individual and even over time in the same individual. For example, one person who previously had climbed Mount Everest later had difficulties at lower altitudes from ascending too rapidly. Dr. Charles Houston, who has done extensive research at high altitudes, says a cautious rate of ascent that would ensure comfort and safety for almost anyone is to take five days to reach 11,000 ft (3350 m) and six more days to reach 15,000 ft (4500 m). Above 15,000 ft (4500 m), climb 500 ft (150 m) a day. However, most parties could safely go at a slightly faster rate, allowing one day of acclimatization (rest) for every 3000 ft (900 m) gained between sleeping sites above 10,000 ft (3000 m). This is feasible only if everyone is on the lookout for the signs and symptoms of maladaptation to high altitudes. If the party acts appropriately should anyone develop altitude illness, serious problems can usually be avoided.

For example, in ascending to Everest Base Camp, Kala Pattar, or anywhere above 15,000 ft (4500 m), allow at least two rest and acclimatization days. One stop could be at 11,000 ft (3350 m), and the other at 14,000 ft (4250 m). On these days, people who feel good could take an excursion to a higher point, but return to sleep at the same altitude as the night before. In Khumbu, a rest day at Namche Bazaar or Tengboche, followed by another at Pheriche, would be the minimum requirement. Then spend a night at Lobuje, and ascend to Kala Pattar the next day, returning to Lobuje for the night. Climb high and sleep low.

If you are on a group trek going to high altitudes, ask how many rest days are built into the schedule and ask how flexible it is. Most deaths from altitude illness in Nepal probably result from group treks adhering to an inflexible schedule with an inadequate number of rest days.

If you are a leader of a trek, take note that the most significant blunder likely to be made by you is to deny that a member's illness or symptoms represent altitude illness. Please take this seriously, as clients are in a more litigious mood these days and have sued leaders, and charges have even been leveled back home.

There are other factors besides a slow rate of ascent that help in acclimatization. A large fluid intake to ensure good hydration is key. Four quarts (liters) or more a day of liquid are usually necessary. Urine volume should always exceed one pint (one-half liter) daily, preferably one quart (one liter). The urine color should be almost clear. A strong yellow color indicates that more fluids should be drunk. Some trekkers and Himalayan climbers find that measuring urine output daily with a small plastic bottle helps ensure adequate hydration. A simple way to measure urine output is to wait until you are absolutely bursting before urinating. The volume is then close to half a liter. Empty a full bladder at least twice a day. One sign of adaptation to altitude is a good natural diuresis (passage of lots of urine). I find myself passing copious quantities of urine some 24 hours after arrival at altitude. If this is not found, be cautious. An easy way to judge the presence of dehydration is to compare heart rates standing and lying down, with a thirty-second interval in between. If the rate is 20 percent greater in the standing position, the individual is significantly dehydrated and should consume more fluids. This can be water, tea, soup, or broth. Alcoholic drinks should be avoided by dehydrated individuals, and at high altitudes by everyone. Besides being detrimental to acclimatization, the effects of alcohol at high altitude may be impossible to distinguish from symptoms of altitude illness.

Proper nutrition is another factor in acclimatization. Caloric intake should be maintained and the diet should be high in carbohydrates. The tasty potatoes found at high altitudes in Nepal are an excellent source of carbohydrates. A good appetite is a sign of acclimatization. Avoid an excessive salt intake at high altitudes; indeed cut back somewhat if you habitually consume a great deal of salt. Don't take salt tablets.

Rest is also important. Overexertion does not help acclimatization. Give up part of your load to Sherpas and other high-altitude dwellers who are already well acclimatized and can carry loads with ease. Avoid going so fast that you are always stopping short of breath with your heart pounding. A rest step and techniques for pacing yourself by checking your heart rate are described in the introduction to Section II. Plan modest objectives for each day so that you will enjoy your stay in the heights.

Many people who frequent the mountains and often make rapid changes in altitude find that forced deep breathing helps reduce the mild symptoms of altitude illness. However, if done to excess, it can produce the hyperventilation syndrome, in which shortness of breath, dizziness, and numbness are present. Breathing in and out of a large paper or plastic bag for a few minutes (sometimes 30 minutes) will relieve these symptoms.

Finally, there are drugs that may help in coping with high altitude in certain situations. Acetazolamide (Diamox™) has been shown to be beneficial in those who fly to high altitudes, and may help the acclimatization process in those walking to altitudes. The dose is 125 to 250 mg by mouth two or three times a day, begun two days before the flight and continued for three days after ascent. The optimum dose has not been established, and currently smaller doses are recommended to lessen side effects. Acetazolamide can also help when begun upon arrival at high altitude by plane and by those walking beginning it at, say, 9000 ft. Even one dose taken at supper may be beneficial. The sustained action preparation (500 mg) is best taken once a day at night. Side effects often noted are an increased urine output, some numbness and tingling in the extremities, and a unusual, perhaps unpalatable taste when drinking carbonated beverages, including beer. Trekkers flying into a high-altitude area such as Lukla, Shyangboche, Langtang, Jomosom, or Manang might consider taking it. Most trekkers probably don't need it, and there is concern that it provides a false sense of security. Users may not heed the early warnings of grave problems and continue ascending to their deaths. Another drug that prevents the symptoms of acute mountain sickness upon exposure to altitude is dexamethasone, a powerful cortisone-like drug. It has no effect on the acclimatization process, and I do *not* recommend trekkers taking it for prevention. However, it may have a place in treating severe symptoms of altitude illness. Other drugs for prevention of altitude illness that have been tried include furosemide, also called frusemide (Lasix™), and antacids. There is no evidence to suggest that they might be helpful.

Personally, I do not use medicines to help me adapt to the altitude. On the other hand, I usually have few problems. If I had repeated, predictable difficulties in Nepal at altitude, I would try acetazolamide, unless I were being helicoptered somewhere up high to do a rescue, in which case I would take dexamethasone, since I would be back down soon.

Most people trekking to high altitudes experience one or more **mild symptoms of altitude illness.** The symptoms include:

- headache
- nausea
- loss of appetite
- mild shortness of breath with exertion
- sleep disturbance
- breathing irregularity, usually during sleep
- dizziness or light-headedness
- mild weakness
- slight swelling of hands and face

As long as the symptoms remain mild, and are only a nuisance, ascent at a modest rate can continue. Symptomatic treatment with medicines may be helpful. If several of the mild symptoms are present and the climber is quite uncomfortable, ascent should be halted and the victim observed closely. If there is no improvement after a few hours, or after a night's rest, descent on foot should continue until the symptoms are relieved. Then ascent at a more gradual rate can be considered.

Serious symptoms of altitude illness are a grave matter. They include:

- marked shortness of breath with only slight exertion
- rapid breathing after resting—twenty-five or more breaths per minute
- wet, bubbly breathing
- severe coughing spasms that limit activity
- coughing up pinkish or rust-colored sputum
- rapid heart rate after resting—110 or more beats per minute
- blueness of face and lips
- low urine output—less than a pint (500 ml) daily
- persistent vomiting (*)
- severe, persistent headache (*)
- gross fatigue or extreme lassitude (*)
- delirium, confusion, and coma (*)
- loss of coordination, staggering (*)

If anyone in your party develops any of these symptoms, he or she should descend IMMEDIATELY, on the back of a porter or animal to avoid undue exertion. This is the most important treatment, and should not be delayed until morning. You may only have a corpse to transport then. The victim should be kept warm and given oxygen if it is available. Give acetazolamide, 250 mg every 8 hours. If dexamethasone is available, and the cerebral symptoms are present as noted above with (*), give 4 mg every 6 hours. After a descent of only a few thousand feet, relief may be dramatic. At the point where relief occurs, or lower, rest a few days. Then consider ascending cautiously again. However, if you have taken dexamethasone for treatment, I do not advise ascending again, since the drug seems to only mask the symptoms of altitude illness which, upon reascending, could get much worse. This is currently unproven, but seems to be the best advice based on limited experience with the drug at altitude.

Judgement is affected by altitude. Hence, possible altitude illness may be denied by the victim and his companions. To guide you, the clearest symptoms of significant altitude illness to watch for in *yourself* are:

- breathlessness at rest
- resting pulse over 110 per minute
- loss of appetite
- unusual fatigue while walking

The clearest ones to watch for in *others* are:

- skipping meals
- antisocial behavior
- the last person to arrive at the destination (i.e., people having difficulties with the walking)

It cannot be stressed too strongly that you *must* descend at the onset of serious symptoms. If in Khumbu, go to the hospital at Kunde, or to the Trekker's Aid Post in Pheriche, if that is on your descent route. A pressure chamber to simulate the effects of descent is available there, as well as other recourses. But don't stop descending in Pheriche unless the victim is considerably better. Trekkers have died in Pheriche from not heeding this guideline. Don't wait for a helicopter to rescue you. Many trekkers, including Olympic athletes, doctors, and experienced climbers, have died in Nepal from altitude illness because they failed to heed symptoms when they occurred. A disproportionate number of physicians, who should know better, have died from altitude illness in Nepal. Finally, it appears that those trekking individually almost never die from altitude illness. Rather it is peer pressure in groups that contributes to deaths among trekkers. Those alone descend early, it seems, while in groups there seems to be a tendency to not hold the party back. Don't be another statistic in this totally preventable problem.

Be aware that there is a new device that might have a remarkable impact in treating serious, potentially fatal, altitude illness. It is the Gamow Bag™, a portable hyperbaric chamber. The victim is placed inside, and then the pressure inside is increased via an air pump to simulate descent of 5000 to 9000 ft. It can be useful for diagnosis, too. If you wonder if someone's symptoms might be due to altitude, put them into the bag and "descend" them 3000 ft or more and see if the symptoms improve. Indeed, as we learn more about this device, it seems that treatment in the bag for an hour may produce pronounced improvement in someone suffering from mild symptoms. This effect may be better than that achieved with the usual drugs. These are only preliminary impressions; more data will be coming in the future.

The device is lightweight (less than 12 pounds including pump) and expensive, but cheaper than the cost of a funeral. I have listed the manufacturer's address in the medical kit section. It would certainly be appropriate to carry for a large trekking group that will spend considerable time up high, where the way down is long and difficult. Indeed, I hope that it will become standard equipment for any group trek to altitude. If you are going on an expensive group trek, ask if they will carry the bag, and if not, why not. Your money should be going to buy life-saving items such as this. The Gamow Bag™ should become standard insurance for all parties to altitude. Also, one altitude "guru" suggests that all guided parties who will sleep above 14,000 ft should carry oxygen as well. Ask your leader about this.

The essential material on altitude illness has already been covered, and what follows is for trekkers who are particularly interested, or who are suffering from altitude illness.

Altitude illnesses observed in Nepal include: acute mountain sickness (AMS), high-altitude pulmonary edema (HAPE), peripheral edema (PE), high-altitude cerebral edema (HACE), high-altitude retinal hemorrhage (HARH), and high-altitude flatus expulsion (HAFE).

AMS commonly comes on after being at high altitudes for one to two days. A variety of symptoms are experienced, most often a persistent headache, usually present on awakening. The mild symptoms listed above also occur. Irregular or periodic breathing during sleep, called Cheynes-Stokes respiration, is common. The rate and depth of respirations increase to a peak, then diminish, stopping altogether for a fraction of a minute, then increasing again. If none of the serious symptoms are present, there is no cause for concern.

Young people seem to be most susceptible to AMS. Physical fitness *per se* is of no benefit. This is true for most altitude illness. The treatment is to deal with each symptom with whatever means you have, and to ascend slowly or rest, depending on the severity of the problem. Acetazolamide, if available, is worth trying in treating the symptoms of AMS. Try a 250 mg tablet at suppertime, and perhaps upon arising to see if it helps the headache and malaise. It may also help ensure a good night's sleep. Do not take sleeping pills at high altitude; they may worsen symptoms and be dangerous. It is important to make sure that mild weakness does not progress to the serious symptoms of extreme fatigue or lassitude in which the person becomes unable to care for himself. Don't leave such a person alone, for the mild condition may progress and the victim can become helpless.

Tests for coordination should be given. An easy one is called tandem walking. See if, after resting, the person can walk a straight line by putting the heel of the advancing foot directly in front of the toe of the back foot. Slight difficulty is tolerable if 12 ft (4 m) can be covered in a straight line. If in doubt, compare the individual with someone who is having no difficulty. Often the rugged terrain will make it more difficult for both to accomplish the maneuver. In exhaustion, hypothermia, or intoxication, mild degrees of loss of coordination (ataxia) can be seen, but there should be no staggering or falling. Another test is to have the person stand, feet together, arms at the side (or held out in front), and eyes closed. If the person sways considerably, significant loss of coordination (ataxia) is present. Again, use an unaffected member of the party as a measure. Ataxia is a sign of serious illness, possibly HACE, and the person should descend while he is still able to do so under his own power, but always with someone else who is well. Even if this condition is diagnosed at night, descent should begin immediately. If a Gamow Bag™ is available, place the person in it and descend him.

HAPE, the presence of fluid in the lungs, is a grave illness and is probably present if the respiratory problems on the above serious symptoms list are noted. The heart and breathing rates are useful clues. Do not delay in descending with individuals with these symptoms as death can be only a few hours away. Usually there are also some signs of AMS. Trained people using stethoscopes may hear sounds called rales in the lungs of trekkers with no symptoms. This is common and no cause for alarm. Only the presence of the above symptoms are grounds for descent. It may be difficult to differentiate HAPE from lung infection—in fact, both may be present. If there is any doubt, especially if the person is getting worse, descend. If the Gamow Bag™ is available, put the person in it. Give oxygen if it is available. If the victim seems to be drowning in his fluids, finding some way for him to hang almost upside down and then applying firm, steady pressure to the upper abdomen might help cough up some of the edema fluid and provide temporary relief.

Individuals with chest disease are more susceptible to HAPE, as are people who have previously suffered from it. People under age twenty-five are also more susceptible. Those with upper respiratory infections or common colds are probably not at any increased risk. Oxygen is beneficial and morphine may be, but it appears doubtful that other drugs used to treat pulmonary edema at sea level are effective. Give acetazolamide if you have it. Medical personnel who are carrying nifedipine could administer a 10 mg capsule to the stricken individual, asking him to chew it in a dire emergency. If this pulmonary artery vasodilator helps, it can be taken perhaps hourly for relief. This drug is experimental in this situation and should not be used by nonphysicians, for there are potentially fatal hypotensive side effects. This information is provided for physicians who must use their clinical judgement in deciding whether to use it. Descent for all must be undertaken and is best done without exertion, say on the back of a porter or a yak.

PE—swelling around the eyes, face, hands, feet, or ankles—is present in some degree in many visitors to high altitudes. Women seem to be affected more than men, but this doesn't appear to be related to the menstrual cycle or to taking birth control pills. The hands are the part of the body most often affected. This can also be caused by carrying a heavy pack with tight shoulder straps that affect venous return. Rings on the fingers and constricting clothing or pack straps should be removed or loosened. Swelling of the feet and ankles should be treated by rest and elevation of the legs. Facial swelling, especially if severe enough to shut the eyes, requires descent. In general, check for other symptoms, and if any of the serious ones are present, descend. Otherwise, if the swelling is not especially uncomfortable or disabling, cautious ascent can continue. But such swelling can be an early indication of failure of the body to adapt to high altitudes. A diuretic to increase urination can be administered if swelling is a problem, but again, watch for serious symptoms.

HACE, or swelling of the brain, is a serious disorder that has killed quite a few in Nepal. It usually occurs after a week or more at high altitudes and begins with mild symptoms that progress to the serious ones. Usually the heart and lung symptoms are not prominent. Characteristic features are severe lassitude, lack of coordination (as demonstrated under AMS), and total apathy, leading to coma and death. Do not leave such a person alone, assuming that he is tired. A good night's sleep is not the answer. You may find a corpse in the morning. Check for ataxia (loss of coordination) and descend. If you have a Gamow Bag™, use it—it may be a lifesaver. Give acetazolamide and dexamethasone if you have it, 4 mg every 6 hours. Oxygen is beneficial too. Those trained in the use of an ophthalmoscope may detect papilledema, a late sign. Difficulty with the tandem walking test is much more reliable as an early sign.

HARH, or bleeding in the retina of the eye, is more common at extreme altitudes. But it does happen to trekkers occasionally and usually is symptomless unless the vision clouds somewhat or the bleeding is near the macula (center of visual acuity) in the eye. Double vision or noticeable blind spots are sufficient cause for descent. Vision clears and bleeding in the retina resolves at lower altitudes.

HAFE, the production of increased amounts of intestinal gas, seems endemic up high. This ailment, although not serious, does cause problems for the sufferer and to those around him. There is no known treatment or effective prevention.

All this may seem frightening to the trekker bound for the heights, but the information has to be put in perspective. If you have previous high-altitude experience, you have some idea of what to expect (though altitude illness continues to strike groups led by Himalayan "experts"). If you have not been to high altitudes, don't be scared away from enjoying the mountains of Nepal. Be prudent. Ascend at a rate appropriate for the entire party—that is, at the rate appropriate for the individual having the greatest difficulty. Know the symptoms of altitude illness and what to do about them. If descent becomes necessary for some members of the party, make sure they are not sent down alone, but are cared for by responsible, informed people. Don't always assume that your hired employees understand altitude illness. There have been too many incidents in the past when people with obvious serious altitude illness were put into tents to rest unobserved and were discovered dead in the morning. With people better informed today, this shouldn't happen. Above all, use common sense. You are not in Nepal to race up to base camp even if it kills you, but to enjoy the country and its people in all their varied beauty. Finally, give yourself permission to not be the high-altitude wanderer, summiter, and pass crosser, should you be one of the many who cannot tolerate high altitudes well. This group includes many renowned climbers and athletes and does not reflect a lack of character or endurance.

FOOT CARE

It is easier to prevent foot problems than to treat them. Well-fitting boots or shoes and proper socks are a must (see chapter 3). Blisters tend to form on the same spots time and time again, so prophylactic early application of moleskin or adhesive tape is beneficial. Tincture of benzoin can be applied to the skin to toughen it. The tape, moleskin, or molefoam (foam with adhesive backing) tends to spread the friction over a larger area and reduce local shear stress between layers of the skin. When you feel a tender or hot spot on the skin while walking, stop and investigate. Put a generous piece of moleskin, foam, or adhesive tape over the area. Don't remove it for several days; otherwise you may pull some skin off with it. Rather than wait for hot spots to develop, begin your trek with padding applied to potential trouble areas. Other products used by trekkers to prevent blisters include Spenco Second Skin™ and plain open-cell foam that is used for packing and cushioning. The latter is cut in pieces about one-half inch to an inch thick and applied next to the skin, held in place over the friction point by the lightweight sock. This is especially useful for toes and irregular areas of the foot where blisters might form. If you are developing blisters, and have other footwear, change to it and see if this eliminates hot spots.

It is important to keep the feet dry. Moist feet are more prone to blisters. Change socks frequently in hot weather and do not wash or soak your feet too often. By keeping feet dry, you develop callouses over pressure points, and this protects your feet against blisters. Sometimes callouses can get too thick and cause painful problems. Soaking them in warm water will soften them, and they can sometimes be peeled back with a knife.

Once a blister has formed, there are two schools of thought on what to do. Some advocate leaving an intact blister alone, in fact protecting it by cutting a hole the same diameter as the blister in a piece of moleskin or foam and applying that around the blister. Several thicknesses may be necessary in order to have the padding level with the top of the blister. Eventually the blister will go away of its own accord. The alternative is to drain the blister with a needle. Sterilize the needle in a flame until it turns red hot and allow it to cool. The needle should be inserted at the edge of the blister right next to the good skin. Then apply a sterile dressing or some moleskin or foam over it. I prefer the latter routine. Finally, if you have any of the biologic dressings that doctors use for wounds, they would be ideal for putting on blisters.

Do not go barefoot in Nepal. The risk of picking up infections is great. Hookworm is spread this way.

STRAINS, SPRAINS, AND SAHIB'S KNEE

As muscles flex, they shorten and move joints by means of tendons that attach to bones. Ligaments are fibrous tissue straps that cross joints and hold them together. Sprains are tears or stretching of ligaments; strains are tears in muscles. The tendons may get stretched, torn, or inflamed too. For most trekkers, the prolonged, continual walking necessary to reach a distant point causes more wear on their musculoskeletal systems than they are used to. If you gradually increase the amount of activity, your body will toughen up and adjust. Even so, the amount of toil can cause problems, especially in those not well conditioned. People who push themselves to walk long distances every day, especially with heavy packs, will find their poorly prepared body protesting. Strains, especially in the thigh and calf muscles, make climbing and descending painful. Knees will rebel, especially on the downhill portions, if the cartilage (the shock-absorbing pads in the joint) gets too much pounding. "Sahib's knee" is the result. Those with weak cartilage lining the kneecap (chondromalacia patellae), women being more commonly afflicted, will especially have pain climbing and descending.

When tired, or not paying attention to the trail, anyone can twist and sprain a joint, most commonly the ankle. Ankle sprains are common when the foot turns inward. The pain can initially be quite severe and make walking difficult. Check for the points of maximum tenderness immediately after the injury. If they are just in front of the outside base of the ankle (lateral malleolus or distal fibula), and just below it, then you probably have the common variety of ankle sprain.

Treatment for strains and sprains is similar. Control internal bleeding by icing or cooling the affected part, and elevate and compress the injured area. Compression can be achieved by means of adhesive tape or an elastic bandage if available. Severe injuries will require rest for a few days. For strains in the bulky muscles of the thigh, there may be little you can do except to lighten the load and ease up on the amount of ground to be covered. This advice applies to sprains as well. Aspirin for pain will help, as will the application of moist heat several days after the injury has occurred.

Individuals with preexisting knee or ankle problems should strengthen the muscles that pull across the joint by doing isometric exercises before they trek. Those with a tendency to ankle sprains will want to wear sturdy, over-the-ankle boots and do exercises to strengthen their peroneal muscles (those on the outside of the lower leg, done by pushing outward with the foot against an immovable object). Others prone to knee injuries will be wise to work on their quadriceps muscles (those on the front of the thigh, by keeping the knee straight and pushing up on a fixed object with the top of the foot—an isometric exercise). Those with knee problems will be better off wearing footwear with shock absorbency in the heel.

Everyone should pay attention to reducing the impact on the descent. Absorb the shock by bending the knee when the lower foot contacts the ground. Take short, choppy strides. Once the quadriceps muscles get into shape, this method is much less tiring than keeping the knee straight. Turn your feet sideways on steep descents. Watch how Nepali porters descend. Be sure to keep your shoes or boots laced tightly over the ankle during descents to avoid toe blisters. If you take long strides with your legs fully extended, the cartilage pads in the knee joint and the supporting ligaments will absorb the shock, predisposing you to "sahib's knee." If this occurs, apply the treatment principles outlined above.

HYPOTHERMIA

This condition, often termed exposure, occurs when loss of body heat exceeds gain, and body core temperature drops. The body gains heat by digesting food, from an external source such as a fire, and through muscular activity, including shivering. Loss occurs through respiration, evaporation, conduction, radiation, and convection. The combination of physical exhaustion and wet or insufficient clothing, compounded by failure to eat, dehydration, and high altitude, can result in death in a very short time, even at temperatures above freezing. People venturing into cold, high regions must take adequate steps to prevent hypothermia, and should be able to recognize its signs and symptoms. Be especially alert to its development in lowland porters, who may be inadequately clothed for cold.

Obese people are better able to insulate their bodies against the cold than are slim individuals—a rare advantage to being overweight. Small adults and children are especially prone to hypothermia.

Initial symptoms of hypothermia are marked shivering and pale skin, followed by poor coordination, apathy, confusion, and fatigue. As temperature drops further, speech becomes slurred, and the victim has difficulty walking. Even at this stage, an external source of heat is needed to warm the victim. Further lowering of core temperature results in cessation of shivering, irrationality, memory lapses, and hallucinations. This is followed by increased muscular rigidity, stupor, and decreased pulse and respiration. Unconsciousness and death soon follow. Symptoms can appear in a few hours after the onset of bad weather, and the situation can quickly progress to the point where the victim cannot perform the functions necessary for survival. Hypothermia is easily diagnosed with a low-reading thermometer. Mild degrees of hypothermia are present when body temperature is below 94° F (34.4° C), most accurately measured rectally.

Treatment consists of applying heat rapidly to the person's body core. Remove wet clothing and put the person in a sleeping bag together with a source of heat—a warm naked person, or rocks warmed by a fire and wrapped in cloth, or hot water bottles. Place these under the armpits, and in the groin. Cover the person's head. If possible, feed the victim warm drinks and sweets if he is conscious and able to swallow. Set up a tent, dig a snow cave, or seek shelter. On one of my treks a companion developed hypothermia on a high rainy pass. Taking turns we carried him down to a pasturing shelter where I put him in my sleeping bag with me to warm him up. He recovered the next day.

FROSTBITE

Frostbite is a condition of frozen body tissues. Fingers, toes, ears, noses, and chins are most commonly affected. Fortunately, it is rare in trekkers because the temperature extremes necessary are not usually encountered for long periods of time. But it has happened, especially on high passes and trekking summits. Inadequate boots, skimpy gloves or mitts, and lack of experience are the most common causes. So-called easy passes can become frostbite traps after unseasonable snowfall. Beware of someone's developing frostbite or hypothermia if your party is moving slowly over easy ground due to fatigue, or is being delayed by route-finding difficulties, or by having to help another member. Prevention is a matter of having adequate clothing and equipment, eating adequate food, and avoiding dehydration and exhaustion. Extreme altitudes increase the potential for the problem, as does a previous history of frostbite. Frostbite can occur at relatively warm temperatures if there is significant wind and if the victims are inadequately equipped and suffer from dehydration and exhaustion. Affected tissues initially become cold, painful, and pale. As the condition progresses, they become numb. The trekker may then forget about the problem, with serious consequences.

An earlier reversible stage is frostnip. At this stage, the affected area becomes numb and white. Treatment consists of rapid rewarming by placing the part against a warm area of the body—an armpit, a hand, the stomach of the victim or another trekker. Once normal color, feeling, and consistency are restored, the part can be used, providing it is not allowed to freeze again. A part of the body that has suffered frostnip before is more likely to get frostnip again. It may be difficult, especially when at altitude and dehydrated, to decide whether the injury is reversible or not. If you have a prostaglandin inhibitor pain medicine, preferably ibuprofen, (aspirin and meclofenamate are others, but acetaminophen is not), it would be prudent to take it.

Once an extremity has become frozen and seriously frostbitten, it is best to keep it that way until help and safety can be reached. A frozen foot can be walked on to leave the cold area. Do not rub snow on the frozen area, nor rub it with your hands. Once feasible, the treatment is rapid rewarming in a water bath between 100° F (37.7° C) and 108° F (42.2° C). Thereafter, the victim requires expert care in a hospital and is not able to walk until treatment is completed. Trekkers are more apt to discover a dark toe or finger after an exhausting day crossing a high snowy pass. At this point, the part has already been rewarmed. Treatment consists of adequate hydration, elevation of the affected part, prevention of further injury, and evacuation. Like most medical problems associated with trekking, prevention is far better than treatment.

HEAT INJURY

Not only does travel in Nepal pose problems in coping with extreme cold, but also in dealing with extreme heat. Both can happen during the same trek, if it is from the hot lowlands to the cold, windy, snowy heights. Heat produced by the body is eliminated mostly by the skin through evaporation of perspiration. Acclimatization to heat takes about a week. When the body becomes able to sweat more without losing more salt, the ability to exercise in a hot environment improves. Maladaptation to heat can be prevented by an adequate intake of fluids and salt. Thirst mechanisms and salt hunger may not work adequately, so extra salt and water should be consumed in hot weather. In humid regions where evaporation is limited, it is a good idea to rest in the shade during the hottest part of the day. Cover the head and wear light-colored clothing to reflect sunlight.

Signs and symptoms of heat exhaustion are a rapid heart rate, faintness, and perhaps nausea, vomiting, and headache. Blood supply to the brain and other organs is inadequate because of shunting of blood to the skin. The patient's temperature is normal. If the victim is treated with shaded rest, fluids, and salt, recovery is usually rapid.

Heat stroke is a failure of the swelling and heat regulation process, usually because of fatigue of the sweat glands themselves. The victim rapidly becomes aware of extreme heat, then becomes confused, uncoordinated (ataxic), delirious, or unconscious. Characteristically, the body temperature is very high, 105° F (40.6° C) or higher. The skin feels hot and dry and does not sweat. Treat immediately by undressing the victim and cooling him by any means available. Immersion in cool water, soaking with wet cloths, and fanning are all appropriate. Massage the limbs vigorously to promote circulation. Continue cooling the body until the temperature is below 102° F (38.9° C). Start cooling again if the temperature rises. The victim should be watched closely for the next few days and strenuous exercise should be avoided.

ACROPHOBIA, VERTIGO, AND BRIDGE AND TRAIL PHOBIAS

These problems are not uncommon among those who trek in Nepal without previous mountain climbing and hiking experience. People with these fears usually choose environments and activities not requiring adjusting to exposure. Individuals living all their lives in the flatlands may not realize that they have this problem. Nevertheless, if you've come to Nepal and find yourself on a wobbly bamboo bridge, or on a ledge with a few hundred feet of drop-off, a few principles might help. Obviously, don't look at the big drop-off, be it the river a hundred feet below your feet, or the bottom of the cliff you are traversing. Instead, focus on a stationary object, say the end of the bridge. If feeling dizzy on a particularly exposed part of the trail, stopping and staring at a fixed object, even your thumb, can help. Don't hesitate for what seems an interminable time before you venture forth. As you walk the difficult portion, say a few verses of a familiar tune, or a prayer or mantra. This will give you an aural focus on the exposure, and you will not let your eyes wander. Breathe slowly, using your diaphragm—that is, pushing your stomach out as you inhale in. Don't stop in the middle and wonder what you are doing, or whether you will make it. A positive mental attitude is the best help. Just believing you can do it will result in it being so.

If you know that there will be a particularly difficult stretch coming up, plan to do it when you are not exhausted. Vertigo is worse when you are tired. Wear shoes that have good traction. This will give sufferers some added confidence. Find companions who are sympathetic. Nepali guides, once they understand the magnitude of the problem, will most likely be more helpful than macho Westerners. I well remember the first bridge that terrified me in 1969. After walking up to it, I realized that if I didn't cross it right then, I never would. I still find some of the bridges breathtaking, but they have improved considerably. And you too will find that each successive exposure will become easier after you find that you made it across the first.

ANIMAL BITES

Loud, threatening dogs are sometimes met along the trail. They rarely attack, but just to be sure, carry a long stick and pass them assertively. I particularly remember the angry dogs in Jubing. Often you meet large Tibetan mastiffs, but they are usually chained, except possibly at night and near herders' camps. If you suspect that there might be an unchained mastiff about, call and get the attention of people at the camps and ask them to chain the dog. The chained ones should never be approached.

In case of an animal bite, treat by washing the site immediately with soap and water as well as a dilute solution of salt and water. Wash and irrigate the wound for 30 minutes or more. In animal experiments, washing alone has been shown to be effective in preventing rabies after innoculation of a wound with rabies virus. Irrigation with a quaternary ammonium solution (cetrimide or benzalkonium chloride, also found in the antiseptic Savlon™) within 12 hours has also been found effective in animal tests. Those who have had rabies vaccine before coming to Nepal face less risk than others but should get post-exposure inoculation as well, although they do not need rabies immune globulin.

If rabies is suspected, speed of evacuation is essential so that the vaccine can be administered as soon as possible. Once symptoms occur in the person bitten, it is too late to begin treatment. The decision to seek help may be difficult if the animal bite is unprovoked and the animal appears healthy. If other animals in the area have been acting strangely recently, there may be an epidemic. In order to contract rabies, it is necessary that the animal's saliva penetrate the skin, either through the bite itself or through a previous wound.

Try to capture the beast and keep it alive for seven to ten days. Impractical advice for most trekkers, but added here for completeness. Actually, you could pass through the village again and check with the animal's owner in that time. If the animal is healthy after that, you do not have to worry about rabies. A dead animal's brain can be examined for rabies by medical personnel, but this is not as reliable as direct observation of a live animal—again, relatively impractical in the reality of Nepal.

Often a dog's bite can be explained considering the circumstances surrounding it. In such cases, it is wise to inquire seven to ten days after the incident to see if the animal has undergone any unusual changes. But in case of an unprovoked, unexplained attack, get yourself and the animal, if possible, to Kathmandu as soon as possible.

I recall two incidents of dog bite occurring during my initial treks in Nepal. Once a person entered a courtyard quickly, and without looking, thrust a leg near a bitch that was nursing her pups. Circumstances explained the bite and the observation of the animal several days later alleviated any worries. Another time, I heard squeaking noises coming from a covered basket and went over to investigate. As I crouched down to look, the mother of the litter in the basket sank her teeth into my posterior! Again, explainable.

In the mountainous regions where yaks are kept, sometimes you may feel threatened by one. If a yak makes an aggressive move, stand your ground, raise your hand, and shout! I'm not sure if this works for buffaloes, as I have not had problems with them.

Leeches, abundant during the monsoon in the forests above 4000 ft (1200 m), are attracted to byproducts of respiration and drop onto you as you pass under them, or crawl up from the ground, or attach as you brush by leaves or rocks. The best way to deal with leeches is to pick them off as soon as they latch on. When you feel a very localized cool sensation anywhere on your skin, stop immediately and investigate. It may be around your ears or neck, or just above your ankle. In leech-prone forests, stop periodically and search. You may find it amusing to tease the critters with your finger as they scan with their suckers while attached to a leaf or rock.

Once attached to your skin, they may often be pulled off. Holding a lighted match or cigarette to them also works well, as does some salt or iodine generously applied. The resulting wound may bleed considerably, a useful feature for improving circulation of reattached body parts that has been rediscovered in the last decade. Control this with pressure and watch for signs of infection later. I no longer recommend any leech repellents, but feel that dealing with individual offenders makes most sense. The usual insect repellents will work, as will dibutyl phthalate solutions applied to clothing around where leeches gain entry.

Ticks can be removed using similar methods. I sometimes enlarge the opening by the head with a sterile knife to remove the critter.

FEVER

This section deals with fever when there is no apparent cause, such as a pneumonia or abscess.

When associated with joint aches, perhaps nausea and vomiting as well as diarrhea, a fever is likely due to a flu-illness. Aspirin and fluid replacement are appropriate. When the fever is severe, and the person very ill, sometimes delirious, enteric or typhoid fever may be the cause. Usually there is no diarrhea. Treat presumptively with ciprofloxacin, norfloxacin or co-trimoxazole (TMP/SMX), if medical help is not available. If traveling in the Tarai, especially before and during the monsoon, periodic fevers might be due to malaria. In that case, and if ciprofloxacin or norfloxacin is not available, try treating with chloroquine phosphate 1 gram (four 250 mg tablets) initially, then half that dose at 6 hours and again at 24 hours. If this doesn't work, and the person remains severely ill, treat for typhoid fever.

SMALL WOUNDS AND INFECTIONS

It is important to clean with soap and water *any* wound that breaks the skin. This means using copious amounts of water, treated or untreated, to flush the wound and remove debris. Avoid using the common antiseptics, as they may damage healthy tissue. If you are using tincture of iodine or povidone iodine for water purification, you might cleanse the skin around the wound with this material. Do not put them into the wound, except possibly the povidone iodine. A large wound should be covered with a sterile dressing, which should be changed periodically until a good clot has formed and healing is well under way. It is then best left uncovered. Small wounds, especially if not gaping or occurring over joints, are best left uncovered. There is less risk of infection.

A wound infection is often the result of contamination and is evident by signs of inflammation (redness, swelling, tenderness, warmth) and pain a day or more after it occurs. They are more common at high altitudes, perhaps because the "resistance" of the body is less there. In this case, soak the wound in hot water for at least 15 minutes. Afterwards, cover it with a sterile dressing. With severe spreading infections, antibiotics should be taken; the cephalosporin or erythromycin are preferable. For abscesses such as boils, the treatment is similar to that for wound infections, except that antibiotics probably do little to help unless the boils are a recurring problem. Drain the abscesses by soaking them in hot water for 15 minutes five or six times a day. They will usually spontaneously open but you may have to assist the process with a sharp knife that has been sterilized by an open flame.

CONSTIPATION

This is not nearly the problem diarrhea can be. However, it is not uncommon in the first few days of a trek, as you get used to the routine. A bulky diet usually prevents difficulties with bowel movements. If constipation does occur, drink plenty of fluids. Try a cup or two of hot water, tea, or coffee upon waking in the morning. In rare cases, mild laxatives may be needed. Better to just wait until the problem works itself out.

HEMORRHOIDS

These irritable dilated veins around the anus are usually a result of constipation. They are not very tender, nor hot, and this distinguishes them from abscesses. They may become larger while trekking, sometimes becoming hard with blood clots (thrombosed). This is not a threat to life, but a nuisance. There are various creams, ointments, and suppositories that may provide some symptomatic relief for uncomfortable hemorrhoids. When they become thrombosed, however, frequent warm sitz baths are the answer.

BURNS, SUNBURNS, AND SNOWBLINDNESS

Burns are common among Nepali infants, who walk or crawl too close to a fire and fall in. The severity of a burn depends on its area, its depth, and its location on the body. So-called first-degree burns are superficial—they do not kill any of the tissue, but produce only redness of the skin. Mild sunburn is a typical example. Second-degree burns are also usually superficial and kill only the upper portion of the skin and cause blisters. In third-degree burns, damage extends through the skin into the underlying tissues. First-degree burns require no treatment, but for the others, wash the area gently with iced or cold water, if possible, and cover with a sterile dressing. Ointments are of no use and may increase the danger of infection. Burns that cover more than 20 percent of the body surface are usually accompanied by shock, which is a serious threat to life. Attempt to get the injured person to drink plenty of fluids; the oral rehydration solution made from Jeeval Jal is best. Aspirin and codeine, two tablets of each every 6 hours, may help relieve pain. There is little else you can do for extensive burns except evacuate the person to medical help.

Sunburn is common among trekkers visiting high altitudes, where there is less atmosphere to filter solar radiation, and where snow and ice can reflect additional radiation. Effective sunscreening agents are listed as contents of the medical kit. Be sure to protect the lips and under the chin and nose when on snow. When sunburn occurs, it should be treated in the same way as any other burn.

Eye protection in the form of dark glasses is needed on snow, and generally at high altitudes. In an emergency, lenses made of cardboard with a thin slit to see through can be used, or a coarse cloth with small slits cut out can be tied over the eyes. Hair combed over the face, a method favored by Sherpas and Tibetans, is effective. Otherwise, snowblindness, a painful temporary condition, can result. The condition gets better in a day or two. Darkness and cold compresses over the eyes may help relieve pain. A poultice of tea leaves can provide some relief too. Patch the eyes tightly so the lids don't move. Use your antibiotic eye drops. For severe pain, take aspirin and codeine, two tablets each, every 6 hours.

COMMON COLD

Upper respiratory infections, including the common cold, are very prevalent in Nepal. Medical science does not offer any widely agreed upon remedies. Linus Pauling, the twice-Nobeled scientist, has popularized taking large doses of vitamin C to prevent a cold, and to cure it, or to modify its symptoms in the early stages. There is no strong evidence to back up his claims, but I use his protocols and find them helpful. He feels that the correct dose needs to be individualized, and that you need to be aware of your body's reactions. Furthermore, when you sense a cold coming on, he recommends taking additional ascorbic acid at that time, again sensing your body's needs. You might start by taking a gram of vitamin C a day and modifying this to suit the response. I like such programs that depend on your being aware of your body.

Other ways of dealing with a common cold include rest, drinking plenty of fluids, and taking aspirin. Do not smoke. Gargle with warm, salty water for a sore throat. Decongestants have been used for years by many people. You might want to try the antihistamine, chlorpheniramine maleate, suggested in the medical kit, at a dose of 4 mg four times a day. I would avoid decongestants containing many different drugs. People with high temperatures should not continue trekking. Investigate the cause for the fever. Normal temperature is 98.6° F (37° C), but there is little reason for concern if temperatures measured orally remain below 100° F (39° C) and the person feels pretty strong.

COUGHING

Coughing normally brings up sputum and is beneficial in ridding the body of it. Sometimes, however, an annoying cough occurs that does not produce sputum, even after a few days. If this happens, take one or two tablets of codeine (30 mg) every 6 hours for a day or two. On a recent trek, with my inevitable common cold degenerating into a nonproductive cough that kept me hacking at night, I decided to follow my own advice. Eureka, it worked! Do not attempt to suppress those coughs that produce some sputum. Read the section on altitude illness to make sure you are not dealing with a form of it. General measures in treating an annoying cough include drinking plenty of fluids and breathing moist air. The latter is difficult in dry mountain areas. Steam inhalation, that is, getting a kettle of boiling water and putting it inside a tent or under a blanket and breathing the water vapor, may help. Hard candy or throat lozenges may provide some relief at night.

In addition to altitude illness, serious coughing could be due to a pneumonia. An affected individual would have high fevers, sputum thick with pus and possibly streaked with blood (but not frothy), and often localized chest pain that is most severe at the end of a deep breath. The sick person is usually too ill to travel. Treatment consists of antibiotics, aspirin for high fever and pain, and plenty of fluids.

Other commonly encountered causes of coughs are colds and bronchitis. Bronchitis features inflammation of the airways in the lungs, the hallmark of which is the production of plenty of sputum through coughing. The sputum is usually yellow, or green, but in those with asthma it is usually clear. Sufferers are less sick than those with pneumonia, rarely have fevers, and if they have chest discomfort, it is more likely to be central, resulting from the prolonged coughing. If the cough is persistent, and you have had bronchitis before, you might try a week's course of antibiotics.

CONJUNCTIVITIS AND EYE PROBLEMS

Conjunctivitis is an inflammation of the delicate membrane that covers the surface of the eye and the undersurface of the eyelid. The eye appears red and the blood vessels on its surface are engorged. The flow of tears is increased, and material may be crusted in the margins of the eyelids and eyelashes. Irritation from the ubiquitous smoke in Nepali homes is a common cause, especially among the Nepalis. Apply ophthalmic antibiotic ointment or solution beneath the lower eyelid next to the eye every 4 hours until the symptoms disappear.

If you wear contact lenses, at the first sign of any eye irritation that is distinct from the irritation caused by dirty lenses, you should remove them and apply the antibiotic solution. In cases of problems persisting, especially if the eye is very sensitive to the light, patch it for 24 hours.

You may find your lenses need less frequent cleaning while trekking, since Nepal's hill and mountain air is quite clean. But don't neglect regular cleaning. Disposable contact lenses may be the solution in Nepal to cleaning them. Once, while getting up in the night to answer the call up in the high dry air, my lens dried out, and I had to remove it. I used my iodized water to rehydrate it and replaced it in my eye. Some irritation persisted for an hour or so, presumably caused by the iodine residue. Better to carry some commercial normal saline for this purpose.

GYNECOLOGIC PROBLEMS

Women plagued with vaginal yeast infections when taking antibiotics might bring along appropriate vaginal suppositories. Those prone to urinary infections could consider carrying extra medicine for this problem. These individuals should make sure to urinate right after sexual intercourse, often a preventive measure for recurrent infection. Women who decide to take prophylactic antibiotics for diarrhea should not have urinary infections unless harboring resistant organisms.

Trekking is very strenuous and women who have been on the trail for many months may find that their menstrual periods stop. This is not serious; providing they are not pregnant, periods should resume again with lessened activity. Vaginal bleeding may be profuse after one or two missed periods and will necessitate resting until the bleeding stops. Note that tampons or sanitary napkins are not available in the hills.

Heavy bleeding in a pregnant woman demands prompt medical attention, as does modest bleeding if accompanied by fever, light-headedness, pelvic cramps, or pain. If you are having profuse vaginal bleeding and there is not even the remotest chance that you could be pregnant, and you are far from any medical facility, you could try the following treatment. *Caution: if you are pregnant, this treatment could harm the fetus.* Take a birth control pill, if you have them, four times a day for five days. Bleeding should stop in a day or so.

After stopping the pills, you should have a menstrual period within a week. If you don't, it is possible that you are pregnant and would need a termination since the hormone pills you have taken could harm the fetus. If bleeding doesn't stop, then prompt attention is warranted. An alternative to taking birth control pills for this is to take meclofenamate, the anti-inflammatory medicine suggested.

Pelvic pain can have serious consequences if accompanied by fever (possibly due to an infection in the fallopian tubes), or associated with pregnancy. This latter possibility can be easily overlooked and there could be a tubal gestation. Sometimes this could be associated with vaginal bleeding. A leaking tubal pregnancy is a distinct possibility if defecation is also very painful. The only treatment for a tubal pregnancy is surgical. Seek help immediately. If pain accompanied by fever is the predominant symptom, and you have had PID (pelvic inflammatory disease), or an infection in your tubes before, it is conceivable this has occurred, or recurred. Again, a precise diagnosis is important, but if there are no medical facilities, you could take an antibiotic. Tetracycline, doxycycline, or erythromycin would be the best choices from the drug list. If pelvic discomfort is accompanied by frequent and burning urination, sometimes with associated back pain, a urinary tract infection could be the cause. An antibiotic, especially co-trimoxazole, would be the treatment of choice. If you have co-trimoxazole, take two double-strength tablets as one dose.

WORMS

You probably won't be bothered by a worm infection while in Nepal. But your porters may tell you they have passed worms. It is likely that there are more inside. A broad-spectrum worm medicine such as mebendazole (mentioned in the medical kit list) may be of some benefit. The porters will, however, get reinfected. Mebendazole is also a good drug to try if your porter complains of abdominal pain. Do not pass it out to villagers, for reasons explained in the previous chapter. And be sure to get your own stool examined when you return home if you have symptoms. Trekkers do pick up worm infections. Although the common roundworm will die of old age and you will be rid of him if you avoid reinfection, this is not necessarily true of other intestinal parasites. Roundworms do not cause diarrhea, and in my personal experience, the discomfort is that of recurring, wandering, sharp pains in the abdomen that last seconds.

APPENDICITIS

Sometimes trekkers out in the remote hills worry about appendicitis. The chances of it occurring are very slight, so this information is offered only for your peace of mind. The pain usually starts in the mid-abdomen, soon shifts to the right lower quadrant, and becomes accompanied by nausea. Persistent diarrhea is rare with appendicitis. In a case where appendicitis is suspected, give fluids and an antibiotic, and evacuate the patient. Cases of acute appendicitis may respond to antibiotics and even improve without treatment.

HEARTBURN

This is not uncommon among those prone to it, and others as well, especially if they try to eat a Nepali diet in porter quantities. The burning is most likely to occur when on the trail soon after a meal. Better to eat smaller amounts. Don't fasten your pack waistband right after meals. Antacids may help, too. The liquid preparations are best in doses of two tablespoons every hour for symptomatic relief. Some preparations are available in Kathmandu. It is of course possible that the pain of heartburn could signify a heart attack. Such a person will look and act very sick, perhaps perspire profusely, and need gentle evacuation.

DENTAL PROBLEMS

Most dental problems are unlikely among trekkers if they see a dentist before going to Nepal. For simple toothache, a small wad of cotton, soaked in oil of cloves and inserted in the appropriate cavity, often relieves pain. Codeine and aspirin, two tablets each every 4 to 6 hours, help relieve severe pain. Abscesses, characterized by swelling of the gums and jaw near the site of the toothache, and often accompanied by fever and chills, as well as persistent hot and cold sensitivity, call for the care of a dentist. In the interim, take an antibiotic.

One possible hazard is breaking a tooth while eating because of the possible presence of small stones in the rice or *daal*. Often the piece of broken tooth may remain attached by a tissue hinge and should probably be left there. Taking pain medicine and avoiding foods of extreme temperature is the best field treatment.

SINUSITIS

Sinusitis is an inflammation of the sinuses, often following a cold. It is characterized by headaches of a dull nature, pain in the sinuses, fever, chills, weakness, and swelling of the facial area. Some or all of these symptoms may be present. For severe symptoms, record the fever and chill temperatures, rest, drink plenty of fluids, take two aspirin every 4 hours for the fever, and use phenylephrine nose drops three times a day. Start an antibiotic if the temperature is less than 97° F (36.0° C) during a chill or more than 101° F (38.3° C) when feverish. This course should be continued for seven days no matter when the symptoms subside. The best antibiotic if you have it is co-trimoxazole, a cephalosporin, or ciprofloxacin.

URINARY TRACT INFECTIONS

These are common in some women, especially after vigorous sexual activity. If you experience burning, frequent urination, passing small amounts of urine, without a fever or back pain, and are not pregnant, take co-trimoxazole, two tablets once, or ciprofloxacin 3 grams, once, or the cephalosporin or tetracycline for a week. If you have a fever, or back pain, or are pregnant, in addition to the above symptoms, take any of the recommended antibiotics in its appropriate dose for a week.

PSYCHOLOGICAL AND EMOTIONAL PROBLEMS

> *But at times I wondered if I had not come a long way only to find that what I really sought was something I left behind.*
> Tom Hornbein, *Everest, The West Ridge*

Trekkers and travelers to exotic countries can, and sometimes do, have emotional problems adjusting. Reasons are many: being separated from friends and familiar places; adjusting to a very different environment; being seemingly surrounded by poverty, filth, and disease; realizing that you are essentially alone a week or two from "civilization" and 15,000 mi (24,000 km) from home; being sick and not eating well; being dirty and unkempt; consuming recreational drugs; and realizing that trekking is not all it was cracked up to be. (I can well remember squatting in the bush with diarrhea on the first few days of my first trek in Nepal on my first journey away from North America and pondering whether this was my reaction to being separated from my familiar environment.)

As with most health matters, prevention is the key to not getting "burned out." Steps for prevention depend on the individual. For some, it may be ensuring that you are with friends, with whom you can share the experience. For those who are fastidious in their personal habits, it may mean a daily bath, shaving every day, or every other day, keeping hair combed, and putting on a clean change of clothes every few days. Sometimes the daily routine of constant walking, eating, and sleeping is too much. Take rest days every now and then and pamper yourself. For some it may mean acceptance of the reality that the schedule they have set for themselves is too ambitious, or that difficulties in adjusting to altitude will prevent them from getting to that famous viewpoint or crossing that pass. For all, it should include being aware of what is in store during the trek and being prepared for it psychologically as well as physically.

What if you are getting quite depressed or close to a "nervous breakdown"? First do some familiar, relaxing, comforting routines, such as bathing, shaving, washing your clothes, or putting on clean ones. If alone, find other trekkers to join. If carrying a heavy load, hire a porter. If sick and weak, rest and eat better foods frequently during the day. If consuming marijuana and other mood-altering drugs, stop them. If appalled by the conditions in Nepal and among the Nepalis, take comfort in the fact that you can leave if you choose. If your mood does not improve, head back to Kathmandu or Pokhara by plane if possible. But be careful not to end up waiting a week for a plane when you could have walked in three days. If you have trouble adjusting to conditions in Nepal, don't go to India.

Few people end up having to curtail their treks in Nepal for these reasons. Rather, many will undergo a "culture shock" upon returning home as, based on their experience in Nepal, they question the values of the environment they have grown up in. But trekking in Nepal is not for everyone. If it isn't for you, don't despair. There are many other superb activities elsewhere waiting for you.

> *Oh mommy, take me home.*
>
> Mantra of the burned-out trekker

Emergency Care and Rescue Facilities

Nepal's health plan involves setting up hospitals staffed by physicians in each of the seventy-five districts. They are intended to provide secondary health care. Primary health care is provided by health posts scattered throughout each district. These are staffed by paramedical personnel and provide basic facilities. Tertiary care is provided by a few major hospitals throughout the country, with the best in Kathmandu. However, to date, district hospitals have not been set up in all district centers. None of these can provide health care to a standard that even approximates that available at home.

If an emergency occurs, try to enlist the help of Nepalis. If in a district center, contact the CDO (Chief District Officer), who will usually be fluent in English. Otherwise, seek out elected officials. Schoolteachers may also be helpful.

A seriously ill person can be carried by a porter, a horse, or a yak. You or your fellow trekkers can carry the person, too. I have been amazed at the resources that can be mustered in the most desperate of circumstances.

If faced with a life-threatening emergency in the hills, you must choose between trying to reach one of the hospitals or clinics listed here and trying to get word to Kathmandu to affect an air rescue. If an air rescue is necessary, head for a STOL landing strip if one is near, or send to Kathmandu for a helicopter. Most STOL airstrips do not have frequent or even regular service, so a fixed-wing aircraft should be sent for. Air rescue by fixed-wing aircraft is usually impossible during the monsoon, except from a few strips, such as Jumla and Pokhara.

HOSPITALS, AID POSTS, AIRSTRIPS, AND RADIO STATIONS

Kathmandu

There are several choices for trekkers seeking health care services. Check with your embassy for advice. Many travelers use the CIWEC international clinic (phone 228531), in Baluwatar, across from the Russian Embassy. Another facility is the Nepal International Clinic, between Durbar Marg and Naxal (phone 412842). The offspring of the United Mission Shanta Bhawan Hospital is now the Patan Hospital in Lagankhel (Patan). It is now mostly run by Nepalis, and offers good care. Many Nepali doctors are well trained and very competent and could be seen in their private clinics. There is Tribhuvan University Teaching Hospital, in Maharajganj, which is affiliated with Nepal's

Take care, or this might be your ambulance!

medical school and the tertiary referral center, Bir Hospital, across from the Tundikhel.

Helambu, Gosainkund, Langtang

The only facilities available are at the government hospital in Trisuli, where there is also a radio and telephone to Kathmandu. A STOL strip is located near Kyangjin, in the Langtang Valley. The nearest radio station is on the Bhote Kosi at Rasuwa Garhi on the Tibetan border, or in Dhunche. The national park headquarters in Dhunche has a radio set. In winter, the STOL strip in Thamgmojet across the Bhote Kosi may be the only other recourse. There is also a little-used strip at Likhu near Trisuli.

North of Pokhara

There is a regional government hospital, radio service to Kathmandu, and an airport in Pokhara. Radio stations are located in Chame, Kusma, Baglung, Beni, Jomosom, Besisahar, and Manang. STOL strips are found in Jomosom, Hongde, and in Balewa (south of Baglung, across the river from Kusma). There are district hospitals in Baglung, Besisahar, and Jomosom. A Trekker's Aid Post operated by the Himalayan Rescue station at Manang is staffed by a doctor during much of the popular trekking season. A small aid project staffed by a French doctor in Tatopani could provide assistance.

Solu-Khumbu and Rolwaling

There are radio stations at Jiri, Namche Bazaar, Tengboche, Pheriche, Lobuje, Salleri, Charikot (south of Rolwaling), and Lamobagar (north of the Rolwaling River). STOL strips are found at Jiri, Phaphlu, Lukla, and Shyangboche. There are government health facilities in Jiri, Namche Bazaar, Phaphlu, and Charikot. A hospital built by Sir Edmund Hillary and staffed by foreign physicians is found in Kunde. There is a Trekker's Aid Post operated by the Himalayan Rescue Association at Pheriche. It is staffed by a doctor during most of the trekking season.

From Namche Bazaar toward Darjeeling

There are radio stations at Chainpur, Khanbar, Taplejung, Phidem, Bhojpur, Terhathum, Dhankuta, Dharan, Ilam, and Chandragari, and STOL strips at Tumlingtar, Lamidanda, Bhojpur, Chandragari, and Taplejung. There are government hospitals in Chainpur, Taplejung, Bhojpur, and Dhankuta.

Pokhara to Kathmandu

In addition to the facilities in Pokhara and Trisuli already mentioned above, there are radio stations in Gorkha and Kuncha and a government hospital at Gorkha. The United Mission runs a hospital at Ampipal.

Western Nepal

In addition to the facilities in Baglung and Beni already mentioned above, there are radio stations in Dunai, Sumduwa (Shey Phoksumdo National Park headquarters), Jumla, and Tansen. There are radio stations at the Royal Dhorpatan Hunting Reserve post in Dhorpatan, Chaumri Pharm, and Goatichaur. STOL strips are found at Dhorpatan, Jumla, Jufal, and Chhaaujhari. The Dhorpatan strip has not been used for several years, and it is doubtful if a plane would land there now. There is a government hospital in Jumla.

Chitwan

The park communication system includes a base set at Kasara and a field set at Saura.

The radio stations listed here are civilian operated, part of the telecommunication systems at district centers, or army, police, HRA, or national park posts. The civilian messages are delivered through the Telecommunication Central Office in Kathmandu. In addition, there are other wireless systems in operation listed here, but their use is normally restricted. In an emergency, it may be possible to use them. Ask at police check posts or army installations, and expect that you may have some difficulty locating the radio transmitter station. Be aware that there is now a radio linkup between each national park and Kathmandu. Also, each district center should have a phone link with Kathmandu.

EMERGENCY MESSAGES AND RESCUES

In writing a message and organizing a rescue, it is important to provide the proper information and make sure it reaches the proper place. It is wise to send several messages to different organizations to ensure that at least one is delivered. Write them up beforehand, and take extra time to make sure they are comprehensible by nonnative English speakers. Addresses should be as specific as possible to speed delivery. The phone numbers of the agencies and rescue facilities should be rechecked once you reach Kathmandu; there have been many changes recently, as the phone system gets modernized. Rescue messages should be sent to one or more of these (redundancy helps ensure that one message will arrive):
- The trekking agency that organized the trek, if applicable.
- Royal Nepal Airlines Corporation, Charter Division, RNAC Building, New Road, Kathmandu (phone 220757, extension 197, or 214628).
- For helicopter rescues, VVIP Flight, phone 414670, 415341, or the Royal Nepal Army, phone 413297 or 413290.
- The embassy or consulate of the victim.
- Himalayan Rescue Association, G.P.O. Box 435, Ghantaghar, Kathmandu (phone 418755).

The message should contain the following information:
- Degree of urgency. **Most Immediate** means death is likely within 24 hours. **As Soon As Possible** is used for all other cases in which helicopter rescue is justified.
- The location, including whether the victim will remain in one place or be moved down along a particular route. If the pickup place is above 10,000 ft

(3000 m), give the altitude. If it is lower, and you know it, include that data, too. Generally, 17,000 ft (5000 m) is the limit for helicopter pickups. Describe the pickup point in relation to other nameable features, and if you can, give the town, ward number, village development council *(gAU bikaas chhetra),* and district.

• Medical information, including the type of sickness or injury, and whether oxygen or a stretcher (as for back injuries) is needed.

• Whether a doctor is at the scene, and whether one might be required from Kathmandu. It may be difficult to send a physician along, and usually is not necessary, since the evacuation will bring the victim to medical attention.

• The name, nationality, age, and sex of all people to be evacuated.

• The sender's name and organization, along with information on the method and source of payment for the rescue. Generally, RNAC will not fly rescues without written assurance of payment. This can sometimes be provided by the embassy of the victim.

Be aware that in sending a message, you will usually not be able to verify that it has been actually transmitted, but be politely persistent and concerned. Ask that the message be sent now; there is usually an extra charge for this. At district centers where you can phone, there is a better chance that you will be able to verify reception and get a feeling for what will happen.

A rescue can take several days, especially if a runner has to be sent with the message, or if there is airplane trouble. It is wise to move the person along the route, waiting each day until 10:00 A.M. to start. In each sleeping place, a large, smoky fire should be built each morning, and a landing site cleared and marked with a large x, preferably using international orange garments or a colorful sleeping bag or tent. If you have a mirror to signal with, use it. If you are directing a helicopter to land, stand at the end of the "pad" with your back to the wind, and wear brightly colored clothing so that you are easily seen.

Once the helicopter is preparing to land, remove the signal garment or sleeping bag and any other material that may be blown around by the rotor downdraft while the helicopter is approaching or leaving. Do not signal a helicopter unless you can direct it to the victim. Locating the stricken party from the air can be quite difficult and pointless waving has resulted in dangerous landings, increased costs, and delay in evacuating a severely ill patient. Approach and leave the helicopter in a crouched position, always in view of the pilot and never toward the rear of the helicopter, and only after the pilot has signaled you to do so. You will rarely have a flat landing site, so on uneven ground, always approach and leave on the downhill side. When boarding, carry any material horizontally, below waist level, and never on your shoulder. Secure any loose articles of clothing before you approach.

The cost of a helicopter rescue is high—an hour of helicopter time costs over U.S. $600. This has to be borne by the party involved, unless rescue insurance has been taken out previously. Some trekkers might wish to obtain a comprehensive travel, accident, and rescue insurance policy before they leave home. If you have not dealt with a trekking agency, it may be prudent to make yourself known at your country's embassy in Kathmandu, in case they receive a rescue telegram. Westerners working in remote areas in Nepal have posted bonds in Kathmandu to pay for a rescue, should it be needed. It all depends on your acceptance of risk. Approximately 75 people are helicopter rescued for every 100,000 trekking permits issued.

In the tragic event that a porter or trekker dies, be aware that RNAC will not transport corpses on their planes. You might be able to charter a helicopter or carry the body out, though you may find it very difficult to hire porters to do this. However, even chartered helicopters may not transport the body, as some trekking parties have discovered when faced with a tragedy. It is best to cremate the body. If possible, this should be witnessed, preferably by a local policeman, village headman, or person not associated with your trek. Record the victim's name and address, as well as those of any witnesses, remove all valuables, and keep the ashes for relatives. If Westerners die, realize that even in Kathmandu there are no public cemeteries, mortuaries, or even a morgue. If you do get the body to Kathmandu, further difficulties in transporting it to your homeland ensue. The body must be embalmed, and there is no regular service to accomplish this. Enquire at the CIWEC Clinic in Kathmandu, at phone 410983.

The risk of death while trekking in Nepal has been studied, and it is estimated to be 15 per 100,000 trekking permits issued. Your risk of death staying at home is certainly higher!

The Jaljala and the south face of Gurja Himal

SECTION II

THE ROUTES

Dara, perched high above the Mayagdi Khola in Western Nepal

Following the
Route Descriptions

No one goes so far or so fast as the man who does not know where he is going.

H. W. Tilman, *Nepal
Himalaya*

In the trail descriptions that follow, treks are not set out on a day-to-day basis. Instead of adhering to a schedule, each party can adjust for long rests or interesting diversions. Those committed to straight traveling can count on covering about 5 to 7 hours of the given route times in a day, allowing a 2-hour food stop during mid-morning. In winter there is less daylight than at other times. Also, if you have many porters, shorter distances will be covered.

In the route descriptions that follow, the times listed between points are actual walking times, generally those I took myself. They *do not* include any rests. This has been strictly adhered to by using a chronograph. Over most of the trails I carried a moderately heavy pack. I almost never walked the segments in these times. Like everyone else, I rested, photographed, talked with the people, and so forth.

The times are fairly uniform in that, if a person takes 90 minutes to cover a stretch listed as taking an hour, then it will take him one and a half times as long as the time listed to cover any other stretch—providing the same pace is maintained. Some people have commented that they find the times too long, while most find them too short. The latter is usually because they do not subtract rest times from the total. The times are in boldface in descriptions to make them easier to total for a particular stretch. Times not in boldface are either noted for additional information, or deal with a side trip. These estimations help trekkers know what to expect and thus find the way more easily, and they make it easier to plan where to eat and spend nights.

At the end of each description of a major route, I have prepared a graph of cumulative walking times (excluding stops and rests) and altitudes from the start of the trek to significant points along the way. This does not include trail variations or side trips. Each graph tries to depict the high and low points along a trek, to give you an estimate of the effort required. Note that the abscissa (horizontal scale) is *not* horizontal distance (miles or kilometers), but hours of walking per the text. Until someone runs an odometer over the trails in Nepal (and it won't be me), you'll have to judge for yourself how far the trails go. By reading off altitudes and times between points, you can estimate your night stopping points.

Be aware that for many trekking routes, the distance is measured in number of camps (or days) necessary for large parties of trekkers accompanied by numerous porters to complete the route. I do not follow this convention here, to allow trekkers to plan the days as they wish, and to allow for individual preferences. Camp days make sense for large groups who need space for tents and allowance made for the porters to carry the loads the required distance.

Experienced trekkers find that often the first day on the trail seems fast. The next two or three days can be slow and painful. As the body strengthens and adjusts to the pace, the miles and hills seem to go by more effortlessly.

Everyone should learn the rest step for ascents. As you advance your uphill foot, plant it and then, before transferring your weight to it, consciously rest briefly with your weight on your downhill foot. Do this continuously and the hills come easier. Try to coordinate your breathing with your steps. That is, breathe in on raising the left foot and out on raising the right. Or breathe in on raising each foot, if the ascent is very steep. This will also make the ascent less tiring. It is better to take several short steps up, rather than one long one, just as for going down.

Here's how the leader of the first ascent of Rum Doodle, at 40,000½ ft, did it:

> *I tried to remember all I had read about climbing at such heights. I took one step, then waited for 10 minutes. This I understood was essential; our predecessors were unanimous about it: one step, then 10 minutes rest, or seven in an emergency. I found it more difficult than I had anticipated. To remain in one position for 10 minutes was not all easy. First, I tended to fall over sideways; then I got cramp in the calf; then my nose started to itch; then my foot started to vibrate and had to be held down by both hands. This was very tiring, and when I crouched to hold my foot I was lower than I had been before making the step, which caused me to wonder whether I was gaining height or losing it; and the mental strain was so great that I lost control of myself and fell off my step. . . .*

W. E. Bowman, The Ascent of Rum Doodle

On descents, tighten your shoe- or bootlaces so that your toes are not crammed into the front of the boot with each step. Take short steps, bending your knees to absorb the energy of the descent. Be limber. Watch the porters to see how they walk. People can easily get knee problems by not descending with bent knees. Knee injuries take a long time to heal and can be quite disabling if they occur many days away from the road.

An effective way to gauge your pace is to monitor your pulse by placing your fingertips on a wrist or neck artery, or to use a computerized pulse monitor. Maximal heart rate can be determined by a sustained strenuous activity for a short time (for instance, running at full speed for 1½ mi or 3 km, bicycling up a steep hill, or running on a treadmill). About 60 or 70 percent of the heart rate after such exercise is an appropriate target pulse for such activity. Try maintaining your pace to produce this heart rate or less, and see if you fatigue easily. Most people following this method find a speed that produces an optimal heart rate (related to oxygen consumption) which they can maintain without getting short of breath or fatigued. This may help you maintain a pace without tiring, especially climbing uphill. Many people, myself included, find this too technical and just walk at a comfortable pace.

During a walk of many weeks in such spectacular country, it is easy to let your mind wander from the task at hand, to daydream or gaze at people, mountains, or scenes. You must *always* pay attention to the trail in front of you and where you put your feet. This may sound obvious, but too many careless trekkers have had serious accidents or falls, and even lost their lives. As veteran trekker Hugh Swift puts it so well, "Look when you look, walk when you walk." When passing animals on the trail, keep to the uphill side, where the fall is much shorter should you be nudged by a yak or buffalo. Trekkers have been seriously injured by not following this advice. Drivers of yak trains want you to pass on the downhill side of yaks. They feel the yaks are spooked less by this. I wouldn't, unless the downhill side is perfectly safe!

In the mountainous regions where yaks are kept, sometimes you may feel threatened by one. If a yak makes an aggressive move, stand your ground, raise your hand, and shout! I'm not sure if this works for buffaloes, as I have not had problems with them. Near high-altitude herders, *goTh,* and other shelters, be aware that Tibetan mastiffs might be loose. When you see an occupied *goTh,* make some noise first and the herder will usually chain the dog.

At rest stops, drink fluids and elevate your feet. Take off your shoes, remove the insoles, and let the sweat dry off your feet, socks, insoles, and shoes. Don't point your feet at any Nepali. Do not roll rocks off trails to see how far they go. This is especially important if traveling with children who may be eager to do this. People, animals, and villages are almost always downhill!

The altitudes listed in the descriptions are taken from several sources, including recent maps whose accuracy can be trusted and my own altimeter. I initially used a Thommen instrument, but most recently use a Casio Alti-Depth™ or Citizen Altichron™ watch with altimeter for all but the highest readings, which are still taken on the Thommen. The readings have not been corrected for temperature changes, but they are adequate to indicate the order of climbing or descending.

Ascent rates of 2000 ft (600 m) per hour are difficult to maintain for any length of time. Most trekkers find 1000 ft (300 m) per hour a reasonable rate if the trail is good and they climb easily. Similarly, a descent rate of 1500 ft (450 m) per hour is reasonable. Altitudes are usually converted from feet into meters and are not rounded off; they are only approximations at best and can be in error by a few hundred feet. Altitudes of most towns in the hills are difficult to interpret accurately since several hundred feet of elevation may separate the highest and lowest parts of a town.

Routes are described in one direction only. They can easily be followed in the opposite direction. The time for the trip in the reverse direction can be figured approximately if altitude is to be gained or lost and the rate of ascent or descent is taken into consideration.

Directions in the trail descriptions are given with reference to the compass. In addition, right- and left-hand sides of rivers are indicated to avoid confusion. **Right and left refer to the (true) right and (true) left banks when** *facing downstream.* Compass directions, for the most part, are general and may be a little off in some places. However, they are adequate for finding your way.

Often there are branches off the main trails that lead to houses. You'll quickly discover if you've taken one of these. Sometimes if you follow large trekking groups, you may find direction arrows scratched in the ground or on rocks to help indicate the way. Nepalis do not do this for themselves, it seems.

Local village governments are improving trails because of the increasing popularity of trekking. Improved trails may take different routes from those described here, and routes can shift in popularity for a variety of reasons. I have walked most of the trails described in this book at least twice. Notable changes range from improvements in some trails to erosion and damage on others, and finding more villages and settlements catering to trekkers along the popular routes. Landslides on steep valley-floor trails result in almost cyclical rerouting over a period of years to decades.

Along the popular trekking trails, it is likely that you will find many more hotels, tea shops, lodges, etc. in places where I haven't reported them. Local people are responding to the increased demands of tourism. It is hard to know what to call a hotel, or a tea shop, or a lodge. I have tried to use the term *bhaTTi* to refer to a traditional Nepali inn, one used by local people, but as an area becomes popular with trekkers, these are often the first to cater to outsiders. Consider all the other terms to be used interchangeably. Trekking times change also, usually decreasing as the trails improve through use. Please note down any changes or new information and send it to me in care of the publisher.

A *chautaara,* referred to in the trail descriptions, is a rectangular rock platform with a ledge for resting your load. Sometimes a pipal and a banyan tree are planted side by side in the center. In the east, you are as likely to find wooden benches. You can look forward to these welcome structures, found on many of the well-traveled routes. A *chorten* is a Buddhist religious structure, often cubical, with carved tablets. The term entrance *chorten* refers to a covered gateway or arch decorated with Buddhist motifs. A *stupa* is a very large *chorten. Mani* walls are rectangular and made of stone tablets carved with mantras and prayers.

Names of towns and villages are taken from two sources: maps and other documents, and my phonetic rendering of the names I heard. I try to spell the names according to the principles in my language book, so you may find my spellings differ from those found on signboards, though occasionally I will list some local English spellings.

Place names in Nepal are not unique. There are many Bhote Kosi's (rivers from Tibet), Beni's (junctions of two rivers), Phedi's (foot of hill), and Deorali's (passes). In addition, some villages may be called by two different names, but this should not cause much confusion in actual practice. Finally, as facilities that cater to trekkers are built in remote mountain regions, they may take on English names, albeit pronounced in a confusing Nepali fashion.

The pronunciation and transliteration guide at the end of this introduction indicates the correct way to pronounce the place names. It is important to place the stress on the first syllable of most words, for instance, Kathmandu, Pokhara, and Tengboche. The meaning of capital letters occurring within words is explained in the language section at the back of the book. Place names and other proper nouns are capitalized in spite of the transliteration system. The only place names that would be capitalized if the transliteration scheme were followed strictly are *RaRa, Dumre, AAbu Khaireni,* and *RiRi.* The correct spelling of Kathmandu in this transliteration system is kaaThmaanDu, but for the sake of convenience, the common spelling is used.

In the route descriptions, the names of some towns are in boldface. They are usually large, well-known places whose names the trekker should use when asking the way. Usually food and accommodations are available there. This should help you plan your journey. No recommendations for places to stay are given. These change constantly, and there is no way I can evaluate them, or describe them in Travlish, that evanescent dialect found in traditional guidebooks. You are advised to ask other trekkers about the latest finds, which, depending on your point of view, might be places to avoid.

In the interests of keeping the book to a manageable size, I have attempted to streamline the descriptions to leave out unnecessary details.

Even if you ask the way, there are times when you might get lost, especially along the less trekker-frequented trails. If this happens, it is preferable to backtrack to a place that you know, rather than bushwhack ahead. If faced with an unknown trail junction, refer to the general route description, and apply it to the topography in your situation to arrive at a decision. Go off, and see if the trail seems to be going where you expect it to.

Many trekkers have found their greatest enjoyment from finding new trails little used by foreigners. After you get the hang of it, don't be afraid to venture forth on undescribed terrain, especially if you are trekking independently. Encouraging you to explore on your own, without route descriptions at hand, may be the best advice I can provide.

Enterprising Nepalis and Tibetans sell artifacts along popular trails.

6 Helambu, Gosainkund, and Langtang

(Map No. 1, Page 165)

If you walk the trails of Nepal, you will know what Buddhist dharma is all about.

Tengboche Rimpoche

These regions are the ones most convenient to Kathmandu. Beginning from Kathmandu, the basic trek through the Helambu region makes a circuit from Pati Bhanjyang. There is an alternative exit from Talamarang to the Kathmandu–Kodari road. Visits can be made to Gosainkund and Langtang, beginning at Trisuli to the northwest of Kathmandu and via routes linking them with Helambu. An alternative route goes to Langtang with the return via Gosainkund and Helambu. Langtang, Gosainkund, and the northern part of Helambu have been designated a national park with headquarters at Dhunche village.

Helambu

Helambu or Helmu is the name of a region at the northern end of the Malemchi Khola valley. The Helambu trek starts from **Sundarijal,** a small dam and hydroelectric station in the northeast corner of the Kathmandu Valley. More precisely, it begins west of Sundarijal at the end of the auto road, where the large water pipe comes out of the hill.

There is now bus service to Sundarijal. A taxi can also be hired. The cheapest way to go there is by bus from Kathmandu to Baudha. Stay on the bus until it reaches the turnaround point several hundred yards east of the *stupa.* At this point the road forks—the right branch going to Sankhu, and the left to Sundarijal. Begin on this left fork and walk **2 to 3 hours** along the level road until it forks again near the edge of the valley. The left fork goes a short distance to a gate and the water treatment plant. Follow the right fork until it ends near a large water pipe. Cross under the pipe and proceed along its west side. Much of the way is up stairs. The trail reaches a clearing with an open building in **30 minutes.** Continue until you come to a school on your left. Then just beyond, turn left to cross over the dam of a water reservoir (5200 ft, 1585 m). Cross the dam and continue uphill, crossing the watershed management road, which winds around the hillside.

Climb through wet, subtropical forest to an oak forest, and on to **Mulkharka** (5800 ft, 1768 m), a scattered *Tamang* village. The trail continues up, first in open country, then in oak forest, and reaches the few houses of Chaubas

(7525 ft, 2233 m) in **1½ hours.** The trail then ascends for another **30 minutes** to a pass, Burlang Bhanjyang (8000 ft, 2438 m), with a few houses below it on the north side. This pass marks Kathmandu Valley's rim, here known as the Shivapuri ridge. The trail descends through a pleasant oak forest, past some houses on the left, Chisapani (7200 ft, 2194 m), to a flat portion where another trail joins from the right. In clear weather there are good views of the Himalaya to the north. In the spring rhododendrons bloom here. The trail continues to descend through open farmland to reach **Pati Bhanjyang** (5800 ft, 1768 m), sitting in a saddle **1¾ hours** from the pass. There is a police check post here.

From here, there is a choice of two routes. One continues along the general ridge system heading north, and eventually descends east to the Sherpa village of Malemchigaon. The other heads east, descends to the Malemchi Khola, and proceeds up its east (left) bank toward Tarke Ghyang, situated opposite Malemchigaon on the east side of the river. The ridge route goes much higher (almost to 12,000 ft, 3658 m) than the other route, and there may be snow on its upper portions in the late winter or early spring. There are no permanent villages between Kutumsang and Malemchigaon on this route, but if you leave Kutumsang in the morning, you should reach Malemchigaon that evening. This part of the route offers excellent views of the mountains. If it clouds over, as often happens late in the day, consider spending a night up high in a *goTh* or shelter used for pasturing animals. Then hope for good views the next morning.

The circuit to the north along the ridge and the return via the east side of the Malemchi Khola valley is described. But if the weather is bad, it is wise to head up the east (left) side of the Malemchi Khola and then, if conditions have improved, to return via the high route. In this case, follow the directions in reverse.

To head north from Pati Bhanjyang, climb up the north side of the hill forming the saddle to the left of a long house. Shortly (100 ft, 30 m), the trail forks. The right fork heads to Thakani, a *Tamang* village, and beyond to the Talamarang Khola and Malemchi Khola. This is where it meets the return path.

Take the left fork instead, climb a little, and contour for **30 minutes** to reach another saddle (5800 ft, 1768 m). Continue climbing north for **1¼ hours** to the town of **Chipling** (7100 ft, 2165 m), scattered along the hillside. Climb on, taking the uppermost fork at major junctions, up to 8050 ft (2453 m), then begin descending through the oak forest to **Gul Bhanjyang** (7025 ft, 2142 m), a *Tamang* village **1¾ hours** from Chipling. The trail is not very direct over this portion. A few minutes north of the town, reach a clearing and a trail junction where the left fork contours while the right climbs near the ridge. Take the right fork. Almost **1 hour** beyond Gul Bhanjyang at 7975 ft (2430 m), there is another fork. Take the left fork up to 8350 ft (2545 m) just west of the summit of the hill and descend to the few houses and trekker lodges at **Kutumsang** (8100 ft, 2469 m), situated in a pass. Reach it in **1¾ hours.** At the pass, you can take the right fork and contour for **10 minutes** to **Bolumje,** with more houses. There are no permanent villages between this town and Malemchigaon, a day away.

HELAMBU, GOSAINKUND, LANGTANG
MAP NO. 1

From Kutumsang or Bolumje the trail ascends the hill to the north. From Bolumje, pass two *chorten* then reach a *mani* wall (8250 ft, 2515 m) in **10 minutes.** Climb through a prickly-leaved oak forest that becomes a rhododendron-and-fir forest in its upper reaches. Reach a notch containing three *chorten* (10,600 ft, 3230 m) after climbing for 2½ **hours,** mostly on the east side of the main ridge. If starting from Kutumsang, the trail initially keeps close to the ridge crest. Just beyond the notch is a clearing. Continue, keeping more level, on the west side of the ridge. Another clearing containing some *goTh* (10,450 ft, 3185 m) is reached in **30 minutes.** At the north end of the clearing, a little to the west, there is a fresh-water spring. Water can be difficult to find along this ridge during dry weather. From here on, there are two route choices. One keeps close to the ridge crest, the Turin Danda, while the other contours over portions on the west side.

From the clearing, contour on the west side to reach **MangegoTh** (10,775 ft, 3285 m) in **30 minutes.** This is the largest group of *goTh* before Tharepati, and also the site of an army guard post. There may also be a permanent trekker hotel constructed here. Continue north on the east side through pleasant rhododendron forests. Cross over to the west side in **15 minutes,** then contour to reach some *goTh* (11,125 ft, 3390 m) in less than **30 minutes.** Continue on the west side to the ridge crest in another **45 minutes.** A few minutes beyond in a notch on the ridge (11,800 ft, 3597 m), you can look across the valley to the east and see a tight cluster of houses some 3000 ft (913 m) below you. If this town of Tarke Ghyang is east-southeast of you (slightly south of east or about 117°), you are in the correct notch. The notch is north of a *chorten* and there is now a *goTh* there, as well as a *chorten* with some faint trail markers in blue paint indicating that heading left leads to Gosainkund Lakes and right to Malemchigaon. If the village of Tarke Ghyang cannot be seen because of bad weather or haze, or if you are unsure, continue north along the trail to the left of a minor summit. Then, if in 15 minutes you cross the crest of the ridge to the west side and see two clusters of *goTh,* Tharepati, 100 ft (30 m) below, you had the correct notch. Currently, there are simple hotels operating in Tharepati during the trekking seasons. Backtrack to the notch. This part of the trail may be confusing to trekkers. There are many trails on this portion from Bolumje to Tharepati, so the specific one you take may be different from those described. Keep to the ridge crest for the most part. There may still be some signs in English to help locate the trails.

You can reach the notch in some 5 hours from Kutumsang, and in clear weather you should have fine views of the mountains. As mentioned before, consider spending a night in one of the *goTh* en route to enjoy views in the morning. If, instead of descending from the notch, you continue to the two clusters of *goTh* called Tharepati (11,800 ft, 3597 m) and then beyond to the north, the trail leads to the Gosainkund Lakes in a day.

To continue to Malemchigaon and the villages of upper Helambu, descend east from the notch mentioned above along a cut, but at times indistinct, steep trail. Eventually you enter a rocky streambed (9600 ft, 2926 m). Follow it down about 200 ft (61 m). About **1½ hours** from the notch, at 9400 ft (2865 m), you reach a clearing with a few *goTh* and, beyond, a fork in which the right branch descends to cross a tributary (8265 ft, 2520 m) after **40 minutes.** A short climb brings you to **Malemchigaon** (8400 ft, 2560 m).

The people here call themselves Sherpas, but their relationship with the Sherpas of Solu-Khumbu is distant. The dialects spoken are also different. Here you will find a *gomba* on the east end of the town, and the interesting rock home of a hermit on the west end.

There are no more towns farther up this valley, so to go to Tarke Ghyang, proceed down to the south of the *gomba* through an entrance *chorten* and descend a small ridge. About 1000 ft (304 m) below, there are some large rocks, and farther below, a large bridge over the Malemchi Khola. Reach it (6200 ft, 1890 m) in **1 hour** from Malemchigaon. Cross to the east (left) bank and head up southward to a *chorten*. Here, turn east and climb a little until a trail branches to the right across some terraces. Continue, mostly contouring but climbing a little, and cross two tributaries. After the second crossing, the trail rises more directly, and **1 hour** from the bridge, reaches a small treeless *chautaara* (7200 ft, 2194 m). Another 1000 ft (304 m) of vertical climbing brings you to a *chorten* and, shortly beyond, to a tight cluster of houses called **Tarke Ghyang,** another Sherpa village (8400 ft, 2560 m), **1¼ hours** from the *chautaara.* The town's name means "temple of the 100 horses" and was taken from the name of a temple established in 1727 by a lama who was called by the king of Kantipur to stop an epidemic in Kathmandu. As his reward the lama asked for 100 horses, which he brought here. The local temple, rebuilt in 1969, follows the Bhutanese style.

From Tarke Ghyang you can head east up past the schoolhouse and then north for three days to reach the Ganja La, a high pass (16,805 ft, 5123 m) leading to the Langtang Valley. Food, shelter, and fuel have to be carried, and the party should be equipped for snow climbing. This route is described in the reverse direction later in this chapter. The other route from Tarke Ghyang follows the river southward.

To take this route, head south at the low end of the village past the large new *gomba* and rows of *mani* walls to cross a stream. Take the lower fork just beyond, and after **1 hour,** cross a tributary (7000 ft, 2134 m) to **Kakani,** a small scattered Sherpa village (6750 ft, 2058 m) **30 minutes** after the tributary. Upon rounding the next ridge crest, you reach a clearing in the oak forest with *chorten, mani* walls, and an entrance *chorten.* Descend from here into the valley of the next tributary. Rather than head east to cross the tributary upstream from the main river, the trail descends near the ridge past a large *chorten.* In **1½ hours** from Kakani, you reach **Thimbu,** another scattered Sherpa and *Tamang* village (5000 ft, 1524 m). Below it, the trail descends for **15 minutes** to cross the next tributary (4550 ft, 1486 m).

The trail now follows the east (left) bank of the Malemchi Khola, close to the water for the most part, but rising occasionally to clear difficult stretches. The forest is again subtropical. In less than **1 hour,** descend to a suspension bridge across the river (4050 ft, 1234 m). Do not cross it, but continue on the east (left) bank, crossing several tributaries along the way. About **1½ hours** beyond the first suspension bridge, you come to the third bridge (3500 ft, 1067 m). Cross this to the west (right) bank and continue south on a wide trail that was once a road but is now in disrepair. There is an interesting-looking Brahman village (Sarha) on the right, and **1¼ hours** beyond the suspension bridge, you pass high above another. Then shortly, you descend to **Talamarang** (3150 ft, 960 m), a town with shops and tea houses.

There are two route choices from here. One ascends the tributary lying south of the village to rejoin the outward-bound route at Pati Bhanjyang. The other continues south along the west (right) bank of the Malemchi Khola to Siptaghat, where there is a road and bus service to Banepaa and on to Kathmandu. This route takes only 4 hours to the road, remains quite level, and follows a wide path almost suitable for a jeep. The other route follows an illdefined trail up a riverbed for several hours and involves a vertical ascent of 4700 ft (1433 m), followed by a descent of 2700 ft (823 m) to the Kathmandu

Valley. This route takes 8 to 9 hours to Sundarijal and should be taken if bad weather prevents you from having good views of the peaks on the way to Pati Bhanjyang, or if you are traveling in the spring, when the lower route is much hotter.

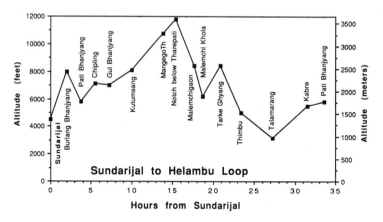

RETURN VIA PATI BHANJYANG

To return from Talamarang via Pati Bhanjyang, cross the suspension bridge over the tributary, the Talamarang Khola, and head west up its south (right) bank. There is a direct trail, which is difficult to find, up the ridge to Thakani. Instead stay close to the river most of the time. Try to follow a small trail that meanders about the river and crisscrosses it irregularly. The forest is chir pine and *chilaune* again. Almost **3 hours** later (4700 t, 1433 m), cross a large landslide through which a prominent tributary from the south flows. **Half an hour** beyond, on the south (right) bank of the Talamarang Khola near the hill to the south, you come to a small water-operated mill (4750 ft, 1448 m). A trail rises near the mill and essentially climbs the ridge north of the tributary valley mentioned before. Follow the trail to the *Tamang* village of **Kabre** (5500 ft, 1676 m), which is **45 minutes** from the riverbed.

Continue along the ridge through oak forest past another *Tamang* village. Take the right fork beyond to head west and rise to a *chautaara* (6050 ft, 1844 m) **30 minutes** from **Kabre.** The trail continues to ascend and reaches a ridge crest (6200 ft, 1890 m) in **20 minutes** near the *Tamang* village of **Thakani.** There are good distant views from here in clear weather. The trail now crosses to the south side of the ridge and contours, heading west, for **1¼ hours** to the trail you took on the way out, just north of Pati Bhanjyang. Descend to **Pati Bhanjyang** in a **few minutes** and retrace the route described earlier to Sundarijal.

RETURN VIA PANCHKHAL

To proceed to the Kathmandu–Kodari road from Talamarang, cross the bridge over the tributary and continue south on a wide trail. Vehicles have succeeded in motoring most of the way on the road, but presently it is not in good repair. There are large boulders and washouts obstructing the way. You are in sal forest and noncultivated areas for the most part.

Follow the west (right) bank of the Malemchi Khola for **1½ hours** until you see a large suspension bridge over the river and a cluster of houses on the west (right) bank. This is **Malemchi Pul Bazaar** (2775 ft, 846 m). Another **1¼ hours** brings you to **Bahunepati** (2660 ft, 811 m), the largest bazaar en route, and the road. A further **1¼ hours** along the much wider valley brings you near another suspension bridge, which spans almost the entire valley floor. There is a town, **Talabasi** (also called **Siptaghat**) (2575 ft, 785 m), at the west end of the bridge. There is now a bus service from Siptaghat to Banepaa and on to Kathmandu.

Gosainkund

Here is the description of a trek from Trisuli, up the Trisuli Valley to the sacred lakes of Gosainkund and beyond to Helambu. Such a circuit may be about the best possible short trek from Kathmandu. It takes a minimum of a week, and food for two or three days must be carried.

Trisuli, the old staging point for this trek, can be reached from Kathmandu on foot in a day and a half, or by bus in 4 to 5 hours from Pakanajol in the northwest corner of Kathmandu. From Trisuli you used to proceed north up the east (left) or west (right) bank of the river. Most trekkers these days, however, take a bus from Trisuli that goes north up a new road through Syabrubensi and into the Ganesh Himal area. Get off in **Dhunche,** the headquarters of the Langtang National Park.

If you took the traditional walking route from Trisuli, you would pass through the villages of Betrawati, Bogata, Manigaon, Ramche, Grang Thare, and Bokajhunga before reaching Dhunche.

Dhunche (6450 ft, 1966 m) is a major village at the junction of the Trisuli Khola and the Bhote Kosi. There are shops and a police check post here. It is also the district center for Rasuwa District. Pay the park entrance fee at the Langtang National Park headquarters here.

From Dhunche, the current trail follows the motor road down to the Trisuli Khola, which drains Gosainkund, and crosses it to the north (right) bank. The bridge washed out in the summer of 1988, and is being rebuilt. Continue to the first stream after crossing the bridge and take the trail that heads up the bank. Climb up the gully to reach the crest and the trail junction. Take the right-hand fork, climbing to the east, and follow it for approximately **5 hours** to Sing Gomba (10,675 ft, 3254 m). Pass through oak forests to reach an impressive fir-and-rhododendron forest.

It is a climb of 8700 ft (2652 m) to the pass. The first 4300 ft (1311 m) are rather steep and there is little water. At junctions, take the upper fork. The pleasant, easy-to-follow trail passes through hillsides ablaze with rhododendrons in season. There are no permanent settlements until you reach the Helambu region, about a three-day trek (in good weather) beyond Dhunche.

One of several methods for spinning wool

Sing Gomba is inhabited during the less severe part of the year, when people there can provide food and shelter for trekkers. An HMG cheese factory is located there.

From the *gomba*, head east along the south side of the ridge, following a wide trail. At first, where there was once a big burn, the slope is covered with *Piptanthus nepalensis* shrubs with yellow flowers. Then the trail enters a rhododendron-and-fir forest, and crosses to the north side of the ridge. In 1¼ **hours,** reach a *goTh* (11,550 ft, 3520 m), where the trail is joined by the one coming up from Syabru. (If coming from Syabru, take the trail up the ridge from the village, past a water-driven prayer wheel, and follow a faint trail to gain the ridge here.) There is now a tea shop/hotel here open during the peak of the trekking season. Continue for **45 minutes** on the north side to the few *goTh* called Laurebina (12,800 ft, 3901 m). Water is scarce here. Again, there may be a seasonal hotel. In good weather there are views of Himalchuli, Peak 29, Manaslu, and Ganesh Himal to the west, Tibet to the north, and Langtang Himal to the northeast. Climb on, reaching a *chautaara* with poles sticking out of it (13,000 ft, 3962 m), then in a little over **30 minutes,** cross the ridge to the south side (13,600 ft, 4145 m). Beyond, you begin to see the lakes. The first is Bhutkunda, followed by Nagkunda, and then Gosainkunda. This third lake (14,374 ft, 4381 m) is reached in **45 minutes.** There are several stone huts on the north shore, and one may be operated as a trekker lodge at peak trekking times. There is also a national park guard post.

Every year during the full moon between mid-July and mid-August, thousands of pilgrims and devotees come to bathe in this lake and to pay homage to Shiva. There are several legends, all similar, concerning the formation of this lake and its significance. One story is that the gods were churning the ocean, hoping to obtain from it the water of immortality. Some poison arose from the seas, and Shiva, realizing that the poison might harm the gods, drank it. The poison caused him a great deal of pain and thirst, as well as a blue discoloration of his neck. To relieve the fever and suffering, Shiva traveled to the snows of Gosainkund. He thrust his trident, or *trisul,* into the mountainside and three streams of water sprang forth which collected in the hollow beneath, producing the Gosainkund Lake. Shiva stretched along the lake's edge and drank its waters, quenching his thirst. There is an oval-shaped rock beneath the surface near the center of the lake. Worshipers say they can see Shiva reclining on a bed of serpents there.

In good weather, consider climbing the hill to the north for a view. To continue to Helambu, contour the lake and ascend past four more lakes (Bhairunkunda, Saraswatikunda, Dudhkunda, and Surjekunda—often they may be covered with ice) to the Laurebina Pass (15,100 ft, 4602 m) in **1 hour.**

From the pass, descend to the valley below, which tends southeast, veering northeast to the left side, where there is a trail junction. The right-hand trail leads down to stone *goTh* frames (13,000 ft, 3962 m), about **1 hour** from the pass. The left-hand trail contours high around the northeast side of the valley, eventually coming out on the ridge above Tharepati. This is a new trail built as a "work for food" scheme and is supposed to be much quicker than the old trail. It traverses steep country, and part of it had fallen away in 1988. Don't take it if there has been a recent snowfall.

If taking the old trail, from the stone *goTh* frames (13,000 ft, 3962 m) descend a ridge with a waterfall on your left. There is a campsite (11,900 ft, 3627 m) **45 minutes** farther. There may be a temporary tea shop/hotel for trekkers in this area during the popular season, but don't count on it. Soon the trail crosses a stream and passes another picturesque waterfall. About **45 minutes** from the first campsite, there is another under the overhanging rocks of Gopte (11,700 ft, 3566 m). The notch (11,675 ft, 3559 m) you saw earlier is reached in **45**

minutes. Some **45 minutes** later, there are more overhanging rocks. Some trekking agency people and park staff call this Gopte, and again there may be a temporary tea shop/hotel here during peak periods. The trail continues through beautiful rhododendron forests and in **30 minutes** crosses a tributary from the north (10,550 ft, 3216 m) to ascend through juniper woods. It reaches a series of *goTh* called Tharepati (11,500 ft, 3505 m) just below the ridge west of the Malemchi Khola in another **1¼ hours.** Several of these *goTh* may be set up as simple hotels during peak season. The others may also be used to stay in if unlocked. There are good views to the north from the crest of the ridge. A trail proceeds north near the crest, and leads over a high pass to the Langtang Valley.

From the ridge (11,875 ft, 3620 m) above the *goTh,* the trail follows the crest to the southeast and drops into a notch (11,800 ft, 3597 m), from which Tarke Ghyang is visible to the east-southeast as a tight cluster of houses on the east side of the Malemchi Khola valley, some 3000 ft (913 m) below you. To the south is a hill with a *chorten.* There are two choices now: descend from the notch to Malemchigaon, or head south along the main ridge to Kutumsang. Both of these trails have been described earlier.

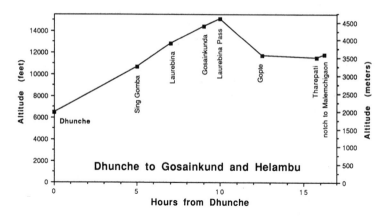

Langtang

Langtang is a valley nestled in the Himalaya. It is best to carry some food in order to be able to explore the upper part of the valley. First the trip from Trisuli to Langtang, then several side trips up the valley, are described. There is a high pass, the Ganja La, which links Langtang with Helambu. A brief description of this route is given; going with a person familiar with this route is advised. Return routes to avoid backtracking from Langtang, and linkups with Gosainkund, complete the description. An interesting and informative recent account of this area is given in Andrew R. Hall's "Preliminary Report on the Langtang Region" (see appendix B).

To go to Langtang, follow the route already described to Dhunche in the Gosainkund section. Pay the national park entrance fee in Dhunche. From Dhunche (6450 ft, 1966 m) follow the road to **Bharku** (6050 ft, 1844 m), reached in **1 hour.** Very soon, after Bharku, take the trail leading off up the hill on your right toward Syabru.

To proceed on the new route, continue contouring and rising beyond Bharku through pleasant chir pine and rhododendron forests. Round a bend to a rest spot (7550 ft, 2301 m) with the first views up the Langtang Valley after **2¼ hours.** Contour and descend another **45 minutes** to **Syabru** (6950 ft, 2118 m), a village strung out along a ridge. From Syabru there are trails ascending to Sing Gomba (3 to 4 hours) and to Gosainkund (about 7 hours). If taking this trail to Sing Gomba, there may be some temporary tea shop/hotel establishments, the first a substantial one 1 hour above Syabru, and the next one, much more temporary, at the *goTh* where the trail reaches the ridge crest after climbing up through the forest.

There are no permanent settlements for at least a day's walk beyond Syabru, but during peak trekking season, there are hotels and tea shops that cater to trekkers. Shelter can also be found under rocks, but food must be carried if you are there outside of the popular trekking times. To continue to Langtang, drop and contour across wheat fields to the east. Then descend and cross to the east (right) bank of a tributary (6375 ft, 1943 m) from the Gosainkund Lekh after **45 minutes.** Climb up a bit to reach the first of many tea shop/hotels. Then descend through a forest and a massive landslide that occurred in the summer of 1987, to reach the Langtang Khola (5450 ft, 1661 m) in **45 minutes.** Soon after reaching the river there is another tea shop/hotel. A trail and several bridges cross the Langtang Khola and lead downstream to Syabrubensi. This difficult trail is passable only in the dry season, but can provide another route of return from the valley.

Continue upstream along the south (left) bank through a quite impressive gorge. In **1 hour,** reach a rock shelter, another tea shop/hotel, and cross a nearby tributary (6325 ft, 1928 m). Another **45 minutes** brings you to a bridge (6700 ft, 2042 m) that is crossed to the north (right) bank. There is now a substantial trekker lodge here and rock shelters suitable for camping. The trail continues climbing through rhododendron and prickly-leaved oak forests, to meet the old trail (7825 ft, 2385 m) from Syabrubensi in 1 hour. This older trail keeps high on the north side of the valley before descending to Syabrubensi. It is described later. At the junction is another new lodge.

Notice how much drier it is on this side of the valley, which—because it faces south—receives more sunlight. Continue on up the valley, which widens out. **Half an hour** farther there are several substantial lodges, at a place known as **Lama Hotel** for the first such, as well as space for camping. A **1½ hour**'s climb brings you to **Ghumnachowk** (Trekker's Corner), also called Riverside, with a lodge and campsites. Another **1½ hour's** climb brings you to the valley floor and **Ghora Tabela** (9450 ft, 2880 m). This was once a Tibetan resettlement project and may not have any permanent residents, but your permits will probably be checked here. A trekkers' lodge may be in operation. Beyond, on the south side of the valley, are larch forests that turn golden yellow in the autumn.

Continue up the valley, passing several temporary settlements now converted to seasonal tea shop/hotels, then cross a tributary below a monastery after **1½ hours.** This active monastery is interesting and worth a visit. Note the glacier-worn *U* shape of the valley here, in contrast to the water-worn *V* shape of the valley below Ghora Tabela. Another **30 minutes** brings you to beautiful **Langtang** village (11,483 ft, 3500 m). Tourist facilities have been constructed here. Continue on up a moraine to cross a tributary (11,800 ft, 3597 m) after another **1¼ hours.** The views become better with further progress and, looking back, you can see the impressive Langtang Himal. Another **20 minutes** brings you to a trail fork (12,075 ft, 3680 m). The left fork goes to Kyangjin Gomba. Shortly beyond, on the right fork, is the HMG cheese factory and the summer pasturing settlements of **Kyangjin** (12,300 ft, 3749 m). Food and lodging can usually be arranged at the lodge here.

UPPER LANGTANG VALLEY

From Kyangjin there are several worthwhile excursions. You can head north to reach the glacier and icefall in less than 3 hours. Climb the lateral moraine to the left of the glacier. Or 1 hour's climb to the north up a small hill provides a good view. An hour beyond is Point 4773 m (15,660 ft) on the Austrian map, an even more spectacular viewpoint. You can also proceed farther up the main valley. The STOL airstrip (12,425 ft, 3786 m), in a state of disrepair, is 30 minutes beyond Kyangjin, in the valley floor. There are many possibilities for short climbs, mostly to the north. There is another cheese factory at Yala, a 3½-hour climb from Kyangjin. A small summit with outstanding views can be reached from the factory.

To go to Yala, head east from Kyangjin, and after about 10 minutes, contour the hillside to the north, reaching a few *goTh* in 1 hour. Another hour's contouring and climbing brings you to another series of *goTh* (13,650 ft, 4160 m). Round the ridge crest and contour another slope for **30 minutes** to another ridge (14,400 ft, 4389 m). Climb north beside a small stream to reach the buildings at Yala (15,200 ft, 4633 m) in less than **1 hour.** To reach Tsergo Ri (some call this Yala Peak), an excellent viewpoint, head west from Yala, or continue circling the hill, reaching the prayer flag-festooned summit (16,353 ft, 4984 m) in **2 hours.** To the south, you can see the Ganja La, a pass leading into Helambu. The surrounding peaks are quite spectacular. Many short climbs may suggest themselves to the experienced.

From Kyangjin, you can also head up the valley to Langsisa, the next to the last of the summer pasturing settlements. Cross an alluvial fan (12,250 ft, 3734 m) **20 minutes** beyond and reach the airstrip, crossing its western end. In less than **30 minutes,** reach the north (right) bank of the Langtang Khola and continue upstream. Another **45 minutes** brings you to a summer settlement (12,500 ft, 3810 m), and another **hour** brings you to a second. Big lateral and terminal moraines of the West Langtang Glacier loom ahead. Contour around its south terminus and reach the lone hut of **Langsisa** (13,400 ft, 4084 m) in another **hour.** Ahead lies the main Langtang Glacier, and the Tibetan border, a hard day's climb away (some trekking maps are grossly in error regarding the border). To the south lies beautiful Buddha Peak and the terminus of the East Langtang Glacier. Up this valley lies a difficult pass leading to the region east of Helambu. It was probably first crossed by H. W. Tilman in 1949. There are many places to explore.

There is a big reddish rock at Langsisa which, according to legend, is that color because a holy man living outside the valley lost his yak and trailed it to this place. The yak died here, however, and the lama, wanting its hide, skinned it and spread the skin on a rock to dry. But the skin stuck and remains there on the rock to this day! This is the legend of the discovery of the Langtang Valley. *Lang* means "yak," and *tang* means "to follow," hence the name. Also, a few miles up the valley to the southeast, two big rock gendarmes stand a hundred feet above the glacier. They are said to represent two Buddhist saints, Shakya Muni and Guru Rimpoche.

There are several possible linkup routes to avoid backtracking. From below Ghora Tabela, you can cross the Langtang Khola and ascend to the Chedang yak pastures and Laurebina on the main trail to Gosainkunda. This takes **two days** and requires a guide who is quite familiar with the route. You can also reach Malemchigaon from Chedang. From Syabru you can ask the way to Gosainkunda and to Sing Gomba. For experienced parties, the Ganja La leads to Helambu. This pass is normally possible from May to November, or sometimes longer in dry years. Food, fuel, and shelter for four to five days must be carried. It is necessary to have someone along who is familiar with the route, as it is quite easy to get lost in poor weather.

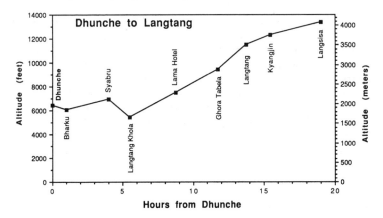

THE GANJA LA

To cross the Ganja La from Langtang Valley, follow the main route from Kyangjin to Langtang for a few hundred yards (meters) down the old moraine to where the trail swings west down the valley. Another trail leads off near here and continues straight on down to the Langtang Khola, which can be crossed by a log bridge between massive boulders. Then upstream on the south (right) bank are a few huts and meadows. Pick up a trail at the edge of the forest behind the meadows and climb in an easterly (upriver) direction through birch-and-rhododendron forest, then rhododendron scrub, to come out at the stone huts and pastures of Ngegang (14,450 ft, 4404 m) in **2 hours.** Stay here, or at a site 30 minutes further, where there may be water.

Another **4 or more hours** brings you to the pass, which may be difficult to see from below. Basically, you continue easterly, climbing steeply for the first 1½ to 2 hours, and contouring till you reach the slopes of the moraine and a glacier, below the pass. Keep to the west side of the valley coming down from the pass. The last 100 ft (30 m) to the pass (16,805 ft, 5122 m) is a scramble, either on rock, or on mixed rock and snow, depending on the conditions. Mountaineering experience, with the ability to use a rope and ice ax, is necessary here.

At the pass, descend steeply over scree for several hundred feet to reach more gradual broken rock. Keep to the eastern side of the basin, at times on the crest of a moraine, avoiding the glacier. In **2 to 3 hours,** reach a cairn. Then descend steeply over easier ground, on a trail, to a small meadow where there may be a stream. This takes less than **30 minutes,** and the site may be a suitable campsite. Keep to the east side of a mossy rock, and enter the left (northeast) side of the Yangri Khola valley. Reach meadows with old *goTh* in **1 to 1½ hours** from the previous campsite. Cross a tributary of the Yangri Khola here to the right side. Ascend on a faint trail to some more meadows and keep high up on the east side of the ridge, passing several broken-down *goTh*. There is little water along this route most of the time, but several possible campsites. Avoid trail forks descending into the valley to the east.

Reach Kelchung, a series of *goTh* in poor repair, in **2 to 3 hours.** Continue south, crossing several shoulders, for the most part tending to the east side of the main ridge. Staying high on the main ridge, reach Dukpu (13,200 ft, 4023 m), a group of *goTh* in better shape, located near scrub, in another **3 to 4 hours.** Contour and then ascend to a notch to the northeast of a prominent hill, where there are prayer flags and cairns, in **1 hour.** Enter fine rhododendron forests, crossing and recrossing the ridge crest. Pass through a clearing with a hut (10,900 ft, 3322 m) in **1 hour. An hour** beyond is a trail fork, the right heading to Malemchigaon. Take the left branch toward Tarke Ghyang, reaching it after **2 to 3 hours,** the last part a steep descent. Routes linking Tarke Ghyang with Kathmandu have been described in the Helambu section of this chapter.

LANGTANG TO SYABRUBENSI

If you came to Langtang without visiting Syabrubensi, consider varying your exit to Trisuli slightly by following the Langtang Valley downstream, high on the north side, to Syabrubensi. Descend on the usual trail from Ghora Tabela, and after **1 hour,** pass a bridge over the Langtang Khola (8625 ft, 2629 m). The bridge can be used to reach Gosainkunda via Chedang yak pastures as mentioned earlier. However, continue down to reach the trail junction (7850 ft,

2393 m) in another **45 minutes.** The left fork descends to the bridge and Syabru. The right fork ascends through open, steep country where you might spot some interesting animals, such as goral or serow. The trail passes a lodge and descends to the few houses of Syarpa or **Syarpagaon** (8225 ft, 2507 m) in another **hour.** Continue contouring and climbing on the steep valley wall for **2 hours** until you round a ridge to an oak-and-blue pine forest and the valley of the main Bhote Kosi. A **30- to 45-minute** descent brings you to **Khangjung** (7250 ft, 2210 m), a scattered village with cultivated fields. At the lower end, the trail forks near a water source and *mani.* The right fork heads north to Rasuwa Garhi, while the left descends through terraces into chir pine forest to Mangal (4900 ft, 1494 m), near the bottom of the Bhote Kosi valley, in a little over **1 hour.** Head downstream (south) from here, following the main trail on the east (left) bank of the Bhote Kosi for **30 minutes** to **Syabrubensi** (4650 ft, 1417 m). This large town contains a settlement of Tibetan refugees, as well as *BhoTiya,* who call themselves *Tamang.* The road from Trisuli comes to this town, so a bus can be taken back.

There are some hot springs near here that can be used for bathing. To reach them, cross the main suspension bridge over the Bhote Kosi and head downstream on the west (right) bank for about 10 minutes to a small hot spring. There are other bigger ones below.

SYABRUBENSI TO SING GOMBA

From Syabrubensi, cross the suspension bridge over the Langtang Khola to its south (left) bank. Heading upstream from here, you can take a trail to Syabru and on to Sing Gomba or Gosainkunda. Or you can walk for less than **10 minutes** downstream on the Bhote Kosi, take a left fork before some *mani* walls, and climb for about 6 hours to Sing Gomba and Chauchan Bari, the HMG cheese factory (10,625 ft, 3239 m). This could provide a pleasant side trip for those basically retracing their steps to Trisuli, or it would be appropriate for trekkers who wish to visit the Gosainkund Lakes and cross over to Helambu. If taking this fork, climb steeply through chir pine forest to a *chorten* (6950 ft, 2118 m) in **2 hours.** Another **15 minutes** brings you to a clearing with another *chorten* and good views north and west. Continue through wheat fields to **Bhrabal** (7450 ft, 2271 m) in a few minutes. About 125 ft (40 m) above this pleasant village, the trail intersects the trail from Bharku to Syabru at a *chautaara* and *mani* wall. However, continue climbing steeply up to the ridge, leaving terraces (8950 ft, 2728 m) after another **1½ hours** and climbing through oak forest. In **1 hour** reach a clearing (10,250 ft, 3124 m) where the trail from Syabru joins. There are good views up the Langtang Valley and to the west. Climb for a minute, then take the right fork, which contours through blue pine forest to reach a clearing (10,450 ft, 3185 m) in **30 minutes.** Here the trail to Gosainkunda, beginning from across the Trisuli Khola at Dhunche, enters. Do not climb, but continue contouring through an impressive fir-and-rhododendron forest to reach **Sing Gomba** and the cheese factory, Chauchan Bari (10,625 ft, 3239 m), in **30 minutes.** Accommodation can be arranged here. The trail beyond to Gosainkunda has already been described.

Machhapuchhre, from just north of Pokhara

7 North of Pokhara

(Map No. 3, Page 183)

If there be a Paradise on earth, it is now, it is now, it is now!
Wilfred Noyce, describing the
area above NagDAADa in
Climbing the Fish's Tail

Pokhara, a very scenic spot itself, can be the starting point for at least four treks described in this book. The three described in this chapter are: the traditional trek to Thak Khola, Jomosom, and Muktinath; the trek to Manang starting at Dumre east of Pokhara; and the trip to the Annapurna Sanctuary. It is possible to combine all three in a circuit of the Annapurna massif with a visit to the so-called sanctuary. Such a trek combines spectacular mountain scenery with incredible ethnic and cultural diversity and traverses through very different ecological life zones. This is justifiably a classic trek, among the world's best.

Many people take shorter journeys from Pokhara.

To Thak Khola and Muktinath

The trek from Pokhara to Jomosom on the Kali Gandaki, or the Thak Khola, as the river is called in its northern portions, is perhaps one of the easiest, most comfortable, and certainly the most popular trek in Nepal. There is relatively little climbing, cooked food and lodging are easily available along the entire route, and the terrain is more varied than on any other trek of comparable length. Although the route passes among some of the highest mountains in the world, the scenery may not be as exciting as in, say, Khumbu. There are, however, several side trips that take the trekker up and out of the valleys and closer to the main Himalaya. Muktinath, a Hindu and Buddhist pilgrimage site, is a day's walk north of Jomosom.

Unless you plan a side trip to one of the uninhabited areas, there is no need to take food or shelter. Hotels in most villages offer food and accommodations that are more "Western" in style, though they are certainly primitive by modern tourist standards. These places are run by the *Newar, Thakali, Gurung,* and *Magar* ethnic groups.

Transportation from Kathmandu to Pokhara is available daily by air (RNAC) and by road, and from India by road. You could take a plane to or from Jomosom to avoid backtracking, but this is not worth doing, since backtracking will increase your understanding and enjoyment of the area. Furthermore, it is difficult to get a seat on a scheduled flight to or from Jomosom.

Flights are often canceled due to bad weather and the high winds.

As more roads are built, the question of using them arises. A road is being constructed from Pokhara all the way to Baglung and Beni. It goes at least as far as KAAre now, will go through Lumle soon, and cross the Modi Khola below Birethanti. Currently, it is difficult to get a vehicle to KAAre, but this should change in the future. Popular trails may change because of its alignment. If you prefer to walk but don't want to share the road with heavily laden jeeps, take the trail to NagDAADa from Phewa Tal, the lake at Pokhara. Or better still, trek to Dhampus from Suikhet, and then go on to Landrung, cross to Ghandruk, and head over to GhoRepani. See page 199 for a description of the route to NagDAADa in the reverse direction, and page 205 for the route from GhoRepani to Ghandruk. My first trek in 1969 began from the airstrip in Pokhara because there was no road.

From the **Pokhara** airstrip (2713 ft, 827 m) you can now board a bus or taxi to Mahendra Pul in the downtown area. The bus from Kathmandu also brings you here. From Mahendra Pul take a bus or taxi to the Shining Hospital. Or you can walk. To do so, continue up to the upper end of the bazaar where the road descends a short hill. Near its bottom, 1 hour from the airstrip, turn left and head toward the Multi-Purpose High School and the Shining Hospital (the Quonset huts in the field to your right). The first such nongovernmental facility established in Nepal, Shining Hospital has now merged with the Gandaki Anchal Hospital, which lies off the road to the south of Mahendra Pul. You may be able to hire a jeep to KAAre at Shining Hospital, but more likely, you will get one to Phedi, below NagDAADa.

To walk, continue north above the right fork of the Seti Khola and, after passing a river junction, cross the tributary Yamdi Khola to its left bank (3075 ft, 937 m). A Chinese hydroelectric project is under construction here. After passing through the small settlement of Yamdi, pass below the **Hyangja Tibetan Camp** (3325 ft, 1013 m) **1 hour** from the Shining Hospital. Food and lodging are available, and the handicraft center is well worth visiting. If you haven't seen a carpet factory in action, be sure to see the one here. The trail heads on to the town of **Hyangja** (3600 ft, 1097 m) in **40 minutes,** then enters the long, wide Yamdi Khola valley, the floor of which is a series of irrigated rice paddies. Depending on the season, the route either goes through the paddies or follows the road on the northeast side of the valley. **Suikhet** (meaning "irrigated fields") is the name given to the small settlement where the valley, after narrowing, opens up (3650 ft, 1113 m) to a few tea shops. **Phedi** (meaning "foot of hill") is at the bottom of the hill to the south (3700 ft, 1128 m). Reached just after crossing the Yamdi Khola, this area is at the western end of the paddies about **1 hour** from Hyangja.

From Phedi, climb the hill through sal forest to the south, crossing the road several times to reach **NagDAADa** (4782 ft, 1458 m) on the ridge **1 hour** from Phedi. The trail then goes west along the ridge. Phewa Tal, the lake at Pokhara, is visible to the southeast. There are stunning views of Machhapuchhre and the Annapurna range. Either on the way out or on the return trip, spend a night near here or near Chandrakot to get morning views of the range. NagDAADa, meaning "sharp ridge like a nose," is an appropriate name for

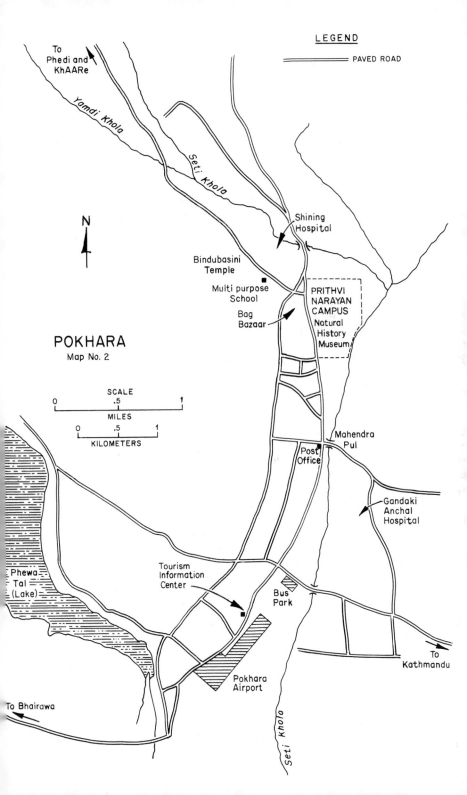

this town. NauDAADa, usually spelled Naudanda by Westerners, means "nine ridges" and is clearly not the correct name. NauDAADa is a village on the road south of Pokhara. But the incorrect name is the common one here. Unfortunately, though once an idyllic town, NagDAADa is now a dusty, dirty town, with construction vehicles passing through.

About 25 minutes west of where you reach the ridge (5000 ft, 1524 m), the trail to Kusma forks left. But to go on to Chandrakot, keep close to the ridge on the trail or road, and bear northwest through countryside reminiscent of Scottish highlands. Pass through Paundur (5650 ft, 1722 m) to the village of **KAAre** (5700 ft, 1737 m), which is in a pass. Continue through Jaljala (5275 ft, 1608 m) and **Lumle** (5300 ft, 1615 m) to **Chandrakot** (5250 ft, 1600 m) at the west end of the ridge. Reach KAAre in **1½ hours** from NagDAADa, Lumle in another **45 minutes,** and Chandrakot in another **30 minutes.** Lumle is the site of a British agricultural development project where former Gurkha soldiers are trained in farming. It has one of the highest rainfalls in Nepal.

The views from Chandrakot, as from NagDAADa, are unforgettable. You will cross the Modi Khola, which flows south between the peaks Annapurna South and Machhapuchhre shortly. The Annapurna Sanctuary, which lies up river inside the gate formed by Machhapuchhre and Hiunchuli, the peak east of Annapurna South, is a worthwhile side trip.

The trail descends to the Modi Khola, follows its east (left) bank southward a short distance to a suspension bridge, and crosses to the prosperous town of **Birethanti** (3600 ft, 1097 m) **1¼ hours** from Chandrakot. This is a good place to stock up on supplies, because prices go up the farther you get from Pokhara. From here, one trail heads up the Modi Khola on its west (right) bank toward the Annapurna Sanctuary. The trail to Thak Khola heads west. Just up from the town by a picturesque waterfall is a cool pool on the Bhurungdi Khola. If you swim here, be sure to wear clothing in order not to offend the Nepalis. Follow the Bhurungdi Khola westward, at first through forests. Stay on its northeast (left) bank, passing a steel suspension bridge. Cross several tributaries, then pass through two settlements, Lamthali and Sudame. In times of low water, the trail may even cross the main river to avoid steep areas. Do what the locals are doing, but stay on the northeast (left) bank except for these short diversions. **Hille** (5600 ft, 1524 m) is reached in **2 hours,** and shortly beyond is **TirkheDUgaa** (5175 ft, 1577 m). Farther on, the branches of the Bhurungdi Khola are crossed on several bridges (5075 ft, 1547 m). The steepest climb so far, up to **Ulleri** (6800 ft, 2073 m), takes **2 hours** from Hille.

If you want to pace the climb, there are 3767 steps to ascend to Ulleri; trekker Lance Hart counted them! Note the handsome slate roofs on the village houses. Near the last house is the new stone commemorating the death of a Dutch trekker. Higher up, at a *chautaara* on the left, is a worn rock tablet faintly inscribed as follows: "Once, sweet, bright joy, like their lost children, an Ulleri child." It is a memorial to 18-month-old Ben, the son of anthropologist John Hitchcock. Ben died here in 1961 while his father was doing field work.

From Ulleri, the trail climbs steadily, enters lush oak forest, and crosses numerous small streams. It is a great place for bird-watching. An hour above

Ulleri you come to Banthanti (7775 ft, 2307 m), meaning "a place in the forest," and 1½ hours later to Nayathanti (8550 ft, 2606 m), literally meaning "new place." New lodges in both villages cater to the great numbers of trekkers passing through in recent years. Lone trekkers have been attacked in this forest. If by yourself, hire a porter or join up with others. This caution applies all the way to Chitre.

The trail emerges at **GhoRepani** (9250 ft, 2819 m), a cluster of hotels below the pass some **3 hours** from Ulleri. GhoRepani, meaning "horse water," is now a far cry from the one building I saw on my first trek in Nepal in 1969. Then it truly was a watering place for the horse caravans that traveled between Pokhara and Mustang. There are more hotels at the pass, GhoRepani Deorali, which is 200 ft (61 m) higher than the town. Trekkers should make certain they catch the views, either from the pass itself, which is now incredibly deforested, or from east or west of the pass. On my first trek, there were no views from the pass, as it was in a dense rhododendron forest!

Poon (Pun) Hill (10,478 ft, 3194 m) on the ridge to the west is a popular viewpoint. Reach the hill in less than 1 hour. Signs point the way to Poon Hill from GhoRepani and from the pass. Make sure you take all the water you can to Poon Hill, as sources there are very limited. There are no facilities there. Views of Dhaulagiri and the Kali Gandaki gorge are best in the early morning. From the pass, a trail follows the ridge to the east to link with the trail from Ghandruk. The views to the east along the ridge are very impressive too. This route, which will be described later, offers a different return to Pokhara for those who have traveled north from Ulleri.

To continue to Thak Khola, descend through rhododendron forest, then prickly-leaved oak, to cultivated areas. Facilities begin 300 ft (91 m) below the pass. Reach the right fork to Ghandruk (8020 ft, 2444 m), with **Chitre** below, and **PhalaTe** (7400 ft, 2256 m), before reaching **Sikha** (6820 ft, 2079 m) in a notch that is **2 hours** from the pass. This unforgettable descent offers views of the immense south face of Dhaulagiri to the north. There are plenty of facilities all along here. Reach **Ghara** (6000 ft, 1828 m) less than **1 hour** from Sikha.

Continue through a notch now called Durbin Danda ("binocular ridge"), and descend steeply to the south (left) bank of the Ghar Khola. Cross it on a wooden bridge (3850 ft, 1173 m) and reach the few houses called Ghar Khola above the junction of the Ghar Khola and the Kali Gandaki. As the junction of two rivers, this area is sacred and has a little temple below. The trail to Beni continues south on the east (left) bank of the Kali Gandaki. But you should head upstream, cross the Kali Gandaki on a suspension bridge, and go on to **Tatopani** (3900 ft, 1189 m) **1½ hours** from Ghara. Nilgiri is the summit in the valley floor. If you head up to Kagbeni, you will go around it to the north side!

The police check post is in the south end of town. There are substantial tourist facilities here and many shops. Several lodge keepers here have installed bio-gas plants to operate their stoves and lights, as much an energy-conservation measure as an economic one. Another has installed a hydro-generator to power the electric lights in his hotel. Soon there will be a new 1000-kilowatt mini hydro-generator upstream.

Tatopani, a prosperous *Thakali* town, takes its name (taato paani, literally "hot water") from the hot springs located along the banks of the river, near the middle of town, reached by a trail to the river bank. There are currently two excellent pools, one very hot and the other hot. Don't foul the water with soap. Wash in the effluent below the pools, or in the river, rinse and then soak in the hot water. Be discreet and modest, as the Nepalis are.

Head north from Tatopani, pass the few houses of Nagdhunga and then Jalkale, near the junction of the Miristi Khola and the Kali Gandaki. Beyond is BhuiTe, where a suspension bridge leads to the hydroelectric project on the east side. Stay on the west (right) bank of the Kali Gandaki and pass through Sukebagar to reach **Dana** (4600 ft, 1402 m) by the Ghatte Khola. This wealthy, stretched-out town is reached in about **1½ hours** from Tatopani. Continue on the west (right) bank to Titar, then climb to the few houses of **Rupse Chhaharo** (5350 ft, 1631 m), named after the waterfall above the bridge. Rupse Chhaharo is reached in **1¼ hours** from Dana.

There are two route choices beyond: taking the east (left) or west (right) bank. The east-side trail is currently the more used and is probably safer in the monsoon, but inquire locally about conditions. The more spectacular west-side route, rebuilt in 1982, suffered a serious slide in 1988 and is awaiting further repairs.

To follow the east-side trail between Rupse Chhaharo and Ghasa, fork right just after the bridge at the waterfall. Descend to cross the Kali Gandaki on a wooden bridge (5360 ft, 1634 m) at a narrow point in the gorge. Head upstream, keeping close to the powerful torrent, and go through a big slide area to Kopche Pani, with several small clusters of tea houses (5500 ft, 1676 m), in **30 minutes.** A further **hour's** steep climb on a scree-boulder trail brings you to a similar spot, Pahiro Tabla (meaning "landslide place," 6400 ft, 1951 m). As you go along, look for the trail on the west side and the ancient pilgrim trails above it. Along the way, you may see monkeys in the forests. In another **45 minutes,** reach the suspension bridge and trail junction (6400 ft, 1951 m) a few minutes below Ghasa.

On the west-side route, climb above the tea houses of Rupse Chhaharo to reach Kabre (5600 ft, 1707 m) in less than 30 minutes. Kabre is the northernmost village inhabited by hill castes in the Kali Gandaki valley. From Kabre, continue north along the steep cliffside to where the valley narrows spectacularly and the cascading river torrent resounds across the canyon walls. Probably the world's steepest and deepest large gorge, the gradient to the summit of Dhaulagiri is more than 1 mi (1.6 km) vertical to 1 mi (1.6 km) horizontal (1:1.05 to be exact). The steepest part, however, is south of the line between the two summits. Just beyond the main gorge you can see the old trail, cut like a three-sided tunnel into the wall. Above it are older pilgrimage routes. Pilgrims traveled this dangerous trail to Muktinath as long ago as 300 B.C. Beyond the most impressive narrow section, the trail crosses a boulder-strewn flat and reaches a *chautaara,* where the east-side trail rejoins it 2 hours from Kabre and a few minutes south of Ghasa.

It takes 30 minutes to get through **Ghasa** (6700 ft, 2040 m), a sprawling, flat-roofed *Thakali* village in the middle of which an army barrack sits.

Note how remarkably the land has changed over this short stretch, as the climate becomes colder and drier. To the south, you may see lizards through-out the year, but from here northward none are seen in the cold season. Sim-ilarly, as you head north, you will encounter more pine forests and fewer broad-leaved trees. The houses beyond here have flat roofs because there is less rainfall. The changes will be even more dramatic farther along.

To continue north from Ghasa, cross a tributary, and pass through Kaiku and the few houses of Gumaaune (literally "walking around"). There is a huge landslide scar on the east side. Reach a cement suspension bridge over the Lete Khola (8000 ft, 2438 m), a tributary from the west, and cross it to a lodge. **Lete** (8100 ft, 2469 m), some 30 minutes beyond, is **2 hours** from Ghasa. There is a trail coming in from the southwest before you cross the Lete Khola. It offers a high route over the south shoulder of Dhaulagiri to Beni. Annapurna I, the first 8000-meter peak ever climbed, can be seen to the east from Lete. Again, note the change in ecology; Lete gets 124 mm (49 inches) of rain a year while a mere half day to the north, Tukche gets only 20 mm (8 inches).

Heading north, pass the police check post in the spread-out village of Lete, which then blends into **Kalopani** (8300 ft, 2530 m). Sunsets from Kalopani and Lete are memorable. Cross a tributary north of town to reach your choice of two bridges over the Kali Gandaki in **30 minutes** from lower Lete. In the dry season, cross it if there is a good temporary bridge to cross back over the Kali Gandaki farther upstream. Check what others are doing. If you cross to the east (left) bank here, the trail passes through Dhampu and KokheThAATi before crossing a series of bridges back to the west (right) bank just below **Larjung** (8400 ft, 2560 m) **2 hours** from Kalopani.

In the monsoon, or if you wish to reach the area below the southeast Dhaulagiri Icefall, stay on the west (right) bank and cross a river delta with its alluvial fan to reach the few houses of Chatang in 30 minutes. Just beyond is a *chautaara* with a plaque commemorating the 1969 Dhaulagiri tragedy, in which seven members of an American expedition were killed in an ice ava-lanche. The trail to the icefall cuts off left just to the north. If continuing on to Larjung, cross another tributary, enter a pine-and-juniper forest, then cross the broad delta of the Ghatte Khola, wading where necessary, to rejoin the forest. Larjung is just beyond, perhaps 1¾ hours from Kalopani. To the west is the in-credibly foreshortened summit of Dhaulagiri, almost 3.5 mi (5.5 km) higher.

From Larjung, head north, cross a tributary, and in a few minutes enter the fascinating town of **Khobang** (8400 ft, 2560 m). The trail passes through a tunnel, and doors to the houses open off it. The village is thus protected from the strong winds that blow up the valley almost every afternoon. The northern, open segment of the series of settlements is called Kanti. Cross another tribu-tary, either on a temporary bridge or upstream on a more substantial one. **Tuk-che** (8500 ft, 2591 m), a historically important town, is **1 hour** beyond Khobang.

Tukche was once an important center for the trade of Nepali grain for Ti-betan salt through the valley of the Thak Khola. *Thakali Subbha,* or customs contractors, controlled it and exacted taxes at Tukche in the summer and at Dana in the winter. The handsome architecture and great wood carving in Tuk-che attests to the importance of this town. By the middle of this century compe-

Clockwise from upper left: *winnowing grain by letting the wind blow away the chaff; harvesting rice by hand; a disabled man weaves a* Doko.

tition had reduced this trade, and the enterprising *Thakali* turned their attention south and became more involved in business ventures around Pokhara and in the Tarai. Their spread throughout many of the trade routes in Nepal resulted in the establishment of many *bhaTTi* even before trekking became popular. With the coming of foreigners, the *Thakali* developed hotel facilities for them, and many of their family homes have been developed into lodges. I urge you to try to find a traditional *bhaTTi* and sample a good Nepali meal of *daal bhaat tarkaari* (lentils, rice, and vegetables) or at least have such a meal in a tourist restaurant. The *Thakali* seem to prosper in whatever they turn to. In comparing my visits to this region twenty years apart, I find the improvements impressive —water systems, latrines, more schools (indeed, *functioning* schools), better trails, more varieties of crops, and cleaner homes. Of course, all is relative. If this region strikes you as destitute and dirty, what would you think of the poor areas of Nepal? *Thakali* have always exhibited a strong ethnic group consciousness, and Thak Khola is their homeland. Many of the towns have been electrified through the installation of a mini–hydroelectric generator across from Khobang that produces 200 kilowatts.

A strong wind blows from the south up the valley, beginning in the late morning and lasting most of the day. This is probably caused when the air mass over the plateau to the north warms, rises, and creates a pressure difference. The best time to head south is in the early morning when the wind is from the north. As you go up the valley from Tukche, notice that there is relatively little vegetation on the valley floor itself, but there are trees and forests on the walls. The valley floor is in a rain shadow due to the strong winds. When the wind is blowing, you may notice that there are no clouds over the center of the valley, but clouds do hang on the sides.

A trail to Dhampus Pass (described later) goes up the hill to the west of the *gomba* at Tukche. For variety, you could cross the Thak Khola north of Tukche and visit Chhimgaon, and Chaira, and recross below Marpha. Most people will stay on the west bank to reach **Marpha** (8750 ft, 2667 m) in **1½ hours.** About 15 minutes before Marpha, pass by the Marpha Agricultural Farm, which has introduced new crops into the area. You may be able to purchase fresh fruit and vegetables in season at the most reasonable prices in the area.

Marpha, a charming town, has a fine sewer system—a series of canals flowing down the streets. Marpha's inhabitants call themselves *PaunchgaaUle,* people ethnically similar to the *Thakali.* There are plenty of choices for accommodation and food here. Some of the hotels in Marpha, and also in Jomosom, advertise pony rides as far as Muktinath. The foot-weary trekker may welcome the opportunity to change his mode of travel. Dhampus Pass can also be reached from Marpha.

To continue upstream, leave the town through the *chorten* and cross first a tributary, then the Pongkyu Khola, another alluvial fan, with a water mill, which flows from the west. Along the trail you will see willow plantations, part of a reforestation project. The town of Syang is beyond, and its monastery is up the hill a bit farther. On certain days during late October to early December, monks stage dance festivals in the *gomba* of Marpha, Syang, and Tukche.

Somewhat similar to the *Mani-rimdu* festivals of Solu-Khumbu, they are definitely worth seeing. The Nepali name for such a festival is *dyokyapsi*.

Cross a tributary farther up the valley, and reach **Jomosom** (8900 ft, 2713
m), the center for Mustang District, 1½ **hours** from Marpha. There is a STOL
airstrip here with scheduled service to Kathmandu. But because of the winds,
service can be unreliable. Winter winds regularly reach thirty to forty knots,
with gusts to seventy! Other facilities include banks, a hospital, rather luxurious food and accommodations with solar water heaters, a bakery, and, of
course, a police check post. This town has prospered immensely over the years
and has expanded to both sides of the river to provide space for the many government employees and offices. Many of the pony caravans bring food to
Jomosom to feed the bureaucracy.

The countryside to the north is very arid, not unlike the Tibetan Plateau
farther north. To the south, Dhaulagiri impressively guards the Thak Khola
valley. It is much less foreshortened than at Larjung. To the east, across the
river on a shelf of land, is the town of Thinigaon (9500 ft, 2897 m), reached in
30 minutes from Jomosom. The inhabitants are technically not Buddhists
(though they may say otherwise) but followers of Bon-po, the ancient religion
that antedated Tibetan Buddhism. Up the valley east of Thinigaon is Tilicho
Pass and Tilicho Tal. The latter, at 16,140 ft (4919 m), is one of the highest,
most spectacular lakes in the world. Once open to trekking, this area has been
closed to access from the west because of a Nepali army camp this side of the
pass, used for mountain warfare training. You might have noticed their "R &
R" facilities in Jomosom.

To continue on to Kagbeni and Muktinath, you can travel on either side,
depending on the condition of a temporary bridge over the Kali Gandaki. If
you stay on the east (left) side, you will either have to climb to avoid wading
the separate rivulets of the river, or stay on the valley floor close to the river
and probably get your feet wet. If you take the west (right) bank trail, there
may be a temporary bridge crossing upstream. Either way, in 1½ hours reach
the trail junction of Chyancha-Lhrenba (9050 ft, 2758 m). This place is known
locally as Eklai BhaTTi, meaning "lonely inn."

The left fork continues up the river to **Kagbeni** (9200 ft, 2804 m) in 30
minutes, while the right ascends out of the valley and heads more directly to
Muktinath. The right fork reaches the junction (10,350 ft, 3155 m) of the trail
from Kagbeni to Muktinath in 1½ hours.

The name Kagbeni aptly reflects the town's character—*kak* means
"blockade" in the local dialect, and *beni* means "junction of two rivers." And
this citadel does effectively block the valley. River junctions are especially sacred to the local people. Since the town is at the confluence of trails from the
north, south, east, and west, the ancient king who sat here could control and
tax the exchange of grain from the south and wool and salt from the north. The
ruins of his palace, which can still be seen, are a reminder of the ancient kingdoms that predated the unification of Nepal. Some scholars believe the family
that ruled here was related to the ancient kings of Jumla. The Sakyapa monastery here is run down, but worth a visit. You may see two large terra-cotta images of the protector deities of the town—a male at the north end and the

remains of a female at the south. This mingling of old animistic beliefs with those of the more developed religions is common in Nepal. People here call themselves *Gurung,* but are clearly not the same as the *Gurung* to the south. People from Tibet who have settled in Nepal often call themselves *Gurung* to facilitate assimilation. This practice has continued with the recent immigration of Tibetan refugees in the 1980s.

The impressive folding of the cliffs west of town illustrates the powerful forces of orogeny. You can just make out the crest of the Thorung La up the valley to the east of town. Try to make out Kagbeni from the pass. The trail to Mustang and the kingdom of Lo crosses the Kali Gandaki here and heads up the west (right) bank. There is a police check post in Kagbeni, at the northern limit for trekkers.

To go to Muktinath from Kagbeni, cross the Dzong Khola, the tributary from the east, and head east through terraces to the trail's junction (10,350 ft, 3155 m) with the trail from Chyancha-Lhrenba in 1½ hours.

Whether you go to Kagbeni, or not, it will take **3 to 3½ hours** to reach the junction from Jomosom. Continue east, noting the caves on the north side of the valley. So ancient are these caves that no one remembers if they were used by hermits or troglodytes. On a clear day, the walk can be ethereal, as the dry valley sparkles and the north wall seems suspended close to you. Climb to **Khingar,** the old part of town north of the trail. Continue to **Jharkot** (11,850 ft, 3612 m), a crumbling but still impressive fortress perched on a ridge **1½ hours** from the trail junction above Kagbeni. Jharkot, called Dzar by Tibetans, is believed to have been the home of the ruling house of this valley. Note how some houses around the ruins of the fort are made of blocks of earth.

Continue climbing and contouring, often staying near an irrigation trough. Along the trail there are little piles of stones made by pilgrims returning from Muktinath in hopes of obtaining a better reincarnation. Go on to **Ranipauwa** (12,200 ft, 3718 m), a village of sorts, with a large rest house for pilgrims, and many hotels. It is **40 minutes** from Jharkot. Across the valley you can see the extensive ruins of Dzong ("castle" in Tibetan) and the town built around it, the original seat of the king of this valley. **Muktinath** (12,475 ft, 3802 m) is less than **10 minutes** farther. Dhaulagiri looms impressively to the south. Trekkers are not allowed to stay inside the fenced compound. The considerable cement poured here recently has decidedly changed the character of this previously locally cared-for sacred spot.

Muktinath, located in a poplar grove, is a sacred shrine and pilgrimage site for Hindus and Buddhists. The *Mahabharata,* the ancient Hindu epic written about 300 B.C., mentions Muktinath as Shaligrama because of its ammonite fossils called *shaligrams.* Brahma, the creator, made an offering here by lighting a fire on water. You can see this miracle (burning natural gas) in a small Buddhist shrine *(gomba)* below the main Hindu temple *(mandir).*

Hindus named the site Muktichhetra, meaning "place of salvation," because they believed that bathing there gives salvation after death. Springs are piped into 108 water spouts in the shape of boars' heads near the temple dedicated to Vishnu, the focal point for Hindus. Because Buddha is the eighth incarnation of Vishnu, the Hindus tolerate the Buddhists here. The Buddhists consider the image of Vishnu in this typically *Newar* style temple as the Bodhisattva Avalokiteshwara. Vishnu is in the shape of an icon as well as a large ammonite fossil. The same fossil image is worshiped by Buddhists as Gawa Jogpa, the "serpent deity."

The miraculous fire revered by Buddhists and Hindus burns on water, stones, and earth, and is inside the Jwala Mai Temple, south of the police check post. Natural gas jets burn in small recesses curtained under the altar to Avalokiteshwara. On the left the earth burns, in the middle water burns, and on the right the stone burns. One flame has died out; only two remain lighted. Your Sherpas and other Buddhist porters may ask you for a bottle to take some of the "water that burns" with them. Be sure to leave an offering of money for temple upkeep.

Padmasambhava, who brought Buddhism to Tibet in the eighth century, is believed to have meditated here. His "footprints" are on a rock in the northwest corner of this sacred place. On their way to Tibet, the eighty-four *siddha* ("great magicians") left their pilgrim staffs, which grew into the poplars at the site. You will find many old *chorten* and temples cared for by Nyingmapa nuns or old women from the nearby villages. A full moon is an especially auspicious time to visit Muktinath. In the full moon of August–September, thousands of pilgrims arrive for the main religious festival. At about the same time, local Tibetan villagers of the valley hold a great horse festival called *Yartung*—a time of horse racing, gambling, and general merriment. With its themes of "food, sex, and violence," it bears a striking resemblance to the European Carnival, according to Charles Ramble, who writes about "The Muktinath Yartung: A Tibetan harvest festival in its social and historical context," in *L'Ethnographie*, LXXXIII, 221–245, 1987.

Many people from Mustang and other areas come to sell handicrafts to the pilgrims. Some sell the *shaligram,* a mollusk fossil called an ammonite, from a period roughly 140 to 165 million years ago. These objects, treasured for worship by Hindus, are said to represent several deities, principally those associated with Vishnu, the Lord of Salvation. You are apt to find them along the flats north of Jomosom.

To the east is the Thorung La Pass (17,700 ft, 5416 m), which leads to Manang. Crossing the pass from Muktinath to Manang is more difficult than crossing in the other direction, for in the dry season there are few if any suitable campsites with water on this side of the pass. It is a very long day to ascend from Muktinath to the pass and then to descend to the first campsite on the other side. In season, there may be a hotel for trekkers partway up. Altitude illness may jeopardize those who are unacclimatized. Crossing from Manang, on the other hand, is easier because of the comparatively long time spent at high altitudes before approaching the pass, and because of the higher campsites below the east side of the pass. The pass is often crossed from Muktinath, but it certainly is more difficult and hazardous. Under no condition should you ascend from either direction unless the entire party, including porters, is well equipped to camp in snow should a storm arise. The trail descriptions for the

Manang to Muktinath crossing are given with the Manang section later in this chapter.

On the return journey, consider some variations, such as returning to Marpha via Thinigaon, which is approached from Jomosom on the east (left) bank of the river; returning to Pokhara by following the Kali Gandaki south from Tatopani past Beni, Baglung, Kusma, and east to Pokhara; returning from Chitre to Ghandruk and Dhampus; and returning from NagDAADa by going to Phewa Tal. These last three variations are described in greater detail later, but first some side trips out of the Thak Khola valley are described. All are strenuous trips to substantial altitudes where food, fuel, and shelter must be carried. At certain times of the year, snow can make the trips almost impossible. Parties should be prepared for cold at any time of the year. It is always best to have someone along who is familiar with the route. You could climb out of the valley at other points and get good views of the mountains.

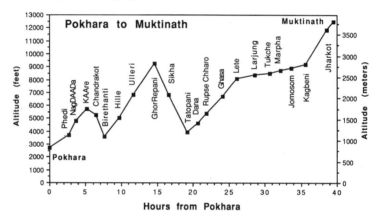

DHAMPUS PASS

Dhampus Pass (17,000 ft, 5184 m) connects the valley of the Thak Khola with Hidden Valley. It lies beyond the treeline and is often snowed in. Huts used for pasturing yaks can be used for shelter and cooking en route to the pass. There are no facilities at the pass. Carry food, fuel, and shelter. Temperatures below freezing can always be expected and in the winter months the temperature drops below 0° F (−18° C). A trip to the pass is ideal for those who want a more intense experience of the mountains. Reach it from Tukche or Marpha by going to some yak huts (13,000 ft, 3962 m) the first day, and to the pass the next. This may be too rapid an ascent for many people. If you are unprepared to spend a night at the pass, you could go up and return to the yak huts in a day.

To trek from Tukche to Dhampus Pass, go to the large open field at the north end of the village. Just behind the village, to the east, is a steep earth cliff. Follow a plainly defined switchback trail to the top and continue along the ridge behind the cliff. You pass through scattered apricot trees and horse pasturage for 1 mi (1.6 km) to arrive at the base of a high rock cliff. Keeping well to the east, the trail ascends this steep but not technically difficult cliff and comes out just above where the ridge plunges down to the Kali Gandaki far below. You are now on the end of the ridge defining the north side of the Dhampus Khola. There are fantastic views up the Kali Gandaki toward Mustang, and a panorama from Tilicho Peak in the east round through the Nilgiris, the Annapurnas, and Dhaulagiri to Tukche Peak in the southwest.

Up to this point, the trail is fairly well defined. But on the ridge it degenerates into myriad cow and yak trails, and you are pretty much on your own. Continue up the north side of the ridge for about 2 hours until you come to a low point (relatively speaking), then cross the south (Dhampus Khola) side of the ridge. Looking up the Dhampus Khola valley, you can see a large rock ridge going off your ridge and dropping steeply into the Khola. It is perpendicular to your line of travel. Traverse upward slightly toward this ridge to a wide trail, which takes you around and behind the ridge. This is the main trail to the upper portion of the Dhampus Khola valley, and is used by local herders taking their yaks up to graze during the summer. Yak yogurt is delicious—during the warm season you should try to buy some at the herders' huts along the way.

After crossing the rock ridge, climb obliquely upward by obvious routes to Dhampus Pass, which is not visible at this point. If there is any possibility of cloudy weather, hire a local man from Tukche as a guide. Once clouds settle in, it is very easy to get lost. If fog becomes a problem, don't descend to the Dhampus Khola to escape, since the Khola is impassable due to rock cliffs in its lower portions. If you become confused in a fog, stay up high and traverse eastward back toward Marpha or Tukche. Again, be sure to descend if severe symptoms of altitude sickness come on.

Beyond the pass, you can descend into the upper (southern) end of Hidden Valley for excellent views of Dhaulagiri's north face and the glaciated pass called French Pass, which lies between Dhaulagiri and its sister peak to the west, Dhaula Himal. You may see the remains of a plane near the pass, the Swiss Pilatus Porter that crashed in 1961 while ferrying people and loads from Pokhara for the Dhaulagiri Expedition. You may encounter semiwild yak herds, snow leopards, and mountain sheep in Hidden Valley.

DHAULAGIRI ICEFALL

The area below the east Dhaulagiri Icefall abounds with yak pastures and was the location of the 1969 American Base Camp. At a lower altitude than Dhampus Pass, it has correspondingly less severe conditions. The views of the mountains are excellent, possibly better than at Dhampus Pass.

To reach this area, proceed from the trail junction north of the few houses of Chatang between Kalopani and Larjung. The trail leaves the valley near a *chautaara* with a plaque commemorating the seven members of the 1969 American Expedition to Dhaulagiri who died in an ice avalanche. Again, it is best to hire a local guide. The area below the icefall (12,400 ft, 3780 m) can be reached in a day from the Kali Gandaki. Beware of avalanches in the vicinity of the icefall.

NORTH ANNAPURNA BASE CAMP

The route to the original Annapurna Base Camp was discovered by the 1950 French Expedition to Annapurna led by Maurice Herzog. The French first tried to climb Dhaulagiri, but found it beyond their capabilities, and instead tried to find a way to the base of Annapurna. They had difficulty getting there from the Kali Gandaki, and the route still has a bad reputation. It is seldom used except by shepherds and mountaineering expeditions. However, in the relatively snow-free early fall and late spring, the route is neither very difficult nor dangerous. The trail is often indistinct and traverses steep grassy slopes. Porters do not like this trail, but it is certainly no worse than little-used trails in many other areas of mountain wilderness.

The views along the way are spectacular. As the trail climbs steeply out of the Kali Gandaki valley, the incredible gorge becomes more and more impressive. The views of Dhaulagiri and Annapurna from the crest of the ridge separating the Kali Gandaki from the Miristi Khola are breathtaking. Only from this perch (14,000 ft, 4267 m), some 7000 ft (2134 m) above the valley floor, can you appreciate just how high these mountains are. From the foreshortened view from Kalopani, it is hard to believe that Dhaulagiri is the sixth highest mountain in the world. If you venture beyond the base camp toward Camp One, on the north side of Annapurna, you can appreciate the impressive features of that side of the mountain.

There are neither villages nor shelter from Chhoya onward, so you must be self-sufficient for at least five days. It is best to hire someone from Chhoya to show the way. In times of high water, it may be impossible to cross the Miristi Khola and reach the base camp without building a bridge, an undertaking most trekkers prefer to avoid. But with the increasing number of expeditions to Annapurna, the chance of finding a usable bridge is good. Check beforehand to find out if there has been a recent expedition. In low water, the river can be forded with some difficulty downstream. If there is no bridge, consider at least climbing to the height of land for the spectacular views.

If you are coming from the south, turn off the regular trail just after crossing the Lete Khola on a new suspension bridge. Keep close to the Kali Gandaki for some 10 minutes before crossing the tumultuous river on a wooden bridge to reach Chhoya (8000 ft, 2484 m). If you are coming from the north, take a left fork a few minutes before reaching Lete and after passing through Upala Lete (8150 ft, 2484 m). This left fork takes you through a beautiful pine forest before you descend slightly in 10 minutes to the same wooden bridge to Chhoya. You can get provisions in Chhoya or in Lete. From Chhoya, cross the delta of the Polje Khola and ascend to the few houses of Poljedanda (8175 ft, 2492 m). Then turn right and head southeast to the few more houses of Deorali (8275 ft, 2522 m) 30 minutes from Chhoya. This is the last village on the route. Here the trail forks left and you contour above fields to enter the valley

Camp below the west face of Annapurna near Thula Bugin

of the Tangdung or Bhutra Khola, a little more than 30 minutes later. Contour below a small waterfall of a tributary to the main river (8075 ft, 2461 m) after a short, steep descent through forest. The river is 1¼ hours from Deorali. There should be a wooden bridge here unless it has been washed out during the monsoon. Fill up all your water containers as you may not get another chance during the next day.

The next section of the trail ascends 6000 ft (1829 m) and is unrelentingly steep. There are few suitable campsites until near the end of the climb. After crossing to the southeast (left) bank, ascend a cliff and enter a mixed broadleaved forest. The trail is easy to follow and the forest is pleasant. There are occasional vistas to inspire the weary. In the upper reaches you find areas of bamboo, then rhododendron, fir, and birch forests. In 2½ hours, reach a saddle called Kal Ghiu (11,000 ft, 3383 m). Some trekking groups call this place Jungle Camp. Camping is possible here if you can find water down the other side of the saddle. Keep close to the crest of the ridge as you pass several notches. Enjoy the rhododendrons in bloom in the spring. After keeping to the southeast side of the ridge and leaving the forest, the trail becomes fainter, reaches a minor ridge crest (12,600 ft, 3840 m), and crosses over to the northwest side. Keep climbing to a prominent notch with a *chorten* (13,350 ft, 4069 m) some 2 hours from Kal Ghiu. The views of Dhaulagiri are unforgettable.

The slope eases off now, and continues over more moderate grazing slopes to a place near a ridge crest called Sano Bugin (13,950 ft, 4252 m), where herders stay during the monsoon. There are rock walls here that the herders convert to shelters with the use of bamboo mats. If there is no snow to melt, water may be difficult to obtain. The gigantic west face of Annapurna, climbed by Reinhold Messner in 1985, is before you. Head north along the ridge crest, or on the west side. The trail is marked with slabs of rock standing on end. In 1 hour, reach another ridge crest (14,375 ft, 4382 m) and cross to the southeast side of the ridge. This may be the "*passage du avril 27*" that Herzog's expedition discovered in order to get to the base of Annapurna. You are now in the drainage area of the Miristi Khola, the river that enters the Kali Gandaki above Tatopani.

Continue contouring for a few minutes to Thulo Bugin (14,300 ft, 4359 m), where herders stay. There is a small shrine here. Contour, crossing several tributaries of the Hum Khola, a tributary of the Miristi. The last stream (13,375 ft, 4077 m), reached in 30 minutes, is a little tricky to cross. Climb on, at first gradually, then more steeply, to reach a flat area sometimes called Bal Khola (14,650 ft, 4465 m) in 1¾ hours. Camp here, for there are few other suitable places until the river is reached. The west face of Annapurna looms before you. Local people do not venture much beyond here in their tending of sheep and goats.

Descend and round a ridge crest to the canyon of the Miristi Khola proper. The river is almost a mile below you, yet its roar can be heard. Continue on steep grassy slopes and pass an overhanging rock (14,075 ft, 4290 m) suitable for camping, 45 minutes from the high point. Descend more steeply on grass, cross a stream, and go down into shrubbery until it appears that a 1000 ft (300 m) cliff will block the way to the valley floor. The trail heads west to a break in the rock wall, and descends through the break to the river (11,500 ft, 3505 m) 1½ hours from the overhanging rock. The gorge at the bottom is most impressive and gives a feeling of relative isolation. Head upstream on the northwest (right) bank. The dense shrubs may make travel difficult. There are campsites by some sand near a widening in the river (11,575 ft, 3528 m), where it may be possible to ford in low water. Otherwise, head upstream for 10 minutes to a narrowing where there may be a bridge. Cross the river, if possible, and camp on the other side if it is late.

Once on the southeast (left) bank of the Miristi Khola, follow the trail upstream. The vegetation soon disappears as altitude and erosion increase. The trail becomes indistinct in the moraine. As the valley opens up, bear right to the east and leave the river bottom to climb the moraine to a vague shelf. Continue beyond to a small glacial lake in the terminal moraine of the North Annapurna Glacier. Cross its outflow to the right and climb the lateral moraine to the left. There are views of the Nilgiris to the west. The base camp for the various attempts to climb Annapurna from the north is on a flat shelf of land (14,300 ft, 4359 m) to the north of the glacier. There is a steep drop-off to the glacier valley to the south and east. The base camp is reached in 3 to 4 hours from the crossing of the Miristi Khola.

The view of Annapurna I from the base camp is minimal. Better views can be obtained by contouring and climbing to the east to a grassy knoll from which much of the north face can be seen. You could also proceed toward Camp I by dropping from the shelf and climbing along the lateral moraine of the glacier to 16,000 ft (4877 m). Exploratory and climbing journeys will suggest themselves to those with experience. The Great Barrier, an impressive wall of mountains to the north, separates you from Tilicho Tal. Be sure to take enough food to stay awhile and enjoy this unforgettable area.

TILICHO TAL

Currently, approach to the lake is restricted from the west because the area is used as a mountain warfare training ground for the Royal Nepal Army. It is possible to reach it from the Manang side, however, and that is mentioned further on. In case this restriction is relaxed in the future, the route is described here.

To reach Tilicho Tal from Thak Khola proceed up the trail from Thinigaon (9500 ft, 2895 m). The trail winds up the north side of the valley, leading to the pass to the east. There is little or no water along the lower part of the route. Pass through rhododendron, fir, and birch forests to reach alpine vegetation. Soon after crossing two tributaries, the trail leads to a *goTh* (14,000 ft, 2468 m) some 6 hours from Thinigaon. Another day takes you over the Tilicho Pass (16,730 ft, 5100 m) to the majestic ice walls beyond. The pass itself is not clearly seen from the *goTh*. It is glaciated, so those who are not equipped for ice climbing may prefer to head up one of the gullies north of the pass. The climb is higher, up to 17,500 ft (5334 m) or so, but the route is preferable for most parties. A trip to the lake and climbs of nearby summits are rewarding. The lake is often frozen. Trekkers attempting to climb up to the lake from the valley in two days must be especially watchful for signs and symp-

Tilicho Tal and the Great Barrier

toms of altitude sickness. They should descend at the first signs of severe symptoms. You can also reach the lake from the east, heading up from Khangsar in Manang.

TATOPANI TO POKHARA VIA BENI

The return to Pokhara from Tatopani via Beni mentioned earlier involves less climbing. It is not advisable to go this way in late spring as it is much hotter than on the higher route. To proceed from Tatopani, cross the suspension bridge to the east (left) bank of the Kali Gandaki and cross the wooden bridge over the Ghar Khola to its south (left) bank to rejoin the Kali Gandaki. Proceed south on its east (left) bank.

After several hours on the trail, which in places is carved into the rock cliff and passes through subtropical valley forests, cross to the west (right) bank at Tiplyang (3400 ft, 1037 m) and climb high up the west (right) bank. Eventually descend to Ranipauwa (3900 ft, 1189 m), also called Galeshwar, and cross the tributary RahughaT Khola. Ranipauwa, some 6 hours from Tatopani, is the site of the annual *mela* (fair) that is usually in mid-November or early December.

An hour after crossing the tributary, come to a suspension bridge over the Kali Gandaki, just before Beni (2700 ft, 823 m), the administrative center for Mayagdi District. If spending the night in Beni, it is preferable to stay near the bridge (Kali Pul), where the breeze will keep mosquitoes away and there may be less noise. The trail from Beni to Kusma, and then either to NagDAADa, or NauDAADa, and beyond to Pokhara, is described in reverse in chapter 10. Of the two choices, the NagDAADa way is more scenic, but more crowded.

There are two routes from NagDAADa to Pokhara. One, the route of ascent from the Yamdi Khola via Suikhet, enters Pokhara from the north and will probably be little used because of the presence of the road. The other goes along the ridge crest east of NagDAADa to the town of Sarangkot (5200 ft, 1585 m). There is now a road from Pokhara to Sarangkot. But consider walking to Phewa Tal, and taking a boat to the business end of the lake. About 30 minutes east of NagDAADa, you reach a point on the ridge crest from which all the peaks from Dhaulagiri to Manaslu and Himalchuli can be seen. Soon after, descend to the west end of Phewa Tal (2500 ft, 762 m). Here there are some lodges and restaurants. You could follow its north shore to the airstrip. Often you can hire a dugout to ferry you across, and it is advisable to bargain for a local, rather than a sahib, fare. It takes about 2 or more hours to reach the lake from NagDAADa and another hour to walk to the airstrip. There is also a trail from Sarangkot to the north end of Pokhara, reaching the main trail just north of Shining Hospital, near the Bindubasini temple.

The Modi Khola and the Annapurna Sanctuary

Walking the uphill staircases in Gurung *country is a mantra*.
Trekker Anne Outwater

The term Annapurna Sanctuary, coined by outsiders, denotes the high basin southwest of Annapurna and the headwaters of the Modi Khola. This vast amphitheater, surrounded by Himalayan giants, was explored by Jimmy Roberts in 1956 and brought to the attention of the Western world by the British Expedition to Machhapuchhre in 1957. The gigantic mountains named for the goddesses Annapurna and Gangapurna, important figures in Hindu myth and folklore, justify calling it a sanctuary. Its gate, the deep gorge between the peaks Hiunchuli and Machhapuchhre, marks a natural division between the dense rain forest and bamboo jungle of the narrow Modi Khola river valley and the scattered summits and immense walls of the mountain fortress inside. This area is also referred to as the Annapurna Base Camp and the Machhapuchhre Base Camp.

Trekking possibilities are varied. Those without time to head up to Thak Khola can make a circuit from Pokhara into the Sanctuary, in less than ten days, with little backtracking. However, to enjoy the route and the Sanctuary itself without feeling rushed, plan to take two weeks. This area can be easily combined with the entire Annapurna circuit or with a trek to Jomosom that offers various link-up possibilities.

The route up the Modi Khola has always had a reputation among porters for being slippery and difficult. Indeed, back in 1969, on my first journey there, I had to chase after my porter, who ran ahead 3 hours toward Pokhara, rather than risk the possibility of going up the Modi Khola. Of course, when I had asked him previously about going up there, he said nothing in order to not disappoint me! While lodges and inns that cater to the trekker now exist outside the inhabited areas, the trail hasn't changed much. It is often wet, and in the steep and slippery places a fall could be disastrous. But the trail never lived up to its old reputation; the route to the North Annapurna Base Camp is a much more serious undertaking.

Now you can hope to find cooked food and lodging along the entire route. During winter months, snowfall may make the trip difficult or impossible, and avalanche hazard can increase the risk. When there is little traffic, you can't count on the innkeepers being there, so ask at Chomro before venturing forth.

This is the homeland of the *Gurung* people, an ethnic group renowned for bravery in the Gurkhas. They speak their own unwritten language, a member of the Sino-Tibetan family, and names of villages don't transliterate accurately into Nepali. Hence the variations in spelling that you will see on signboards here. Is it Ghandrung or Ghandruk? Landrung or Landruk? Chomro or Chomrong? Kyumunu, Kimrong, Kymnu, Kyumnu, or Kimnu? I try to use the Annapurna Conservation Area Project spellings.

For those traveling from Pokhara, one access route to the Sanctuary leaves the trail (described on page 182) at Chandrakot. This is not a popular approach, as more people head there from GhoRepani, or Dhampus. A route from Phedi could be followed in the opposite direction as part of the circuit from Pokhara. If coming from the Thak Khola region, you could leave the standard trail at GhoRepani or Chitre. These options will be described in the Chomro to Suikhet section, along with a route from the Sanctuary to Pokhara through Dhampus.

CHANDRAKOT TO ANNAPURNA SANCTUARY

Begin at the *chautaara* at **Chandrakot** (5250 ft, 1600 m) but instead of descending, contour north by some fields, passing through a fault in the rock to reach a *chautaara* in **30 minutes.** Take the left fork into an oak forest, reaching another fork **25 minutes** later. The right branch heads over the ridge to Dhampus. Instead, go straight and descend to the few houses of Pathalikhet

(4750 ft, 1448 m) **5 minutes** beyond. Continue through a tributary valley past more homes and descend into a larger tributary valley. Cross its river **22 minutes** later. Climb up and pass through the scattered houses of WAAD. At the junction 30 minutes beyond (4700 ft, 1432 m), take the left fork. Here you appear to leave the main trail, which is a series of steps that go to Landrung and offer another route to the Sanctuary. But here I recommend you take the left fork and go via Ghandruk, an impressive *Gurung* village, and bypass Ghandruk on the return. The left fork contours a bit, then drops to the valley floor in an oak-forested tributary valley. Reach a suspension bridge over the Modi Khola (3875 ft, 1181 m) in **20 minutes.** Cross it to the right to the few houses of **Ghandruk Besi** (meaning "foot of Ghandruk"). If coming from Birethanti, keep close to the river and, passing fields and forests, reach this point in 1 hour.

Head upstream on the Modi Khola, cross a tributary (4125 ft, 1257 m), and begin a long climb along a remarkable staircase to reach **Thamel** (5600 ft, 1707 m) in **70 minutes** from the Modi Khola. There are a few hotels here in this entrance to *Gurung* country. Another **15 minutes** beyond are the few houses of Kimche (5775 ft, 1760 m). A trail forks left here to TirkheDUgaa in the headwaters of the Bhurungdi Khola, on the way to GhoRepani. Along the way, you would pass through the villages of Moriya, Dhansing, and Sabet, taking some 4 hours to reach TirkheDUgaa. You could travel from Thak Khola by this route instead of one of the other trails from GhoRepani or Chitre.

From Kimche, cross a tributary a few minutes later and continue on these magnificent steps. Imagine the effort it took to construct them! Those coming from Landrung will join this trail just beyond a *chautaara* and by a *goTh* on the right side (6300 ft, 1920 m) 30 minutes beyond Kimche. Ahead is the large, affluent *Gurung* village of Ghandruk. Their wealth comes from handsome pensions provided to *Gurungs* who have served as Gurkhas in the British Army. This income was one of several factors that changed their primary livelihood from herding and hunting to sedentary farming.

Reach **Ghandruk** (6600 ft, 2012 m) in **40 minutes** from Kimche. At the upper end of Ghandruk, the trail leads to Banthanti and GhoRepani, at least a day's walk. You can also join this trail by heading upstream by Kimrong Khola in the next major tributary valley to the north. These will be described below. It takes **15 minutes** to pass through Ghandruk, and along the way you may be upset or pleased to hear the whistle of progress—a diesel-powered rice mill, an example of private enterprise. Sometimes, *Gurung* dancing and singing can be staged for trekkers willing to pay.

Leave the town, cross a tributary and mostly contour through fields and oak forest in a side draw to reach Kimrong Danda (7400 ft, 2255 m), a prominent notch with houses and lodges, 1 hour beyond Ghandruk. Descend into the valley of the Kyumnu Khola (also called Kimrong, Kymnu, Kyumnu, Kimnu) on a trail much improved over the one I got lost on in 1969. Just below the crest of the ridge take the right fork and descend steeply to reach the river in **45 minutes** (5940 ft, 1810 m). A trail, described below, heads upstream in this tributary valley to reach GhoRepani and Chitre. Cross to the left bank and ascend to the few lodges of Kimrong Khola just beyond. Now climb steeply up

the hillside and traverse east higher up to enter the Modi Khola valley at
Daaulu (7160 ft, 2182 m) **70 minutes** from the Kyumnu Khola crossing.

At this junction of the two valleys, there are several lodges for trekkers as
well as signs pointing out the routes. On the return you can take the right fork
here and descend the spur below, cross the river beyond, and reach Landrung
directly. This pleasant, direct route from Pokhara is now possible, thanks to a
bridge over the Modi Khola.

But to head to Chomro, contour and climb to enter the tributary valley
draining the south side of Annapurna South (left) and Hiunchuli (right), the
major peaks before you. Descend to **Chomro** (also called Chomrong), a prosperous *Gurung* village (6725 ft, 2050 m), reached in **30 minutes** from Daaulu.
Pass the school 400 ft (122 m) above the center of town. There are many
large hotels for trekkers here. You can rent climbing equipment and down
jackets as well.

As mentioned before, there are lodges beyond that cater to the independent trekker during the peak season. There were none in 1969. There is no
permanent habitation there, so trekkers coming out of season will have to be
self-sufficient.

From Chomro descend northward to cross the main tributary on a new
suspension bridge (6200 ft, 1890 m) **20 minutes** beyond. Climb through terraces and the few houses of Kilche (6700 ft, 2042 m) to contour and enter the
main Modi Khola valley, which you will follow for the next two days. The trail
was previously used only by shepherds, who drove their flocks of sheep and
goats up during the monsoon to browse in the forests and the shrubbery above
treeline.

You reach a *goTh* and a tea shop/hotel upon entering the main valley
(7625 ft, 2324 m) **1½ hours** beyond the suspension bridge. Contour along a
reasonable trail in an oak-and-rhododendron forest, reaching growths of bamboo as you go further up the valley. Tibesa (8050 ft, 2454 m), **45 minutes** beyond, may provide services. Reach **Kuldi** (8200 ft, 2499 m) in **25 minutes** as
you go through increasingly dense forest. In 1969, there was an empty stone
hut here, the only such structure on the entire route. Now there are several
inns. The trail drops slightly from here and then appears transformed into the
stone staircases of the *Gurung* villages to the south, but with the addition of
drainage ditches!

Above the main trail, reached by two feeder trails, is the former site of a
British experimental sheep-breeding project that functioned for about ten
years. The handsome, sturdy buildings in this picturesque setting have been
converted to a tourist hotel. There is another hotel just before this point as well.

The main mountain visible at the head of the valley is Annapurna III;
Machhapuchhre, the "fish-tail" mountain whose name has been obvious for
several days now, is off to the right. After you leave this improved trail, descend over a series of slabs, which require care to negotiate. Enter a dense
bamboo rain forest. The area around Pokhara and south of the main Himalaya
receives considerably more rainfall than almost any place in Nepal. South of
Pokhara the Mahabharat Lekh, the range of hills above the Tarai, is lower and

Machhapuchhre, from near the Annapurna Base Camp

doesn't block the northerly flow of moisture. The trail is always wet in this jungle.

Reach a clearing and some lodges, Bamboo, in **35 minutes** (7700 ft, 2347 m). Cross several substantial tributaries. The third has an overhanging rock upstream that could serve as a shelter in a pinch. Eventually, you reach Dovan (8550 ft, 2606 m), with several inns, in **1 hour and 20 minutes.** The rhododendrons festooned with moss in the forest beyond are gigantic. There are hemlocks too but, because of excess rainfall, not as many as elsewhere at this elevation.

The Modi Khola seems much closer as you wend your way through the jungle. Across the valley, some 30 to 40 minutes later, you'll see streams of water plunging thousands of feet into the river. At a very slight rise at the neck of the gorge, called Deorali (8950 ft, 2728 m), 35 minutes after Dovan, you'll find a small rock shrine (Panchenin Barha) and strips of colored cloth. Local custom dictates prohibiting buffalo, chicken, eggs, or pork north of here, or else risking the anger of the mountain gods, whose revenge will be sickness and death in your party. Nepalis explain the misfortune that has befallen some trekking groups and mountaineering expeditions in the Sanctuary by breach of this custom. Just beyond is a spot where you can stand closer to the center of the valley to see the torrent rushing below you and the weeping wall across from you. Shortly beyond, the forest opens slightly and again, by venturing closer to the river from the main trail, you'll see a 100 ft waterfall thundering down this canyon.

Continue to a clearing, called Hotel Himalaya, and its lodges (9425 ft,

2873 m), 1 hour beyond Dovan. After another stretch of dense forest, the valley begins to open up. In **45 minutes** reach **Hinko** (10,300 ft, 3139 m), a large overhanging rock housing an inn.

The next hour or more of trail is subject to avalanches. You may find the remains of some near the trail. After heavy snowfall above, which may be rain along the trail, the safest course may be to wait a few days for the slopes to clear. Since none of the avalanche slopes can be easily seen from the valley floor, it is difficult to be sure when it is safe to proceed. If up in the Sanctuary, wait a few days if food supplies allow. Be aware that trekkers have been buried by avalanches along here.

Cross several streams and reach another Deorali (10,600 ft, 3231 m) **35 minutes** from Hinko, where there are several lodges. Notice the beautiful birch forests across the valley. Most of the trees have been cut on this side. You come to the inn at Bagara (10,825 ft, 3300 m) in **30 minutes.** As you proceed along, you can admire before you the triangular snow-and-rock face of Gangapurna, which has actually been climbed.

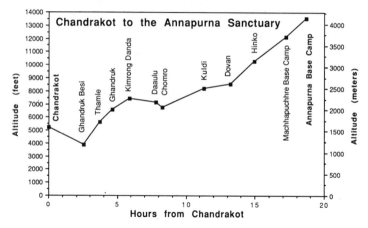

Suddenly, you cross the imaginary gates and are inside the Sanctuary! A stream flows in from the west and a large grass-covered moraine is ahead of you, with more grassy slopes beyond. Reach a shelf with several inns, so-called Machhapuchhre Base Camp (12,150 ft, 3703 m) in **1¼ hours.** There has not been a legally sanctioned expedition to sacred Machhapuchhre since 1957, and that one stopped short of the summit. The west face of Machhapuchhre looms above you, but the other views are limited to Annapurna South to the west.

Be cognizant of the rapid gain in altitude, but if conditions permit, try to stay higher, to gain better views. The trail heads west in a trough between the moraine and the north slopes of Hiunchuli. In 1 hour, the halfway point to the Annapurna Base Camp is reached (12,925 ft, 3939 m). The views are much better from here, but are even more spectacular further on, at the Annapurna Base Camp, where food and shelter are available during peak season. This flat area (13,550 ft, 4130 m) was first used by the British in their climb of the South Face of Annapurna in 1970. It is the coldest and windiest of all places to stay, but is well worth it if you are acclimatized and suitably equipped. Venture beyond to the crest of the moraine to gaze upon the awesome mountain walls. From left to right they are: Hiunchuli, Annapurna South, Fang, Annapurna, Annapurna III, and Machhapuchhre. Tent Peak and Fluted Peak, rising above the hills to the north, complete the unforgettable panorama. Wander around and feel at peace with the earth.

People with time and equipment may want to venture across the rubble-covered glacier to the north and explore further.

GHOREPANI TO GHANDRUK AND CHOMRO

The route keeps high, traversing the ridge system to reach Ghandruk. Begin at GhoRepani Deorali (9450 ft, 2880 m), and head east through the forest, keeping close to the ridge. Reach a clearing (10,360 ft, 3158 m), in **40 minutes,** with an immense panoramic view from Machhapuchhre to beyond Gurja Himal that rivals that from Poon Hill. Climb a little more, and before descending to the next notch, you can see east to Annapurna II, and Himalchuli. Reach this pass, **Deorali** (10,160 ft, 3097 m), in another **40 minutes.** Here the

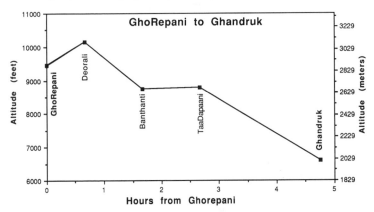

trail mentioned earlier in the descent from GhoRepani to Tatopani, which heads south from Chitre, joins, and offers another route to Ghandruk. There are several inns here. Head south to descend a steep gully that is treacherous when wet or icy. Pass another lodge, and switchback by a tiny waterfall in a moss-festooned rhododendron forest till you reach **Banthanti** (8740 ft, 2664 m) beneath a steep cliff in **1 hour.**

Continue traversing east and descending, passing another lodge in 15 minutes, then a campsite by a stream, before climbing up to **TaaDapaani** (meaning ''far water,'' 8800 ft, 2682 m), beautifully situated in a notch, in **1 hour.** All of the facilities at these places where there is no farmland have been set up for trekkers. There was no sign of habitation here twenty years ago. Just below the pass, to the southeast, there is a trail fork, with the right branch going to Ghandruk, the left to Chomro. Both options will be described.

To go to Ghandruk, take the right fork through rhododendron forest to BhAIsi Kharka ("buffalo pasture," 8260 ft, 2518 m) in **35 minutes,** then continue a descending traverse in a narrow valley to Sitke (7120 ft, 2170 m) in **1 hour.** Reach the upper portion of Ghandruk in a further **30 minutes,** and descend to lodges. The Annapurna Conservation Area Project offices, where there is an informative exhibit on the area, are on a spur near the lower end of town (6480 ft, 1975 m).

If taking the left fork at TaaDapaani to go to Chomro, descend and head northeast. Reach MelAAje (7260 ft, 2213 m) in **50 minutes** and fork right at the school, climb the fence, and descend very steeply among terraces to the Kyumnu Khola. Head downstream to a suspension bridge to meet the trail coming from Ghandruk (5940 ft, 1810 m) in **30 minutes.** The way to Daaulu and Chomro has already been described above.

CHOMRO TO SUIKHET

This route avoids some backtracking and is now feasible because a new bridge has been constructed over the Modi Khola. It could be followed in reverse as a direct route to the Sanctuary.

From Chomro return to **Daaulu** (7160 ft, 2182 m), above the spur of mostly terraced land that appears to jut out into the Modi Khola valley. Take the left fork that descends steeply, going around and through terraced fields of millet. Take the steepest choice at trail forks. Near the spur of land, which is just a shoulder of the Kyumnu Khola valley, cross a fence to keep to the crest of the spur. Reach the few houses of **Chinu** (5660 ft, 1725 m), **40 minutes** from the junction. This is a settlement of *Jaishi* Brahmans. There is a hot spring near the river about 15 minutes' walk north, and a sign points the way.

Beyond, the main trail drops on the south side of the spur, heading toward the Kyumnu Khola. Just before reaching it, fork left to a log bridge (5180 ft, 1579 m), some **15 minutes** from Chinu. Cross the tributary and climb up the south bank pass, called Samrung, and then return to the Modi Khola valley at around 5425 ft (1653 m). Reach forest and go almost all the way around a small side valley before dropping down to the lodges at **Himalkyo** (5050 ft, 1539 m), some **35 minutes** from the previous bridge. Popularly called New Bridge, or Naya Pul for the now old structure 100 ft (30 m) below, the *Gurung* name meaning "water from the snows" is much more appropriate.

Cross the Modi Khola to the left bank and head downstream, past ChiURe, then climb and contour, reaching terraces. An **hour** from Himalkyo, cross a suspension bridge over a tributary (5175 ft, 1577 m). Some **5 minutes** beyond, reach the main trail from Landrung to Ghandruk (5325 ft, 1623 m), by a lodge. A short climb brings you to **Landrung,** a large *Gurung* settlement. At a fork in the middle of town (5340 ft, 1628 m) take the right branch to contour southward.

The trail heads down the valley to climb out of it into the Pokhara drainage. Leave Landrung, and contour south through several tributary valleys to reach **Tolka** (5660 ft, 1725 m) in **45 minutes.** Continue through more lodges of Tolka in the Bhichok or Ghirsung Khola valley. Cross this tributary to the left bank and climb out of the valley to **Bhichok Deorali** (6880 ft, 2097 m) in **1 hour.** There are now plenty of facilities for trekkers along here, and it is difficult to get lost. Continue in the same direction you have been walking and cross to the opposite (east) side of the ridge to contour above the Indi Khola valley. Descend slightly to the lodges and tea shops at **Potana** (6460 ft, 1969 m) in **30 minutes.** Shortly beyond, the trail forks. The right fork, which goes

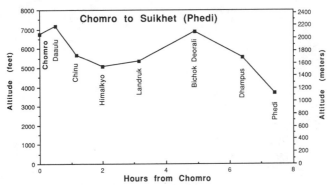

through forest to KAAre, comes out at the pass just to the west. This route may be a useful link, depending on your plans.

To return to Pokhara via Dhampus, don't take the right fork, but continue and descend, reaching fields on the north side of a ridge in the Indi Khola valley in 30 minutes. The village of **Dhampus** is spread out farther along the north side of this ridge. Reach the far end of town (5560 ft, 1695 m) in 1 hour from Potana. The views of the giants to the north are worth waiting for if the weather is bad. You can continue along the ridge to Dhital, Henjakot, and Astam before descending to Suikhet at a narrowing in the Yamdi Khola valley. Those wishing longer views along the ridge will enjoy taking this route.

Most trekkers will want to descend, following the stairs, joining trails coming in from the right. Keep close to the crest of the hill, along terraces. Reach a *chautaara* 35 minutes below (4575 ft, 1394 m) and descend into forests of *chilaune* trees. *Chilaune* means "itch" in Nepali, and if you rub sap of this tree on your skin, you will learn how it got its name. As you drop down to the Yamdi Khola valley floor, you'll be impressed with this uncut forest so close to Pokhara. The people of Dhampus have traditionally protected this forest, and governmental programs are only now realizing that this traditional, social forestry should be encouraged. Reach the valley floor (3750 ft, 1143 m) and the road to NagDAADa in **45 minutes** from Dhampus. Depending on the service on the road, you may have to cross the stream, heading east (downstream) to Phedi to get motorized transport, or may decide to walk the rest of the way.

If taking this trail in reverse, look for the small (50 ft, 15 m) waterfall on the north side of the valley, near the start of the climb. The trail begins a few minutes beyond.

Thrashing grain beneath the Annapurnas

To Manang and Over the Thorung La

The Manang area was only recently opened to trekkers. It offers many of the same attractions of a trek to Jomosom via Thak Khola, except that the Marsyangdi Khola valley lacks the strong winds and associated dry vegetation near the river. Furthermore, the area does not abound with *Thakali bhaTTi,* and the clang-clong of horse bells of long caravans won't be heard as often. On the other hand, the *Manangba,* the people of Manang, are a most worldly ethnic group and some of the men may have traveled farther on the globe than you. The mountain scenery is perhaps more breathtaking than on the other side, if only because the peaks in the open Manang Valley are closer.

Enjoy it all. Cross the Thorung La Pass and circle the Annapurna massif. It is a walk of over 150 mi (240 km), but the rewards certainly compensate for the effort. The circuit takes at least three weeks, perhaps a week more than just walking to Manang and then retracing your steps, but this includes time for some diversions. There are now primitive inns temporarily set up on both sides of the pass so it is possible to cross without being self-sufficient, though storms may make it difficult to reach one. A number of trekkers have died because they pushed on in storms when not adequately prepared with food, clothing, and shelter. Serious frostbite is not uncommon among trekkers who are inadequately prepared and lack mountain judgement. Crossings can be difficult or impossible if there is deep, soft snow on the pass. Such conditions can be expected from January to March, and often longer. Storms can threaten the party at any time, and it is prudent to wait them out or turn back rather than risk lives.

The route is described from Dumre on the Kathmandu–Pokhara road. You could begin by walking directly from Pokhara to intersect the trail described here at either Khudi or near Tarkughat. The Khudi-to-Pokhara route is described briefly here.

The basic route description is very simple. The entire trek is spent going up the Marsyangdi Khola to its headwaters, and then crossing a pass to reach the Kali Gandaki drainage.

Dumre (1500 ft, 457 m) is reached in some 5 hours by bus from Kathmandu, or 2½ hours from Pokhara (more or less, depending on road conditions). Board the bus in Pokhara at Mahendra Pul or at the main bus terminal at Chhaina Chowk, just east of the town-airport road junction, on the south side of the Kathmandu–Pokhara road. In Kathmandu the staging area is near the post office at Sundhara, where buses leave early in the morning, or at the main bus terminal just east of the Tundikhel. (The bus terminals are often called *bas parak,* "bus park.")

Dumre is one of the many towns that have sprung up along the road to serve the needs of travelers, traders, and villagers. It is a principal staging area for people arriving and departing for the hinterland of the Marsyangdi Khola. This is a place to purchase a range of provisions at reasonable prices, although more and more, goods can be bought at main towns along the dry-weather feeder road that parallels the Marsyangdi Khola on the west bank and goes to Besisahar. Porters can be hired at Dumre or at the terminus of the feeder road, and sometimes a guide may also be engaged.

The feeder road is passable for four-wheel-drive vehicles from October to May or June, depending on weather conditions. Jeeps may be hired on a "reserve" basis (expensive) or you can pay by the seat (crowded but inexpensive). There is usually a nominal charge for baggage in addition to the seat charge. Taking a vehicle along the road saves two or more days of walking, but the rugged trucks and wagons take their toll as they pitch and heave. Larger and taller people are advised to keep their centers of gravity as low as possible.

Those wishing to trek the entire way (and avoid the road) should get off the bus at Bimalnagar, east of Dumre. Cross the suspension bridge and walk up the east side of the Marsyangdi Khola. You can rejoin the trail described here at either Tarkughat, PhalenksAAghu, or Besisahar, or you can stay on the east side all the way to Syange. Bimalnagar to PhalenksAAghu takes about 8 hours.

From **Dumre** (1440 ft, 439 m) head north on the feeder road and cross the Naahaalaa Khola by a series of rocks to the north (left) bank and continue uphill. The trail follows the road except for shortcuts, which provide pleasant relief. In **15 minutes** turn right, off the road, and enter a subtropical deciduous forest. Then climb to the first few houses of Bhansar (1650 ft, 503 m) in **10 minutes.** Continue past dwellings until you reach a *chautaara* in the center of town; go on for some **15 minutes** to reach an oil mill (fuel-driven, it whistles when operating). Turn right here toward the Marsyangdi Khola, which you will continue to follow for many days. Pass a police check post. The trail stays well above the west (right) bank and reaches the small town of Barabise (1650 ft, 504 m) in **20 minutes.** Reach Chambas (1759 ft, 533 m) in **45 minutes,** then **Turture** (1725 ft, 526 m) in another **45 minutes.** Turture sits above a suspension bridge over the Marsyangdi Khola.

Walk through Turture bazaar and descend at the north end to cross the Paundi Khola; continue north along the west (right) bank of the Marsyangdi Khola. Just north of the Paundi Khola, on the banks of the Marsyangdi Khola, is a large sandy beach, good for tent camping. Tenters are advised to be cautious along this route (and on many others); there are many reported cases of robberies (principally by slitting tents during the night and extracting rucksacks, cameras, money, clothes, shoes, and other items).

North of Turture the trail passes through many small hamlets, including Tharpani (1875 ft, 556 m), in **1 hour.** Beyond there are fewer settlements and more farmland until **1 hour** later you come to the new town of Kalimati. Below and across from you, on the east (left) bank of the Marsyangdi Khola, you can see the town of Tarkughat.

To go to Manang, follow the feeder road north, and in 30 minutes cross a suspension bridge over a tributary, the Paundi Khola (same name as the river near Turture). Climb up to reach Paundi Dhik (1900 ft, 579 m) a few minutes later. There is a good swimming place under the bridge (*paundi* means "swim"). The road goes out across the fields. Stay on the trail through this small town. Don't take the left fork at the top end of the few shops, but continue north along the west edge of the fields. The trail soon rejoins the road, sometimes staying with it, sometimes avoiding it on shortcuts. Reach opposite the large tributary, the Dardi Khola, that you see joining the Marsyangdi Khola on the east (left) bank, in **50 minutes. An hour** farther, cross another tributary to **Udipur** (2450 ft, 747 m) **5 minutes** beyond. The forests that remain are tropical sal, but have been cut extensively. Continue on to the rapidly growing village of **Bhote Wodar** (also called Suidibar).

In **30 minutes** the trail reaches **PhalenksAAghu.** Follow the road through the high part of this town, unless you want to cross the Marsyangdi Khola here, in which case you should descend into the old town by the bridge. The name PhalenksAAghu comes from the English word "plank" and the Nepali word for a rather primitive bridge, *sAAghu.* There was once a plank bridge here, and the name stuck. Such combinations of Nepali and English words can often cause difficulty when they are pronounced with a Nepali accent or spelled in the local script. Another name for this town is Dalal, meaning "black market," a reference to activities of an earlier time.

An alternative trail here crosses the bridge and ascends the east (left) bank of the river to rejoin the other trail above Bhulbhule. This east (left) bank route is slightly shorter than the west (right) bank route and has more spectacular views. In the winter, many *Manangba* camp and trade on this side of the river. Trekkers who want to use the well-supplied shops at Besisahar might consider a combination route, following the west (right) bank to Besisahar, crossing the river there and taking the left-hand fork to join the east (left) bank route; or, following the east (left) bank trail from PhalenksAAghu, crossing back to the west (right) bank at Besisahar. The west (right) bank trail may be preferable, however, because the road is being built on this side, where there are more eating and lodging places. The east (left) bank trail is described as an alternative, following the west (right) bank description. Another variation, or even a side trip, is to cross the Marsyangdi Khola here and climb to the lakes on the Baahra Pokhari Lekh for fine views of Manaslu, Peak 29, and Himalchuli. You could even head north from the lakes to rejoin the main riverside route a day beyond. The route from PhalenksAAghu to Baahra Pokhara takes about two days of steady climbing.

If you don't cross the suspension bridge at PhalenksAAghu, continue on up the west (right) bank through stands of wet subtropical forest (good birding, and even a squirrel or two may be seen, especially on early mornings). The trail on to Besisahar generally follows the feeder road. Reach a small town, Nadiwal (2650 ft, 808 m), in **45 minutes.** Take the shortcut right, down, and across a small stream, then continue along the wide roadbed to Bakunde (2675 ft, 815 m) in another **30 minutes.** You will see the large buildings and roofs of Besisahar in the distance. Descend to cross a tributary stream in **45 minutes,** then ascend to **Besisahar** (2700 ft, 823 m) **15 minutes** beyond. The old Lamjung Darbar, a palace fortress, once the center of a princely state, is high on the ridge southwest of the town. Besisahar has two sections; the main part of town is 5 minutes beyond, across a small stream. This major town, situated on a shelf of land above the Marsyangdi Khola, is the Lamjung District headquarters and the site of a police check post, where you might be asked to show your trekking permit. The town also has a district hospital, prison, high school, government offices, shops, lodges, and electricity. It is a real "boom town" in every sense, with new construction visible on all sides of the old bazaar. The feeder road ends here.

The bridge across the Marsyangdi Khola to the east (left) bank is reached by a trail that turns off near the south end of the main old bazaar, near the hospital. It can be used by those taking the east (left) bank trail from PhalenksAAghu, or by going to Bhulbhule on the east (left) side of the valley.

To proceed from **Besisahar** (2700 ft, 823 m) on the west (right) bank, continue north through town to the end of the wide roadbed. The peak up the valley is Gyahi Kang. Descend from the shelf and cross the tributary PoDjo Khola some **15 minutes** later. Climb up steeply and then contour in wet subtropical forest and rice fields to Tanaute (2800 ft, 853 m) in **15 minutes.** Just beyond, fork right, to contour, rather than climb. Continue north above the Marsyangdi Khola to the Khudi Khola, a main tributary stream that drains the east end of the Lamjung Himal. Reach the old suspension bridge in **70 minutes.** The mountains up to the northeast are Ngadi Chuli and Baudha Himal. Either cross the old bridge (2600 ft, 792 m) or ascend 10 minutes upstream to cross a new suspension bridge and return from "new Khudi" (Naya Khudi) at the new bridge site. On the east (left) bank of the Khudi Khola, pass through **Khudi** to rejoin the Marsyangdi River trail. The Marsyangdi valley turns, narrows, and changes character now.

If returning from Manang, you might consider walking directly to Pokhara from Khudi and avoiding Dumre. This route takes three days. The trail goes from Khudi to Baglung Pani, through Lamagaon, across the Badam Khola to Nalma, and across the Midam Khola, passing Kala Pattar to Begnas Tal, the lake in the eastern part of the Pokhara Valley. Most of the villages passed are inhabited by people of the *Gurung* ethnic group, who farm the high hills and raise sheep. Trekkers wishing to meet few other foreigners should consider this route.

To reach Manang from Khudi, continue up the Marsyangdi north (right) bank northeastward, and pass above the Khudi school stone pillar and tree nursery. Continue along the Marsyangdi Khola another **20 minutes** to a long suspension bridge (2720 ft, 829 m). Bagartol refers to the hotels and houses on this side. Cross to the south (left) bank to **Bhulbhule.**

To take the alternative route from PhalenksAAghu to Bhulbhule, cross the bridge at PhalenksAAghu and climb the hill for **10 minutes** to the fields above. The trail winds its way through fields, sometimes diverging into several trails. The villages are pleasant and the sights lovely. In midwinter, you may see a temporary potters' encampment here, *Newar* from Kathmandu Valley who have come for generations to sites like this in the middle hills to extract clay and make pots for sale in the surrounding villages.

After **1½ hours,** the trail drops down into a steep ravine with a stone staircase leading in and out on both sides. Then it traverses along a steeper slope with fine views across the valley to the high mountains beyond. **Twenty minutes** from the ravine is the bridge crossing the Marsyangdi Khola to Besisahar. Several trails drop down to the river; take the one that traverses the slope and continue to another lookout (Deskadanda) **20 minutes** beyond. It is another **1¼ hours** to the big pipal tree and small village of Simbachaur, and an additional **1 hour and 20 minutes** to Bhulbhule. The trail from the opposite north (right) bank joins here at the bridge, which enters the middle part of Bhulbhule. There are a few shops in Bhulbhule, and also the first lodges operated by *Manangba,* who have moved down here from the upper Marsyangdi valley.

The most-traveled route now continues eastward out of Bhulbhule along the south (left) bank of the Marsyangdi Khola; later it turns northward again.

Continue upstream from Bhulbhule and pass the first beautiful, thin waterfall on your right. I'll let you discover the rest! Below it is a fine pool for bathing— much better than the main river. Beyond, fork left, rather than climbing up the stairs, except in the monsoon. Pass Tarante, and just beyond, fork left, rather than climbing.

An **hour** from Bhulbhule, reach **Ngadi** (3000 ft, 914 m), on the banks of a small tributary stream. There is more town beyond, and you reach a suspension bridge (3060 ft, 933 m) over the Ngadi Khola in **10 minutes.** Cross it to the right bank of the Ngadi Khola, and take the left of the two trails, which heads over to the Marsyangdi Khola on a wide trail. Cross a landslide via a detour. If the landslide is no longer visible, then the Nepalis have rebuilt the area, something that foreign experts have realized is the common way the peasant farmers deal with these land movements. Beyond, climb through Lampata, to reach **Bahundanda** (literally meaning "Brahman hill"), on the right of a prominent brow at a saddle (4300 ft, 1311 m) **1 hour** from the crossing of the Ngadi Khola. There is a police check post here and good views to the north if the weather is clear. On the high hills all around are *Gurung* settlements. There is an undeveloped hot springs (taato paani) at the edge of the Marsyangdi Khola, below the knob of Bahundanda hill, but it is a steep descent (and return ascent) and takes some time and effort to find. Ask locally for the way.

Descend into another tributary valley and in **45 minutes** cross its river on a cantilever bridge (3700 ft, 1128 m). Ascend to the main river valley and follow the trail beautifully carved out of the rock wall of the valley. Pass the houses and lodges of Khanegaon (3900 ft, 1189 m) in **30 minutes,** and contour to the first houses of **Shyange** (3725 ft, 1136 m) in **30 minutes.** Arrive at the large suspension bridge over the Marsyangdi (3700 ft, 1128 m) and cross it to the west (right) bank to pass through more of **Shyange.**

The gorge now becomes narrower and the trail rises and falls. There are overhanging rocks that can provide campsites. The trail continues 1¼ **hours** to the village of **Jagat** (4400 ft, 1341 m)—also called Gadi Jagat or Chote— situated in a saddle in the forest. This used to be an old customs post for the salt trade with Tibet and is inhabited mostly by *BhoTiya.*

The trail continues up and down and has detours to avoid slide areas. An **hour** beyond Jagat, reach the small settlement of **Chamje** (4560 ft, 1390 m), which has a large overhanging rock between two groups of houses, both with lodges. There are many changes in the people, architecture, and vegetation as you head upstream. Houses are now built of rocks, the vegetation is less tropical, and the culture is more Tibetanlike.

Just beyond the town, the gorge is very impressive. Descend for less than **10 minutes** and cross to the east (left) bank of the Marsyangdi Khola on a suspension bridge (4420 ft, 1347 m) on which the upstream upper cable has loosened. It is quite safe, providing you stay away from that side. The forests are temperate broad-leaved, with bamboo. Continue upstream, usually high above the river, for almost 1½ **hours** until you emerge from the gorge with its torrent below. An ancient landslide from the mountain to the east filled the gorge here, creating a lake that has become silted in above. The river itself flows buried beneath the rubble and is muffled but not seen.

Enter a broad, pleasant, flat valley with a somewhat quieter river. There are a few houses, then a suspension bridge across the river that isn't taken. You have entered Manang District. Continue ahead to the houses of **Tal** in the center of the flat valley (5460 ft, 1664 m) in **1½ hours** from Chamje. Tal, meaning "lake" in Nepali, refers to the prehistoric one. There is a police check post here. Try to spend a night here, for there is nowhere else along the trek quite like it. The area of Manang to the north is called Gyasumdo, meaning "meeting place of the three highways." It is inhabited partly by *BhoTiya,* who are primarily agro-pastoralists. These people were the real trans-Himalayan traders of the region until 1959 or 1960 when the trade closed after the Chinese takeover of Tibet. Nareshwar Jang Gurung wrote an interesting survey on Manang (see appendix B).

The former way went along the east bank, crossing to the west just before Dharapani. However, there have been serious landslides on a portion of this route, resulting in loss of life, and it has fallen into disuse. The current route is to cross a cantilever bridge (5540 ft, 1689 m) 30 minutes north of Tal. Pass a few houses, then proceed on a section that has been blasted out of the rock along the right (west) bank. In **45 minutes** come to a new, long suspension bridge (5960 ft, 1817 m) and cross to the left (east) bank of the Marsyangdi and Khotro, which has a few lodges. In **20 minutes** cross back to the west bank (6100 ft, 1859 m). **Five minutes** beyond is **Dharapani** (6180 ft, 1884 m).

Continue on upstream and note the valley coming in from the northeast some **10 minutes** beyond. It comes down from the Larkya Pass and leads north of Manaslu to the Buri Gandaki. The village of Thonje, which in *Gurung* means "pine trees growing on a flat place," lies at the confluence of the Dudh Khola and the Marsyangdi Khola. Don't fork right to cross the wooden cantilever bridge over the Marsyangdi Khola upstream of the river junction. There is more village and a police check post here. Some **10 minutes** beyond the confluence, take the lower fork—the upper leads to some higher villages.

A pleasant **30-minute** walk brings you around the corner to the town of **Bagarchap** (6900 ft, 2103 m)—meaning "butcher's place." This town has flat-roofed houses, indicating that rainfall is less here because the monsoon clouds have unloaded some of their water to the south. The waterworks flowing through the town are unusual—you will see nothing remotely similar until you reach Marpha in the Thak Khola across the Annapurna range to the west. The Diki Gomba of the Nyingmapa sect has handsome frescoes on its walls and is worth a visit. There are views of the Annapurnas and part of Lamjung Himal.

Just beyond the town, take the left fork and do not go down to the cantilever bridge crossing the Marsyangdi Khola. Then fork right on a wider trail **17 minutes** from town and come to Danakyu (7140 ft, 2176 m) **15 minutes** beyond. There are a few lodges in this new town. Continue in the picturesquely narrow valley of temperate mixed broad-leaved forest.

You may see four light-colored diamond shapes on the rock to the left, near the middle part of the waterfall above the only concrete cantilever bridge I can recall in these parts. Local legend holds that a lama painted these auspicious symbols centuries ago. Unlike similar valleys in eastern Nepal, there are not many rhododendron trees along the trail.

Come up to **Chaumrikharka** (7380 ft, 2249 m), with its few houses and a lodge, in **45 minutes.** Timung and the trail to the Namun Bhanjyang is 1 hour above here. This high pass crosses the Himalayan barrier east of Lamjung Himal. Once heavily traveled, it is now only occasionally used by *Gurung* shepherds who pasture their sheep and goats on the high slopes. The newly constructed trail along the Marsyangdi Khola has replaced the dangerous old river bottom route that people avoided by taking the strenuous high route.

Continue to **Lattemarang** (7720 ft, 2353 m) in **30 minutes.** Across the river, reached by a bridge that heads off between the two groups of lodges, are several hot springs. Fork left after you cross the bridge and reach the two pools.

Twenty minutes later is Tanshe Beshi, a lone house. Keep on the left bank and fork right on a bigger trail in 25 minutes, and reach **Koto** (less often called Qupar, 8300 ft, 2530 m) in **1¼ hour** from Lattemarang. The prominent tributary valley heading north is the Nar Khola, which drains the region called Nar Phu, whose inhabitants are traditionally pastoralists. Don't take the right fork heading there, just beyond the police check post in the upper part of Koto. The valley walls here might remind you of Yosemite.

To continue to Manang, enter **Chame** (8580 ft, 2615 m) in less than **30 minutes.** Note the unusual entrance *chorten* containing Hindu elements, the result of being a government town, the district center for Manang. It has a bank, electricity, and many shops. The nongovernmental people live at the west end of town, where there is a *gomba*. At the far end of town, first cross a tributary from the south, then the main Marsyangdi Khola, on either a cantilever or suspension bridge (8620 ft, 2627 m) to the north (left) bank. There are more houses here as well as some (poorly maintained in 1989) hot springs right at the river's edge about 200 yards (200 meters) south of the bridge over the Marsyangdi Khola on the north (left) bank, beyond a lodge about as far as you can go downstream.

Go up the valley past more Chame, to **Taleku** (8960 ft, 2731 m) in **30 minutes.** Continue in the unrelentingly narrow valley of pine, hemlock, and cypress forest, almost 1 hour to **Bhratang** (9340 ft, 2847 m).

There used to be a *Khampa* village situated across the valley from here. These Tibetan refugee warriors settled here after the Chinese occupation of Tibet in 1959. They built several bridges; when I first journeyed up here, the bridge here was still in use, and had remnants of a gate used to maintain control over traffic in the valley. You still might see its remnants in the river bed some 15 minutes upstream. The only remaining *Khampa* bridge is below Phedi. The former village had a huge meeting hall for strategy sessions. The *Khampa* were all resettled in 1975 and the town was eventually destroyed, only to be rebuilt on the other side of the river to serve trekkers.

Head upstream on a new trail carved out of the narrow canyon walls, through hemlock-and-pine forest. Cross again to the south (right) bank in **35**

minutes on your choice of a suspension or cantilever bridge (9740 ft, 2969 m), then climb into a serene pine, hemlock, and fir forest. After the days in the gorge, you can appreciate the beauty and silence of these **45 minutes.** Pass a rest house, a rock cairn memorial, and a clearing. Then reach a house and lodge at Dhukur Pokhari Danda (10,200 ft, 3109 m).

Just beyond the *mani* wall, if you fork right, the trail goes directly to a bridge over the Marsyangdi Khola to the north (left) bank (10,220 ft, 3115 m). Then you climb directly to upper Pisang. The left fork keeps to the valley floor and lower Pisang. Take this trail, and reach lower **Pisang** (10,280 ft, 3133 m) in **45 minutes.** This town is now mostly a collection of lodges. You can cross the river at the western part, fork right, and climb up to upper Pisang (10,600 ft, 3231 m), where there is a *gomba* and amazing views of Annapurna II. An essential side trip.

You are now in the dry, arid region of Manang called Nyesyang. Since it is in the rain shadow of the Himalaya, which acts as a barrier to the wet monsoon clouds from the south, the area gets little rain in the summer. Snow falls here in the winter and remains on the ground much of the time. The men are traders and part-time farmers, and the women are full-time farmers. There is comparatively little animal husbandry. In the winter many leave for warmer places. You may meet many young men with considerable facility in English who have traveled far and wide in Asia. They may try to sell or trade almost anything. The people of Nyesyang were granted special trading privileges by the King about 180 years ago. This included passports and import and export facilities. These privileges have been extended to all the people of Manang District. Initially they traded local items for manufactured goods, usually in India and Burma, but more recently they have begun using hard currency from the export of expensive items to import machines and other manufactured goods from most South Asian countries. The resultant seasonal migration means less development of agriculture and animal husbandry. So you won't see many herds of yak, sheep, or goats at the higher elevations. These people are thus quite dependent on food imports.

From lower Pisang there are basically two routes, which join up in the valley below the village of Braga. The direct route keeps to the valley floor, staying mostly on the south (right) side. The other trail ascends on the north side of the valley to reach several villages on the north (left) side of the valley. The views of the mountains from this route are more impressive than from the floor, and the villages are quite interesting, but it takes perhaps 2 hours more to reach Braga. You will find fewer facilities here and, as well, fewer trekkers.

For the lower route, start from lower Pisang, cross a tributary from the south, just beyond, and regain the main Marsyangdi by a row of *mani* walls, and continue on its south (right) bank. Climb to a ridge crest, Ngoro Danda (11,060 ft, 3371 m), in **45 minutes.** Villagers may stay here and sell refreshments and souvenirs to trekkers. **Hongde** (or Ongre, Omdhe, HumDe, or Hongre, 11,060 ft, 3371 m), a sprawling new settlement with an airstrip at its upper end, is reached in another **45 minutes.** The RNAC office is here along

The immense north face of Annapurna II, from a house balcony in Pisang

with a police check post. Continue along, on a two-lane highway, to cross another tributary from the south in **20 minutes.** Here, nearing completion, is a
hydroelectric project to provide electricity for upper Manang Valley. Some **20
minutes** later, cross the Marsyangdi Khola (11,160 ft, 3401 m). Ascend along
the north (left) bank 10 minutes to Munchi (11,240 ft, 3426 m), a dilapidated
series of houses where the high, north-side route joins the main valley route.
Stay on the north (left) bank of the Marsyangdi, and in **30 minutes,** come to
the base of **Braga** (11,320 ft, 3450 m). There is a cooperative hotel below the
village, but few facilities in the town perched above.

The high, north-side route begins in lower Pisang. Like many villages
here, the town is constructed using flat roofs. The roof of one house serves as
the yard or open area of the house above it. There is a long, handsome wall of
prayer wheels in an open space below a little-used *gòmba*. To head up the valley on the north side, cross the Marsyangdi Khola (10,260 ft, 3127 m) and immediately fork left to head upstream. Cross a tributary (10,800 ft, 3292 m) and
contour in a pleasant pine-and-juniper forest. Pass above a small green lake,
and contour to a long *mani* wall. Then descend to cross a tributary (10,775 ft,
3284 m) a little over **30 minutes** from Pisang. Take the upper fork and begin a
steep climb for 1 hour to **Ghyaru** (12,050 ft, 3673 m). Spectacular views of
Annapurnas II and III and Gangapurna are the main attractions, along with the
dark, tunnellike streets of the town. Contour out of the town to the west, cross

a tributary (12,075 ft, 3680 m), and reach a ridge crest (12,375 ft, 3772 m) some 100 ft (30 m) above some ruins, perhaps of an old fort, in **45 minutes.** Rest here and enjoy the views of Gangapurna, Glacier Dome, and Tilicho Peak to the west. North of Tilicho Peak lies the "great frozen lake," named by Herzog, although it is out of view from here. If you cross the Thorung La Pass, you will eventually return to Pokhara by heading well north and then west of this peak.

Continue contouring, cross a tributary, and pass three trails joining yours on the left. Cross another tributary to **Ngawal** (11,975 ft, 3650 m) **45 minutes** from the ruins. Descend to cross a tributary in a few minutes, then continue descending, avoiding a left fork (11,625 ft, 3543 m) 10 minutes beyond town. Descend to the valley floor (11,325 ft, 3452 m) and, in **1¼ hours** from Ngawal, reach the few houses of Munchi (11,425 ft, 3482 m). Here the trail meets the main lower trail from Pisang. **Braga** is 30 minutes away.

Braga, a large and interesting village, is the seat of the oldest monastery in the area. The *gomba* is perhaps 900 years old, and belongs to the Kargyupa sect of Tibetan Buddhism. Like most of the *gomba* in this region, it is not very active, but is well worth a visit, for it contains some unique works of art and is spectacularly situated. The *Konyer* (custodian) will show you around, sometimes with varying amounts of patience. The main temple holds 108 terra-cotta statues, each about 2 ft (60 cm) high, arranged in rows along three of the four walls. They represent the Kargyupa lineage and much more. There is another three-story temple above this main building. The temple is described in detail in David Snellgrove's *Himalayan Pilgrimage* (see appendix B).

The village of **Manang** (11,480 ft, 3499 m) is **30 minutes** beyond Braga. Between two tributaries along the way, on a ridge to the north, lies the Bod-zo *gomba*. Reach this *gomba* by climbing upstream before crossing the second of the series of tributaries. Head up the valley for 30 minutes to the ridge crest (11,750 ft, 3581 m). Directly to the north of it, across a tributary, is the new Kargyupa *gomba*. Before going to either of these, try to determine if the key bearer is around.

You can restock your provisions in Manang, although prices are quite high. The Himalayan Rescue Association's post is here, and daily lectures on altitude illness are held. If you are planning to cross the Thorung La and reach the Kali Gandaki (river) to the west, it is important to spend a day or two acclimatizing here before proceeding. If you have flown to Manang, you should spend at least three or four days in this region before attempting to cross the pass. In addition, it is advisable to spend an additional night at Letdar, before going on to Phedi. Acclimatization days are best spent being active and climbing to high elevations for views, but returning to lower altitudes to sleep. There are many suitable hikes on both sides of the valley. These extra acclimatization days may be unnecessary for some, or not long enough for others. They are guidelines on how to proceed with less risk.

For people traveling without food or tents, it is now possible to cross the pass relying on local facilities, except during the winter, when crossing the pass is a mountaineering endeavor. However, it is best to bring some extra food from Manang. Ask here if Phedi is set up to provide services.

There are several "rest day" activities possible. Perhaps you may see an archery contest or a horse race! An hour above the town, there is a lama who likes to receive visitors and give blessings. Manang itself is spectacularly perched across from a glacial lake formed by water from Gangapurna and Annapurna III. Cross the Marsyangdi below town by the school and fork right to go up to the lake. Go around it and visit the caves at the foot of the icefall. Or climb up the lateral moraine on its southeast side for good views of the Chulu peaks and Manang.

A good half-day hike is a circuit to Khangsar, the last town before Tilicho Tal. A visit here may give a glimpse of what the region was like before Westerners invaded. To get there, go through Manang, and then 3 minutes beyond, where you pass a *mani* wall with prayer wheels, fork left and descend to the bridge by the river. Cross it and head upstream to climb to a shelf. Contour into the valley of the Khangsar Khola and cross a small slide area. Continue through a serene forest, eventually descending to cross the Khangsar Khola. Ascend to Khangsar (12,180 ft, 3712 m), 1½ hours from Manang. To return, keep high on the north side of the valley until you reach a plateau, and then descend its north side to cross the Marsyangdi and head downstream to the bridge you crossed before.

Beyond Khangsar is the impressive north face of Tilicho Peak. An approach to the lake has been described from the Kali Gandaki side. It can also be reached from Khangsar in two days. On the new trail, it takes about 4 hours to reach a base camp, where there is water.

A further 3 hours' climb will bring you to the crest of the moraine. The lake can be seen from beyond there. In bad weather it can be difficult to find the lake from the east. It is frozen in winter, and periods of thaw vary from year to year.

To proceed from Manang over the Thorung La, cross a tributary below a falls northwest of Manang and climb up to Tengi (11,950 ft, 3642 m) in **30 minutes.** This last permanent settlement below the pass has few tourist facilities. Climb gradually to reach some *goTh* and a hotel at Ghunsang (12,725 ft, 3879 m) an **1 hour. Ten minutes** farther is a higher settlement of *goTh* and another hotel, called Thora. The trail has now turned northwest up the valley of the Jargeng Khola. Pass some *goTh,* cross small tributaries, and contour along pleasant meadows with occasional birch groves. If you are here early in the morning or late in the afternoon, look for herds of blue sheep, which may descend for water. Reach Yak Kharka (13,020 ft, 3968 m) in **1½ hours,** with a hotel there, and one 10 minutes before. Letdar (13,700 ft, 4176 m) is **1¼ hours** from Yak Kharka. The original two-story shelter is beyond the two hotels. It is possible to hire a horse from here to the summit of the pass. People have been put on a horse only to arrive higher up unconscious and moribund from altitude illness. Acclimatizing and walking is safer.

Do not attempt to cross the pass unless all of the party, including the porters, are equipped for cold and bad weather. If the weather is threatening, do not proceed. Lives of trekkers and porters have been needlessly lost on this pass because parties proceeded in bad weather. Recently, many people have been crossing the pass wearing running shoes and other light footwear. If you do not carry proper boots, at least recognize that there is risk of frostbite should a storm occur. I have seen trekkers get serious frostbite on this pass. Losing fingers and toes is a big price to pay! If stuck with poor footwear, in bad conditions, and unwilling to turn back, wrap your feet in plastic socks as a vapor barrier. This may help, but there are no guarantees.

From Letdar, climb, pass above a tarn, contour, and then descend to the river by a covered wooden cantilever bridge (14,000 ft, 4267 m) in **45 minutes.** Tall people should watch their heads on this last remaining *Khampa* bridge!

Cross to the west (right) bank of the Jargeng Khola, and climb and contour upstream to reach the riverbed and campsite (14,450 ft, 4404 m), called **Phedi**—meaning "foot of hill"—in **45 minutes** from the bridge. There are lodges another **15 minutes** up the hill (14,660 ft, 4468 m) during the trekking season.

At the hotel, you must pay for everything as you order it, since in the past trekkers have run off without paying. A lucky trekker might spot a snow leopard near here at dusk! Trekkers are often advised to leave at ungodly early hours, such as 3:00 or 4:00 A.M., to avoid the strong winds that are said to blow later in the day. Leave at daybreak. It takes a long day to cross the pass, but doing the first quarter in the dark is unnecessarily tiring, and stumbles and falls can result in injury, fatigue, and getting wet, which can lead to hypothermia and frostbite higher up. As well, the wind is too variable to predict.

The trail now leaves the river valley, which continues northwest and then ascends west. In dry weather, water can be scarce the next day, so fill up. There are no good campsites with water beyond the pass unless you camp on snow in the appropriate season. In early-season snow (November–December), or early spring conditions (March–April), don't underestimate the difficulties of proceeding, especially if you don't have mountaineering experience. In deep snow, an ice ax, ski pole, or walking stick are helpful. Some parties bring a stove with them to melt snow and rehydrate along the way.

From Phedi, ascend to a notch (15,725 ft, 4793 m) in **1¼ hours** and head left (west), traversing to the base of a prominent lateral moraine (15,900 ft, 4846 m) in **30 minutes.** Reach its crest (16,050 ft, 4892 m) a few minutes later and continue west along less steep terrain. After many false crests, reach the Thorung La Pass (17,700 ft, 5416 m) in **2 hours** if you are adequately acclimatized. A large cairn marks the pass, but it may be almost entirely covered with snow. The pass is exhilarating in that it is an abrupt transition from one major Himalayan valley to another, but views from the pass are probably less impressive than those on either side. Far below you to the west is the Kali Gandaki. Those with sharp eyes and binoculars can pick out the green oasis of Kagbeni.

The descent from the pass is gradual at first and follows the middle of the valley for the first hour. It becomes considerably steeper and keeps to the south side of the valley on scree. The first campsites, with some *goTh,* called Thante (14,450 ft, 4404 m), are some 2 hours down from the pass just after crossing a tributary to the right. Locals are only here during the monsoon. In the dry season, after and just before the monsoon, when all the snow has melted, there is no water available, necessitating a further descent. There are more *goTh* frames around 13,720 ft (4182 m), but the nearest lodge or inn is Chatar Puk,

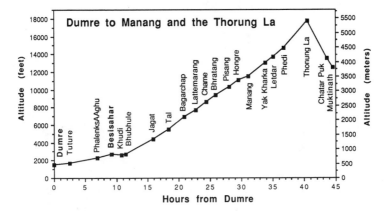

or Chambar (13,500 ft, 4115 m), perhaps **3 hours** from the pass. Just as at Phedi, there will be no one here in the middle of the winter—if you are coming up from Muktinath at that time, ask there first. Since fewer people cross the pass from this side, there is not a great deal of sleeping space, compared to the Phedi side. Cross a tributary (which may be dry) to the left (it flows from the south) and descend to a major tributary in the valley floor (12,650 ft, 3856 m). Cross it to the south (left) bank and ascend a bit to continue down the main valley. Reach Muktinath (12,460 ft, 3798 m) after rounding a corner **1 hour** from Chatar Puk.

To continue, reverse the trail descriptions given earlier for the trek from Pokhara to Muktinath.

Ama Dablang looms over Khumjung

8 Solu-Khumbu (The Everest Region)

Because it's there.

Replied George Mallory, one of the first climbers to attempt Everest, when asked why he wanted to climb it. He disappeared into a cloud near the summit in 1924.

There are several possible ways of reaching Solu-Khumbu District of Nepal. The classic way to Khumbu, the northernmost part of the district, is to walk from Kathmandu. But since roads continue to be built ever closer to Khumbu, this route, beginning at Kathmandu, is never used. Someday a road may reach Namche Bazaar! Lamosangu or Dolalghat, on the Kathmandu–Kodari road, were the traditional staging areas until recently. A road has now been built to Jiri from Lamosangu. Most trekkers walking in will take the road as far as possible.

There are STOL airstrips in several places along the way, and aircraft charters can be arranged. The airstrips are at Phaphlu in Solu, three days' walk, and at Lukla, a day's walk from Namche Bazaar. There are now regularly scheduled flights by Royal Nepal Airlines to Lukla and Phaphlu. In addition, a strip has been constructed above Namche Bazaar. It is called Shyangboche and is used by visitors to the luxury Everest View Hotel in Khumjung (if it is in operation), and to a certain extent by trekkers.

As mentioned earlier, rapid ascent to high altitudes can be dangerous, even fatal. For some people, rapid ascent to even 10,000 ft (3100 m) has been disastrous. Lukla is at 9275 ft (2827 m) and the airstrip at Shyangboche is at 12,435 ft (3790 m). Hence it is best to walk to Khumbu and arrange to fly out, if you want to fly partway. If you must fly in, fly to Phaphlu or Lukla and ascend gradually. In winter, few landings are made at Lukla or Shyangboche because of snow. Often it is difficult to walk into Lukla and get a flight out, sometimes even with a confirmed reservation! Thus most trekkers flying one leg tend to fly in to Lukla and accept the added risk of altitude illness.

If you are walking both ways, the journey from Kathmandu to Khumbu can be combined with the trek from Khumbu to Ilam District in eastern Nepal, followed by air transportation to Kathmandu. Or you can go by jeep and train to Darjeeling. This is described in chapter 9. You can also reach and leave the Khumbu region via Rolwaling to the east by crossing a high glaciated pass, the Trashi Labsta. This long crossing is somewhat hazardous and requires some mountaineering skills and equipment and considerable stamina. The route is described in chapter 11.

To Solu-Khumbu
(Map No. 4, Page 225)

Although there are few close views of the mountains until you get to Khumbu, the walk from Jiri to Khumbu is recommended as an introduction to the hills of Nepal and their inhabitants. A few pleasant diversions along the way are described. Average walking time to Namche Bazaar is seven to nine days. Local people have been known to take much less time, but they traveled all day and sometimes at night. After all, a curvilinear distance of 80 mi (128 km) is involved, but with switchbacks and diversions in the trail, it is about 150 mi (240 km) of walking from Lamosangu to Namche Bazaar. Furthermore, the trip involves a series of ascents that total 35,200 ft (10,724 m) and a series of descents that total 26,100 ft (7954 m). You more than climb Everest along the way, but it is well worth it.

Generally speaking, the main rivers run south and are separated by high ridges, so the route is a succession of ups and downs, often following tributaries flowing east and west. Compared to the trek between Pokhara and Kathmandu, which also goes against the grain of the land, the ridges and valleys are much higher and the climbs and descents are more strenuous.

In the past, *bhaTTi* and tea shops were rare along the route except near Khumbu, but this is no longer the case since the trail has become quite popular with Westerners. There is usually no difficulty in obtaining cooked food along the way, but it is wise to carry some food with you. Shelter should also pose no problem.

Take the bus heading to Jiri, which leaves from the staging area north of the Kathmandu city hall, east of Tundikhel. The ride takes most of a day.

From **Jiri** (6250 ft, 1905 m) there are two choices. One route passes through Those, a *Newar* bazaar and a town with many shops, where you can replenish your supplies. The other route ascends higher and offers distant views of mountains.

The route from Jiri through Those follows the west (right) bank of the Jiri Khola south to about 6125 ft (1867 m), crosses to the east (left) bank, and ascends, passing near the village of Kune (6775 ft, 2064 m) to join the trail from Sikri Khola that avoids Jiri. The trail continues to a notch marked with *chorten* (8800 ft, 2070 m) in a chir pine-and-oak forest and then descends, passing the settlement of Kattike to the south, to the Khimti Khola (5750 ft, 1753 m), which is followed on its west (right) bank to a suspension bridge. Cross it and follow the river north to **Those** (5775 ft, 1760 m). From Jiri to Those takes **2½ to 3 hours.** From Those, follow the river on its east (left) bank, walking upstream for **1½ hours** to **Shivalaya** (5900 ft, 1800 m).

To take the more popular high route from Jiri, climb the east side of the Jiri Valley in a rhododendron forest to reach a pass (7875 ft, 2400 m) after **1½ hours.** Then descend to a bridge over the Yelung Khola. As you drop down, notice the cliffs on the north side, and look for beehives. In late spring, villag-

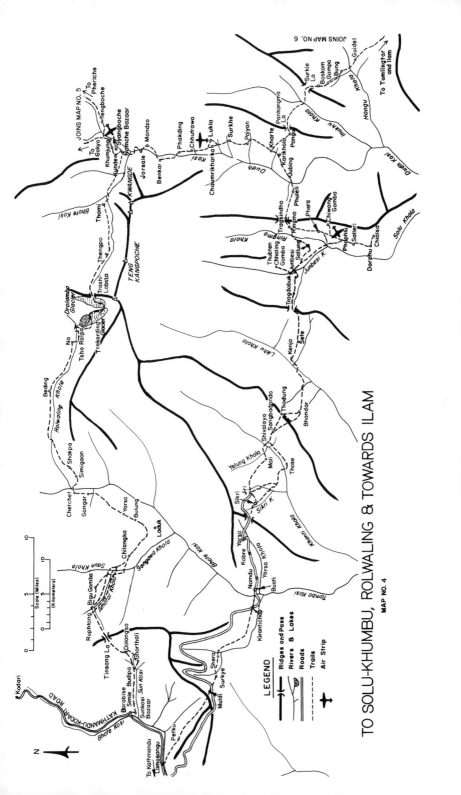

TO SOLU-KHUMBU, ROLWALING & TOWARDS ILAM

MAP NO. 4

LEGEND
- Ridges and Pass
- Rivers & Lakes
- Roads
- Trails
- Air Strip

Scale (Miles)
0   5   10
(Kilometers)
0   5   10

JOINS MAP NO. 5

JOINS MAP NO. 6

ers will dangle on rope ladders to harvest honey from them. Cross the bridge to the northeast (left) bank and go on to a suspension bridge over the Khimti Khola. **Shivalaya** (5900 ft, 1800 m), the village on the other side, is **1½ hours** from the pass.

All the route choices end up at Shivalaya. From here the trail climbs steeply up the ridge to the scattered village of **Sangbadanda** with its school-house (7350 ft, 2240 m) in **1¾ hours.** Just up from the schoolhouse, the trail branches. If you take the right fork, shortly beyond is Kasourbas and the begin-nings of Sherpa settlement. The left branch heads up past the village of Buldanda (8200 ft, 2500 m) to the cheese factory at Thodung (10,140 ft, 3091 m) about 2¾ hours from Sangbadanda. Besides buying cheese here, you can get a good view of Gaurishankar to the north. This peak (23,459 ft, 7150 m) was once thought to be the highest in the world since it was visible from afar. Thodung is definitely a worthwhile detour. There is a monastery 30 minutes south of the cheese factory. To rejoin the regular route, head south along the ridge to the pass (8900 ft, 2713 m), reaching it in 1 hour.

The direct trail to the pass, the right fork, continues along the north side of the valley of the Mohabir Khola, crossing numerous tributaries and entering a rhododendron-and-broad-leaved forest until the pass (8900 ft, 2713 m) is reached. It takes **1¾ hours** to reach the pass from Sangbadanda. There are now tea shops and lodges run by Sherpas at the pass, and also one of the largest col-lections of *mani* walls in Nepal. From the pass, take the left fork. The trail de-scends into the beautiful, lush valley to the east and heads toward the two large *stupa* by a small *gomba* at the town of **Bhandar** (7200 ft, 2194 m), which is called Changma by Sherpas. This walk takes **1 hour** and brings you into the area populated by Sherpas.

From the scattered village of Bhandar, descend the fertile plateau toward a notch to cross a river (6600 ft, 2012 m) on a covered bridge. Just beyond, take the fork to the far left. Then go on through forests and terraces to cross the Surma Khola (5100 ft, 1555 m) to its north (left) bank. Continue to the Likhu Khola and cross it on the second suspension bridge (5060 ft, 1543 m) to its east (left) bank. It takes **2 hours** to reach the river from Bhandar, then less than **1 hour** walking upstream along its east (left) bank through broad-leaved forest to reach the Kenja Khola, which is crossed to **Kenja** (5360 ft, 1634 m).

The biggest climb of the journey so far, up to the Lamjura Pass (11,580 ft, 3530 m), begins behind the town and follows a ridge more or less on its south side through oak forest to the small settlement of **Sete** (8450 ft, 2575 m), which has a small *gomba* above it. Be sure to obtain water from the streams crossing the trail below Sete, as there is little until you have descended the other side of the pass. It takes **2¼ to 3 hours** to reach Sete from Kenja. Be-yond, the trail continues along the ridge in a prickly-leaved oak forest. Reach the few houses of Dakchu (9350 ft, 2850 m) 1 hour beyond. A recently in-stalled water-supply system may be functioning here. Goyun (10,350 ft, 3155 m) is a small cluster of tea shops 1 hour beyond. The trail passes through im-pressive stands of fir. The ridge you have been following meets the main ridge striking north–south, and you fork left at a *mani* wall (11,300 ft, 3444 m).

Contour in a splendid rhododendron grove to reach the pass. There are now tea shops and lodges along the way to the pass. During the monsoon, people use makeshift shelters along the way to churn milk into butter or *ghiu*. The pass (11,582 ft, 3530 m) is **3 to 4 hours** from Sete. Despite the height of the pass, there is no view of the mountains, but those with time and energy can climb the peak north of the pass (13,159 ft, 4010 m) for views in good weather.

From the Lamjura Pass, the trail descends through a fir-and-rhododendron forest and emerges at **Tragdobuk,** also called Taktor (9380 ft, 2860 m), in **1½ hours.** Continue on the north side of the valley, round a notch, and drop down to the town of **Junbesi** (8775 ft, 2675 m) in 1 hour. The Serlo Monastery above the village is quite active. The monks print ancient Buddhist texts from woodblocks.

About 1½ hours off the main trail to the north of Junbesi lies Thubten Chholing Gomba, an active monastery with 150 monks. The abbot there, Tulshig Rimpoche, was formerly at the Rongbuk Monastery on the northern slopes of Mount Everest in Tibet. It is a rare privilege to have an audience with him. The small *gomba* is exquisitely painted and definitely worth seeing. To reach it, head north from Junbesi past some *chorten* and *mani* walls to a bridge (9000 ft, 2743 m) over the main Junbesi Khola, 30 minutes from town. Continue up the east (left) bank until you spot the monastery on a shelf above you to the east. Follow the main trail past fine Sherpa homes until you are just about under the *gomba* and head directly up to it. The town of Mobung is nearby. The *gomba* is 1 to 1½ hours from Junbesi. *Rhythms of a Himalayan Village* is a most informative book about this area.

From Junbesi you can also head south to the major Solu towns of Salleri and Phaphlu and to a Tibetan resettlement center at Chialsa. This area is described later in this chapter. The *Shorong/Hinku* map of the Research Scheme Nepal Himalaya covers the trek from here to Namche Bazaar.

To continue to Namche Bazaar from Junbesi, cross the Junbesi Khola on a bridge below the *stupa* (8700 ft, 2552 m) and take the extreme left or upper trail up the valley to the south. The trail passes through blue pine forest to rhododendron-and-prickly-leaved oak forest typical of the western midland forest described in chapter 12. Such forests are often found on south-facing slopes in this region. After reaching open country, round the crest (10,000 ft, 3048 m) of the Sallung ridge, from which you can see Mount Everest on a clear day! Head north up the valley of the Ringmo Khola to the town of Sallung (9700 ft, 2953 m), about **2 hours** from Junbesi.

From here, the trail descends through oak forests to cross two tributaries, then the main river of the Ringmo Khola (8525 ft, 2599 m). The trail then ascends to the few houses of **Ringmo** (9200 ft, 2805 m), **1½ hours** from Sallung. Here, enterprising Sherpas may serve you apple juice. En route, the trail branches after crossing the river. The right branch heads south to Phaphlu. This region is described later. From Ringmo, the wide trail ascends east through juniper woods past some rectangular *mani* walls to Tragsindho La pass

(10,075 ft, 3071 m) with *chorten, mani* walls, prayer flags, and hotels. To the south, 450 ft (137 m) below, there is a cheese factory on the west side of the river. You probably will have seen signs pointing the way there. To the east is the valley of the Dudh Kosi, which you will follow north to Khumbu. Meanwhile, 460 ft (140 m) below you is Tragsindho Monastery. To reach it, take the left branch of the trail at the junction 100 ft (30 m) below the pass on the east side. The other trail passes above the monastery and rejoins the monastery trail 100 ft (30 m) below the *gomba.* It takes **45 minutes** to reach the pass from Ringmo and another **15 minutes** to reach the Gelugpa monastery, which is considerably enlarged and much more active than during my first visit in 1969.

From Tragsindho, the trail forks right, descends to the southeast, passes through forests, and emerges at the Sherpa village of **Manidingma** (Nuntale) (7200 ft, 2194 m) in **1½ hours.** Beyond, descend past terraces into oak forests to emerge at a bridge over the Dudh Kosi (4900 ft, 1493 m) **1½ hours** from Manidingma.

The trail crosses the river to the east (left) bank and heads north to reach Namche Bazaar in three days. Sometimes the trail is over a mile above the river, which falls through a steep gorge. This part of Solu-Khumbu is called Pharak. There have been many improvements in agriculture in Pharak over the years. You may notice fruit trees and many varieties of vegetables. The main trail north of here is being continuously improved and may vary from the descriptions in this book. Ask locally for the latest routes.

Follow the river for a while through forests, then climb through terraces to reach the *Rai* village of **Jubing** (5500 ft, 1676 m) in **40 minutes.** This is your only opportunity along this trek to see a settlement of these people who populate so much of eastern Nepal. The British found the *Rai* to be excellent soldiers and actively recruited them as Gurkhas. Climb through the village, round a ridge, and aim for the prominent notch in front of you. From the notch (6900 ft, 2103 m), contour to the village of **Karikhola** (6575 ft, 2004 m) inhabited by Sherpas, *Rai,* and *Magar.* Karikhola is **1½ hours** from Jubing. The *Magar* hail from western Nepal, settling here generations ago. They no longer speak their native language.

Cross the bridge over the Kari Khola, take the right fork, and ascend its north (right) bank through the scattered settlement of Kharte. The trail continues to climb through this tributary valley into prickly-leaved oak-and-rhododendron forest, where langur monkeys may be occasionally seen. Traditionally, the route ascended to the ridge crest, Khari La (10,100 ft, 3078 m), which was **3 hours** from Karikhola. At this point, you were almost a mile above the Dudh Kosi. Unlike the gorge of the Kali Gandaki, in central Nepal, you passed well above the steep slopes.

The next tributary valley to the north has to be traversed. Descend 1000 ft (305 m) and cross the tributary after **1 hour.** Continue on the north side of the valley to reach **Poiyan** (9175 ft, 2796 m) in **30 minutes.** Again, continue to the crest of a ridge, Chutok La (9662 ft, 2945 m), leading down to the Dudh Kosi and again enter the valley of another tributary. Shortly after beginning a steep descent, you can see the buildings and STOL landing strip at Lukla, almost due north, as well as the sacred mountain Khumbiyula at the head of the valley.

The village of **Surkhe** (7525 ft, 2293 m) at the bridge crossing the tributary below is **2 hours** from Poiyan.

The trail now leaves this tributary valley and heads more directly north toward the town of Chaumrikharka, another scattered village. Along the way, pass the fork to Lukla (7850 ft, 2393 m), 30 minutes beyond Surkhe. This junction is reached just before the main trail crosses a stream on a small cantilever bridge. The STOL field (9350 ft, 2850 m) is 1 hour from here. Before ascending to **Chaumrikharka** (8500 ft, 2591 m, to 8900 ft, 2713 m) the main trail crosses a spectacular deep gorge with a high waterfall (7900 ft, 2408 m). Upper Chaumrikharka (8700 ft, 2652 m), with three large slopes and a *gomba*, is **1¾ hours** from Surkhe. From here on, the going is easier; the major climbs are over. The trail from Chaumrikharka (which means "pastures for yak-cow cross-breeds") passes through pleasant fields and ascends to a small ridge (8775 ft, 2674 m), where the trail to the north from Lukla joins the main trail up the Dudh Kosi valley at **Choplung,** a recently built town **30 minutes** from Chaumrikharka.

Lukla (9350 ft, 2860 m) has become a major trekking center over the years. The name Lukla means "place with many goats and sheep," but clearly things have changed! In addition to the airstrip nestled among spectacular mountains, there are now many hotels featuring food and accommodations varying from slightly more expensive than the cheapest in nearby places to quite luxurious and, of course, expensive. Many trekkers try to fly into Lukla, tour Khumbu, and fly out. There never seem to be enough flights out of Lukla to prevent bottlenecks, and bad weather can cause delays of several days or even a week or more. If planning to fly out, whether or not you have a "confirmed" seat, try to find the RNAC agent, and get on the list. Sometimes several hundred trekkers of many nationalities may find themselves stranded at Lukla. Many of them have come to Nepal to escape the pressures of their jobs and homes. Yet when they find themselves missing flights to Kathmandu to return to their jobs and homes, they can become very difficult to contend with. Patience wears thin and tempers flare. Although it may be comical to those who remain calm, such displays project an unfortunate image of the visitors to the rather relaxed natives.

These problems can be prevented by avoiding Lukla as a point of pickup by air. Shyangboche, farther north, is certainly no better, for there are no scheduled flights. However, Phaphlu, an airstrip perhaps two days farther from Khumbu, has fewer logistical problems, and the prosperous area of Solu visited en route is quite pleasant. The airstrip at Phaphlu has been enlarged to enable Twin Otter aircraft to land. Walking out toward Jiri is time-consuming, but especially worthwhile if you have never traveled this route before. Walking out to the south is another possibility. Flights back to Kathmandu can be arranged from the STOL strips at Lamidanda and Rumjatar, two towns near the route. You can also continue south to the Tarai and either link up with the East–West Highway and go to Kathmandu, or fly from major towns, such as Janakpur. Or you could go southeast to Dharan or Ilam. (This route is described in chapter 9.) Finally, you could walk out of Khumbu by crossing the high and potentially dangerous Trashi Labsta, a pass to the west of Thami, and return to Kathmandu via Rolwaling. Only well-equipped parties of experienced mountaineers should attempt this route.

To proceed from Lukla to Khumbu, head north and join the main trail at **Choplung**. (All trekkers heading to Khumbu, whether on foot from Kathmandu, or by plane, will end up at Choplung.) To proceed from there, head north, crossing another tributary (8850 ft, 2698 m) with a beautiful peak at its head and a lodge at the bridge. Soon, come to a bridge over the Dudh Kosi, with the village of Ghat (8350 ft, 2545 m) on both banks. There are hotels here. Proceed on the east (left) bank through to **Phakding** (8700 ft, 2652 m), now expanded to both sides of the river. Phakding is **1½ hours** from Choplung and 2½ hours from Lukla. Here, cross to the west (right) bank (8600 ft, 2621 m) of the Dudh Kosi. Continue through blue pine-and-rhododendron forests to the village of **Benkar** (8875 ft, 2905 m), which is reached in 1 hour from Phakding. Watch for large, hanging, tonguelike beehives just beyond a waterfall on the east (left) bank cliffs opposite you in this steep-walled canyon. In a short while, cross to the east (left) bank and climb up through Chumowa. Here you may notice extensive vegetable farms as well as a Japanese hotel. The vegetables grown here are excellent. Cross another tributary, the Kyangshar Khola (9100 ft, 2773 m), before climbing up a cleft in the canyon wall to **Mondzo** (9300 ft, 2835 m) about **45 minutes** from Benkar. Enter Sagarmatha (Everest) National Park here and pay the entrance fee. The trail then descends in a cleft to the left of a huge rock and crosses to the west (right) bank of the Dudh Kosi on a large suspension bridge to reach **Jorsale** (9100 ft, 2774 m) in **45 minutes.** Although this is the last village before Namche Bazaar, there are now tea shops and lodges scattered on the way to Namche. You can see the route on the *Khumbu Himal* map of the Research Scheme Nepal Himalaya. Jorsale is called Thumbug on this map.

Continue up the west bank through blue pine forests to a new bridge that crosses again to the east (left) bank. This area has had the bridges rebuilt several times because of large floods, most recently in 1985. I expect there will be more changes in the future, and that you will have no difficulty finding the way. The latest trail proceeds above the confluence of the Bhote Kosi from the west and the Dudh Kosi from the east, to cross the east fork to its west (right) bank. The climb to Namche Bazaar begins. Some 500 ft (152 m) up the crest of the prow, Everest can be seen behind the Lhotse–Nuptse ridge. Water has even been piped to this point, and beyond there is a tea shop. At some point, this route will change, because another bridge will be constructed over the Dudh Kosi to take a less steep route. **Namche Bazaar** (11,300 ft, 3446 m) is **2 or 2½ hours** from Jorsale. You are now in Khumbu. Sherpas run the stores, hotels, and restaurants. Prices are high but most staples are available. Old expedition food and equipment are available in the shops. The headquarters of Sagarmatha National Park is in Namche, with an excellent museum on the hill to the east. General regulations of the national parks are discussed in chapter 3. You and your party must carry and use only nonwood fuel during your stay in the park.

Namche Bazaar is a remarkable town. In the autumn of 1983, a small hydroelectric generating station built on the stream flowing out of town began producing electricity for lighting and a few other services. Lights are turned off at 10:00 P.M. currently. As the administrative center for Khumbu, Namche Bazaar has many officials and offices, including a police check post. Many of the officials are lowlanders who would rather be elsewhere, though they do enjoy the good things about Namche Bazaar—the clean air, good water, and impressive views. Namche Bazaar used to be a trading center, where grain from the south was exchanged for salt from Tibet, and it remains a trading center even though the salt trade has ended. The weekly market, held on Saturday, is colorful and well worth seeing, and there are a lot of interesting shops. Enterprising Sherpas have set up hotels with hot showers and a variety of foods. It is a good place to rejuvenate after the rigors of the heights. If you find Namche too commercial, stay in Kunde or Khumjung. But spend at least one night in Namche to become acclimated.

Khumbu
(Map No. 5, Page 233)

To arrive by foot in Sherpa country is to gain some insight into what it was like for the Israelites to reach the promised land.
Mike Thompson,
anthropologist and climber

You should not regard Namche Bazaar or Tengboche as the turnaround point on the trek. There are enough things to do in Khumbu to occupy two or three weeks. Four main river valleys can be explored, each with spectacular mountain scenery. You can visit two monasteries and at least three village *gomba*. And perhaps most appealing are the Sherpa people and their culture. If you have employed a Sherpa whose home is in Khumbu, you will most likely be given the hospitality of his home. Those fortunate enough to be in Khumbu during the full moon in May or November–December may see *Mani-rimdu,* the Sherpa drama festival depicting the victory of Buddhism over Bon. The May production is usually at the Thami Monastery and the November–December one at the Tengboche Monastery. Several of the trips possible in Khumbu are described here.

TO EVEREST BASE CAMP

From Namche Bazaar the trail rises to the saddle to the east, where the Sagarmatha National Park museum (11,550 ft, 3520 m) sits. You could head northwest to Shyangboche from here. Instead, contour high above the Dudh Kosi until, by some large boulders (11,800 ft, 3597 m), this trail joins the one from Khumjung. The trail continues through forests of blue pine and rhododendron, passing below the village of Trashinga and through the houses of Levishasa and the forest nursery to the Dudh Kosi (10,650 ft, 3247 m), where there is a small settlement called **Pungo Tenga,** with several mills, a series of water-driven prayer wheels, and some hotels, on the far left bank. It is **2 hours** from Namche Bazaar. The trail climbs past the prayer wheels through very pleasant forest, with occasional impressive views of Kangtega, to **Tengboche** (12,887 ft, 3867 m), about **2 hours** from the river. The portion from Namche to Tengboche is approximately 12 mi (19 km). The forest of pine, fir, black juniper, and rhododendron en route is remarkable. Early in the morning or late in the afternoon, if you are quiet, you may be able to spot a musk deer along here. Across the valley to the south, there are silver birch forests, which grow well on the colder north slopes.

Look for blood pheasants feeding near Tengboche in the morning. As from so many places in Khumbu, the views from Tengboche are spectacular. What a place for a monastery! It was founded in 1916, and the building completed three years later, but the main temple was destroyed in the 1934 earthquake. The monastery was electrified in 1988, and on January 12, 1989, the *gomba* burned to the ground. It has been rebuilt with foreign and local funding. The monks follow the Nyingmapa sect of Buddhism. Sometimes respects can be paid to the venerable abbot. When visiting the abbot, be sure to offer him a ceremonial scarf or *kata* obtained from another monk. A donation from each visitor is appreciated. The abbot has built a Sherpa cultural center. There are several choices for food and lodging. The park maintains guest houses for trekkers and also latrines or *chaarpi*.

From Tengboche the trail heads east and descends slightly past the nunnery at Deboche (12,325 ft, 3757 m) and the few houses at Milingo, all the while in a fine forest of rhododendrons that are spectacular in bloom. Where you have a choice, take the lower trail. These trees are festooned with moss lower down. Pass immense trunks of juniper, which bespeak the extensive forests that once existed here. Continue to the river, the Imja Khola, and cross it at a narrowing on a suspension bridge (12,400 ft, 3780 m), from which you get a spectacular view of Ama Dablang. This is 35 minutes from Tengboche. Some 5 or 10 minutes beyond, near some *mani* stones, the trail forks. The left (higher) fork ascends to the Pangboche Gomba (13,075 ft, 3985 m), and upper Pangboche, while the right goes directly to the village of lower **Pangboche** (12,800 ft, 3901 m) some **1½ hours** and 3 mi (4.8 km) from Tengboche. The *gomba,* the oldest in Khumbu, was built some 300 years ago at the time that Buddhism is said to have been introduced into Khumbu. According to legend, a venerable old lama tore out his hair and cast it around the *gomba*. The large black juniper trees surrounding it sprouted from those hairs. They are so large because it is forbidden to cut them. The *gomba* contains some yeti relics—a scalp and some bones—which you can see for a few rupees. Residents here are especially sensitive to intrusions by camera-wielding trekkers.

Continue northeast from either the village itself or from the *gomba,* and reach a trail fork at a *mani* wall (13,725 ft, 4183 m) **1½ hours** beyond Pangboche. The right fork goes toward Dingboche, while the left, slightly less prominent fork climbs past one hut to the crest of a small ridge (14,050 ft, 4282 m), from which Pheriche can be seen. Descend a short distance to the bridge over the Khumbu Khola (13,875 ft, 4229 m) and cross it to the west (left) bank to reach **Pheriche** (13,950 ft, 4252 m) in some **2 or 3 hours** and 3 mi (4.8 km) from Pangboche, depending on acclimatization.

Pheriche, once a *yersa* or temporary yak-herding area, is now settled

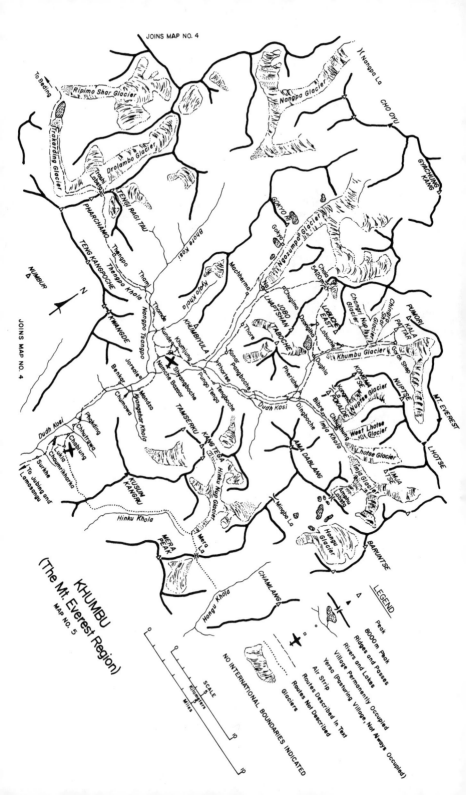

Cresting the ridge above Dughla, with Ama Dablang wrapped in clouds

throughout the winter—entirely because of the trekking traffic. It is a very different place from the one I encountered on my first visit in 1969. There are hotels built from blocks of sod, a garbage dump, and some latrines. Pheriche is usually crowded with people, although solitude can be found nearby. There is a Trekker's Aid Post, which was set up by the Himalayan Rescue Association in 1973. The post does research on altitude illness as well as providing medical care to trekkers and porters. A pressure chamber is being used here to treat altitude illness. Of course, it is even better to prevent it by slow acclimatization. Every party should spend two nights, or at least a complete day and night, at Pheriche. During the day spent here, an ascent or hike is an especially good idea. You could spend this day going to Dingboche and farther east up the Imja Khola, as described later. Or you could climb the ridge to the northeast to as high as 17,000 ft (5030 m) for views of Makalu to the east and of nearby summits. There is a hermitage on the way. You could also recross the Khumbu Khola and climb up on the shoulders of Taboche to the west. Or simply do the next day's walk, but return to Pheriche for the night. If you are already bothered by the altitude, it may be best to walk along the valley floor or just rest! Check the section on altitude illness in chapter 5.

To go on to the foot of Everest, continue north from Pheriche along the flats past the *yersa* of Phuling Karpo, then turn northeast up a grassy lateral moraine of the Khumbu Glacier. If coming from Dingboche, there is a high route that doesn't descend to Pheriche, as mentioned later. The route crosses its crest, descends to cross a glacial stream emerging from the snout of the glacier, which is covered by the moraine (15,025 ft, 4579 m), and ascends to the lodges at **Dughla** (15,075 ft, 4593 m). It takes **1½ hours** to reach Dughla from Pheriche, a distance of 3 mi (4.8 km). Climb to pass to the right of stone memorials on a ridge crest. These are built for climbers killed on expeditions to nearby summits, mostly Everest. There were none here when I first walked up this valley in 1969! The trail then contours on the west side of the glacier. After crossing another stream of meltwater, the trail heads northeast to the tea shops of **Lobuche** (16,175 ft, 4930 m), situated below the terminal moraine of a tributary glacier. Lobuche is about **1½ hours** and a little over 2 mi (3.2 km) from Dughla. A climb to the ridge crest to the west provides fine views, especially at sunset.

There is shelter beyond Lobuche. Several stone huts at Gorak Shep cater to trekkers in the autumn and spring. It is possible to use Lobuche as a base to climb to Kala Pattar for views and to return the same day. This is advisable to avoid altitude problems.

To the southeast of Lobuche lies a pass, the Kongma La (18,135 ft, 5527 m). A good side trip is to cross the Khumbu Glacier, ascend the pass, and head south to Bibre as described later. This trip takes a very long, strenuous day, and requires confidence on rock. Pokalde Peak, south of the pass, could also be climbed.

Beyond Lobuche the trail follows a trough beside the Khumbu Glacier, then climbs through the terminal moraine of another tributary glacier. From a high point here the rubble-covered hill of Kala Pattar, in front of Pumori, can be seen, and at its base, a lake that is often frozen. Those planning to go to Gorak Shep, at the northeast end of the lake, should descend to the sands and contour the lake on its northeast shore to the rock monuments to persons who have died nearby. **Gorak Shep** (17,000 ft, 5184 m) is reached in **2½ to 3 hours** and 3 mi (4.8 km) from Lobuche. You can no doubt see Tibetan snow cocks here and approach them quite closely. Gorak Shep is the starting point for the world's highest marathon race, the Everest Marathon, which has been run in 1987, and in 1989 to Namche Bazaar. Data from it has allowed me to quote trail mileage figures.

The cairn of upper **Kala Pattar** (18,450 ft, 5623 m), to the north of the rounded hill that is the surveyed point of Kala Pattar, can be reached in **1½ hours** from Gorak Shep by ascending directly and keeping slightly to the northeast. You can see the South Col of Everest from here, as well as the immense west and south faces. This is certainly one of the most majestic mountain viewpoints in the world. Alternatively, by proceeding from the terminal moraine, you can head directly up to Kala Pattar without going to Gorak Shep. It may be difficult to find the "trail" through the moraine, especially if there has been a recent snowfall. Trail sense is an asset, though small cairns mark the way.

The world's highest mountain was named after Sir George Everest, the head of the Survey of India from 1823 to 1843. Sherpas use its Tibetan name, Chomolongma, which means "Goddess of the Wind." Sagarmatha, its Nepali name, means "The Forehead of the Sky" or "Churning Stick of the Ocean of Existence," from a Sanskrit interpretation. It was first climbed in 1953 by Sir Edmund Hillary and Tenzing Norgay.

The sites of the various base camps used for climbing Everest are close to the foot of the Khumbu Icefall (17,575 ft, 5357 m) and can be reached from Gorak Shep in a few hours by venturing over the rubble-covered surface of the Khumbu Glacier. Many trekkers find the serac formations along the glacier a fascinating change from the majestic mountain walls. As you approach the first evidence of base camp garbage, note that recent base camps are 1 hour or so beyond, right at the foot of the Khumbu Icefall. If you are here when no expedition is climbing Everest, it may be tedious and time-consuming to find the exact location. Even if there is an expedition there and you are not following a supply team, it is easy to get lost and wander about. It is possible to visit the base camps from Lobuche and return the same long day if you are well acclimatized.

Better views of the Khumbu Icefall and the other side of the Lhotse–Nuptse Wall can be obtained by climbing up the southeast ridge of Pumori. This ridge is reached by going partway to the base camps and turning northwest. Do not go out on the Khumbu Glacier to reach the ridge; stay on the lateral moraine. You will be able to see the North Col of Everest before encountering technical difficulties. Lhotse can also be seen. The view of the massive hulk of Everest is not as good from here as from Kala Pattar. Gorak Shep is the best base for this trip.

You can vary your return trip in several ways. Crossing the Chugima Pass offers one route. You can also take a trail on the left side of the Imja Khola, crossing it below where the Khumbu (or Pheriche) Khola enters. Cross back

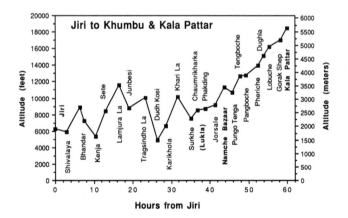

before Pangboche, or continue on the south side to meet the trail to Tengboche.

The times given for the journey beyond Namche Bazaar are quite variable. They depend upon the weather conditions as well as the fitness and acclimatization of the party. Allow at least five days to reach Kala Pattar from Tengboche. Hire local porters to carry your loads since they can handle the altitude much better than you. If you are going to high altitudes, be prepared for cold winds and snow. It is most important to heed the warning signs of altitude sickness described in chapter 5. Many trekkers have died in this region because they did not do so.

UP THE IMJA KHOLA

There are several ways to reach Dingboche, depending on where you happen to be. If coming from Pangboche, and heading directly to Dingboche, it is best to avoid going to Pheriche, which is generally cold and windy.

At the trail junction by the confluence of the Khumbu and Imja Kholas, about 1½ hours from Pangboche, take the right-hand branch (the left goes to Pheriche as described above). Descend and cross the Khumbu Khola, then climb above the Imja Khola to reach old moraine terraces. Continue heading east into the Imja valley, climbing gently to reach the outer fields of Dingboche. Follow the stone-walled path through the fields to reach lodges on the far side of the village in about 2 to 3 hours from Pangboche.

Reach Dingboche as described above or climb up and over the ridge (14,250 ft, 4343 m) behind Pheriche and descend to it in 30 minutes. You can also take a shortcut from Lobuche by crossing the stream that emanates from the snout of the Khumbu Glacier and climbing up the lateral moraine. Then follow a trail that contours to the south, passing the small temporary village of Dusa before dropping down to Dingboche. This third possibility is the quickest route from Lobuche.

From a little west of Dingboche you can climb up to Nangkartshang Gomba (15,430 ft, 4703 m) in 1½ hours for fine views of Makalu to the east.

Sharing a picture book with a Sherpa family in Khumjung

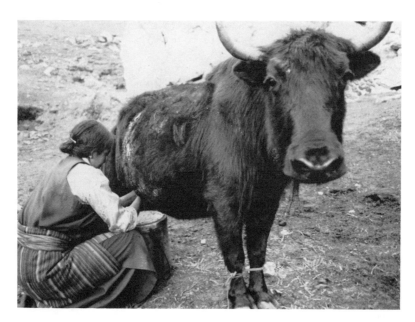

Milking a nak *(female yak) at Lobuche*

This is a detour if you are going to Chhukhung, but you could then head east to join the trail coming from Dingboche at Bibre (15,000 ft, 4571 m). Bibre is reached in 1½ hours from Dingboche by the direct route. The trail continues east, crossing numerous streams that flow from the Nuptse and Lhotse Glaciers, to a number of yak huts or *yersa* at Chhukhung (15,535 ft, 4734 m) perhaps 1½ hours after Bibre.

You can now see Ama Dablang's east face. It is worthwhile to spend a day or two traveling around to the east and to the northeast for close views of the incredible Lhotse–Nuptse Wall. The *Khumbu Himal* map is very useful here and suggests many hikes. Imja Tse (Island Peak), a trekking summit, is northeast of Chhukhung.

KHUMJUNG AND KUNDE

The STOL strip called Shyangboche (12,205 ft, 3720 m) is carved out of a shelf of land. Reach it less than 1 hour from Namche Bazaar, taking the trail that climbs past the *gomba*. The government yak-breeding farm 5 to 10 minutes to the northwest is recognized by an impressive fence enclosing it. Often the yaks and *naks* (females) may be pastured much higher. The farm is attempting to preserve and maintain good genetic stocks necessary for the crossbreeding programs in which hearty *chAUmri* (cross between cow and yak) are developed. You can proceed past the preserve to the northwest, climbing to a crest (12,700 ft, 3871 m) in peaceful juniper forests and descending to Kunde (12,600 ft, 3841 m) 30 minutes from Shyangboche. The north end of this town is the site of Kunde Hospital, built by the Himalayan Trust established by Sir Edmund Hillary.

To reach Khumjung, the "sister city" of Kunde, you can either traverse east from Kunde, or go directly from Shyangboche by climbing northeast from the airstrip past a large *chorten* in a blue pine forest. Descend past the Himalayan Trust school to the potato fields below Khumjung (12,400 ft, 3780 m). A village *gomba* in a juniper grove to the north contains yeti relics that can be seen for a donation. The yeti scalp was sent around the world in 1960 to test its authenticity. The famed Sherpa artist Kappa Pasang lives in Khumjung.

Of final interest is the Everest View Hotel, beautifully situated on a shelf (12,700 ft, 3870 m). To visit this place, there is a trail from the lower end of the airstrip, but the main trail is the one leading southeast from the large *chorten* above the top end of the airstrip. It climbs gently across the hillside above the side of the airstrip to reach the ridge crest, then turns sharply north above the Dudh Kosi and traverses under the ridge crest to reach the hotel. The trail from the lower end of the airstrip joins this main trail at the ridge crest. Or you can reach it from the *stupa* at the eastern end of the potato fields of Khumjung. It has been recently reopened after a decade of major problems, including weather, transportation, water, and energy sources, not to mention the hazards of rapid ascent to altitude from Kathmandu by plane!

Much has changed in this area since my first visit. Immediately noticeable are the new houses with Western-style windows, corrugated tin roofs, and chimneys. People are much more cautious with their use of firewood since it is so time-consuming to search for it. Families have a greater variety of Western goods. Mountaineering equipment and clothes are often used rather than the traditional items. Indeed, the school bell at Khumjung is an old oxygen cylinder. Wealth is more often measured in terms of equipment and money rather than traditionally in the size of yak and sheep herds. Of course the general level of education is quite good, and there are many Sherpas who are fluent in English. Many Sherpa families now prefer to live in Kathmandu and can afford to send their children to private schools there. The economic pressures of tourism have turned potato fields into lodges below Khumjung. And it is not uncommon to find widows caring for children and looking after homes. Mountaineering expeditions take their toll and the Sherpas as an ethnic group were never large in number. It was traditional for a family to send the youngest child to the monastery, but now such practices are less common. Some of the changes are for the good, and some are questionable. No matter how we perceive it, the Sherpas feel their lot is better now.

TO GOKYO

The trip up the Dudh Kosi from Khumjung takes you to summer yak-grazing country, to beautiful small lakes, and to the foot of Cho Oyu and Gyachung Kang peaks. The trail goes northeast of the *stupa* at the east end of Khumjung and climbs along the side of Khumbiyula, crossing a rocky prominence to a crest of a ridge (13,000 ft, 3992 m), where there is a *stupa,* some lodges, and a fantastic view. This takes **2 hours** from Khumjung. Above you, on the slopes of Khumbiyula, watch for a herd of Himalayan tahr (called *goral*

At a puja *in a village* gomba

by locals). Phortse is across the river. The trail descends steeply to near the river (11,950 ft, 3643 m), where there is a tea shop. Take the left fork at junctions, as those to the right descend and cross the river to Phortse. The trail heads north and, after an hour or so, Cho Oyu is visible. You cross many spectacular waterfalls that are frozen in winter. Many landslides have occurred on both sides of this steep valley. After emerging from the woods, the trail passes several summer yak herding huts, or *yersa,* including Tongba (13,175 ft, 4015 m), Gyele, and **Dole** (13,400 ft, 4084 m) where there are now lodges. It takes **2¾ hours** from the *stupa* on the ridge crest to Gyele. The next *yersa* at Lhabarma is far from water, but it is available at the one after that, Luza. Because this valley has not developed traditional resting points, such as Pheriche on the way to the foot of Everest, people are ascending too rapidly. Serious altitude illness is occurring more often here, while the incidence on the way to Everest has declined. Be prudent and take the time to rest a day or two.

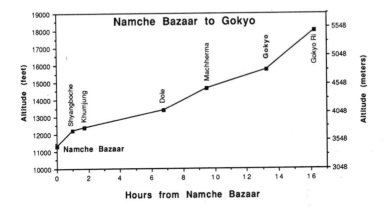

From Gyele, Lhabarma (14,200 ft, 4328 m) is reached in less than **1 hour** and Luza (14,400 ft, 4390 m) is another **hour.** In the next tributary valley is **Machherma** (14,650 ft, 4465 m), another **45 minutes** away; there are now lodges here. Go on for 1 hour to Pangka (14,925 ft, 4548 m), but here again, there is no water near. From Pangka, descend slightly, following one of the melted glacial rivers that flow down the west side of the Ngozumpa Glacier, which is to the east now. The trail crosses this river at a narrowing and soon emerges at the first of several small lakes (15,450 ft, 4709 m) **1½ hours** beyond Pangka. Another **45 minutes** brings you to the next lake, or *tsho,* with the *yersa* Longpanga at its northern end. There is no good shelter here, so continue for another **30 minutes** to the third lake (sometimes called Dudh Pokhari) and the *yersa* of **Gokyo** (15,720 ft, 4791 m) on its east shore.

From Gokyo, Cho Oyu looms to the north. There are several places to go for views. Currently the most popular is to ascend the ridge to the northwest to a small summit (17,990 ft, 5483 m). This climb takes 2 to 3 hours for those well acclimatized and provides an excellent panorama from Cho Oyu, to Everest, to Lhotse, and all the way to Makalu. Some trekkers consider the view from this Kala Pattar (or Gokyo Ri), as it is called, better than from the one above Gorak Shep. Alternatively, you can follow the trail north between the lateral moraine of the glacier and the hills to the west until you reach the next lake (16,150 ft, 4923 m) where, near its east shore, there are some roofless huts, about 1½ hours from Gokyo. A climb of a few hundred feet up the hill to the north of the lake provides fine views. You could also continue another 1½ hours to the last lake. The *Khumbu Himal* map may suggest many other hikes. You could return from Gokyo by following the east side of the valley, reaching it from below the snout of the glacier at Pangka. Or you could cross the glacier directly east of Gokyo. Alternatively, you could follow the route described below in reverse to reach the Khumbu Glacier and the foot of Everest.

PASS 5420 METERS (CHUGIMA)

For people who want to combine visits to the Everest Base Camp region with one to the upper reaches of the Dudh Kosi beneath Cho Oyu without extensive backtracking, this pass is a scenic and enjoyable route. It does involve a short glacier crossing, for which a rope and ice ax are advisable; however, there are no serious dangers or technical difficulties. In the process, you circumnavigate Jobo Lhaptshan (21,128 ft, 6440 m) and Taboche (20,869 ft, 6367 m) for excellent views of Cho Oyu to the north.

Be aware that fresh snowfall on the pass seriously increases the difficulty and the risk of frostbite. If you do not have enough experience to be sure that the new snow will not cause problems, consider skipping the pass. In the autumn of 1982, snowfall resulted in at least five trip-ending cases of frostbite, and some trekkers suffered permanent damage. At that time, renowned mountaineer Reinhold Messner assessed the conditions and elected to avoid the pass and go around via Phortse!

To descend from the Everest Base Camp area, follow the trail down below Lobuche some **15 to 30 minutes** as far as the stream crossing on the lateral moraine (16,000 ft, 4877 m), but instead of crossing it, contour along a trail on the side of the valley, eventually turning northwest into the valley of the pass. You can thus stay at a high elevation instead of descending to the shores of the lake below you (Tshola Tsho). Cross the main stream that feeds into the lake higher up. Pick the trail up again near the stream crossing if it has been lost. The trail ascends to the *yersa* of Dzonglha (15,869 ft, 4843 m), beautifully situated on a shelf of land with fine views in every direction. It is about **2½ hours** or more from Lobuche. This is a very good spot to camp, either in tents or in the huts. The feeling of sitting under the north face of Jobo Lhaptshan is unforgettable.

Alternatively, if approaching this area from the south, go to Dughla and follow the trail slightly below it before bearing west to the small trail that skirts the end of the Tshola Glacier moraine, which has almost blocked the valley and formed the Tshola Tsho (lake) above it. Reach the end of the lake (14,804 ft, 4512 m)—it is ice-covered in November—in **30 minutes.** The best camping spot for spectacular views is near here, but the only huts are some distance farther on. The trail follows the north shore of the lake and rises gradually until it reaches Tsholo Og (15,306 ft, 4665 m), a *yersa* of three huts, in **45 minutes.** All are unoccupied and locked in winter. Water must be carried from a stream **10 minutes** farther on. Dzonglha is another **hour** up the faint trail. Above this *yersa,* the trail is less distinct, and although there is no further shelter, there are signs of people using the pass.

Cross a small crest just above Dzonglha and descend slightly into the gentle valley coming down from the glacier in the pass to the northwest. The pass, sometimes called Chugima or Cho La by locals, is the 17,783 ft (5420 m) crossing marked on the Schneider *Khumbu Himal* map. There is a small trail aiming for the glacier-smoothed rock to the east of the glacier itself. The moraine at the head of the valley is reached in 1 hour from Dzonglha. Ascend to the right of the glacier, sometimes on loose rock, sometimes on large slabs with handsome grain, until you reach a small valley or moat between the rock and the glacier. Eventually, gain the glacier around 17,350 ft (5285 m). Keep to its south side and ascend steeply at first (30) on the snow-covered surface. Watch for crevasses. During the monsoon the surface may be bare ice and require crampons. The glacier levels out and the pass (17,783 ft, 5420 m) is reached in perhaps **2½ hours** from Dzonglha. A new valley and new vistas open up before you. From the pass there are no views of the giants, but an opportunity to appreciate the lesser, often more beautiful, mountains. Those with experience and equipment may want to scramble up the snow to the minor summit to the south.

The descent on the west side of the pass heads south, initially down steep, hard snow, then onto variegated talus. Beware of ice avalanches and loose rock from the hanging glacier on the peak marked "5686 m" on the Schneider map. Reach the valley floor, with its boulders and hummocks. If heading to Gokyo, you can bear west without losing much altitude, then descend to cross the Ngozumpa Glacier. If heading south, continue along the trail through the boulders and hummocks near the main stream in the rather flat valley. Near the end of the shelf there are caves by the stone fences of Chugimo (16,175 ft, 4930 m). They are suitable for shelter or camping. Reach them in **2 to 3 hours** from the pass. As you leave the flats, follow the trail on the north (left) side of the stream and reach Dragnag, a beautiful *yersa* (15,100 ft, 4602 m) within sight of the terminal moraine of the Ngozumpa Glacier in **45 minutes.** Cross the river on a rock bridge to the south (left) bank. The river may be concealed beneath it. Don't descend, but contour **15 minutes** to a *yersa* called Tsom (15,000 ft, 4572 m), labeled Gonglha on the *Khumbu Himal* map. Alternatively, you could descend from Dragnag to Na (14,435 ft, 4400 m), labeled Tsoshung on the map, which is below the tongue of the glacier. From here, you can join the route described earlier, on the west (right) bank of the Dudh Kosi, by crossing the stream west of Na and contouring gently up to the south to reach the shelf above the river in **30 minutes.** Before you proceed, note the view of the impressive south face of Cho Oyu to the north.

To head south to Phortse on the east side of the valley, continue contouring below Tsom, crossing a tributary to reach Thare (14,250 ft, 4343 m) in **45 minutes.** Another **30 minutes** of climbing brings you to Thore (14,435 ft, 4400 m), which is probably the spot marked Thare on the Schneider *Khumbu Himal* map. Names do get confusing in Khumbu, especially since names on the Schneider map are Tibetan for the most part, while the inhabitants are Sherpa, and the initial surveyors were Indian! Fortunately the route is completely straightforward. After a couple of tributaries, the *yersa* of Konar (13,425 ft, 4092 m), near another tributary, is reached in **1½ hours.** There is no permanent habitation along this valley before Phortse. All of the huts along the route are in excellent condition, and the area is very beautiful—perhaps there is a relationship to the paucity of trekkers.

Continue into a handsome juniper-and-birch forest to a tributary that is the source of the Phortse water supply. Continue through rhododendrons to upper

Phortse (12,140 ft, 3700 m), some **45 minutes** from Konar. Phortse is the impressively perched village you have probably seen from the south. It dominates the entrance to the valley you have descended. To leave Phortse, descend through the fine forest to the west to the Dudh Kosi (11,200 ft, 3414 m) in **30 minutes** and ascend to meet the trail from Khumjung to Gokyo, which has already been described, in another **30 minutes.**

TO THAMI

The trail to Thami begins at Namche Bazaar and heads west without going behind the *gomba,* as the other trail does. You can also take the trail heading west from Shyangboche before the descent to Namche Bazaar. The trail contours the Nangpo Tsangpo Valley, passing Phurte (11,400 ft, 3475 m), then crossing the main tributary from the north, the Kyajo Khola (11,200 ft, 3414 m), at the small town of Kyajo. Continue on to **Thamo** (11,300 ft, 3444 m) 1½ hours from Namche Bazaar or less from Shyangboche. To the north above the trail is the town of Mende, where there is a new monastery with an English-speaking *Rimpoche* (reincarnate abbot). Westerners sometimes study there. Proceed to **Thomde** (11,500 ft, 3505 m) where a miniature hydroelectric project is being planned to provide electricity to Khumbu. The trail continues to follow the river and crosses it (11,550 ft, 3520 m) some 45 minutes beyond Thamo to ascend on its south (right) bank. Pass through pleasant forests and reach the Thengpo Khola, flowing east from the Trashi Labsta Pass. Cross it to the north (left) bank (12,075 ft, 3880 m) and ascend a small hill to the north to the valley flats and the town of **Thami** (12,400 ft, 3780 m) 1 hour from Thomde. There is a small hill just to the north of Thami, beyond which you are not permitted to go. To the north up the main riverbed lies the Nangpa La (18,753 ft, 5716 m), an important pass into Tibet that was once the popular trading route. To the west of Thami, where the hill behind the town terminates at the base of a cliff, is a monastery (12,925 ft, 3940 m) worth visiting. Farther to the east at the head of the valley is the Trashi Labsta, a high pass (18,885 ft, 5755 m) leading west to the Rolwaling Valley. It is described in chapter 11.

Solu
(Map No. 4, Page 225)

Those with sufficient time should consider visiting the towns of southern Solu. This region is inhabited by Sherpas who have migrated south from Khumbu and settled where it is much easier to farm and live. They are generally wealthier than their northern counterparts, and signs of this wealth are readily apparent. Another attraction of this area is a successful Tibetan camp at Chialsa.

People who are heading to Khumbu, but who wish to detour to this region, must leave the regular route at Junbesi, while those returning to Kathmandu should turn off from Ringmo, or possibly from Phuleli.

From **Junbesi,** cross the bridge below the *stupa* and take the right fork of the level trail that follows above the northeast (left) bank of the Junbesi Khola.

In less than 30 minutes you come to **Khamje** (8525 ft, 2599 m). Continue along the river until it flows in the Dudhkunda Khola, also called the Solu Khola, and cross this river (7725 ft, 2355 m) to its east (left) bank. Head south, following close to the river for the most part, until a shack (7480 ft, 2250 m) is reached. The trail rises beyond the shack and soon joins the main north–south trail higher on the east bank, at a magnificent house with a private *gomba* (8100 ft, 2469 m) in **Phaphlu**. This walk takes about 2 hours from Khamje. The impressive forests are mostly prickly-leaved oak. A hospital has been built here by Sir Edmund Hillary. Head south for about 45 minutes to **Salleri** (7700 ft, 2347 m), the district center of Solu-Khumbu. Along the way, pass the Phaphlu airstrip (7775 ft, 2370 m). From a distance Salleri is reminiscent of a Wild West town. The name Salleri means "pine forest." Another 15 minutes to the south is **Dorphu** (7500 ft, 2256 m), where a colorful market is held every Saturday. To visit the Tibetan camp at **Chialsa,** follow the trail to the southeast from Dorphu for a little over 1 hour. It continues climbing above most of the houses to the camp (9000 ft, 2743 m). Be sure to visit the carpet-manufacturing center.

Another attraction of the area is **Chiwong Gomba** (9700 ft, 2953 m), a monastery spectacularly situated high on a cliff overlooking Phaphlu and Salleri. It can be reached by heading north from Chialsa for some 3 to 4 hours. Trekkers heading south from Ringmo can get to it more directly. It could also be reached from the bridge over the Dudhkunda, from which a trail heads directly up to join the main north–south trail on the east side of the valley at 8200 ft (2500 m). From here, head south and shortly take the fork to the left heading to Chiwong. The *gomba* is well described in *Buddhist Himalaya* (see appendix B). The *Mani-rimdu* dance/drama festival is staged here in the autumn.

To reach this area on your return from Khumbu, head south from **Ringmo.** The trail branches left from the one to Sallung at 9050 ft (2758 m), just below the town, and goes south on a wide path. After contouring through a forest, the trail passes through the attractive town of **Phera** (8300 ft, 2530 m) 1¾ hours from Ringmo. Beyond, take the left branch, since the right descends to the river and then to Junbesi. Continue on the main trail, passing the turnoff to the left to Chiwong Gomba and reaching **Phaphlu** in 2 hours. The rest of the route has been described. There is also a route heading directly over the ridge from Phuleli to Chialsa.

Sunset on Kumbakarna Himal (Jannu), from Gurja

9 Eastern Nepal

Eastern Nepal is characterized by different hill ethnic groups from those in the central and western regions, more development efforts in the hills, and perhaps a higher standard of living. Much of the difference is attributable to several factors. The east receives more rainfall generally, and this increases agricultural productivity; proximity to Darjeeling has always resulted in a greater awareness of the outside world; the Gurkhas, the soldiers recruited for service in the British army, traditionally came from four ethnic groups, two of which, the *Rai* and *Limbu,* are concentrated in this region. As a consequence, the eastern Tarai was the first segment to be developed; large cities first appeared here, and construction on the East–West Highway was begun in the east. Air links were also concentrated here. By contrast, the inhabitants of the mountains have tended to maintain their links with Tibet, and have shared in development to a lesser extent. Ethnically, these people are somewhat apart from the Sherpas around Khumbu, though they may often call themselves Sherpas.

For a trekker, this area is attractive because it is little visited by tourists, the rhododendron forests are perhaps the most spectacular in Nepal, and the mountain scenery offers new vistas. There are essentially none of the trekker lodges and inns that characterize the region north of Pokhara, as well as the way to Everest. Travelers here must be either self-sufficient or able to live in a modified Nepali style. The high mountain regions are pretty well uninhabited and so those venturing there must be entirely self-sufficient. There are no organized help or rescue facilities like those in Manang or in Khumbu.

Three trekking regions are described here. One focuses on Kangchenjunga, and the second is a different route to Khumbu, traversing from the eastern hills. The latter way can be used as an exit from Khumbu as well. Finally, a trek to Makalu Base Camp is described.

Kangchenjunga Base Camp
(Map No. 6, Page 249)

A circuit of sorts will be described, starting in Kathmandu, traveling by air to Tumlingtar, crossing the Milke Danda to the valley of the Tamur Khola to reach the Ghunsa Khola, the major river draining the northwest side of the Kangchenjunga Himal. This torrent is followed upstream to near its source, where the base camp is located on the north side of Kangchenjunga. Then after retracing your steps partway, back as far as Ghunsa, the route will take you to the south side of the massif, crossing a high pass. From there, you head south to reach Taplejung, the district center for the northeast corner of Nepal. In contrast to the outbound route, this one is primarily a high traverse that only occasionally follows roaring river bottoms. The return rejoins the major ridge, the Milke Danda, and follows it south to reach the road at Basantapur, where vehicles can take you to the Tarai. Options then include returning to Kathmandu by road, or flying from Biratnagar.

Such a trip will take at least three and a half weeks, though four to five weeks is preferable. It can be shortened by trying to fly in and out through Taplejung, but this may be difficult to arrange, and schedules and arrivals can be erratic. Such a course misses out on traveling through some fascinating middle hill country and the unforgettable long-distance views from the Milke Danda. Those wishing a more denture-rattling journey can take vehicles from Kathmandu to Basantapur on the road north of Dharan, or to somewhere north of Phidem on the road north of Ilam. Currently the former road is preferred, but the road north of Ilam will eventually reach Taplejung, and will probably double back to join the other road at Basantapur. More bone-jarring opportunities.

For those with less time, consider an itinerary that starts with a flight from Kathmandu to Taplejung, proceeds to the south side of Kangchenjunga, crosses the Mirgin La to visit the north side, and then descends to meet the road at Basantapur. At any rate, there are many possibilities for travel in this region.

Trekker lodges and tourist facilities have yet to be developed, and trekkers can get a permit for the Kangchenjunga Base Camp (the area beyond Taplejung) only by going through an approved trekking agency. You may be able to have such an agency get the permit for you and allow you to travel without many porters. You could live with Nepali people for the most part, but to get to the base camps, you must be self-sufficient. Of course, below this high mountain area, a special permit is not necessary and you can travel in any style you wish.

TUMLINGTAR TO GHUNSA

To begin, fly to **Tumlingtar** (1500 ft, 457 m), a broad, flat plateau on the left (east) bank of the Arun Khola. Further to the east, a landing strip is located on a convenient shelf of the valley of the Sabaaya Khola. There are hotels on the eastern side of the airstrip, and surprisingly, you see modern electric wires and sturdy metal poles. There is a hydroelectric project downstream, and the juice is routed north to the district center Sankusabha District at KhAADbari as well as to Chainpur, east from here. If stuck here waiting for a plane back to Kathmandu, you can wander over the main river, and perhaps take an army ferry boat across it. It can even be swum. If impatiently stuck here, you might consider walking south to Hille, and reaching the road to Basantapur. It takes a long day, and then a half-day trip to Dharan, hopefully to catch an overnight bus to Kathmandu. (Before heading east, stock up on oranges at the airstrip, as they become scarcer for a few days.)

From the airstrip, head south along the main trail, and pass many laden porters as they head north to the district center from Hille. When the road is completed up the Arun, the importance of this major route will diminish. Reach a few houses in **15 to 20 minutes,** the last habitation before a significant climb. Shortly beyond, take a left fork (the right goes to Hille), to descend a rocky gully from the plateau to the major valley of the Sabaaya Khola. Arrive at its junction with the HEwAg Khola, a lesser river from the northeast. You

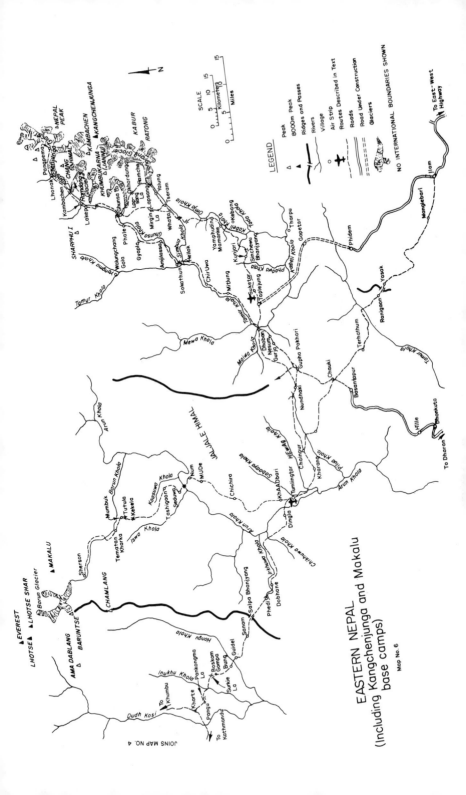

EASTERN NEPAL
(Including Kangchenjunga and Makalu base camps)

Map No. 6

JOINS MAP NO. 4

LEGEND

△ Peak
▲ 8000m Peak
━ Ridges and Passes
Rivers
○ Village
✈ Air Strip
━ ━ Routes Described in Text
Roads
══ Road Under Construction
Glaciers

NO INTERNATIONAL BOUNDARIES SHOWN

SCALE

0 5 10 15 Kilometers
0 5 10 15 Miles

N

arrive on the right bank after **10 minutes.** There is no bridge, so you have to either ford at an appropriate spot, or take a brief, exhilarating ferry ride across (1100 ft, 335 m), eventually ending up on the left bank of the HEwAg Khola, and crossing another tiny stream to its right bank. There is really only one main trail to find; it climbs up the hillside to the east.

Climb up through forest and then farmland, reaching a house, which is part of a scattered village, Gahate (2100 ft, 640 m), and soon some views of the Khumbu Himal to the northwest. Reach the ridge crest and a *bhaTTi* at Luwakot (3125 ft, 952 m) in 1¼ hours from the river ford below. Continue on up another ridge crest to the pleasant town of **Kharang** (4335 ft, 1321 m) reached in **2¼ hours** from the ford. Climb west along the ridge, reaching a fork in 30 minutes and taking either the left fork trail that climbs more, or the right fork that passes above some houses, enters a bamboo thicket, and soon gives you views of Chainpur in a pass ahead. As you descend a ridge crest toward this major city, you enter a new suburb, Katari Gaon (4375 ft, 1333 m), a little over **1 hour** from Kharang.

Another **20 minutes'** descent brings you to the field at the eastern end of **Chainpur** (4300 ft, 1311 m), a beautiful, ridge-crest *Newar* bazaar. Plan so as to have enough time to explore and savor this wonderful offspring of Kathmandu, where traditional craftsmen continue their brass work.

These artisans from the Shakya clan of the Kathmandu (their ancestors moved here eons ago) continue the centuries-old process of making the attractive small brass vessels Nepalis drink from and take to the fields. Here the wax-covered molds are carved on a hand-driven lathe, encased in a clay-dung coating, heated in an oven to extract the wax, then baked. When ready, molten brass is poured into the mold. After cooling, the molds are broken open to remove the vessel, which is finished on the hand-driven lathe. Complicated designs are made in separate parts, which are later joined together. The decorated patterns are made by a similar process, adding wax elements with the designs embossed into the wax mold. Later the artwork is completed with fine tools. The other major center for this craft in the east is in Bhojpur. It is sold by weight. Interestingly, the biggest consumers of this dying art are in the Kathmandu Valley, where the urban people have a taste for this fine craftsmanship. Elsewhere in Nepal, cheaply produced stainless steel, aluminum, and plastic ware, as well as discarded tin cans, have become commonplace. If you don't wish to buy examples of their work here and carry it with you, it is available in Kathmandu, at of course much higher prices.

Continue on by taking a right fork at a clearing in the center of town, before you encounter the brass workers, and keep near the ridge crest to pass south of a Buddhist temple at the high eastern end of the town ridge (4525 ft, 1379 m). The trail climbs the ridge, passes south of the houses of Okharbhote (or DAgigaon) **15 minutes** from town, and then enters broad-leaved forest, meeting a trail coming in from the left by a water faucet **35 minutes** from Okharbhote (5075 ft, 1546 m). **Fifteen minutes** beyond is the town of **Pokhari** (4950 ft, 1508 m), a few houses in a saddle on the ridge. Here you see the first *chorten*, bespeaking a former Buddhist presence. Follow the crest trail, pass above the few houses of Mayam, and follow the route on the north side of

The Sakya Newar *artisans at Chainpur work brass on a hand-driven lathe.*

the valley of the Pilua Khola, the river to the south. Tanglewa, a *bhaTTi* and a few houses (5150 ft 1570 m), is 1 hour beyond Pokhari. The scattered houses beyond belong to the village of **Chitlang,** and the trail wanders in and out of tributary valleys until you reach a suspension bridge over the Pilua Khola (4450 ft, 1356 m) **2½ hours** from Pokhari. Cross it to the left bank and pass by some stalls used for a market every Tuesday. A steep climb follows, to the scattered town of **Nundhaki** (5350 ft, 1631 m), a little over 30 minutes from the bridge. In Nundhaki, climb up in the valley above the YAUra Khola (you are on its right bank) and on the south side of the ridge. Reach the crest of this spur, and follow it to a school with a prominent field (6350 ft, 1935 m), some **45 minutes** above where you first come to the town. Along the way, you have probably noticed what appear to be coffins set on prominent parts of the hillsides. These are *Limbu* graves, with the dead interred in the stone-and-concrete structures. Various sizes suggest the ages of the deceased. Traditionally, there are four tiers of stones for a male, three for a female. The cement is inscribed with the name and age of the person.

There are two trails beyond to choose from. The more direct one climbs steeply to the northeast. It crosses the major ridge separating the Arun Khola valley from that of the Tamur Khola (to the east) at a place called the Milke Danda. (In fact, that is the name for the ridge crest along this portion, but is used locally to indicate the pass crossing.) The trail then descends to Dhoban, on the Tamur below Taplejung. The other trail, less used by locals, ascends more easterly to reach the ridge crest at an idyllic lake setting called Gupha Pokhari. Both have views; the latter takes longer, but offers a convenient place to break the journey at the ridge crest, since there is a recent settlement with hotels at the lake. The views, however, are better the farther south you are, since Jannu appears more separated from the Kangchenjunga massif, and Everest peers out from behind Lhotse Shar. Indeed, this subsidiary summit hides the earth's high point when you are up this close, but still at a relatively low altitude in comparison to the Himalaya. The main trail north from the current road head at Basantapur follows the ridge crest to Gupha Pokhari, and then descends to Dhoban. From Gupha, you could walk the ridge crest north as well, to join the other trail from Nundhaki and avoid the major trade trail from the road. No matter which trail you choose, the distant views from the ridge of Everest, Makalu, Kangchenjunga, and the lesser peaks are outstanding.

The route from Nundhaki to Gupha Pokhari and beyond to Dhoban will be described here. At the school field in Nundhaki, the left major fork climbs steeply up to the Milke Danda. Take the right fork, which ascends more gradually at this point, to Gupha Pokhari. The trail climbs but mostly contours through forest, crossing a tributary below a waterfall (6340 ft, 1932 m) in **50 minutes** from Nundhaki. Just beyond is another tributary and the few houses of Bhittri. Continue on fairly level trail to cross two branches of the YAUra Khola, **15 minutes** beyond, on cantilever bridges below a recent slide (6675 ft, 2034 m). Climb up through terraces to reach the houses of DAADa Kharka (7050 ft, 2149 m), in **15 minutes.** This is the last settlement before Gupha Pokhari. If you climb up into the forest in the morning or evening, perhaps you might spot a leopard, or maybe see some tracks or fresh spoor. Cross a tributary (8850 ft, 2697 m) in **1 hour,** but this may be dry in late spring.

The trail is not very prominent, but there is little to do but climb to reach the ridge crest and the serene lake of **Gupha Pokhari** (9525 ft, 2903 m) in another **30 minutes.** The recent settlement, with hotels, is on the other side of the rock-fenced lake. The water all comes from the dammed, stagnant pond. Even locals take to boiling it, since they recognize illness coming from drinking it straight! Views of the Kangchenjunga (to the east) and Khumbu Himal (to the west) are distant but outstanding, especially at sunrise and sunset. It is hard to see Everest itself, because it is hidden by Lhotse Shar, the subsidiary summit of Lhotse. From the southeast, the face of Everest is all snow covered, and very different from the conventional views. It becomes easier to make out as you head south, toward Basantapur.

From Gupha, you can head south to the current road head at Basantapur; this will be described later. You can also head north to join the other trail crossing the Milke Danda, which forks from Nundhaki. However, the direct trail to Dhoban, which the heavily leaden porters ferrying supplies to Taplejung use, will be described here. There are always choices, and here you have one. The old trail dropped to the east a few hundred feet, then contoured and climbed to a ridge crest of gneiss and schist (9725 ft, 2964 m) 1 hour from Gupha. Some 15 minutes before reaching this small pass, and 300 ft (91 m) below, you meet a newly cut trail entering from the left. If you want to take this more direct route with more ups and downs, instead of dropping to the east from Gupha, head north along the pleasant ridge crest for about 10 minutes to a right-hand fork, which heads off to the northeast. The other trail heads north along the Milke Danda to join the previously mentioned trail from Nundhaki. It also continues north, following the wild ridge crest for many days, into the Jaljale Himal. This would be a great monsoon walk when the highlands would be full of yaks pasturing.

Either way from Gupha, you end up at the small pass **1 hour** beyond, and then drop 50 ft (15 m) to reach the temporary tea houses of Akar Deorali, the name of the pass above you. These tea houses, set up to service the porters who carry loads from Basantapur to Taplejung, may disappear when the road to Taplejung is finished. The next **2 hours** are spent on a spur in mixed rhododendron forest, with occasional clearings and temporary tea houses; one comes up in 45 minutes at Buje Deorali (9325 ft, 2842 m). About 30 minutes beyond is Fokde (8525 ft, 2598 m), and you reach the few houses at Mulpakuri (8460 ft, 2578 m) in another 30 minutes. In less than **1 hour,** you come out of the forest to reach terraces and substantial houses, and the spread-out settlement of **Gurja** (6825 ft, 2080 m). Consider spending a night here for the sunsets on the Kangchenjunga massif. You can look across the Tamur Khola valley at Taplejung, the airstrip above it, and the all too common road scars.

Continuing on the main trail below Gurja, reach the few tea houses of Chedarpati and then the scattered village of **Nesum** (5125 ft, 1562 m), **1 hour** from Gurja. Keep descending to Bhajogara (3125 ft, 952 m), a small town 1 hour beyond.

You approach Dhoban (2150 ft, 655 m), a large town at the confluence of the Maiwa Khola valley, which enters from the west, and Tamur Khola, the major river draining the snows to the north. Meet power lines from a hydroelectric project on the Tamur south of here. **Dhoban** is reached in **70 minutes** from Nesum. If you crossed the Milke Danda north of Gupha Pokhari, you will enter Dhoban by descending in the Maiwa Khola valley. This is the last major town en route, with banks, a lot of stores, and the chance to stock up on supplies, unless you climb up to Taplejung on the other side of the valley. There is a police check post here. For those wishing to camp, the area near the confluence of the two rivers is a pleasant site.

As you pass through Dhoban, you reach the right bank of the Maiwa Khola and then cross it on a suspension bridge to another collection of houses and hotels on the north (left) bank. Head east to the large suspension bridge over the roaring Tamur, and cross it to the left bank. Immediately after crossing the bridge, you meet a staircase heading up. This leads to Taplejung, and would be the route to take if you wanted to head to the south side of the Kangchenjunga massif first. However, the route described here leads to the north side of the range, and the trail to it diverges left immediately after crossing the bridge, before climbing any stairs. It is indistinct, and you cross some bushes to descend to the Tamur Khola. Sometimes a trek guide has inscribed an arrow pointing left just at the end of the bridge to help his clients find it. Arrows like this were common in 1988, when the area first opened. Since Nepalis do not do this for themselves, the arrows can probably be followed with some confidence if you are heading up to Kangchenjunga.

Head north on the left bank of the Tamur, following the small trail through rice paddies close to the main torrent. Soon you see another major confluence ahead, that of the Mewa Khola from the north, and the Tamur Khola from the northeast. There is a suspension bridge over the Mewa Khola above the confluence, which, luckily, you don't have to make your way to! (I was confused coming up here the first time and thought we would somehow have to make it across to it. An impossibility to be sure.)

There are no large villages along the route for the next several days. You'll understand why as you encounter the difficult terrain and sense the tension in this roaring river-valley bottom. Furthermore, there has been no active trade to support, either historically (as existed in the Thak Khola between Tibet and Nepal), or currently (as between the Pokhara and the lower Mustang regions). If you want to reach more houses and villages along the way, you'll usually have to climb out of the valley bottom to reach farmland above.

Reach the confluence in **30 minutes** from the last bridge crossing, and then head up the left bank of the Tamur. Boulder-hop and cross tributaries as the trail gets a little more prominent. Sometimes it wanders along sandy flats, other times climbs into subtropical forest to avoid steep sections the river has carved or to bypass slides in this eroding valley. But you stay close to the bottom of this wild, roaring river for the next several days. Where you have choices in the trail, and no arrow or person to indicate the way, take the choice that keeps you closest to the river bottom. Reach the few houses of Tumma (2700 ft, 823 m) in **1½ hours** from the confluence, then pass above a suspension bridge (it is not crossed on this route), and go by a few more tea houses. An hour later, you cross a tributary (2800 ft, 853 m) in a slide area, then climb steeply up the debris on the right bank to rejoin the main valley to enter **Mitlung** (3025 ft, 922 m), a town with a few shops, **30 minutes** later.

Continue along the southeast side of the river valley, on the narrow trail. In **45 minutes,** cross a tributary (the Sisne Khola) either by the suspension bridge upstream, or in low water by hopping rocks (3075 ft, 937 m). Pass above a newly built suspension bridge **40 minutes** beyond, just before reaching the town of **SInwa** (3225 ft, 983 m), with some shops. An **hour** beyond, come to a bamboo suspension bridge over the Tamur (3525 ft, 1074 m), which (thank God) you don't have to cross unless you want a frightful feeling of adventure. In less than **30 minutes,** you pass by a tall cascading waterfall on the other side of the gorge, and in **1 hour and 35 minutes** from SInwa, you reach a powerful narrowing in the river where a big boulder splits the flow into two halves. The trail traverses a slide (3825 ft, 1166 m), and there are tall cliffs on the opposite side of the valley. Notice that on these overhanging portions there are large beehives. Nepal's so-called honey hunters dangle from bamboo ladders and cut down portions of the hives for honey. (See Eric Valli and Diane Summers's outstanding photo-essay *Honey Hunters of Nepal* for the details.)

Proceed almost another **hour** to **ChirUwa** (4175 ft, 1272 m); the village has one shop, and is by a suspension bridge, which isn't crossed. Beyond you pass some overhanging cliffs and enticing fault caves. An hour from ChirUwa, cross another tributary to the right bank on a suspension bridge (4550 ft, 1387 m), and notice that the main valley is heading east now. Some 15 minutes beyond, the valley opens up, and you come to a new suspension bridge across the Tamur, which is not crossed. Up the hillside to the south is the scattered village of Topletok. The trail over the next section has been considerably improved due to the efforts of the local village development council. **Two hours** from ChirUwa cross a tributary, the ThAkyak Khola (4900 ft, 1493 m), on a suspension bridge and again notice the scattered houses of ThAkyak on the hillside above you. Climb up a spur to the lone bamboo hut of Chilaune (5225 ft, 1593 m), **20 minutes** beyond. *Chilaune* means itch, and also is the name of a tree found near here which is produces the same irritation.

Continue high above the valley in a forest, and a little over 20 minutes beyond, don't take the left fork that goes to a suspension bridge over the Tamur. However, 5 minutes beyond, do take the lesser left fork, rather than the bigger trail that climbs to the town of Hellok, unless you want to go there to spend the night or get food. The left fork descends to near the river again and crosses a fresh landslide to enter the valley of the Simbua Khola, which drains the southwest side of Kangchenjunga. You reach the recently constructed Hellok suspension bridge (5200 ft, 1585 m), **45 minutes** from Chilaune, and cross it to the right bank. The town of Hellok is above the bridge on the south side.

Immediately after crossing the river, turn left, and contour north into the main Tamur valley. Almost immediately meet another side valley from the northeast, that of the Ghunsa Khola. Reach a suspension bridge, which has seen better days, over this river. Cross it to the right bank of the Ghunsa Khola, your companion for the next week or so. The bridge (5225 ft, 1593 m) is **30 minutes** from the Hellok one. Again, if you want to reach Sokathun, a *BhoTiya* village, turn left and climb up. The more direct way heads right after crossing the bridge to continue upstream on the right bank. (If you go to Sokathun, you join this trail a little higher up.)

The next day or two is spent in this wild, steep valley, usually high up on its side, on a surprisingly narrow and exposed trail. There are few habitations. You encounter numerous delightful waterfalls. If you return via the southern route I suggest, you'll look down upon this valley from a high ridge—quite a contrast.

Climb up, and in a little over 1 hour, pass under a waterfall that seems surprisingly warm—there must be a hot spring above that partly feeds it. There is another waterfall shortly beyond and high above. Climb up a fault between a large cliff (on the right) and the main valley to reach Ghaiya Bari, a few houses scattered 800 ft (243 m) between each other on the steep hillside. Continue on to the upper few structures (6725 ft, 2050 m), some 1¾ **hours** from the bridge. The trail then climbs up 1000 ft (305 m) and traverses one of the steepest valleys you'll find an open trail on in Nepal. Don't let your mind wander from your feet and sense of balance. The exposure is fierce, and slides you traverse remind you that active erosion is taking place. Because of its steepness and northerly aspect, I doubt it was ever forested—unlike the opposite side, which receives more rainfall. Pass by yet another impressive waterfall, to reach **Amjilassa** (8250 ft, 2514 m), a few houses, 2½ **hours** from Ghaiya Bari. You are leaving the hill Nepal culture behind, and entering the *BhoTiya* domain of the mountain region.

Continue traversing the valley, which is now less nerve-racking, and head north. There is more vegetation, bamboo, oak forest, and higher up, some rhododendron. And always, wonderful waterfalls. There are many tributaries to cross. At times the trail is close to the river, but often climbs and descends to circumvent obstacles. There are no campsites along this difficult portion, and again, like the trail before Amjilassa, this section is best done when well rested. Finally, reach the houses of **Gyapla** (8875 ft, 2705 m) in 3¼ **hours** from Amjilassa. Just up the trail a bit there is a thin waterfall on the Ghunsa Khola. You notice burned stumps on the hillside above, from a 1981 fire. An important reminder of the precarious balance of which you are a part.

Just beyond Gyapla, cross a tributary, head east again, enter an impressive forest, and take a right fork 30 minutes beyond the village. Continue crossing tributaries, at times near the main river, and notice that the valley has opened up a little, easing the tension of walking in the narrow river bottom. The bridges and trails have become more substantial, because *chAUmris* are taken along here. Notice the fir forests, especially on the east side of the valley. Climb up to the sprawling *BhoTiya* settlement of **Phale** (10,475 ft, 3193 m), in 2½ **hours** from Gyapla. Here there is a settlement of Tibetan refugees, and many people of Ghunsa move down here during the winter. There is a *gomba* at the upper end of town. Descend to cross the Yangma Khola (11,000 ft, 3353 m) 30 minutes beyond the *gomba*.

Here you first meet larch forests, along with juniper and rhododendron. The larches are golden in the autumn, a delightful sight that is rare in most of Nepal. They are common in Bhutan and Sikkim, but only sporadically reported in a few other places in Nepal. Enjoy them all the way up to Kambachen.

To continue to Ghunsa, come to a pair of restful benches across the trail at about the halfway point (11,025 ft, 3360 m), and then continue close to the right bank of the Ghunsa Khola. Beyond, you come to a left fork, which heads to the *gomba;* but you should continue to the wooden cantilever bridge over the main river (11,225 ft, 3421 m), 1 **hour** from Phale. Cross it to the left bank and climb up to the village of **Ghunsa** (11,300 ft, 3444 m), some **10 minutes** beyond. The police check post is just on your right as you reach the bench the town sits on.

Ghunsa is a traditional *BhoTiya* settlement of sturdy wooden houses, surrounded by potato fields and magnificent forests. These isolated people have been little affected by tourism. Their values center around their yak herds, which will be found pastured up as far as Pangpema beneath the north face of Kangchenjunga during the summer months, or down as far as Phale during the winter. Indeed, in the middle of winter, the village may seem deserted. People have moved "south" to Phale, leaving only the police to shiver here, although you may find Tibetans tending yak herds farther up the valley. But there is no permanent settlement beyond. No major trade routes traverse this area. The lack of substantial numbers of trekkers and climbers presents an outwardly different culture than is found in, say, Khumbu. Don't expect to be able to buy much here, other than inexpensive potatoes and costly rice (rice is expensive because of substantial transport costs).

The altitude is probably having an affect on you here. It is a good place to take a rest day. Explore the *gomba* or the wonderful forests. The best side trip to the latter is an excursion toward the Lapsang La, the high pass leading to the south side of the Kangchenjunga massif. This will be described with the other pass leading to the south side.

GHUNSA TO PANGPEMA AND THE NORTH KANGCHENJUNGA BASE CAMP

The route to Pangpema, a summer yak pasture and the site of the North Kangchenjunga Base Camp, takes at least three days from Ghunsa and involves a further elevation gain of over 5500 ft (1676 m), so trekkers must watch for signs of altitude illness and be ready to descend should serious ones occur. There is no food available beyond Ghunsa. There are sturdy huts in Kambachen and Lakep, but these are all locked. The only other structures are rock walls for erecting the yak-hair Tibetan-style tents used by yak herders. So tents for trekkers are necessary, unless this route gets popular and locals construct lodges.

Head northeast, up the valley from Ghunsa. Avoid the right fork that climbs into a forest, but cross a small tributary above a tiny bluff festooned with prayer flags, then go by a fenced-in pasture. Admire the rhododendrons, larch, and huge fir trees in this impressive forest. Cross a tributary to its right bank 1¼ hours after leaving Ghunsa on a wide log bridge made for yak herds. Kabur, not Jannu, is the mountain up at the headwaters of this tributary. Eventually descend to the main river, reach a wide cantilever bridge, and cross the Ghunsa Khola to its right bank **2 hours** from Ghunsa (12,450 ft, 3795 m). Proceed along to Lapuk Kharka, another pasture, 10 minutes beyond. There are rock overhangs here that would make good shelter. Enter an idyllic rhododendron- and juniper-forested valley, which ends all too soon as you cross a tributary with a spectacular waterfall at its head 15 minutes from Lapuk Kharka (12,900 ft, 3932 m). Just beyond is Lapu Kong, a flat pasture area. Along the way, the birch tress festooned with hanging lichens are memorable. Take the lower fork beyond, as the upper goes to higher yak pastures. The impressive

Yalung Kang's north face, from near Lhonak

summit to the east-northeast is Kambachen. But as you ascend further, it disappears and you see Jannu, or Khumbukarna Himal.

The next part of the trail crosses a slide area, another indication of the active orogeny still going on. Sometimes the slopes are active, and boulders can roll down, usually in the early morning when the sun melts the ice "glue." If you hear activity, it is best to cross one at a time, with someone spotting for missiles. It is not a place to gawk at Jannu—you'll have plenty of opportunity for this later. Across the slide, descend a little to the lone house of Lakep (13,450 ft, 4099 m), **1¼ hours** from the crossing of the Ghunsa Khola.

Lakep is the place to be awestruck by Jannu's northwest face. Sunsets are particularly grand. This rock stock, reminiscent of Ama Dablang in the Khumbu area, pokes into the sky only a little short of the magical 8000 m mark. Its altitude is 25,294 ft (7710 m). Jannu was first climbed by the French in 1962 from the south, and now has been ascended several times by the difficult side you see here, climbers reaching the rock at the top by its left (north) ridge. Parties of trekkers might wish to head up to the base camp used for these climbs on the north side. The route actually branches off beyond Ghunsa, before crossing the river and proceeding up the Jannu or Khumbukarna glaciers.

The mountain is called Khumbukarna (its official name) by locals, especially in the south, and Jannu by others. The only problem with camping at Lakep is that water is far away at the river below. Twenty minutes away is Kambachen, a large summer settlement of sturdy stone huts, with easy water, but alas, less impressive views, as all but the rock stock of Jannu is hidden.

From Lakep on, look for blue sheep in the mornings and afternoons. In the middle of winter they will come down here, usually browsing on grass within reach of cliffs and rocks that offer protection. The herds migrate up the valley to stay near Pangpema during the summer.

Reach Kambachen by heading around the next bend to the northeast, and descending to cross two tributary streams (the Nupchu Khola) from the north 15 minutes beyond (13,450 ft, 4099 m). No matter where you spend the night, take time to explore. A rest day to acclimatize might be in order. Wander up the Nupchu Khola valley. In the dead of winter, you might find Tibetan snow cocks here (in warmer seasons, they head up the main valley).

Climb up the hill behind Kambachen and continue along the northeast side of the main valley, reaching the potato fields of Lungba Chemu, then another pasture, before traversing scree and boulders near the river. Pass below a spectacular waterfall and follow the trail up through the boulder field along the river. A cairn, located where the trail levels off above, may be visible to the keen eye. After climbing up from the river, continue along a fairly flat trail. Avoid the animal trails and herder trails used to get to yak pastures. Reach Ramdang Kharka (15,025 ft, 4579 m), another pasture with a small *chorten* situated across from another impressive mountain face, that of Kambachen. This is **2¼ hours** from the huts at Kambachen. This impressive mountain, like Jannu, is a mere 25,925 ft (7902 m), and therefore short of the 8000 m dividing line that compels climbers. It was first ascended in 1974 from the side you see from here, first by Polish and then Yugoslavian expeditions. The route proceeded to the ridge west of the summit via the valley between Jannu and Kambachen, up the Ramdang Glacier in front of you.

Up the main valley, you may have seen a lone pillar (gendarme) on the south side of the valley, set off from Chang Himal. Lhonak is across the Kangchenjunga Glacier from it. To reach it, the trail descends an old lateral moraine, crosses a river from the north (possibly difficult, depending on the conditions), then crests another old lateral moraine before coming to the sandy valley from the north. Descend to the yak-herding area of Lhonak (15,700 ft, 4785 m), some **1½ hours** from Ramdang Kharka. You may find some yak herders in their tents here even during winter. The yaks seem content to scratch at the sparse grass found at that time. Notice that the surrounding rock is primarily gneiss; as you proceed, you will encounter granitic elements.

The foot of the north side of Kangchenjunga, which remains hidden still, is finally seen at Pangpema, a summer yak pasture and the base camp for ascents from the north. You can either pack your supplies up there and camp, or make a day trip from Lhonak. For those who are well acclimatized, it is a glorious place to spend the night. Make your decision on how well the slowest members of the party are acclimatizing, and on how well-clothed the porters are.

To proceed, continue on up the flats from Lhonak, cross some wet areas, descend an old moraine slide, and walk in a trough, sometimes strolling on pleasant grassy slopes, other times dealing with the occasional boulder. An **hour and a half** from Lhonak, reach a big plateau with an impressive boulder in the center. This is Jorju (16,475 ft, 5021 m). As you continue up valley, Kangchenjunga begins to come into view; it has been well hidden by its neighbors up to now. Reach the shelf of Pangpema (16,875 ft, 5143 m), where there are some rock walls for herders' tents, in 1 hour from Jorju. Kangchenjunga's north face is immense, just like the rest of the mountain. This massif is probably the second largest mountain mass in the world. (Mount Logan in the Yukon Territory of Canada is reputed to be the bulkiest!) The face you see has been climbed on the left (east) side, first by an Indian expedition in 1977. "Kangchenjunga" is a Sikkimese name, roughly translating to "The five treasures of the great snow." It is considered a god and a protector by the people of Sikkim to the east.

There are many options for side trips. At least climb up the hillside to the north. If you ascend the boulder ridge crest that bounds the Ginsang Glacier from the north some 700 ft (213 m), you'll come to a plateau with even more impressive views of Kangchenjunga's face. You can continue higher for a more panoramic sense of the area. Or head northwest, where you may find a small lake at about the same altitude. There are plenty of choices for following the glacier valleys to the north and east. It would be grand to make a circuit of the entire Kangchenjunga massif, but political considerations and international boundaries make this impossible at present. In retracing your steps, you'll probably admire the lesser summits, such as the rock spires of Sharpu III below Kambachen, and have more time and patience to stalk blue sheep. If you are well acclimatized, you can do the trip to Ghunsa in two very long days, but spend three and enjoy it.

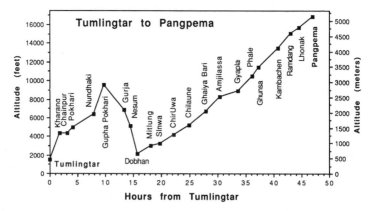

GHUNSA TO THE SOUTH SIDE OF KANGCHENJUNGA

Besides returning from Ghunsa down the Ghunsa Khola valley, the way you came, there are two other feasible exits that head over to the south side of Kangchenjunga. These allow you the option of visiting the base camps there, and give you a return to Taplejung, where there is an airstrip, to which, eventually, a completed road will reach. The two exits both cross high passes from Ghunsa and arrive in the Yalung Glacier–Simbua Khola valley.

The higher route crosses the Lapsang La, a 17,250 ft (5258 m) pass, to reach the herding area of Lapsang near the snout of the Yalung Glacier. En route, it heads up to the Yamatari Glacier, crosses its moraine, and ascends the valley of the Lasampa Glacier to the pass. The way is loose and rocky and requires two days' travel, with an intermediate camp at the Lumba Sumba Kharka, across from the Yamatari Glacier lateral moraine. This route is not recommended because of the additional altitude gain, the lack of views, the length, and the increased difficulties on the trail, especially for the porters. If you plan to do it, hiring extra porters to carry loads makes sense. Snowfall can make the way hazardous.

The lower route, essentially a high-ridge, upper-valley traverse, is exhilarating, and can be done in a long day. If you wish to break it up into two, which would be more enjoyable, there are suitable camping sites but no wood. Parties should be self-sufficient in fuel. There are several names for points reached, including Sinion La, Tama La, and Mirgin La. The maximum altitude reached is 15,250 ft (4648 m). This is the route locals use for getting back and forth. It also has a bonus: a more complete view of Jannu from the southwest than the former route. If you climb above the trail near the high point, you can also see the Khumbu Himal peaks and Makalu. On the descent toward Tseram, there are panoramic views of the south face of Kangchenjunga, and surrounding peaks. Finally, there are two exit options that allow a more direct route for parties not wanting to get to the base camp on the south side of Kangchenjunga.

To proceed on this lower route, climb up behind the schoolhouse at the south end of Ghunsa into a forest to reach a fork **10 minutes** beyond (11,500 ft, 3505 m). The left fork goes to the Lapsang La; going partway up can make a pleasant day hike for people adjusting to the altitude at Ghunsa, and provides some closer views of the west side of Jannu.

To take this day hike, first ascend a serene juniper, rhododendron, and fir forest, keeping to a ridge crest within the woods that is probably an old lateral moraine. Seventy minutes beyond the fork, reach the right bank of a stream (13075 ft, 3985 m), cross, and ascend to a yak pasture. Crest and ascend a lateral moraine and begin to see Jannu. In 30 minutes, fork right to descend the loose moraine to the river draining the Yamatari Glacier and find a spot to cross it (13,700 ft, 4176 m) to its left bank. Now ascend the other loose lateral moraine to its crest. You can either proceed along this moraine toward Jannu, or descend to the yak pastures of Lumba Sumba Kharka (13,800 ft, 4206 m). Further efforts toward the Lapsang La are not very rewarding.

To follow the other route south, take the right fork at the junction shortly beyond Ghunsa, and reach the Yamatari Khola, which you cross to its left bank. Just beyond is the pasture called Yamatari. Make sure you get water here. Find the trail into the forest at the end of the corral area and follow it to the forested crest of another old lateral moraine. The route then climbs steeply on the impressive, rhododendron-forested side of the valley to reach a prayer-flag-festooned spot on the open ridge crest (12,950 ft, 3947 m) in **1¼ hours** from the fork. Called the Tama Lasi, it is not really a pass. Proceed up near the ridge crest, and then on its right (west) side. Look down on your route up the Ghunsa Khola valley—Phale and Gyapla are easily spotted. To the north is the Yangma Khola valley, which leads to the Nango La, the pass connecting Ghunsa with Wallungchung Gola.

The ascending traverse is serene. Reach a spring in 45 minutes (13,400 ft, 4084 m), just below a ridge crest called Tynuma, which you cross into another draw to the south. I well recall the exotic ambrosia along here. Continue along to Mani Bhuk (13,975 ft, 4259 m), a fine campsite with a pleasant stream, **1½ hours** from the Tama Lasi. Eventually, Jannu's west face pops up above a ridge behind you. An hour beyond Mani Bhuk, you reach a level area (14,325 ft, 4366 m), after which you leave the views of Jannu. In some seasons, if water is available, this would be an idyllic spot to camp. If not, continue up to another notch (15,250 ft, 4648 m), which leads into a very different series of valleys.

After more pleasant traverses, you reach a small draw with a prominent spire (gendarme) and attendant Sphinxlike consort, called Menda Puja (15,250 ft, 4648 m), up the valley. Notice the many rock cairns along here. Local people feel the gendarme is a deity and make cairn offerings to it. Finally, reach the last ridge crest (15,250 ft, 4648 m), also called Menda Puja, and per haps Sinion La, in **2 hours and 10 minutes** from Mani Bhuk. At this point, you can look down into the Simbua Khola valley to see a fork in the trail. The left fork traverses and then descends to the yak pastures at Tseram. This is the choice for those planning to see the south side of Kangchenjunga close up. The right fork descends more directly into the valley, and would suit those wanting a more direct exit.

The right-fork trail will be described. Descend, and reach some scree, pretty much the first such rubble along this trail. Below you are two lakes. The trail drops to pass to the south of the lower lake, which is called the Tsojung Tanga (14,300 ft, 4358 m) and marked Chhudung Pokhari on the recent Survey of India maps. Reach it in **40 minutes** from the pass. There are a few rock monuments out in the lake, a sign of its sanctity to the locals. To continue, descend steeply, first a small spur, and then a side valley, to reach the forest. At a fork in the forest (12,400 ft, 3779 m), turn right to traverse rather than heading down more steeply, to eventually reach the main trail up the right bank of the Simbua Khola by a small stream (11,800 ft, 3596 m), **1¼ hours** from the lake. If you turn left here, you will reach Tseram in 2½ hours. But turn right, and head downstream to cross a tributary just beyond on a log bridge (11,715 ft, 3571 m) to reach the half-roofed hut of Whata **10 minutes** beyond.

THE SOUTH SIDE OF KANGCHENJUNGA

The south side of Kangchenjunga presents a rugged, somewhat more open valley that sees less local presence than the north side because of its distance from permanent habitation. But it is similarly used as yak-pasturing grounds, and because of the southerly exposure and increased rainfall, it gets better grass growth. It was the focus of attempts to explore and first climb the mountain in the early 1950s. The route of the first successful ascent of the mountain by the British in 1955 went up the Simbua Khola valley. If this area is your goal and you are crossing the Mirgin La, described above, then instead of dropping right from the Sinion La, traverse northeast and descend to Tseram. If you are coming up from Taplejung, following the directions in reverse, then head up to Tseram from Whata, which is described below. Be aware that there is no food or shelter available beyond Yamphudin, so all parties must be self-sufficient. This includes carrying fuel, since these magnificent forests *must* be preserved.

From Whata, proceed up the valley floor in larch forests with some rhododendron, like those near Ghunsa, eventually reaching the two large terraces of Tseram, (12,700 ft, 3870 m), in **3 hours.** You may find some caves here to stay in. The other fork of the Sinion La trail comes in just above the upper terrace, where there may be water for camping. Nearby is the small shrine of Devi Than. It is said that if you pray there once a year, your prayers will be answered. The major mountain massif up the valley is Kabur. Across the Simbua Khola to the southeast is the valley of the Yamagaachha Khola, which heads up to the Kang La, a 16,580 ft (5053 m) pass into Sikkim. It was used by outsiders as an early approach to this side of the mountain.

To continue on, head upstream on the same right bank in a broader valley, climbing rapidly at first, reaching Yalung (13,550 ft, 4130 m) after **1 hour,** just after crossing a stream. The forests below Yalung are the last woods and porters may want to carry wood from there, but I advise that the party be self-sufficient in fuel. Yalung, with a stone hut and potato fields, is below the terminus of the large valley glacier of the same name. There are striking views of Kabur, Kabur Dome, and Ratong. Climb on to Lapsang (14,540 ft, 4432 m), in **2 hours.** The trail keeps to the plateau between the lateral moraine of the glacier and the steep valley wall, near where the Simbua Khola also flows. The trail from the Lapsang La, mentioned before, comes in here from the north, and there is a small pond. However, neither the trail nor the pass is visible from the main trail. The path continues climbing over the plateau, coming to a small pond and then continuing another **hour** to Ramche (14,700 ft, 4480 m). There is a large meadow here as well as a stone hut, and beyond there is a *chorten*. Views of Koktang, Ratong, and the Kabur Dome, the massif to the east, are most impressive. You may see blue sheep along here, the only place besides Dhorpatan where they may exist south of the main Himalayan chain. Tibetan snow cocks can be seen in this valley, too.

From Ramche, the trail gently ascends along the ridge above the moraine of the Yalung Glacier. About an **hour** above Ramche, the trail rounds a corner to the left and you can see the main mass of Kangchenjunga. If you then climb up to the crest of the ridge above the moraine, you will find a good trail that continues along the edge of the moraine. After about **1 hour** on that trail, there is a spectacular panorama of the Kangchenjunga massif and the edge of the Jannu ridge.

The trail heads more northerly, to Okhordung (15,520 ft, 4730 m), labeled Oktang on some maps, reached in a further **1½ hours.** From the *chorten* there, on the lateral moraine, there is a grand panoramic view of the Kangchenjunga massif, including Jannu, which looks quite different up close from this angle than it does from the north and southwest. Climbers can head up a ridge on a small peak to the west, reaching 17,700 ft (5395 m) in some three hours, for even better views. To reach this peak, turn left before the *chorten* and skirt the first group of rocks on the right. Then head left, behind the rocks, and follow the ridge to the top, being careful on the loose rocks higher up. To head on toward the actual base camps of Kangchenjunga climbing expeditions, you have to cross the Yalung Glacier and head onto the slopes of Ratong. The way is difficult, especially for those unfamiliar with unstable, rubble-covered ice, and the views are not better, except perhaps of Jannu.

All the times along here, of course, depend on the state of acclimatization of the party. Those who have already visited the north side and been acclimatized there will be much quicker than those coming up from the south. Be prepared to take your time.

SOUTH KANGCHENJUNGA TO TAPLEJUNG

The return to Taplejung from Whata will be described. This becomes the exit from the south side of Kangchenjunga for trekkers. To identify Whata, the half-roofed hut, look directly across the main valley, up a tributary valley to a forked peak. To proceed, go southwest, keeping close to the eroded bank of the raging torrent of the Simbua Khola. In **1¼ hours** from the junction at Whata, the trail crosses a small tributary and heads inland to a rhododendron forest for a respite. In another **½ hour**, at a slight clearing called Toronten, don't continue along the forested trail, but fork left to descend to a wooden cantilever bridge over the Simbua Khola (9,950 ft, 3033 m) and cross it to the left bank.

Head downstream on the much wetter side of the valley, as you notice more bamboo growth. In 15 minutes, you begin to climb out of the main valley, traversing an impressive fir forest. A half-hour later, cross a stream, the last running water for some time, and continue traversing and climbing in a small side valley to reach a clearing at Thangsetang (10,350 ft, 3155 m), used as a midway point in dried cheese *(churpi)* trade. This is **1¼ hours** from the Simbua Khola crossing. Climb up through a rhododendron-birch forest to reach more open slopes and a kind of pass, Lassi Than (11,425 ft, 3482 m). The actual pass is a little lower down, but the trail avoids the low point, 125 feet below, which is more hazardous. Continue on to the southwest, to a clearing and the pasture of Lassi (11,375 ft, 3467 m), **1 hour** from Thangsetang. With the now-distant views of Jannu behind you, this is a spectacular spot to camp, but water may be hard to find. It is available about a half-hour's descent directly to the southeast, below the pass.

There is also a fine viewpoint of the south side of Kangchenjunga, which is reached by taking the ridge-crest trail that heads northeast from where you meet the ridge at Lassi Than. After a 35-minute walk through rhododendron forest, you come to a rock outcropping (12,150 ft, 3703 m). A brief scramble to the small summit gives great views of Jannu and Kangchenjunga. The peak to the west of Jannu is Sharpu I. You can look back at Makalu, the white pyramid, before reaching this point.

The south face of Kangchenjunga

To head on from Lassi, continue for ½ **hour** along the trail in a rhododendron forest to a clearing called Lamite (10,750 ft, 3276 m). Another ½ **hour** down in a bamboo forest and you come to Chitre (9725 ft, 2964 m), another clearing, with little chance of finding water in the dry season. Continue into an oak forest, and just before coming out of it, **20 minutes** beyond Chitre, fork right (9150 ft, 2789 m), to stay in the woods. After a clearing, the trail switchbacks along a new, slippery, pebble trail. Finally reach water, as you cross a tributary on stepping stones (7475 ft, 2278 m), to its right bank. Traverse along to Tzenday Portok, a *chautaara* a ½ **hour** beyond.

This area has farm fields without terraces, which you also notice across the valley, to the southeast. It is an example of slash-and-burn agriculture, where every five years or so the area is burned and one crop of corn is grown. The land lies dormant for another five years. Population and food pressures have resulted in the use of more marginal lands in this manner. To do otherwise would require these slopes to be terraced. Further pressures on the land might result in terracing at some future date.

Here, I took the right, lesser fork, which descended to a pool below a waterfall in 10 minutes. To reach it, however, you have to descend some 30 ft (10 m) on a cliff. It has good foot and hand holds, as well as a vine rope to hold on to, but it is a scramble. The payoff is that the pool could provide a cool, refreshing bath. Cross the tributary to the right (6900 ft, 2103 m) and climb up a faint trail, which then traverses and ascends. A high trail joins this one ½ hour beyond; take the lower left fork just before the main trail coming up from the bridge is reached on the right.

If you take the left fork from Tzenday Portok, the trail descends a spur to cross the Tzenday Khola to the right bank on a cantilever bridge and then ascends.

Either way, the settlement of **Yamphudin,** the first since Ghunsa, is just beyond (6825 ft, 2080 m), less than **1 hour** from the *chautaara* called Tzenday Portok. The people here are mostly *BhoTiya* like those in Ghunsa, but as you head along towards Taplejung, *Limbu* predominate and the town names reflect their different linguistic origins. These villages are usually quite scattered; denser collections of houses usually reflect the presence of other ethnic groups.

From Yamphudin there is a trail to Hellok at the junction of the Tamur and Ghunsa Kholas. This takes one long day, and climbs to 12,850 ft (3916 m). It could be used to give you access to a different arrival or departure route. Also, you might consider not going to Taplejung, but heading south more directly to reach the road at Ghopethar. The point at which to branch off is noted in the trail descriptions below. When regular road service is established to Ghopethar, this will be a faster exit than walking to Taplejung, unless you have confirmed plane reservations out from there. Of course, eventually the road will be completed to Taplejung, and reliable service established from there. There would then be little reason to go to Ghopethar. The important point is to be aware of the options; local people will know what the status of the roads is at any time.

The trail now for the most part travels through farmland. To continue from Yamphudin, descend through town to a spur and meet trails coming from the right and then from the left. Descend to the Kabeli Khola valley floor, and cross a tributary en route. Reach it in some 35 minutes from town. You are on the right bank, and should follow the river downstream. The main trail then climbs over a steep part of the valley, and there, at **45 minutes** from Yamphudin, just beyond a *chautaara* (5500 ft, 1676 m), there is a left fork that descends to a suspension bridge over the main river. This would be the fork to take if you were heading to Ghopethar.

This route would take two days, and follow the Kabeli Khola for the most part. The towns along the way are Kebang, Barundin, Dandagaon, Panchami, Tharpu, and then Ghopethar.

To continue to Taplejung, however, take the right fork and climb up a bit to traverse in and out of side valleys of the Kabeli Khola. This is done for almost two days, before descending to Taplejung. At forks, always choose the more prominent or bigger trail. After traversing along the main trail for **1½ hours** from the *chautaara,* you cross a tributary from the north, either on a suspension bridge, or on stepping stones below. The first houses of **Mamanke** (6075 ft, 1852 m) are **15 minutes** beyond, but the school is on a spur almost ½ **hour** further. Notice how schools are almost always sited on the land most unsuited for agriculture.

The trail then descends and traverses to cross a major tributary, the Takshewa Khola, to the right on a suspension bridge. Climb up to the few houses and shops of Pumpe (6150 ft, 1874 m), **1 hour** from the school. Continue traversing, mostly in mixed broad-leaved forest with some rhododendron. A half hour beyond is an arboreal surprise for this region: some pine trees! These are the three-needle chir pine, *Pinus rhoxburghi,* called *KhoTe Salla* by Nepalis. Almost an hour beyond Pumpe are two small but idyllic waterfalls you pass.

Pass above the scattered *Limbu* houses of Yampung, then round a spur and reach the town of Pum Pung (6050 ft, 1844 m), **1½ hours** from Pumpe. This town is referred to as Funfun on some trekker maps, a decidedly difficult *Limbu* name to exactly pin down. Here you finally leave the Kabeli Khola valley and enter the tributary valley of the Nangden Khola. The traverse continues, crossing below a waterfall in a fault with pleasant, shallow pools below. Shortly beyond is a weeping wall, then another tributary to cross on a log bridge, before the steep climb up to Kheshewa (6450 ft, 1966 m). It is reached in **1¼ hours** from Pum Pung.

Ascend to a small pass, **Sinchewu Bhanjyang** (7050 ft, 2149 m), where there are some tea shops. This is **45 minutes** from Kheshewa. The Kangchenjunga massif is seen behind you. The trail to Taplejung turns right here to descend into the Phaawa Khola valley. At a *chautaara* on the notch of a spur, some 25 minutes beyond, head down the other side, and 15 minutes later reach the first houses of **Kunjari** (6325 ft, 1928 m).

Upon reaching some shops, turn left and continue down a spur, reaching a few covered stalls in **1 hour** from Sinchewu Bhanjyang (5700 ft, 1737 m). There is a market here on the first day of the Nepali month *(sAAgrAti).* The school is just below. Descend to the suspension bridge over the Phaawa Khola in another ½ **hour.** Cross it to the right (4700 ft, 1432 m), then climb up the other side. **Half an hour** later, take the left fork and reach **Simbu** (5600 ft, 1707 m), **10 minutes** beyond. Continue climbing and traversing, and in a half-hour, fork right to climb rather than traverse (6175 ft, 1882 m). Round a spur crest, head into another tributary valley, and proceed to the scattered village of Tam Mewa (6325 ft, 1928 m), **10 minutes** beyond. Just before coming to a school, fork right to climb rather than heading lower to reach the school. Here begins a long, ascending traverse in this valley.

Pass several streams in a draw to reach a house in **1 hour and 10 minutes** (7475 ft, 2278 m). Climb into an oak forest to reach a spur crest **10 minutes** beyond (8675 ft, 2644 m), but there is another **1¼ hours** of climbing, till you reach an open, lofty area (8700 ft, 2652 m). Here you see Makalu to the west, as well as the Jaljale Himal. Traverse a little further to a crossroads, where five trails converge. You head southwest on a forested ridge, taking some stairs up from the junction. Cross to the northwest side of the ridge, on a very wide, almost jeepable road, and enter an open area. As you walk down this hillside, you can look back at the Kangchenjunga range you were so intimately connected with not so long ago.

The walk down is a restful contrast from the endless forest to the crest. Soon you reach a modern fence, and beyond is the airstrip of **Suketar, 30 minutes** from the crossroads. The top of the runway is 8000 ft (2438 m). There are several hotels here, and a sense that much expansion will take place here. The district center and large bazaar of **Taplejung** is another **30 to 60 minutes** beyond. Some hotels are below the hospital (5850 ft, 1783 m). The dense collection of shops is a little further below. There is a weekly market on Saturdays, held near the district army headquarters, south of the main bazaar. There is a police check post here where you should register. The road from Ilam to Taplejung will be completed soon. Future plans call for it to link up with the road to Basantapur, on the ridge dividing the Tamur and Arun Kholas.

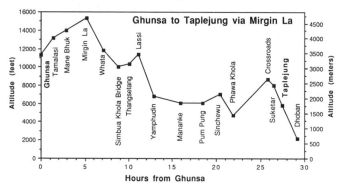

LINKS FROM TAPLEJUNG WITH THE ROAD

Taplejung to Basantapur

The trail to Dhoban and the segment from Gupha Pokhari will be described, to allow you to link up with the road to Dharan. Even when regular bus service is established to Taplejung, I would advise walking the trail south from Gupha Pokhari. It is a most pleasant day, spent along a ridge crest for the most part, with views of the Khumbu Himal and Everest massif, as well as the Kangchenjunga region.

From Taplejung, descend past the primary school (5800 ft, 1768 m). Follow a big trail to **Deolinge,** some houses with a school (3675 ft, 1120 m), an hour from Taplejung. Twenty minutes below are the tea houses of Nangesuri (2975 ft, 907 m), and as you approach the suspension bridge over the Tamur, across from Dhoban, there are a few more tea shops. The bridge is **1 hour and 40 minutes** from Taplejung (2125 ft 648 m).

The trail from Gupha Pokhari to Dhoban has already been described, so those descriptions can be followed in reverse.

———

The trail segment from Gupha Pokhari to Basantapur will now be documented. From Gupha Pokhari (9950 ft, 3033 m), head south to reach Korunga, a few tea houses on the ridge crest (10,075 ft, 3071 m), **½ hour** beyond. Like almost all the settlements along this portion to Basantapur, they are temporary, set up to serve the porter traffic to Taplejung. How they will change once regular road service is established to Taplejung is unclear.

Cross a ridge crest to reach Lam Pokhari, **15 minutes** beyond. There are two quiet lakes here to contemplate. The next collection of tea houses is

Balukop (9650 ft, 2941 m), 20 minutes further. Then Sirmani, before reaching **Manglabari** (9100 ft, 2774 m), **1 hour** from Lam Pokhari. Climb up a bit, and contour on the west side of the ridge crest, before reaching **Chauki** (9250 ft, 2819 m), **35 minutes** further.

The views of the Khumbu Himal are impressive, but it is hard for the un-initiated to pick out Mount Everest. Certainly the locals all along here tend to point to Makalu when asked where Everest is. Further north, around Gupha Pokhari, it is especially hard to make it out, since it is blocked by Lhotse Shar.

Continue on to Madan Sing, then Phedi, and begin a climb to Jinjuri Deorali, a few tea houses just below a notch where the trail crosses to the south side of the ridge. This spot (10,100 ft, 3078 m) is **1 hour and 10 minutes** from Chauki. Alas, the mountain views are over for now. Below, you can see the substantial town of Basantapur, and the road. Traverse along the southeast side of a ridge, to reach Durpani, then Dur, and finally Deorali in a notch, all collections of tea houses. At Deorali (8850 ft, 2697 m), **1 hour** from Jinjuri Deorali, you end the traverse, and turn left to head south. Reach **Basantapur** (7950 ft, 2423 m) in another **45 minutes.** The odyssey is over.

Taplejung to Phedim

The following brief trail description by Neil Vigilante takes another alternative from Taplejung that descends the eastern part of the zone to Phedim, where a vehicle can be taken to Ilam and south. It takes from two to three days, and accommodation and food is limited until you are close to Phedim. You have to ask directions most of the way. Eventually the road will reach Taplejung, and few people will want to walk the distance.

Leaving Taplejung, one can follow the partially completed roadbed or the well-used foot trail. Ask for directions to either near the main market area where they both begin. The foot trail begins well defined and maintained, but deteriorates after approximately half a day due to the road construction. Reach the suspension bridge over the Kabioli Khola; the small village set up to cater to the road crew across the river is Ang Bung. The trail crisscrosses the road as you climb behind Ang Bung, and after an hour or two, at a saddle, the trail forks. Go right off the main trail, down through a forested area, then ascend to Muktara. There are a school and tea shops at the top. Eventually you reach the road closer to the river and the suspension bridge below Phedim. Reach Phedim, where there is a check post. Vehicles are available at the far end of town to Ilam, and there are several morning buses, though you can walk in a very long day. If walking, the route would take you through Sukie Pokhari and Saukijang.

Tumlingtar toward Khumbu
(Maps No. 6, Page 249, and No. 4, Page 225)

The following route description provides an alternative to getting to Khumbu and the Everest region. It is close to the original route taken by outsiders in 1949, and was for many years the principle path to the Everest region. It does not have quite as many ups and downs as the way from Jiri, and is much less popular with trekkers. It also offers an excellent way of varying your route of exit from Khumbu, especially if the plane situation is out of control in Lukla. Some trekkers have been doing a "grand traverse," starting in Kathmandu, going to Everest, then leaving this way, going to the Makalu Base Camp, and finishing up with the Kangchenjunga circuit. This is at least a two-month odyssey, but what a glorious gambol! It is described below, beginning with a flight to Tumlingtar from Kathmandu. You could also take the road to Hille, and walk from there. If leaving Khumbu, and ending up in Tumlingtar, you could then proceed further east through Chainpur and Terhathum and end up in Ilam. The route to Chainpur is described in the above section (in "Tumlingtar to Ghunsa"). The way further east from Chainpur, which traverses the midland hills, is described at the end of this section.

TUMLINGTAR TO KHARTE

Fly to **Tumlingtar** (1500 ft, 457 m), a broad, flat plateau on the east (left) bank of the Arun Khola. Once there, spend the night in the hopes of getting the spectacular early-morning views of Makalu and Chamlang to the north. To head to Khumbu, head north for ¾ **hour** and fork left at a *chautaara* (ask the way here) to drop steeply northwest down to the Arun Khola (1000 ft, 305 m). Head up river on its left bank.

There are two trails: a monsoon track that proceeds up higher, and the more usual valley-bottom trail. It is usually quite hot here, and if you care to swim or bathe in the river, beware of powerful currents. Reach the suspension bridge in **3½ to 4 hours.** Cross (1200 ft, 366 m) to Khatteghat on the southwest (right) bank. Continue upstream on a rice paddy trail to the Chikhuwa Khola, in ½ **hour.** Cross it to the north (left) bank and ascend a major ridge system to the northwest, climbing out of the valley of the Arun Khola.

Ask the way at junctions for the trail to Phedi. Gain the ridge crest (3000 ft, 914 m) in 3 hours and traverse north to descend into the south side of the Irkhuwa Khola valley. Cross it on a wooden cantilever bridge at 2200 ft (671 m) in an hour. Trails exist on both sides of the Irkhuwa Khola; ask which is the best this year. It depends on which bamboo bridges remain from the last monsoon. Continue up the Irkhuwa Khola, reaching the village of **Dobhane** in **4 hours** from the crossing of the Chikhuwa Khola. Cross several tributaries to reach **Phedi** (4900 ft, 1493 m), a large *Rai* village on the prow between the Irkhuwa Khola to the west and the Sabu Khola to the north. There is a hotel here, **3 hours** from Dobhane.

Climb up steeply through Phedi to the ridge crest to the northwest towards Salpa Bhanjyang. A spectacular causeway brings you to a group of *goTh,* Tamdse Dingma, in a meadow with a pond (9300 ft, 2835 m). It is **5 to 6 hours** from Phedi. There are campsites here, but the pond may be dry in the spring.

A **half-hour** above the pond there are also good campsites with water near more *goTh.* A further hour will bring you to Salpa Bhanjyang (11,018 ft, 3349 m), with its large *chorten* and good views of Numbur and Katang to the north.

Descend steeply through dense coniferous forest to cross the Lidung Khola to the north (right) side and traverse to the Sherpa village of **Sanam** (8530 ft, 2600 m) in **2 hours** from the pass. There are lodges here.

Stay high, traversing above the river to round a ridge promontory, and see the large *Rai* village of **Guidel** (6560 ft, 2000 m) directly below you. This village is **2 hours** from Sanam. Camp at the school, or stay in a *bhaTTi*. Then descend very steeply to cross the Hongu Khola to the northwest (right) bank on a suspension bridge (4318 ft, 1316 m). Ascend through the large hillside village of **Bung** (5250 ft, 1600 m). Reach it in **1½ hours** from Guidel. Continue up through the village and head north to Lenji Kharka and on to Boskom Gompa in **3½ hours** from lower Bung. Once a beautiful Buddhist monastery, it is now in disrepair. One monk remains at this wonderful site.

Reach a promontory with a *chorten* in **½ hour.** Climb through rhododendron forests to the Surkie La (10,122 ft, 3085 m), some **2 hours** from Boskom Gompa. A steep, slick, rocky descent follows. Reach the meadows past the *bhaTTi* at **Nachi Dingma** (8531 ft, 2600 m) in **¾ hour.** Traverse and descend through the pastoral village of **Gai Kharka.** Continue descending to cross the suspension bridge (6090 ft, 1856 m) of the Inukhu Khola to the west (right) bank. The trail on both sides is extremely steep and exposed. It is **1½ hours** from Nachi Dingma.

Climb very steeply to the ridge crest at the Sherpa village of **Shibuche** (8858 ft, 2700 m), where there are several tea shops. This takes **2 hours.** Head west up the ridge crest and traverse over to the Pangkongma La (10,410 ft, 3173 m) in **1½ hours.** Descend past the *gomba* to Pangkongma, or **Pangu** (9338 ft, 2846 m), in **¾ hour.** If heading toward Everest, take the right-hand fork and traverse to Kharte in **3 hours.** You can now follow the trek descriptions in chapter 8 to Khumbu, or perhaps continue west toward Kathmandu.

CHAINPUR TO ILAM

This route description allows a trekker who is in Chainpur to continue traversing the middle hills to Ilam. Once there, you can head south to the main East–West Highway and either return to Kathmandu or, as described at the end of this section, head on to perhaps Darjeeling. This route was done in 1972, and I'm not sure how accurately the description reflects the conditions today. The region is heavily populated, a road now passes west of Terhathum, and the traveler will have little difficulty asking the way.

Reach Chainpur as described in the Tumlingtar to Ghunsa section at the beginning of this chapter. Leaving **Chainpur,** the trail now descends for ¾ **hour** and crosses the Pilua Khola. Then it ascends for **1¼ hours** to **Madi** at about the same elevation as Chainpur. Now proceed on a level trail to the right to reach **Palomadi** in another **hour.** Both Palomadi and Alimela are also called Mulkharka. Another **hour** on level ground brings you to **Alimela,** from which it is only a short descent and climb to reach a crossing of the Maya Khola in **½ hour.** Then climb through the widely scattered village of **Umling** and eventually to the pass over the Mungabori Lekh in **2½ hours.** This last part is through an extremely beautiful meadow and forest, with a few tea shops 15 minutes before the pass. Now the trail descends rather gradually and follows the long ridge stretching out to Terhathum. The road to Basantapur is crossed. Pass through the rather pleasant village of **Jirikimpti** in **2 hours** and keep fairly level on either side of the ridge to reach **Terhathum** in another **hour.** This is a

Sherpa girl trying on her mother's jewelry (photo by Jeff Greenwald)

dense little bazaar town with three parallel streets and district offices.

The trail to Ilam now continues down the left side of the ridge to **Keorimi** in **1½ hours.** Beyond, it goes down more steeply on the end of the ridge into the furnace-hot valley of the Tamur Khola. The river is reached in **1½ hours.** Go upstream for 10 minutes to where a man in a dugout boat can take you across the river for a small charge, or go half an hour farther upstream and walk across the bridge for free. From either place, there is a stiff climb of some

3 hours to Ranigaon. If you cross by the dugout, go to the small, extremely steep direct trail just opposite the landing place of the boat. It becomes somewhat cooler after a one-hour climb. From the saddle at **Ranigaon,** it is ½ **hour** up the left side of the ridge to **Yasak,** a small Brahman bazaar town.

Another **hour** of reasonably level going brings you to **Milkrode.** Its high school is visible from afar. **Two more hours** of traversing the left side of the hill eventually bring you to a stream. Once across the stream, the trail finally goes steeply up through a village to the barren crest of the Mahabharat Lekh in **2 hours.** Follow this crest to the left for **1 hour,** taking the right fork at the base of a small hill shortly after a tea shop. The bazaar town of Manglebari is visible across a valley. Descend to the stream and follow it until the trail gradually goes diagonally up and crosses various streams and ridges to reach **Manglebari** in **4 hours.** It is now only **4 hours** to **Ilam.** Along the way, descend to a small stream, then climb slightly before descending a long way to the stream at the base of the Ilam hill, an hour from the town.

For the first time in many weeks, you will see jeeps. From Ilam, take a morning bus to Birtamod, on the East–West Highway. To return to Kathmandu by bus or plane, go either to Biratnagar, where there are daily flights, or to Bhadrapur, where there are fewer air connections. It is possible to motor directly to Kathmandu overnight. But to proceed to Darjeeling, take a bus east to Kakarbhitta, which is located on the border. Pass through customs and take a 1-hour jeep ride to Siliguri. From Siliguri, you can take a train, a jeep, or a bus to Darjeeling, or you can go via jeep or bus to Kalimpong, or to Gantok, Sikkim. Most vehicles leave early in the morning or around noon. You must check beforehand to make sure that border crossings from Nepal to India are permitted here for foreigners—this was not permitted in 1989. Permits for Sikkim and Darjeeling must be applied for many weeks in advance.

Makalu Base Camp
(Map No. 6, Page 249)

The route described here begins at the airstrip in Tumlingtar and reaches the base camp on the south side of the main massif. If coming from Khumbu, you could join this route at Seduwa by leaving the trail from Khumbu at Menpang, and heading up the west (left) bank of the Arun. There are other possible link-ups, including taking the road to Hille, and walking to Tumlingtar.

Begin at the airstrip in **Tumlingtar** (1500 ft, 457 m) and follow the main trade route north towards KhAADbari, the district center. The way follows the plateau that divides the Arun Khola to the west and the Sabaaya Khola to the east, and climbs the populated ridge crest. Reach the *Newar* bazaar and district center of **KhAADbari** (3500 ft, 1067 m) in 2¾ **hours.** In addition to a police check post, many shops, hotels, and a hospital, there is a Wednesday market here.

Continue climbing on the ridge to Mane Bhanjyang (3800 ft, 1158 m), where you can choose to either continue near the ridge crest to the northwest, or divert north along the terraced hillside through the scattered settlements of

Gairipangma. Either way, in **3½ hours,** you reach BhoTebas (5700 ft, 1737 m) below a crest. Climb up to a pass (6200 ft, 1890 m), then head northeast along a ridge crest to reach the tiny village of **Chichira** (6300 ft, 1920 m) in **2 hours and 10 minutes.** Here there are some tea shops and supplies. Continue to Kuwapani. Along the way, as you look north, you can see Makalu and much of the journey for the next few days. Pass a bivouac cave. The trail crosses and recrosses the ridge crest reaching 7000 ft (2133 m) before dropping to the few simple houses of **MUDe** (6800 ft, 2073 m) in **2 hours and 50 minutes** from Chichira.

Descend gradually, staying mainly on the west side of the ridge, and reach **Num** (5000 ft, 1524 m) in **1½ hours** from MUDe. Immediately to the west of the school, the trail drops into a series of steep switchbacks through terraced fields to the Arun Khola. Reach it in **1½ hours** from Num, then cross the suspension bridge (2250 ft, 686 m) to the right bank, taking care on the narrow, slippery floorboards. Climb up the eroded right bank to reach terraces and pass through the houses of Rumruma, and reach **Seduwa** (4900 ft, 1493 m) in **2 hours** from the bridge. More trekker-oriented facilities are being built here. On your return to the airstrip at Tumlingtar, you could take a three-and-a-half-day alternative, keeping on this side of the Arun on the traditional trade route, which has fallen into disuse in sections, but is definitely devoid of Westerners. You need to ask directions as you go.

From Seduwa, the main track angles diagonally up right (north) and across open, terraced fields to a *mani* wall and the single house on the ridge crest, which separates the Arun drainage from the Kaasuwa Khola. Reach the *mani* wall in **1½ hours** from Seduwa. You can see the uppermost limits of agriculture from here, and the cluster of a dozen bamboo huts comprising Tashigaon. The trail continues to contour and rise slightly all the way to reach **Tashigaon** (6750 ft, 2057 m) in **2 hours.**

For a slightly shorter way to Tashigaon, which requires some route finding, you can climb the slopes above Seduwa on a less well-defined trail that works its way up through the fields to the Sherpa village of Nashigaon (you can see Hindu and Buddhist influences in the small *gompa* there—not uncommon in such a transition zone). This more direct route then moves over to the east to a heavily wooded ridge through which the trail wanders to reach Tashigaon. Consider this way on one leg, to put some variety in the route, and to appreciate minimally disturbed cloud forest.

Tashigaon (literally, "luck village"), is the last settlement on the trek to base camp. You must be self-sufficient in food, fuel, and shelter from here on. The area beyond is used by shepherds for the most part. Groups usually hire porters here who are familiar with the way beyond. These people are especially helpful in locating water where there seems to be none. The town, comprised mostly of bamboo-and-thatch houses, was the subject of a fine documentary film done by Kurt Diemberger and Julie Tullis. There are now some tourist facilities, and basic meals put together from whatever leftover expedition food items are available. You may be able to purchase these and kerosene, but come well equipped.

The trail now heads into a lovely cloud forest, and 20 minutes beyond, you cross the last creek for a couple of days! The way continues to climb steeply in forest, and until you break out on the main ridge separating the Kashuwa Khola and the Iswa Khola valleys, there are no views. Reach Kaungma, the first major leveling of the ridge, where there is a "dry" camp with a small bivouac cave immediately below the grazing area in **5 hours** from Tashigaon. A further **2 hours** will bring you to a lovely little tarn campsite (13,150 ft, 4008 m), just below Shipton Pass. You would be advised to camp lower down to avoid altitude illness, however. At the top of the first knoll from Kaungma, the world suddenly opens up with great views of Chamlang (23,999 ft, 7317 m) and Peak 6 (22,103 ft, 6739 m), while Makalu (27,817 ft, 8481 m) and Kangchenjunga (the prominent peak off to the east) are clearly visible. From the above-mentioned tarn, the trail angles up and is forced left by rock bands toward Shipton Pass. The pass itself is actually two passes, the first known locally as Kekela (13,875 ft, 4229 m), and the second, Tutula (13,725 ft, 4183 m), with a rather large tarn with a *chorten* and prayer flags in between. From the Kekela, descend north to the austere lake, then continue due north again on a switchback trail to the Tutula. This pass is **1 hour** north of the

Tarn campsite in the moonlight below Shipton Pass; Peaks 6 and 7 behind (photo by Patrick Morrow)

"campsite" tarn on the south side of the complex.

Try to memorize the features here, since the terrain opens up at this point and it could be difficult to find the way back in poor visibility. Although not technically difficult, this region is the crux of the route to the base camp, and you could get lost here in whiteout conditions. As well, if a snowstorm hits this pass, be ready to recognize avalanche hazards, and make sure the entire party is equipped with food, fuel, clothing, and shelter. Porters and trekkers have died here because of mountain weather.

From the Tutula, the path drops gently at first, enters rhododendron forest, and contours to the campsite at Mumbuk (11,475 ft, 3498 m), just a short distance after a stream, one of many encountered north of the pass to here. There is a cave, used by porters, down slope between the tent sites and the creek. Reach it in **2 hours** from the pass.

Beyond Mumbuk, the trail plunges steeply down a dry watercourse for 700 ft (213 m) and, shortly before it reaches the Barun Khola, swings left, heading upstream on the right bank. The trail sticks close to the Barun Khola from this point on, swinging upstream to parallel it on the south side for the next couple of days. Another campsite, "lower Mumbuk," located just as the trail comes close to the river, provides simple shelter in a cave, as well as a few tent platforms. Shortly thereafter, the trail crosses an active rock slide just above the river. This dangerous section may be bypassed in the future by planned trail reconstruction. As you approach the grass-covered plain of Yangri Kharka, **2½ hours** from Mumbuk, you are reaching the alpine region, with increasingly spectacular views of the northeast side of Peak 6 and its ice-covered neighbors. At the end of a large meadow, the trail takes an unexpected turn directly up a creek bed and eventually climbs directly up the fan of a gentle avalanche path, through scrub alders. Just as it starts to cut diagonally back down toward the creek you will see the solitary hut and prayer flags at Nehe Kharka (12,000 ft, 3657 m). This hut, which sits in a clearing beneath a towering cirque of black, moss-covered granite, clearly is physically and spiritually well protected. It is **2½ hours** from Yangri Kharka.

Most campsites from this spot on offer a lot of sun, which is welcomed in the early hours in this ever-increasing gain in altitude and cold. Shortly after leaving this idyllic spot, the trail crosses the river to the left bank on a sturdy bridge (the one and only crossing of the Barun Khola, at this writing). Then climb steeply through a splendid mixed forest of rhododendrons and mature spruce. When the trail breaks out onto open scrub and grassy slopes there is a bivouac cave at the base of the cliff straight ahead. The trail now ascends alpine terrain and roughly parallels the river all the way to base camp. Waterfalls stream down for hundreds of feet on either side of the granite-walled valley, and there's even one emerging from a cave 328 ft (100 m) off the ground, pouring down a sheer cliff. Amazingly, the scenery continues to improve. You can now see the backsides of the peaks you've been looking at in the early days of the trek. Pyramid Peak (22,402 ft, 6830 m), Peak 4 (22,041 ft, 6720 m), Chamlang, Peak 6, Peak 3 (21,244 ft, 6477 m), and Peak 5 (21,005 ft, 6404 m). Ramara, the large *mani* wall where the trail breaks into a dozen ill-defined ones contouring the grassy slope, is reached in **3 hours** from Nehe Kharka. There is a roofless stone enclosure here that is used by shepherds.

Take the uppermost trail, which becomes more defined as it hits the ridge on the skyline. Soon after, the trail hugs the Barun Khola (near its headwaters), which is much reduced in size at this point. Within sight of the Lower Barun Glacier, you come upon white sand platforms 450 ft (138 m) past a clear stream that enters from the right, and where there is a shallow bivouac cave called Merick. At this point, you are in true alpine conditions, well above treeline. There are more shallow caves 600 ft (183 m) beyond. You have made it onto the Schneider *Khumbu Himal* map. The altitude has slowed you down at this point, and the walk across the moraine flats toward the roofless sheep pens at Sherson (15,485 ft, 4720 m) seems to take longer than it should, so plan to get here in **2 hours** from Ramara. The base camp is situated just south of the snout of the Barun Glacier, at 15,825 ft (4823 m), **1 hour** from Sherson. The mountain was first climbed by the French in 1955. They headed northwest of here to cross a col to reach the north side of the mountain. Its name is taken from Maha-kala, meaning the great black one, clearly appropriate for this rocky massif.

The upper half of Makalu's impressive south face rears its head above an intervening ridge, and you are truly entering the throne room of the gods! You can walk north, along a loose, rubbly moraine that ascends gently to the base camp of Makalu, skirting a ridge coming off it, in a couple of hours. Consider taking a tent directly up this intervening ridge, to the north, above Sherson to a huge, flat plain at 17,390 ft (5300 m), for an ultra-spectacular campsite with a full view of Makalu. You would need to melt snow for water there. Just a half hour's walk from the campsite toward the imposing south face and southeast ridge of Makalu, across a gentle plateau, will being you to views of the unfamiliar back sides of Lhotse and Everest. You can see the flanks of their ridges reaching down into Tibet. You may have seen this snow summit from the Milke Danda, far to the south. It may be difficult to convince yourself that this is the same mountain you saw in Khumbu. From the campsite, you could also drop down to the north to cross the frozen surface of a 1200 ft (400 m) wide lake and ascend a peak for great views north. Or you could head up the Barun Glacier, or rather in the valley between it and the moraine to the southwest. There are a lot of choices in the high Himalaya, more than enough to take your breath away.

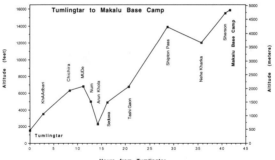

Marijuana seeds are pressed into oil at Rigi

10 Western Nepal

The fact that I could find almost no other information about the north-west of the country convinced me that that was where I should go.

John Pilkington, *Into Thin Air*

Western Nepal, the region west of the Kali Gandaki river, offers a chance to visit fascinating country and people and is a good choice for the trekker who has done the popular treks. It is more difficult to travel here than in the more trekker-frequented east. Except for the Dhorpatan–Tansen circuit, food and accommodations are difficult to obtain. Either going with an agency or organizing porters yourself makes sense in most places here. Very few people in the area speak English, trails tend to be more difficult, and the country is more rugged. Furthermore, except for the region around Dhaulagiri, the Himalayan scenery in this part of Nepal is less impressive than in the east. It is more difficult to get the feeling of being in the mountains that Khumbu, Kangchenjunga, Makalu, the Thorung La region, and Langtang provide. But for the seeker of impressive forests, rugged, sometimes stark terrain, and fascinating people with unusual customs, the west may be the best.

Three treks will be described. Many, many others are possible. First, a circuit from Pokhara to Dhorpatan and then on to Tansen. This trek involves few logistic problems, and only a moderate pass must be crossed. If there is snow, an alternative route is described that will avoid it, although it requires some backtracking. Next, a newly opened area in Dolpo, Nepal's "Hidden Land," is described, starting from Dhorpatan and walking to Jumla, the district center for Karnali Zone. Finally, a trek out of Jumla to RaRa Lake National Park completes our look at Nepal's Wild West!

Dhorpatan–Tansen Circuit
(Maps No. 3, Page 183, and No. 7, Page 280)

A circuit from Pokhara to Dhorpatan with the return through Tansen offers a pleasant trek through mixed country and views of impressive mountains. The spacious Dhorpatan Valley is refreshing in this tangled country, and there are many intriguing side trips. In the winter, snow can make the crossing of the Jaljala, a moderate pass into Dhorpatan, difficult if not impossible for a few days, so an alternative route is described that crosses a lower pass. The turnoff for this is several days before the Jaljala, at Baglung, so an early decision must be made. Food and lodging is available along most of the way. There might be a problem on the last day, near the Jaljala, so food should be carried for that.

There are several options for starting this trek. You could fly to Balewa south of Baglung on regular RNAC flights from Pokhara and walk from there.

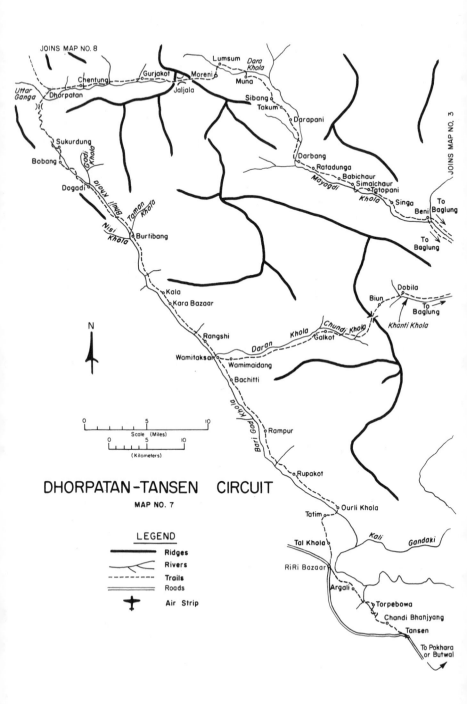

Lumsum

Dara Khola

Chentung

Gurjakot

Moreni

Muna

Uttar Ganga

Dhorpatan

Jaljala

Sibang

Takum

Darapani

Sukurdung

Godi Khola

Darbang

Ratadunga

Bobang

Babichaur

Simalchaur

Myagdi

Tatopani

Dogadi

Nisi Khola

Toman Khola

Khola

Singa

Beni

To Baglung

Burtibang

To Baglung

Kala

Biun

Dobila

Kara Bazaar

To Baglung

Khanti Khola

N

Rangshi

Daran

Khola

Chundi Khola

Galkot

Wamitaksar

Wamimaidang

Bachitti

0 5 10
Scale (Miles)

0 5 10
(Kilometers)

Bari Gad

Khola

Rampur

DHORPATAN -TANSEN CIRCUIT

MAP NO. 7

Rupakot

Ourli Khola

Tatim

LEGEND

Tal Khola

Kali Gandaki

RiRi Bazaar

Argali

Torpebowa

Chandi Bhanjyang

Tansen

To Pokhara
or Butwal

Ridges

Rivers

Trails

Roads

Air Strip

If starting from Pokhara, you could walk or drive to NagDAADa, on the popular route to Thak Khola, and proceed off the beaten path from there. When the road eventually reaches Kusma and Beni, that will shorten the journey by several days. An entry point is NauDAADA, 1½ hours south on the Siddhartha Rajmarg, the road from Pokhara to Butwal. (This is not the same as the town of NagDAADa, which is on the way to GhoRepani.) Finally, you could take the same bus all the way to Tansen and do the circuit in reverse. I find some people doing this late in the monsoon, or just after it, hoping to get better views on the Jaljala if they arrive there a little later.

POKHARA TO DHORPATAN VIA JALJALA

The first beginning will be from Pokhara to Suikhet and NagDAADa; then the alternative, from NauDAADa, south of Pokhara, will be described. Both routes join at Kusma.

Pokhara to Kusma via NagDAADa

The first part of the trek crosses the crest between Pokhara and the Modi Khola valley to the west. Get to NagDAADa (4782 ft, 1458 m) from Pokhara, as described in chapter 7. The road from Pokhara reaches the ridge at this point, and the once-idyllic town with spectacular views at sunrise and sunset is now also a road stop. From here, it is best to continue along the road, though you can keep to the old trail through the town, along the ridge crest. In **25 minutes** from NagDAADa, leave the road at 5000 ft (1524 m), and fork left to reach the spread-out Brahman-*Chhetri* village of **PaaUdur** (4940 ft, 1506 m). Continue a further level **45 minutes** and just at the edge of the village, fork right and contour (the left fork descends). The trail keeps to the right of a reforestation project fence, then crosses it, forks left to descend, crosses a stream, and re-ascends to reach the original trail. Either way, you reach the few homes of Kaauli in **30 minutes.** Just beyond are the first houses of Bhadaauri, and you climb to the pass and village of **Bhadaauri Deorali** (5460 ft, 1664 m) in **30 minutes.** Here there are hotels, and views.

Head west, contouring (there is a more direct trail that descends, but there are no facilities along it), to reach the scattered village of Saliyan (5460 ft, 1664 m) in **40 minutes** and eventually pass through in **30 minutes.** Traverse a slide, descend a spur, pass the few houses of Jaigaon, and continue in a pine forest to reach the school and village of Tamarjung (4280 ft, 1304 m) in another **50 minutes.** Higher up, across the valley, you will notice either the road scar or completed road, depending on progress. You have been in the Rati Khola valley, and heading to the Modi Khola. Pass through **Tilhaar,** another scattered Brahman-*Chhetri* village (3660 ft, 1116 m), and beyond at a *chautaara,* **1 hour** from Tamarjung, fork right (the left goes down and crosses the Rati Khola on a suspension bridge). Pass under a water line that spans the Rati Khola, and keep to the sandy right bank for the most part, through substantial subtropical forests, to reach Gijaan in another **hour.**

Reach the confluence of the Rati Khola and main Modi Khola near where the smaller Jaare Khola joins from the east, in **20 minutes** from Gijaan. **Dobila** is in the valley bottom; the hotels are on the left bank. Cross the Modi Khola (2860 ft, 871 m) to the right, then turn right and ascend a spur to reach Chhuwa (3300 ft, 1006 m). Continue downstream through Kariya to reach **Kusma** (3100 ft, 945 m), the administrative center *(sadar mukam)* for Parbat District, **1½ hours** from crossing the Modi Khola. This town, like most district centers, has grown immensely in the last decade. In 1989, it took me quite some time to find the old town I remembered from the mid-seventies!

At this point, you have reached the valley of the Kali Gandaki, one of Nepal's major rivers, which cuts one of the deepest gorges in the world to the north of here. The route proceeds north up this valley to Beni, and then heads west up a tributary valley. If you took the trail from NauDAADa, south of Pokhara, you will join the description here, at Kusma. Unseen, on a shelf across the river here, at Balewa, is an airstrip used by RNAC for its daily flights from Pokhara.

Pokhara to Kusma via NauDAADa

Take the bus to NauDAADa as described above. From **NauDAADa** (3600 ft, 1097 m), head west and contour, then descend to the south to a tributary from the north. It can be crossed directly or, in high water, **10 minutes** upstream at a bridge. On the east (right) bank, reach **Seti Dovan** (2950 ft, 900 m), a large bazaar town **45 minutes** from NauDAADa. Continue west above the north (left) bank of the Andhi Khola to **Rangatani** (3100 ft, 945 m) in **30 minutes.** Cross the suspension bridge here and follow the south (right) bank during the high water. Either bank can be followed in low water. Continue upstream to **Chilaunabata** (3600 ft, 1097 m) in **1½ hours,** then to **Phedi** (3850 ft, 1173 m) in another **1½ hours.** There are usually three fords of the river, at places that depend on the river level. This is a main route and the trail is easy to find. Beyond Phedi, begin a steep ascent to the pass and town of **Karkineta** (5350 ft, 1631 m) after **1½ to 2 hours.**

The descent to the Modi Khola now begins. Head southwest from the pass and descend through **Potebar** and **Phedi** to reach **Yamdi** (3000 ft, 914 m) in **1½ hours.** Stay on the east (left) bank of the river for **30 minutes,** then ford the river to its east (right) bank. Contour the rice paddies and ascend a small bamboo-forested gully. Continue to Ghandichaur (2875 ft, 876 m) in **30 minutes.** Ascend to a large suspension bridge over the Modi Khola (2400 ft, 732 m) in **30 minutes.** Cross to the west (right) bank and ascend for **30 minutes** to **Kusma** (3100 ft, 945 m).

Kusma to Dhorpatan via Jaljala

Proceed from Kusma by heading north, past the statue of former King Mahendra in the lower part of town, and through the old town to Chamurke, where the trail leaves the shelf and descends to the roaring river. Head up its left bank to the large bazaar of **Armadi** (2620 ft, 799 m), **1 hour** from Kusma. Beyond is Naya Pul (new bridge), with its bridge north of town, but continue on the east bank, through the spread-out village of Shastradara, to reach **Khaniyaghaat** (2740 ft, 835 m) in **1¾ hours** from Armadi. Here there is a bridge across the Kali Gandaki that leads to Baglung, on a shelf above the

Sheets of so-called rice paper (actually made from a shrub) set out to dry, from below Beni

river, is the administrative center for Baglung District, which has a hospital. Views of the south face of Dhaulagiri are particularly impressive from here.

People flying to the Baglung airstrip at Balewa (3325 ft, 1013 m) proceed north up the valley, and in **2½ hours** descend to cross the Kante Khola (2800 ft, 853 m) to its north (left) bank and ascend to **Baglung** (3150 ft, 960 m) in another **30 minutes.**

To go on to Beni, you could cross the river here and head up its west bank, but the east side is currently a little easier. Along here, you may see villagers making so-called rice paper from the bark of the *Daphne bholua* shrub, (called *baruwa* or *kagat pate* in Nepali), which is collected up in the high hills here. The bark is pounded into a pulp, and the paper is made from the slurry that settles on a screen and dries in the sun. It is traditionally used in Kathmandu, and you can buy cards and stationary made from it there. If you see a family making some, ask to buy a few sheets locally.

Continue north up the east bank, through Jimire, to **Pharse, in 1 hour.** Here there is a suspension bridge (2720 ft, 829 m) over the Kali Gandaki. Decide whether to cross it, depending on the weather and time of day and whether you want to be in the sun. Assuming you crossed it to avoid the afternoon sun, your route will head north and pass through the towns of Taremaregaon, Ratnaachaur, Lamogara, TAAgnebagar, and Jaremare, before coming to the Mayagdi Khola in **1½ hours.** Here you cross the suspension bridge (2700 ft, 823 m) and reach **Beni,** the large town and administrative center for Mayagdi

District. The way west now heads up the Mayagdi Khola valley for several days before crossing the Jaljala to leave this major drainage system and enter that of the Bheri Khola. You could also continue north up the Kali Gandaki and reach Tatopani, with its hordes of trekkers, and go on to Thak Khola, between Annapurna and Dhaulagiri.

Proceed west, up the left bank of the Mayagdi Khola, past a cable car over the river. The new government buildings here were designed by the winner of an architectural competition held in Kathmandu. Pass many small villages, including Chutreni, Ghorsang, and Baguwa, to **Singhaa** (2800 ft, 914 m), reached in **1¼ hours** from Beni. In **30 minutes,** reach the first houses of **Tatopani,** and after crossing a tributary, pass above a hot springs pool, where men bathe up to 4:00 P.M. and women after. Like similar places in other parts of the world, people with arthritis and other complaints have moved here to soak and soothe. The main part of town (2920 ft, 890 m) is **10 minutes** beyond. Below this part of town, by the river, are more hot springs emanating from the rocks, where you can wash. At the upper end of town there is a suspension bridge that you cross to the right and in **15 minutes** regain the northeast bank on another bridge to reach Simalchaur (3100 ft, 945 m).

Continue heading up valley, staying on the left bank, and not crossing any bridges over the main river, to reach **Babiachaur** (3220 ft, 981 m) in **1 hour.** Upstream, pass through Ranamang, Shastradara, and Baloti to reach Rata-Dhunga (meaning "red rock") in a further hour. Continue on the same left bank, through Poteni, and reach the lone hut of Dharkharka in another **35 minutes,** where the trail now forks right to climb up above the huge landslide you have been seeing on the south bank.

This slide rumbled for 5 minutes in September 1988, claiming the lives of over 100 people. The rock and debris washed across the river, taking out the trail on the north bank. Such major events are now considered more likely due to tectonic (mountain-building) forces than to deforestation. When I used to journey up this valley in the mid-seventies, there was a major slide before RataDhunga that I couldn't find in 1989. Nepalis are quick to rebuild the slides, to reclaim farmland, so I expect that eventually even this scar will be invisible and the trail will not detour.

The detour climbs 300 ft (91 m) through terraces, crosses and follows an irrigation canal, contours, and then descends to the large town of **Darbang** (3520 ft, 1073 m) in **40 minutes.** You cross the Mayagdi Khola to the west (right) bank, and local villagers may collect a tax for porters crossing here. Go past the few more hotels in the village and head north to reach Phedi, the few houses at the foot of the climb to Dharapani, in **30 minutes.** Cross the tributary Daanga Khola on a suspension bridge upstream, or on rocks at low water, and pick up the trail that climbs the ridge. As you ascend, join a trail coming in from the right and reach the crest of the ridge. As you climb, on the right is subtropical forest and on the drier left, chir pine. This results from the marked climatological changes on either side of the ridge. Reach the spectacularly situated town of **Dharapani** (5125 ft, 1562 m) in **1 hour.** Dhaulagiri is the massive mountain to the north, and off to the west is Gurja Himal. Between lie

Dhaulagiri IV and V. Hope to get views (unfettered by clouds) here in the morning or evening. Don't despair, I had been by here several times in the mid-seventies, and it wasn't until recently that I saw the mountains clearly.

The trail now contours high above the river, as it heads northwest toward the watershed. The views along this stretch are some of the finest in Nepal. Reach **Takum** (5500 ft, 1676 m), another idyllic setting, in **1 hour.** The predominant ethnic groups in this region are *Magar, Chhetri, Kaami, Damai* and *Bahun.* Continue contouring through Sibang, then climb up to Maachhim. As you round a bend by a *chautaara* (6600 ft, 2112 m) and begin to head northwest up the tributary Dara Khola, you can look north up the Mayagdi Khola valley, which drains the west side of Dhaulagiri. A strenuous high trek encircles the sixth highest mountain in the world by crossing French Pass at the headwaters of this valley.

Continue on to sprawling Phaleagaon (6200 ft, 1890 m) in **1½ hours** where, at the outskirts, there is a recently constructed water mill run by an efficient turbine. During the trade embargo with India in 1989, the noisy diesel mills were laid to rest, and traditional mills flourished. As you head up, notice that you are at the altitude limit of rice cultivation. However, nearer to Jumla, it will be growing almost 2000 ft (610 m) higher! **Muna** (6460 ft, 1969 m), is **45 minutes** beyond. You have to take the uphill fork after you leave Phaleagaon, or you will pass below the village and head directly to the bridge over the Dara Khola. Across the valley is the spectacularly perched village of Dara.

Reach the suspension bridge (6200 ft, 1990 m) over the Dara Khola in **15 minutes** and cross it to the left bank. Climb up to enter a side valley and reach the single house of Narja Khola (7060 ft, 2152 m) in **35 minutes.** Cross the tributary and reach a trail junction (7220 ft, 2201 m) **10 minutes** later. The right fork heads to Lulang, Gurjaakhaani, and the Gurja Himal region. But to head on to Dhorpatan, take the left fork. Pass above the houses of Lumsum to reach a hotel in **25 minutes** (7180 ft, 2188 m). Ask to find out if the next village is occupied and whether food is available, if you need to. Cross the Dara Khola again in **20 minutes,** to the right bank, and head upstream to cross another tributary. Immediately turn left and begin to climb to **Moreni** (lowest at 7820 ft, 2383 m). The few houses, scattered 700 ft (213 m) up the hillside, are reached in some **40 minutes,** and they may be unoccupied in the middle of winter as the people descend to Lumsum. There may be little water along the way, so fill up at the valley bottom. Moreni is the last place to get food before Dhorpatan.

The trail heads southwest, reaching prickly-leaved oak forests, then rhododendron and birch higher up. After **2½ hours,** you reach a cluster of prayer flags and a *chorten* (11,200 ft, 3414 m). Continue to the west (don't take the left fork), pass a small spring, and reach the broad, flat plateau of Jaljala a few minutes later at a *chautaara.* The panorama from here takes in Machhapuchhre all the way to Churen Himal. Sunsets are supreme. There are some *goTh,* used in the monsoon by people from Muna as they pasture their animals on the lush grass.

From Jaljala, follow the trail on the left (south) side of the plateau, and don't descend into the river valley to the north. Descend some 15 minutes to reach a small saddle point (11,000 ft, 3353 m) that is the actual watershed between the Kali Gandaki and the Bheri-Karnali. Head for the valley *V* shape, through the pastures, and pass below a group of *goTh* to reach a lone stone one in **30 minutes** from the *chautaara*. Beyond, cross to the right bank of the Uttar Ganga ("north river"), which you will follow to Dhorpatan, and continue down valley. Don't cross the cantilever bridge over the river 30 minutes beyond, but enjoy the rhododendron and juniper forests on the north side of the valley. Reach an open area with *goTh* in **1½ hours** from the lone stone *goTh*. GurjaakoT (9900 ft, 3017 m), the next cluster of *goTh* on this side of the valley, is **20 minutes** beyond. From here, cross several tributaries of the Simudar Khola on wooden bridges. As a variant side trip, you could head up this tributary valley, cross a pass and get to Gurjaakhaani, and then head back to Lulang and Muna.

In **30 minutes** from the Simudar Khola, head upstream in another tributary valley to cross the Gur Gad to its right bank on a suspension bridge. Rejoin the main valley, and reach the beginning of the broad Dhorpatan Valley. The way keeps to the drier north side and reaches **Chentung** (9660 ft, 2944 m) and a few hotels in another **hour.** The main Tibetan village is across the tributary. The Bon-po *gompa* of this village, behind you on the hillside, follows the tradition that predated the introduction of Buddhism to Tibet. It has been much changed, so it is difficult to tell adherents apart. The best way is to see which

Maikot, a Kham Magar *village west of Yamakhar*

direction they spin their prayer wheels and circumambulate *mani* walls. Many of the settlements here and beyond, on the north side of the valley, date from the influx of Tibetan refugees in 1959–60.

Continue west and reach Nauthar, also called Chisapani, in **35 minutes.** Here Nepalis come up from the south in the summer to grow potatoes and pasture animals. This agro-pastoral style of life is followed by many Nepalis in these parts as they farm the lowlands in the winter, grow rice in the summer, and move up with their animals to the high country in the monsoon. Cross the next tributary and go on through another Tibetan settlement before descending to the flat area called Giraaund (9325 ft, 2842 m), meaning "ground," the local term for an airstrip. Reach it in a further **30 minutes.** The airstrip is overgrown with vegetation; planes haven't landed here for several years. Before you reach the flats, pass below the Wildlife Conservation and Hunting Office, where they will ask to see your permits. They monitor the trophy hunting for blue sheep that goes on north of here.

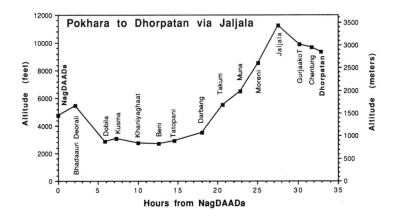

AROUND DHORPATAN

Dhorpatan is the name of the area, an unusually broad, flat valley in this rugged hill country. It was once a lake that was filled in. Many Nepalis from villages to the east, south, and west live here during the summer months, when they grow potatoes and pasture animals. Their settlements are seen along the perimeter of the valley, especially on its southern aspect, and at Nauthar.

Although there are few views from the valley floor (Annapurna South can be seen some 35 mi or 56 km to the east), easy climbs of the surrounding hills provide unparalleled views. You can travel a few days to the north into blue sheep country, or up into the snows of the western Dhaulagiri range. The base camps of the various expeditions at the head of the Ghustung Khola are worth visiting. Also, the route northwest to Dolpo will be described. Food and shelter must be carried for all these trips to the north.

To the west and northwest live the *Kham Magar,* an ethnic group with many animistic and shamanistic traditions. Food and shelter are difficult to obtain in this area and are best carried. A four- to five-day circuit through this region can be most interesting. After a long day down the Uttar Ganga you reach the villages of Taka and Shera, where the flat-roofed houses are reminiscent of Thak Khola or of areas further west. Cross the ridge up the tributary valley to the north and descend to Hukum (Hugaon), and go beyond to Maikot, on the north side of the Pelma Khola, in another very long day. The third day takes you through Puchhargaon and Yamakhar, where you meet the trail described below to Dolpo, which you can backtrack to Dhorpatan.

Those with less time should at least walk up one of the hills surrounding the valley for a view. The ridge crest directly south of the airstrip is the easiest viewpoint, and takes less than 2 hours via one of its north-facing spurs. The view from here in clear weather extends beyond Langtang in the east! The hill to the north of the valley (13,600 ft, 4145 m) can be reached in 3 to 4 hours from the airstrip. Surtibang, the "writing desk" hill to the southwest, is an excellent viewpoint. Reach it by heading west for 30 minutes as the valley narrows to a bridge over the Uttar Ganga. Cross and ascend to the top (13,300 ft, 4054 m), in 4 hours from the airstrip. Hiunchuli Patan is visible to the west. Finally, the highest of the peaks surrounding the valley, Phagune Dhuri (15,500 ft, 4724 m), lying to the northwest, can be reached from the Phagune Danda pass, which is described in the route to Dolpo.

DHORPATAN TO TANSEN

To head south to Tansen from Giraaund, go south across the valley toward the obvious pass. Depending on the year, there may be small bridges over the Uttar Ganga, but it is often necessary to wade. Pick up the trail from the east and reach the pass (9625 ft, 2934 m) in **30 minutes.** You could also head west through Shelpaki, cross the bridge to Nabe, and head toward the pass that way. Descend from the pass to a stream, and at 9300 ft (2835 m) begin crossing a series of six small bridges over the stream for the next 600 ft (185 m). Continue descending on the northeast (left) bank of the Bhuji Khola to reach Dowal (7600 ft, 2316 m) in **1 to 1½ hours** from the pass. This is the first permanent settlement. Typical terraced Nepali country lies ahead. The forest is prickly-leaved oak. In 1 hour, cross and recross the river and ascend slightly to **Sukurdung** (6700 ft, 2042 m), where there is a post box. Beyond the large schoolhouse, the trail crosses to the southwest (right) bank of the Bhuji Khola and descends slightly to **Bobang** (5800 ft, 1768 m) in **45 minutes.** Continue descending after a level stretch, and cross to the east (left) bank (5200 ft, 1585 m) of the Bhuji Khola in **30 minutes.** In **15 minutes** reach another suspension bridge (5052 ft, 1532 m) and cross to the west (right) bank. In another **15 minutes,** reach a covered bridge at **Dogadi** (4775 ft, 1455 m). Bypass another covered bridge and a suspension bridge, then cross to the east (left) bank on a suspension bridge (4250 ft, 1295 m) in **45 minutes.** Reach another suspension bridge (3600 ft, 1097 m) over the Taman Khola, a tributary to the east, and cross it to **Burtibang,** a large town with a police check post, reached in **1 hour.** From here the trail keeps to the east (left) bank for almost two days.

Continue along the Bhuji Khola, climbing somewhat through Renam to the small town of **Bingetti** (3400 ft, 1036 m) **2 hours** beyond Burtibang. Cross a tributary from the east, the Bing Khola, on a suspension bridge (3100 ft, 945

m) and reach **Kala** (2950 ft, 900 m), a large town, in another **30 minutes.** Keep on the east (left) side of the river and enter **Kara Bazaar** (2850 ft, 869 m) in 1 hour. Pass through Balua (2700 ft, 823 m) in another **45 minutes** and, **20 minutes** later, cross the Labdi Khola, another tributary. Climb through a sal forest before descending to **Rangshi** (2575 ft, 785 m) in 1 hour. The main river is now called the Bari Gad. Another **30 minutes** brings you to the bridge (2500 ft, 762 m) crossing the Daran Khola from the east. Just beyond, a left fork ascends to Wamitaksar. Baglung can be reached in a very long day. The route from Baglung to here is described later.

To continue to Tansen, pass through Sutti and reach **Bachitti** (2325 ft, 709 m) in **1½ hours.** The trail continues along rice paddies through Laureshimal, Jorkale, and Abachor, crosses a tributary from the east, and reaches **Rampur** (2150 ft, 655 m), a large bazaar, in **2¼ hours.** Continue through Mojua and cross a tributary from the east to reach **Ourli Khola** (2075 ft, 632 m) in **3¼ hours.** Cross the main river to its southwest (right) bank, then climb up steeply for **1¼ hours** to **Tatim** (3700 ft, 1128 m).

Keep climbing, take the left fork after passing through the town, and round a ridge jutting to the east (4475 ft, 1364 m). Dhaulagiri and Churen Himal can be seen from here. Enter chir pine forest, then drop slightly to a saddle and the town of **Ghiubesi** (4300 ft, 1311 m) 1 hour from Tatim. Enter a small, beautiful valley and go left through Chauraata (4500 ft, 1372 m) in **20 minutes.** Descend to the west, pass through **Pataunje Pani** (4400 ft, 1341 m) and drop steeply into a widening valley to reach the town and river of **Tal Khola** (2500 ft, 762 m) in **45 minutes.** Continue dropping down on the west (right) side of the valley to 2275 ft (693 m) before climbing out of the valley and heading downstream above the west (right) bank. Drop into the valley of the Kali Gandaki and descend to the large town of **RiRi Bazaar** (1550 ft, 472 m), **1¾ hours** from Tal Khola. There is now a road from Tansen to here with jeeps available.

If you want to walk all the way to Tansen, go through town, cross the RiRi Khola to its south (right) bank, and climb above the west (right) bank of the Kali Gandaki through Oruan Pokhari and Sattari Pokhari to reach **Argana** (2350 ft, 716 m) in **45 minutes.** Descend into another valley to reach **Argali** (2175 ft, 663 m) in **30 minutes.** There is a side trail heading off to the left of the fountain and *chautaara* in this village. It leads to a palace built in 1947 as a retirement home for then Prime Minister Juddha Shumshere J. B. Rana. It is worth a detour.

Continue shortly beyond Argali to the Gurung Khola (2025 ft, 617 m). Cross to the south (right) bank and follow the river upstream. Pass through Torpebowa (2400 ft, 732 m) in **30 minutes,** then cross to the east (left) bank and climb for **15 minutes** to Tirap (2675 ft, 815 m). Cross the river three times and reach Rossuas (3625 ft, 1105 m) in 1 hour. The town of **Gurung Khola** (4325 ft, 1318 m) is **30 minutes** beyond. Soon you see a pipe and a tunnel through the hill, but keep climbing for **15 minutes** to **Chandi Bhanjyang** (4625 ft, 1410 m). Enter a new valley and turn right (west) to contour the Shrinagar ridge on a wide trail. The trail passes through a few small settlements before it crosses the ridge to the south and drops into **Tansen** (4650 ft,

1417 m), the district center for Palpa, in **1 hour.** The head of the road is at the lower end of town. Buses leave for Pokhara in the morning. It is also possible to take a bus south to Butwal and Bhairawa. Be sure to catch the view of the mountains from the ridge behind Tansen. There are also many interesting temples in Tansen. The book *Palpa As You Like It* (see trekking in appendix B) is informative.

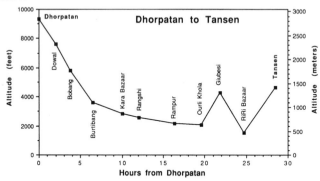

DHORPATAN TO JUMLA THROUGH DOLPO

(Map No. 8, Page 291)

The next section describes the long route to Jumla through the recently opened southern part of Dolpo District. A side trip to the pristine lake at Phoksumdo, coupled with the crossing of the Kaagmaara La (a high pass) to avoid backtracking, is described. Trekking parties are required to be self-sufficient in food and fuel, and to go through a trekking agency. In the monsoon, you might be able to hire horses at Dhorpatan to carry loads to Tarakot.

The first part of the trip crosses a major ridge to reach the Pelma Khola, then crosses another ridge to reach the same river system higher up. Then the crest of this part of the Himalaya is crossed to reach Dolpo and the upper reaches of the Thulo Bheri river system. There are only two small, poor villages along this four- to five-day walk.

The description starts at Giraaund, just down from the Wildlife Conservation and Hunting Office. Cross a small stream and climb up a short hill to Shelpaki, the houses spread out on a shelf above the valley floor, and continue west. You see a low-lying notch to the northwest, and fork right about 15 minutes beyond Giraaund. If you miss it, there is a more direct trail up to the notch, and you can go cross-country up to the trail that climbs more gradually to it. Reach the notch (10,120 ft, 3084 m), **1 hour** from Giraaund. Descend slightly to a plateau, and head toward the main Phagune Khola valley heading north up to the Phagune Danda pass. You proceed up the east (left) side of this valley lower down, reaching the main river in another **1½ hours,** crossing to the west (right) bank at 12,020 ft (3664 m) in another ½ **hour.** You then leave the river and climb up the valley wall to reach the pass (13,300 ft, 4054 m) in a further **45 minutes.** Hopefully, weather will permit you to enjoy the panorama from Putha Hiunchuli to the north, to Dhaulagiri in the east.

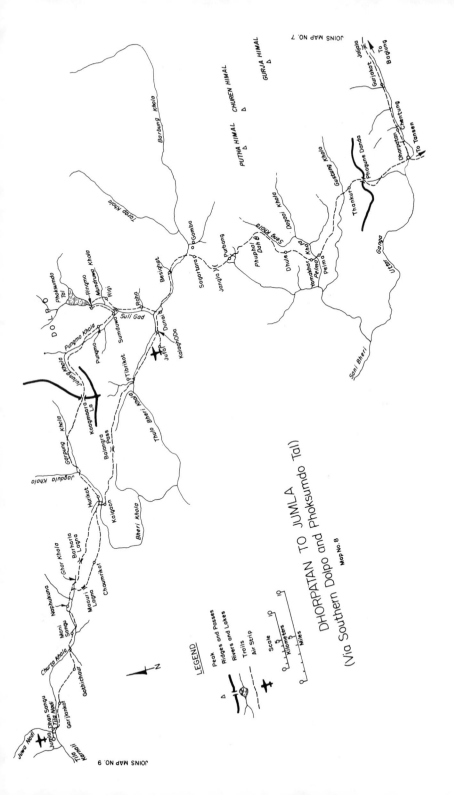

DHORPATAN TO JUMLA
(Via Southern Dolpo and Phoksumdo Tal)

Map No. 8

LEGEND

△ Peak
▬ Ridges and Passes
〰 Rivers and Lakes
--- Trails
✈ Air Strip

Scale
Kilometers
Miles

N

To Baglung
Jaljala
To Tansen

GURJA HIMAL △
CHUREN HIMAL △
PUTTHA HIMAL △

Guriakot
Chentung
Dhorpatan
Phagune Danda
Thankur

Gustung Khola
Uttar Ganga
Seni Bheri
Ganga

Phupha Dah
Pelma
Dhule
Dosaoi Khola
Yamakhar Khola
Pelmo
Seng Khola

Barbung Khola
Tarap Khola

Phoksumdo Tal
Ringmo
Rigi
Mudruma Khola
Suli Gad
DOLPO
Pungmo Khola
Pungmo
Sumduwa
Roha
Besishat
Sagartara
Gomba
Juphal
Dunai
Jangla
Purhang
Tibrikot
Thulo Bheri Khola
KalagHODa

Juljul Khola
Koagmara La
Balangra Pass
Garpung Khola
Jagdula Khola
Hurikot
Kaigaon
Bheri Khola

Barharia Lagna
Maauri Lagna
Chaurikot
Ghar Khola
Naphukuna
Mani Sangu
Churta Khola
Gothichaur
Garjankot
Dhan Sangu
Juwa
Tila Nadi
Jula
Tila Nadi
Karnali
Juwa Nadi

Look for blue sheep in the early morning and late afternoon to the north of the pass as you contour and descend in open country. In 1 hour, round the bend to the west and you can see the isolated peak of Hiunchuli Patan, and then descend into rhododendron-and-birch forest. Reach a *goTh* and then descend a spur into the Ghustung Valley, ending the steep portion at Thankur, a broad, flat valley (10,800 ft, 3292 m) with several *goTh,* in almost **2 hours** from the pass. There are few suitable campsites for another 3 hours, and even there, water may be lacking.

Cross the small stream at Thankur to the left bank and head downstream on the left bank of the main Ghustung Khola valley. Descend through a magnificent forest to reach the river in **70 minutes,** and cross it on a cantilever bridge (9100 ft, 2774 m). Climb steeply on the much drier north side to the ridge crest, passing a few streams, which may be dry in the spring. The trail heads west and keeps high to reach an open area and *goTh* frames (Kami Danda, 10,280 ft, 3134 m) in **1¾ hours** from the river. In another **45 minutes,** after a descent, reach a *chorten* (9800 ft, 2987 m) and look down upon the only villages for a few days, and gaze north toward the pass you will cross. Continue down to reach **Pelma** (8300 ft, 2530 m) in **45 minutes.** This flat-roofed village and the one across the valley are populated by *Kham Magar,* a fascinating ethnic group who continue shamanistic traditions closest to the classic Northern Siberian custom.

Descend to the gorge of the Pelma Khola and cross to the right bank (7620 ft, 2322 m) in another **15 minutes.** Ascend slightly and head downstream to pick up a trail after crossing a tributary that climbs steeply to **Yamakhar** (8200 ft, 2499 m) in **30 minutes.** Near the top of the village, the trail to Jangla forks right, while that to Puchhargaon and Maikot heads left and downstream. Take the right fork and switchback some forty-six times; the trail then levels out somewhat and ascends to the north to reach Askyur (9660 ft, 2944 m) in **1 hour.** Here there are fields and *goTh* tended by *Kham* villagers from Maikot. Climb up for 15 minutes (10,240 ft, 3121 m) to traverse over to a ridge, rather than climbing up farther. Descend and wind around the hillside to the left and traverse across it, then join a more prominent trail that descends steeply at first, then more gradually to cross a tributary stream 20 minutes later. Ascend gradually to reach the crest of a spur above Shengam, where there are some fields and *goTh* (10,180 ft, 3103 m) tended by Pelma people.

Contour, then descend through a deciduous forest into a flat draw with a stream that you follow up on its right bank. Cross and recross it several times in a cold, mysterious, narrow canyon with caves that could be used as shelter in a pinch. End up ascending on the right bank to reach **Dhule** (10,920 ft, 3328 m), in **2 hours** from Askyur. This semipermanent settlement serves the Nepali traffic over the Jangla, and *Kham* people from Maikot and Pelma stay here, except in the dead of winter. There are possible sites for camping. There is no water for a long stretch beyond.

Climb up another 400 ft (122 m) to a notch, traverse left, and reach a ridge crest, which you follow north out of the woods to reach a *chautaara* (12,420 ft, 3785 m) in **1 hour.** Traverse northwest across a hillside, then climb to a pass (12,900 ft, 3932 m) in **1 hour.** Descend into the wild Sheng Khola

Top: *Pounding* marsha *to separate the seeds, in Tarakot*
Above: *Protector deities, or* komba, *in Tarakot*

valley, passing rock overhangs that could be used for camping, and reach a tributary (12,140 ft, 3700 m) in **45 minutes.** Look for blue sheep near the cliffs. Along the west (right) bank, pass above a flat area suitable for camping (12,800 ft, 3901 m) in **1 hour.** About **15 minutes** beyond, take the left fork (12,940 m, 3950 m). The way up the valley floor would cross the river beyond, and head east over the crest to Gurjaakhaani. Ascend to the north for **45 minutes** to reach a crest (14,160 ft, 4316 m) with Phuphal Dah, a small pond, just below.

Head northwest in open country over a small pass, then on the left bank of a stream to reach a saddle (14,760 ft, 4499 m) in **45 minutes.** Descend into the drainage system of the Saunre Khola, reaching the major tributary at 13,000 ft (3962 m) in **1¼ hours.** Cross it to the right and begin the final climb to the Jangla. **Ten minutes'** climb brings you to Purbang (13,160 ft, 4011 m), where there is a steel rigging system for a *goTh* that was installed around 1975 by the Nepali government as a shelter for Nepalis crossing the pass. The metal roof blew off ten years later. This entire area is monsoon pasturage.

Climb up to another crest (Majala, 14,200 ft, 4328 m), descend slightly to the last tributary, and be sure to fill every container with water here. Ascend to the Jangla (14,840 ft, 4523 m), reached in **2 hours** from Purbang if everyone is well acclimatized. Add a stone to the cairn as you enter Dolpo District. Descend to the north, keeping to the east side of the valley, heading over to a notch (13,300 ft, 4054 m) in **1 hour.** There is another, less-used trail, forking left, up high, that heads off northwest to reach Dunai.

Descend steeply northeast from the notch and enter an oak, then pine, forest, reaching Samtiling (9960 ft, 3036 m) in **1½ hours,** where there is a *gomba.* This region, called Tichurong, is populated by people calling themselves *Magar,* with those in three villages speaking Kaike. Read Jim Fisher's *Trans Himalayan Traders* for more information on their life. Descend to **Sagartara** (9120 ft, 2780 m) in **20 minutes.** Below to the east is strategically situated Tarakot, once the fort town controlling access through here, and across the tributary valley to the east is Gomba, with its monastery. Both are worth visiting. Notice that the terraces are constructed differently from those you left. Rice, needing irrigation, can't be grown here.

There is a high route from that goes north up the Tarap Khola to Tarap (in 2 to 3 days) and then west over two high passes to Phoksumdo Tal. Permission for this is occasionally granted to trekkers.

To continue on to Dunai, you descend to the main river and follow it west. From Sagartara, begin at the walnut trees below town and fork left to traverse west and drop down, passing above Ruma and reaching the valley floor (7800 ft, 2377 m), where there is a police check post, in **30 minutes.** Head downstream on the left bank of the Thulo Bheri Khola for a few minutes to reach a massive concrete suspension bridge (7680 ft, 2341 m), which you cross to the right bank, and then head downstream. Keep to the valley floor and descend close to the torrent. There are several possible campsites along here. Reach the Rishi Khola from the north in **1½ hours.** Cross it either here or upstream, and reach the few houses of **Besighat** (7500 ft, 2286 m). Head west in a pleasant pine forest and reach a cantilever bridge (7140 ft, 2176 m) in **1¼**

hours, which you cross to the left bank of the Thulo Bheri. Head downstream, passing Menosara in another **30 minutes,** to reach **Dunai** (6920 ft, 2109 m), the administrative headquarters for Dolpo District. You will note that there is quite a different atmosphere in government towns from that in peasant villages.

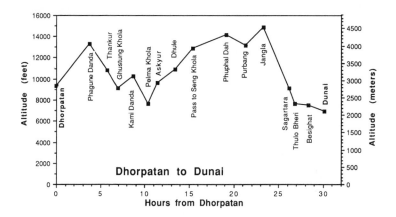

From Dunai there are two route choices, both of which are described. To go to Phoksumdo Tal and beyond, over the Kaagmaara La toward Jumla, you cross the river and climb up the valley to reach the Suli Gad valley, which you follow to the lake. To head directly to Jumla, continue down valley on the left bank of the Thulo Bheri. This will also take you to the Jufal airstrip (called Dolpa on RNAC schedules). Snow can make the crossing of the Kaagmaara La impossible, and can force you to backtrack to Dunai to take the lower route. This description follows below.

Dunai to Phoksumdo Tal and over the Kaagmaara La

> *These villagers dwell in one of the most glorious places on earth without being remotely aware of it. But how should they be? It is we who have somehow grown weary of the benefits of modern life, who can tarry in such a place with keen enjoyment. We imagine that we should be content with the simplicity of their life, scheming how we would improve this within proper limits.*
>
> David Snellgrove, *Himalayan Pilgrimage,* speaking of Phoksumdo Tal

Cross one of the bridges at Dunai to the right bank of the Thulo Bheri and head downstream, forking right after 10 minutes to climb up to a spur (8180 ft, 2493 m) in **1 hour** from Dunai. Enter the Suli Gad valley and traverse through sage, bypassing a few Himalaya deodar trees as you contour into a tributary valley and see the small village of Parla across on the north side. Cross the stream (8220 ft, 2505 m) in this valley in **30 minutes** and get water here. Climb, rather than contouring, to the village. Enter the next steep tributary valley upstream, that of the Phokso Khola, and reach the few houses of Pun Alduwa, and Eklai Tigho just beyond. Finding water is a problem for camping here. Cross the Phokso Khola in **1½ hours** from the previous tributary (9400 ft, 2865 m). Reach the outskirts of **Roha** (9660 ft, 2944 m), in **15 minutes.** This village is populated by *Matwali Chhetri,* who have more animistic traditions than the lower-elevation Hindu peoples. Notice the protector deities, called *komba,* on the houses. There is a Devi temple up above the village. Water is difficult here, too.

Pick up the trail at the lower west side of town and contour north, passing the stream, which is the town's water supply! Fork left (9520 ft, 2902 m) in **30 minutes** in an open area, and continue, rounding a bend into a glade with spruce and cypress trees in a steep tributary valley in **40 minutes.** Descend to a sturdy cantilever bridge, which is crossed to the right bank (8660 ft, 2639 m). Just beyond is **Anke,** the few buildings at the entrance to Shey Phoksumdo National Park (8720 ft, 2658 m). Pay the fee here.

Climb up and traverse into the main valley and reach the few Tibetan houses of Chepka (8600 ft, 2621 m) in **45 minutes.** The trail leaves the valley floor in less than 30 minutes, climbs up, then enters a tributary valley and descends under a large, dripping overhang to cross the stream (9360 ft, 2853 m) in **1¼ hours** from Chepka. Just beyond is an overhang suitable for shelter but too small for camping. Regain the main valley and ascend to 10,540 ft (3212 m) in an open, wider valley, where there are a few houses below, after **2 hours.** Enter a birch glade and descend steeply to reach the river and a rock causeway. Continue upstream to a bridge (9800 ft, 2987 m), across the Suli Gad, in another **hour.** If you cross it and head downstream a bit, you reach the few houses of RiAAjic.

To continue to Phoksumdo Tal, head upstream on the east (left) bank, passing a field on the left in **45 minutes** that is used for camping by trekkers (9940 ft, 3030 m). A minute north of this, find a little wooden bench with a big, flat rock as a backrest, and enjoy this seat!

Five minutes further, come to a major junction, where the Pungmo Khola, which drains the Kaagmaara La to the west, joins the Suli Gad, which drains Phoksumdo. You can head up either the east or west bank of the Suli Gad valley. The west is more direct, while the east gives a different perspective on Nepal's biggest waterfall, which drains the lake. The west bank route also passes through an interesting village. Go up one side and come down the other! Sumduwa, the headquarters of the national park and an army encampment, is a short climb up after crossing the river here. The way up the east and down the west is described.

Fork right at the sign by the bridge over the Suli Gad above the confluence. Head up its east (left) bank, passing another bridge over the river 10 minutes beyond. This is the place to cross if you want to ascend the west side of the valley. Shortly beyond is perhaps a better campsite than the one below the wooden bench because of views to the north. Traverse above some fields and climb up to a notch with a *chorten.* Here the trail heads east into the Mundruwa

Khola valley, and soon you can look back and see the source of the roar, the magnificent waterfall. Continue along to **Rigi** (10,800 ft, 3292 m), **1¼ hours** from the confluence. It is also called Morwa, and Mondro, and provides a winter retreat for some people from Ringmo at the lake. The trail to Tarap heads east up the south side of the valley, reaching it after crossing two high passes, the Baga La (16,569 ft, 5050 m), and the Numa La (16,897 ft, 5150 m), in two days.

Descend **15 minutes** to reach the Mundruwa Khola and cross it to the north (right) bank (10,700 ft, 3261 m). Just beyond, climb, head down valley slightly, and less than 10 minutes from the crossing, fork right to climb. The left fork takes a lower route to the lake. Climb steeply and, in 30 minutes, reach a trail joining from the east. Gain a crest at 12,320 ft (3755 m) in **1 hour.** Here a high trail (mentioned above) from the east joins. Traverse north on the west side of a small valley of pine and juniper. Reach the height of land (12,460 ft, 3798 m), and see the falls again, and just beyond, the lake. Cross the river draining the lake (11,900 ft, 3627 m) in another **30 minutes,** and climb up through the entrance *chorten* to **Ringmo** (11,940 ft, 3639 m) at its southern end. The local name for it is Tso-wa or "lakeside."

The unearthly, azure blue waters of the Phoksumdo Tal change color constantly with the sun and clouds. Majestic small summits ring the water, and the entire area affords a peacefulness found in few other places. There is a Bon-po monastery by the water to the southeast of the lake that must be visited.

The monastery at serene Phoksumdo Tal

The trail to Shey is fixed to struts on the west side of the lake, but local officials will not permit you to venture forth on it. So, alas, you currently have to retrace your steps. To head down the west side of the valley, leave Ringmo by going past the school and its entrance *chorten* up on the right bank of the river. Follow the river, and look for musk deer in the forest before reaching an open crest (12,380 ft, 3773 m) with views of the falls after **35 minutes.** Descend to the winter houses of Palam (10,000 ft, 3048 m) in another **35 minutes.** Reach the park headquarters at Sumduwa (10,260 ft, 3127 m) in another **hour.** If you are not ascending the Kaagmaara La there is little reason to go to the headquarters, and you could cross back over to the east (left) bank of the Suli Gad.

From Sumduwa, head up the north (left) bank of the Pungmo Khola for **1¼ hours** to reach **Pungmo** (10,840 ft, 3304 m). This is the last inhabited place before the pass, though in the warmer months people will be found up quite high. A further **30 minutes** beyond is KAAru (11,200 ft, 3414 m), with substantial houses. In another **45 minutes** is a lone house in a flat area that makes a good campsite. Cross to the west (right) bank of the Pungmo Khola (12,020 ft, 3664 m) **15 minutes** beyond, and continue up valley, keeping to the same side. Head west beyond the confluence of the Pungmo Khola from the north, keeping to what is now called the Julung Khola. Reach Phedi, the bottom of the hill, and summer pastures (13,950 ft, 4252 m), in **2 hours.** There may be blue sheep along here. The route now heads south and climbs to the Kaagmaara La (16,780 ft, 5114 m), in another **3 hours.** *Kaag* means "crow" in Nepali, while *maara,* "death"; Khumbu's Gorak Shep is Sherpa for the same thing.

From the pass, the descent angles down along a rocky slope into the valley of the Garpung Khola, keeping to its south (left) bank. There is a campsite (another "Phedi") at 13,120 ft (3999 m) in **2½ hours.** Continue to the bridge (12,150 ft, 3703 m) near the treeline, crossing the river to its right, in **1 hour.** Recross it again (10,400 ft, 3170 m) in another **hour.** Head downstream, below the junction with the Jagdula Khola, and recross it (9450 ft, 2880 m), to the north (right) bank in **45 minutes.** At the national park boundary, along the Jagdula Khola, there is an army camp with a radio. Another **2 hours** along the Jagdula Khola valley will bring you **Hurikot** (8500 ft, 2591 m).

There is a choice of routes at this point, depending on whether you want to take a direct, uninhabited, ridge route to cross the *lekh* at the Barharla Lagna, also called the Barbaria Lekh (14,050 ft, 4282 m), or a lower, longer, more populated route to cross at the Maauri Lagna (12,850 ft, 3916 m). Certainly in the middle of winter, the lower crossing is preferred, while the higher would be better in the monsoon. The lower is described.

From Hurikot, follow the river valley to the bridge across from **Kaigaon** (8740 ft, 2664 m) in **45 minutes.** There is a school, up the way. Keep to the right bank of the Jagdula Khola and pass by Topgaon, then on to Majgaon (9560 ft, 2914 m), at the school, in **1 hour** from the bridge. These villages are all in **Rimi** village development council. Reach Jharkot, and continue on in a tributary valley to reach a notch (10,280 ft, 3133 m) in **1¼ hours** from the school. Descend northwest in another tributary valley, cross the stream, and reach **Chaumrikot** (10,200 ft, 3109 m) in **45 minutes.** Keep traversing west, crossing tributaries, then head northwest and climb up toward the pass. Leave behind the views of the Dhaulagiri peaks, and reach the Maauri Lagna ("bee pass") (12,850 ft, 3916 m), in **3 hours** from Chaumrikot. Here you leave behind the Bheri drainage and enter that of the Karnali. These rivers join down in Surkhet District. Way off to the northwest is the massive peak of Saipal. To the northeast are the lower summits of Kang Chunne and Wedge Peak.

Descend steeply to the north on switchbacks and reach the Ghar Khola (11,540 ft, 3517 m) in **30 minutes.** Cross it to the right bank. The trail over the Barharla Lagna comes in here. Head down valley, contouring then angling out of the bottom of the valley to the north, crossing a tributary, the Gumaiya Khola, to the right bank, and come up to a fairly flat area suitable for camping (11,060 ft, 3371 m) in **30 minutes.** Continue down valley, soon passing another campsite, and reach **Chhurta** (also called **Naphukuna,** 10,200 ft, 3109 m), a Tibetan *drokpa* (nomad) village, in another **hour.** The *gomba* above here is worth a visit. Just beyond, pass through more of the town, which looks distinctively Nepali in contrast, to reach a bridge over the Chhurta Khola in **30 minutes** (9700 ft, 2956 m). There are spots for camping here.

Cross the river to the left bank and continue downstream, not taking any uphill forks or crossing the river again until you reach a log bridge (9240 ft, 2816 m), **1 hour** later. Cross to the right bank and reach Mani Sangu (9100 ft, 2774 m) in **20 minutes.** Don't cross the bridge here, but continue on the right bank of the main valley, which heads northwest and opens up delightfully. Cross to the left bank on a large cantilever bridge (9020 ft, 2749 m) in **40 minutes.** Continue downstream, and soon head west up the right bank of the Gothichaur Khola a short way. Cross to the left bank via a little island (9000 ft, 2743 m), where there are a series of mills, in **15 minutes.**

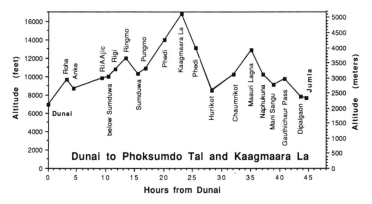

Head up the valley and emerge from the narrow canyon into a broad valley. Head northwest to pass above the Gothichaur Sheep Breeding Farm, which has been active since the early 1970s trying to introduce Australian breeds of sheep and improved grass. Years ago, planes landed here. Before you leave this area, sit and gaze at the solitude around. Just before the fence for the farm, below you, is a pillar that is hundreds of years old. Some say it dates from the Hindu epic the *Mahabharata,* and was built by Panchpanta, perhaps two thousand years ago. Gothichaur used to be a grazing area and is remarkable in being so verdant yet unsettled.

Ascend to a pass (9723 ft, 2963 m) in **1 hour** from the river crossing. Head northwest in another idyllic pastoral valley and in **1 hour** join a major trail from the right that comes from Gothigaon. In a few minutes, reach the first few houses of **Garjlankot** (8600 ft, 2621 m), and cross to the left bank there. The main valley of the Babila Khola enters to the north. Traverse on the south side of this valley. Note that they grow rice at this altitude—quite a contrast with the regions south of the Himalaya! Continue through more houses of Garjlankot, especially a cluster situated strategically in a notch near the center of the valley, reached in **30 minutes.** The main river is called the Tila Nadi here; you follow it to Jumla. Meet electric poles and wires, and pass through Dipalgaon (7840 ft, 2390 m) after **45 minutes.**

Cross the Tila Nadi to the right in **30 minutes** and come up to the small town of Dhan Sangu, situated at the junction with the Juwa Nadi. Here there are several Hindu temples, common at river junctions, which are considered sacred. They are to the deities Shiva, Ganesh, and Mahadev. You are not likely to see the *komba* (also called *dokpa*) or protector deity, on houses anymore. Continue through the suburbs to **Jumla** (7640 ft, 2329 m) in another **30 minutes.** Just before, at the few houses of Kali Khola, if you fork right, you will climb up to the airstrip (7660 ft, 2335 m). Here there are hotels, shops, and a hospital, as well as a strong government and development presence.

Dunai to Kaigaon via Tibrikot

To take the low route to Kaigaon, and then on to Jumla, do not cross the bridge at Dunai. If you are backtracking from Phoksumdo Tal, do not try to cross the Suri Gad above its confluence with the Bheri (there is a bridge there), but retrace your steps to Dunai. The trail to Tibrikot on the south side of the valley is much easier. The route heads up the Bheri to a tributary, and follows that valley up across a pass and down into the next drainage system.

From Dunai, head northwest along the sandy left bank of the Bheri Khola, and reach the few houses of Dhupichaur, named after the cypress trees near the river, in **30 minutes.** Pass through Rupcheghat at the crossing of the Rup Gad, and then come to the few houses of **KalaghODa** (6740 ft, 2054 m) in less than **1 hour.** Here the trail to the airstrip at Jufal forks left and climbs to reach it in 1½ hours. But keep to the barren valley floor, pass Bhertigaon on an alluvial flat, and eventually reach the few houses of Supani (6660 ft, 2030 m) after **2½ hours.**

There is a choice of trails beyond here. One goes to Likhu and avoids Tibrikot, while the other goes to this historically strategic site. The Tibrikot trail is described. Reach a new suspension bridge (6600 ft, 2012 m), and cross it to the right bank of the Thulo Bheri. Fork right a few minutes beyond (the left fork is the Likhu trail), cross the Galli Gad tributary, and climb. Reach **KoT** or **TibrikoT** (7020 ft, 2140 m) in **25 minutes** from Supani. To the south of the notch is presumably the old fort of a former king who could watch everything and everyone from there. It is now a temple to Tripureshsundari Devi. The town is now scattered in three nondescript clusters. Descend to the Chhal Gad, the tributary from the north, in **10 minutes** and cross it to the right bank (6860 ft, 2091 m). Be sure to get water here.

Head downstream a bit, and begin the climb up to the northwest. Pass a number of little shrines that bespeak the animistic feel of this area. Reach the crest of the spur in 1 hour, and then keep to it. Eventually, keep to the north side of the Khorain Khola valley and pass above the villages of Koragaon and Kamigaon. Halfway between them, just above the trail, noticed if you look back, is a segmented stone pillar that dates back to the old kingdom here. Pass through the bottom of Dagine (9760 ft, 2975 m) in **2½ hours** from the Chhal Gad crossing and then climb, eventually going into the forested tributary of the Kali Charo ("black bird") river. Cross the river and reenter the main valley to pass below the town of Kaliban ("black forest," 10,140 ft, 3091 m) and cross the tributary in **45 minutes.** When I asked trail directions from the people in Kaliban, they pointed down the hill and said the trail was over by those "forest people" there. I expected to see some wild hunter-gatherers there, and in a sense I did—langur monkeys!

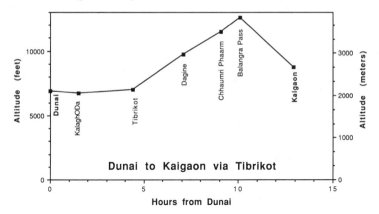

Dunai to Kaigaon via Tibrikot

Continue up the valley another **1¼ hours** to reach the **Chhaumri Pharam** (11,480 ft, 3499 m). Officials at this yak-breeding project may let you stay in their guest house. To head on to the Balangra Pass (12,590 ft, 3837 m), either contour up high, or go through the forest, for **1 hour.** Descend to the west, keeping to the north side of the valley on a wide trail, passing by a tiny spring. Unlike the major Thulo Bheri cutting the landscape to the east, the western side of the pass is a jumble of ridges. In **1½ hours** take the right fork (10,850 ft, 3307 m) by a tiny stream, rather than the left fork, which passes below the lone house of Chiplaaina. In less than **20 minutes** reach a small notch (10,820 ft, 3298 m) and fork right to descend steeply into the Garpunk Khola valley (the left fork contours).

The descent to **Kaigaon** (8740 ft, 2664 m at the bridge) takes **1 hour.**

You can fork either way halfway down, depending on whether you want to arrive at the bridge or pass through the upper part of town. On the left fork, you pass a few sheds with colored bits of cloth: temples to Masta, the local protector deity. To proceed on to Jumla, pick up the trail description at Kaigaon above.

Jumla—RaRa Lake Circuit
(Map No. 9, Page 303)

At the southern edge of Mugu District, at an altitude of almost 10,000 ft (3050 m), lies RaRa, the largest lake in Nepal. It has a circumference of almost 8 mi (13 km) and is nestled between heavily forested, steep-sided ridges that thrust up from the fault lines that riddle this section of the foot of the Himalaya.

RNAC operates scheduled flights to Jumla (7660 ft, 2335 m), the headquarters of Karnali Zone. It is situated in a broad valley three days' walk south of RaRa. Most flights originate from Nepalganj to the south, but there are less frequent direct flights from Kathmandu. It is possible to trek to Jumla from Pokhara, more than a two-week trip, but most people fly there. One can also trek to Jumla from Surkhet to the south, to where there is a road. This takes about a week. Either of these might be viable alternatives for getting out of Jumla at the end of the trek. Finally, you could walk there from Khaptad National Park, another week's journey.

First, the usual route from Jumla to RaRa is described. There are two variations. Most people do well to take the longer route—at least if traveling without a guide familiar with the shorter *lekh* route. Then the return route described follows a little-used trail to Sinja, an interesting, historic town. From here, a former trade and communication route leads to Jumla. Some food must be carried no matter which route you take.

Rice, wheat, potatoes, or beans may sometimes be available in the bazaar in Jumla, but food shortages are a recurring problem in this whole area. As far as possible, all supplies required for trekking should be brought from Kathmandu. Porters can be hired locally, but English-speaking ones are very rare. It is almost essential to carry a tent when trekking in this area. Most of the people along this trek are *Thakuri,* the King's caste. They are loathe to allow anyone below their caste to enter or stay in their homes.

As mentioned, there are regular flights to Jumla by RNAC, but it is difficult to arrange return flights, either in Kathmandu or in Jumla. Once you arrive in Jumla, see the RNAC representative immediately to confirm your return flight. If you are stuck in Jumla, and unable to make direct connections to Kathmandu because of frequent "rice" charters into Jumla, it is easier to get a seat out on one going back to Nepalganj. There are daily flights to Kathmandu from Nepalganj. It is also possible to walk seven days south to Surkhet and fly from there, or drive to Nepalganj.

JUMLA & RARA LAKE

MAP NO. 9

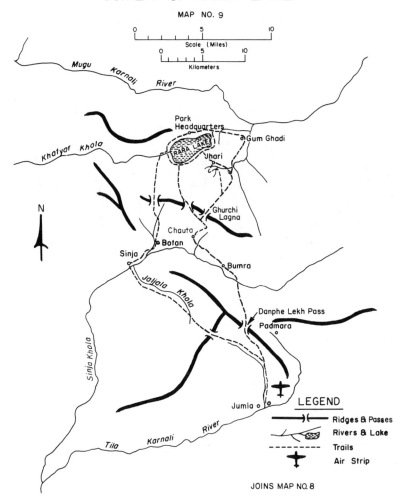

JOINS MAP NO. 8

JUMLA TO RARA LAKE

Looking north from the Jumla Bazaar you can see most of the trail to the top of Danphe Lekh. The trail goes to the left of the highest point of this *lekh*.

Head out of the main bazaar from Jumla (7640 ft, 2329 m), on a wide trail along the east (left) bank of the stream heading north. Stay on this side more or less all the time until the climbing begins. The trail up this valley passes next to

These **Magar** *girls have stuffed cigarette papers in the ear lobes to stretch them, a sign of beauty*

the buildings of a large technical school on the way to the pass. After **1 hour** begin the ascent from the valley floor, climbing toward the right. The trail rises through a series of cultivated fields, passes close to a few scattered houses, and ascends steadily for over **1 hour.** While still well below the main treeline, the trail rises steeply for about **15 minutes,** crosses a small stream, and enters one of the few clusters of blue pine trees on the open stretch of hillside. Near this spot—above the trail and slightly off to the right—is a campsite with a fresh-water spring (9000 ft, 2743 m), a good place to rest and cook your morning meal. This is the last water before the pass.

Ascending out of the trees, the trail opens out onto wide meadows rising gently to the north. **Fifteen minutes** beyond the trees, the trail forks near some stone huts. Take the less obvious right fork and, shortly after, reenter the forest. (The left fork is a more level main route to Sinja.) The trail emerges into high meadows, visible earlier from below, in **1½ hours** from the fork. Another **hour** on increasingly difficult rocky terrain brings you to the pass, the Danphe Lekh (12,100 ft, 3688 m). The summit is marked with a small *chorten*. There is a small peak to your left (13,715 ft, 4180 m), and another to your right (13,807 ft, 4224 m). From this point you should have a fine view back down over the Jumla Valley to the 15,000 ft (4500 m) ridges to the south. There is no northern view until you cross the top of the pass.

From the *chorten,* follow the trail across the top of the ridge, winding through patchy forest to the north before dropping again into open meadows.

Note carefully the spot where you emerge from the trees. If you come back this way, it is very easy to miss the opening. If you climb straight on over these meadows, you reach a different pass that leads to the village of Padmara to the southeast, and a much longer walk back to Jumla.

Leave the meadows, cross a small stream, follow the trail into the trees, and descend rapidly through dense, mixed forest for **2 hours.** Notice the magnificent birch trees, the bark of which is collected for use as paper. And keep your eyes open for a *DAAphe*—the multicolored national bird of Nepal.

Near the end of the descent, the trail drops very steeply to the Sinja Khola, which is immediately crossed by a substantial log bridge (8900 ft, 2713 m). Turning west, proceed along the north (right) bank of the river. Within the next hour choose any suitable campsite along the valley floor by the river.

Approximately **1 hour** from the bridge, the trail rises from the riverbed to pass near the village of **Bumra** (9350 ft, 2850 m). An alternative campsite could be in the vicinity of the village. Supplies, such as eggs or firewood, can sometimes be procured.

From Bumra, continue along the side of the hill, proceeding about 500 ft (150 m) above the river. Pass just above another small village within **15 minutes.** After another **15 minutes,** descend steeply to cross a small stream entering the main river from the north. On the valley floor, cross the main stream (9250 ft, 2819 m), and immediately climb steeply again for **30 minutes** to regain your former altitude. Within another **hour,** descend again to cross another stream entering from the north. At the foot of this descent, huddled beneath the steep rock walls on the far side of the stream, stand the few houses of **Chauta** (9000 ft, 2743 m). Splendid clay *chilim* (pipes) are made in this area, and are sometimes sold at one of the hotels here.

From Chauta, head north, following the trail gently uphill and crisscrossing the stream, the Ghauta Khola, in a steep, narrow valley. A pleasant walk through groves of large walnut trees takes you to a small *dharmsala,* or resting place, with a good, clear-flowing spring. Reach some isolated cultivated fields in 1 hour. In another 15 minutes the trail passes out of the trees and, leaving the course of the stream, swings left onto the high, open pastures. You are now climbing again to the pass of Ghurchi Lagna.

The wide trail proceeds almost directly westward, rising across a broad, grassy valley that runs almost at right angles to the final ridge. After you pass groups of large boulders for 30 minutes, the valley you are following splits into two distinct valleys. One heads northwest, and the other, containing the main trail, goes slightly northeast. The main trail heads up the right valley, climbing more or less north to the pass of the Ghurchi Lagna (11,300 ft, 3444 m), which is marked by a small stone *chorten.* The pass is some **3 hours** from Chauta.

There is now a new trail to RaRa from the pass. Descend 30 minutes, and take an obvious new trail branching to the left, and traversing without losing much height, through young pine forest. Cross a couple of meadows and then descend steeply to a clear stream. Cross this stream and continue northwest above another valley and stream, which is eventually crossed before making a final climb to **Jhari** (8350 ft, 2545 m) some **5 or 6 hours** from the pass.

On the older trail from the Ghurchi Lagna pass, descend north again into forest. Some 5 minutes below the top is a *dharmsala* near a small stream. From here the trail is difficult, dropping very steeply away from the stream over a series of rocky outcrops. It descends in and out of belts of trees and emerges almost 2 hours later. Traverse for another 30 minutes to the village of Pina (8000 ft, 2438 m). Pass a water source and suitable campsites on the way to the village. About 5 minutes before the village, you pass Pina's only hotel, an isolated house directly on the main trail. If you are lucky, it may be open for business. The hotel is open only about half the year, generally during the spring and monsoon.

The village of Pina is grouped into upper and lower clusters, which are connected by an intricate maze of paths through the fields. The main trail from lower Pina proceeds in the direction of the river below, reaching Gum Ghadi (6500 ft, 1981 m) in about 3 hours. This is the government headquarters and police check post for Mugu District. One trail from Gum Ghadi cuts back, ascending steeply to the northern ridge of RaRa. The other trail from the village continues dropping steeply to the Mugu Karnali river, the gateway to the trails into Humla and Mugu.

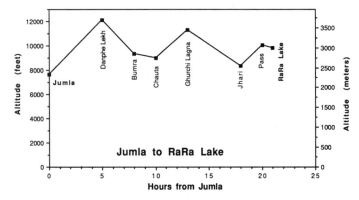

To proceed most directly to RaRa from Pina, take the new trail that splits from the main trail about 10 minutes above the hotel. It passes through upper Pina after beginning on the side of a valley at the edge of the village. To find the trail when descending from the Ghurchi Lagna pass, take the left fork at the first stream you come to after leaving the pass, a few minutes outside of Pina. Bearing to the left, the trail traverses the side of this westward-heading valley, passes through cultivated fields for 30 minutes, and gradually meets the valley floor and a stream at the end of the traverse. Cross this small stream by a mill (7500 ft, 2286 m) and climb again for 15 minutes before dropping almost immediately to the main valley stream. Follow the stream for another 30 minutes through more fields in an ever-narrowing valley. Cross the stream on a substantial wooden bridge and climb steeply to the north for 30 minutes to the village of Jhari (8350 ft, 2530 m).

Continue up through the village of Jhari to the north, pass some huge cedars, climb again through the forest, and emerge after about **2 hours** onto high, open pasture. Cross the easily gained summit (10,050 ft, 3063 m) and emerge at the "airstrip" on the south side of RaRa Lake (9800 ft, 2987 m). The airstrip, the only flat area around the shores of the lake, is no longer used. Directly across, toward the northwestern side of the lake, is the newer building of the national park headquarters, and staff and army houses.

RARA

The area surrounding the lake, which was designated a national park in 1975, offers spectacular scenery, although views of snow-capped peaks are limited. Magnificent examples of fir, pine, spruce, juniper, cedar, birch, and rhododendron are found in the forest. Wildlife, including bears, cats, wolves, and deer, has been observed in the area. Around the shores of the lake are some fine "Malla Stones"—pillars of rock bearing Devanagari inscriptions and figures of the sun and moon. The inscriptions probably date from the Malla kings, who reigned over much of the western Himalayan region in the twelfth century.

The best camping areas are on the lake's south side, which has much more diverse topography and vegetation than the north side. Meadowlands, virgin spruce forest, and some streams on the southwest corner of the lake make for ideal camping.

Legend and folklore provide the bulk of knowledge about RaRa Lake. The villagers believe it is at least 1800 ft (550 m) deep. They feel it is fed from underground springs flowing from the Mugu Karnali river, which is located about 1800 ft (550 m) downhill from the lake on the other side of the north *lekh*. Given its size and location near one of the main trade routes to Tibet, it is surprising that the lake does not have greater historical or religious significance. Unlike many Himalayan lakes, it is not a pilgrimage site. An annual festival in July and August commemorates the intervention of the great god Thakur, who changed the direction of the outlet of the lake. Firing an arrow to the west, he opened the western hill to form the present outlet, and taking huge quantities of earth, he filled in the eastern outlet and stamped it firmly with his great feet. His footprints, embedded in a rock, are visible to this day at the eastern end of the lake. They are the festival's main objects of interest—other than the attractive dancers and the local brew.

The lake's inaccessible location has kept many of its secrets undiscovered. The potential for discovery may be one of the most exciting aspects of this trek.

RARA TO JUMLA VIA SINJA

You can return by taking a less-traveled, longer route through Sinja, the historical summer capital of the Malla Kingdom (twelfth to fourteenth centuries). Food, shelter, and a good map or a local guide familiar with the route are necessary.

The trails you take are Nepal's highways

From the park headquarters (9900 ft, 3018 m), take the shore trail southwest to the lake outlet, the Khatyar Khola (9780 ft, 2981 m), also called the Nisha Khola, in **45 minutes.** Do not cross the bridge here, but continue down the north (right) bank for **30 minutes** then cross the stream on a log bridge. One trail continues west on the south (left) bank of the *khola* after ascending a 100 ft (30 m) knoll. Instead, take the left fork (heading south) up a small valley. Climb through the woods on a sometimes indefinite trail that keeps to the western side of the valley. Reach a meadow with a *goTh* (10,740 ft, 3274 m) on a crest in **1 hour.**

Continue south, climbing steeply through oak, then birch, then rhododendron forests, to reach an alpine ridge (12,500 ft, 3810 m) in **2½ hours.** Above to the left is Chuchuemara Danda. Traverse on its west shoulder for **15 minutes** and come out on a saddle above the Ghatta Khola. Descend 500 ft (150 m) to the headwaters of the river and continue down through the valley for 1 hour to GhorasAI, site of the army guard post (10,500 ft, 3200 m), in **1½ hours** from the saddle. Here the stream turns southwest. This is an appropriate and beautiful place to camp.

From GhorasAl, the trail at first heads down the right side of the valley, then soon crosses to the left, where it is very flat, to the top of the moraine wall. It recrosses the stream here and descends very steeply on the right-hand side. Botan can be seen ahead on the left-hand slopes of the valley. Regardless of trails heading off to the right in the general direction of Sinja, stay in this valley, taking the fork that keeps you closest to the Sinja Khola, until you reach it.

There is an excellent campsite at the confluence of the Jaljala and Sinja Kholas. Just below here, the Sinja Khola goes through a narrow gorge. The top end of Sinja village is at the lower end of this gorge, a further 15 minutes' walk. Reach **Sinja** (8000 ft, 2438 m) in **4 hours** from GhorasAl. A bridge across the Sinja Khola at this point (top end of the village and lower end of the gorge) is crossed to pick up the trail heading up the Jaljala Khola. Food and lodging are difficult to find in Sinja, even for porters.

Sinja lies in a highly cultivated valley. To the south, on a prominent knoll, are the remains of the former capitol of this area. It is presently the site of a temple, Kankasundri. This area is well worth visiting by climbing the 400 ft (120 m) to the top of the knoll.

To return to Jumla, follow the historical route between Sinja and Kalanga, the old name for Jumla. The two-day route through beautiful forests ascends a river valley to a *lekh* and descends to Jumla. A camp roughly halfway on the crest of the *lekh* (11,500 ft, 3505 m) is ideal.

From Sinja ascend the Jaljala Khola to the southeast, keeping to the south (left) bank on a very good, clear trail for **6 hours** to reach the high point. On the far watershed, the trail descends through forests and pastures south to Jumla (7640 ft, 2329 m) in less than **4 hours.**

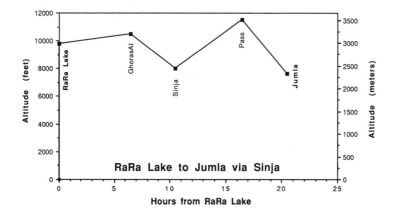

Crossing the Bheri Khola in a dugout

11 Other Treks

Two roads diverged in a wood, and I—
I took the one less travelled by,
And that has made all the difference.

Robert Frost

Two other treks are described in this chapter. One is an exit from Khumbu to Rolwaling and on to Kathmandu. Finally, there is a trip through the Tarai to Chitwan National Park, home of much interesting wildlife.

Thami to Rolwaling and Barabise via the Trashi Labsta

This is a spectacular high route that leaves Khumbu via a glaciated pass and reaches the Rolwaling Valley to the east and its major settlement, Beding, in a minimum of four days. There are no villages or shelters along the way and the route is dangerous even in the best of conditions. Only experienced mountaineers should attempt it, and then only with a party that includes some Sherpas who have been over it before. The entire party, including all the porters, must be equipped for severe conditions of cold and high altitude. Since it is necessary to camp on ice, parties should carry tents and fuel for everyone as well as ice-climbing equipment (ice ax, rope, crampons, and ice screws). Under ideal conditions, the crossing need not require technical climbing, but such conditions cannot be counted on. Storms are to be expected, and food for at least five days should be carried in order to be able to wait out bad weather. Temperatures below freezing are always encountered. Crossings have been made at all times of the year, but the best time is probably April to early December. Falling rock is the danger most often encountered. Ice avalanches are also possible. Many people have died attempting this crossing, but competent, well-equipped parties should have little trouble. Sherpas even take yaks over it! You must be very aware of the hazards of rapid ascent to altitude and of hypothermia. There are no quick escape routes, especially on the Rolwaling side of the pass, should altitude illness become serious.

The route is described from Thami to Rolwaling, thus offering a route out of Khumbu that avoids the traffic jams at Lukla. This direction is also preferable because parties attempting the crossing have usually acclimatized first in Khumbu. Furthermore, if altitude problems strike on the ascent, it is easier to retreat to lower altitudes from this side than from the other side, where technically difficult terrain and long glaciers must be negotiated. The times listed here, of course, depend on the acclimatization of the party.

From **Thami** (12,500 ft, 3810 m), described in chapter 8, head west, passing below the monastery to reach a *yersa,* Kure (13,875 ft, 4229 m), in **70 minutes.** The next *yersa* (14,050 ft, 4282 m) is **10 minutes** beyond. Proceed as the valley of the Thami or Thengpo Khola opens up and admire the peaks on its south side, especially the north face of Teng Kangpoche. The extensive *yersa* of Thengpo (14,175 ft, 4321 m) is reached in **25 minutes.** Climb through the various fenced-in fields of this *yersa* and continue up the north side of the valley. Traverse a rock slide from the north to the end of the slide (15,465 ft, 4714 m), **1⅓ hours** from lower Thengpo. The best views east, including the west face of Makalu behind Ama Dablang, are along here. Continue on a grassy slope, then begin climbing a loose moraine to reach a flat area suitable for camping (15,910 ft, 4849 m) in **30 minutes.** Climb the moraine for **1 hour** to Ngole (16,745 ft, 5104 m), located below an icefall to the north. Ngole, which has tent sites and overhanging rocks for shelter, is protected from the icefall and is a good place to camp below the pass. In order to avoid rockfall off the southern slopes of Tengi Ragi Tau, the peak to the north, it is wisest to ascend beyond here in the early morning. There is another possible campsite (17,150 ft, 5227 m) **30 minutes** beyond. Below and to the south a lake lies in the moraine.

Continue climbing beyond this last site on snow or rock, as the season dictates, to another level area (17,700 ft, 5395 m) in **30 minutes.** Some **15 minutes'** more climbing, closer to the face of Tengi Ragi Tau, brings you to yet another small campsite (17,850 ft, 5441 m). These last two campsites are not entirely protected from rockfall, a hazard that varies with the time of year. Be on the lookout for serious symptoms of altitude illness, and descend if they occur.

The icefall before you, which has been visible for some time, is from the Trashi Labsta Pass. Ascend a scree slope to the northeast of the icefall and traverse to a sheltered spot (18,250 ft, 5563 m) under the rock face of Tengi Ragi Tau in another **30 minutes.** If coming from Rolwaling, this sheltered spot could be an appropriate place to pitch a tent and camp. It is safer to camp lower, but you should not descend late in the day if much rock is falling. To proceed over the pass, climb on snow east of the icefall to a long, more gradual slope. There are sheltered spots under overhanging rocks under the face of Tengi Ragi Tau, but it is not a good idea to camp this high, because the risk of altitude illness is greater. Better to sleep low and climb high. Proceed west to the height of land and the Trashi Labsta Pass (18,882 ft, 5755 m)—the name means "luck-bringing prayer flags"—in another **45 minutes.** There is a cairn with prayer flags at the pass. The times listed here are actual traveling times, and most parties take at least half a day from Ngole to here when rests are included. New vistas open up to the west, but the views to the east are limited to Teng Kangpoche. Directly south is the peak Pharchamo (20,582 ft, 6273 m), a trekking summit.

The descent is over a snow-covered, moderately steep glacier with crevasses, and requires roped travel and the ability to do crevasse rescues. The route may take you near the cliffs to the north—where there may be a potential rockfall hazard. Reach the Drolambo Glacier (17,850 ft, 5440 m) in perhaps

45 minutes. Parties wishing to explore further can get plenty of ideas from the Schneider map. Note that the route marked on Schneider's *Rolwaling Himal* map is not the one described here, as the marked route (which is perhaps more hazardous) is no longer in use. The route in use when you cross could be different. Thus it is advisable to have along a Sherpa familiar with the current way.

Head south along the Drolambo, proceeding near a medial moraine. It is safest to camp above the icefall that lies at the snout of the Drolambo, which in turn lies above the Trakarding Glacier. Camping here will enable you to get an early start and minimize the danger of rockfall from the medial moraines. A campsite (17,750 ft, 5410 m) can be found in about **30 minutes** after reaching the valley glacier. Unlike the narrow upper part of the eastern side of the Trashi Labsta, the country here is open.

Continue descending the Drolambo, staying east of the first medial moraine and of an icefall that you pass in **30 minutes.** Most likely you can travel in a trough that is easy and quite safe, providing you have made an early start and the sun hasn't hit the walls. Late in the day the ice-bound rocks loosen and you may feel like a target in a shooting gallery in the middle of a waterfall! In the usual trough, there is one steep ice step, perhaps 40 to 50 ft (15 m) high, where it is best to belay the party down. Crampons, ice axes, rope, and ice

A chorten *in the misty Rolwaling gorge*

screws are usually necessary. Descend carefully on snow and ice-covered rock, keeping close to the rock face to the right to avoid falling rocks and ice. In **2½ to 3 hours** from the camp above, reach a spectacular rocky spur (16,950 ft, 5166 m) below the icefall on the Drolambo, but still considerably above the Trakarding Glacier below. There are plenty of campsites here that are safe from falling rock and ice. If ascending to the pass from Rolwaling, it would be prudent to camp here if you arrive late in the day, unless it is very cold and the rocks are frozen in place. If there is no sound of falling rock when you stop here on the way to the pass, it is probably fairly safe to continue. Along the way, there are several points where your porters might appreciate a rope to use as a handline.

The Trakarding Glacier is the long, rubble-covered ice river flowing northwest below you. It is reached in **30 minutes** from the spur (16,125 ft, 4915 m). Rock overhangs that provide shelter should be apparent. Traverse northwest under the icefall of the Drolambo Glacier to a campsite called Thakar (16,075 ft, 4900 m) in **15 minutes.** There are few if any good campsites on the extensive moraine of the glacier until the lake is passed. Finding water is also a problem. Keeping close to the northwest side of the glacier, follow an indistinct trail marked with cairns. There is sometimes falling rock from the northwest, so be cautious. The going is slow along this moraine. Occasional rock overhangs are passed that would make possible campsites.

About halfway toward the big lake—Tsho Rolpa or Chu Pokhari—the current route crosses the dry Trakarding Glacier to the southwest side and ascends the moraine to a shelf or pasture, Kyidug Kangma (15,682 ft, 4780 m), where you could camp, providing water is available. This is **2 to 3 hours** from the rock overhangs. The route used to follow the northeast side of the glacier and cross the lake on that side, but the moraine along the lake has become virtually impassable. From Kyidug Kangma follow the trail up steeply to the 4886 m (16,830 ft) high point marked on the Schneider *Rolwaling Himal* map. Descend into a trough with pleasant pastures and streams once you reach Kabug (14,875 ft, 4534 m), where there are overhanging shelters you can camp under. Reach it in **1½ hours** from Kyidug Kangma. Proceed along more friendly terrain to reach the terminal moraine of the Ripimo Shar Glacier.

Descend just beyond to pass through a small *yersa* of unroofed frames, Sangma (14,175 ft, 4321 m), reached in ¾ **hour.** Descend to cross the outflow (13,900 ft, 4237 m) of the lake to the left a few minutes later. Descend the broad valley and enjoy the fragrant shrubs. In **30 minutes** cross to the north (right) bank of the Rolwaling Khola (13,725 ft, 4163 m). There is a route to the south over the ridge via the Yalung La, a pass to the Khare Khola. But continue on the usual route and reach the west end of the settlement of Na and the limit of the glaciated valley. Downstream, the Rolwaling Valley is a sharp, river-worn *V.* Na is a large *yersa* at the base of an impressive peak to the north. It is occupied by inhabitants of Beding part of the year, depending on the potato harvest. The Sherpas of Rolwaling believe that their valley was formed by the sweep of a giant horse and plow guided by Padmasamblava, who brought Buddhism to Tibet from India. According to one source, *rolwa* means "a furrow," while *ling* is "a country." Another meaning for *Rolwaling* is "the place where the *dakini* play." They also feel it is one of the eight *beyul*, or "hidden valleys," in the Himalaya. Because of this, they do not allow anyone to kill animals in the valley.

Descend 125 ft (38 m) to the lower part of Na and in 1 hour reach rhododendron and juniper forests, a pleasant contrast to the barren landscape above the lake. Pass through another *yersa*, Dokare (12,575 ft, 3833 m), 15 minutes later and continue to **Beding** (12,120 ft, 3694 m), **1½ hours** from Na. This is the main settlement for the Sherpa inhabitants of the Rolwaling Valley. It is located in a narrow gorge and gets little direct sunlight. There is no farmland nor mountain view, save that of Gaurishankar before you reach the village. The *gomba* here is impressively located and worth visiting to see the fine paintings. There is a school built by Sir Edmund Hillary and some interesting flour mills. People wishing to take a side trip with a view of spectacular Menlungtse (Jobo Garu on the Schneider map) can ascend to the Manlung La in a day and a half from Beding if they are already acclimatized. There is some trade to Palbugthang and Thumphug over this pass during the summer—mostly rice exchanged for Tibetan salt.

Leave Beding and pass through a *yersa* (11,975 ft, 3650 m) in **10 minutes.** Then cross a tributary (11,875 ft, 3584 m) in another **10 minutes.** This river, the Gaurishankar Khola, has eroded a gap in the wall, allowing a pretty waterfall to cascade through. Just beyond is a *yersa*, Chumlgalgya, and there are two more in **5 and 10 minutes** respectively (the last at 11,700 ft, 3566 m). The trail continues into a pleasant fir, rhododendron, and birch forest and descends in 20 minutes to a small sanctuary (11,275 ft, 3437 m) dedicated to the Nepali deities Sita Mahadev and Kanchi Mahadev. A cantilever bridge here to the south (left) bank of the Rolwaling Khola is the beginning of a trail that leads to the Daldung La. It offers a higher route out of the Rolwaling Valley to use in the monsoon, when the main route may be too wet. Don't take it unless so advised by the locals. Continue in forest for **35 minutes** until you cross a tributary from the north. Here there is a good, though very foreshortened, view of Gaurishankar to the north. Some **10 minutes** beyond, come to a covered bridge crossing the Rolwaling Khola (10,200 ft, 3108 m). Cross to the south (left) bank and keep to the south side of the narrow valley. Notice how everything is much greener and lusher here, perhaps because this north-facing slope receives less direct sun. In addition to the deciduous vegetation, there are impressive fir trees.

Continue on the south side above the valley floor and enter a burned area (9350 ft, 2850 m) in **35 minutes.** Some **20 minutes** beyond reach some steep slabs (9150 ft, 2789 m). Leave the riverbed and ascend the slabs along an impressive, locally made ramp. Reach a clearing in **30 minutes**—you are still in the burn, which has more growth the farther west you go. **Ten minutes** beyond is a campsite under an overhanging rock, and nearby is a fault cave. Continue high on the side of the valley to stands of oak. Pass under a swirling waterfall (9175 ft, 2797 m) **1 hour** beyond the slabs. Continue contouring for almost **1 hour** before descending to reach the few *goTh* of Shakpa (8700 ft, 2652 m).

Descend in less than **1 hour** to the village of **Simigaon** (6550 ft, 1996 m). Sherpas and hill Nepalis inhabit this lush oasis, which has interesting fruits and vegetables in addition to the predominant millet fields.

Descend steeply to the river, the Bhote Kosi, passing under some large rock overhangs. Cross to the east (right) bank on a suspension bridge (5000 ft, 1524 m) **45 minutes** from Simigaon. The trail rises above difficult stretches of an impressive gorge to the south. Traverse the few fields of Chetchet 15 minutes beyond and admire the falls that tumble at least 300 ft (100 m) down the east (right) bank. Some **35 minutes** beyond Chetchet, the trail forks. The lower fork keeps close to the river and is suitable during low water. The upper fork is for use during the monsoon. In **30 minutes** the valley widens and in its floor ahead is the village of **Gongar** (4525 ft, 1410 m). Cross the Gongar Khola, a tributary from the west, to the trail fork beyond. The left fork keeps close to the river and goes to Charikot. You can take it to join the usual Everest Base Camp route from Lamosangu. The right fork, described here, ascends and heads to Barabise. Climb on a spur through terraces to a *chautaara* (5150 ft, 1570 m) **30 minutes** from Gongar. Contour and cross two tributaries in **30 minutes.** Climb another **25 minutes** to a Shiva sanctuary (5825 ft, 1775 m) to the left of the trail. Surrounded by a rock wall, this sanctuary contains a few bells and innumerable tridents of iron in various shapes and sizes. Climb another 30 minutes to **Thare** (6475 ft, 1974 m), a scattered *Tamang* village. It is not marked on Schneider's *Lapchi Kang* map.

Continue contouring to **Dulang** (6225 ft, 1897 m), the next scattered village. Another **50 minutes** brings you to the ridge where the Warang school (6600 ft, 2012 m) is located. Enjoy the views of Gaurishankar to the northeast. Pass through the settlement of **Yarsa** (6225 ft, 1897 m) **25 minutes** beyond, then contour and descend for **20 minutes** to cross the Warang Khola (5775 ft, 1760 m). Contour another **25 minutes** to the scattered village of Bulung (5850 ft, 1783 m). Continue to a high clearing, the site of the local middle school (6335 ft, 1931 m), some **25 minutes** beyond. You are now leaving the valley of the Bhote Kosi for the tributary valley of the Sangawa Khola. Contour for **45 minutes** to a *stupa*, then a *chautaara* with Tibetan-style religious paintings. Pass above the scattered village of Laduk and reach the school situated above it (6810 ft, 2075 m) in **20 minutes.** Don't climb beyond, but take the lower fork and descend slightly. Cross a recent slide, then the Thuran Khola (6260 ft, 1908 m) in another **1¼ hours.** Above you is the town of Charsaba, but the main trail ascends and contours below it. Beyond a main ridge, the town of Chilangka (6310 ft, 1923 m) is reached in **65 minutes.** Descend past another small slide and cross the Jorang Khola (5585 ft, 1702 m) in **25 minutes.** Contour through chir pine forest to reach **Lading** (5835 ft, 1778 m) in **50 minutes.**

Beyond there is a choice of routes. The left fork descends to the river (the Saun Khola), crosses it to the east (right) bank on a log bridge, ascends near a tributary (the Amatal Khola), and passes the village of Amatal to the few houses of Ruphtang (7670 ft, 2335 m) in approximately 4 hours. This route is more direct than the other, but it avoids the climb up to Bigu Gomba, one of the most fascinating Buddhist nunneries in Nepal.

To head to Bigu Gomba, also known locally as Tashi Gomba, don't descend the Saun or Sangawa Khola, but contour around a ridge and descend to the Samling Khola, a tributary from the north. Cross it on a cantilever bridge (5710 ft, 1710 m) to the west (right) bank in **45 minutes.** Begin climbing up to **Bigu Gomba.** The entire terraced hillside has numerous houses and is called Bigu. It takes **2 hours** or more to reach the actual nunnery (8235 ft, 2310 m), a long, white building in front of the temple itself, which is set among juniper trees. This nunnery was built around 1933 and houses some thirty-six nuns, most of them Sherpas. It is unusual because its east and west walls are lined with interlacing statues of Avalokiteshwara, each with eleven heads and a thousand arms, hands, and eyes. You are not allowed to photograph the inside of the *gomba.* This convent of the Kargyupa sect was described by Christoph von Furer-Haimendorf in "A Nunnery in Nepal" (see appendix B).

To leave Bigu, traverse north on a high trail, then contour and drop to join a main trail west of the *gomba* near three *stupa* (7895 ft, 2406 m) in less than **30 minutes.** Continue until you spot Ruptang, one house on top of a small hill; take a left fork to descend and cross a tributary from the north on a covered bridge by some mills (7460 ft, 2275 m). Climb the hill to **Ruptang** (7680 ft, 2335 m) **30 minutes** from the *stupa.* This may be the last habitation below the pass, the Tinsang La. Climb beyond, steeply at first, then more gradually in a forest of prickly-leaved oak. There is a tea shop (8740 ft, 2664 m) some 55 minutes above Ruptang. Continue climbing in impressive fir forest with numerous campsites. There is a *goTh* (10,240 ft, 3121 m) **2 hours** from Ruptang, and a pleasant stream some 500 ft (150 m) higher. The pass itself (10,890 ft, 3319 m), with several *goTh* nearby, is **30 minutes** beyond. The view of the Himalaya, although somewhat distant, is breathtaking. The tower of Chobo Bamare is quite close.

From the pass, descend into rhododendron-and-fir forest that becomes almost pure rhododendron forest lower down, then blends again into prickly-leaved oak forest. A small *gomba* above **Dolangsa** (8165 ft, 2489 m) is reached in **65 minutes** from the pass. There are many variations in the route down the Sun Kosi river to its junction with the Bhote Kosi below Barabise. You can head south through Nangarpa and cross the main river west of Gorthali before proceeding along its north (right) bank. Or you can keep to the north side of the valley, crossing tributaries and going below a pretty waterfall (7390 ft, 2252 m) **65 minutes** beyond the *gomba.* Beyond, you can continue contouring, or you can descend closer to the river. If descending, reach **Kabre** (5265 ft, 1605 m) in **70 minutes** from the waterfall. Continue west, crossing a tributary from the north on an old suspension bridge (3890 ft, 1185 m) in 35 minutes. Contour another **10 minutes** to the first stores of **Budipa** (3790 ft, 1155 m). The main trail continues contouring about 500 ft (150 m) above the main river and passes through the scattered houses of **Simle** (3550 ft, 1080 m) in **55 minutes.** The solace and freedom from the noises of the twentieth century are almost over. Horns can soon be heard. The trail rounds a ridge to descend to **Barabise** (2690 ft, 820 m) on the west (left) bank of the Bhote Kosi in 45 minutes. Buses leave this staging center for Kathmandu periodically during the day.

There is another high pass leading out of the upper Rolwaling Valley, the Yalung La (17,422 ft, 5310 m). The descent is made to the southwest to Suri Dhoban. Inquire at Beding for a guide.

An alternative route from Rolwaling branches from Simigaon, and instead of crossing to the west (right) bank of the Bhote Kosi, heads south on its east (left) bank, passing through Tashinam to Manthali (3450 ft, 1080 m), approximately one day from Simigaon. The Sieri Khola, a tributary from the east, is crossed en route. Continue on the east (left) bank of the main valley and cross the Suri (or Khare) Khola at Suri Dhoban (3215 ft, 990 m). Continue to Tyanku in a day. Cross the main river, the Tamba or Bhote Kosi, at Biguti (3150 ft, 960 m) and climb up to Dolakha (5580 ft, 1700 m), which has several interesting temples. Shortly beyond, reach Charikot (6560 ft, 2000 m), less than a day from Tyanku. The main trail to Solu-Khumbu is soon intersected; Lamosangu is a day and a half farther. This trail is somewhat shorter than the higher Tinsang La trail, but less scenic.

Chitwan National Park

(Map No. 10, Page 319)

Chitwan National Park, covering 360 sq mi (932 sq km), some 60 mi (96 km) southwest of Kathmandu, is perhaps the best place in Nepal to see jungle wildlife. Tours to the park can be arranged by several commercial agencies (see Addresses in appendix A). The usual format includes round trip by air, elephant rides, stays at either a jungle lodge or a tent camp, hikes, boat rides, and animal observation. Rhinos are usually seen and occasionally a leopard or tiger. These tours are quite expensive, but for those who can afford them, well worth it.

But for the cost-conscious and adventuresome trekker-tourist, there is another way to see the park. Travel independently to Saura on the outskirts of the park and arrange it all yourself. For such a visit allow at least two days in the park and two days for round-trip travel from Kathmandu. If you start from Birjung, coming overland from India, the travel time can be shortened and made a part of your journey to Kathmandu. The best season to visit Chitwan is from October to April. From February onward is probably the best time to see wildlife.

Since the airport at Bharatpur has been closed, the usual way to reach the park from Kathmandu is by bus from Narayangarh. There is a new road from Mugling, on the Kathmandu–Pokhara Highway, to Narayangarh that shortens the travel time considerably. Then take a bus or truck east toward HetauDa along the East–West Highway. Get off at TaDi Bazaar. Sometimes, buses leave Kathmandu for Birjung by way of Narayangarh. These are the most convenient because you can get off right at TaDi Bazaar and do not have to change vehicles at Narayangarh.

From TaDi Bazaar it is usually easy to arrange a ride in a jeep or oxcart to Saura, now that the locals have caught on to tourism. By this route it is easy to

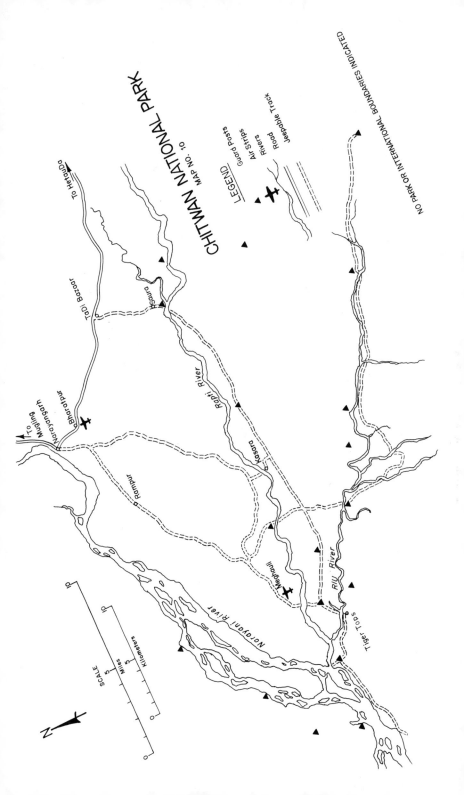

CHITWAN NATIONAL PARK
MAP NO. 10

LEGEND

Guard Posts ▲
Air Strips ✈
Rivers
Road Track
Jeepable Track

NO PARK OR INTERNATIONAL BOUNDARIES INDICATED

To Hetauda
To Muglng
Tadi Bazaar
Narayangarh
Bharatpur
Saura
Rampur
Kasara
Meghauli
Rapti River
Riu River
Narayani River
Tiger Tops

SCALE
Miles
Kilometers

N

reach Saura in one day from Kathmandu. Those coming from Birjung should first go to HetauDa and then take a bus heading west toward Narayangarh. Get off at TaDi Bazaar.

It is also possible to reach the park by flying to Meghauli, but this town is far from Saura and offers very little opportunity for independent travel. There is a road from Bharatpur to Meghauli, and buses leave Bharatpur early in the morning.

Saura (properly written Sauraha), a small village located at the northeast corner of the park, is the starting point for visits. Simple accommodations, campsites, and Nepali food are available. There are also several hotels, and more emphasis is being placed on meeting the needs of the independent tourist. A modern campground has been constructed, and there is a small shelter. Water is available in the nearby Rapti River or from local wells. Although some wood may be available locally, campers are encouraged to bring their own stoves and fuel to help curb deforestation. In Saura there is a guard station, park offices, visitor's center, and museum. A permit must be obtained to enter the park. Payment of the entrance fee does not include the services of a guide, but private guides are available for hire.

Elephants can be rented at the park offices. Usually two or three people ride one elephant and the trip lasts 1½ hours. On such a ride in the park you may see rhinoceroses, spotted deer, sambar, rhesus monkeys, peafowl, and jungle fowl.

Another interesting adventure is to ride canoes down the Rapti River, which can be arranged at the Saura park office. The 12 mi (20 km) trip down the river to Kasara, the park headquarters, takes about 3½ hours. This may be difficult to do as the canoes must be poled back up the river. A special permit is required. There are no hotel or dining facilities at the headquarters, but camping is allowed. There is a museum there as well as a gharial (crocodile) breeding project. A longer trip downstream, lasting 5 to 6 hours, brings you to within a 1-hour walk of the Tiger Tops Hotel. The best time for this trip is late October to February. Along the way you see many interesting birds and crocodiles. You must walk back. There are regular boat trips going down the Rapti River for 1 hour. Since you must walk back to Saura, you are required to take a guide with you.

A popular trip is to go partway down the Rapti by canoe and make a side excursion east up a small stream, where crocodiles are normally seen sleeping on the banks from mid-October to mid-March. At the Tiger Tops Hotel, you may be able to arrange elephant rides with the management, but this is less likely for budget-conscious tourists. You might be able to hitch a ride back from the hotel in a jeep, but it is usually necessary to walk back to Saura, a very long (23.6 mi, 38 km) day. This could be dangerous because you must walk through long stretches of grassland inhabited by rhinos. En route, pass two guard posts, then a sign pointing to the park headquarters and a small museum 0.25 mi (0.4 km) off to the left. Pass two more guard posts before reaching Saura. It could be necessary, or interesting, to spend a night at a guard post.

One way to mount an elephant

Several blinds *(machaan)* for observing animals have been constructed in the jungle, usually next to waterholes. Ask at the park office in Saura for a guide. They can be reached by elephant or on foot. Consider spending a night at one to observe the active feeding times and to hear the nocturnal sounds of the jungle. The view is best during a full moon. Animals can be seen undisturbed rather than flushed out, as when riding on elephants. Lucky trekkers have seen tigers and leopards, and most people observe rhinos, wild boar, deer, monkeys, and colorful birds.

Finally, you can walk in the jungle. It is not advisable to wander through dense jungle on foot without a qualified guide. Insist on seeing a guide's certificate before hiring him. Rhinos and sloth bear are the main hazards. Rhinos are quite common in forests, grasslands, and water. Their sight is poor, but their sense of smell is excellent. You can be on top of a rhino before noticing it. They do charge people, and are amazingly fast and agile. Females with calves will attack without provocation. If a rhino charges, climb the nearest tree immediately. If there are no trees, run in an arc, as rhinos usually charge in a straight line. Best of all, avoid walking in tall grasslands. I believe that some tourists have been killed by rhinos—certainly local people get killed every year. There have been fatal attacks from tigers, and sloth bears are also very dangerous.

VEGETATION AND ANIMALS

Most of Chitwan National Park is covered with sal forests, the climax forest of the higher elevations in the park. There are small areas on the highest ridges where chir pine occurs, but sal predominates, becoming best developed below the base of the hills. Sal is a hard, heavy, slow-growing species, typically reaching 80 to 100 feet. It is valuable as the principal commercial species of southern Nepal.

Low regions of the park are subject to flooding and are dominated by tall grass species. There are over fifty species of grasses, and *Saccharum* and *Phragmites* are common. Stable tracts near the large rivers are covered by a distinct riverine forest characterized by the red silk cotton tree, or simal *(Bombax ceiba)*. The massive red flowers of this tree make a remarkable display in January and February. These trees, when young, have a thorny bark, while older ones grow large buttresses at their bases. Some of its common associates are *belar (Trewia nudiflora), sissu (Dalbergia sissoo),* and more occasionally, the Flame of the Forest, *palaas (Butea monosperma),* which provides beautiful floral displays in spring.

Vegetative cover is at a maximum just following the monsoon. By March and April, grazing, cutting, and burning have reduced the cover to a relative minimum until the rains bring growth again in late June. Thus, from February on is a good time to see wildlife.

Perhaps the greatest attraction of the Chitwan area is its wildlife. The one-horned rhinoceros is the most conspicuous of the large species. It is estimated that there are perhaps 350 rhinos in the area. Rhinos prefer riverine and grassland habitats, seeking the shelter of the forest during the hot months. In May and June they may often be seen in considerable congregations at wallows or waterholes, where they seek relief from the heat.

Another of the more famous species of the park is the royal Bengal tiger. While research being carried out in the area indicates that tigers may spend considerable time near areas of human activity, they are seldom observed except by careful effort or fortunate chance.

The large gaur (wild ox) is found in the hilly areas of the park. At least four species of deer, including chital, or spotted deer, hog deer, barking deer,

A musician of the Tarai plays a shehnai.

and sambar, occur in the lower parts of the forest and grasslands. The hog deer stays near the short grass along the river banks. They are an important prey species of the tiger.

Other mammals that occur in the park include sloth bear, leopard, fishing cat, jungle cat, jackal, wild boar, otter, langur and rhesus macaque monkeys, several kinds of mongooses, and several species of civet cats. During periods of high water the Gangetic dolphin is seen in the large rivers.

Reptiles include large crocodiles—the fish-eating gharial, common in the Narayani River, and the mugger, found in the Narayani and in ponds near the river. Numerous species of snake are found in the park, including the king cobra, common krait, rat snake, and Indian python.

Birds are the most conspicuous fauna of the park, with over 400 visitor and resident species. Among the larger species are peafowl, red jungle fowl, Bengal florican, black partridge, giant hornbill, white-backed vulture, gray-headed fishing eagle, crested serpent eagle, and several species of stork and egret. Waterfowl, such as the Brahminy duck and barheaded goose, come to winter along the rivers.

Many smaller birds occur as well. The most colorful and conspicuous are parakeets, kingfishers, woodpeckers, pigeons, and bee-eaters. Songbirds are common, with the black-headed oriole among the best known. There are over 100 species of butterflies in the park, including some of the largest ones, as well as the largest recorded moth.

Visitors should be aware that heavy, uncontrolled use of the park out of Saura is creating considerable pressure on the habitat. The same cautions regarding conservation of fragile alpine areas of Nepal apply here.

THE COUNTRY AND THE PEOPLE

A Sherpa house up the Imja Khola; the canisters contain tOmba, *a fermented mash (photo by Pat Morrow).*

At certain altitudes and temperatures, lizards may be seen.

12 Natural History

To a person uninstructed in natural history, his country or seaside stroll is a walk through a gallery filled with wonderful works of art, nine-tenths of which have their faces turned to the wall.

Thomas Huxley

GEOLOGY
by Daniel Schelling*

According to the theory of plate tectonics, the Himalayan arc has formed as a result of the "collision" between the Indian subcontinent and Asia. Prior to approximately 180 million years ago all the present-day "southern" continents, including South America, Africa, Australia, Antarctica, the Arabian Peninsula, and the Indian subcontinent, formed one large, southern-hemisphere "supercontinent" known as Gandwanaland. A vast ocean, the Tethys Sea, separated the northern margins of Africa and India from the southern margin of Laurasia, the northern hemisphere supercontinent composed of Asia, Europe, and North America. About 180 million years ago Gandwanaland began to break apart. Between 75 and 80 million years ago the Indian subcontinent, containing present-day India, Pakistan, Nepal, Bangladesh, and Sri Lanka, broke away from Antarctica and began its northward "drift" toward Asia. The Indian Ocean, which separates India and Antarctica, began opening up through sea-floor spreading along the mid-Indian Ocean Ridge at this time. India and Antarctica traveled away from each other at an initial rate of about 16 cm per year, separating the two continents a distance of 3200 km over the next 20 million years. While to the south of India new oceanic crust was being produced at the mid-ocean ridge and the Indian Ocean was being created, to the north of the Indian continent the Tethys Sea was closing and the oceanic crust underlying the Tethys Sea was being subducted (consumed) beneath Tibet.

About 55 million years ago the Indian subcontinent slammed into Tibetan and southern Asia. Sea-floor spreading has continued in the Indian Ocean since the collision, and India has continued to move northward relative to Tibet and Asia. With the Indian subcontinent plowing into Tibet and southern Asia, something has had to give. The result has been the crumpling-up, folding, faulting, and uplift of the northern margin of the Indian subcontinent to form

---

* Since 1983 Daniel Schelling has been actively involved in Himalayan geological research, doing his doctoral research on the geology of the Rolwaling and the eastern Nepal Himalaya. Presently, he is studying the geology of far-eastern Nepal as a research fellow of Hokkaido University in Sapporo, Japan.

the Himalaya, as well as the uplift of the Tibetan plateau.

Today, four different physiographic (geographic) and geologic divisions of the Himalaya are recognized. These are, from north to south, the Tibetan Himalaya, Higher Himalaya, Lesser Himalaya, and Sub-Himalaya. North of the Tibetan Himalaya lies the Tibetan Block or micro-continent; south of the

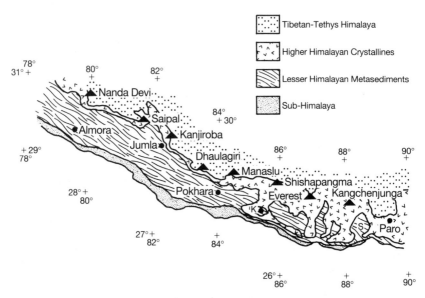

Figure 1. Map of the central Himalaya, showing the four tectonic zones; K = Kathmandu, S = Sikkim (from Pecher and Le Fort, 1986)

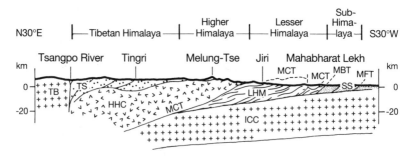

Figure 2. Crustal-scale cross-section of southern Tibet and eastern Nepal; TB = Tibetan Block north of the Indus–Tsangpo Suture, TS = Tethyan Sediments of the Tibetan Himalaya, HHC = Higher Himalaya Crystalline rocks, LHM = Lesser Himalayan Metasedimentary rocks, SS = Siwalik Series sediments of the Sub-Himalaya, ICC = Indian Continental Crust, MCT = Main Central Thrust, MBT = Main Boundary Thrust, MFT = Main Frontal Thrust (from Brunel, 1986, and Schelling, 1989)

Sub-Himalaya lie the Ganges Plain and Indian subcontinent (figs. 1 and 2).

The northern boundary of the Tibetan Himalaya is the **Indus–Tsangpo Suture,** along which the Indus and Tsangpo rivers flow. The Indus–Tsangpo Suture is the actual collision zone and boundary between the Indian subcontinent and the Tibetan micro-continent. Along some sections of the Indus–Tsangpo Suture, oceanic crust and sub-crustal mantle have been squeezed up between the Indian and Tibetan continents and thrust over the oceanic sediments of the Tibetan Himalaya. This oceanic crust, along with the Tethyan sediments of the Tibetan Himalaya, is all that remains of the Tethys Sea today.

The **Tibetan** or **Tethys Himalaya** lie between the Indus and Tsangpo rivers to the north and the high summits of the Higher Himalaya, which form the backbone of the Himalayan range (e.g., Mount Everest, Annapurna, and Dhaulagiri), to the south. The Tibetan Himalaya include the Tibetan Marginal Range, a range of mountains which lie to the north of the High Himalayan peaks and includes the Dolpo, Mustang, and Manang regions of central Nepal as well as the Tingri region of southern Tibet. The Tibetan Himalaya are composed of Cambrian to Eocene sediments, which were deposited in the Tethys Sea between 500 and 55 million years ago on both the northern margin of the Indian continent (the continental platform underlain by Higher Himalayan rocks) and in the deep ocean basin between the Indian and Asian continents. These oceanic sediments include limestones, sandstones, and shales, and contain abundant fossils, including brachiopods, oysters, occasional plant fossils, and the famous Upper Jurassic ammonites found in profusion around the sacred area of Muktinath. The Nilgiri Limestones (named after the peak of Nilgiri in the Annapurna region) were deposited in the Tethys Sea during the Ordovician period (500 to 435 million years ago); they presently form the summits of Nilgiri and the Annapurnas and are found on the northern flanks of Dhaulagiri. Similar early Paleozoic sediments cap the summits of Mount Everest, Lhotse, Kanjiroba, and Nanda Devi; thus it is true that many of the highest summits of the world are capped by rocks that were once deposited in an ocean. Since these early Paleozoic Tethyan sediments in the Annapurna and Everest regions lie at the base of a 12-km-thick sequence of Tethyan sediments, and since the summits of these mountains are presently over 8 km high, these sediments have been uplifted some 20 km since the onset of the Himalayan orogeny (mountain-building event) 55 million years ago. During the Himalayan orogeny, the Tethyan sediments have been extensively faulted and folded; this can be seen between Marpha and Muktinath, and north of Manang in the Annapurna region.

The physiographic **Higher Himalaya** includes the high mountains of the Himalaya proper (e.g., Kangchenjunga, Makalu, Everest, Cho Oyu, Shishapangma, Manaslu, Annapurna, Dhaulagiri, Kanjiroba, Api, Saipal, etc.) and the valleys within the high mountains. The Higher Himalaya are generally considered to include those regions with altitudes over 4000 m that lie south of the Tibetan Plateau and the Tibetan Marginal Range. Geologically, the Higher Himalaya consist of highly metamorphosed and extensively deformed schists and gneisses (crystalline rocks). These rocks were the original Precambrian continental crust of the northern margin of the Indian continent. (The Tethyan sediments of the Tibetan Himalaya were deposited upon these Higher Himalayan rocks). About 25 million years ago, a deep, east–west-trending fracture formed within the Indian continental crust. The continental crust on the north side of the fracture (the Higher Himalayan rocks) was shoved over the continental crust and its sedimentary cover rocks south of the fracture (the Lesser Himalayan rocks). The Higher Himalayan crystalline rocks (to the north) were thrust over the Lesser Himalayan sedimentary rocks (to the south) along a fault known as the Main Central Thrust. The Main Central Thrust is the geological boundary between the Higher Himalaya and the Lesser Himalaya. Higher Himalayan rocks have been thrust over the Lesser Himalayan sediments a minimum of 100 km into eastern Nepal. Between 25 and 10 million years ago, at about the same time as thrusting was taking place along the Main Central Thrust, very high temperatures in the Higher Himalayan rocks melted the schists and gneisses, forming large granite bodies in many of the Higher Himalayan Peaks. These granites can be seen on Makalu, Everest, Lhotse, Shishapangma, and Manaslu.

The Physiographic **Lesser** (or Lower) **Himalaya** are divided into two distinct regions in Nepal: the Middle Mountains and the Mahabharat Lekh. South of the Higher Himalaya lie the heavily inhabited Middle Mountains, from which almost all treks to the Higher Himalaya begin. Elevations in the Middle Mountains range from a few hundred meters in the valleys (e.g., Tumlingtar at an elevation of 457 m) to 4000 m on the ridges. The Middle Mountains are dissected by major south-flowing rivers, such as the Karnali, Kali Gandaki, and Arun rivers. The ridges that come off of the southern flanks of the Higher Himalaya also trend roughly north–south. The Mahabharat Lekh, an east–west-trending range of hills with summit elevations of 2000 to 2500 m, runs the whole length of Nepal south of the Middle Mountains and north of the Siwalik Hills. The Mahabharat Lekh can be seen south of Kathmandu and the Kathmandu–Pokhara road, and is breached by the Trisuli-Narayani river, along which the road from Kathmandu to Narayangarh and India runs.

Much of the physiographic Lesser Himalaya are underlain by rocks belonging to the geologic Lesser Himalaya. The geologic Lesser Himalaya consist of variously metamorphosed and deformed sediments that were deposited in an inland basin from Precambrian times (more than 570 million years ago) up to about 50 or 60 million years ago. The original sediments of the Lesser Himalaya included shales, sandstones, conglomerates, limestone, and some acid-volcanic rocks. During the last 25 to 30 million years, these were metamorphosed to form the slates, phyllites, metaquartzites, marbles, and granitic augen-gneisses that make up the Lesser Himalaya today. Practically no fossils are seen in the Lesser Himalayan metasediments. It is interesting to note that the hills encircling Kathmandu, and the Mahabharat Lekh in eastern Nepal, which belong to the physiographic Lesser Himalaya, are actually composed of Higher Himalayan rocks—schists, gneisses and granites—which have been thrust over the Lesser Himalayan sediments along the Main Central Thrust.

The **Sub-Himalaya** is the geologic name for the Siwalik Hills, the foothills of the Himalaya lying between the Mahabharat Lekh to the north and the Indo-Gangetic Plains of north India to the south. These hills rarely exceed

1200 m in elevation. The Siwalik Hills are composed entirely of shales, sandstones, and conglomerates less than 20 million years old, which are the product of the erosion of the rising Himalaya to the north. Thus the Siwalik Series sediments record the uplift of the Himalaya. The Siwalik sediments contain scattered fossils of crocodiles, rhinoceroses, and elephants, all present-day inhabitants of the few wild regions left in the Himalayan foothills, such as Royal Chitwan National Park. Presently, the Lesser Himalaya, including the Mahabharat Lekh, are being uplifted and thrust southward over the Sub-Himalayan Siwalik Hills; the Siwalik Hills are being uplifted and thrust southward over the Ganges plain.

While the Himalayan orogeny has been active for the last 55 million years, the present-day landforms of the Himalaya are the result of tectonic and erosional activity that has taken place during the last 1.6 million years (the Pleistocene and Holocene epochs). This includes the glacial activity that has carved out the mountain slopes and the *U*-shaped valleys of the Higher Himalaya and the Tibetan Marginal Range above approximately 3800 m; the erosional activity of water that has produced the deep, *V*-shaped valleys of the Higher and Lesser Himalaya, including the Arun and Kali Gandaki valleys, which vie for the honor of "deepest valley in the world"; the recent uplift of the Mahabharat Lekh, which has forced all the rivers of Nepal, except the Arun River, to turn abruptly from their north–south orientations to east–west orientations as they flow out of the Higher Himalaya or Tibetan Marginal Range; and the formation of, and subsequent drying up of, a number of lakes lying on the north side of the Mahabharat Lekh, including the Quaternary Kathmandu Lake, which has been uplifted and drained during the last 10,000 years to form the Kathmandu Valley.

Of particular interest are the numerous major rivers that originate on the Tibetan Plateau and within the Tibetan Marginal Range that cut through the High Himalaya. Why doesn't the highest mountain range in the world, the Himalaya, form a hydrologic divide? These Himalayan rivers were flowing southwards off of the Tibetan Plateau onto the plains of north India prior to the uplift of the Higher Himalaya. The erosive power of these rivers has kept pace with the uplift of the Himalaya, cutting spectacular gorges through the Higher Himalaya as fast as the tectonic forces of the region could lift up the summits of the great Himalayan peaks. The Kali Gandaki, Arun, Bhahmaputra, and Indus rivers are all examples of rivers that have maintained their original positions, and cut impressive valleys, during the uplift of the Himalaya.

The Himalaya remains a tectonically active region today. The magnitude of the present-day tectonic forces in the Himalayan region is demonstrated by the numerous earthquakes felt in the Himalaya, including the devastating "Great Earthquake" of 1934, which destroyed much of Kathmandu, and the more recent earthquake of August 22, 1988, which caused landslides, destroyed homes, and killed hundreds of people throughout eastern Nepal. As India keeps plowing northward into Tibet and southern Asia, the Himalayan orogeny continues, and the Higher, Lesser, and Sub-Himalaya continue to be uplifted and pushed southward (relative to north India) at rates of several millimeters per year.

Climate

Nepal has a monsoon climate. The heavy rains of the monsoon occur from June to September, and begin in the eastern parts—two to three weeks can separate the onset of the monsoon in the east from that in the west. Similarly, more rain falls in the east. At high altitudes, above about 20,000 ft (6000 m), there is snow rather than rain. In addition, a less well-defined winter monsoon occurs from December to the end of March. This precipitation takes the form of snow at altitudes above about 8000 ft (2440 m).

The monsoon is caused by the movement of moist air north and west from the Bay of Bengal. As the moist air rises, it cools and condenses as rain. This precipitation falls on the southern side of the main Himalayan range. Generally there is less at higher altitudes, since the clouds have already given up much moisture at the lower altitudes. When the resulting dry air mass crosses the Himalaya, it has very little moisture left to deposit on the northern sides. A rain screen thus exists on the north sides of the Himalaya, producing the xerophytic conditions in Dolpo and Mustang.

The winter rains enable Nepalis to grow a second crop at lower altitudes. Generally, crops are grown up to the altitude at which clouds hang during the monsoon, as the clouds limit the amount of sun available. Local factors are immensely important in determining the rainfall and climate. Rain falling on north and west faces evaporates less, and more rain falls on steeper slopes, so there tends to be greater variety in the flora in these areas. Shady areas also have a more varied vegetation. While trekking, observe the changes in vegetation on different terrain, and try to predict local climatic factors that produce them.

FLORA AND FAUNA
by Carol Inskipp*

Nepal's Species—Richness

Nepal has a remarkably high diversity of flora and fauna considering its small size. There are over 830 species of birds, more than 600 of butterflies, and about 6500 of flowering plants.

Nepal's species—richness can be partly attributed to the country's extremely varied climate and topography. The altitudinal range is greater than in any other country, ranging from almost sea level to the highest point on earth, Mount Everest. In the lowlands, such as in Royal Chitwan National Park, there are tropical forests, which support the greatest number of species. Here can be

---

* The author of this section is an ornithologist, nature conservationist, and writer with a special interest in the birds of Nepal. Since 1977 she has made many trips to the country studying birds with her husband, Tim. Together they wrote the standard work on the distribution of birds of Nepal. Carol has also written other books and articles on Nepali birds and their conservation.

found some of the Indian subcontinent's large mammals, including the Indian rhinoceros and tiger. At the other extreme is the alpine zone of the high peaks, which holds the smallest number of species. Among these is the Tibetan snow cock, a large gamebird that normally summers above 4500 m.

The other major factor contributing to Nepal's species–richness is its position of overlap between Asia's two great biogeographic realms—the Oriental and Palearctic. Palearctic species originating in Europe and northern Asia are dominant in the Himalaya. For example, birds include accentors, redstarts, and rosefinches. Primulas, gentians, and edelweiss flower in the alpine grasslands, attracting Apollo butterflies. Oriental species are the most common in the tropical and subtropical zones of southern Nepal. Hornbills feed in large fruiting trees of the forest canopy while gaudy pittas search the leaf litter below, and large, colorful butterflies, such as the yellow and black birdwings, flutter past.

MAJOR HABITAT TYPES

Nepal's major natural habitat types are forests, grasslands and wetlands. Nepal has rather few wetlands, but their ecological diversity is very great. For instance, a total of over 160 indigenous species of fish have been recorded. There are three major river systems, which are fed by the Himalayan snows and glaciers: the Kosi, Kali Gandaki, and Karnali. Other wetlands include a number of small lakes scattered throughout the country. The Kosi Barrage area, a large expanse of open water, marshes, grasslands, and scrub lying in the Kosi's flood plain in the far eastern lowlands, is by far the most valuable wetland in the country. It is internationally important as a staging point for migrant water birds. Over 50,000 ducks are estimated to be there in February.

Only small areas remain of the country's lowland grasslands and almost all of these lie within protected forest areas. They are important for a number of threatened animals, including the swamp deer, Indian rhinoceros, and two of the world's most endangered bustards, the Bengal and lesser floricans. In spring and summer a mass of colorful flowers bloom on alpine grasslands. A number of mammals, such as the bharal and common goral, depend on these grasslands for grazing and in turn they form the vital prey of the threatened snow leopard.

Forests form the major natural vegetation of Nepal. In his classic work *Forests of Nepal*, Adam Stainton identified thirty-five different forest types— an extraordinarily high number for such a small country. These include dry coniferous forests on the northern Himalayan slopes, rhododendron shrubberies in the subalpine zone, temperate oak forests draped in mosses, and lush, wet tropical jungles. The main reason Nepal is of great value for birds is because of its forests. There are as many as 124 species of breeding birds for which the country may hold significant world populations. Nearly all of these are dependent on forests. Nepal's forests also support a rich variety of mammals, although those in the Himalaya have been little studied so far. Relatively few species have adapted to habitats heavily modified or created by people, such as gardens, scrub, and cultivation. Most of them are widespread and common, such as the Asian magpie robin and jungle crow, while many animals dependent on natural habitats are declining.

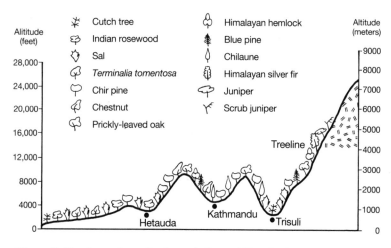

Figure 3. North-south profile through Central Nepal, showing altitudinal forest distributions

The Kali Gandaki Valley—A Great Biogeographic Divide

When trekking up the Kali Gandaki valley to Thak Khola, you experience changes in flora and fauna that are more dramatic than anywhere else in Nepal. For example, in one day you can climb down from the arid Tibetan steppe flora at Tukche through temperate coniferous forests to reach the humid subtropical zone around Tatopani. The Kali Gandaki has cut the world's deepest river gorge right through the Himalaya. The river runs from the Tibetan plateau to the north, through almost the center of Nepal and the middle of the Himalaya.

The valley is a biogeographic divide for Himalayan flora and fauna. Forests to the west of the valley are generally drier and have fewer plant species than eastern forests. In their field guide *Birds of Nepal,* the Flemings point out that the Kali Gandaki is a very distinctive break in bird distribution. Some species, such as the fire-tailed myzornis and the brown parrotbill, are restricted to the valley and further east, while others, the cheer pheasant for instance, only breed in the valley and westwards. Forests to the east of the valley are significantly richer in bird species than western forests, even taking into account that western forests are relatively poorly recorded.

OBSERVING PLANTS AND ANIMALS

Flowers *[phul]*

The main flowering season in the Himalaya is from mid-March to the end of May, while the period between November and late March is a good time to look for flowering plants in the lowlands.

Birds *[charo]*

The period between mid-March and the end of May is excellent for birds because many residents and summer visitors are at a peak of activity. Late May is the best time to bird-watch on the high-altitude treks, such as those to Langtang and Solu-Khumbu. Although it is very hot, late April is exciting for bird-watching at Chitwan, and probably other lowland forests, because large numbers of migrants are passing through the lowlands on their way to the hills and most summer visitors have arrived, while a few winter visitors still remain.

Between December and mid-March is a very interesting time due to Nepal's numerous winter visitors. Look for birds while you trek to Thak Khola and around Annapurna. In October and November small numbers of passage migrants can be seen flying south along the Himalayan valleys. In recent years, thousands of birds of prey have been reported northwest of Pokhara, moving west along the southern edge of the Himalaya.

When bird-watching remember that most birds are active early in the morning and that their movements are affected by the sun. Slopes bathed in sunshine attract birds away from slopes in the shade, except during hot midday periods, when birds tend to be inactive. When walking in forest you may hardly see any birds for several hours. This is because most birds from one area of forest often join together to form a fast-moving party of different species.

Mammals *[pashu, janaawar]*

In general, mammals can be seen throughout the year, although the best months are March to May in the lowland, protected forests of Chitwan, Sukla Phanta, and Bardia. During these months the regrowth of grasses after the annual grass-burning attracts large numbers of herbivores, and with them their predators.

Unlike birds, mammals are usually difficult to see in Nepal. Many of them are only active at night and are usually silent. The first 2- or 3-hour period after sunrise is a productive time to look for nocturnal mammals. They are often still active then and the trail is more likely to be undisturbed. Most mammals are shy and wary of people, so dress in clothes that blend in with your surroundings. Greens or browns are suitable in forest, and pale colors in the Himalaya when they are snow-covered. Remember to be silent and to walk lightly, with slow body movements. Large carnivores and some other mammals, notably the Indian rhinoceros and sloth bear, are potentially dangerous and should never be approached.

Insects *[kira]*

June to September is the best time for insects, but the monsoon weather will present difficulties in finding them. Many species can be seen in other months—for example, many butterflies *[putali]* emerge in March and April, becoming abundant by May and June.

Conservation Measures

PROTECTED AREAS

Nepal has an extensive protected-area system, which now covers 7.4 percent of the country. The country's Department of National Parks and Wildlife Conservation (DNPWC) is aiming to protect representative samples of the country's ecosystems. The majority of these are well represented, although there are a few important omissions, notably subtropical broad-leaved forest.

The task of protecting such a large proportion of the country is formidable. Besides a lack of finances and equipment, the DNPWC faces other problems. Many protected areas are remote and are only accessible by air or on foot. The rugged terrain of the Himalayan protected areas makes coverage problematical. Nepal has a national conservation strategy that aims to strike a balance between the needs of people and those of nature—which are ultimately the same. However, there is widespread ignorance among local people of the value of protected areas as providers of precious resources and as part of their heritage. Practicing conservation education in a country where most of the population lives in widely dispersed small villages is very difficult.

The King Mahendra Trust for Nature Conservation is responsible for managing the Annapurna Conservation Area. The measures the Trust is taking are both innovative and successful. The aim is to balance the needs of the local people, trekkers, and the natural environment. The Trust, established in 1982, is a nongovernmental, nonprofit, independent organization. It aims to conserve and manage natural resources in order to improve the quality of life of the Nepali people.

Royal Chitwan National Park *(Area 932 sq km)* and Parsa Wildlife Reserve *(Area 499 sq km)*

Chitwan, the first park in Nepal, was established in 1973 and lies in the central lowlands. Parsa is adjacent to Chitwan and was designated in 1984. Together they comprise sal and riverine forests and grasslands, and extend into the Siwalik Hills, which are forested with chir pine and sal. Chitwan is famous for its large mammals, which include tiger, leopard, Indian rhinoceros, and gaur. Bird species recorded at Chitwan total 489, a larger number than in any of Nepal's other protected areas. The park also supports a larger number of nationally threatened birds than the others.

Langtang National Park *(Area 1710 sq km)*

Langtang National Park lies in the central Himalayan region and contains a wide range of habitats, from subtropical to alpine. It is especially important for upper temperate and subalpine species, such as pheasants. Mammals include the lesser panda, Himalayan musk deer, and Himalayan tahr. In spring there is a rich variety of butterflies and flowers.

Sagarmatha National Park *(Area 1148 sq km)*

The Sagarmatha National Park, a World Heritage Site, is situated in Solu-Khumbu District in the northeast. The park is an easy place to see high-altitude species, such as Himalayan monal and Tibetan snow cock.

Makalu-Barun National Park *(Area approximately 1400 sq km)*

The proposed Makalu-Barun National Park, an extension of Sagarmatha National Park, lies to the east in the Arun valley watershed. This valley is clothed in dense forests hardly touched by people and is rich in wildlife. Two new bird species for Nepal have been found there in recent years, the slaty-bellied tesia and spotted wren-babbler.

RaRa Lake National Park *(Area 106 sq km)*

A small mountain park in the northwest that includes Nepal's largest lake, RaRa, the park is dominated by magnificent coniferous forests. Like the rest of western Nepal, RaRa Lake National Park is relatively species-poor compared to the east. However, because the west is under-recorded, a visit should prove exciting, as there is a good chance of finding something new. RaRa also provides opportunities to see some western Nepal specialties, such as the cheer pheasant and white-throated tit. The lake is a useful staging point for migrating waterbirds overflying the Himalaya. Grasslands bordering the lake are full of colorful flowers in spring and summer.

Shey Phoksumdo National Park *(Area 3555 sq km)*

Shey Phoksumdo National Park, the largest of Nepal's protected areas, lies mainly in the trans-Himalayan region in the northwest. Birds are typical of those in the Tibetan plateau, and include Tibetan partridge and Hume's ground jay. The snow leopard and bharal occur. Foreigners are allowed access to the southern part of the park.

Khaptad National Park *(Area 225 sq km)*

Khaptad is an isolated massif reaching 3100 m; it lies in far western Nepal south of the main Himalayan chain. Beautiful oak and rhododendron forests cover the slopes, and the rolling plateau on top consists of coniferous forests interspersed with grasslands. There is an interesting variety of bird species present, including the satyr tragopan pheasant and great parrotbill. The meadows are covered in a mass of flowers in spring and summer. Khaptad is nationally renowned for its medicinal herbs.

Royal Bardia National Park *(Area 968 sq km)*

Bardia is situated in midwestern Nepal. It extends from the lowlands, which contain sal and riverine forests and grasslands, into the Siwalik Hills, which are covered in chir pine and stunted sal. Mammals include tiger, swamp deer, and the recently introduced Indian rhinoceros. Birds include some western specialties, such as the white-naped woodpecker.

Royal Sukla Phanta Wildlife Reserve *(Area 155 sq km)*

Sukla Phanta lies in the lowlands of the extreme southwest and consists of sal forests and extensive grasslands (*phanta* means "grassland"). The reserve is important for grassland wildlife, notably its large herd of swamp deer, the threatened hispid hare, Bengal florican, and swamp francolin. Except for a wildlife camp on the outskirts, there are few facilities for visitors at present.

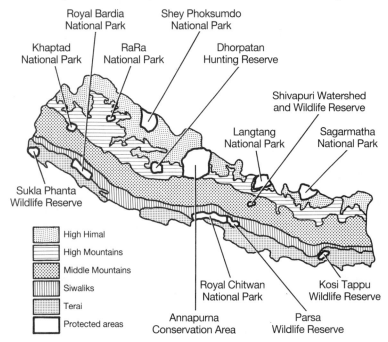

Figure 4. Nepal's protected areas and main physiographic zones

Kosi Tappu Wildlife Reserve *(Area 175 sq km)*

Kosi Tappu lies in the Kosi River plain in the southeastern lowlands. The reserve consists of extensive marshes, grasslands, degraded scrub, and riverine forest. It supports some of the few remaining herds of the wild water buffalo, although they have interbred with the domestic buffalo. The reserve is a valuable wintering area and staging point for migrating birds, especially wildfowl, waders, gulls, and terns.

Shivapuri Watershed and Wildlife Reserve *(Area 145 sq km)*

Shivapuri lies on the northern side of the Kathmandu Valley. Only about half of the watershed is still forested and supports rare Nepali bird species, including the yellow-bellied bush-warbler and gray-sided laughing-thrush.

Annapurna Conservation Area *(Area 2660 sq km)*

The Annapurna Conservation Area lies north of Pokhara in central Nepal and includes the Himalayan biogeographical divide, the Kali Gandaki valley. The conservation area therefore supports species from both the eastern and western Himalaya, as well as flora and fauna typical of the trans-Himalayan zone. The high total of 441 bird species has been recorded. A wide variety of mammals occur, including the lesser panda, snow leopard, Himalayan musk deer, and bharal.

Dhorpatan Hunting Reserve *(Area 1325 sq km)*

This hunting reserve lies in Baglung District in west-central Nepal. There is controlled harvesting of the blue sheep population by foreign trophy hunters. Forests are mainly temperate and subalpine and are dominated by conifers. There is a good population of the cheer pheasant; the satyr tragopan also occurs.

OTHER CONSERVATION MEASURES

In recent years there has been a great increase in reforestation, and some forestry projects have been successful. For instance, the Nepal-Australia Forestry Project has gained much local trust and support. The overall impact in the country has, however, been very small. There are now large areas of degraded, low-density forest in Nepal. Up to now most effort has been put into tree-planting, but protection of some severely depleted forests has resulted in dramatic recoveries. This indicates that there is enormous potential to improve Nepal's forest cover by managing such forests better through controls on cutting and grazing, and through enrichment planting.

THREATS

Habitat loss

The major threats facing wildlife in Nepal are the loss and deterioration of the country's forests. The Nepalis depend on forests for fuel, animal fodder, medical herbs, bamboo for making baskets, and a host of other basic materials. As the population continues to increase, the forests can no longer meet the requirements of the people. In recent times this has been most pronounced in the Tarai, but loss has also occurred in the hills, as people clear land for agriculture to support the increasing population.

In some places however, and mainly in Nepal's well-visited protected areas, such as Sagarmatha and Langtang national parks and the Annapurna Conservation Area, trekkers and mountaineering expeditions are making the problems much worse. Dr. Hemanta Mishra of the King Mahendra Trust for Nature Conservation discovered that a tourist trekker uses nearly five times more fuel than a local Sherpa in Khumbu. The forests that are suffering are some of the best for wildlife in Nepal. An example is the forests along the trail between GhoRepani and Ghandruk in the Annapurna Conservation Area, a route once almost never used by local people. A huge, unbroken oak-and-rhododendron forest covered the surrounding ridges, supporting such rare species as the lesser panda and the orange-rumped honeyguide. In recent years the trail has become a popular trekking route, and an increasing number of large forest clearings have been created by tourist lodges. Another important consideration is that many of the forests and shrubberies being depleted by tourists lie in the subalpine zone, and are especially sensitive because they grow extremely slowly.

During your visit to Nepal's protected areas there are many ways in which you can help to ensure that you do not damage the environment (see chapter 4).

Hunting

Hunting poses an additional threat to some mammals and birds, although in most cases habitat loss is much more serious. One exception is the delightful Himalayan musk deer. Populations of this small deer are now much depleted as a result of overexploitation to obtain a strong-smelling secretion called musk, which is produced by the male. This is highly prized as perfume and is worth more than its weight in gold. The snow leopard, one of the world's rarest and most endangered mammals, is also threatened by hunting despite protection. This large cat has a beautiful, thick, spotted coat of soft gray and white fur, which is highly sought after to meet the demands of the fashion industry. Depletion in numbers of its prey (mainly bharal) are, however, thought to pose a much greater threat to its survival. Local hunting pressures on pheasants can be very high, such as in the Himalaya south of Annapurna. *Rhacophorus* frogs are hunted intensively near some villages because their dried extracts are thought to cure typhoid and high fever.

Fauna and Flora of Nepal's Climatic Zones

In the short space of this chapter it is only possible to cover a small proportion of Nepal's numerous plants and animals. You will need field guides to identify the majority of birds, butterflies, and plant species. Recommended guides for birds are Fleming et al. (1984); for butterflies, Smith (1989); for trees, Storrs (1984); for flowering plants, Polunin and Stainton (1987). Books covering mammals include Gurung (1983), Inskipp (1989), Mishra and Mierow (1976), and Prater (1980). See appendix B for details. Some of the animals and plants which you are most likely to encounter on treks, and some others of special interest, are described below under the climatic zones where you have the greatest opportunity to see them. Do remember, however, that many Himalayan birds and mammals are altitudinal migrants, which descend to lower elevations in winter, especially after the onset of harsh weather conditions. Nepali names are given where possible.

Left: *An open-billed stork, Chitwan National Park*

Right: *The spiny, pink* Morina longifolia *blooms in the late spring (photo by Mary Lynn Hanley).*

TROPICAL ZONE (246–328 ft/75–1000 m)

Most Nepal treks start higher up than the tropical zone. Tropical areas you trek through are likely to be well cultivated, with a much-reduced variety of animals and plants. An excellent way of seeing Nepal's rich variety of tropical wildlife is to visit either the Royal Chitwan or Royal Bardia National Park. K. K. Gurung's book *Heart of the Jungle* provides a detailed and interesting account of wildlife at Chitwan.

SUBTROPICAL ZONE (3300–6500 ft/1000–2000 m in the west, to 5500 ft/1700 m in the east)

Extensive forests of chir pine *(Pinus roxburghii, [khoTe salla])* occur throughout the subtropical zone in western Nepal and on drier slopes in the east. The forests are typically open, with no understory, because of frequent fires. Chir pine is a conifer with needles arranged in clusters of three. Broad-leaved, evergreen forests of *Schima wallichii [chilaune]* and chestnut *(Casta-nopsis indica, [Dalne katus])* once covered much of subtropical central and eastern Nepal. Almost all of them have either been converted to agriculture or are much depleted, as they lie in regions of highest population density. Both species have oblong-elliptical, leathery leaves, alternately arranged on the twigs. The chestnut has silvery-gray fissured bark, while that of *Schima* is dark gray and rugged. The chestnut has a prickly-covered fruit. Riverine forest with *Toona spp* (compound leaves divided into eight to thirty pairs of leaflets) and *Albizia spp,* or Nepali alder *(Alnus nipalensis, [utis]),* often grow along streams. The alder has elliptical leaves alternately arranged on the twigs, and the fruits resemble miniature fir cones. Alder also frequently colonizes abandoned cultivation and landslips. There are small areas of evergreen forest in the far east. The showy, large, red flowers of the silk cotton tree *(Bombax malabaricum,* syn. *B. ceiba, [simaal])* are a characteristic feature of the subtropical zone in spring. The flowers are clustered toward the ends of bare horizontal branches, and are alive with mynahs, sunbirds, drongos, bulbuls, and other birds that feed on nectar. This tall, deciduous tree has branches that grow out from the trunk in regular whorls.

Birds

The natural variety of fauna and flora in the subtropical zone is much reduced because of human interference. Despite this, birds are conspicuous.

Birds of prey. Birds of prey either kill other animals or feed on their bodies. Nepal has over seventy species, including twenty-one owls. Egyptian vulture *(Neophron percnopterus,* length 60 cm) is a familiar small vulture around villages. It has a wedge-shaped tail. The adult is white with black flight feathers and yellow head (immature is brownish). It also occurs in tropical and temperate zones. The steppe eagle *(Aquila nipalensis,* length 74–81 cm) is a large eagle with long, broad wings and medium-long tail. From below, while in flight, it looks dark brown with one or two white wing bars across the undersides of its wings. It is a common winter visitor between September and April, and occurs from tropical to alpine zones.

Pigeons and Doves. Nepal has twenty species of pigeons and doves. The spotted dove *(Streptopelia chinensis,* length 30 cm), a pale brown dove spotted white above, is one of the commonest species. It occurs in gardens, cultivation, and forest; also occurs in tropical and temperate zones.

Cuckoos *[koili]* and Barbets. Its call monotonously repeated all day in spring and summer, the barbet usually remains hidden in tree tops. The blue-throated barbet *(Megalaima asiatica,* length 22 cm), green with blue throat and face and red forehead, makes a loud "chuperup." It also occurs in tropical and temperate zones. The coppersmith (or crimson-breasted) barbet *(Megalaima haemacephala,* length 14 cm), greenish with yellow throat and reddish breast, makes a metallic note said to resemble a coppersmith beating on metal. It also occurs in the tropical zone. The Indian cuckoo *(Cuculus micropterus, [kaphal pakyo],* length 33 cm), like several other cuckoo species, is grayish above and on the throat, with the rest of the underparts barred black and white. It occurs in tropical and temperate zones. Its bubbling call sounds like "one more bottle." It calls all night, as does the common hawk cuckoo or brainfever bird (*Hierococcyx varius,* length 34 cm), which is gray above and mottled or barred brown below. It occurs in the tropical zone. Calls start slowly and accelerate to a high pitch.

Bulbuls. Nepal has nine species of these medium-sized, crested, confiding birds with cheery calls. They associate in noisy parties, often perched conspicuously on tops of shrubs and trees. The white-cheeked bulbul (*Pycnonotus leucogenys,* length 20 cm) has white cheeks, yellow vent, and the crest curved forward. The red-vented bulbul (*Pycnonotus cafer,* length 23 cm) is a dark bird with pale rump and red vent. The black (or gray) bulbul (*Hypsipetes madagascariensis,* length 24 cm) is all black with bright red bill and legs. All three species also occur in tropical and temperate zones.

Minivets. Nepal has six species of these long-tailed, brightly colored arboreal birds. Long-tailed minivet (*Pericrocotus ethologus,* [*Ranichara],* length 18 cm) males are red and black, females yellow and black. Flocks often perch on tree tops and twitter to each other as they fly from tree to tree. They occur in the temperate zone. The Asian magpie robin (*Copsychus saularis,* length 19 cm) is a long-tailed, black-and-white robin. The male is black above, on throat and breast, and rest of underparts; the wing bar and outer tail coverts are white. In the female, black is replaced by gray. Common in gardens, it has a sweet song of short repeated phrases. The spiny babbler (*Turdoides nipalensis,* length 24 cm) is Nepal's only endemic bird. It is very secretive and rarely seen, but fairly common in thick scrub. Grayish brown and streaked, with a long tail, it also occurs in temperate zone.

Laughing-thrushes. Nepal has sixteen species, well named for their bursts of laughter. They keep well hidden as they move through dense vegetation. Gregarious, they forage noisily on the ground. The white-crested laughing-thrush (*Garrulax leucocephalus,* length 33 cm), rufous and brown with all-white crest, throat, and breast, and black band through the eye, also occurs in the temperate zone.

The gray (or Himalayan) treepie (*Dendrocitta formosae,* [*kokula],* length 40 cm) is long-tailed, with a strong bill and legs. It is dark gray with white wing patches and rufous vent. Noisy and gregarious, it calls its Nepali name; also found in temperate zone.

Starlings and mynahs. Nepal has ten species. The common mynah (*Acridotheres tristis,* length 24 cm) is a familiar and abundant species around gardens, cultivation, and habitation. Dark brown with a glossy black head, bare yellow patch around the eye, and yellow bill and legs (a white wing patch shows in flight), it is noisy, sociable, and aggressive, like other starlings and mynahs. It also occurs in tropical and temperate zones.

Mammals

Mammals are especially inconspicuous in the subtropical zone. The jungle cat (*Felis chaus,* [*ban biralo],* head and body length 60 cm), highly adaptable, is found in a wide variety of habitats, ranging from village outskirts to open country and forest edges. Its coat is pale brownish gray, legs long with dark stripes, tail ringed and tipped black. It also occurs in tropical zone.

The Indian gray mongoose *(Herpestes edwardsi, [naauri musa],* length 90 cm) has a gray coat and a tail as long as the rest of its body. It hunts snakes, inhabits cultivation and open scrub forest, and also occurs in tropical and temperate zones.

Amphibians and Reptiles

Little is known about Nepali amphibians and reptiles. They are primarily found in the warmer tropical and subtropical zones. A total of thirty-six species of amphibians, including frogs *[bhyaguto],* toads, newts, and a caecilian, have been recorded so far. One of the commonest is the aptly named skittering frog *(Rana cyanophlyctis),* which can float and skip over the water surface. The six-fingered frog *(Rana hexadactyla)* is the largest Nepali amphibian. Not aquatic, it is reported to feed on mice, shrews, birds, and lizards. In the breeding season it calls deep "oong-awang" throughout the night. Reptile species total eighty and include crocodiles, turtles, lizards, skinks, and geckos. Snakes *[sAAp, sarpa]* are elusive; most are nonpoisonous. One of the commonest is the buff-striped keelback *(Amphiesma stolata),* which occurs in grassy areas near cultivation. It is olive-green or brown above with black spots or bars intersected with buff stripes. Lizards *[chepaaro]* are more obvious and can often be seen basking in the sun on stone walls or rocks. A familiar lizard is the Himalayan rock lizard *(Agama tuberculata).* It is coarsely scaled, has a long tail, and is generally colored brown with black spots; breeding males have blue throats.

Insects

Insects are particularly abundant in the subtropical zone. Common butterflies include the plain and common tigers and blue and peacock pansies (all four also in tropical and temperate zones), and common Indian crow (also tropical zone). Large and especially colorful species occur, such as the golden birdwing (also tropical and temperate zones), Paris peacock, and glassy bluebottle (also temperate zone). The orange oakleaf, as its name implies, closely resembles an oak leaf when its wings are closed; it is also found in tropical and temperate zones. There is a bewildering variety of other butterfly groups with evocative names such as sailers, sergeants, windmills, and jezebels.

Cicadas are large insects that resemble the color and pattern of the tree bark on which they live. Countless numbers make a prolonged, monotonous trilling in the forest. The noise is so loud that it has a deafening effect. Males sing by vibrating a membrane to attract females, which are incapable of making sounds. There are at least four distinct sounds. One is a low-frequency rattle made by the *[shechshelli],* another the continuous pitch made by the *[jaaUkiri],* one sounding almost electronic, and a fourth that is wavering and intermittent. Cicadas also occur in tropical and temperate zones.

Fireflies *(Lampyridae, [junkiri])* are tiny beetles. Wingless females resemble larvae and are also called glow worms. At night, winged males flash lights on and off in flight during their courtship display. Lighting is produced by special glands in the abdomen. Each species has a distinctive glow. They also occur in tropical and temperate zones.

Stick insects *(Phasmida)* have slender bodies up to 20 cm long, usually green or brown. They resemble twigs or branches amazingly well, and stay motionless at the first sign of danger.

Praying mantids *(Dictyoptera)* are so called because, when waiting for prey, they hold their forelegs folded in front as if in prayer. Any insect, lizard, or small bird that comes by is snapped up with lightning speed by the vicelike grip of the forelegs. They also occur in tropical and temperate zones.

TEMPERATE ZONE

The temperate zone can be divided into the lower temperate zone (approximately 6500–9000 ft/2000–2700 m in the west and 5500–8000 ft/1700–2400 m in the east) and upper temperate zone (9000–10,200 ft/2700–3100 m in the west and center and 7800–9200 ft/2400–2800 m in the east). Oak, rhododendron, and fir forests dominate the zone. Upper temperate forests are much less disturbed than those lower down, especially those in the west, because they mainly lie below the limit of cultivation.

In wetter parts of the lower temperate region there are mixed broad-leaves with abundant laurels *(Lauracea)* and oaks (broad-leaved evergreens with acorns): *Quercus lamellosa [bAshi, shaalshi, gogane],* a very large tree with massive spreading crown, and alternate, toothed, oval leaves with dark green uppersides and bluish green undersides, in the east; and *Q. floribunda [belekharmendo],* with small, leathery, spiny-margined leaves, in the west. Drier, lower temperate forests consist of *Q. lanata [bAnjh],* with leaves dark shiny green above and rust-colored below; *Q. leucotrichophora,* with undersides of leaves covered in dense, white, woolly hairs; and Himalayan blue pine *(Pinus wallichiana, [gobre sallaa]),* a conifer with clusters of long, cylindrical cones and drooping, gray-green needles in clusters of five.

Rhododendrons *[lali gurAAs]* are common in the upper temperate zone in the center and east, either as the dominant tree or scattered among other forest types. They grow as shrubs or trees and are broad-leaved evergreens with shiny, leathery leaves. The rhododendron is the national flower. The gorgeous flowers, colored red, pink, and white, are the most conspicuous Himalayan feature in this and the subalpine zones.

Forests of prickly-leaved oak *(Q. semecarpifolia [karsu]),* with leathery, sometimes prickly leaves and globular fruits that have concave cups, occur throughout the upper temperate region, especially on south-facing slopes. Mixed broad-leaved forests grow in wetter places, while coniferous forests occur in the west.

Look for Himalayan blue pine; Himalayan hemlock *(Tsuga dumosa, [tingre sallo]),* a conifer with distinctive small, egg-shaped cones and flat needles that are dark green on the top and silvery white underneath, in two rows; and others, including Himalayan silver fir *(Abies pindrow, [talis patra],* which has flat needles with two whitish lines on their undersides spread around the branchlets, and west Himalayan spruce *(Picea smithiana, [jhule sallaa]),* a floppy-looking tree with vaguely four-sided, pendulous branches, and needles arranged in a spiral, leaving scars where they have fallen off. In the drainage of the Thulo Bheri and Karnali, look for the Himalayan cedar, or deodar *(Cedrus deodara, [deodaar])*, with its pyramidal crown and three-sided needles mostly scattered in tufts on the branches, and cones that have fan-shaped scales. Also limited to the west is Himalayan cypress *(Cupressus torulosa, [raj sallo,* or *dhupi])*, a large tree with pyramidal crown, horizontal to up-sloping branches, small, flat, triangular leaves that overlap each other closely, tiny cones, and gray-brown bark that peels off in strips. The larch *(Larix griffithiana, [lekh sallo])*, a deciduous tree, golden in autumn, is found in dry inner valleys of the northeast corner as well as in northcentral Nepal.

Bamboo *[bAAs] (Bambusa spp* and *Arundinaria spp, [nigaalo])* flourishes in very high rainfall areas. In a few places, such as in the Modi Khola valley on the Annapurna Sanctuary trek, it forms dense stands up to 7 m high. Elsewhere, bamboo occurs in the forest understory. The damper forests of the center and east are draped in mosses and lichens. In spring, beautiful epiphytic orchids, such as the white *Coelogyne,* bloom on the tree trunks. Ferns and numerous wildflowers, including fritillaries, primulas, and many orchids *[andashaya]*, grow in damp ravines and along streams.

Note the following associations: Himalayan fir in rhododendron-oak forests on northern slopes, and with prickly-leaved oak on southern aspects; west Himalayan spruce in the drier region around Jumla, but as far east as Ganesh Himal; Himalayan hemlock almost exclusively on northern aspects.

Birds

Birds of prey. The Himalayan griffon vulture *(Gyps himalayensis,* length 122 cm), like most vulture species, has long, broad wings and a short, broad tail. It sails majestically on motionless wings over mountains and valleys searching for food. From below, adults show white underparts and forewing and a dark trailing edge to the wing; immatures are dark brown. Occurs from subtropical to alpine zones.

Pheasants. Nepal is famous for its variety of Himalayan pheasants. There are six species, all of which can be seen in the Annapurna Conservation Area. Forests above Ghasa (on the trek to Thak Khola) are especially productive. Most are shy and difficult to see unless you flush them from the forest. They call frequently in spring. The Kalij pheasant *(Lophura leucomelana, [kalij]*, length 60–68 cm) inhabits all types of forest with dense undergrowth, especially near water, and also occurs in subtropical and tropical zones. The male is mainly black with a long tail and red on the face; the female is reddish brown with a shorter tail. The Koklass pheasant *(Pucrasia macrolopha, [phokras]*, length 52–61 cm) inhabits oak and conifer forests from the Modi Khola valley westward. The male is dark, with a long crest and tail, black head, and white ear patch. The female is brownish, with a shorter crest and tail. It crows loudly at dawn. The satyr tragopan, or crimson-horned pheasant *(Tragopan satyra, [monal]*, length 59–68 cm), is found in damp oak and rhododendron forests with dense undergrowth, and occurs above Syabru and near Sing Gomba (on the Langtang and Gosainkund treks.) The male is bright red, spotted with white and with a blue wattle; the female is mottled brown. In spring, it makes a strange, mammallike "waaa" noise at dawn and dusk.

Cuckoos and Barbets. Cuckoos and barbets call repeatedly in spring and summer while concealing themselves in tree tops. The great barbet (*Megalaima virens,* length 32 cm) has a large yellow bill, dark head, and red vent. It sings a duet with its mate: he repeats "pir-ao," while she replies with a trilled "pur." It occurs in oak forests; it is also found in subtropical zone. The common (or Eurasian) cuckoo (*Cuculus canorus,* length 33 cm) is a familiar bird in Europe. It sings its English name. Found in open wooded country, it also occurs in tropical, subtropical, and subalpine zones. The oriental (or Himalayan) cuckoo (*Cuculus saturatus,* length 33 cm) makes a monotonous "oop-oop" call. The appearance of both species is similar to Indian cuckoo (see Subtropical Zone). The large hawk cuckoo (*Cuculus sparverioides,* length 38 cm) has a call and appearance similar to common hawk cuckoo, but is larger and occurs at higher altitudes. The latter two species are found in oak-rhododendron forests. The orange-rumped (or Himalayan) honeyguide (*Indicator xanthonotus, [maurichara],* length 15 cm) is a drab, sparrowlike bird, which is remarkable for its ability to digest beeswax. It will defend the nest of the giant honey bee from other honeyguides, and can be seen on cliffs north of Ghasa (on the Thak Khola trek) and near Syabru and Lama Lodge (on the Langtang trek).

Warblers. Over sixty warbler species occur in Nepal; about thirty of them inhabit temperate forests. Small yellow, green, or brown birds with thin bills, they are constantly on the move. They hover in front of branches, flick their wings, and make short flights to catch insects.

Flycatchers. Nepal has thirty species. Most are summer visitors to the Himalaya. Typically, they sit upright and motionless on a branch, making sallies into flight to catch insects. The verditer flycatcher (*Muscicapa thalassina,* length 15 cm) is one of most conspicuous and common flycatchers. The male is brilliant greenish blue with a black line in front of the eye; the female is duller. It also occurs in subtropical zone.

Babblers. Babblers make up one of the largest Nepali bird families, with over seventy species. They are more similar in behavior than appearance. In general, they have short, rounded wings and long tails and bills; they are highly vocal, gregarious, and secretive. Laughing-thrushes are babblers. The white-throated laughing-thrush (*Garrulax albogularis, [setokanthe bhyakuro],* length 28 cm) is olive-brown with a large white throat. The black-faced laughing-thrush (*Garrulax affinis,* length 28 cm) is brownish with a black-and-white face pattern. It inhabits oak-rhododendron and conifer forests, and also occurs in the subalpine zone. The black-capped sibia (*Heterophasia capistrata, [kalotauke sibia],* length 23 cm) is one of most conspicuous and common babblers in oak-rhododendron forests. Orange-brown with small black crest, it has a loud, clear, ringing, repeated whistle.

Tits. Nepal has fourteen species of these small, gregarious, active birds, which cling acrobatically to branches. The coal tit *(Parus ater)* and spot-

Blue sheep, prey of the snow leopard, on the north side of Kangchenjunga (photo by Robin Houston)

winged black tit (*Parus melanolophus,* length 11 cm) are both crested black with dark gray upperparts, black bib, and white cheeks. The coal tit occurs in the east; the spot-winged black tit replaces it in the west. Found in coniferous forests, both also occur in subalpine zone.

Sunbirds. Nepal has seven species of sunbirds. Small, active, long-tailed birds with long decurved bills, they feed on nectar and insects among flowers. The green-tailed (or Nepal) sunbird (*Aethopyga nipalensis, [bungechara],* length 10–15 cm) is found in oak-rhododendron forests. The male has bright iridescent colors, with a green head and yellow below and on the rump; the female is drab olive green.

The jungle crow (*Corvus macrorhynchus,* length 43–50 cm) is an all-black crow with a heavy bill. Usually associated with habitation, it occurs in open country, cultivation, and forest, from tropical to alpine zones.

Mammals

The gray langur (*Presbytis entellus, [bAAdar],* head and body length 60–75 cm) is long tailed and long limbed, with silver-gray fur and a distinctive black face. Troops inhabit forests and feed on leaves, flowers, and fruits. Easily seen on the Thak Khola trek near Ghasa and GhoRepani, it occurs from tropical to alpine zones.

The lesser (or red) panda (*Ailurus fulgens, [hobre],* head and body length 60 cm) is rich chestnut above with white face, dark legs, and a long, ringed tail. A forest dweller, it is nocturnal, remaining in treetops during the day. It has been seen in Langtang National Park and between GhoRepani and Ghandruk in Annapurna Conservation Area.

The yellow-throated marten (*Martes flavigula, [malsapro],* length 45–60 cm), a lithe, arboreal predator, has a yellow throat and a long tail that makes up over a third of its length. It also occurs in subtropical zone.

The leopard (*Panthera pardus, [chituwaa]*, length 185–215 cm) is rarely seen, but not uncommon; you may find tracks on the trail. Found in open country, scrub, dense forest, and near villages, it also occurs in tropical and subtropical zones.

The Himalayan musk deer (*Moschus chrysogaster, [kasturi mriga]*, shoulder height 50 cm) is a small deer with large, rounded ears. The male has long upper teeth that form tusks. Now rare because of persecution, it inhabits upper temperate and subalpine forests and shrubberies.

The Indian muntjac (*Muntiacus muntjak, [mriga]*, male shoulder height 50–75 cm) is also known as the barking deer after its distinctive barking alarm call, which sounds remarkably like a dog. It inhabits forests and forest edges, especially rocky ravines, and also occurs in tropical and subtropical zones.

The mainland serow (*Capricornis sumatraensis, [thar]*, male shoulder height 100–110 cm) is a thickset, goatlike mammal. Chestnut or blackish, usually solitary, it occurs in thickly forested ravines and steep slopes.

Amphibians and reptiles are poorly represented in the temperate zone and at higher altitudes.

Insects

The temperate zone is rich in insects, although there is less variety than in the subtropical zone. Temperate-zone species include praying mantids, fireflies, cicadas, beetles, bugs, bees, ants, moths, butterflies, and others.

Butterflies are most common in open forests, forest clearings, and grassland. Common species include the common windmill (also found in the tropical zone), Indian fritillary (also occurs down to the tropical zone), painted lady, Indian red admiral, and Indian tortoiseshell (the last three species common from the tropical to subalpine zones). The giant honey bee *(pis dorsata, [mauri])* is a large bee that forms highly sophisticated colonies. Common in the Himalaya, it makes a distinctively shaped hive—a single exposed sheet of wax hanging down from beneath a rock overhang or ledge.

SUBALPINE ZONE (10,000–13,800 ft/3000–4200 m in the west, to 12,500 ft/3800 m in the east)

Forests of Himalayan silver fir *(Abies spectabilis)* are widespread and are often superseded above 11,500 ft (3500 m) by birch *(Betula utilis, [bhaj patra])*, which grows up to the treeline. Birch is deciduous, with oval leaves that are woolly-haired below, and white to gray-brown bark. Rhododendron forests or shrubberies often replace other forests in wetter places, while junipers *(Juniperus spp)*, coniferous shrubs with berrylike, fleshy fruit, occur in drier areas. Bamboo *(Arundinaria spp* and *Bambusa spp)* is common in the understory of high rainfall areas and sometimes forms pure stands. Some of the least disturbed forests occur in this zone, although trekkers and mountaineers are posing severe threats.

Birds

Birds of prey. The lammergeier, or bearded vulture (*Gypaetus barbatus, [giddha],* length 122 cm), a magnificent vulture, has a characteristic wedge-shaped tail. Rusty-white on the head and below, dark brown above, it drops bones from a height to splinter them on rocks below and then feeds on the bone marrow. It soars along mountain slopes on motionless wings with hardly a wing beat; it occurs from subtropical to alpine zones.

Pheasants. Himalayan monal, or Impeyan pheasant (*Lophophorus impejanus, [Danphe],* length 72 cm), is Nepal's national bird. The male has nine iridescent colors, but at a distance looks black; the female is dull, brown-mottled buff. Both sexes have white rumps and brown tails. It summers on grassy slopes above the treeline and winters in oak-rhododendron forests. It is easily seen on the Gosainkund trek and in Sagarmatha National Park.

The blood pheasant (*Ithaginis cruentus, [chilme],* length 46 cm), a small short-tailed pheasant, is often tame and curious. The male is pale gray, green, and red; the female is reddish brown. Both sexes have red legs. It is found in rhododendron, juniper, or bamboo; there is a tame flock around Tengboche monastery in Sagarmatha National Park.

Redstarts. Nepal has seven species of redstarts, which are robinlike, insectivorous, altitudinal migrants. They perch conspicuously, with an upright stance, on tops of bushes and flick their tails up and down. The blue-fronted redstart (*Phoenicurus frontalis,* length 16 cm) is one of the most common Nepali redstarts. The male has a blue head and is dark orange below; the female is pale brown. Both sexes can be identified by the chestnut tail, tipped black. It breeds in shrubberies and above treeline in the trans-Himalayan region, descending to forests and fields in winter.

Sunbird. The fire-tailed sunbird (*Aethopyga ignicauda,* length 20 cm) breeds in rhododendron shrubberies and winters mainly in temperate forests. The breeding male has a very long red tail, a red mantle, and is yellow on the rump and below. The female is mainly olive gray, yellowish on the belly.

Rosefinches. The twelve Nepali species of this gregarious, small bird with a thick bill breed in late summer in shrubberies, or above the treeline in the alpine zone, then descend in winter, mainly to temperate or subtropical forests and grasslands. Males are mainly pink and usually have a pink rump, females are streaked brown. The pink-browed rosefinch (*Carpodacus rhodochrous,* length 14.5 cm) is one of Nepal's most common rosefinches. The male has a distinctive broad pink eyebrow and warm-brown-streaked mantle. The female has a buff eyebrow.

Mammals

The Asiatic black bear (*Selenarctos thibetanus, [himali kaalo bhaalu],* length 140–170 cm) is all black with a creamy V on the chest. A powerful and potentially dangerous animal, it is seldom seen. Active between dusk and dawn, it inhabits subalpine forests in summer and descends to temperate or subtropical forests in winter.

The common goral (*Nemorhaedus goral, [goral]*, shoulder height 65–70 cm) is one of the goat-antelopes. Found singly or in small groups on steep grass- and rock-covered slopes, it can be seen on Gosainkund and Helambu treks.

The Himalayan tahr (*Hemitragus jemlahicus, [jhaaral]*, male shoulder height 90–100 cm) is a large goat with a black face. The male has a shaggy shoulder ruff. It grazes in herds at 12,000 ft (3660 m) and below, on precipitous slopes and in dense forests and scrub, and can be seen above Langtang village and around Phortse and Pungo Tenga in Sagarmatha National Park.

Royle's pika, also known as the mouse hare (*Ochotona roylei, [musa kharayo]*, length 15–20 cm), is a delightful small mammal. It has a short muzzle, small ears, and no visible tail. It lives above the treeline in open country among rocks, and can be seen on the Gosainkund trail, at Lobuche, and along the trail above Pheriche in Sagarmatha National Park.

ALPINE ZONE *(12,500 ft/3800 m in the east and 13,800 ft/ 4200 m in the west)*

The alpine zone lies between the treeline and the region of perpetual snow. Shrubs grow above the treeline up to 16,000 ft (4870 m), with rhododendrons abundant in the east and junipers in the west. In the northwest and north of the Dhaulagiri–Annapurna massif, there is extensive steppe country dominated by *Caragana*, a low, spiny shrub typical of the Tibetan plateau. Flowers in both the subalpine and alpine grasslands produce spectacular colorful displays in late spring and summer. There is an amazing diversity of plants: gentians, anemones, saxifrages, geraniums, primulas, cinquefoils, and many others. Isolated plants are common up to 18,000 ft (5500 m).

Birds

Snow cocks *(Tetraogallus spp)* are represented by two Nepali species. Large, mainly gray gamebirds, they frequent steep grassy slopes and stony ridges up to 18,000–19,700 ft (5500–6000 m) in summer, then descend to the subalpine zone in winter. They escape from people by running uphill. These birds can be seen on the Muktinath side of the Thorung La pass on the Annapurna Circuit and in Sagarmatha National Park.

The snow pigeon (*Columba leuconota*, length 34 cm), a pale gray and white pigeon with a black head, occurs in flocks on rocky cliffs. It may descend to 5000 ft (1500 m) in severe winter conditions.

Most of the nine Nepali species of pipits (*Anthus spp*, length 14–23 cm) inhabit grasslands. Slim, brown, and streaked, they run or walk quickly, and have both an undulating flight and song flight.

Accentors (*Prunellidae*, length 15–16 cm), of which Nepal has seven species, resemble sparrows, but have sharp, pointed bills. Most are drab gray or brown and heavily streaked above. They feed quietly on the ground, often in small groups in winter. Look for them on grassy and rocky slopes or, in winter, open forest.

The grandala (*Grandala coelicolor,* length 23 cm) belongs to the thrush family. The male is deep, brilliant purple-blue; the female is brown with a white wing patch. It forms flocks of several hundred birds in winter, and inhabits rocky slopes and stony alpine meadows. It can be seen on Laurebina pass on the Gosainkund trek and between Dole and Gokyo in Sagarmatha National Park.

Choughs in Nepal include the red-billed chough (*Pyrrhocorax pyrrhocorax,* length 46 cm) and the alpine, or yellow-billed, chough (*Pyrrhocorax graculus,* length 40 cm). Both are all black, except that the former has a red bill and legs, and the latter, yellow. Behavior and appearance are crowlike: sociable and noisy. They engage in fantastic aerial acrobatics.

Mammals

The snow leopard (*Panthera uncia, [hIU chituwa],* length 100–110 cm) is one of the Himalaya's most elusive animals. It occurs above the treeline, mainly in the trans-Himalayan region near the Tibetan border. Well-adapted for life at high altitudes, it has a long, thick coat. There have been recent sightings by trekkers near Thorung Phedi, north of Manang, south of the Ganja La, and in the Kangchenjunga region.

The Himalayan marmot (*Marmota bobak, [himali marmot],* length 60 cm) has a distinctive squat build, medium tail, and very small ears. Large colonies live in deep burrows in the open country of the trans-Himalayan region.

The blue sheep, or bharal (*Pseudois nayaur, [bhaaral],* shoulder height 90 cm), is intermediate in appearance between sheep and goats. It has long backward-curving horns. Herds of ten to fifty graze on grass slopes between treeline and snowline, usually within cover of rock cliffs, rarely descending below 12,000 ft (3660 m) in winter. It can be seen in Manang District east of Thorung La pass on the Annapurna circuit, near Kangchenjunga, or north of Dhorpatan.

Butterflies

In spring and summer, butterflies are common in subalpine and alpine zones, feeding on the nectar of blooming flowers. Common blue Apollo, Queen of Spain fritillary, and common yellow swallowtail are frequently seen; the latter two species are also found in subtropical and temperate zones.

AEOLIAN ZONE

This is the region where snow lies permanently, although much terrain is not covered because snow accumulates unevenly. A. F. R. Wollaston, writing in *Mount Everest, The Reconnaissance, 1921,* records the highest flowering plant species as a small, white-flowering sandwort *(Arenaria bryophylla)* at 20,277 ft (6180 m). Some invertebrates make their homes at even higher altitudes. Large populations of fairy shrimp have been reported in glacial pools at 19,000 ft (5790 m), for example. Insects, such as snow fleas *(Proistoma)* and some carabid beetles, feed on pollen grains, spores, seeds, dead spiders, and insects uplifted on air currents from the distant plains of India. Permanent life even exists at the highest point on earth: samples of soil and snow collected on the summit of Everest were found to contain micro-organisms. Birds and mammals are brief visitors to the high peaks and passes. Flocks of bar-headed geese *(Anser indicus)* have been seen flying over the summit of Everest at over 30,500 ft (9300 m). Mountaineering expeditions have reported alpine choughs scavenging from tents above 26,900 ft (8200 m).

STREAM BIRDS

Several conspicuous bird species can be found along fast-flowing streams throughout Nepal.

The ibisbill *(Ibidorhyncha struthersi,* length 39 cm) is a gray wader with black forehead and face and a long decurved red bill. Shy, it breeds in gravelly river beds, such as those near Kyangjin in upper Langtang Valley. It winters on stony river beds in foothills.

The brown dipper *(Cinclus pallasii, [dubulke charo]* length 20 cm), a plump, all-brown, short-tailed bird that bobs up and down while standing on boulders, can feed by walking underwater on the stream bed.

The plumbeous redstart *(Rhyacornis fuliginosus,* length 14 cm) is robin-like. It constantly pumps its tail up and down and makes short flights after insects flying over the water. The male is slate blue with a reddish tail; the female is pale gray with a white rump.

The white-capped redstart, or river chat *(Chaimarrornis leucocephalus, [taukecharo],* length 19 cm) is a handsome maroon and black bird with a contrasting white cap. Both sexes are alike in appearance. It fans and pumps its tail as it flies from one rock to another.

The blue whistling thrush *(Myiophoneus caeruleus, [kalchande],* length 33 cm) is a blue-black thrush with a yellow bill. It has a beautiful whistling song and harsh alarm call, both of which penetrate the sound of rushing water.

Nepal has four species of forktails *(Enicurus spp, [kholedobi],* length 13–27 cm). Black and white birds with long, forked tails, they are shy and fly off quickly, making a harsh alarm call, when disturbed. Three species can be readily seen along Bhurungdi Khola near Birethanti on the Thak Khola trek.

DOMESTIC ANIMALS

Two domestic animals you are likely to see when trekking are the yak and the water buffalo.

The yak *(Bos grunniens, [chAUmri gaai],* male shoulder height 200 cm) is vital to people living at high altitudes, such as in Sagarmatha National Park. It carries loads, pulls plows, and provides milk, meat, hair, and hides. Very well adapted to high elevations, with a thick coat and large lungs, it is closely related to the wild yak, which is still thought to live in the high Himalaya on the Tibetan border. The female is known as *nak.* Commonly used hybrids (crossed with cattle) are called *dzum* (cows) and *zopkio* (bulls).

The water buffalo *(Bubalus bubalis, [bhAIsi],* male shoulder height 170 cm) is found at lower altitudes than the yak. Apart from shorter horns, it is very similar in appearance to the wild buffalo, which is now restricted in Nepal to Kosi Tappu Reserve and is a potentially dangerous animal. It is essential to the life of Nepalis at lower altitudes in similar ways to the yak.

Tharu *transplanting rice in Surkhet*

13 Hill and Mountain Peoples of Nepal

by Donald A. Messerschmidt*

Nepal has always been a meeting ground for different people and cultures.

Dor Bahadur Bista, Nepali
anthropologist

Nepal is a land of great diversity. Its social, cultural, religious, geographical, floral, and faunal varieties fascinate and challenge the imagination. The diversity across the land is quickly seen and felt by trekkers and travelers. In a relatively short distance (although it may be days of arduous walking) a trekker can leave the low, subtropical Tarai forests and ascend northward into the high alpine meadows. The *Tarai-wala* (a person of the Tarai) is left behind for the *PahAARi* (hillsman), the *Lekhali* (person of the high country), the *goThaalo* (alpine herdsman), and the *BhoTiya* (Tibetan) of the hills and mountains.

Variations in social and cultural expression seem to parallel the physical, geographic, and biotic changes associated with altitude and latitude. The trekker sees an ever-changing variety of farmsteads, villages, and bazaars; passes the shrines of Hindu, Buddhist, and animist; encounters farmer, trader, storekeeper, pilgrim, innkeeper, and herder; and notes changes in the architecture of homes and religious edifices. The colorfully diverse expressions of human adaptation to the Himalaya are unexpectedly fascinating for a land to which most visitors come expecting only spectacular mountains, smiling guides, yak herds, and pagodalike temples.

Nepal has dozens of ethnic and caste groups, each differentiated by unique aspects of language, dress, locale, lifestyle, house style, economy, and

---

* The author of this chapter is an anthropologist who advised me on trekking before I first came to the Himalaya and who has continued to provide information on Nepal for subsequent editions of this book. His first experience in Nepal was with the Peace Corps in 1963. He has worked in community development, taught in the American school in Kathmandu, studied the *Gurungs* of west-central Nepal for his Ph.D., led treks and study tours, conducted research, and participated in scientific forums on the Himalaya. Currently, he is working in Pokhara as a social forestry advisor to Yale University and Nepal's Institute of Forestry. "People," he says with conviction, "are the most important resource to work with when it comes to conserving and managing the Himalayan environment." The section on jewelry comes from the studies of anthropologist Bronwen Bledsoe, whose interest in Nepal began on a college study tour led by Donald Messerschmidt; it has been updated by Hannelore Gabriel.

religion. At one level of analysis, however, certain elements of uniformity tend to knit all the diversity together. Take language. It divides Nepalis into two major camps: those who speak Nepali as their mother tongue—primarily the caste groups—and those who speak languages identified by linguists as part of the Bodic division of Sino-Tibetan (sometimes called Tibeto-Burman)—that is, the hill ethnic groups and those of close Tibetan affinities. At another level, however, language draws them together; most Nepalis, regardless of local dialect, speak Nepali in the public forums of trade, education, government, and daily encounters with outsiders. (In some places English has become the second major language of the land.)

Another of the more visible attributes of uniformity in Nepal is a marked association between cultural groups and the altitude/latitude where they traditionally live. Each distinct group can be identified in great part by the ecological niche it occupies. Each niche is characterized by similarities in dress, house style, religious expression, patterns of trade, and subsistence. Caste groups, for example, tend to occupy the lower valleys in dispersed settlements, where they raise rice on irrigated paddy fields. Ethnic groups tend to cluster in nucleated villages on higher, more northerly ridges, where they raise upland crops such as millet, corn, barley, and wheat. Each depends upon the other for exchange of produce and for other economic, social, and religious interaction. In addition, Nepal's rich cultural heritage has been heavily influenced and sometimes irrevocably changed by the recent influx of tourism, education, technology, mass communications, and other aspects of modernization.

In the brief anthropological description of Nepal that follows, the many ethnic and caste groups are described in terms of differences and similarities to one another. It is inevitable in a generalized discussion that much of the uniqueness of the people is blurred, and descriptions are given that do not fit all situations. The discussion focuses on those peoples most often met on trails in the hills and mountains. Because few trekkers travel in the Tarai valleys and plains adjacent to India, discussion of the peoples of that region is omitted. The intent here is to provide the trekker with enough general information to better understand and appreciate the sights seen and the people met while trekking. An abbreviated list of hill and mountain peoples is provided, and some major festivals of Nepal are described at the end of the chapter.

Religion

Nepali religion is based on two "great" or "high" traditions—Hinduism and Buddhism—each undergirded by expressions of local "little" traditions of animism and shamanism. (Of course, practitioners of the latter do not necessarily see their religion in this way; the dichotomy is only for purposes of analysis.) Since only a very small percentage of Nepalis are. Muslim, or "Musalman," they will not be considered here.

"Hinduism is not a religion, but a way of life," states ethnologist A. W. MacDonald. This seems evident from observing the devout in Nepal. Hinduism is rooted in the texts of the ancient Vedas dating to 2000 B.C. As it evolved, three main deities became focal: Brahma the creator, Vishnu the pre-

This man from Dolpo has woven his hair into a hat.

server, and Shiva the destroyer. In their varied manifestations they pervade daily ritual and symbolize the cycle of life. There are no basic dogmas, no qualities that define a Hindu, except perhaps whether that person employs a Brahman as a priest. It is left to each individual to decide the form of his or her worship. The caste system is a fundamental aspect of Hinduism. An individual who aspires to rebirth in a higher caste must live a proper life in his present caste. This precept has exerted a significant stabilizing effect on Indian and Nepali societies. Caste etiquette was codified as law in Nepal in the Muluki Ain of 1854. Although this law has now been repealed, it still governs behavior.

Buddhism, on the other hand, is more a philosophy than a religion. Founded by the disciples of Siddhartha Gautama, born at Lumbini in Nepal's Tarai around 623 B.C., Buddhism is based on the four noble truths: Existence is suffering, craving and attachment cause suffering, the attainment of nirvana is an end to this suffering, and there is a path to nirvana, the eightfold way. These are: right views, right resolve, right speech, right action, right livelihood, right effort, right mindfulness, and right concentration. Buddhism depends on the institution of a monastery and monks. The Buddhist community supports a monastery and derives strength from it. Meditation and observance of moral precepts are the foundations of Buddhist practice. To trekkers, the recitation of the esoteric mantra *Om mani padme hum,* and the spinning of prayer wheels, are examples of meditative practice observed by the common folk.

In Nepal, Hinduism is reflected both in the system of caste, which defines social status, and in a subsistence economy based on rice agriculture and a highly ritualized cattle culture (cow worship). Buddhism, principally the Mahayana ("Great Vehicle") Tibetan form, with strong tantric expression, is found among the *BhoTiya* people of the northern border area. Vajrayana Buddhism is practiced by Buddhist *Newar* of Kathmandu Valley. Buddhism and Hinduism tend to blend in many settings, such as the Kathmandu Valley, where indigenous *Newar* practice both religions, side by side and intermixed. The various local expressions of these two religions, and of animism and shamanism, are so conceptually interwoven that it would take much more than this short account to untangle and explain them accurately and clearly.

Animism and shamanism are concerned respectively with spirits that exist in nature and with the human condition, body and soul, alive or departed. Animistic beliefs and shamanic ritual permeate both of the "high" cultures of Buddhism and Hinduism. At virtually every wayside shrine, in almost every religious rite, in ceremonies performed by lay people as well as by Hindu temple priests *(pujaari),* Buddhist priests *(lama),* or village shaman *(jhAAkri),* you will see some form of worship *(pujaa)* focusing on both the animate and inanimate objects of nature. Funerals, rites of passage, and curing ceremonies are all richly ornamented with the animist's and shaman's concern for placating local spirits and natural forces. If you happen upon a religious ceremony, your presence may be offensive (your proximity to food preparation or to hallowed ground, for example, may be deemed ritually polluting). As you observe ritual events, be aware of the sensitivities of the officiants and participants. And open your senses to the fullness of their expression, especially to the sometimes awesome respect shown for nature—to the moon, earth, fire, water, and air; to cow dung and smoky incense; to cow's urine and curds; to the blood sacrifice of chickens, pigeons, goats, and buffalo. Therein you will begin to glimpse a very close association between villager and nature, a necessary relationship that many people, caught up in the frenetic pace of the modern world elsewhere, seem to have forgotten or have uncaringly abandoned.

History

The Himalaya has always been viewed, it seems, as a safe haven for immigrants and refugees. One large movement of peoples into Nepal dates from the twelfth to fifteenth centuries A.D., when many Hindus—particularly of Rajput origins—fled the Indian plains during the Mughal invasion. Some refugees settled in the Kathmandu Valley, but great numbers remained more rural, populating the lower valleys and hills all across the land. The *PahAARi* people of the adjacent India hills (Kumaon and Garhwal, just west of Nepal) are culturally, physically, and linguistically the "cousin-brothers" of the Nepali caste hillsmen who date from this refugee invasion.

The refugee arrivals were mostly *Brahman* (priest caste) and *Chhetri* (warrior caste, known as *Kshatriya* in India), along with low-caste crafts people and menial laborers. They encountered a local population of *Khas* people and many ethnic groups, with whom they intermixed to various degrees—linguistically, economically, religiously, and socially. The caste Hindu migrants brought certain strong social and cultural traditions—a status hierarchy, language, religion, and a rice- and cattle-based economy that, blended with the local lifestyle and world view, formed what is today's unique Nepali national culture.

Nepali history until the Gorkha Conquest of the eighteenth century A.D. is one of petty principalities. These small hill kingdoms fell into two groups—the *baaisi raja,* or twenty-two kingdoms, of western Nepal, and the *chaubisi raja,* or twenty-four kingdoms, of central Nepal (between the Kali Gandaki and the Trisuli rivers). Many treks of central and western Nepal pass through these former kingdoms, and if you are observant you can see remnants of fortresses *(koT)* on many of the higher hilltops. The most famous fortress, now a sacred temple site, is the "Gorkha Darbar" (Gorkha palace) above Gorkha Bazaar in central Nepal. Others are found in high places along the Marsyangdi River trail (e.g., Lamjung Darbar, just west of Besisahar), near Pokhara (Kingdom of Kaski), and along the Kali Gandaki river just north of Beni (Rakhu). The famous Malla Kingdom of far west Nepal encompassed parts of western Tibet and was so strong that it influenced political events as far east as the upper Kali Gandaki valley. The west Nepal Mallas (not to be confused with the later Malla rulers of Kathmandu's three city-states) ruled from about the twelfth to fourteenth centuries A.D. They were apparently related to the *Khas* people, an ancient group whose presence as a power in the region had profound effects on all of Nepal's subsequent social history. They ruled simultaneously with the arrival of the migrant Rajputs. The fighting forces for these Nepali kingdoms were conscripted from local ethnic populations, such as the *Magar* and the *Gurung*.

It should be noted that various kingdoms of western Tibet, Ladakh, and Kashmir also had influence on northern Nepali affairs, particularly in the region of Jumla (far northwest) and Mustang (north central). Many Tibetan fortresses *(dzong)* may be seen in the northern border areas. The history of these regions is only now beginning to be rediscovered by scholars. The ancient alliances and influences of these many principalities, Nepali and Tibetan, are still felt in the internal political workings of the present-day kingdom of Nepal. And the silent and empty ruins speak to a rich and yet little-studied feudal past—part of its untapped sociohistoric and archaeological heritage.

The small central hill kingdom of Gorkha eventually became the most famous under its eighteenth-century leader Prithvinarayan Shah. His grandiose plans were to unify the Himalaya into one great mountain state. In the 1760s he laid siege to the Malla *Newar* city-states of Kathmandu, PaaTan, and BhatgAAU (Bhaktapur), and ultimately went on to control a vast territory, from Bhutan on the east to Kashmir on the west, parts of southern Tibet on the north, and territories of the British East India Company on the south. By the early 1800s, however, this Gorkha conquest was halted by the British, and the Gorkha domain was cut back to approximately its present boundaries. The British were so impressed with the fighting abilities of the Gorkha hillsmen, however, that they chose not to subjugate the kingdom. Instead, they allowed it to remain independent and a source of the warriors of Gorkha, whom they called Gurkhas, for the British army. The present Shah kings of Nepal are the direct descendants of Prithvinarayan Shah of Gorkha.

Nepali Cultures

The inhabitants of Nepal can be classified culturally into three general groups: Hindu castes, ethnic groups of the hills, and northern border people.

HINDU CASTES

The Hindu castes are called by the general term *PahAARi* (people of the hills). They inhabit the middle hills and lower valleys, generally below 6000 ft (1800 m). Each caste has an ascribed profession, but many people no longer follow the rules.

High Castes

Today this group includes peasant farmers, civil servants, money lenders, and school teachers, as well as people following the traditional caste occupations.

Bahun (Brahman)—the traditional priest caste. In former times, the Brahmans did not handle plows or eat certain prohibited foods (e.g., onions, tomatoes, certain kinds of meat) or drink alcohol. These days, however, many of these prohibitions are ignored, even the rule against drinking. Some of these rules are still followed in the more remote and traditional rural areas. Brahmans can be grouped into those from the east *(Purbiya)* and those from the west *(Kumaon)*. Offspring of irregular unions among Brahmans are termed *Jaishi Bahun*.

Chhetri—the traditional warrior caste. It includes much the same occupations as the Brahmans, as well as soldiers in the Gurkha armies. The King's family is *Thakuri,* a subcaste of *Chhetri*. The term *Matwali Chhetri* ("those who drink liquor") refers to western peoples who are not given the sacred thread characteristic of the "twice born" castes of Brahman and *Chhetri*.

Menial Castes

Many men and women of the three lower menial castes no longer pursue blacksmithing, shoemaking, or tailoring, but work as day laborers on the land of others or as porters for large trekking parties or merchant-traders.

Damai or *Darji*—tailors and musicians for Hindu weddings and festivals.

Kaami—ironworkers, toolmakers, and sometimes silversmiths and goldsmiths *(Sunar)*.

Saarki—cobblers and leatherworkers.

(These are the main castes found in the Nepali hills. Many other caste groups are found among the *Newar,* below, and in the Tarai regions.)

ETHNIC GROUPS OF THE HILLS

The ethnic groups of the hills have been in the Himalaya somewhat longer, it is thought, than the Hindu castes. They are descendants of several waves of migration from the north and northeast. These groups tend to cluster between 6000 ft (1800 m) and 9000 ft (2700 m).

Newar—merchants, civil servants, craftspeople and artists in wood, brass, and bronze, and farmers of the Kathmandu Valley and the hill bazaars. Many are hotel keepers. *Newar* society is stratified into numerous castes and subcastes modeled after the Hindu caste system. The *Newar* practice both Hinduism and Buddhism, and their communities typically have many well-endowed temples and monastic compounds.

Kiranti (Rai and *Limbu)*—peasant hill people of east Nepal. *Rai* villages are found as far west and north as Solu District on the Mount Everest trek. Some are Gurkha soldiers. *Limbu Kiranti* are also found in neighboring Darjeeling District in India, where they are employed on tea plantations.

Tamang—peasant farmers, day laborers, and porters of east and central Nepal. They are particularly numerous around the Kathmandu Valley and the upper Trisuli Valley, and are frequently seen carrying incredibly large loads on the trails of west-central Nepal. The *Tamang* are predominantly Buddhist.

Magar—peasant farmers of central and west Nepal. Some of their villages can be seen on the hillsides above the Kali Gandaki river in upper Myagdi District, and some live as far north as southern Dolpo and Mustang Districts. *Magar* join the Gurkha armies, and are recruited to the oil fields of the Persian Gulf. *Magar* are much influenced by Hinduism.

Gurung—peasant farmers and shepherds of central Nepal. They generally live higher than their *Magar* neighbors. Many *Gurung* are Gurkha soldiers, and some have recently become successful businesspeople in and around Pokhara, in central Nepal. They practice Buddhism (in the northernmost vil-

An old Gurung *woman*

lages), Hinduism (in the lower villages), and their own ancient shamanism. *Gurung* are commonly seen in Lamjung, Parbat, and Kaski Districts on the Manang, Jomosom, Ghandruk, and Annapurna Sanctuary treks. In Gorkha District live the *Ghale* people, a prominent *Gurung* clan.

Sunwar and *Jirel*—small groups of peasant farmers east of the Kathmandu Valley.

Thakali—farmers and mountain herdspeople, traders, and businesspeople of Thak Khola in central Nepal. They are often found trading or keeping inns and hotels in and around Pokhara and surrounding Districts as far south as the Tarai. They are aggressive entrepreneurs, former salt merchants of the Kali Gandaki trade corridor to Tibet. This small group has made a large impact on the economy of central and north-central Nepal. They are strongly influenced by Tibetan Buddhism and their own ancient shamanism.

(*Gurung, Tamang,* and *Thakali* are closely interrelated linguistically and culturally but display different adaptations according to the local ecology and their own histories.)

NORTHERN BORDER PEOPLES, OR BHOTIYA

Like the ethnic groups of the hills, these people came to Nepal from the north and northeast long before the arrival of the Hindu castes from the south. They inhabit the northern valleys and mountainsides, usually above 9000 ft (2700 m), and are the true "Himalayan highlanders." Their sociocultural, linguistic, and religious affinities are clearly with Tibet. They are Buddhist and pursue economies such as high-altitude farming, long-distance trade, yak and sheep husbandry, and, more recently, portering and guiding for trekking and mountaineering parties. In north-central Nepal, most of the pony-train drivers are *BhoTiya* villagers from upper Mustang District and around Muktinath. Since 1959, many Tibetan nationals have migrated as refugees into Nepal. They live in camps in the Kathmandu and Pokhara valleys and in east Nepal, and as traders and laborers in some of the northern border towns, especially in the Thak Khola region of Mustang District. Many of these newly arrived Tibetans have intermarried with local *BhoTiya* and are virtually indistinguishable from them.

BhoTiya ethnic names usually reflect the places where they live; the attached suffixes *-ba, -pa,* or *-le* mean, simply, "people of." Listed as they occur from east to far west Nepal, across the arc of the great Himalaya, they include: *Lhomi* (upper Arun river); *Sherpa,* i.e., Shar-ba (Solu-Khumbu, Rolwaling, and Helambu); Langtang *BhoTiya* (Langtang valley north of Kathmandu); *Nupri-ba* (northern Gorkha District, upper Buri Gandaki river); *Manangba* and *Nar BhoTiya* (Manang District, upper Marsyangdi river); *BaragaaUle* (Muktinath valley); *Lopa* (Mustang District, north of Muktinath and Thak Khola region); *Dolpa* and *Tarap BhoTiya* (Dolpa District, northwest of Thak Khola); *Mugu BhoTiya* (Mugu–Karnali valley); and *Limi-ba* (Limi valley, northwest of Jumla). There are other *BhoTiya* peoples in small, high-altitude valleys. Some northern-area peoples appear to be *BhoTiya* in their dress and house styles; certain *Gurung* (in southern Manang District, for example); the *Tarali* (a northern Magar people in southern Dolpa District), and the *Byansi* (far northwest corner of Nepal) all reflect *BhoTiya* cultural affinities.

Some *BhoTiya* peoples, perhaps as many as 50 percent from areas like Muktinath and Mustang, for example, migrate south on trading trips during the cold winter months, when you may encounter them along the main north–south trails. Many are itinerant peddlers (of high-mountain herbs and spices, woolen scarves, leather goods, and various trinkets and costume jewelry). Others are much more sophisticated traders or smugglers. The *Manangba,* for example, are reputed to have become quite rich at smuggling gold, electronic consumer goods, and fancy clothing into the country from Hong Kong and Southeast Asia. There are many *BhoTiya* peoples dwelling in the Thamel district of Kathmandu.

Human Geography

The Nepali people may also be grouped geographically in four regions: the Kathmandu Valley, east Nepal, central Nepal, and west and far west Nepal.

PEOPLES OF THE KATHMANDU VALLEY

The early inhabitants of the Kathmandu Valley were farmers and herders. The indigenous *Newar* are a mixture of those peoples and other migrants who found their way, over the centuries, to this fertile basin. Each conqueror of the valley, some from the eastern hills of Nepal (of *Kiranti* stock) and some from north India, added to the cultural heritage to make the ethnologically rich *Newar* culture and society of today. *Newar* make up the bulk of the merchants and shopkeepers (alongside more recently arrived Indian merchants) in the three cities of Kathmandu, PaaTan, and BhatgAAU (Bhaktapur). *Newar* are also the predominant shopkeepers in outlying rural bazaars and, throughout the country, make up a considerable percentage of the Nepali civil service.

The Kathmandu Valley is also populated by large numbers of Brahmans and *Chhetri*. They too are farmers and many have become professional and civil servants in the capital city.

Other peoples often seen on the streets of the capital are Hindu peddlers from the Tarai, *Tamang* hill people who work as coolies and day laborers, *BhoTiya* (including many Sherpas) from the north, *Gurung* and *Magar* from central and west Nepal, and *Kiranti (Rai* and *Limbu)* from east Nepal. Since 1959, many Tibetan refugees have also settled in the valley. Monks and other Tibetan men and women are found in the Buddhist temples and monasteries of Baudhnath and Swayambhunath, on the outskirts of Kathmandu, and at the refugee and handicraft center at Jawalakhel, near PaaTan. Tibetan handicrafts—especially articles of woolen clothing and colorful carpets—are well known to tourists in Nepal and in the export marts of Europe and America.

In medieval times, *Newar* craftsmen developed the distinct architectural and decorative motifs and religious arts of the valley and, not insignificantly, of Tibetan Buddhism as well. They became active traders when, for centuries, a main trade route between India and Tibet passed through Kathmandu and BhatgAAU. In time, *Newar* extended their craftsmanship and business enterprises to Lhasa and other Tibetan trade centers. After the defeat of their valley kingdoms by the Shah rulers from Gorkha in 1769, the *Newar* proceeded to take economic advantage of the Gorkha conquest. As Gorkha military and administrative outposts were established to tie the new Himalayan kingdom together, *Newar* merchants went along to set up shops. They created many of the hill bazaars that trekkers encounter throughout Nepal, and they continue to serve as suppliers for many of the still remote government outposts.

Not all *Newar* are businessmen or civil servants. Members of one subgroup known as *Jyapu* are seen tilling the vast fields of rice, wheat, and vegetables in the valley. Others are stone and wood carvers, carpenters, potters, goldsmiths, blacksmiths, butchers, and Hindu or Buddhist temple priests. *Newar* peasant communities are even occasionally found in the outlying dis-

Cleaning millet with a nanglo

tricts. Most *Newar,* no matter how far dispersed, try to keep kinship and ritual ties with the Kathmandu Valley because it is their homeland.

PEOPLES OF EASTERN NEPAL

The east is the indigenous home to *Kiranti* people *(Rai* and *Limbu), Tamang, Sunwar,* and *Jirel* people at the middle elevations, and to more recently arrived Brahmans and *Chhetri,* who arrived in the wake of the Gorkha conquest of the eighteenth century. Sherpa, *Lhomi,* and other *BhoTiya* people populate the high valleys of eastern Nepal, up to 14,000 ft (4000 m).

The *Kiranti* live in the easternmost districts, and are found even around Darjeeling in West Bengal. Like the *Gurung* and *Magar* farther west, the *Kiranti* are renowned for their exploits in the British and Indian Gurkha armies. They speak a number of interrelated dialects that are often unintelligible from one watershed village to the next.

Kiranti economy is fairly self-sufficient. (The description that follows fits the Nepali hill peoples in general.) Rice is raised in lower, well-watered fields. Upland crops, such as corn, millet, barley, wheat, and potatoes, are raised on higher, drier, and steeper or terraced hillsides. No mechanized farm equipment is found in the hills (except an occasional threshing machine or rice mill). Tilling is done either by hand with a short-handled hoe (seen most often in the Kathmandu Valley), or with bullocks pulling iron-tipped wooden plows. All hillsmen eat what they raise, and market what little surplus they may have. Some supplement their incomes by selling oranges or fish. The wealthier may engage in moneylending. Others work seasonally in neighboring India as porters, Gurkha soldiers, policemen, or watchmen. In the far eastern hills bordering the Darjeeling District of West Bengal, there are tea plantations—Nepal's own brand of Ilam tea is exceptionally tasty. Many *Limbu* work the tea plantations on both sides of the border. Some hillsmen make and sell bamboo baskets and mats, and where sheep are raised on the higher slopes, the people weave and sell the woolen blankets, rugs, and feltlike capes and jackets that are often seen in Kathmandu's street bazaar. Trekkers are most likely to encounter *Kiranti-Rai* along the lower trail through Solu District on the trek to Mount Everest, and around Makalu and Kangchenjunga.

The *Tamang,* a very large and widespread hill group, are among the most recent groups to have settled along the northern border regions and higher hills, having come, it appears, from farther north and east. *Tamang* have retained much of their Tibetan and Buddhist heritage. They have many villages all around the Kathmandu Valley, especially north, toward Helambu, and east, on the Mount Everest trek. They also populate the upper Trisuli Valley, on the Langtang trek. *Tamang* are well known to Himalayan climbers, who hire them for the long haul into base camps. At the higher elevations, however, the Sherpas tend to dominate the portering.

Eastward, toward Mount Everest, there are also small ethnic enclaves of the *Sunwar* and the *Jirel* peoples. *Sunwar* inhabit the Likhu and Khimti valleys. Some of them have been recruited into Gurkha British and Indian regiments. The *Jirel* are found in the Jiri and Sikri valleys. These groups are difficult to distinguish initially from surrounding hill peasants.

Next to the Gurkha soldiers of Nepal, it is perhaps the Sherpas, famous as mountain guides and porters, who have attracted the most worldwide attention. Some Sherpas dwell in the remote Rolwaling valley, and as far west as Helambu region north of Kathmandu, but the most renowned come from the villages of Shar-Khumbu (Solu-Khumbu), along the upper valley of the Dudh Kosi and its tributaries, in the Mount Everest region. Sherpas are relatively recent immigrants to Nepal. Pangboche, their oldest village and one of the highest in the world, is thought to have been built a little over 300 years ago. The Sherpas speak a Tibetan dialect, dress like their Tibetan neighbors—or often like Western trekkers—and live as traders and agro-pastoralists, farming their high fields (mostly potatoes, wheat, barley, and buckwheat) and herding yak and sheep in alpine pastures up to 17,000 ft (5000 m). Their region is divided into three subregions: Solu, Pharak, and Khumbu. Solu, at the south, includes such villages as Junbesi and Phaphlu, and the monastery at Chiwong, in picturesque valleys at approximately 9000 ft (2700 m). Pharak is situated between Solu and Khumbu along the steep banks of the Dudh Kosi. Most Sherpa mountaineers hail from Khumbu, the highest and most northerly of the three regions, at elevations of 11,000 ft (3300 m) and up. Their villages include Namche Bazaar, Thami, Khumjung, Kunde, and Pangboche, as well as the famous and beautiful Buddhist monastery of Tengboche. Among the Sherpas, the practice of Tibetan Lamaism remains strong.

Their religion gives Sherpas a concern for all living things and for their Western clients on treks and expeditions. Their warmth of character, shared by many Himalayan peoples, is perhaps best displayed in their sense of hospitality. Visitors to a Sherpa house are considered guests of honor, for whom nothing is spared (sometimes to the point of embarrassment for Westerners). The best response to an outpouring of generosity by a Sherpa, or any Nepali host, is reciprocity—your own generosity and care in their regard.

Sherpa names of men often reflect the day of the week on which the boy was born. Nima on Sunday, Dawa on Monday, Mingma on Tuesday, Lhakpa on Wednesday, Phurbu on Thursday, Pasang on Friday, and Pemba on Saturday. Like any tradition, this one is not strictly adhered to.

The Sherpas have received considerable attention from anthropologists, mountaineer-writers, and traveling journalists, so we need not go into detail here (see appendix B). One facet of Sherpa culture not often described in the literature is the Namche Bazaar Saturday market, which is interesting from a traveler's perspective because of the chance to see several ethnic groups and a wide variety of local handicrafts and trade goods on display. If traveling toward Namche Bazaar immediately before a Saturday, trekkers may see many groups of lowlanders, mostly *Rai* and a few Brahman and *Chhetri,* carrying baskets of produce such as rice, corn, and fruits to sell or trade for highland produce such as wheat, wool, potatoes, *ghiu* (clarified butter, or *ghee*), and other animal byproducts. This is part of the natural economic exchange that keeps each community supplied with the produce of the other. The lowlanders are easily singled out by their style of dress (light, tie-across Nepali shirts and baggy trousers that fit snugly at the calves) from the Sherpas and Tibetans. Sherpa and Tibetan men, by comparison, prefer heavy woolen cloaks and trousers, with leather or woolen boots. And these days, some dress in down jackets as well. At the market itself, Tibetan boots and handicrafts of silver, wool, and leather are displayed. A market day is a lively occasion, a time when Tibetans, Sherpas, *Rai,* and others (including Western visitors) intermingle to trade, gossip, eat, drink, and even dance and sing in a spirited, sharing atmosphere.

The *BhoTiya* people east of Makalu, out to Kangchenjunga, sometimes call themselves Sherpa, sometimes not. Generally their language is Tibetan, which is distinct from the Sherpa dialect of Solu-Khumbu.

PEOPLES OF CENTRAL NEPAL

Central Nepal is the region extending from the Kathmandu Valley westward to, and just beyond, Pokhara. It is the home of Brahman, *Chhetri, Magar* and *Gurung* peoples, and of a number of northern border peoples, including the *Thakali* of the Thak Khola region of the Mustang District. The Brahman and *Chhetri* people are encountered especially in the lower valleys. Look for them in the vicinity of the old Gorkha kingdom and along the lower Marsyangdi valley trail. *Newar* bazaars line the road between Kathmandu and Po-khara, and many other caste and ethnic people have been attracted to these new settlements. The *Gurung* inhabit the higher slopes of the Annapurna, Lamjung, Himal Chuli, and Ganesh Himalaya massifs. There are many *Tamang* in the region as well, often indistinguishable from the *Gurung*. The *Magar* people live widely scattered, in both lower and higher hill areas.

The *Gurung* are most prominent on high ridges and upper valleys below the Annapurna and Himal Chuli massifs north and east of Pokhara, eastward beyond Gorkha. They are an enterprising upland farming and herding people; their sheep herds are often seen along the Manang trail on the Marsyangdi river route. They are subdivided into many clans, but except for the *Ghale* (pro-nounced like "golly"), who prefer to use the clan name, most call themselves, simply, *Gurung*. They, like their *Magar* counterparts, occupy some of the most inaccessible villages, high on the mountainsides above the trekking routes. Young *Gurung* men are often encountered as porters; older *Gurung* of distinction may have served in the Gurkha regiments, and many have interest-ing tales of exploits from World War II. If you happen to stop at a *Gurung* vil-lage for the night, you might see their colorful dances, or other ritual or festival activities, some of which display very ancient characteristics. Especially inter-esting are *Gurung* funerary rituals (called *arghun*), which are described later.

Tibetan *BhoTiya* groups of northern central Nepal come from Nupri (northern Gorkha District, upper Buri Gandaki river), Manang (upper Mar-syangdi river), Lo-Manthang (upper Kali Gandaki river), and from Dolpo and Tarap (north of the Dhaulagiri massif). During the winter months, large num-bers of these high-mountain peoples trek south to the lower hills and are often encountered in and around bazaar towns, where they engage in trade and some-times run inns and small shops. Many of the pony and donkey trains encoun-tered along the Thak Khola trek route are operated by *BhoTiya* men from LoManthang region, northern Thak Khola, and the valley of Muktinath, all in northern Mustang District.

The Thak Khola trek passes through villages of several ethnic and caste groups. Pokhara, the starting point for many central and west Nepal treks, is inhabited by all sorts of peoples—Brahman, *Chhetri, Newar, Gurung, Thakali, BhoTiya,* Tibetans, and many menial castes, as well as newcomers from the Nepali Tarai lowlands and from India. The surrounding hills are dot-ted with *Gurung* villages. The wealth of ex-Gurkha soldiers among them is ob-vious from their large, cut-stone houses with slate or corrugated metal roofs. There is a Tibetan refugee settlement at Pardi, near the Pokhara airport, and another at Hyangja, a half-hour walk north of the main Pokhara bazaar. Trek-king north, one may encounter Hindu caste settlements at first, to be replaced on the higher hills by the ethnic *Gurung* and *Magar*.

The *Magar* are farmers and herdsmen who live along the tributaries of the Kali Gandaki river in Myagdi District both north, west, and southwest of Beni. *Magar* villages situated under the Dhaulagiri Himal seem to cling like postage stamps to the high cliffs. In some regions, indigenous *Magar* call themselves by clan names, such as *Pun, Chantel, Kaiki,* and *Tarali. Pun Magar* are re-nowned for rock-cutting skills, which are visible along the Kali Gandaki river trail. Some of the more northerly trails were cut out of the cliffs in the 1950s by

A beguiling Nepali

Tibetan refugee *Khamba*. *Chantel Magar,* who also dwell below the south face of the Dhaulagiri massif, are herdsmen and farmers who are noted also for their skills in local copper mining. The culture of the northernmost *Magar,* the *Tarali* of Dolpo District, blends into that of the *BhoTiya*.

Above the dramatic gorge of the Kali Gandaki, north from the town of

Ghasa, is the region known as Thak Khola. *Thakali* villages line the route north along the high Kali Gandaki valley. Their language is very close to *Gurung* and *Tamang,* but their cultural history has been more influenced by Tibet. The *Thakali* are noted for their strong trading spirit, which they developed as middlemen in the formerly very active Nepal–Tibet rice and salt trade through their region. The largest town until recently was Tukche, the center of the *Thakali* ethnic culture and, for many decades earlier in this century, the regional center of the Tibetan salt trade. Since 1959, when the Tibetan border trade diminished, the Tibetan salt business has come to a virtual standstill in Thak Khola, and many *Thakali* have turned southward for other economic opportunities. Today, Jomosom, the district center north of Tukche, is much larger and at times Tukche appears almost abandoned. Some *Thakali* have dropped their Tibetan and Buddhist predilections and have adopted Nepali culture and Hinduism. Some have moved permanently out of Thak Khola to take advantage of business ventures in the larger bazaars and trade centers of Nepal.

Despite their uniform appearances, Thak Khola is actually the home of two similar ethnic groups, and one quite distinct group. The *Thakali* proper live between Ghasa and Tukche. North of them, and virtually indistinguishable, are a people known as *PaunchgaaUle* (which literally means "people of the five villages"—Marpha, Syang, Chiwong, Cherok, and Jomosom-Thini). The *PaunchgaaUle* sometimes call themselves *Thakali* but intermarriage between them and their "true" *Thakali* neighbors is not condoned. The third group are a *BhoTiya* people who inhabit the valley of Muktinath, from Kagbeni east to the Muktinath shrine at the base of Thorung Pass. They are also sometimes called the *BaragaaUle,* or "people of the twelve villages." Muktinath is a special place to these *BhoTiya* people, as it is a Hindu-Buddhist shrine of great significance. There are many religious observances throughout the year that attract Hindu and Buddhist pilgrims. The most important event to local Buddhists is the celebration of the *Yartung* festival in the fail, when the animals have been brought down from the high pastures for the winter. *Yartung* is highlighted by horse racing and great revelry. For Hindus, one of the largest events of the year falls on the occasion of Janai Purnima, the "full moon day *(purnima)* of the sacred cord *(janai)*." The sacred cord is worn by men of the highest twice-born Hindu castes, as a sign of their privileged social status and religious sanctity. More about Muktinath as a sacred center is given in the section on the Thak Khola trek.

Finally, north of Muktinath Valley, there are the *Lopa,* the *BhoTiya* people of upper Mustang District, in what was once the petty kingdom of Mustang. Their lives center around high, dry-land agriculture on oasislike farmland wherever nearby streams can be diverted for irrigation water, and they follow pastoral pursuits with sheep, goats, and yak. In winter, many of them migrate south as traders and pony drivers. These people are Tibetan Buddhists, and some practice the pre-Buddhist religion called Bon. There are a number of small monasteries of both religions throughout Thak Khola and upper Mustang. In their northernmost walled town of Manthang lives the king of the *Lopa,* the Raja of Mustang, whose allegiance is firmly with the government in Kathmandu.

PEOPLES OF WESTERN AND FAR WESTERN NEPAL

West and far west Nepal are less known to anthropologists than other parts of the country for several reasons—the difficulty of travel in the area, the remoteness from centers of trade and government, and the relatively low population, sparse settlement, and dearth of ethnic groups. These hills are drier, and the people suffer from more difficult environmental circumstances; their production is lower and it takes much more land to support the average family. The great distances and time involved to travel from either the Tarai towns to the south or the capital at Kathmandu also explain our relatively poor understanding of this region.

Part of the west is the home of the *Magar,* but only as far as the Sallyan District. Beyond that to the western border with India, Hindu caste groups predominate. In great measure these Hindu villagers are closely related to the *PahAARi* (hill people) of Almora, Kumaon, and Garhwal in the neighboring Indian sub-Himalaya. The Nepali language here blends into the central *PahAARi* dialect of north India, and to some extent there is greater sociocultural interaction with Indian neighbors than with the peoples of central Nepal or Kathmandu. In recent years the national government has taken a more active interest in the problems and potential of the far west. There has been a concerted effort to further integrate and unite all of the Nepali people as one nation and to improve the local standard of living.

Living north of the Hindu caste groups of the west and far west are more of the *BhoTiya* people, named after particular valleys in which they live, such as Limi, Mugu, Tarap, and Dolpo. Some of these have only recently been studied by anthropologists, and most accounts of them are found only in scholarly journals and dissertations.

This region offers some spectacular treks, particularly to the lakes (RaRa and Phoksumdo) and mountains. And there are equally interesting social systems, cultural patterns, and historic and archaeological reminders of the past.

This is the land of the ancient Malla Kingdom of the Karnali river basin. This region is literally littered with many of the cultural and historic artifacts of the Malla era, the twelfth to fourteenth centuries A.D. At one time, the Malla Kingdom included portions of western Tibet as well. After its decline, the *baaisi raja* (twenty-two kingdoms) of west Nepal emerged and were not ceded to the expanding Gorkha kingdom until the nineteenth century. (Historians have postulated a relationship between the Malla kings of west Nepal and those of the Kathmandu Valley just prior to the eighteenth-century Gorkha conquest, but there is no consensus.)

Along the former "royal highway" of the Malla Kingdom of west Nepal, a walking route stretching north from the inner Tarai through Jumla and into Tibet, there are various inscribed stones that scholars have used to determine the nature and extent of the Malla domain. And there are ancient shrines to be seen throughout western Nepal dedicated to the prominent local deity called "*Masta.*" On some trails in the west, one may see carved wooden spirit effigies, festooned with bells, flowers, and strips of colored cloth, set out to appease the spirits that haunt each locale. Trekkers are admonished—*please*—to respect local customs here and throughout Nepal and to refrain from handling

This man vowed to keep his arm in the air for the rest of his life to atone for his sins; his long fingernails attest to his perseverance.

or taking souvenirs beyond what can be captured on film. Much of what is seen and admired here is sacred, and local feeling toward holy objects is not unlike the reverence and respect Westerners feel in the sanctuaries of the great cathedrals of Europe, or in their hometown churches and synagogues.

One fascinating cultural feature of some of the more northerly dwelling Hindus of this region is their apparent "Tibetanization." Unlike elsewhere in Nepal, some *Chhetri* and *Thakuri* of the west and far west are indistinguishable at first glance from their Buddhist *BhoTiya* neighbors. They wear the same style of clothing, construct similar flat-roofed houses, and pursue the same patterns of trade and subsistence economy. Their way of living is unlike that of their more "pure" Hindu caste neighbors to the south and east, who look down upon them in some respects. The *BhoTiya* cultural attributes noted here, and wherever they occur among non-*BhoTiya* people in Nepal, are reflections of the northern mountain environment.

There are also many true *BhoTiya* encountered on the trails of this region, along the Bheri and Karnali river routes, for example. They are typically high-mountain dwellers of Tibetan racial and cultural affinities who prefer to spend their winters in the warmer, lower southlands of Nepal. At times, in the fall and spring, the trekker may encounter a kaleidoscope of people in caravans, including *Byansi* ethnic traders, who live mostly in the Indian frontier district of Almora, and in adjacent border regions of far west Nepal.

The salt trade was once a flourishing business here. Salt from the great salt lakes of western Tibet was procured from Tibetan traders, then traded through several hands for cereal grain and other commodities in Nepal and India. Today, traders deal more often in wood products, animal byproducts (butter, hides), and cereal grains, as well as numerous manufactured goods, mostly of Indian origin.

Besides traders, the traveler may encounter devout Hindu pilgrims wending their way northward through far west Nepal. Their destinations are the sacred Mount Kailas and Lake Manasarowar, in western Tibet.

Despite the growth of tourism and travel throughout Nepal, and the government's increasing investment in rural development (new roads, schools, and other basic services), Nepal's west and far west districts remain remote from the national center. It is a region as exotic and romantic as its curious-sounding place names: Dang, Dandeldhura, RaRa, Limi, Mugu, and Humla.

Religious Festivals and Sacred Observances

SECULAR FESTIVALS

Several national holidays are celebrated throughout the country. The most colorful, from the standpoint of national culture and the prospect of photography, is *Prajaatantra Divas,* or Nepali National Day, February 19. It is highlighted by parades on the Tundikhel (parade ground) in the center of Kathmandu. National ethnic groups, dancing troupes, the military, and various peasant, class, and cooperative organizations participate, all dressed in their traditional finery. There is much pomp and splendor.

At least three different New Year celebrations are held in Nepal annually. The Lunar New Year begins in the Nepali month of Baisakh (mid-April). The Tibetan New Year, called *Losar,* usually falls in February. It is heralded by feasting and celebration among the Tibetan community. The traditional *Newar* New Year falls in October and is celebrated by the preparation and sale of great amounts of sweet cakes and candies, and with colorful decorations throughout the streets of Kathmandu, PaaTan, and BhatgAAU.

Among the secular festivals in the hills, one of the most interesting is *Yartung* at Muktinath (Thak Khola trek). *Yartung* signals the return from the highlands of the animals, which are pastured in the lower valleys during the coming winter. It occurs in the fall and sometimes coincides with the full-moon day of *Janai Purnima,* a Hindu sacred occasion (below). *Yartung* annually attracts the majority of *BhoTiya* people from throughout upper Thak Khola, northern Mustang, and neighboring Manang District (over the Thorung Pass). The participants wear their traditional ethnic dress. Horse racing at Ranipauwa, about 0.5 mi (0.8 km) below the Muktinath shrine, is the main event, along with drinking, dancing, gambling, and a generally merry and festive good time. (See Buddhist Festivals, below.)

The *Yartung* is a kind of fair or *mela.* These rural fairs are countrywide and occur throughout the year at various locations. Many are held in the spring and in the fall after the harvest. Fairs are traditionally associated with local rural shrines, quite often for Hindus at the confluence *(beni)* of two sacred rivers or simply on the bank *(ghaaT)* of a sacred river. They usually coincide with a religious occasion, and include worship at a local shrine. Some *mela* are quite large and last several days, attracting people from surrounding districts. Others are quite brief and limited to a small region.

HINDU FESTIVALS

Hindu festivals are celebrated in the Kathmandu Valley and in many hill bazaars and villages. Only a few of the many smaller local festivals are mentioned here. Information about them and the exact dates of all festivals, which are reckoned by the lunar cycle, can be obtained in Kathmandu. The following Nepali words are often used in relation to certain festivals and religious occasions:

ekadasi, the eleventh day of every fortnight during the lunar year, is observed by fasting, worship, and ceremonial bathing.

jaatraa means festival or fair.

yaatraa is more specifically a religious occasion that attracts pilgrims (*jaatraa* and *yaatraa* are sometimes used interchangeably).

pujaa means worship.

A *Tikaa* is a mark of religious and decorative significance on the forehead of Hindus. They are given and received, particularly at festival and religious occasions, to express good wishes, friendship, respect, and honor. When a Hindu visits a temple or shrine, he or she often takes *Tikaa* from the officiating priest. One day each year, during the religious observance of *DasAAI,* the King gives *Tikaa* to the general populace. Outside of Kathmandu, the headman of a village substitutes for the King on this day of honor.

The major Hindu holidays include:

Shiva Raatri, literally "Shiva's Night," is observed in February at Pashupatinath, a famous large Hindu temple on the banks of the Bagmati river in the Kathmandu Valley, northeast of the capital city. This festival attracts thousands of pilgrims from all over Nepal, the Tarai, and India, who walk, fly, or ride buses into the valley for the occasion. The Nepal army parades on the Tundikhel, and bonfires burn for several nights.

Holi is celebrated in early March. Its climax is on the full-moon day, when red powder is thrown and passersby are doused with colored water. It is not a day to wear one's best clothes, unless you were expecting to have them cleaned immediately anyway!

GhoRa Jaatra, held in late March, includes horse racing and athletic events on the Kathmandu Tundikhel.

Janai Purnima (or *Janai Purne*) is the full-moon day of the late monsoon season (usually August) on which high-caste Hindus bathe ceremonially and men ritually change their sacred threads *(janai),* which are worn over the left shoulder. In addition, on this day priests give yellow threads, worn on the wrist for good luck until the *Tihaar* festival, to all who wish them. Hardy and pious Hindus take pilgrimages on this day to bathe and worship at some of the high Himalayan lakes, such as Gosainkunda, north of Kathmandu, and to other equally auspicious holy sites, such as Muktinath in northeastern Thak Khola. In Kathmandu, large numbers gather at the water tank of Kumbeshwar in Lalitpur, a site that has religious affinities with Gosainkunda.

Indra Jaatraa lasts eight days at the end of September and beginning of October. The center of activity in Kathmandu is Hanuman Dhoka (the square near the old royal palace in Kathmandu), but preparations can be seen at various other places for many days prior to the main celebration. A tall pole is erected and a golden elephant is placed there, attracting worshipers with offerings of sweets, fruit, and flowers. The festival also features dancing troupes and drama productions. Families pay special tribute to those members who have died during the past years, parading through the streets carrying burning lamps and incense and chanting religious hymns. Various manifestations of the god Indra are shown throughout the city, the most famous being the huge head of Bhairab, at Indrachok, and the metal head gilded with gold, at Hanuman Dhoka. Each evening the temples of Hanuman Dhoka and the old palaces are lit with numerous oil lamps.

This festival and many others are especially important to the *Newar* people, and are celebrated in remote bazaars throughout the country. Travelers who happen to be in a *Newar* bazaar during *Indra Jaatraa* will see colorful masked street dancers who are thought to become possessed.

In Kathmandu, on *Raths Jaatraa,* the day before the full moon of *Indra Jaatraa,* thousands of Nepalis crowd the streets to glimpse the "Living Goddess," Kumari, and two "Living Gods," Ganesh and Bhairab, as they are paraded in ancient temple carts through the lower part of the city. The young virgin deity and her two boy attendants are especially selected from the *Bada* subcaste (silversmiths and goldsmiths) of the *Newar.* Kumari is considered the protectoress of the Kathmandu Valley.

DasAAl (*Dusserah* in India) lasts for ten days at the time of the new moon in mid-October. This is Nepal's most important festival. It commemorates the legendary victory of the goddess Durga (Kali) over the evil demon-buffalo, Mahisashur. One highlight is the ceremonial decapitating of buffaloes at the *koT* (fort) near Hanuman Dhoka on the ninth day of the festival. The tenth day, called *Vijaya Dasami* (literally, "Victorious Tenth Day") is the day of the *Tikaa* ceremony, and symbolizes victory by extermination of the demon-buffalo by Durga. On this day, the King and Queen receive citizens at the royal palace, where they give *Tikaa,* and village leaders dispense *Tikaa* to their constituents in the hinterlands. Schools and government offices are closed during

DasAAI, and the holiday is considered a time for family reunions all over the country. On rural trails, one will see women and children returning to their *maiti ghar* (or mother's home) during the time of *DasAAI* and/or during *Tihaar,* which follows. At this time of year, the Kathmandu Tundikhel is alive with goats and sheep brought into the valley from northern districts, and with buffalo from the Tarai. These animals are for sale, and are ultimately used in the necessary sacrifices and feasting of the occasion. The whole *DasAAI* season is one of feasting and merrymaking.

Tihaar or *Diwali* is a five-day festival in mid-November. The last three days are the most interesting. The third day is *Lakshmi Pujaa,* dedicated to Lakshmi, goddess of wealth and associated with light. Houses are trimmed with hundreds of tiny oil lamps, which transform Kathmandu into a beautifully lit city at night. Lakshmi's blessings are invoked, and a new business year is officially begun. In *Newar* communities, the streets are overhung with paper lanterns that are lit each evening. During *Tihaar* various creatures, including humans, are singled out for attention—on the first day, the crow; on the second day, the dog; on the third day, the cow; and on the fourth day, the bull. On the final day, *Bhaai Tikaa,* sisters ceremonially give their brothers *Tikaa* on the foreheads and wish them prosperity and long life. This is the only time of the year when public gambling is condoned, and you will see many crowds around groups of *juwaa* (cowrie shell) players, or card players. During this season, girls and boys also carol in the streets and alleyways of towns and villages. Girls carol on the night of *Lakshmi Pujaa,* and boys carol on the next night. A popular treat during *Tihaar* is the rice-flour doughnut, called *sel roti.* Finally, among the *Newar* merchant community, *Tihaar* marks the beginning of their New Year, and *Newar* bazaars, in particular, are festooned with decorations and crowded with well-wishers and merrymakers. At this time, the sweet shops are overflowing with pastries and candy treats.

Both *DasAAI* and *Tihaar* mark the end of the farming season, the bringing in of the harvest, and new beginnings. This time of year is especially joyous for individuals and families alike, and most people prefer to be at home with relatives and friends.

BUDDHIST FESTIVALS

Buddhist festivals are celebrated among the Tibetan and Buddhist *Newar* communities in the Kathmandu Valley and in outlying districts where these people are found. Secular and religious festivals among Buddhists are commonly celebrated in the northern border districts, the principal domain of Nepali Tibetans *(BhoTiya).* Buddhist festivals include:

Losar, the Tibetan New Year, in mid-February. There are festive activities at Baudhnath and Swayambhunath temples in the Kathmandu Valley, and at the Tibetan refugee center near PaaTan. Festivals are also held in outlying Tibetan refugee communities, such as in the Pokhara Valley, in Langtang Valley, and at Chialsa. Buddhist pilgrims visit the big temples and monasteries at this time, and family reunions—with feasting, drinking, and dancing—highlight home life.

Buddha's Birthday in May is a solemn occasion. Foreign dignitaries are usually invited to observances during the day at Swayambhunath, where Tibetan and *Newar* Buddhist monks perform elaborate rituals in their brightly colored robes. Observances are also held in other Buddhist temples and monasteries. Prayer flags fly overhead, and at night the Swayambhunath hilltop is brightly lit. The celebration of Buddha's Birthday is less elaborate in outlying Buddhist communities, where observances at the local *gomba* or monastery are common.

Dalai Lama's Birthday, on July 6, is a time for prayer, invocation of blessings, and feasting, especially by Tibetan refugees. For some refugees it is a time of patriotic expressions in remembrance of former times, when the Dalai Lama was the supreme ruler of Tibet. Prayer flags fly overhead, and within the monasteries, butter lamps are lit in the name of the Dalai Lama. Prayers are said for his long life and good health.

Mani-rimdu is a Sherpa dance drama performed in the Khumbu region. It is held annually at Tengboche and Chiwong monasteries during November or early December and at Thami each May. Although usually held during the full moon, this is sometimes scheduled at a more auspicious time, so inquire in Kathmandu and along the way to learn when it will take place. This colorful, uniquely Sherpa festival has its origins in ancient Tibetan theatrical genres. The performers are monks, but the occasion is highlighted by much gaiety and feasting by monks and lay spectators alike.

Yartung is a horse festival held annually at the end of the monsoon (August or early September) on the race grounds of Ranipauwa, adjacent to the Muktinath pilgrimage site in Mustang District. *BhoTiya* people from all over BaragaaU (Muktinath or Dzong river valley), and Lo-Manthang (upper Mustang), and some from Manang (east of Mustang) and Dolpo (west) attend. The men of BaragaaU region compete in a day of horse racing, a raucous occasion spiced by drinking and gambling in tents set up on the hills around the small community below Muktinath. The day begins with processions of laymen and monks in colorful attire, some riding equally decorated horses, from each of the surrounding villages. The monks lead the processions to circle the Muktinath shrine, before the secular fun starts. Frequently, *Yartung* coincides with the Hindu pilgrimage of *Janai Purnima,* adding to the number of people present at the shrine during the day.

Other Festive Events

WEDDINGS

Hindu weddings can be observed almost any time, but most are held during the months of January and February. Wedding parties can be observed traveling to and from the bride's house, sometimes over a long distance and for several days. In rural villages, weddings are loud, colorful affairs accompanied by hornpipers, drummers, and dancers. Wealthy city weddings often include professional bands, and the house where the wedding feast is held is decorated with strings of lights at night. Hindu marriages are traditionally arranged by the parents of the couple; horoscopes are compared by a priest, and an auspicious date is set. Dowries are often demanded, and can be quite expensive. Child marriage, now prohibited, was traditionally the norm among orthodox Hindus.

Buddhist weddings in the hills and mountains are less elaborate, more relaxed affairs, with great attention paid to ostentatious display and reciprocity in gift giving. Among Sherpas, for example, a wedding is preceded, sometimes years earlier, by betrothal rites and often by the birth of a child. There is much beer drinking and dancing. Monks from a nearby monastery attend to the actual ceremonial activities.

Today, throughout Nepal, the customs surrounding the securing of a marriage partner are greatly relaxed compared with the past. Love marriage and marriage between castes and ethnic groups are not uncommon. Nonetheless, arranged marriages of alliance between families in proper caste or ethnic categories are still contracted, especially among the more traditional and orthodox people.

FUNERALS

Funerals can be observed in the city and countryside at any time. Most Nepalis burn the dead, preferably at the riverside *(ghaaT),* within a few hours of death. Hill villagers, far from the river, prefer prominent hillsides on which to burn or bury the dead. Funeral parties are obvious from the presence of a white-shrouded corpse carried on a bier either prone or bound tightly into a sitting position. Male relatives at the funeral typically shave their heads; women frequently loosen their hair, letting it hang unadorned down the back. Drumming is uncommon, except on the occasion of post-funerary ceremonies held sometimes months after death to celebrate the passage of the deceased's spirit into the afterlife. Such post-funerary rituals are common, for example, among the hill ethnic groups such as the *Gurung, Tamang,* and *Thakali.* These are occasions for great feasting, dancing, drinking, and serious and ancient religious rituals conducted by shamans and Bon or Buddhist monks. Such post-funerary events are sometimes known in Nepali as *arghun* in the hills of west and west-central Nepal.

PILGRIMAGE

The Himalaya are a great attraction to Nepali, Tibetan, and Indian pilgrims. Pilgrimage sites are common—a high "milk lake" *(dudh pokhari* or *kunda),* the confluence *(beni)* of sacred rivers, or an especially prominent shrine or temple. Some of the most famous pilgrimage sites for Hindus are at Gosainkunda, Dudh Pokhari, Panch Pokhari, and Baahra Pokhari. Muktinath and several other high-mountain shrines are sacred pilgrimage attractions to Hindus and Buddhists alike. Likewise, there are many shrines and temples within the Kathmandu Valley—Swayambhunath, for one—that are sacred to both religious groups. Baudhnath and Pashupatinath, on the outskirts of Kathmandu city, are especially sacred to Buddhists and Hindus respectively.

Pilgrims come to Nepal from all over southern Asia, and as travel conditions allow, from Tibet. Hindu holy men stand out clearly by their attire (or relative lack of attire, as the case may be). The occasion of *Shiva Raatri* is especially significant both to holy men and Indian lay pilgrims, who flock to the

Kathmandu Valley. Sometimes holy men may be encountered who are observing vows of silence; they sometimes go for as long as twelve years without speaking.

Lay pilgrims are commonly seen throughout the year on popular routes to the high-mountain shrines or lakes. For example, there are many seasonal events that attract pilgrims to and from Muktinath shrine above Thak Khola. Many of them have planned for years to come to a certain Himalayan Shaivite or Vaishnavite shrine (devoted to Shiva and Vishnu respectively). Others seem to come on the spur of the moment: some to cleanse themselves from sin or bad luck; others, just for the pleasure of doing something different and unusual, or to see the country. For Hindus, water is an essential element at pilgrim shrines, and bathing is a central feature of the ritual observances. Sometimes Hindu and Buddhist shrines offer other attractions as well, such as natural gas fires, the presence of sacred fossils, hot springs, an ice cave, a sacred footprint or other holy mark or memory of the gods, or a rich mythology of sacred events that adds to the attractiveness of a place. Legendary accounts of sacred pilgrimage sites and events in the Himalaya are recorded in the ancient literature of Hinduism, some works dating back over two thousand years.

Jewelry

Jewelry and other body decoration is another fascinating aspect of Nepali culture that attracts the attention of visitors. As in most societies, jewelry is used for decoration; for women, it is their inalienable property and their dowry.

Such decoration shows affluence, but there is perhaps less individuality and idiosyncratic expression in jewelry worn by a particular ethnic group in an area than in some modern cultures. Nepali people are modest and disapprove of too much self-pride. At festivals and weddings, however, it is appropriate and necessary to wear all one has, for Nepal is very much a public culture.

Wearing jewelry is "auspicious" for women, who wear it at their ears, neck, and wrists. The religious implications are many, to honor is to adorn: men, their wives and daughters; hosts, their guests, with *kata* (scarves) and *maalaa* (flowers); and devotees, their gods, with red powder, *kata, maalaa,* and jewelry; and *stupa* and mountain passes, with prayer flags and flowers.

Many styles are borrowed freely from adjacent groups. Occasional indicators of ethnicity are found: *Newar* never pierce noses; caste Hindus always do; only Sherpas and other *BhoTiya* wear striped aprons and the big silver hook clasps to hold them.

Jewelry is almost always handmade by a goldsmith. The metal is paid for by weight, and a small fee for craftsmanship. The gold, usually very pure, represents a safe investment.

Women pierce the nose on the left side (the female side) in the Hindu castes, and insert a discreet stud. Many hill ethnic groups—*Tamang, Gurung, Magar, Rai, Limbu,* and Hindus—pierce the left nostril and septum. You may find a ring on the left side, or a flat or dome-shaped plate of gold, with or without a colored stone. While the latter may be glass, or plastic because of its attractive color, the gold is usually real and quite pure. Brass or alloy is occasionally seen.

Ears are pierced early in life, as earrings are considered auspicious and gold helps the ears to hear *dharma* and the mind to understand it. There is great variety in the ornaments worn on earlobes, with no clear representational design. Some earrings will have *makar* (dragon) heads on either side, similar to the fish design of old water fountains. Large, up to 3-inch (8 cm) diameter, lightweight gold earrings, held stiff by their rim (*chepTisun,* meaning flat gold) are worn by *Tamang, Magar,* and *Gurung,* especially.

In the hills, many groups (except Sherpas and other *BhoTiya*) wear large *dhungri* through the stiff center cartilage of the ear. These may be so heavy that the ears flop over, a traditional sign of beauty among some peoples. The ear rims of some individuals may also have as many as eighteen to twenty tiny holes for carrying little rings. Some men, notably the *Jyapu,* pierce the right (male) side of the ear, high up. *BhoTiya* men and women wear coral and turquoise on strings through the earlobes.

Necklace designs are shared among many groups. There may be large gold beads, lac-filled for strength and lightness, strung with coral, glass, or layers of velvet circles between them. While the necklaces were once silver, the trend is away from it to gold.

A *tilhari,* a long, cylindrical, repoussé gold bead that hangs in the center of a few to a hundred strands of fine colored glass beads (seed beads), is worn by married Hindu women. Red, followed by green, are the most popular color beads.

The most commonly worn necklaces are composed of multiple strands of small glass beads *(pote)*. With the availability of Czechoslovakian and Japanese beads, color choices number in the hundreds. Necklaces may be choker length with just a few strands, or may hang to the hips and have numerous strands.

The most significant color is red, the color of marriage and fertility. Among the Hindu castes, the bridegroom places a necklace of red *pote* around the bride's neck. This application of red *pote* in combination with the application of red powder *(sindur)* in the part of the hair constitutes the most important act in the wedding ceremony. The red beads are the sign of a woman whose husband is alive. When a woman becomes widowed, the beads are discarded.

BhoTiya wear big pieces of coral (often imitation) and turquoise (almost always real) as well as large black and white *dzi* beads. *Dzi* protect the wearer from stroke and lightning. They are believed to have a supernatural origin as creatures (worms) which were petrified by the contamination of human touch, but retain some of their supernatural power. *BhoTiya* will also wear prayer boxes of gold and silver, often with bits of turquoise and fine filigree work. Colored, knotted strings, blessings from lamas, are also worn.

Many women wear bangles of gold, silver, and Indian glass on the wrists. Red is the most auspicious color, and the clinking is considered mildly erotic. Ankles are less commonly decorated than in the past. The *Tharu* in the Tarai may wear hollow or solid heavy anklets. Hill ethnic groups used to wear dragonlike *(makar* or *singha mukh)* designs. Anklets display high relief when

A Tharu *woman dressed in her finest*

new, but wear down over the years to become almost smooth. Some may wear similar pieces on the wrist. Gold, a divine metal, sacred to Vishnu, is rarely worn below the waist (the more impure part of the body), so these are usually silver. Anklets are currently out of fashion except among guides.

A plain *Tikaa* of red or yellow powder is an essential part of *pujaa* (worship) for men and women. Black ones guard against spirits. Fancy ones are worn by women as decoration or makeup.

Colored powder, usually red and orange, is put on images of gods, thrown at *Holi,* and slapped on cheeks at festivals. This custom of Hindu origin is a sign of reverence that pleases the gods and delights people by expressing their connection with one another and with the gods.

Children, who need protection from the "evil eye" of witches and from ghosts and spirits, wear black *gaajal* at the eyes and black strings at the neck, wrists, ankles, and waist. Similarly, silver anklets are thought to help their legs grow straight. Amulets with mantra papers are worn at the neck. *Rudaaksha* (seeds of *Eleocarpus ganitrus*) are a sign of respect to Shiva, while *Narasimha* images of copper protect against lightning and fright.

APPENDICES

A local comb in use

A.   Addresses

The following addresses could be helpful for organizing a trek in Nepal. Naturally, businesses come and go, and addresses change, but these will at least provide a place for the reader to start. Be aware that as the phone system in Kathmandu undergoes modernization, phone numbers continue to change. Before you go on a trek with a particular company, verify their phone number, address, and cable address. Inclusion in this list does not imply endorsement by the author or publisher. There is little regulation of trekking agencies in Nepal, so standards of performance vary widely. The list of trekking agents is taken from a recent list of the Trekking Agents Association of Nepal. To address a letter, write the company's name, post box, town (Kathmandu unless otherwise stated), and Nepal, on the envelope. The first address shown is an example of a complete address. Fax numbers are shown in parentheses. To dial from the United States, use prefix 977-1.

Trekking Agencies

Above the Clouds Trekking
Thamel
Box 2230, Kathmandu
NEPAL
Cable: Clouds
phone 416909 (416923)

Adventure Nepal Trekking
Tridevi Marg, Kesar Mahal
Box 915
Cable: Advent
phone 412508

Adventure Tenzing Trekking
Lazimpat
Box 3647
phone 414405

Ama Dablam Trekking
Lazimpat
Box 3035
Cable: Amadablam
phone 410219 (416029)

Annapurna Journeys
Durbar Marg
Box 1415
Cable: Annatours
phone 223536

Annapurna Trekking and Mountaineering
Durbar Marg
Box 795
Cable: Amtrek
phone 222999 (228890)

Asian Trekking
Thamel, Tridevi Marg
Box 3022
phone 412821

Atlas Trekking
Thamel
Box 4545
phone 225158

Cho-Oyu Trekking
Lazimpat
Box 4515
phone 418890 (414184)

Chomolhari Trekking
Durbar Marg
Box 1519
phone 222422

Cosmo Treks
Lazimpat
Box 2541
phone 416226

Everest Express Trekking
Durbar Marg
Box 482
phone 220759

Everest Trekking
Kamaladi
Box 1676
phone 220558

Four Season Trekking
Jyatha
Box 2369
phone 214237

Ganesh Himal Trekking
Thamel
Box 3858
phone 414185

Glacier Safari Treks
Thamel
Box 2402
phone 412116

Great Himalayan Adventure
Kantipath
Box 1033
Cable: Himventure
phone 216144

Guides for All Season Trekking
Gairidhara
Box 3776
phone 415841

Highland Sherpa Trekking
Thamel
Box 3597
phone 226389 (222026)

Himalaya Expeditions
Thamel
Box 105
phone 522770

Himalayan Adventures
Lazimpat
Box 1946
phone 414344

Himalayan Explorers
Jyatha, Thamel
Box 1737
phone 226142

Himalayan Horizons
Box 35, **Pokhara**
phone 253

Himalayan Journeys
Kantipath
Box 989
phone 226139 (227068)

Himalayan Shangrila Treks
Maitidevi
Box 221
phone 222160

Hiunchuli Treks
Jyatha, Thamel
Box 3725
phone 225371

International Trekkers
Narayanhity Marg
Box 1273
Cable: Intrek
phone 418594

In Wilderness Trekking
Baudhnath
Box 3043
phone 410760

Jai Himal Trekking
Durbar Marg
Box 3017
phone 221707

Journeys Mountaineering & Trekking
Kantipath
Box 2034
phone 225969 (414243)

Khumbi-ila Mountaineering & Trekking
Kamal Pokhari
Box 731
Cable: Khumbila
phone 413166

Lama Excursions
Durbar Marg
Box 2482
phone 220186

Lamjung Trekking & Expeditions
Kantipath
Box 1436
phone 220598 (226820)

Last Frontiers Trekking
Lainchaur
Box 881
phone 416146

Machhapuchhre Trekking
Thamel
Box 3880
phone 227207

Malla Treks
Lekhnath Marg
Box 787
Cable: Mallotel
phone 418389 (418382)

Mandala Trekking
Kantipath
Box 4573
phone 228600

Menuka Treks & Expeditions
Thamel
Box 3769
phone 411847

Mountain Adventure Trekking
Thamel
Box 3440
phone 414910 (418382)

Mountain River Adventure Trekking
Durbar Marg
Box 1945

Mountain Travel
Narayan Chour, Naxal
Box 170
phone 414508 (419126)

Natraj Trekking
Kantipath
Box 495
phone 226644

Nepal Himal Treks
Kesar Himal, Tridevi Marg
Box 4528
phone 411949 (227229, 418382)

Nepal Trek House
Patan Gate, Lalitpur
Box 1357
phone 526990 (521291)

Nepal Treks & Natural History Expeditions
Ganga Path
Box 459
phone 222511

Overseas Adventure Trekking
Thamel
Box 1017
phone 411045

Rover Treks & Expeditions
Naxal, Nagpokhari
Box 1081
Cáble: Rovertrek
phone 414373

Sagarmatha Trekking
Kantipath
Box 2236
phone 226639

Sherpa Cooperative Trekking
Durbar Marg
Box 1338
phone 224068

Sherpa Society
Chabahil
Box 1566
phone 470361 (470153)

Sherpa Trekking Service
Kamaladi, Ghantaghar
Box 500
Cable: Sherpatrek
phone 220423 (222026)

Snow Leopard Treks
Naxal
Box 1785
phone 414719

Summit Nepal Trekking
Kupondole Height, Lalitpur
Box 1406
phone 525408 (523737)

Tawache Trekking
Jyatha, Thamel
Box 2924
phone 227295

Tenzing Trekking & Mountaineering
Thamel
Box 1542
phone 220988

Thamserku Trekking
Sonam Expedition Service
Jyatha
Box 3124
phone 226645

Tip & Top Trekking
Gyaneshwar
Box 1760
Cable: Toptrek
phone 414781

Trans Himalayan Trekking
Durbar Marg
Box 283 Cable: Transeview
phone 224854

Trekking International
Lekhnath Marg, Thamel
Box 4431
phone 226939 (417877)

Treks & Expeditions Services
The Square, Kamal Pokhari
Box 3057
Cable: Treks
phone 412231

Venture Treks & Expeditions
Kantipath
Box 3968
phone 221585

White Magic Trekking
Tridevi Marg
Sanchayakjosh Building, Rm 123
Box 3356
phone 226885

Wilderness Experience
Kantipath
Box 4065
Cable: Wilderness
phone 220534

Yangrima Trekking
Kantipath
Box 2951
phone 225608 (227628)

Yeti Mountaineering & Trekking
Ramshah Path
Box 1034
phone 410899

Yeti Trekking
Kantipath
Box 2488
phone 225982

Nepal Book Dealers (Kathmandu)

Himalayan Book Center
Bagh Bazaar
Box 1339
phone 224191

Himalayan Booksellers
Ghantaghar
Box 528
phone 225484

Ratna Book Distributors
Bagh Bazaar
Box 1080
phone 213026

Tiwari's Pilgrims Book House
Thamel
Box 3872
phone 416744

B. Further Reading

Many people come, looking, looking...
some people come, see.

Dawa Tenzing, a Sherpa

I love Nepal. Ever since I first saw her in 1969, I have wanted to know all about her. The first experience led to questions, and answers to those lead to still more questions. By now I have come to know a little about much of her, but the spell has not waned. I want to share her with you. Maximum enjoyment will come through familiarity with her history, her culture, her geography, and her people. And as time passes, you see the changes with her development. While this book is primarily concerned with the practical matters related to trekking, a kind of Kama Sutra, you will want to know more about her personality, in its diverse aspects. Reading helps.

Most of the books in the annotated list below focus on areas outside of the Kathmandu Valley, and should help the trekker learn more about the various regions of this country. I have included much more material than might be considered appropriate for the casual encounter, but the interests of the peripatetic lover can often be far-ranging and lofty.

The books listed are either still in print, recently reprinted, or recently out of print. Those out of print can sometimes be purchased in Kathmandu. In an attempt to save space, I have cut out some material that was in previous editions. Books published in Nepal can normally only be purchased there. Some sources for ordering books by mail are listed in the Addresses section of appendix A. I urge you to buy books in Kathmandu, before you leave Nepal. Books are often cheaper and easier to find there than at home, and you will avoid the hassle of mail-ordering them later. Many of these volumes can be read at the Tribhuvan University Library in Kirtipur, Kathmandu.

General

Hagen, Toni. *Nepal: The Kingdom of the Himalayas.* Berne: Kummerley and Frey, 1980. A large-scale, illustrated book by the first man to travel widely through the country.

Hoefer, Hans Johannes. *Nepal.* Hong Kong: Apa Productions, 1990. One of the Insight Guides series, with contributions by experts; currently, it is the best general guidebook to Nepal.

Rieffel, Robert. *Nepal Namaste.* Kathmandu: Sahayogi Press, 1987. A detailed general guide to Nepal.

Shirahata, Shiro. *Nepal Himalaya.* San Francisco, Heian International, 1983. A photographic record of the awesome mountains by view camera.

Stein, R. A. *Tibetan Civilization.* Stanford, California: Stanford University Press, 1972. The more you know about Tibet as it once was, the better you'll understand the people of northern Nepal.

Tilman, H. W. *Nepal Himalaya.* Cambridge: University Press, 1952. An account by the first trekker in Nepal, with journeys to Langtang, Annapurna, and the Everest Region. It has been reprinted in his compendium: *The Seven Mountain Travel Books.*

Anthropology

Anderson, Mary M. *The Festivals of Nepal*. London: George Allen & Unwin, 1971. Mostly concerned with Kathmandu, but also helpful for the hills.

Aziz, Barbara Nimri. *Tibetan Frontier Families*. New Delhi: Vikas, 1978. A good source of information on Tibetan social life.

Bista, Dor Bahadur. *People of Nepal*. Kathmandu: Ratna Pustak Bhandar, 1974. Presents an excellent synopsis of most of the ethnic groups found in Nepal. If a trekker were to restrict himself to one book in this category, this should be it.

Dorje, Rinjing. *Food in Tibetan Life*. London: Prospect Books, 1985. Some insight into culinary practices and philosophy as it affects Tibetans, and by analogy, the highlanders of Nepal.

Fisher, James F. *Sherpas: Reflection on Change in Himalayan Nepal*. Berkeley: University of California Press, 1990. A look at this legendary ethnic group seen through their eyes, interpreted by an anthropologist who first worked among them in 1964.

———. *Trans-Himalayan Traders: Economy, Society, and Culture in Northwest Nepal*. Berkeley: University of California Press, 1986. A look at the *Tarali* people in southern Dolpo.

Kunwar, Ramesh Raj. *Fire of Himal: An Anthropological Study of the Sherpas of Nepal Himalayan Region*. New Delhi: Nirala Publications, 1989. A distillation of much information on these people.

Macdonald, Alexander W. *Essays on the Ethnology of Nepal and South Asia*. Kathmandu: Ratna Pustak Bhandar, 1975. A far-ranging collection of material dealing with music, castes, and healing, among other essays.

Macfarlane, Alan, and Gurung Indrabahadur. *Gurungs of Nepal (A Guide to the Gurungs)*. Kathmandu: Ratna Pustak Bhandar, 1990. A concise synopsis.

Messerschmidt, Donald A. *The Gurungs of Nepal*. Warminster: Aris & Phillips, 1976. An excellent description of the social and political organization of these people.

Ortner, Sherry B. *Sherpas through Their Rituals*. Cambridge: Cambridge University Press, 1978. Useful for descriptions of Sherpa hospitality.

———. *High Religion: A Cultural and Political History of Sherpa Buddhism*. Princeton: Princeton University Press, 1989.

Rakesh, Ram Dayal. *Folk Culture of Nepal: An Analytical Study*. Jaipur: Nirala Publications, 1990. Some insightful information on *Tharu, Magar,* and *Gurung* sociology.

Von Furer-Haimendorf, Christoph. *Asian Highland Societies*. New Delhi: Sterling Publishers, 1981. A series of modern essays by distinguished anthropologists.

———. *Himalayan Traders*. London: John Murray, 1975. A look at changes in the economic patterns of Nepal's high-altitude dwellers.

———. *The Sherpas of Nepal, Buddhist Highlanders*. New Delhi: Sterling Publishers, 1979. The classic account.

Art

Aran, Lydia. *The Art of Nepal*. Kathmandu: Sahayogi Prakashan, 1978. Deals primarily with the Kathmandu Valley, as do most books on Nepali art. It is also a useful guide to the art of this country seen through the religions.

Sharma, Prayag Raj. *Preliminary Study of the Art and Architecture of the Karnali Basin, West Nepal*. Paris: Centre National de la Recherche Scientifique (CNRS), 1972. One of the few art studies pertaining to Nepal outside the Kathmandu Valley.

Singh, Madanjeet. *Himalayan Art*. London: Macmillan, 1968. A survey of most of the Himalayan region with beautiful reproductions. There is a paperback edition published by UNESCO.

Crafts, Development, Economics, Environment, and Geography

Blaikie, Piers; Cameron, John; and Seddon, David. *Nepal in Crisis*. New Delhi: Oxford University Press, 1980. A radical look at the development problems facing Nepal today, focusing on the building of roads.

Blair, Katherine D. *Four Villages: Architecture in Nepal*. Los Angeles: Craft and Folk Art Museum, 1983. An insightful look at structures and social ecology.

Blamont, Denis, and Toffin, Gerard. *Architecture, milieu et societe en Himalaya*. Paris: CNRS, 1988. Informative papers.

Dunsmore, Susi. *The Nettle in Nepal: A Cottage Industry*. Surbiton, England: Land Resources Development Council, 1985. About weaving a variety of materials from the plant trekkers despise.

―――. *Weaving in Nepal: Dhaka-Topi cloth*. London: Overseas Development Natural Resources Institute, 1990. A look at weaving the cloth for the traditional cap worn by Nepali men.

Gajurel, C. L., and Vaidya, K. K. *Traditional Arts and Crafts of Nepal*. New Delhi: S. Chand, 1984. Invaluable for understanding many of the folk processes going on around you.

Ives, Jack D., and Messerli, Bruno. *The Himalayan Dilemma: Reconciling development and conservation*. London: Routledge, 1989. An insightful, scholarly look at the myth of environmental degradation in the Himalaya. Is there a crisis or not? The most significant recent publication on Nepal. Essential reading for all Nepal cognoscenti.

Kuløy, Hullvard Kare. *Tibetan Rugs*. Bangkok: White Orchid Press, 1982. A compendium of this traditional craft, it has helpful explanations of designs.

Seddon, David. *Nepal, A State of Poverty*. New Delhi: Vikas, 1984.

Shrestha, Chandra Bahadur. *Cultural Geography of Nepal*. Bhaktapur, Nepal: K. K. Shrestha and K. L. Joshi, 1981. The seminal account.

Swiss Association for Technical Assistance in Nepal. *Mountain Environment and Development*. Kathmandu: SATA, 1976. A collection of essays on the Swiss development experience in Nepal.

Toffin, Gerard. *L'Homme et la Maison en Himalaya*. Paris: CNRS, 1981. A collection of articles on village architecture in diverse areas of Nepal, mostly.

Tuting, Ludmilla, and Dixit, Kunda. *BIKAS-BINAS/Development-Destruction? The Change in Life and Environment of the Himalaya.* Munich: Geobuch, 1986. A collection of reprints dealing with changes in Nepal.

History

Regmi, Mahesh Chandra. *A Study in Nepali Economic History, 1768–1846.* New Delhi: Manjusri, 1971. Invaluable for understanding how life in the hills evolved.

———. *Thatched Huts and Stucco Palaces.* New Delhi: Vikas, 1978. More on economic history of the nineteenth century.

Snellgrove, David, and Richardson, Hugh. *A Cultural History of Tibet.* Boulder, Colorado: Prajna Press, 1980. Another example of a work dealing with Tibet that helps you understand Nepal's highlanders.

Stiller, L. F. *The Rise of the House of Gorkha.* New Delhi: Manjusri, 1973. Provides an understanding of the problems involved in unifying Nepal in the 1700s.

———. *The Silent Cry.* Kathmandu: Sahayogi Prakashan, 1976. A continuation of the author's study of the growth of unity in Nepal. It covers the pre-Rana period, 1816 to 1839.

Language

Adhikary, Kamal R. *A Concise English-Nepali Dictionary (with transliteration and Devanagari).* Kathmandu: self-published, 1988. A very useful help to the trekker who has mastered the basics.

Bell, Charles A. *English-Tibetan Colloquial Dictionary.* Calcutta: Sripati Ghosh, 1977. A reprlnt of the 1920 edition; it is not very helpful without language instruction.

Bezruchka, Stephen. *Nepali for Trekkers.* Seattle: The Mountaineers Books, 1991. A book and accompanying language tape that is essential for all trekkers.

Bloomfield, Andrew, and Tshering, Yanki. *Tibetan Phrasebook* and *Tibetan Phrasebook Tapes.* Ithaca, New York: Snow Lion, 1987. A useful beginning.

Clark, T.W. *Introduction to Nepali.* London: School of Oriental and African Studies, 1977. The only formal text. It is difficult to use, but valuable to those seeking a good knowledge of the language.

Formi, Daniel. *Le Petit Trekker: Francais/Anglais/Nepalais.* Kathmandu, 1990. A French phrasebook.

Goldstein, Melvyn C. *Tibetan for Beginners and Travellers.* Kathmandu: Ratna Pustak Bhandar, 1982. It is a place to start, but you need a teacher.

———. *Tibet Phrasebook.* South Yarra, Australia: Lonely Planet, 1987. Another resource.

Hari, Anna Mari. *Conversational Nepali.* Kathmandu: Summer Institute of Linguistics, 1971. An excellent situational course, though not practical for use while trekking. A reprinting is planned.

Karki, Tika B., and Shrestha, Chij K. *Basic Course in Spoken Nepali*. Kathmandu: published by the authors, 1979. Written for Peace Corps volunteers; stresses the situational approach. It may be useful for the serious trekker. Chij Shrestha's language institute in Naxal is also a source for language lessons.

Matthews, David J. *A Course in Nepali*. London: School of Oriental and African Studies, 1984. Another useful formal text for those seeking an in-depth study.

Meerendonk, M. *Basic Gurkhali Dictionary*. Singapore: published by the author, 1960. An excellent, dated, pocket dictionary. Some grammar is needed to use it.

Sherpa, Phinjo. *Sherpa Nepali English*. Kathmandu: published by the author, n.d. The first resource on the Sherpa language.

Terrell, Grace M., and Krishna B. Pradhan. *A Small World of Words*. Kathmandu, 1990. A pocket-sized Nepali–English and English–Nepali dictionary; its usefulness is limited by its unfortunate design.

Literature

Dixit, Mani. *Come Tomorrow*. Kathmandu: Sajha Prakashan, 1980. A novel about the Gurkhas by a current, prolific writer.

Rana, Diamond Shumshere. *Wake of the White Tiger*. Kathmandu: Mrs. Balika Rana, 1984. An English translation of this popular historical novel.

Rubin, David. *Nepali Visions, Nepali Dreams*. New York: Columbia University Press, 1980. Translations of and commentary on the poems of the late Laxmiprasad Devkota, perhaps Nepal's finest poet.

Natural History

Bhatt, Dibya Deo. *Natural History and Economic Botany of Nepal*. Calcutta: Orient Longmans, 1977. An excellent survey, with a wealth of detail.

Daniel, J. C. *The Book of Indian Reptiles*. Bombay: Bombay Natural History Society, 1983. Color photos and plenty of information for the herpetophile.

Fleming, Robert L., Jr. *The General Ecology, Flora, and Fauna of Midland Nepal*. Kathmandu: Tribhuvan University Press, 1977. A useful synthesis.

Fleming, Robert L., Sr.; Fleming, Robert L., Jr.; and Bangdel, Lain. *Birds of Nepal*. Kathmandu: Avalok, 1984. The comprehensive field guide. It can be ordered from Mrs. Vern Beieler, 1028 Crestwood Street, Wenatchee, WA 98801 U.S.A.

Gurung, K. K. *Heart of the Jungle: The Wildlife of Chitwan Nepal*. London: Andre Deutsch, 1983. Recommended for every visitor to Chitwan.

Hillard, Darla. *Vanishing Tracks: Four Years Among the Snow Leopards of Nepal*. New York: Arbor House, 1989. A study of these cats in the region northeast of Jumla.

Inskipp, Carol. *A Birdwatcher's Guide to Nepal*. Sandy, Great Britain: Bird Watchers' Guides, 1988. This useful book describes treks in terms of the birds to be seen there and gives descriptions of bird walks in specific areas.

————. *A Popular Guide to the Birds and Mammals of the Annapurna Conservation Area*. Kathmandu: ACAP, 1989. A brief look at the commonly seen creatures around Annapurna.

————. *Nepal's Forest Birds: Their status and conservation*. Cambridge: International Council for Bird Preservation, 1989. A resource for the serious birder—a synthesis of forest types and the birds inhabiting them, as well as detailed check lists of birds for parks and regions.

Inskipp, Carol, and Inskipp, Tim. *A Guide to the Birds of Nepal*. Beckenham, England: Christopher Helm, 1991. Not a pocket field guide, this monograph includes range and distribution maps of species, aids for identifying difficult birds, and information on bird-watching areas. A complement to the Fleming guide for the keen birder.

McKenzie, D. P., and Slater, J. G. "The evolution of the Indian Ocean," *Scientific American* (May 1973), 228: 62–72. Excellent discussion on plate tectonics and the Himalaya.

Mcdougal, Charles. *The Face of the Tiger*. London: Rivington Books, 1977. An ethnographiclike study of the Chitwan tiger.

Mierow, Dorothy, and Shrestha, Tirtha Bahadur. *Himalayan Flowers and Trees*. Kathmandu: Sahayogi Prakashan, 1978. Pictorial material to aid in identifying plants. The notes in the back are helpful.

Mishra, Hemanta Raj, and Mierow, Dorothy. *Wild Animals of Nepal*. Kathmandu: Ratna Pustak Bhandar, 1976. A useful species survey with line drawings.

Molnar, Peter. "The Geologic History and Structure of the Himalaya," *American Scientist* (March–April 1986), 74: 144–154. The next resource (after reading Geology in chapter 12) to extend the story.

Molnar, Peter, and Tapponnier, Paul. "The Collision between India and Eurasia," *Scientific American* (April 1977), 226: 30–41. Another look at the orogeny of the Himalaya.

Polunin, Oleg, and Stainton, Adam. *Concise Flowers of the Himalaya*. Delhi: Oxford University Press, 1987. A portable wealth of photographs and descriptions of the most common species, listed in the 1984 work.

————. *Flowers of the Himalaya*. Delhi: Oxford University Press, 1984. Together with Stainton's supplement, the best photographic record of flowering plants.

Prater, S. H. *The Book of Indian Animals*. Bombay: Bombay Natural History Society, 1980. Useful descriptions.

Regmi, Puskal Prasad. *An Introduction to Nepalese Food Plants*. Kathmandu: Royal Nepal Academy, 1982. Very helpful to those trying to identify exotic foods.

Schaller, George. *Stones of Silence: Journeys in the Himalaya*. New York: Viking Press, 1980. A book on the wild cats, sheep, and goats of the Himalaya. It is a fascinating synthesis of the author's observations and feelings about this ecosystem.

Shrestha, Bam Prasad. *Forest Plants of Nepal.* Kathmandu: Educational Enterprise, 1989. For the serious botanist.

Shrestha, Keshab Nepali. *Nepali Names for Plants.* Kathmandu: Natural History Museum, 1984. A compilation arranged by Nepali names with indexes. It is one more tool in trying to understand Nepal's prodigious flora.

Shrestha, Tirtha Bahadur. *Ecology and Vegetation of North-West Nepal.* Kathmandu: Royal Nepal Academy, 1982. Useful to trekkers venturing forth from Jumla. I hope that similar publications dealing with the rest of Nepal follow.

———. *Gymnosperms of Nepal.* Paris: CNRS, 1974. A useful guide to the identification of conifers.

Smith, Colin. *Butterflies of Nepal (Central Himalaya).* Bangkok: Tecpress, 1989. The long-awaited guide, with color photos, to all the species in Nepal!

———. *Beautiful Butterflies.* Kathmandu, 1990. An introduction with color photos.

Stainton, Adam. *Flowers of the Himalaya: A Supplement.* Delhi: Oxford University Press, 1988. More photographs and species to extend the seminal work of Polunin and Stainton.

Stainton, J. D. A. *Forests of Nepal.* London: John Murray, 1972. A detailed survey requiring knowledge of specific species.

Stocklin, J. "Geology of Nepal and its regional frame," *Jour. Geol. Soc., London,* (1980) 137: 1–34. Excellent technical resource.

Storrs, Adrian, and Storrs, Jimmie. *Discovering Trees in Nepal and the Himalayas.* Kathmandu: Sahayogi Press, 1984. A description of many of the species a trekker could see, together with black and white photographs. Unfortunately, there are important omissions, such as juniper and larch. There is no simple key to finding the write-up on a specimen in the field, so study of the book is needed.

———. *Enjoy Trees: A simple guide to some of the trees and shrubs found in Nepal.* Kathmandu: Sahayogi Press, 1987. A site guide to trees found, especially around the Kathmandu Valley, with helpful color photos. Also covers some of the roads in central Nepal and Chitwan.

Political Science

Mihaly, Eugene Bramer. *Foreign Aid and Politics in Nepal.* London: Oxford University Press, 1965. An early study. His conclusions may be valid today.

Rose, Leo E. *Nepal Strategy for Survival.* Berkeley: University of California Press, 1971. A political history.

Regional

Chorlton, Windsor. *Cloud-Dwellers of the Himalayas: The Bhotia.* Amsterdam: Time-Life Books, 1982. A photodocumentary of life in Nar-Phu.

Coburn, Broughton. *Nepali aama: Portrait of a Nepalese Hill Woman.* Santa Barbara, California: Ross-Erikson, 1982. A sensitive look at life in a *Gurung* village, told by an old woman.

Downs, Hugh R. *Rhythms of a Himalayan Village*. New York: Harper and Row, 1980. A photodocumentary of a Sherpa village in Solu—a most helpful book for understanding *Mani-rimdu* and how Sherpas may view their land.

Gurung, Nareshwar Jang. "An Introduction to the Socio-Economic Structure of Manang District." *Kailash* (1976) 4:295–308. Helpful to understand the *Manangba*.

Hall, Andrew R. "Preliminary Report on the Langtang Region." *Contributions to Nepalese Studies* (June 1978) 5:51–68. An ecological analysis.

Jefferies, Margaret, and Clarbrough, Margaret. *Sagarmatha, Mother of the Universe: The Story of Mount Everest National Park*. Auckland: Cobb/Horwood, 1986. The best single source of information on the Khumbu.

Jest, Corneille. *Dolpo: Communautes de Langue Tibetaine du Nepal*. Paris: CNRS, 1975. A monograph on this area, which has recently partially opened up for trekkers.

———. *Monuments of Northern Nepal*. Paris: UNESCO, 1981. Helpful for the trekker to Thak Khola, Muktinath, Helambu, and Solu-Khumbu.

———. *Tarap*. Paris: Seuil, 1974. A photodocumentary of life in a Dolpo valley.

Mishra, Hemanta R., and Margaret Jefferies. *Royal Chitwan National Park: Wildlife Heritage of Nepal*. Seattle: The Mountaineers, 1991. Also published by David Bateman, Ltd., New Zealand. The best single guide to Chitwan.

Sestini, Valerio, and Somigli, Enzo. *Sherpa Architecture*. Paris: UNESCO, 1978. A record of this tradition, which is changing due to modern influences.

Shepherd, Gary. *Life Among the Magars*. Kathmandu: Sahayogi Press, 1982. The experience of a Summer Institute of Linguistics family living among this ethnic group.

Valli, Eric, and Summers, Diane. *Honey Hunters of Nepal*. London: Thames and Hudson, 1988. An outstanding photo essay of *Gurungs* who hang from bamboo ladders and obtain honey from the large tonguelike hives you may have seen on your treks!

Van Spengen, Win. "The Nyishanga of Manang: Geographical Perspective on the Rise of a Nepalese Trading Community." *Kailash* (1987) 13: 131–278. An informative look at these world travelers.

Zangbu, Ngawang Tenzing, and Klatzel, Frances. *Stories and Customs of the Sherpas*. Kathmandu: Khumbu Cultural Conservation Committee, 1988. A concise, helpful booklet.

Religion

Anderson, Wait. *Open Secrets: A Western Guide to Tibetan Buddhism*. New York: Viking, 1979; Penguin, 1980. Some may find this modern approach useful.

Bernbaum, Edwin. *The Way to Shambhala*. New York: Anchor Press, 1980. An exploration of the myth of the mystical kingdom hidden behind the Himalaya, believed in by many of Nepal's highlanders.

Blofeld, John. *The Tantric Mysticism of Tibet*. Boulder, Colorado: Prajna Press, 1982.

Conze, Edward. *Buddhism, Its Essence and Development*. Oxford: Bruno Cassirer 1951; New York: Harper & Row, 1959. A classic work on the basics.

Detmold, Geogrey, and Rubel, Mary. *The Gods and Goddesses of Nepal*. Kathmandu: Ratna Pustak Bhandar, 1979. Deals primarily with the Kathmandu Valley. But it is nevertheless very useful for Nepal in general.

Jerstad, L. G. *Mani-rimdu, Sherpa Dance Drama*. Seattle: University of Washington Press, 1969. Useful for an understanding of the festival. It also contains introductory chapters on religion and the Sherpas.

Sen, K. M. *Hinduism*. Harmondsworth: Penguin Books, 1961.

Snellgrove, David. *Buddhist Himalaya*. Oxford: Bruno Cassirer, 1957. An understanding of Buddhism is a prerequisite for this book. It deals with the Solu-Khumbu region and the Buddhism of Sherpas and of Kathmandu.

Tucci, Giuseppe. *The Religions of Tibet*. London: Routledge & Kegan Paul; and New Delhi: Allied, 1980. A comprehensive detailed account.

Von Furer-Haimendorf, Christoph. "A Nunnery in Nepal," *Kailash* (1976) 4:121–154. Deals with Bigu Gomba in a scholarly fashion.

Waddel, L. A. *The Buddhism of Tibet or Lamaism*. Cambridge: W. Heffer, 1967. A reprint of a 1895 book that describes the religion and its practices.

Zaehner, R. C. *Hinduism*. London: Oxford University Press, 1966.

Travelogues

Allen, Linda Buchanan. *High Mountain Challenge: a guide for young mountaineers*. Boston: Appalachian Mountain Club, 1989. An account of a trek and trekking-peak climb in Khumbu, with basic mountaineering information, suited for teenagers.

Antin, Parker, and Weiss, Phyllis W. *Himalayan Odyssey: The Perilous Trek to Western Nepal*. New York: Donald I. Fine, 1990. An engrossing account.

Brook, Elaine, and Donnelly, Julie. *The Windhorse*. London: Jonothan Cape, 1986. A travelogue by a blind lady that opens our eyes!

Crane, Richard, and Crane, Adrian. *Running the Himalayas*. London: New English Library, 1984.

Deutschle, Phil. *The Two-Year Mountain*. New York: Universe Books, 1986. An allegory of a Nepal Peace Corps volunteer's climb.

Dingle, Graeme, and Hillary, Peter. *First Across the Roof of the World*. Auckland: Hodder and Stoughton, 1982. The story of an ambitious trekking traverse along the length of the Himalaya.

Greenwald, Jeff. *Shopping for Buddhas*. San Francisco: Harper and Row, 1990. A Kathmandu-centered allegory that offers a modern perspective on matters both serious and sweet.

Gurung, Harka. *Nature and Culture: Random Reflections*. Kathmandu, 1989. A collection of essays.

———. *Vignettes of Nepal*. Kathmandu: Sajha Prakashan, 1980. An account of a

Nepali geographer's many treks in his country's remote regions. It is a source of inspiration for the veteran trekker looking for new horizons.

O'Connor, Bill. *Adventure Treks: Nepal.* Wiltshire: Crowood Press, 1990. Not a guidebook, but a personal narrative, mostly of climbs and the treks to them.

Pilkington, John. *Into Thin Air.* London: George Allen & Unwin, 1985. An account of a trek west to Jumla below Dolpo.

Pye-Smith, Charlie. *Travels in Nepal: The Sequestered Kingdom.* London: Aurum Press, 1988. A recent visitor's view of diverse aspects.

Rowell, Galen. *Many people come, looking, looking.* Seattle: The Mountaineers, 1980. A beautifully photographed look at trekking and climbing in the Himalaya.

Snellgrove, David. *Himalayan Pilgrimage.* Boulder, Colorado: Prajna Press, 1981. A chronicle of travel through north-central and northwestern Nepal in the 1950s. Though scholars question his observations about hill regions, his wide range of interests and acute powers of observation make for fascinating reading.

Tucci, Giuseppe. *Journey to Mustang, 1952.* Kathmandu: Ratna Pustak Bhandar, 1977. Much of this early journey describes the popular trek to Jomosom. Read it to sense the changes.

Trekking

Armington, Stan. *Trekking in the Nepal Himalaya.* South Yarra, Australia: Lonely Planet, 1985. Treks described on a day-by-day basis.

Byers III, Alton C. *Treks on the Kathmandu Valley Rim.* Kathmandu: Sahayogi Press, 1987.

Chester, Jonathan. *The Himalayan Experience: An introduction to trekking and climbing in the Himalaya.* Brookvale: Simon & Schuster Australia, 1989. A photo survey.

Gurung, Harka. *Maps of Nepal.* Bangkok: White Orchid Press, 1983. A detailed look at the history of cartography in Nepal. A catalogue—of no help for route finding.

Iozawa, Tomoya. *Trekking in the Himalayas.* Tokyo: Yama-Kei; and Bombay: Allied, 1980. Has good color photographs, sketches, detailed drawings, and maps of popular trekking areas. The English text is disappointing.

Kaplan, Amy R. *The Nepal Trekker's Handbook.* New Haven, Connecticut: Mustang, 1989. A misleading title, but with general information about trekking.

Kasajoo, Vinaya Kumar. *Palpa As You Like It.* Tansen, Nepal: Kumar Press, 1988. An attempt to put this district on the tourist map.

Lall, Kesar. *Nepalese Customs and Manners.* Kathmandu: Ratna Pustak Bhandar, 1990. Useful information.

Nakano, Toru. *Trekking in Nepal.* Union City, CA: Heian International Inc., 1985. A translation of a Japanese book, containing brief descriptions with maps and photographs of many treks in eastern and central Nepal.

O'Connor, Bill. *The Trekking Peaks of Nepal*. Seattle: Cloudcap Press, 1989. Also published in Great Britain by Crowood Press. A detailed guide to the eighteen summits.

Rana, Greta; Haberli, Christian; and Gerard, Neville. *Dolakha: Trekking and Sightseeing off the Beaten Track*. Kathmandu: Integrated Hill Development Project, 1984. A delightful guide to an easily visited area that does not see many tourists.

Swift, Hugh. *Trekking in Nepal, West Tibet, and Bhutan*. San Francisco: Sierra Club, 1989. Ambitious in scope, it is enjoyable to read. An appetizer rather than a detailed guide, it gives general information about the routes.

Trekking Medicine

Auerbach, Paul S., and Geehr, Edward C. *Management of Wilderness and Environmental Emergencies*. St. Louis, Missouri: C. V. Mosby, 1989. A thorough reference oriented toward health professionals.

Bezruchka, Stephen. *The Pocket Doctor: Your Ticket to Good Health While Traveling*. Seattle: The Mountaineers, 1988. An inexpensive, small, carry-along book to help you prepare and deal with health problems while traveling.

Hackett, Peter. *Mountain Sickness: Prevention, Recognition, and Treatment*. New York: American Alpine Club, 1980. A small, useful booklet. The author is at the forefront of clinical high-altitude knowledge.

Houston, Charles. *Going Higher*. Boston: Little Brown, 1987. Invaluable for understanding what is going on inside you as you climb. The author is the dean of researchers into human diseases of altitude.

Nahlen, Bernard L., *et. al.* "International travel and the child younger than two years: II. Recommendations for prevention of travelers' diarrhea and malaria chemoprophylaxis." *Pediatric Infectious Diseases* (1989) 8: 735–739. A useful reference for your doctor if he or she doesn't often deal with this subject.

Preblud, Stephen R., *et. al.* "International travel and the child younger than two years: I. Recommendations for immunization." *Pediatric Infectious Diseases* (1989) 8: 416–425. Another useful reference for your doctor.

Shlim, David R., and Houston, Robin. "Helicopter Rescues and Deaths Among Trekkers in Nepal" *Jr. Am. Med. Assoc.* (February 17, 1989) 261: 1017–1019. A paper that confirms the relative safety of this activity.

Steele, Peter. *Medical Handbook for Mountaineers*. London: Constable, 1988. Comparable to *Medicine for Mountaineering* listed below, reflecting a British–Canadian point of view.

Ward, Michael P.; Milledge, James S.; and West, John B. *High Altitude Medicine and Physiology*. Philadelphia: University of Pennsylvania Press. 1989. An excellent survey of problems associated with cold and high altitudes. Although it covers therapeutics, this tome is not a carry-along guide.

Wilkerson, James A. *Medicine for Mountaineering*. Seattle: The Mountaineers, 1985. A practical book designed for the layman, yet dealing with the entire spectrum of medical problems encountered in the mountains.

PERIODICALS ON NEPAL

A new publication, titled *Himal,* deals with Himalayan development and environmental issues in a broad context. It is produced, by and large, by Nepalis and other Himalayan nationals, along with other contributors. It sports a unique design, with theme issues, follow-ups on previous issues, abstracts of other publications, and a feature from a yeti perspective appropriately titled "Abominably Yours." You won't find it on the newsstand, but can subscribe by contacting Himal Associates, G.P.O. Box 42, Lalitpur, Nepal.

Scholars might find the *Himalayan Research Bulletin* a useful medium for exchange. Membership in the Nepal Studies Association will bring copies. Contact the Southern Asian Institute, School of International and Public Affairs, Columbia University, New York, NY 10027, U.S.A.

The best source of diverse information on Nepal is the weekly *Nepal Press Digest,* from Regmi Ville, Lazimpat, Kathmandu.

Individuals wishing to keep current on Tibetan affairs might subscribe to *Tibetan Review,* by contacting The Editor, D-11, East of Kailash, New Delhi, 110 065, India.

Finally, people wishing to understand development issues in a broad sense might look at *The New Internationalist,* a British publication reporting on issues of world poverty and inequality. Its somewhat radical point of view is quite different from the usual Western press, as it focuses on problems that are contributed to by the powerful nations. Subscription inquiries can be directed to P.O. Box 1143, Lewiston, NY 14092, U.S.A.

A crew of porters makes the annual trip to a bazaar to replenish supplies for their village.

C.   Questions to Ponder While Trekking

They have everything that money can buy, and they still want
something. That you can't buy with money.
Chundak Tenzing

This Nepali friend of mine from remote northeast Nepal had been educated as a doctor, and had lived for a time in North America. He made this remark when asked about his impression of people there.

Nepal provides marvelous food for thought. A manifold society with almost unfathomable ethnic diversity is layered over landscapes varying from tropical rain forest to snowy heights and desert. Paradoxically, the forces that shape Nepal are essentially very simple: its people endeavor to survive, while the land attempts to self-destruct through natural erosive forces.

There are too many facets to Nepal for an outsider to absorb in a single trip—or a lifetime. When I first came to Nepal, attracted by the incredible mountains, I was partially blinded to the people living among them. After spending more time in Nepal, however, I found the people—the culture, their ways of surviving in this harsh, upturned land—at least as interesting as the great peaks themselves. Once, some years ago, while I was working in western Nepal, a trekking group of expatriate schoolchildren from Kathmandu and Barry Mateer, their teacher, visited my project. They peppered me with good questions about the work being done there. Indeed, I later learned that each of them had been given a list of questions to report on after their trek. But the questions they were asking me were not from the list. The listed questions had merely heightened their curiosity.

I wish to share similar questions with you, to use as you see fit. Please don't try to read all of them at once. But when the urge strikes, perhaps after a few days on the trail, you might read a few to see how they sit. They are not a test or catechism, but one way perhaps of organizing the myriad impressions and observations that are accumulated during an extended trek in Nepal. There are no real answers for many of the questions, but I have occasionally indicated directions in which you may find it helpful to proceed.

Why are some villages composed of clustered houses, reminiscent of downtown Kathmandu, while others have dwellings either widely scattered over the hillside, or within shouting distance? What factors influence this diversity? (Ethnic group? Terrain?) Why are some villages close to the main trail, while others avoid it? Why do some villages near the trail have shops, while others don't? Why do homes and villages face the directions they do? How have people adapted their town plan to the environment?

Some villages have decorative adornment, such as painting on walls, or carved windows. Yet this is absent in others nearby. Why?

Have you noticed lines of communication in villages that follow an organized pattern? (Town crier?) What influence does the transistor radio have? What happens if a printed note or letter arrives? What evidence do you see of modern improvements to people's houses? How well maintained are they? What nonlocally produced materials are required for building? Who builds and maintains bridges, trails, water systems, other community projects? Why do so many of them seem in disrepair?

Have you taken trails in high-mountain areas without signs of much tourism and found the trails and bridges much better than lower down, where there may be more people traffic? Why?

What evidence is there of governmental influence in remote areas? Can you imagine any recording of vital events (births, deaths)? Do you see many calendars in use? How many of the Nepali people you pass know the day, date, and year? How do people keep track of time?

Do you see a great deal of illness as you travel? Is this what you expected? Among which age group is the greatest sickness and mortality? Whom do you think are the greatest consumers of health care? What are the greatest obstacles to better health among the Nepalis? What practices do the people undertake that promote good health? Are there differences in this regard among ethnic groups? What are the most constructive steps that can be taken to improve the health of the Nepalis?

Who makes up the household? What happens to old people, the mentally retarded, the physically handicapped? How much evidence of alcoholism do you see? How much leisure time do people have and how do they spend it? Is there much obesity? How are bodies disposed of? Can you identify a person's caste or ethnic group without asking? What factors go into your hunch? (Facial and body hair? Facial shape? Eye folds? Jewelry? Dress? The way people interact with others? Where they locate their village? The kind of work they do?)

Do people wear makeup? Which sexes or ethnic groups? What materials do they apply? Do you see mirrors? Are people concerned about their appearance as much as you expected? How physically close can people be to one another without feeling uncomfortable? What about eye contact, body language, posturing, and physical contact? Is there much physical display of affection?

What distinctions do you see between gender roles and identity? What kind of work do men do? Women? Who does what work and how does this vary with ethnic groups? What do children do most of the day? What do they play with? Do they cry as often as you might expect? Do you see them sucking their thumbs? At what age are children weaned? How many children go to school? Mostly boys or girls? Are they in school during harvest times, or other periods of intense farm work? Where are the village schools built? How many of them function? Are the classes held inside the building? What supplies does the school have? What means of learning are used? How much teaching is done by chanting? What jobs are available to the educated?

What is the role of young unmarried women? Do you ever see them alone, or are they always in groups? Do you ever see them talking to single men? How do teenagers entertain themselves? What are the status and role of old people?

How much evidence is there of religious activity in the hills? Are there daily practices? How does this vary among ethnic groups in the same area? Do you see statues, symbols, or idols that don't seem to belong to one of the two major religions in Nepal?

What styles of walking and carrying loads do you see among the Nepali people? Slow, steady pace? Many stops? What do they do when they stop? Estimate the weight of the heaviest porter load you see and compare it with his or her body weight. Try lifting it with the tumpline. Compare a porter's foot, especially one walking barefoot, with your own—its shape, position of the toes, etc. Your little toe probably curls under. Why?

Observe the age ranges of Nepali people who undertake long journeys. Does this this reflect the proportions present in the population? Do women undertake long trips?

What role do pets have in Nepali people's lives? Do you see many cats? What do Nepalis feed their pets and how do they treat them? Are they affectionate toward them in ways you would expect?

What domestic animals are given status in the community? How big are they compared to similar breeds in your home country? Who cares for them? What evidence of disease do you see? In what parts of the country do they keep pigs regularly? Why aren't there more horses? What parts of the animals do they use? At what age can a child begin tending an animal? Are wild animals hunted? With what? Which animals are feared? What parts of wild animals are used?

Some terraces are buttressed by rocks and others are not. Why? What crops are planted there? What crop patterns produce maximum productivity for the land? Do you see evidence of periodic slash-and-burn agriculture? What are the altitude limits for certain crops and animals? For what purposes are irrigation systems used, besides watering crops? How are they controlled? Do most of the farmers own the land they are working, or are they sharecroppers?

What is a typical day like for an average person in the hills? How does this differ for men and women? How much do people rest? What are the sleeping arrangements in Nepali homes? What do people seem to talk about with one another?

What kinds of goods are available in local stores? On the main trekking trails, what goods are purchased by the local inhabitants? Which are staples and which are luxuries? What is produced locally and what is imported? How dependent are the hill and mountain people on imported goods? What crafts are produced locally? Compare the use of the wheel in your society and in a remote area of Nepal.

Reflect on the friendliness of trekkers in different areas and circumstances— remote areas where few trekkers go, the well-trodden lodge routes, etc. What differences in ecological behavior do you see among trekkers from various countries? Any generalizations?

Do you see any evidence of natural catastrophes? What factors contribute to erosion besides deforestation? What kinds of wood-cutting practices do you see in different areas? Do you see evidence of reforestation? What attempts do you see by the Nepalis to control erosion?

What physical hazards are hill people exposed to as they go about their daily lives? What tools are used, and how did they evolve to their present designs? Which items are made locally and which are imported? Do you suspect that local production has increased, or decreased?

What modern consumer goods do you see in use? What did they replace, and how dependent are the people on them? How has this affected local craftsmen? How important is cash in trading and commerce? What are the major influences on the economy of the region you are passing through? How important are Gurkha pensions in supporting the hill economy? Can this have a deleterious effect? What are the specific and general benefits as well as the negative influences that road building has brought? What will be the changes in this area in ten years? Twenty years? How can you influence those changes positively?

What changes can you see that have resulted from modern development? What would be the major development effects you could make if you were the King? What problems would you foresee?

Discuss with innkeepers and villagers your concerns about conservation of Nepal's resources. Ask them about plans for the future in their area. Would they want to install a portable electric generator as some, where electricity is not planned, have stated? How would you feel about modern conveniences that might change the experience of trekking?

What do the Nepali people you meet have that you don't? Materially? Otherwise? What do you think they would most like to have of yours? What about your encounter do you think they talk about among themselves after you have left?

Why do Nepali people seem to cling to old ways that may, on reflection, seem to be foolish or counterproductive? If your return home from Nepal was suddenly made impossible, which of your cultural trappings would you cling to most tenaciously? Which would you insist on passing on to your children and grandchildren? If you had to live in the Nepali village you are in, what changes would you want to make? Would you be successful? What would be the hardest part of adapting? What would be the joys of staying here?

Fifty or a hundred years from now, imagine going through a Nepali museum showing artifacts of particular villages you have been through. Compare this imagined trip to one through a North American Indian Tribal museum you may have taken recently, or (as I did), a Ukrainian outdoor museum. Does tourism in Nepal replay the history of the white man coming to North America and changing the lives of the natives by economic and cultural exploitation?

Compare the situation in your country of the differences between the poor and the well-off with that in Nepal. How much wealthier are the well-off in your country compared to the poor there? In Nepal? Look at aspects like diet, leisure time, luxury goods, or ability to get around.

If you have traveled in other mountain areas of the Himalaya, how do your experiences there compare with those in Nepal? If you have been to Tibet, how do you relate to the Tibetans there, and those in Nepal? Is there is distinct Nepali character, a Nepali spirit, or is it just a piece of a larger Himalayan mosaic?

D. After Trekking in Nepal, What Next?

Nepal is growing up and so am I.

Some people who travel to Nepal for the first time are smitten, hopelessly in love with one of the poorest countries in the world. These Nepaleptics want a more serious experience with Nepal than is provided by tourism. Numerous requests come my way for further information on opportunities for such deeper involvement. In the following pages I have listed various possibilities, ranging from contributing to worthwhile projects in Nepal to having a more intense learning encounter to working there.

The remainder of this section has information on activities related to trekking. These include mountaineering, especially ascending the so-called trekking peaks, which, though not as tall as the giants that put Nepal on the map, provide challenges for many climbers. River rafting and bicycling have become popular; details are provided to help people wishing to pursue these activities there.

INTENSIVE STUDY IN NEPAL

The Experiment in International Living's School for International Training, Kipling Road, Brattleboro, VT 05301, U.S.A., or G.P.O. Box 1373, Kathmandu, Nepal, phone 414516.

The University of Wisconsin College Year in Nepal Program, South Asian Studies, University of Wisconsin, Madison, WI 54306, U.S.A., or G.P.O. Box 3059, Kathmandu, phone 215560.

World College West, G.P.O. Box 3725, Kathmandu, phone 413281.

WORTHWHILE PROJECTS TO SUPPORT

Many trekkers want to help Nepal in some way, to begin to repay some of the great wealth they have received by being here.

My criteria for worthwhile projects are somewhat stringent. Projects must spend little for administration, have a large component for local (Nepali) initiative, directly influence the most needy people, be sensitive to reasonable developmental or cultural needs and goals, and be small enough that modest contributions may make some difference. Efforts included here are those that do not get large media coverage. A variety with different foci are included for your consideration. Inclusion here does not guarantee that these criteria have been met, nor does exclusion imply that they haven't. When people send money, they should earmark the specific project on the check. It is difficult to search out such projects, and I would be happy to be kept better informed.

Nepal School Projects

The most remarkable example of a trekker working with the Nepali people to help themselves that I know of is Michael Rojik. On his first trek, this Toronto man realized that while the Sherpas had many admirers and benefactors, the poor *Tamang* porters did not have any. In 1974, he embarked on a selfless project to help build schools in very poor villages within a region that does not derive any economic benefit from tourism. To date, more than sixty schools have been built. Now termed the Nepal School Projects (NSP), it has evolved to become a comprehensive grassroots rural development program with the objective of meeting the "minimum basic needs" of subsistence hill peasants within the poorest and least developed regions of Nepal. These needs include the provision of potable water pipelines, aid in primary-level school construction, vocational training of illiterate and otherwise unemployable young adults, the training of village primary health-care workers, and the provision of free essential medical supplies. All projects are local initiative endeavors planned by the recipient communities, with NSP providing training and technical as well as material aid that cannot be met from local resources. The local participation in each project is substantial. This makes NSP work very cost effective, even by Nepali standards. With the contribution of local materials and labor, the costs of building a village school are on the order of an inexpensive automobile in Canada or the United States!

Nepal School Projects is a registered charitable organization in Canada and all donations are tax deductible. All NSP's development programs receive generous support from the Canadian International Development Agency (CIDA); however, the level of CIDA's support is based on the amount of donations received from the general public. NSP has no paid staff; all administrative work is done by unpaid volunteers. In Nepal, project implementation is supervised by local people. NSP cannot offer employment to expatriates to work on projects in Nepal. Detailed progress reports on NSP's development activities are available on request.

Donations, with checks payable to Nepal School Projects, can be sent to 63 Perivale Crescent, Scarborough, Ontario M1J 2C4, Canada.

World Neighbors

Another organization to consider is a small U.S.-based private development organization called World Neighbors. It receives no government funds, and supports only local Nepali organizations and communities working in reforestation, soil erosion, family planning and health, livestock improvement, and production of local crafts, which give income primarily to women. Some examples of its work are: (1) training village people to organize their own "user groups" for constructing drinking water systems; it provides only materials like pipe, cement, and training, "matched" by local community contributions of labor, portering materials from the road, maintenance, etc., and (2) establishing community nurseries for fodder, fuelwood, and horticulture seedlings, which can be self-sustaining.

Contributions of U.S. $50 can support a villager to produce 1000 seedlings for planting on his (or her) private land, and training for future production, to take the pressure off of overused land. U.S. $500 can build a protected water system for about 20 families!

Contributions are tax deductible in the U.S., and can be made to World Neighbors, 5116 North Portland Avenue, Oklahoma City, OK 73112, earmarked for development activities in Nepal. They can also be made locally in local currency, c/o World Neighbors, P.O. Box 916, Kathmandu, Nepal (phone 411308) and will be receipted in U.S. dollars for purposes of tax deduction if required.

Association for Craft Producers

Association for Craft Producers is a local organization that provides marketing, design, and quality-control support to rural producers of crafts. Hand block printing was a dying traditional craft in Nepal until revived by the association, with new products for old designs. Products, including pillow covers, bedspreads, and sweaters, may be purchased through the nonprofit retail outlet, Dhukuti, which is located across the Bagmati bridge to PaaTan, on the right-hand side before the Himalaya Hotel (in Kupondole). People interested in observing craft production or making arrangements for export can contact the association's design center in Kalimati.

World Education

Literacy, especially maternal literacy, appears to be one of the most important influences on child health, and is generally seen as a major empowering factor in the least developed countries. Nepal has one of the lowest literacy rates of any country in the world. While literacy programs have grown and the primary school system is improving, there is little for people to read in rural Nepali villages, and what exists is written in a Sanskritized form of the language that minimally literate villagers can't read. World Education is working to develop simple, interesting, entertaining, and useful reading material for new literates. Five dollars can produce and distribute reading material for one family, U.S. $25 can provide a village-wall newspaper for 100 villages, and $100 can result in an entire village having a small library. Tax-deductible contributions can be sent to World Education, 210 Lincoln Street, Boston, MA 02111, U.S.A.

Nepal Disabled Assocation

The Swiss-supported Terre des hommes runs the Nursing Home for Disabled Children in Jorpati in the Kathmandu Valley to provide rehabilitation services for children crippled by polio, born with congenital deformities, and most importantly, disfigured by burns and untreated accidents. All services are provided free of charge. The cost of a bed per day here is about U.S. $10 (compare that with your own country!). This project is supported by donations, which can be sent to P.O. Box 2430, Kathmandu, Nepal.

Tengboche Trust

Visitors to Khumbu will wonder what is happening to Sherpa culture. In fact, steps are being taken by the Sherpas themselves to preserve it. Much of the impetus comes from the incarnate Lama at Tengboche, Nawang Tenzing Jangpo. A Sherpa Cultural Center has been constructed there. Funds to support this project can be made payable to Tengboche School, and sent to The Tengboche Trust, P.O. Box 2236, Kathmandu, Nepal.

Ashoka

This nonprofit organization seeks out and supports individuals who have innovative ideas for public service projects and the entrepreneurial drive and aptitude to transform their ideas into reality. These Ashoka Fellows receive a stipend for three years to help pay for their living expenses, freeing them to work on the implementation of their programs. In Nepal, Ashoka Fellows have developed projects for environmental education and protection, education reform, improving public water supplies, introducing modern journalism, providing legal assistance for the poor, and providing community education through street and traditional theater. Contributions are tax deductible and can be sent to Ashoka, 1200 North Nash Street, Arlington, VA 22209, U.S.A. Committees of volunteers in several American cities and London support Ashoka and conduct local education programs. For information, write to the above address, or, in the U.S., call (703) 628-0370.

Himalayan Rescue Assocation

This organization operates the Trekker's Aid Posts in the Khumbu and Manang areas, and its education programs have been partly responsible for the decrease in deaths of trekkers from altitude illness. The association subsists entirely on voluntary funding, supplies, and staffing. Donations can be made at their offices in Thamel, by the Kathmandu Guest House, or to P.O. Box 495, Kathmandu, Nepal.

International Snow Leopard Trust

This organization works with governments, organizations, and individuals to conserve snow leopards (and other high-mountain wildlife) as well as supporting endeavors that improve the lives of people who share its habitat. Members are informed through a newsletter, *Snowline*. Become a member and support their activities by writing to the Trust at 4649 Sunnyside Avenue North, Seattle, WA 98103, U.S.A., phone (206) 632-2421.

King Mahendra Trust for Nature Conservation

KMTNC is an nongovernmental conservation organization that helped establish the Annapurna Conservation Area Project (ACAP), which seeks to link conservation directly with sustainable development. KMTNC was established under the patronage of King Birendra Bir Bikram Shah Dev and is represented by offices in Britain, France, Japan, and the U.S. Besides the Annapurna project, KMTNC supports diverse conservation, research, and education projects in other parts of Nepal. Donations can be sent to the Trust at P.O. Box 3712, Babar Mahal, Kathmandu, Nepal, (phone 223229), or to KMTNC, c/o World Wildlife Fund—USA, 1250 24th Street NW, Washington, DC 20037, phone (202) 293-4800.

Woodlands Mountain Institute

WMI is working with the Department of National Parks and Wildlife Conservation to protect a 3,000 sq km area west of Sagarmatha National Park that encompasses exceptionally rich forests and cultural sites. WMI is also working with the Tibet Autonomous Region and China to protect a 36,000 sq km area extending from beyond Shishapangma in the west to the Kharta Valley in the east, including Mount Chomolongma (as Mount Everest is known in Tibet). Contact Woodlands Mountain Institute, Main and Dogwood Streets, Franklin, WV 26807, U.S.A., phone (304) 358-2401 to donate.

International Trust for Nature Conservation

ITNC supports conservation projects, primarily in Nepal and India. Currently they include the Long Term Tiger Monitoring Project, Pokhara's Pheasant Project, Chitwan Project, and the Mahaguthi Project. Donations, earmarked for specific projects, should be sent to: ITNC, c/o Assistant Director, Royal Geographical Society, 1 Kensington Gore, London SW7 2AR, England.

Save the Children

My initial reaction to this organization was negative, because I felt it inappropriate to single out poor individuals and give them money. The word "poor" is one that the Nepalis now know through their contact with outsiders. Furtherance of that concept will erode their self-respect, which may be their most valuable resource. However, I have come to learn that this organization uses sponsorship as a means of attracting donors, but channels the funds directly into local development projects with considerable village input. No funds go directly to the sponsored child. For some people, helping fund development work by identification with a family and a child is important, and this project provides the means. Contributions are tax deductible in the U.S. For more information, write to Save the Children, 50 Wilton Road, Westport, CT 06880.

Seva Foundation

This band of physicians, ex-hippie activists, mystics, educators, and a clown rally around the rubric of Sixties love and service. In Nepal they have been involved in projects organized through Nepali organizations to prevent blindness, restore sight, and help establish self-sufficiency in eye care. Contributions (tax deductible in the U.S.) can be sent to Seva Foundation, 108 Spring Lake Drive, Chelsea, MI 48118.

Britain Nepal Medical Trust

Set up over twenty years ago by a few British doctors, the trust is involved in tuberculosis and leprosy control in the eastern part of Nepal, and has been involved in other aspects of health-care development as well. Donations can be made to Britain Nepal Medical Trust, Stafford House, 16 East Street, Tonbridge, Kent, TN9 1HG, England.

WORKING IN NEPAL

There are many opportunities but it is not possible to go into great detail here. Many countries have volunteer organizations: Peace Corps, U.S.A.; VSO, United Kingdom; Japanese and German Volunteers, and so forth. There are numerous nongovernmental organizations involved in Nepal, as well as bilateral (government to government) projects. I am most often asked about opportunities to work in the area of health care. One resource I can provide is an article by John Dickinson, "Where Shall John Go? Nepal," in *British Medical Journal,* Volume 2, December 4, 1976, pages 1364–1366. All of the organizations listed there still function.

Physicians with appropriate backgrounds may wish to volunteer their services to the Himalayan Rescue Association's Trekker's Aid Posts. Applicants should send a *curriculum vitae* including credentials, wilderness and/or mountaineering experience, training in high-altitude medicine, site preference (Khumbu or Manang), and reasons for volunteering to: David R. Shlim, M.D., Medical Director, Himalayan Rescue Association, G.P.O. Box 495, Kathmandu, Nepal.

Consider a job teaching English if you have the skills. Others might consider becoming trek leaders, either for foreign agencies contracting with Nepali ones, or with the Nepali ones directly. Being a trek leader requires specific client- and group-oriented skills, not just the ability to navigate the trails of Nepal.

To work in Nepal is, I feel, a rare privilege. The Nepali people are quite capable of dealing with their problems on their own, as they have for countless centuries. It is an extreme form of arrogance to believe that they must have our help. A development project is often a two-edged sword. Sometimes the greatest beneficiaries of these projects are the expatriates who have worked in them. In my own endeavors, I have always felt that I received more from working in Nepal, providing health care, than the people gained from me.

E. Activities Related to Trekking

MOUNTAINEERING

Among the first outsiders to come to Nepal were mountaineers looking for ways onto the highest summits. Much of the early descriptions of the countryside comes from them. The history of climbing on the highest peaks is itself fascinating, and has been well chronicled.

Besides the many expeditionary peaks listed below, there are eighteen minor peaks, called "trekking summits," which can be climbed by trekkers if they get the proper permits. The fact that they are called trekking summits in no ways implies that they are trivial. Some are difficult and dangerous, and a few have only recently had first ascents. These summits are not suitable for trekkers who do not have substantial experience in alpine climbing. Further information on these climbs can be obtained from Bill O'Connor's book *The Trekking Peaks of Nepal* (listed in appendix B), mountaineering journals, trekking agencies, and the climbing community.

To attempt one of these peaks, application must be made to the Nepal Mountaineering Association (NMA), G.P.O. Box 1435, Naxal, Hattisar, Kathmandu, Nepal, phone 411525. Permission is granted for one month, and may be extended. This period applies only to the time spent at or above base camp. Applications are on a first come, first served basis and are not transferable. A fee must be paid, and for groups exceeding ten members an extra charge is levied for each additional climber. The charge for the time extension is 25 percent of the original fee. Fees are payable at the time of application and are nonrefundable. Climbers can apply after they arrive in Nepal.

A Sirdar or guide registered with the NMA must accompany each party. He must be provided with a salary, food, and tent accommodations. If he is required to go above base camp, he must be furnished with climbing equipment and clothing, and insured to Rs. 150,000. High-altitude porters must be insured for Rs 100,000. All climbing must be clean: hardware must be removed and camps left clean. Finally, a report must be submitted to the NMA upon return. Applications should include the climbing fee and the following information: the name of the peak; the period of time for which the permit is requested; the route (peaks can be climbed by any route); the name and nationality of each member of the party; the name, nationality, passport number, and home address of the leader; the appointed representative in Kathmandu (usually a trekking agency); and the name and organization or address of the guide or Sirdar.

The trekking peaks, grouped according to the area and using the term *Himal*, which means range, are:

KHUMBU HIMAL
Imja Tse (Island Peak) (6160 m)
Kwangde (6011 m)
Kusum Kangru (6367 m)
Lobuje (Lobuche) East (6119 m)
Khongma Tse (Mehra Peak) (5820 m)
Mera Peak (6476 m)
Pokalde (5806 m)

ROLWALING HIMAL
Pharchamo (6187 m)
Ramdung (5925 m)

LANGTANG HIMAL
Naya Kanga (5844 m)

GANESH HIMAL	ANNAPURNA HIMAL
Paldor Peak (5928 m)	Singu Chuli (Fluted Peak) (6501 m)
	Hiunchuli (6331 m)
MANANG HIMAL	Mardi Himal (5555 m)
Chulu East (6584 m)	Tharpu Chuli (Tent Peak) (5500 m)
Chulu West (6419 m)	
Pisang (6091 m)	

If you have been to Kala Pattar and other high-altitude trekking destinations in Nepal and are looking for new "summits," are trekking peaks for you? If you are not a mountaineer, by and large the answer is no. While some are not technically difficult, they do involve mountaineering skills, unlike almost all the treks described in this book, which require just walking. Considerable familiarity with climbing on rock, ice, and snow and ice, camping on snow, and the understanding of objective hazards is necessary.

The general rules and regulations for expeditionary peaks are too lengthy to document here. These regulations can be obtained by writing to the Ministry of Tourism, His Majesty's Government, Kathmandu, Nepal. Essentially, a license must be obtained by application to the Ministry of Tourism "with the recommendation of a reputed and recognized mountaineering institution in the appropriate country or the embassy of that country in Nepal." Usually this is the national alpine club, if one exists. A royalty must be paid and the party must take a liaison officer chosen by the government. There are rules governing what he must be provided and paid; these rules also describe his duties and functions. There are similar rules regarding the Sirdar and high-altitude porters. Penalties for disregarding the rules include banishment from Nepal for three to five years or disqualification from climbing in Nepal for five to ten years. An institution that disregards the rules can be disqualified from sponsoring climbs for three years.

RIVER RUNNING

Over the last ten years, many of the great rivers of Nepal have been run by rubber rafts, canoes, kayaks, and other craft. There is nothing unique about rivers in Nepal as far as such activities are concerned. There are the usual difficulties in transporting the boats to the starting point and arranging to have them picked up at the destination. Rivers commonly rafted include the Trisuli and the Gandaki. You can arrange motor transportation to and from these rivers. Another popular choice is the Sun Kosi. You can go by vehicle to the starting point, but you must fly back from Biratnagar after the journey. Rivers like the Bheri, the Marsyangdi, and the Arun offer more challenges because of logistic problems. Others, such as the Karnali, are extremely challenging.

While some professional river runners have done expeditionary trips independently, most people deal with agencies in Nepal that specialize in rafting (see appendix A for addresses).

RUNNING

Running, which has become very popular in the West, has in some measure come to Nepal. While few Nepalis run regularly along the trails, stories abound of incredibly short times taken by Nepalis, usually as mail runners for mountaineering expeditions. Jay Longacre became known in much of Nepal as "The American Runner" for his four-and-a-quarter-day run from Kathmandu to Kala Pattar near the base of Mount Everest, a journey that takes more than fifteen days to trek. Few people will want to challenge that record, but some may wish to combine running with trekking. On some slow group treks, people may wish more exercise. There are now long races in Nepal, including a biannual Everest Marathon. The following information is based on Jay's experiences in Nepal.

Most of the information for trekkers applies also to runners and won't be repeated here. The problems of altitude illness are very important and the cautions in chapter 5 must be heeded. Physical conditioning does not prevent these problems. Runners, if they are alert to the symptoms, should at least be able to descend quickly to safety. If they persist in ascending despite serious symptoms, their risk is certainly greater. However, most runners won't be able to continue running, even with mild symptoms.

One danger of steep mountain running is the possibility of falling off the trail. If a runner stumbles, he should try to fall on his hands and knees onto the dirt. If he tries to remain upright, he may lurch off the trail and down the mountainside. To prevent injury, runners must master the techniques of running downhill. To avoid falling and injuring joints, a runner must shorten his stride, strike heel first with the knee slightly bent, and lean backward as little as possible. Practice it on hills near home first.

Proper shoes and clothing are basics for a pleasant run. Ripple-soled running shoes are preferable to waffle-soled shoes. The latter tend to wear quickly and to grip the trail too well, causing the feet to slide within the shoes. This causes blisters. Running without socks may help prevent blisters, and it enables the runner to walk through water and across rivers easily.

Basically there are two ways of running outside the major cities and towns in Nepal: long solo runs covering two or more days and 50 mi (80 km) or more; and daily runs of more than 1 hour, alone or with a group, along or close to one of the main trekking trails. On long solo runs, you should retain a Sherpa guide (not a porter) to meet you at the end of your run with extra clothes and other needed supplies. On the run itself you need to carry sunscreen, petrolatum jelly, soap, face mask, wool mittens, one suit of long wool underwear, cap with a long bill, nylon all-weather suit, Nepali money, cup, sleeping bag, water bottle, iodine, map, pen, notebook, flashlight, sunglasses, extra clothes, and this book. All of this will fit into a small pack and needn't weigh more than a few pounds. Wear shorts, a tee shirt, and running shoes.

For daily runs along a main trekking route, hire a Sherpa guide to carry your sleeping bag and supplies. He can help by explaining the trails and by leaving earlier to wait for you at difficult or confusing areas. On these daily runs, you need only carry a cup, soap, petrolatum jelly, sunscreen, camera, iodine, and water bottle.

It is important to force yourself to drink frequently to prevent dehydration, even if you don't feel thirsty. It is unlikely you could drink too much.

Runners have greater difficulty with anal irritation than do trekkers. After each bowel movement, wash to help prevent irritation. Use the water in your bottle if necessary.

BICYCLING

Nepal may never be the most popular spot for cycle tourists, but the spectacular scenery, almost traffic-free roads, and curious, hospitable Nepalis make the country a cycling haven. Mountain bikes have become popular in Kathmandu among Nepalis, too. I have reservations about recommending bicycling off the roads used for motor vehicles in Nepal because of the adverse effects on the trails and culture of Nepal. However, if you think bicycling the trails of Nepal may be for you, here are some suggestions gleaned from *girwaalas,* as mountain bikers are called by Nepali cognoscenti.

Touring the country on the rather limited road network is easy enough with any properly outfitted ten-speed bike or, better, on a mountain bike. Riding the trekking routes is feasible, with a mountain bike. Most importantly, the bike you take should be in top running condition, and you should be prepared to handle any mechanical problem that might arise. Although there are now some bicycle shops in Kathmandu that cater to these high-tech creatures, out beyond, you are on your own! Bring along a few spare tubes, a spare tire, extra spokes, brake and gear cables, puncture kit, a pump, and possibly an extra rear derailleur, as well as any tools needed to work on the bike. If you go with a group of cyclists, then you can share the tools, and your individual load will be less.

The choice of a route is important. The route from Kathmandu to Everest goes against the grain of the land, and requires considerable bicycle carrying. Other routes going up the Kali Gandaki, or even the Annapurna circuit, would offer easier stretches. Some cyclists have flown to Lukla and bicycled up from there. This option involves considerably fewer ascents and descents than bicycling all the way from Kathmandu. An estimate from one *girwaala* is that in the Annapurna circuit, you can ride 80 percent of the distance, carrying for 20 percent. On the Kali Gandaki side, the ratio is closer to 60/40, and this seems to be about right for Langtang.

Riding a mountain bike on the trekking trails is not always easy, but it is an interesting and often thrilling alternative to walking. The bike, fitted with a rear pannier carrying your day's needs, should weigh no more than forty pounds. Some cyclists found that panniers are not suitable for the rough trails, and carry a light pack instead. Such a bike, so outfitted, is quite manageable for the motivated trekker to carry and ride. On the rougher sections of the trail, the bike can be carried over your shoulder, or on your back by using a tumpline. Pushing the bike over rough sections is not always easier, but it does give your shoulder or back a rest. The condition of the trail and your level of fitness will determine how much ground you can cover per day. You can expect to go about three-quarters to three times the speed of a walking trekker.

Coordinating your ride with a porter carrying your gear is not a problem. Just plan to meet at points along the day's trek for tea, lunch, and so forth. You must realize, though, that many natives along the trail have never seen a bicycle before, so you'll be a real spectacle—something that might detract from a quiet mountain experience.

A small, light security cable is a good idea to discourage unauthorized test rides when you're not around your bike. If you carry any exposed items that might attract attention, keep an eye on your bicycle, or better still, remove that gear and keep it with you when you leave the vehicle.

Three last tips: invest in a bell—it speaks a universal language. Beware of yaks on the trail; they get very nervous around a bike and may run you off the trail. It is best to stop, dismount on the uphill side of the trail, and let them walk by. The same advice goes for buffaloes and other bovines, though yaks are the most temperamental. Finally, don't forget to ride on the left-hand side of the prayer walls. Happy trails!

F. Glossary of Nepali and Tibetan Words

bhaat	cooked rice
bhaTmaas	soybeans
bhaTTi	traditional Nepali inn
BhoTiya	Buddhist highlander of Nepal
charpi	latrine
chang	locally brewed beer
chAUmri or **zopkio**	a cross between a yak and a cow
chautaara	rectangular resting platform on a trail
chilim	clay pipe for smoking
chorten	Buddhist religious cubical structure
daal	lentil-like sauce poured over rice
daru or **rakshi**	a *Thakali* distilled spirit
dhaarni	measure of weight (approximately 6 lb, or 2.7 kg)
dharmsala	rest house
Doko	conical basket for carrying loads
drokpa	Tibetan nomad
ghiu (ghee in India)	clarified butter
gomba	Tibetan Buddhist temple
goTh	shelter used by shepherds
haatisaar	elephant camp
himaal	mountain (snow peak)
jAAR	locally brewed beer
juTho	socially unacceptable, or polluting
kata	ceremonial scarf of white cheesecloth
khola	river
lekh	hill
loTaa	vessel for carrying water to clean oneself after defecating
maanaa	volume measure (20 oz, 2 ½ cups, or 0.7 l)
machaan	blind for observing animals
mani	prayer
memsahib	honorific title used by Nepalis for female foreigners
naamlo	tumpline
namaskaar	traditional greeting (very polite and formal)
namaste	traditional greeting (less formal)
paathi	volume measure equal to eight
maanaa paau	weight measure (8 oz, or 0.2 kg)
paisaa	smallest denomination of money (0.085 U.S. cents)

rakshi	distilled spirit
rupiyAA (100 paisaa)	100 **paisaa** (about 3.2 cents, at 1991 U.S. exchange rate)
sahib	honorific title used by Nepalis for male foreigners
ser	weight measure equal to four **paau** (2 lb, or 0.8 kg)
taal	lake
thangka	Buddhist scroll painting
tsampa	roasted barley flour, usually consumed by **BhoTiya**
yersa	a cluster of **goTh** in Khumbu, but also applies to other northern regions
zopkio or **chAUmri**	a cross between a yak and a cow

Contents

Nepali for Trekkers

Refusal to accept anybody else's language as worth knowing reflects the same narrow-gauge kind of head, the same stubborn ignorance as that of the fundamentalist I heard about who denounced people speaking in other tongues, saying "If English was good enough for Jesus Christ, it's good enough for them."
The story is apocryphal in both senses.
Flora Lewis

Nepali is an Indo-European language that is easy to learn. Here an attempt is made to introduce the trekker to enough Nepali words and phrases to get by in the hills. It is especially advisable for those trekking without an English-speaking guide to make some effort to learn minimal Nepali. But trekkers constantly tell me how their attempts to speak Nepali even when trekking with guides provide intimate, unforgettable experiences with the country that others, who don't make the effort, miss. Indeed, as more and more Nepalis speak some English, the trekker who tries to speak the native language will be welcomed much more warmly.

The language presented in this section is definitely a basic form of hill Nepali, not at all the language spoken by the educated or the Hindu castes, who use a more Sanskritized form. But it is an appropriate form for the trekker.

I have also produced a 90-minute language tape incorporating all this material, sold together with a pocket-size version of this section. This will enable you to easily carry this section along as you trek and refer to it often. I have talked to trekkers, unaware of who I was, who seemed to be speaking Nepali much better than I would expect a tourist to do, and learned that they had studied from the tape produced for previous editions. These trekkers felt it made a considerable difference in how they were received by their Nepali hosts. While preparing for your trek, use the tape to get a feeling for the sounds of the language and to learn some tape and use it as a reference when needed. Ordering information is at the end of the section.

Besides this material, immersing yourself in the language when in Nepal is the best way to learn it. Consider trading English lessons for Nepali ones with your porters. If you are especially motivated to study when back home, you might extend this section by befriending a Nepali, or a former Peace Corps volunteer, and practicing.

PRONUNCIATION

Nepali is written in Devanagari script, but a system of transliteration to the Roman script is used here. Many of the letters denote their usual sounds and only the special sounds are described.

Stress

The stress usually falls on the first syllable (chaá mal) unless the first syllable has a short vowel and is followed in the second syllable by a long one. Then the stress falls on the second syllable (pa kaaí nos). **The single most common pronunciation error made by the beginning student is NOT putting the emphasis on the first syllable.**

Vowels

a   like the *a* in *balloon*. Never like the *a* in *hat*.

aa   long like the *a* in *father* or *car*.

i   like *ee* in *beer*, the short and long forms pronounced similarly.

u   like *oo* in *mood* or *root*, again with the long and short forms similar. Never like the *u* in *mute*.

e   like *a* in *skate* or like the French *e* in *café*.

ai   a diphthong with the first element like the *a* in *arise* and the second like the *y* in *city*. Together, somewhat like the *ay* in *laying*, but not like the sound of the word *eye*.

like the *u* in *put*.

o   like *o* in *bowl* or *go*.

aau, aai, and **eu**   not diphthongs, but vowels pronounced separately one after the other.

Capitalized Vowels

Capitalized vowels (A,E,I,O,U) indicate nasalization of that sound.

Dental and Retroflex Consonants

The idea with retroflexed consonants is to make the sound further back in the mouth, compared to the dental, which are made much more forward.

t   pronounced unaspirated, with the tip of the tongue on the teeth as in the French *petite*.

T   like the *t* in *little*, with the tongue slightly bent back when it meets the roof of the mouth.

d   dental like the French *d*, in which the blade of the tongue is pressed behind the upper teeth.

D   pronounced with retroflexion of the tongue. Turn the tongue back in the mouth, press the underside of it against the palate, and pronounce the *d* in *dog*.

R   also pronounced with retroflexion of the tongue.

Aspirated Consonants

Nepalis differentiate between aspirated and unaspirated consonants. This is quite difficult for native English speakers. Aspiration is indicated by an *h* following the consonant. Consciously avoid breathing hard or aspirating on the consonants that are not followed by an *h*.

The exception to the above rule in the transliteration scheme employed in this book applies to *ch* and *chh*. Only the latter is aspirated.

chh   press the blade of the tongue behind the upper teeth and try to say *ts*. At the same time exert strong breath pressure so that when the tongue is released from the teeth, there is a loud emission of breath. Listen to a native Nepali speaker. It is like the *tch-h* in *pitch here.*

ch the unaspirated form as in *chalk, Chinese.*

Miscellaneous

k like *c* in *cat.*

y like *y* in *yeast.*

s like *s* in *song.*

j press the blade of the tongue against the upper teeth with the tip of the tongue pointed down and say *j* as in *January.* It is somewhat like *dz* and is especially found in words coming from Tibetan dialects.

ph like *f* in *full.*

p less aspiration than **ph** (more like **p** than **f**).

Other consonants should present little difficulty. When two consonants come together, be sure to pronounce them individually.

GRAMMAR NOTES

Listening to and practicing the sounds of Nepali are basic to communication in the country. Next, you need some vocabulary and the ability to speak in phrases. To help you, lists of useful words and phrases are given later in the section. In addition, too, the language tape offers invaluable assistance. In addition, you can adapt the sample phrases to your particular needs by following the indicated sentence structure and plugging in other words from the vocabulary lists. At some point, however, you may want information on grammar to increase your fluency. You will find such information in this section. You don't have to get bogged down in this material until the need arises because you can do quite well by just learning the sounds and phrases.

Sentence Structure

Subject-object-verb is the usual order in Nepali. This holds true for questions as well; a rising vocal pitch at the end of the sentence indicates the interrogative mode.

Plurals and gender can be neglected by the trekker, as they often are by Nepalis. Verbs are declined and, for the trekker, a few tenses and forms will suffice. Nouns and pronouns used as subjects of transitive verbs in the past tense have the suffix **-le.**

Pronouns

I	**ma**
we	**haami**
he, she, it (familiar)	**u**
he, she (polite)	**uahAA**
they (familiar)	**uniharu**
they (polite)	**wahAAharu**
you (familiar)	**timi**
you (polite)	**tapAAI**

Trekkers should always use the polite forms of address, except with children and animals. I'll never forget the time I addressed a dog using the polite honorific. The laughter roared throughout the entire village.

Verbs

Verbs are listed in the infinitive form, ending in **-nu.** A neutral form used with any pronoun, or noun subject, whose tense is near the present is formed by changing the **u** to **e,** e.g.,

jaanu to **jaane** meaning, go
ma kaaThmaanDu-maa jaane meaning, I am going to Kathmandu;
I Kathmandu to go

or,

tapAAI kahAA jaane? meaning, where are you going?
you where go

Polite imperatives are formed by deleting the -e from the infinitive and adding -os, e.g.,

dinu, to give   in;   chiyaa dinos   meaning, please give tea.
                     tea please give

Negatives can be formed by prefixing na- to the verb, in this imperative form, e.g., naaaunos meaning, don't come.

For the most part, the above verb usage is sufficient for many trekking purposes. More information is included for language lovers, and to help interpret what you hear.

The present tense is made by deleting the -nu from the infinitive and adding one of the following suffixes (the example used is the verb garnu, meaning to do):

	Affirmative	Negative
ma	garchhu	gardinA
haami	garchhAU	gardainAU
u	garchha	gardaina
uhAA	garnu hunchha	garnu hunna
uniharu	garchhan	gardainan
wahAAharu	garnu hunchha	garnu hunna
timi	garchhau	gardainau
tapAAI	garnu hunchha	garnu hunna

There are actually slight differences depending on categorizations of the verb stem, but we shall neglect this detail.

The first perfect participle (e.g. having gone), formed by deleting -nu from the infinitive and adding -eko, can be a general purpose past and present progressive tense. The formation is slightly different for verbs whose infinitives end in -aaunu, -anu, or -unu. The respective forms usually replace with -aaeko, -eko, and -eko. The form of the verb to go, jaanu, is gaeko, and that of the verb to be,

..., is bhaekO. The negatives are formed by prefixing na-, except for bhaekO, which is bhaena. For polite expressions, use the infinitive and bhaeko, or bhaena, e.g.,

tapAAI kahAA baaTa aaunu bhaeko meaning, where have you come from?
you where from to come have

The verb "to be" is special and has two forms. One form has no infinitive; its third person singular is chha, meaning there is or it is, or in the past tense thiyo. It indicates possession, or location. Negatives are chhaina and thiena, respectively, e.g.,

kitaab tyahAA chha meaning, there is the book.
book there is

The other verb to be, hunu, has the present form ho, and the past bhayo, with negatives hoina and bhaena, respectively. It defines, e.g.,

mero desh kaanada ho meaning, I come from Canada.
my country Canada is

Confusion may arise as to which to use, and the full declension is not given. Most Nepalis will understand what you are trying to say.

Future tenses vary depending on the likelihood of the action happening. For the spoken language, the form usually used adds suffixes; using the verb garnu, meaning to do:

I	ma	garUlaa	meaning, I (probably) will do
we	haami	garAUlaa	
he, she (familiar)	u	garlaa	
they (familiar)	uniharu	garlaan	
you (familiar)	timi	garaulaa	

The easiest way to form the negative is to prefix **na-** to the appropriate form of the verb. For the polite forms, use the imperatives mentioned earlier. The form mentioned earlier, ending in **-ne**, is suitable for the future tense as well, e.g.,

kahile   jaane
when   will you go?

Miscellaneous Verbs

The verb **hunchha,** used following an infinitive at the end of an interrogative sentence (indicated by rising voice inflexion) can mean: Is it okay to ———?

ghar   bhitra   aaunu   hunchha?   meaning, can I (implied) go inside the house?
house   inside   to go   is it okay?

To express can or may, in a sense of physical possibility, you use the infinitive end in **-nu** rather than **-na,** and follow it by a form of the verb **saknu** (to be able to do), e.g.,

baaTo   maa   chhirna   sakchha?   meaning, Is it possible to get through
trail   on   to get through   it is possible?   on the trail?

Similarly, to express "must," use the infinitive ending in **-nu,** and the verb **parchha,** e.g.,

bholi   aaram   garnu   parchha   meaning, I (implied) must rest tomorrow
tomorrow   rest   to do   must

The phrases **man parchha** and **man laagchha** both mean like. All of the verbs in this section are used with subjects that have the suffix **-laai,** e.g.,

malaai   Nepal   man   parchha   meaning, I like Nepal
me (to)   Nepal   like

Prepositions

In Nepali, prepositions are *post* positions; that is, they are suffixed to the noun.

in, on, to, at(locating)	**-maa**
to, for	**-laai** (this is also added to the subject of impersonal verbs)

e.g., **ma-laai   paani   chaahinchha**   meaning, I need water
me for   water   needs

for the sake of	**-laagi**
from	**-baaTa**
inside, in	**-bhitra**
around (approximately)	**-tira**
outside	**-bahira**
before	**-agaaDi**
with	**-sita, -sAga**
under, below	**-tala**
of (indicating possession)	**-ko**
after	**-pachhi**

With some pronouns, the word is changed somewhat.

mine	**mero**
whose	**kasko**
yours (familiar)	**timro**
for me	**malaai**
for this	**yasko**
yours (polite)	**tapAAIko**
his, hers (familiar)	**usko**
theirs (polite)	**wahAAko**

With this skeleton of grammar, you should be better able to understand the phrases in this section and modify them to suit your needs.

PRACTICE BEFORE YOU GO

To acquire a language is to learn the spoken utterance. The natural receptive medium is therefore the ear, not the eye. It is an art very much akin to music.
G.G. Rogers, Colloquial Nepali

The following may seem formidable if you are just going on a short trek. Do not be daunted. It is here in case you need it. You will find, however, that a minimal knowledge of the language is indispensable on the trail, where most people normally cannot speak or understand much English, especially if you venture off the usual trekker-frequented routes.

If you have a few days in Kathmandu before you set off, you can practice a little in a familiar and exceedingly helpful environment.

First, ask your hotel receptionist or some friendly waiter in a restaurant to frequent to read the word list to you. Repeat it after him until you get a feel for the pronunciation. This should take about 15 minutes and will probably make you instant friends with your Nepali helper. Then try it out. For example, practice your Nepali in a restaurant. Say:

chiyaa   **dinos**
tea   please give me

or: **bill**   **dinos**
bill   please give me

or: **menu**   **dinos**
menu   please give me

Later when it is time to pay, say:
khaanaa **-ko** **kati?**
food   for   how much

raising your voice pitch at the end of the sentence to indicate a question. Have the person answer in Nepali rather than English. People are usually more than happy to repeat the Nepali number for you and translate it into English. If you feel clumsy or shy about any of this, always smile. It works like magic to ease every situation. Smiling is the Nepali way of getting over tense or slightly embarrassing situations.

When you go to a bazaar and wish to buy an item, point to it and say:

yasko   **kati?**
for this   how much?

The person may answer in Nepali or English, but try to come away from the transaction able to understand the Nepali number.

If you do this each time, you should soon be able to understand spoken Nepali numbers, or at least the main ones. This is a tremendous asset on the trail, where people often do not know the English numbers.

If you do not understand, or want something repeated, say:

hajur
excuse me

By the time you reach this stage, you will already be experiencing the hospitality that even the tiniest knowledge of Nepali inspires.

Now try asking for directions:

paaTan **jaane** **baaTo ho?**
Patan   going to road   is it?

meaning: Is this the road to Patan? On the trail, where there are no road signs, this direction-finding question is essential.

Now add some vocabulary to the skeleton. If you do not want much food, say:

ali ali   dinos
very little   please give

Ask for **dhai** instead of yoghurt, **paani** instead of water. Ask for the time, bargain, use the terms of address.

By asking questions in Kathmandu, you can get used to hearing some of the many types of responses. Basic communication in Nepali will lose some of its terrors, and you will be far more competent in dealing with situations in the non-English-speaking world on the trail.

It's easy. Now go straight to your hotel receptionist and begin reading the word list with him.

There are opportunities for language instruction in Kathmandu. Among organizations that may help you locate instructors or language classes are:

Nepal Studies Center in Naxal, phone 412488
Experiment in International Living in Gyaneshwar, phone 414516
United Mission to Nepal in Thapathali, phone 212179
University of Wisconsin Program, phone 415560
International Community Services in Phora Durbar, phone 222593.
Universal Language Institute, Puthali Sadak, phone 418599, 419443
Horizon Language Institute, Kamaladi, phone 226919, 226548.

While trekking in the hills, trade Nepali lessons for English lessons among people you meet when you stop to eat or sleep.

Word Lists

Food

apple	**syaau**
banana	**keraa**
beans	**simi**
beer	**biyar**
	jAAR (Nepali)
	chang (Tibetan)
	tOmba (fermented millet mash)
biscuits	**biskooT**
bread (loaf of leavened variety)	**pau roti**
(unleavened)	**roti, chapaati**
cabbage	**bandaa kopi**
carrots	**gaajar**
cauliflower	**kaauli**
cheese (dried protein)	**churpi**
chilies	**khursaani**
coffee	**kaphi**
corn	**makai**
cucumber	**kAAkro**
eggs	**phul**
boiled eggs	**umaaleko phul**
feast	**bhoj**
fish	**maachhaa**
flour	**piTho, aaTa**
white flour	**maidaa**
whole wheat flour	**gahUko piTho**
food (usually referring to rice)	**khaanaa, bhansa**
fruit	**phalphul**

garlic	**lasun**	roasted flour	**saatu** (Nepali)
ginger	**aduwaa**		**tsampa** (Tibetan)
greens (spinach)	**saag**	salt	**nun**
guava	**ambaa, belauti**	samosa (Indian food in lower bazaars)	**sIgaaDa**
lemons	**nibuwaa**	snacks	**khaajaa**
lentils	**daal**	soybeans	**bhaTmaas**
limes	**kaagati**	spices	**masalaa**
mangoes	**AAp**	spirits (distilled)	**rakshi**
meat	**maasu**	sugar	**chini**
buffalo	**rAAgoko maasu**	sweets	**miThaai**
chicken	**kukhuraako maasu**	tea	**chiyaa**
goat	**khasiko maasu**	tomatoes	**golbhEDa**
dried goat	**shikaar, sukurti**	vegetables	**tarkaari, sabji**
pig	**sUgurko maasu**	water	**paani**
milk	**dudh**	drinking water	**khaane paani**
millet	**kodo**	boiled water	**umaaleko paani**
noodles	**chaauchaau**	hot water	**taato paani**
noddle soup	**maggi** (actually a brand name)	washing water	**dhune paani**
oil	**tel**	whey	**mAI**
okra	**raamtoriyaa**	yoghurt	**dhai**
onions	**pyaaj**		
oranges (tangerines)	**suntalaa**		
peanuts	**badaam**	**Other Useful Nouns**	
popcorn	**murali makai**		
potatoes	**aalu**	airport	**giraund**
sweet potato	**tarul**	baby	**naani, bachcho**
pumpkin	**pharsi**	basket (for porter)	**Doko**
radish	**mulaa**	bicyclist (Westerner with modern 10-18 speed)	**girwaala**
relish (chutney)	**achaar**		
rice (paddy)	**dhaan**	binoculars	**durbin**
(uncooked but harvested)	**chaamal**	book	**kitaab**
(cooked)	**bhaat**	bottle	**sisi**
rice and lentils	**daal bhaat**		

boy (adolescent)	keTo
bridge (good structure)	pul
(makeshift)	sAAghu
buffalo, male	rAAgo
female	bhAIsi
candle	main-batti
cat	biraalo
carpet (Tibetan)	galenji
cave	wodaar
children	keTaa-keTi
clothes	lugaa
cow	gaai
cup	gilas, kap
curved (referring to trail)	ghumaaune
daughter	chhori
day	din
distance unit (2 mi, 3 km)	kosh
dog	kukur
downhill	oraalo
earthquake	bhUIchaal
elephant	haatti
elephant driver	phanit
expensive	mahAgo
festival	jaatra
fire	aago
firewood	daauraa
flat area	maidhan
floor	bhUI
flower	phul (same as word for egg)
foot	khuTTo
foreigner	bedeshi
fork (table)	kAATaa

fork (of road)	dobaaTo
forest	ban
friend	saathi
my friend	mero saathi
girl (adolescent)	keTi
(younger)	naani
government (of Nepal)	shri pAAch ko sarkaar
help	madat
hill	lekh, pahaaD, DAADa
horse	ghoDaa
hot springs	taato paani
house	ghar
husband	shriman, logne, pati
inn, lodging	bhaTTi
kerosene	maTTitel
knife (small)	chakku
(large, traditional knife of Nepal)	khukuri
lake	pokhari, taal
landslide	pairo
leech	juga
left	baayAA, debre
level, horizontal (of trail)	terso
light (lamp)	batti
load	bhaari
louse (plural, lice)	jumro
luggage (stuff)	saamaan
man	maanchhe
market	bazaar
mat (straw)	gundri
matches	salaai
mattress (foam, in hotel)	Dunlop

medicine	aushadi
mill (for grinding grain)	ghaTTa
mosquito	laamkhuTTe
name	naam
pass	bhanjyang
pasture	buki, kharka
pen (ball point)	kalaam, doT pen
people	maanis
people (members of a trek)	membar
pig	sUgar, (bUgar)
place	ThAAU
plate	thaal
porter	kulli, baariya
pot (for cooking)	dekchi
religion	dharma
rhinoceros	gAIDa
ridge	lekh, DaaDaako Tuppaa
right	daayA, daahine
river	khola, kosi, nadi
road	baaTo
room	koThaa
school	iskul
shelter (temporary)	goTh
shop, store	pasal, dokan
shopkeeper	saahuji
sick	biraami
snow	hIU
snow peak	himaal
soap	saabun
son	chhoro
spoon	chamchaa
stage (camp on trek)	kamp

stone rest spot	chautaara
straight (of trail)	sidhaa, sojho
sun	ghaam
things	chij-bij
toilet	charpi
town	gAAU
trail	baaTo
tree	rukh
trekker (on a group trek)	membar
tumpline	naamlo
uphill	ukaalo
vehicle	gaaDi
village	gAAU
volume unit (2½ cups, 600 ml)	maanaa
waterfall	chhAAga
wife	jhan, shri mati, patni
woman	aaimaaai

Verbs

to ask for	mAAgnu
to ask (a question)	sodhnu
to boil	umaalnu
to buy	kinnu
to carry	boknu
to cook	pakaaunu
to defecate	haaknu
to do	garnu
to eat, drink	khaanu
to forget	birsanu
to fry	bhuTnu

to get	**paaunu**
to give	**dinu**
to go	**jaanu**
to learn	**siknu**
to look for	**khojnu**
to meet	**bheTnu**
to need	**chaahinu**
I need	**chaahinchha, chaaiyo**
to open	**kholnu**
to remember	**samjhanu**
to repeat (do again)	**pheri garnu**
to rest (a burden)	**bisaaunu**
(your body)	**aaraam garnu**
to sell	**bechnu**
to sing a song	**git gaaunu**
to sit, stay, stop	**basnu**
to succeed	**saknu**
it is possible (can be done)	**sakchha**
impossible (cannot be done)	**sakdaaina**
to teach	**sikaaunu**
to understand	**bujhnu**
to wash (face, clothes)	**dhunu**
to wash (body)	**nuhaaunu**
to work	**kaam garnu**

Adjectives and Adverbs

after	**pacchi**
again	**pheri**
all	**sab**
always	**sadhAI**
beautiful	**sundar, sundarai, raamro**
clean	**saphaa**
cold (damp, or of liquids and foods)	**chiso**
(weather)	**jaaDo**
(extreme temperature)	**ThADaa**
delicious	**miTho**
different	**arko**
difficult	**mushkil**
dirty	**phohor**
easy	**sajilo**
far	**TaaDhaa**
good	**raamro**
not good	**raamro chhaina, naraamro**
happy	**khushi**
heavy	**gahrungo**
here	**yahAA**
hot (temperature)	**taato**
(weather)	**gharmi**
(spicy)	**piro**
(climate)	**nyaano**
inside	**bhitra**
little	**ali ali**
long (dimension)	**laamo**
lot (quantity)	**dherai, thupro**
many, much	**dherai**
near	**najik**
new	**naya**
only	**maatrai**
outside	**baahira**
quickly	**chhito**
slowly	**bistaarai**
sour	**amilo**
sweet	**guliyo**

Vocabulary

tasty	miTho
that	tyo
there	tyahAA
this	yo
for this	yasko
where	kahAA
which	kun

Colors

red	raato
yellow	pahElo
green	hariyo
blue	nilo
black	kaalo
white	seto

morning	bihaana
early morning	saberai
afternoon (12:00 noon to 4:00 P.M.)	diuso
evening (4:00 P.M. to 8:00 P.M.)	beluki
night	raati
What time is it?	kati bajyo

Money

small change	paisaa
how much	kati

paisaa is the smallest unit
sukaa = 25 paisaa
mohar = 50 paisaa
rupiyAA = 100 paisaa

Conjunctions

also	pani
and	ani, ra
or	ki
because	kina bhane

Days of the Week

Sunday	aitbaar
Monday	sombaar
Tuesday	mAgalbaar
Wednesday	budhabaar
Thursday	bihibaar
Friday	sukrabaar
Saturday	sanibaar

Time

now	ahile
today	aaja
tomorrow	bholi
day after tomorrow	parshi
yesterday	hijo
minute	minuT
hour	ghanTaa
day	din
week	haptaa

Numbers

#	Nepali	#	Nepali
1	ek	21	ekkaais
2	dui	22	baais
3	tin	23	teis
4	chaar	24	chaubis
5	pAAch	25	paachis
6	chha	26	chhabis
7	saat	27	sattais
8	aaTh	28	aTThaais
9	nau	29	unantis
10	das	30	tis
11	eghaara	40	chaalis
12	baahra	50	pachaas
13	tehra	60	saaThi
14	chaudha	70	sattari
15	pandhra	75	pachhattar
16	sohra	80	ashi
17	satra	90	nabbe
18	aThaara	100	say or ek say
19	unnaais	101	ek say ek
20	bis	200	dui say
		1000	ek hajaar
		100,000	ek laakh
		10,000,000	ek kaRor
		½	aadha
		1½	DeDh
		2½	aDhaai

ENGLISH LOAN WORDS TO NEPALI

These are added to the language almost daily. Surprisingly, they will be the hardest words for a trekker to understand, because the Nepali sounds are not those of the English language. I well remember trying to figure out what a "sati picket" was when a Nepali asked me for one when I was working as a doctor. What he wanted, I learned after much discussion, was a certificate!

QUESTIONS

The basic form is to inflect at the end of the sentence; that is, raise the pitch of your voice on the ending word.

ANSWERS

Nepalis either repeat the verb you have used in your sentence to indicate agreement with you (more frequent), or they use one of the following terms:

it is (definition)	ho
there is (location)	chha
please sit down, stay	basnos
okay (polite)	hunchha
okay (very polite)	haas
okay	hajur
yes	ju
yes	A

To express a negative they might repeat the verb in its negative form:

cannot get	paaindaaina
cannot stay	basnu sakdaaina
not permitted	hundaaina

or they might use the negative form of the verb "to be":

it is not (definition)	hoina
there is not (location)	chhaina
no	ahA
I don't know	khunni

Shaking of the head in a fluid motion can mean yes. You may initially think it means no!

THANK YOU

Westerners are always eager to thank people as part of common courtesy. While Nepali does have a word connoting gratitude (**dhanyabaad**), native speakers do not use it in the sense that we would. Thanking is not a part of their social custom. Indeed, there is ingrained a concept that if they do something for you (or anyone), the doer should be grateful to have the privilege of serving another. You may hear this word used by some trekkers along the popular trails, and the locals are becoming accustomed to hearing it and even using it sometimes, but it is still outside of their custom and they do not use it among themselves. It is best for trekkers to get used to the Nepali social custom of not thanking, except by using the English words where they are understood. Buddhist highlanders in Nepal (*BhoTiya*) do have a word (**thuDichhe** or **thuchhe**) that is used more like our "thank you," but not nearly as often.

PHRASES

No list of phrases can come close to covering all the possibilities a trekker might need or encounter. The English glosses of the Nepali words are placed below them to help you understand the construction of the phrase and to enable you to tailor the phrase you need for your situation by changing words appropriately. In a few instances, I have placed commas in the long phrases to help you know where to pause as you pronounce them. Several series of phrases only have one or two words changed to help you use them to make others. Experiment and see what works best.

What is the name of this town?

yo gAAU -ko naam ke ho?
this town of name what is

Is this the road to Malemchigaon?

yo malemchigAAU jaane
this Malemchigaon going
baaTo ho?
road is this

Where does this trail lead to?

yo baaTo kahAA samma
this trail where up to
jaanchha?
go

Which trail goes to Ringmo?

Ringmo samma kun baato
Ringmo up to which trail
jaanchha?
goes

How many hours to Those?

those-samma kati ghanTaa
Those up to how many hours
laagchha?
does it take

It will take one hour.

ek ghanTaa laagchha
one hour it will take

How many camps to Ghunsa?
(camping days for large groups)

ghunsa -maa kati kamp
Ghunsa to how many camps
laagchha?
will it take

Is there an inn at Tashigaon?

tashigAAU -maa bhaTTi (hoTel)
Tashigaon in inn (western inn)
chha?
is there

Can we get food in Ghunsa?

ghunsa -maa khaanaa sakchha
Ghunsa in food possible
pAAIchha?
can get

Is the trail good enough to take or not?

baaTo -maa chhirnu
road on get through
ki sakdaaina?
or impossible

Is this the main trail?

yo mul baaTo ho?
this main trail it is

I'm scared.

malaai Dar laagchha
me to fear strikes

Impossible, cannot be done.

sakdaaina
impossible

Where are you going?

kahAA jaane?
where go

Where have you come from today?

aaja kahAA baaTa aaunu bhayo?
today where from to go have

Where are you coming from?

kahAA baaTa aaeko?
where from have been coming

Can I come with you?

sAAgaai jaane?
with you go

What is the name of this town?

yo gAAU -ko naam ke ho?
this town of name what is

What is the name of the (next) town on the trail?

yo baaTo-maa kun gAAU
this road on which town
parchha?
must it be

Where is there a weekly market?

haaT bajaar kahAA chha?
market where is there

hoTel hotel
pasal shop

What is your caste? (ethnic group)

tapAAIko jaat ke ho?
your caste what is

(Strictly speaking, it is not polite to ask this, but it may be tolerable from a foreigner who has established friendly relations with a person. The answer "Nepali" usually indicates a low Hindu caste. You will find that as Nepalis practice their English on you, they will ask quite inappropriate questions for a casual encounter.)

The trail going left or the trail going right?

baaTo baayAA jaanchha ki daayAA?
road left goes or right

When is the next vehicle to Phedi?

phedi -maa arko gaaDi kahile jaanchha?
Phedi to next cart when go

I need three tickets to Basantapur.

malaai tin TikaT basantapur jaane gaaDi chaahinchha
me for three tickets Basantapur go vehicle need

I am going to Jomosom.

jomosom -maa jaane
Jomosom to go

Is the trail very uphill?

baaTo dherai ukaalo chha?
trail very uphill is
downhill **oraalo**
level **tirso** or **samtal**

Is there motor service to Taplejung now?

ahile taplejung -maa gaaDi chalchha?
now Taplejung to vehicle moves

When does the vehicle leave Taplejung?

taplejung -baaTa gaaDi kahile jaanchha?
Taplejung from vehicle when go

L28

I came from Ghasa

ghasa baaTa aaeko
Ghasa from have been coming

I must rest here all day tomorrow.

bholi ma din bhari yahAA
tomorrow 1 day whole here
aaram garnu parchha
rest to make must

Let's rest.

aaram garAU
rest let's make

I have to urinate.

pishaab garnu parchha
urine make must
defecate **disaa**
stool

(These questions on elimination are rarely used by adult Nepalis, but are included here in case of illness or other special circumstances.)

TALKING TO PORTERS

Here are some useful words and sentences to aid in making arrangements with porters and in giving them instructions on the trail. To avoid misunderstanding later, arrange these details before setting off: the destination, approximately how many days the porters will be needed, the rate per day and whether it includes food, pay for porters returning without a load, and whether the porters have the necessary equipment, especially if you will be traveling through snow or during the monsoon.

I am going to Namche Bazaar

namche bazaar jane
Namche Bazaar go

I will need porters for one week

ek haptaa- ko kulli chaahinchha
one week for porters need

I will need five porters for two days

dui din samma pAAch kulli chaahinchha
two days up to five porters need

L29

L30

English	Nepali	Gloss
How much per day?	**din-ko kati?**	day for how much?
How much per day with food?	**din-ko kati khaanaa khaaiera**	food eating
How much per day without food?	**din-ko kati khaanaa nakhaaiera**	food not eating
Have you been to Mugu before?	**tapAAI mugu-maa pahile** / **jaanu bhayo?**	you Mugu to before / to go have
Ninety rupees without food is enough	**nabbe rupiyAA khaanaa** / **nakhaaiera pugchha**	ninety rupees food / not eating is enough
For returning, thirty rupees per day is enough	**pharkaaunda din -ko tis** / **rupiyAA pugchha**	returning day for thirty / rupees is enough
Without load	**bhaari chhaina**	load there is not
With load	**bhaari chha**	load there is
After one week	**ek haptaa pachhi**	one week after
Do you have warm clothes?	**nyaano lugaa chha?**	warm clothes is there
Do you have shoes?	**jutta chha?**	shoes is there
Do you have a carrying basket?	**Doko chha?**	carrying basket is there

L30

L31

English	Nepali	Gloss
Please show me your warm clothes tomorrow.	**nyaano lugaa bholi** / **dekhaaunos**	warm clothes tomorrow / please show
Go quickly.	**chhito jaane**	quickly go
Go slowly.	**bistaarai jaane**	slowly go
Walk near me.	**ma sAga jaane**	me with go
We will stop (stay) now	**ahile basne**	now stay
We will stay here.	**yahAA basne**	here stay
We will stop after one hour.	**ek ghanTaa pachhi basne**	one hour after stop
Please ask where to stay.	**kahAA basne sodhnos**	where stay please ask
Please ask about food	**khaanaa-kolaagi sodhnos**	food about please ask
We need firewood	**daauraa chaahinchha**	firewood need
Please cook food.	**khaanaa pakaaunos**	food please cook
tea / bread	**chiyaa** / **roti**	tea / bread
Are you hungry?	**bhok laagchha?**	hunger strikes
I am tired.	**malaai thakaai laagchha**	me to tiredness strikes
Do you want to rest?	**bisaaune ki?**	rest or

L31

This equipment is a loan.

yo saamaan mero rin ho
this kit my loan is

Please give it back after using it.

kaam sake -pachhi phirtaa
work finished after return
dinos
please give

Can I get a horse here to carry me to Muktinath?

ghoDaachaDhera muktinaTh
horse riding Muktinath
samma yahAA paaIchha?
up to here can get

Can you take me to Yamphudin?

malaai yamphudin -maa laanu
me Yamphudin to take
hunchha?
can you

We'll meet you at Tatopani in two hours

haami tatopaani -maa dui
we Tatopani at two
ghanTaa -maa bheTchhAU
hours in will meet

Don't be late, please.

Dhilo nagarnos
late not please make

We may have to travel in snow.

hIU -maa jaanuparchha
snow in to go must
holaa
probably

There are three people in our party

haamro parti -maa tin
our party in three
maanis chhan
people are

Today we will walk to Pelma.

ajaa haami pelma samma
today we pelma up to
hIDchhAU
walk

I am traveling alone.

ma eklai jaanchu
I alone go

We should stop around four o'clock.

haami chaar baje tira baas
we four bells around stay
baschhAU
will sit

It will take two hours.

dui ghanTaa laagchha
two hours strikes

My two children are traveling with us.

mero dui keTaa-keTi
my two children
haami-sAga jaanchan
us with go

Please carry the child in your basket.

bachcho Doko -maa boknos
child basket -in please carry

I want you to wash and dry the diapers.

bachcho-ko mailo kopra
baby of dirty clothes
dhunos
please wash

Wash the dirty diapers in this pan and do not throw the water into the river.

mailo kopra yo karaahi-maa
dirty clothes this pan in
dhunos ra phohor paani
please wash and dirty water
khola -maa naphaalnos
river to not throw please

FINDING A PLACE TO EAT OR STAY

Porters can be very helpful in finding a lodging for you in town, especially if they have been over the trail before. If you are on your own, try these sentences:

Where can I get food?

khaanaa kahAA pAaIchha?
food where get

There.

utaa or tyahAA
there

L34

Here.
yahAA
here

Where is there a hotel?
hoTel kahAA chha ?
hotel where is

Can you cook food for us?
hami-laai khaanaa pakaaunu
us for food to cook
hunchha ki?
can you or

Please sit down.
basnos
please sit

Do you cook on a (kerosene) stove?
isTov -le ki daauraa -le
stove using or wood using
khaanaa pakaaunu hunchha?
food to cook do you

I prefer a hotel that cooks with kerosene (a very complicated phrase, best spoken in three parts separated by commas).
ma khaanaa daauraa -le
I food wood using
pakaaune bADa, maTTitel -le
cooking speaking kerosene using
chalaaune isTov -le pakaaune
moves stove using cooking
hoTel -maa, basna
hotel at staying
man parchha
like (soul strikes)

Does this hotel have a latrine? (toilet)
yo hoTel -maa charpi chha?
this hotel in latrine is there

Can I get food in Manang?
manAg-maa khaanaa
Manang in food
pAAlchha?
get

aalu
potatoes

L35

Where can I stay?
kahAA basne?
where stay

Is there a place to stay in Pangpema?
pAgpema -maa baas pAAlchha?
Pangpema in lodging can get

Are there people in Pangpema now?
ahile pAgpema -maamanchhe
now Pangpema at people
chha?
are there

You cannot stay.
baas paaindaina
stay cannot

Please rest.
aaram garnos
rest please make

May we camp here?
yahAA haami kamp garnu
here we camp to make
hunchha?
is all right?

Where is the toilet?
charpi kahAA chha?
latrine where is

store?
pasal
shop

May we (I) stay in your house?
tapAAlko ghar -maa baas
your house in stay
pAAlchha?
can get

Can I (we) stay here?
yahAA baas pAAlchha?
here stay can get

What days does the plane fly from Taplejung to Kathmandu?
kun baar -maa jahaaj taplejung
which day in plane Taplejung
-dekki Kathmandu -samma
from Kathmandu up to
jaanchha?
goes

How much is the ticket?

Your lodge is very nice.

TikaT   **kati**   **laagchha?**
ticket   how much   does it strike
tapAAI ko hoTel   **dherai raamro**
you   of hotel   very   nice
chha
is

FOOD

Asking for Food at the House

Do you have _____?

yahAA _____ **pAAIchha?**
here _____ can get

Can I get food here?

khaanaa yahAA pAAIchha?
food   here   can get
biskooT
biscuits
chiyaa
tea

Please cook rice and lentils for me.

daal   **bhaat**   **pakaaunos**
lentils   rice   please cook

Please do not make it too spicy.

khaanaa -maa khursaani
food   in   hot peppers
naraakhnos
not please put

I will eat later.

pachhi khaane
after   eat

I will eat in two hours.

dui   **ghanTaa pachhi khaane**
two   hours   after   eat

Please make the tea without milk.

chiyaa -maa dudh na   **haalnos**
tea   in   milk   not   please add
sugar
chini
  sugar

Please cook potatoes for me.

malaai   **aalu**   **pakaaunos**
me for   potatoes   please cook

Can I buy food in Ghunsa?

ghunsa   **-maa khaanaakura**
Ghunsa   in   food stuff
kinna pAAIchha?
buy   can get

Is the food ready?

khaana tayaar bhayo?
food   ready   is

Asking for Food during the Meal

There is a fairly strict Hindu etiquette to be observed while eating. Breach of these rules is grossly insulting. It is wise, therefore, to read about Nepali customs in chapter 4 before you venture to eat in a Nepali home.

Please give me more rice.

bhaat dinos
rice   please give
tarkaari
vegetables

Please give me another cup of tea.

arko   **ek**   **kap chiyaa dinos**
another   one   cup   tea   please give

Give me only a little.

ali ali   **dinos**
a little   please give

It is tasty.

miTho chha
tasty   it is

That is enough.

pugyo
enough

I like daal bhaat.

daal bhaat man   **parchha**
  spirit   becomes

Buying Food to Carry with You

Can I buy uncooked rice?

chaamal kinnu   **pAAIchha?**
rice   to buy   can I
roti
bread

Please give me five maanaas of flour.

pAAch maanaa piTho dinos
five   maanaa   flour   please give

Please give me a fire so I can cook my food.

malaai khaanaa pakaauna aago
me for food to cook fire
dinos
please give

PAYING

How much for this?	**yasko kati?** for this how much
How much for food?	**khaanaa -ko kati?** food for how much
the room?	**baas**
tea?	**chiyaa**
one day?	**ek din**
one maanaa?	**ek maanaa**
I will pay only seven rupees.	**saat rupiyAA maatrai dinchhu** seven rupees only I give
Please give me my change.	**paisaa dinos** money please give
All together, how much?	**jammaai kati laagchha?** altogether how much does it strike?
All right.	
This is too expensive.	**yo jyaadaai mahango chha** this very expensive is
Very well, give it to me.	**la, dinos ta.** there please give (meaningless)

GETTING SOMEONE'S ATTENTION

In Nepal, people address each other using kinship terms whether they are related or not. Rather than grunting or shouting "hey you," here are some more pleasant ways of attracting people's attention. Listen and you will hear Nepalis using these terms all the time.

In addressing a person by name, it is polite to add the suffix **-ji** to the name. When in doubt as to whether the person you address is younger or older than you, use the term for the older. Nepalis use kinship terms in addressing another often.
To get the attention of . . .

a man	**hajur** (this also means *yes, sir* and *I did not hear you*)
a man a little older than you	**o daai** or **daaju** hey older brother
a woman who is a little older than you	**o didi** hey older sister
a man old enough to be your father	**o baabu** hey father
a woman old enough to be your mother	**o aamaai** hey mother
a woman or a girl younger than you	**o bahini** hey younger sister
a man or a boy younger than you	**o bhaai** hey younger brother
Once you have their attention	**namaste**, or more politely, **namaskaar**. Translated literally, this greeting means: "I salute the God in you."

TIME

People like to ask you for the time on the trail, and if you know the first twelve numbers, you can easily answer.

What time is it?	**kati bajyo** how many bells
It is two o'clock.	**dui bajyo** two bells

140

I will go today. | **aaja jaane** today go
tomorrow | **bholi**
now | **ahile**
I will stay for one day. | **ek din basne.** one day stay
one week. | **ek haptaa**
Can we get bread early in the morning? | **roti saberai pAAlchha?** bread early morning get
What day is it today? | **aaja kun baar ho?** today which day is it
Today is Monday. | **aaja sombaar ho** today Monday is
Tomorrow or the next day | **bholi parshi** tomorrow the day after tomorrow
When are you going? | **kahile jaane?** when go

TO BEGGING CHILDREN

Don't beg, it's not good. | **maagnu hUdaina kharaab** to beg should not bad **kaam ho** work is
Begging is bad. | **maagne kharaab chha** begging bad is
I won't give to you. | **dindaina**
No, you shouldn't. | **hUdaina**

MISCELLANEOUS

O.K. (?) (question or answer depending on inflection) | **tik chha (?)** all right there is
How wonderful! | **kati raamro** how much good
What is this? | **yo ke ho?** this what is
What is the name of this? | **yesko naam ke ho?** this of name what is
What is the name of this thing? | **yo chij -ko naam ke ho?** this thing of name what is
bird | **charo**
animal | **janaawar**
tree | **rukh**
plant | **biruwaa**
How do you say "house" in Nepali ? | **nepaali bhaashaa maa kasari** Nepali language in how **house bhanchha?** house say
I only speak a little Nepali. | **ma ali ali nepaali maatrai** I a little Nepali only **bolchhu** I speak
I don't speak Nepali. | **ma nepaali boldinA** I Nepali don't speak
I understood. | **bujhE or bujheko**
I don't understand. | **bujhdinA**
Did you understand? | **bujhnu bhayo?**
Please say it again slowly. | **pheri bistaari bhannos** again slowly please say

141

L42

Please say it again more simply.

tapAAlko kura sajilo
your   words easy
paarera pheri bhannos
causing again please say

What has happened?

ke bhayo?
what has been?

Have a good trip.

raamro sAga jaanos
good with please go

Rest well (an appropriate phrase to say as you leave a Nepali home). We are leaving early tomorrow morning.

raamro sAga basnos
good with please sit
haami bholi bihaana saberai
we tomorrow morning early
jaanchhAU
go

How old are you (young child)?

tapAAlko (timro) umer kati
your   age how much
bhayo?
has been

What is your name (young child)?

tapAAlko (timro) naam ke ho?
your   name what is

My name is Mary.

mero naam mari ho
my name Mary is

My country is America.

mero desh ahmerika ho
my country America is

How many children do you have?

tapAAlko chhorachhori kati
your children how many
chan?
are

L42

L43

I have three children, two sons and a daughter.

mero tin chhorachhori chhan
mine three children are
dui chhora ra euTaa chhori
two sons and one daughter

Is this your mother?

uhAA tapAAlko aamaa ho?
he/she your mother is
baabu
father?

This is my friend.

yo mero saathi ho
this my friend is
shriman
husband
shrimati
wife

You are very beautiful (handsome).

tapAAl dherai raamro chha
you very beautiful are
tapAAlko chhoro dherai
chhori

Your son is very handsome.

raamro chha
your son very
raamro chha
handsome is
chhori
daughter

Have you (young child) seen my traveling companions?

tapAAlle (timile) mero saathi
you   my friend
dekhnu bhayo?
to see

kulli
chhorachhori
porters
children

Did it rain yesterday?

hijo paani paryo?
yesterday water fallen
hIU

Will it rain today?

aaja paani parchha holaa?
today water fall maybe
hIU

snow
snow

L43

I'm sorry.

maaph   garnos
forgiveness please give

Can I help you?

madat diU?
help may I give

Will you help me?

malaai madat dinu hunchha?
to me help to give can you?

I am feeling fine now.

aihile bisek bhayo
now convalescence there has been

I like Nepal.

nepaal man paarchha
Nepal mind causes to become

This is a fine village.

yo gAAU raamro chha
this village good is

Where are you bringing the sheep from?

bheDo kahAA baaTa
sheep where from
lyaaune?
bring

What is in the loads?

bhaarimaa ke chha?
load in what is

Where are you taking the loads?

bhaari kahAA samma
load where up to
lyaaune?
bring

I lost my watch.

mero ghaDi haraaiyo
my watch is lost

I am cold.

malaai jaaDo laagchha
me to cold strikes
garmi
hot

Are you cold?

tapAAI laai jaaDo laagchha?
you to cold strikes

Let's go.

la, jAAU
(la is a meaningless particle that is colloquial.)

What to do? (to be said when there is no viable alternative)

ke garne?
what do (a common expression)

Are you married?

tapAAIko bihaa bhayo?
your wedding has been

I came to Nepal to sight-see.

ma nepaal -maa herna aaeko
I Nepal -to to see came
himaal herna ghumna
see the Himalaya wander
chha?

How are you?

kasto chha?
of what sort are
(about as meaningful as the English phrase!)

Fine

sanchaai
healthy

And you?

tapAAI ni?
you (ni is another meaningless colloquial particle.)

I like rice and lentils very much.

ma laai daal bhaat man paarchha
me to lentils rice mind causes to become

I don't like meat.

malaai maasu man paardaina
me to meat mind doesn't cause to become

Does the dog bite?

kukur tokchha?
dog bites

L45

Do you want to go to Jomosom today?

tapAAIlaai aaja Jomosom-maa
you for today Jomosom to
jaamu man laagchha?
to go mind strikes
(Either **man paarchha** or **man laagchha** are heard, and mean the same.)

I follow the Christian religion.

ma kristiyan dharma maanchhu
I Christian religion accept

What religion are you?

tapAAIko dharma ke ho?
your religion what is

Are you Buddhist

baaudha dharma maanu hunchha?
Buddhist religion accept do you

Don't worry.

dukha maandaaina
pain don't acknowledge

May I please take a picture of you?

tapAAIko phoTo (taswir) khichU?
your picture may I take

Can you sing a song for me?

mero laagi git gaaunu hunchha?
my sake song to sing can you

Is there someone who can dance for me?

mero laagi kasaile naachnu sakinchha?
my sake anybody to dance can

I like your music.

tapAAI baju bajaune man paarchha
you song play like strikes

EMERGENCIES

I am sick.

biraami chhu.
sick I am

I have diarrhea.

malaai dishaa cherchha
me to stool runs

fever

joro laagchha
fever strikes

My foot hurts.

mero khuTTa dukhchha
my foot hurts
chhaati
peT
chest
stomach

My friend is sick.

mero saathi biraami chha.
my friend sick is

Where is a hospital?

aspital kahAA chha?
hospital where is
Thaanaa police post?
aarmi berik army post?
sadar mukaam district headquarters?
aabaa radio? (two way)
hawaai jahaaj giraund airstrip?

I have a message to be radioed to Kathmandu.

kaaThmaanDu -maa pathaaune
Kathmandu to to send
samaachaar chha
message there is

Please send the message now.

ahile samaachaar
now message
pathaaunos
please send

Please take it to Namche.

namche -maa puraaidinos.
Namche to please take

I need a person to carry me.

ma -laai bokne maanche
me for carrying man
chaahiyo
need

Please carry me to Shyangboche.

shyangboche -maa malaai
Shyangboche to me
boknos
please carry.

LANGUAGE TAPE

The language tape and pocket-size edition of this section can be ordered from The Mountaineers Books, 1011 SW Klickitat Way, Suite 107, Seattle, WA 98134; or call 1-800-553-4453 to order with Visa or Mastercard.

To speak a foreign language well . . . we must imitate and mimic the whole time. We must never imagine that our efforts will be laughed at. There are so many dialects . . . that speaking incorrectly does not sound so odd as it might in another country.

G.G. Rogers, *Colloquial Nepali*

INDEX

As I write these last words, my thoughts return to you who were my comrades: the stubborn and indomitable peasants of Nepal. Once more I hear the laughter with which you greeted every hardship. Once more I see you in your bivouacs or about your fires, on forced march or in the trenches, now shivering with wet and cold, now scorched by a pitiless and burning sun. Uncomplaining, you endure hunger and thirst and wounds; and at last, your unwavering lines disappear into the smoke and wrath of battle. Bravest of the brave, most generous of the generous, never had country more faithful friends than you.

Ralph Lilley Turner, author of *Dictionary of the Nepali Language*, describing Gurkhas with whom he served in the British Army. He learned Nepali from these soldiers, and wrote the definitive Nepali dictionary without ever having visited Nepal.

photo by Yvonne Vaucher

STEPHEN BEZRUCHKA first went to Nepal in 1969, drawn by his interest in climbing and a desire to get close to the world's highest summits. He spent a year there between graduate studies in mathematics at Harvard University and the study of medicine at Stanford University, and wrote the first edition of this guide. His fascination with Nepal soon transcended its lofty mountains to focus on the social-cultural matrix that is one of his lifelong passions.

He returned to work in Nepal in the mid-seventies and in the mid-eighties. Initially he helped set up a community health project in western Nepal. Later he developed a remote district hospital as a teaching hospital for Nepali doctors and supervised the first physicians training there.

Stephen Bezruchka has trekked far and wide in Nepal. He has climbed in the far ranges of the earth, including the Yukon, Pakistan, China, and on Everest. He is the author of *The Pocket Doctor: Your Ticket to Good Health while Traveling*. Of Ukrainian descent, he traveled there recently and toured outdoor museums there that reminded him of the way life continues in Nepal today. Mostly between trips to Nepal, he practices medicine in Seattle, but the lure of Nepal, the land and its people, keeps calling him back.

माया नमार्नु होला

This message *(maayaa namaarnu holaa)*, in Nepali script, was written by a Nepali innkeeper on a sign for trekkers seen north of Pokhara in 1978. Underneath it was written in English, "Come Back Again." The literal translation (or Nepali meaning) is "Don't let the love die."